SOCIAL WORK
SPEAKS

9th Edition

NATIONAL ASSOCIATION OF SOCIAL WORKERS
POLICY STATEMENTS

2012–2014

Jeane W. Anastas, PhD, LMSW, *President*

Elizabeth J. Clark, PhD, ACSW, MPH, *Executive Director*

National Association of Social Workers

Published by

NASW PRESS

National Association of Social Workers
Washington, DC

Cheryl Y. Bradley, *Publisher*
Sarah Lowman, *Senior Editor*
John Cassels, *Staff Editor*
Lori J. Holtzinger, *Indexer*

Cover by Metadog Design Group
Interior design by Xcel Graphic Services
Printed and bound by Victor Graphics

Printed in the United States of America

ISBN: 978-0-87101-440-5

Contents

Policy Statement Topic Areas

Adolescents

Adolescent and Young Adult Health
Adolescent Pregnancy and Parenting
Education of Children and Youths
Juvenile Justice and Delinquency Prevention
School Dropout Prevention
School Violence
Youth Suicide

Aging

Aging and Wellness
Client Self-Determination and End-of-Life
  Decisions
End-of-Life Care
Health Care
Hospice Care
Long-Term Care

Behavioral Health

Mental Health

Child Welfare

Child Abuse and Neglect
Family Policy
Family Violence
Foster Care and Adoption
Physical Punishment of Children
Public Child Welfare
Welfare Reform

Community

Community Development
Disasters
Housing
Social Services

Discrimination and Equity Issues

Affirmative Action
Civil Liberties and Justice
Correctional Social Work

Cultural and Linquistic Competence in the
  Social Work Profession
Gender-, Ethnic-, and Race-Based Workplace
  Discrimination
Genetics
Immigrants and Refugees
International Policy on Human Rights
Language and Cultural Diversity in the
  United States
Lesbian, Gay, and Bisexual Issues
Peace and Social Justice
People with Disabilities
Poverty and Economic Justice
Racism
Transgender and Gender Identity Issues
Women in the Social Work Profession
Women's Issues

Education

Early Childhood Care and Services
Education of Children and Youths
Physical Punishment of Children
School Truancy and Dropout Prevention

Employment

Drug Testing in the Workplace
Employee Assistance
Gender-, Ethnic-, and Race-Based Workplace
  Discrimination
Genetics
Homelessness
Housing
Poverty and Economic Justice

Ethnicity and Race

Affirmative Action
Civil Liberties and Justice
Cultural and Linguistic Competence in the
  Social Work Profession
Gender-, Ethnic-, and Race-Based Workplace
  Discrimination
Immigrants and Refugees

Deprofessionalization and Reclassification
Employee Assistance
NASW Code of Ethics
Professional Impairment
Professional Self-Care and Social Work
Public Child Welfare
Rural Social Work
Women in the Social Work Profession

Substance Abuse

Alcohol, Tobacco, and Other Drugs
Drug Testing in the Workplace
Professional Impairment

Violence

Child Abuse and Neglect
Crime Victim Assistance
Family Violence
Physical Punishment of Children
School Violence
Youth Suicide

Policy Statements Approved by the 2011 Delegate Assembly

Adolescent and Young Adult Health
Capital Punishment and the Death Penalty
Community Development
Confidentiality and Information Utilization
Crime Victim Assistance
Employee Assistance
Family Violence
Foster Care and Adoption
Hospice Care
Juvenile Justice and Delinquency Prevention
Mental Health
Parental Kidnapping
Peace and Social Justice
Rural Social Work
School Violence
Social Services
Sovereignty, Rights, and the Well-Being of
    Indigenous Peoples
Voter Participation

Title Changes from the 8th Edition

Adolescent Health is now Adolescent and
    Young Adult Health
Sovereignty and the Health of Indigenous
    Peoples is now Sovereignty, Rights, and the
    Well-Being of Indigenous Peoples

Foreword

The policy statements contained in this book set the parameters for National Association of Social Workers (NASW) positions and actions on a broad range of public and professional issues. *Social Work Speaks* is a comprehensive collection of policies adopted and revised by NASW's key policymaking body, the Delegate Assembly. This edition includes all of the new and revised policies approved by the 2011 NASW Delegate Assembly as well as those approved by previous assemblies.

Since its inception in 1955, NASW's policy statement adoption has been a part of its governance process. The Delegate Assembly, a body of 277 professional social workers representing NASW's diverse membership, meets at regular intervals (every three years since 1981) to set broad parameters for the association's programs and to agree on policy statements that guide advocacy efforts in public policy. The Delegate Assembly is now conducted virtually. Only a few individuals—the president, the facilitators, the parliamentarian, legal counsel, and necessary national staff—are together in Washington, DC. The delegates from all states and U.S. territories log in from their home computers or from a location arranged by their coalition or chapter. Deliberation and voting follow the customary Delegate Assembly process and use *Robert's Rules of Order*. New policy statements are approved, and program priority goals are set. It is an efficient and exciting way to conduct this part of the business of the association.

The involvement of social workers in policy development continues to be important. Increasingly, we participate in a global community in which what happens in one country has repercussions around the world. The population of the United States is more culturally, ethnically, and racially diverse than it has ever been. There is a rapidly aging population and a widening gap between those who are affluent and people living in poverty. At the same time, the recent economic crisis is creating new challenges for human services agencies and organizations. Effective programs are being reevaluated and, in some cases, eliminated due to decreasing revenues from fundraising and earnings on investments. Our social work value systems and our expertise lend themselves to the creation of and advocacy for policies that provide effective solutions in our current world context.

THE PROCESS

The 2011 Delegate Assembly process built on technology innovations used at the Delegate Assembly in 2008. All of the new and revised policy statements were available online for comment by the membership three times before being adopted by the delegates. This allowed members to make suggestions to improve the policies. Policy panels met via online meeting software and teleconferencing, taking comments into account and making necessary revisions. These technology innovations allowed for greater involvement and input from the membership and from the delegates. Consequently, these policy statements represent the collective thinking of thousands of experienced social work practitioners.

LEGISLATIVE ACTIVITY

Before taking a position on any federal legislation, the NASW national office compares the proposed legislative policy with policies in this book. If the proposed legislation is consistent with the thrust of an NASW policy statement or if it contradicts the statement, NASW's position will be readily apparent. However, in many cases, the proposed legislation contains some provisions that support NASW's policies and some that are inconsistent with, or only partially support, the NASW recommendations. In these cases, a decision is not made easily, and other factors must be taken into consideration. NASW then weighs the potential for revising the proposed legislation, the overall value of possible policy gains, political concerns, and other factors before a decision to support the legislation is made. When NASW chapters make decisions on legislative action at the state level, they also review the NASW policy statements to ensure that actions taken are not in conflict with NASW policy.

For social workers to be heard as one voice on federal policy, the national office coordinates action on federal legislation at the national, chapter, unit, and member level. Action may include endorsements for, or opposition to, a bill before Congress; letters to Congress requesting action on a bill; or participation in coalition actions for or against a piece of legislation. Chapters coordinate similar actions on state legislation.

SOCIAL WORK POLICY INSTITUTE

NASW recently created a think tank, the Social Work Policy Institute (SWPI), to strengthen social work's voice in public policy deliberations, inform policymakers through the collection and dissemination of information on social work effectiveness, and create a forum to examine current and future issues in health care and social service delivery. Building on the policies approved by the NASW Delegate Assembly, SWPI will examine issues that relate to the work of social workers, including how to serve people who have multiple or complex needs and how public agencies and other structures deliver health and human services. SWPI hosts think tank symposia on critical issues facing the profession and the clients we serve (for example, end-of-life care, supervisory practice in child welfare, investments in the social work workforce), bringing researchers and frontline social workers together with representatives of government agencies, foundations, and national organizations to study an issue in depth and develop an action agenda that targets research, practice, and policy improvements and workforce development strategies. For more information about SWPI's work, visit http://www.socialworkpolicy.org.

LEGAL ACTION AND THE LEGAL DEFENSE FUND

The NASW Legal Defense Fund initiates or participates in a number of amicus curiae (friend of the court) briefs on critical social policy and professional social work issues. In deciding which cases to support with a brief at the federal or state level, NASW looks to its Delegate Assembly–adopted policy statements for guidance. The policy statements also provide a foundation for comment on federal regulations and proposed federal legislation. For example, NASW filed a brief in the Supreme Court on the issue of whether investigators of child abuse are required to obtain parental consent or a warrant before interviewing students in a school setting. In *Camreta v. Greene*, the U.S. Supreme Court struck down a state ruling that a student's constitutional rights were violated when case workers interviewed her at school. Other cases with positive outcomes in which NASW participated as a friend of the court include the following: *Jackson v. D.C. Board of Elections and Ethics* (ballot initiative not permitted to ban same-sex marriage in Washington, DC); *Florida Department of Children and Families v. In re: Matter of Adoption of X.X.G. and N.R.G.* (Florida ban on same-sex couple adoptions ruled unconstitutional under Florida's equal protection law); *United States v. Arizona* (the state was enjoined from enforcing its immigration law, S.B. 1070, because of the chilling effect on immigrants' capacity to access emergency health services for their children); and *Commonwealth of Virginia v. Sebelius* (a three-judge federal panel for the Fourth Circuit ruled that the Commonwealth of Virginia lacked standing to challenge the 2010 Patient Protection and Affordable Care Act's mandatory health insurance requirement). For more information on the NASW Legal Defense Fund, please visit http://www.socialworkers.org/ldf/default.as.

POLICY STUDY AND ANALYSIS

Social Work Speaks may be used as a text or as supplementary reading for overview, introductory, or macro courses in social and public policy. The book may also serve as an adjunct to a wide range of specialty courses because so many of the policy statements address specific fields of practice.

As an articulation of what one Delegate Assembly viewed as an ideal policy, individual statements are useful for analysis and review. They are excellent resources for classroom discussion and debate, and they can be used to raise questions such as the following:

■ What important issues have practitioners raised in the subject area?

■ Are the issues ones I deem critical?

■ In my opinion, are there major issues that were not considered?

■ Do I concur with NASW's policy stance?

■ What documentation did NASW provide for the conclusions?

■ On what course work, research, other readings, or practice experience do I base my stance?

■ How do the positions compare with the public positions of other groups and organizations on the same subject?

■ How might the statements be improved?

■ How can I use the statements to become a more effective advocate?

For lobbying or analysis, policy statements should be considered in the context of their purpose and the time in which they were adopted. Social workers developed the statements to serve as broad parameters for advocacy work and to help professionals who are concerned with social issues focus their thinking. Nonetheless, because of the breadth of issues and the constantly emerging new information, readers may find that they need more specificity than the statements contain. Contemporary professional literature will serve as an important extension of the policy statements, and NASW national and chapter offices may also provide updated information in many areas (see http://www.socialworkers.org).

As readers use these statements, they may also want to consider new or revised statements that could be presented to the 2014 Delegate Assembly. Social workers who want to be informed and involved in policy analysis, advocacy for social policies, or the formulation of future policy statements will find the ninth edition of *Social Work Speaks* a useful volume.

Jeane W. Anastas, PhD, LMSW
President, NASW

Elizabeth J. Clark, PhD, ACSW, MPH
Executive Director, NASW

PUBLIC AND PROFESSIONAL POLICY STATEMENTS

Adolescent and Young Adult Health

BACKGROUND

Adolescence, the transition period from childhood to adulthood, is a time of tremendous opportunity and promise as well as unique risks and health concerns. The health and well-being of adolescents are critically affected by their experiences during this developmental milestone. The majority of adolescent health problems are preventable, precipitated by environmental and behavioral factors that can mitigate or exacerbate immediate and long-term health consequences (NASW, 2002). The patterns of behavior adolescents develop during these years often influence their health and well-being throughout life.

Improving adolescent health outcomes will require moving beyond a biological approach, toward a broadened understanding of, and attention to, the multiplicity of factors and complexity of circumstances affecting adolescent health and well-being. Improvements in health status will require the collective effort of individuals and communities, social institutions, and the different disciplines involved with adolescents (NASW, 2002).

Critical Adolescent Health Issues

Adolescents are a relatively healthy population, but many in this age group engage in risky behavior; develop unhealthy habits; and experience physical, mental, and behavioral health conditions that can jeopardize their immediate and long-term health (Institute of Medicine [IOM], 2008). Critical adolescent health issues fall into six broad categories: (1) unintentional injury, primarily related to motor vehicle use; (2) violence, including homicide, assault, bullying and other forms of victimization; (3) substance abuse, including tobacco, alcohol and illicit drug use; (4) mental health, including depression and suicide; (5) reproductive health, including pregnancy and sexually transmitted disease; and (6) overweight/obesity and physical inactivity (Centers for Disease Control and Prevention [CDC], 2009a).

Health disparities are present in almost all adolescent health issues and result from multiple factors, including poverty, educational inequalities, and inadequate access to health care. Other risk factors for poor adolescent health outcomes include community norms that condone risky behavior; neighborhood disorganization; family mobility and homelessness; lack of attachment to peers, family, school, and community; family drug use; early and persistent behavior problems, significant grief and loss, and family violence (CDC, 2010). Certain subgroups are at heightened risk. Lesbian, gay, bisexual, and transgender (LGBT) youths experience higher rates of suicide, victimization, risk behavior for HIV infection, and substance abuse, as compared with their heterosexual peers (Advocates for Youth, 2011). Hispanic teenagers have the lowest rates of health insurance among all. children in the United States, resulting in reduced access to ongoing medical care (Kaiser Family Foundation, Commission on Medicaid and the Uninsured, 2010). Prevention efforts for adolescents, particularly efforts targeting disparities, are critical and are directly in the realm of social work practice.

Injury and Violence

Motor vehicle injury is the leading cause of mortality among adolescents and young adults. Substance use is a significant risk factor for motor vehicle crashes involving teenagers. Policies such as graduated driver's licenses are becoming more common and seek to have impact on this issue.

High school students have reported decreased levels of violent behavior since the 1990s (Mulye et al., 2009), but troubling trends remain. The adolescent homicide rate decreased throughout the 1990s, but has since leveled off. Black, male non-Hispanics are disproportionately affected by homicide, both as victims and offenders. In addition, dating violence is an emerging issue for adolescents, with one in four adolescents reporting verbal, physical, emotional, or sexual abuse from a dating partner each year (CDC, 2011a). Bullying, both physical and virtual ("cyber-bullying"), has become a pervasive public health problem, with LGBT and special needs teenagers at particular risk. Prevention of violence and bullying among adolescents requires a balanced effort that addresses the complex underlying factors and builds on the assets of youths, families, and communities (CDC, 2011b).

Mental Health

Mental health issues often appear first in this age group. It is estimated that one in five adolescents experience "significant emotional distress" and one in 10 faces "more serious emotional impairment" (Mulye et al., 2009). Recognizing, diagnosing, and treating adolescents with mental health issues is important given that symptoms of nearly half of all lifetime diagnosable problems appear by age 14 (Kessler et al., 2005). Left untreated, depression and other adolescent mental health concerns can lead to negative consequences, including violence and bullying, increased school dropout rates, and suicide (NASW, 2003).

Suicide is the third leading cause of death for adolescents. The rate of suicide decreased throughout the 1990s, but leveled off at 7.0 in 1999. In 2007, the rate was 6.9 per 100,000 teenagers ages 15 to 19 (National Institute of Mental Health, 2010). Recognizing risk and protective factors is essential when developing adolescent suicide prevention and intervention efforts (NASW, 2009).

Substance Use

In the United States in 2008, almost one-third of adolescents ages 12 to 17 drank alcohol in the past year, around one-fifth used an illicit drug, and almost one-sixth smoked cigarettes (U.S. Department of Health and Human Services, Substance Abuse and Mental Health Services Administration, Office of Applied Studies, 2009). Tobacco use, including cigarette smoking, cigar smoking, and smokeless tobacco use, remains the leading preventable cause of death in the United States. Nearly 90 percent of all adult smokers begin while in their teens, or earlier, and two-thirds become regular, daily smokers before they reach the age of 19 (Campaign for Tobacco-Free Kids, 2011). Alcohol use and binge drinking among adolescents remain major public health concerns. Illicit drug use, as well as prescription and over-the-counter drug abuse, is also a continued threat to adolescent health and well-being.

Pregnancy and Reproductive Health

Since the early 1990s, the teenage pregnancy and birth rates have declined by approximately one-third. The teenage birth rate is now at a record low, as is the national teenage pregnancy rate. However, three in 10 girls in the United States still become pregnant at least once by age 20, resulting in well over 400,000 births to teenage mothers each year. Rates of teenage pregnancy and parenthood in the United States remain far higher than those in other fully developed countries. As in other adolescent health indicators, disparities exist: At least 50 percent of Hispanic and African American teenage girls will become pregnant before the age of 20. Only 19 percent of non-Hispanic white teenage girls under 20 will become pregnant. Research has demonstrated that lowering the rate of teenage pregnancy helps reduce poverty and improve educational achievement, workforce competitiveness, child welfare, and other critical social issues for both parents and children (National Campaign to Prevent Teen and Unplanned Pregnancy, 2011).

Many young people in the United States engage in sexual risk behaviors that, in addition to pregnancy, can result in HIV/AIDS or other sexually transmitted diseases (STDs). In 2009, 46 percent of high school students had ever had sexual intercourse, and 14 percent of high school students had had four or more sex partners during their life (CDC, 2009b). Use of alcohol and other drugs increases the likelihood of risky behaviors, such as unprotected sex (CDC, 2011a).

Chronic Disease

Adolescents are engaging in more behaviors that put them at risk for chronic health conditions. Rates of adolescent obesity are rising, caused in large part by the poor nutritional choices young people often make as they become increasingly autonomous. Another significant cause of obesity is lack of physical exercise, related to sedentary activities, such as video and computer games, and fewer physical education options in schools. Heart disease and diabetes are among the most common consequences of these lifestyle choices. Education for wellness and other preventive strategies would go a long way in lowering the incidence of preventable cases of these diseases, while at the same time improving quality of life and saving on health care costs.

Health Insurance Coverage

Insurance coverage is also an area of concern for this population. Medicaid and the Children's Health Insurance Program (CHIP) have been important sources of health insurance coverage for adolescents. States are required to provide income-eligible adolescents with Medicaid and CHIP coverage until they turn 19. States have the option to extend Medicaid coverage to age 21. However, once children age out of Medicaid or CHIP eligibility, they are typically subject to the much more limited Medicaid eligibility criteria for adults. Young adults who lose Medicaid or CHIP coverage are in danger of becoming uninsured and losing access to their health providers and the medical treatments they may need. High unemployment among older teenagers leaves many particularly vulnerable to becoming uninsured (Kaiser Family Foundation, 2010).

Immigrant teenagers (both documented and undocumented) are the group of children least-likely to have insurance coverage. Undocumented teenagers in almost all cases are ineligible for Medicaid and CHIP (with the exception of preg-

nant teenagers). Legal immigrant teenagers and their families face stiff enrollment barriers to these programs. The result is a perpetuation of heath disparities between immigrant teenagers and their nonimmigrant peers.

ISSUE STATEMENT

Health indicators have shown promising trends for adolescents. Rates of risky behaviors overall have dropped since the early 1990s. However, over the past five years, there has been a leveling off of these developments. In addition, adolescents in different ethnic, racial, and other population groups are disproportionately represented in some of the most troubling adolescent health statistics. Unfortunately, research and policy initiatives to address adolescent health issues continue to rely on a "deficit model," with minimal or no grounding in prevention, youth development, or self-efficacy or responsibility.

Addressing the aspects of disease and public health challenges that are preventable can provide substantial quality of life and economic benefits. The challenge, however, is that for many adolescents, health services are not accessible, acceptable, appropriate, effective, or equitable (IOM, 2008).

Adolescent health issues are largely preventable and can be addressed through behavior modification or through the social environment. Adolescents are strongly influenced by family, schools, peers, and the community. Preventive measures should be developed that enhance family and community involvement, age-appropriate education, and school and peer support, to improve adolescent health.

POLICY STATEMENT

NASW seeks to make adolescent health a national, state, and local policy priority by strengthening adolescent health service delivery systems, with an emphasis on developing programs that

■ include a continuum of evidence-based prevention, early intervention, and treatment approaches to meet the unique physical and behavioral health needs of adolescents.

- promote access to mental and physical health evaluation and treatment in an age-appropriate manner.

- provide medical homes (a primary, ongoing source of medical care) for all adolescents, especially those with special health care needs.

- offer team-based, integrated, multidisciplinary care.

- provide easy accessibility, such as school-based and community-based adolescent health clinics that are available to all adolescents regardless of insurance coverage, ability to pay, or other factors.

- respect the confidentiality and self-determination needs of adolescents and are provided in a culturally appropriate manner.

- offer specialized training to staff on working with vulnerable populations, including LGBT teenagers, and homeless and undocumented youths.

NASW advocates

- full implementation of the Affordable Care Act of 2010, including expansion of Medicaid coverage to all individuals age 19 and over.

- state expansion of Medicaid eligibility up to age 21.

- state adoption of comprehensive Graduated Driver License (GDL) laws, and federal financial incentives for state enactment of comprehensive GDL legislation.

- implementation of comprehensive tobacco-free campus policies and increased tobacco taxes, to prevent and reduce tobacco use and addiction in young people.

- routine inclusion of sexual orientation and gender identity measures in all relevant national, state, and local health and research surveys that cover adolescents, to increase our understanding of the health care needs of LGBT youths.

- increased federal funding for health care workforce training in research-based approaches to adolescent health care.

- implementation of strong gun laws and policies, to prevent adolescents from accessing guns and protect communities from gun violence.

- federal and state policy changes that support nutrition and regular physical activity for adolescents in schools and communities.

- access to affordable and effective family planning services for adolescents, through preservation of teenage pregnancy prevention funding streams and increased funding for Title X programs.

REFERENCES

Advocates for Youth. (2010). *Gay, lesbian, bisexual, transgender, and questioning (GLBTQ) youth: A population in need of understanding and support..* Retrieved from http://www.advocatesforyouth.org/storage/advfy/documents/glbtq_youth%202010.pdf

Campaign for Tobacco-Free Kids. (2011). *Smoking and kids.* Retrieved from http://www.tobaccofreekids.org/research/factsheets/pdf/0001.pdf

Centers for Disease Control and Prevention. (2009a). The national Youth Risk Behavior Survey. Retrieved from http://www.cdc.gov/healthyyouth/yrbs/pdf/us_overview_yrbs.pdf

Centers for Disease Control and Prevention. (2009b). Understanding teen dating violence [Fact sheet]. Retrieved from http://www.cdc.gov/chooserespect/pdfs/TeenDatingViolence2009-a.pdf

Centers for Disease Control and Prevention. (2010, June 4). Youth risk behavior surveillance—United States, 2009. *Morbidity and Mortality Weekly Report.* Retrieved from http://www.cdc.gov/mmwr/pdf/ss/ss5905.pdf

Centers for Disease Control and Prevention. (2011a). *Sexual risk behavior: HIV, STD, & teen pregnancy prevention.* Retrieved from http://www.cdc.gov/healthyyouth/sexualbehaviors/index.htm

Centers for Disease Control and Prevention. (2011b). *Why prevention must be a priority.* Retrieved from http://www.safeyouth.gov/Pages/Prevention_Priority.aspx#a2

Institute of Medicine. (2008). *Adolescent health services: Missing opportunities.* Washington, DC: National Academy of Sciences.

Kaiser Family Foundation, Commission on Medicaid and the Uninsured. (2010). *Aging out of Medicaid: What is the risk of becoming uninsured?* (Publication No: 8057). Washington, DC: Author.

Kessler, R. C., Berglund, P., Demler, O., Jin, R., Merikangas, K. R., & Walters, E. (2005). Lifetime prevalence and age-of-onset distributions of DSM-IV disorders in the National Co-morbidity Survey replication. *Archives of General Psychology, 62,* 593–602.

Mulye, T. P., Park, M. J., Nelson, C. D., Adams, S. H., Irwin, C. E., Jr., & Brindis, C. D. (2009). Trends in adolescent and young adult health in the United States. *Journal of Adolescent Health, 45,* 8–24.

National Association of Social Workers. (2002). *Partners in program planning in adolescent health.* Washington, DC: Author.

National Association of Social Workers. (2003). Practice update: The impact of poverty on adolescent health. *Adolescent Health, 3*(2). Retrieved from http://www.socialworkers.org/practice/adolescent_health/ah0503.pdf

National Association of Social Workers. (2009). *The NASW Shift Project: Suicide prevention for adolescent girls.* Retrieved from http://www.socialworkers.org/practice/adolescent_health/shift/default.asp

National Campaign to Prevent Teen and Unplanned Pregnancy. (2011). *2011 Federal policy agenda.* Retrieved from http://www.thenationalcampaign.org/resources/pdf/Briefly_2011_PolicyAgenda.pdf

National Institute of Mental Health. (2010). *Suicide in the U.S.: Statistics and prevention* [Fact sheet]. Retrieved from http://www.nimh.nih.gov/health/publications/suicide-in-the-us-statistics-and-prevention/index.shtml#children

U.S. Department of Health and Human Services, Substance Abuse and Mental Health Services Administration, Office of Applied Studies. (2009). *Results from the 2008 National Survey on Drug Use and Health: National findings* (HHS Publication No. SMA 09-4434, NSDUH Series H-36). Retrieved from http://oas.samhsa.gov/nsduh/2k8nsduh/2k8Results.cfm

NASW Members with Primary Responsibility for Revision of This Policy

First Draft Revision:

Heather A. McCabe (IN)

Policy Panelists:

Betty Morningstar (MA)
Aline Goodman (NYS)
Steve Burton (WV)
George Baboila (MN)
Deb Hanson (ND)
Lisa Bates (OR)

Policy statement approved by the NASW Delegate Assembly, August 2011. This statement supersedes the policy statement on Adolescent Health approved by the Delegate Assembly in August 2002. For further information, contact the National Association of Social Workers, 750 First Street, NE, Suite 700, Washington, DC 20002-4241. Telephone: 202-408-8600; e-mail: press@naswdc.org

Adolescent Pregnancy and Parenting

BACKGROUND

The social work profession is in a distinctive position to respond to the issues of adolescent pregnancy and parenting. Because social workers assess problems and needs from an ecological perspective considering individual, family, and community factors, and use comprehensive approaches to solving problems, the profession can have a broad effect on issues regarding adolescent pregnancy and parenting. The issues of adolescent pregnancy and parenting are multifaceted and do not have a single root cause. As such, no single methodology exists for affecting adolescent pregnancy prevention, for supporting adolescent parents in parenting their children, or for overcoming the challenges adolescent parents face.

In looking at the issues of adolescent pregnancy and parenting, social work takes into account the medical, social, economic, familial, racial, ethnic, cultural, and all other ecological factors affecting and influencing the adolescent. To better understand the issue, it is valuable to look at where the United States ranks in comparison to other developed, industrialized countries. Despite a large decline over the course of the last 12 years, the United States continues to have the highest adolescent pregnancy rate of industrialized and developed countries (National Campaign to Prevent Teen Pregnancy, 2004). In fact, recent decreases have only moved the U.S. rates to where similar countries were in the 1990s (Darroch, Singh, Frost, & Study Team, 2001). As a point of comparison, the adolescent pregnancy rate of the United States is nearly twice that of Canada and Great Britain (Boonstra, 2002).

Although the rate of adolescent pregnancy in the United States has been declining over the past 15 years, each year almost 750,000 adoles-cent women become pregnant. Almost eight in 10 of these pregnancies are unintended (Alan Guttmacher Institute, 2006a; Boonstra, 2002). In the United States, about 57 percent of adolescent pregnancies result in a birth (Alan Guttmacher Institute, 2006a). The percentage of adolescent males who are involved in pregnancies is small, with only 3 percent of 15-year-olds to 19-year-olds being fathers and only 7 percent of the births each year involving adolescent males (Alan Guttmacher Institute, 2002).

Many teenage women reported that their early sexual experiences resulted from peer pressures, including efforts to sustain a relationship, and were not as pleasurable as had been anticipated (Dodson, n.d.; Luker, 1996). Pregnancies of adolescents aged 15 years and under (approximately 3 percent per year) account for the smallest number of adolescent pregnancies, and these pregnancies are frequently related to sexual exploitation or sexual assault of the adolescent by the present partner or to sexual abuse of the adolescent by other adults in or outside of the family. Seven in 10 girls who had sexual intercourse before age 13 reported the experience was involuntary. The younger the adolescent mother, the more likely that her male partner was 10 or more years older than she (Alan Guttmacher Institute, 1999a). There is also a strong link between adolescent pregnancy and sexual abuse not only for females but also for males (Saewyc, Magee, & Pettingell, 2004).

Like many social issues, adolescent pregnancy and parenting affect minority populations disproportionately. The decline in adolescent pregnancy has been sharpest in the African American population, with the pregnancy rate for 15-year-olds to 19-year-olds declining 40 percent between 1990 and 2002 (Alan Guttmacher

Institute, 2006b), although adolescent pregnancy rates are still highest among African Americans. In births to adolescent mothers, Latinas have the highest rate (83 births per 1,000 girls) compared with African Americans (63 per 1,000) and Caucasians (27 per 1,000) (Kaiser Family Foundation, 2006). Although adolescent Latinas had a slight increase in pregnancy rates from 1991 to 1992, by 2002 the rate was 19 percent lower than in 1990 (Alan Guttmacher Institute, 2006b).

Many factors account for the difference in the adolescent pregnancy rates among Western industrialized countries. Much attention has been paid to the success of countries such as France, Sweden, and Great Britain in preventing and lowering their rates of adolescent pregnancy. The United States could gain valuable knowledge about preventing and addressing the issue of adolescent pregnancy by examining the resources and methods that other industrialized countries use. A common misperception is that other countries have lower rates of sexual activity among their adolescents; however, an examination of rates of sexual activity among adolescents in the United States and other industrialized countries shows little difference in the rates of sexual activity. Indeed, abortion rates are lower in countries such as Great Britain, France, Canada, and Sweden despite having similar sexual activity as the United States. Because rates of sexual activity do not explain higher adolescent pregnancy rates in the United States, other factors must be considered and examined, particularly the significance of contraceptive use among adolescents (Darroch et al., 2001).

Other factors that contribute to the higher rates in the United States include a higher proportion of adolescents growing up in socially and economically disadvantaged situations; lower tolerance of adolescent sexual activity, coupled with limited comprehensive sexuality education for many youth; and challenges to accessing contraceptives and other reproductive health care services (Alan Guttmacher Institute, 2001).

ISSUE STATEMENT

The social work profession has long been concerned about the issues of unintended adolescent pregnancy and adolescent parenting. The implications of adolescent pregnancy and parenting are far reaching and affect not only adolescent parents but also their families and communities. Although there have been dramatic decreases in adolescent pregnancy across the country over the last 12 years, those adolescents and their families affected by an unintended pregnancy continue to face educational, economic, and health challenges. Even though declines in the rates of adolescent pregnancy include all races and ethnicities, adolescent pregnancy affects minority communities in a different and significant way. At times, changes in the political and cultural environment of the country may erode the support necessary to overcome the challenges surrounding adolescent pregnancy, and solutions become controversial, thus hindering professionals from having access to resources to prevent and address adolescent pregnancy.

Reproductive Technology

Advances in reproductive technology have had a major effect on the decline in adolescent pregnancy over the last 12 years. Methods of contraception, including delivery systems that last longer and encourage compliance with the administration of the contraceptive, are responsible for approximately 86 percent of the decline in adolescent pregnancy. This pattern of decline has been observed in other industrialized countries as well (Santelli, Lindberg, Finer, & Singh, 2007). Access to this technology is not without difficulty as more states are considering expanding required parental notification and consent to include birth control methods. Even with the advances in reproductive technology, many communities still lack access to affordable, confidential, publicly funded reproductive health care (Frost, Frohwirth, & Purcell, 2004).

Emergency contraception is an option for reducing adolescent pregnancy, and because it is taken after the act of sexual intercourse it is viable for those adolescents who did not plan to have sex. Although it is available over the counter for women 18 years of age and older, younger females must still access formal medical services to use this method.

Male Involvement

Programming and research on adolescent parents has traditionally focused on adolescent mothers. The stereotypes that adolescent fathers are not involved with their children, are irresponsible, and care only about sexual fulfillment often drive prevention and intervention programming, which may have negative effects on adolescent fathers who want to access resources. The limited data available about adolescent fathers indicate that adolescent fathers want to be and are involved in the lives of their children, even if the involvement does not include financial support (Kimball, 2004). These data suggest that programs must be more inclusive of fathers and that different methods of outreach and engagement are needed to involve them in services and programming

Maternal and Child Health

We know that adolescents access prenatal care later in the pregnancy or sometimes not at all (Child Trends DataBank, 2007). Often this is related to the fear and secrecy that might surround the pregnancy. The lack of prenatal care results in adolescents having negative birth outcomes, with a higher number of preterm births, low birth weights, and infants who die before the age of one (Reichman & Pagnini, 1997). All of these factors have a potential negative effect on the well-being of both the baby and the mother. The ability of adolescents to engage in confidential contraceptive, abortion, and prenatal services without parental consent is critical to the overall health of not only the adolescent but also the pregnancy and, if she chooses to maintain the pregnancy, the baby. When appropriate and acceptable to the adolescent, involvement of a supportive adult may be helpful.

Thirty-four states now require some sort of parental involvement in a minor's decision to have an abortion, up from 18 states in 1991 (Kaiser Family Foundation, 2006). Some states are also exploring consent or notification laws for minors' use of contraceptive services. These efforts would have a negative effect on the prevention of adolescent pregnancy and would create an increase in negative maternal and child outcomes.

Another factor in maternal health is repeat pregnancies. Second pregnancies are an issue for adolescent mothers, with 42 percent becoming pregnant within 24 months of the birth of their first child (Raneri & Wiemann, 2007). The implications of additional children stretch not only to the health and economic well-being of the adolescent mother but also to the potential effect on her ability to parent multiple children.

Educational Attainment and Poverty

The negative effect of an adolescent pregnancy on educational attainment and future employment and earning power is well documented. Adolescent mothers complete high school at much lower rates and go on to college less often than do their childless contemporaries (Hofferth, Reid, & Mott, 2001). Clearly, there is a link between completing high school and college and income stability. Adolescent parenting has a disproportionate effect on those already in poverty and can serve as a tie to that income status over the longer term. In the United States, adolescent mothers "are much more likely to come from poor or low-income families (83 percent) than [are] those who have abortions (61 percent) or teens in general" (Alan Guttmacher Institute, 1999b, p. 4). Adolescent mothers have an increased likelihood of ending up on welfare, with almost one-half receiving welfare benefits within five years of the birth of their first child (National Campaign to Prevent Teen Pregnancy, 2002).

Generational Impact

Adolescent pregnancy has long had a generational effect, with daughters of adolescent mothers being more likely to go on to become adolescent parents themselves—some estimate by 22 percent. The sons of adolescent mothers are also disadvantaged, with 13 percent more likely to end up in prison (National Campaign to Prevent Teen Pregnancy, 2002).

POLICY STATEMENT

Within the context of culturally appropriate and sensitive practice, and on the basis of NASW values and ethical principles, it is the policy of NASW to support and further the following:

■ services that are responsive to the needs and desires (including developmental, ecological, familial, biopsychosocial, mental health) of the client or clients (individual, families, groups, organizations, and communities) being served;

■ services and supports that are safe, legal, affordable, and confidential;

■ comprehensive health education and services for all adolescents;

■ a comprehensive approach to sexuality education for all adolescents, including but not limited to, physiology of sexuality and sexual relations, emotional aspects of romantic relationships, pregnancy prevention (including abstinence and contraception), realistic mock parenting activities;

■ comprehensive family planning services for all adolescents;

■ comprehensive services to adolescents who become pregnant, including but not limited to, health care, education (mainstream and alternative programs to meet all young parents' needs), parenting education and support, social and emotional well-being support (including infant mental health and other mental health services), legal services;

■ adherence to Title IX of the National Education Act that protects pregnant and parenting adolescents from discrimination in the public schools, denial of access to education, and exclusion from participation in school activities because of pregnancy or parenting;

■ comprehensive services to young males who father babies of adolescent mothers, including but not limited to, education (mainstream and alternative programs to meet all young parents' needs), parenting education and support, social and emotional well-being support (including infant mental health and other mental health services), legal services;

■ responsible and nurturing involvement of young fathers in their children's lives from the prenatal period all throughout their lives, when appropriate and possible;

■ comprehensive services to the children of adolescent parents, including but not limited to health care, education, services to promote social and emotional well-being; and

■ financial support that enables rather than hinders adolescent parents' engagement in their primary responsibilities of parenting and completing an education.

REFERENCES

Alan Guttmacher Institute. (1999a). *Teenage pregnancy: Overall trends and state-by-state information*. Washington, DC: Author.

Alan Guttmacher Institute. (1999b). *U.S. teenage pregnancy rate drops another 4% between 1995 and 1996* [Press release]. Washington, DC: Author. Retrieved June 15, 1999, from http://www.guttmacher.org/media/nr/newsrelease_teen_preg.html

Alan Guttmacher Institute. (2001). *Can more progress be made? Teenage sexual and reproductive behavior in developed countries*. Washington, DC and New York: Author.

Alan Guttmacher Institute. (2002). *Their own right: Addressing the sexual and reproductive health of American men*. Washington, DC and New York: Author.

Alan Guttmacher Institute. (2006a). *Facts on American teens' sexual and reproductive health*. Washington, DC and New York: Author.

Alan Guttmacher Institute. (2006b). *U.S. teenage pregnancy statistics national and state trends and trends by race and ethnicity*. New York: Author.

Boonstra, H. (2002). Teen pregnancy: Trends and lessons learned. *Guttmacher Report on Public Policy, 5*(1), 7–10.

Child Trends DataBank. (2007). *Late or no prenatal care*. Washington, DC: Author.

Darroch, J. E., Singh, S., Frost, J. J., & Study Team. (2001). Differences in teenage pregnancy rates among five developed countries: The roles of sexual activity and contraceptive use. *Family Planning Perspectives, 33*(6), 244–250, 281.

Dodson, L. (n.d.). *We could be your daughters: Girls, sexuality and pregnancy in low-income America*. Cambridge, MA: Radcliffe Public Policy Institute.

Frost, J. J., Frohwirth, L., & Purcell, A. (2004). The availability and use of publicly funded family planning clinics: U.S. trends, 1994–2001. *Perspectives on Sexual and Reproductive Health, 36*(5), 206–215.

Hofferth, S. L., Reid, L., & Mott, F. L. (2001). The effects of early childbearing on schooling over time. *Family Planning Perspectives, 33*(5), 259–267.

Kaiser Family Foundation. (2006). *Sexual health statistics for teenagers and young adults in the United States*. Washington, DC: Author.

Kimball, C. (2004). Teen fathers: An introduction. *Prevention Researcher, 11*(4), 3–5.

Luker, K. (1996). *Dubious conceptions: The politics of teenage pregnancy*. Cambridge, MA: Harvard University Press.

National Campaign to Prevent Teen Pregnancy. (2002). *Not just another single issue: Teen pregnancy prevention's link to other critical social issues*. Washington, DC: Author.

National Campaign to Prevent Teen Pregnancy. (2004). *Teen birth rates: How does the United States compare?* Washington, DC: Author.

Raneri, L. G., & Wiemann, C. M. (2007). Social ecological predictors of repeat adolescent pregnancy. *Perspectives on Sexual and Reproductive Health, 39*, 39–47.

Reichman, N. E., & Pagnini, D. L. (1997). Maternal age and birth outcomes: Data from New Jersey. *Family Planning Perspectives, 29*(6), 268–272, 295.

Saewyc, E. M., Magee, L. L., & Pettingell, S. E. (2004). Teenage pregnancy and associated risk behaviors among sexually abused adolescents. *Perspectives on Sexual and Reproductive Health, 36*(3), 98–105.

Santelli, J. S., Lindberg, L. D., Finer, L. B., & Singh, S. (2007). Explaining recent declines in adolescent pregnancy in the United States: The contribution of abstinence and improved contraceptive use. *American Journal of Public Health, 97*, 150–156.

Policy statement approved by the NASW Delegate Assembly, August 2008. This policy statement supersedes the policy statement on Adolescent Pregnancy and Parenting approved by the Delegate Assembly in 1999 and referred by the 2005 Delegate Assembly to the 2008 Delegate Assembly for revision, the policy statement on Adolescent Pregnancy approved by the Assembly in 1993, and the policy statement on Adolescent Pregnancy approved in 1984. For further information, contact the National Association of Social Workers, 750 First Street, NE, Suite 700, Washington, DC 20002-4241. Telephone: 202-408-8600 or 800-638-8799; e-mail: press@naswdc.org

Aging and Wellness

BACKGROUND

The aging of the U.S. population presents social and political implications for both the social work profession and society. Although ageism remains prevalent, the aging of the baby boom generation is challenging biases toward older people. Social workers, other professionals, and the public increasingly understand that old age is a time of continued growth and that older adults contribute significantly to their families, communities, and society. This shift influences gerontological social work practice, education, and research (Social Work Leadership Institute, 2007).

As the U.S. population ages, it is also becoming more racially and ethnically diverse (U.S. Census Bureau, 2005). The proportion of older people who are minorities will increase from 16.4 percent in 2000 to 23.6 percent in 2030 (Administration on Aging, 2006). In addition to race and ethnicity, cultural diversity among older adults is recognized increasingly in geographical location and living arrangements; national origin and civil status; sex, sexual orientation, and gender identity and expression; religious and political beliefs; and physical, psychological, and cognitive ability, among other factors.

Demographers attribute population aging primarily to declining fertility and mortality rates (United Nations, 2002). From 1950 to 2000 the proportion of adults 60 years of age and older increased from 12.1 to 16.3 percent of the U.S. population; this percentage is projected to rise to 26.9 percent by 2050. Similarly, the median age of the population rose from 30.2 to 35.3 years between 1950 and 2000, and is expected to rise to 40.7 years by 2050 (United Nations, 2002; U.S. Census Bureau, n.d., 2001). Globally, the "oldest old"—those 85 years and older—comprise the fastest growing segment of the population (National Institute of Aging & U.S. Department of State, 2007). By 2050 the world will experience a squaring off of the population pyramid: Ninety-four percent of the global population will survive to 60 years (United Nations, 2002; Wan, Sengupta, Velkoff, & DeBarros, 2005).

Although adults are generally living longer, gains in life expectancy are not equally enjoyed by all. For example, a study by Ezzati, Friedman, Kulkarni, and Murray (2008), of all counties in U.S. states, plus the District of Columbia, found that life expectancy actually decreased between 1983 and 1999 in almost 1,000 counties, primarily in rural and low-income areas; within those counties, women experienced the greatest increase in mortality rates (Ezzati et al., 2008).

Even among adults who are living longer, whether *healthy life expectancy*—defined by the World Health Organization (2002) as expected years free of illness, disease, or disability—is increasing remains unclear. In 2005, 42 percent of people 65 years and older reported they had at least one functional limitation, with women reporting higher levels of functional limitations than men (Federal Interagency Forum on Aging-Related Statistics, 2008). Although this number constituted a 7 percent decline from 1992, the overall levels of functional limitation among older adults remained fairly steady between 1997 and 2005. Moreover, percentages of disability increase with age. In 1997, 30.0 percent of people 65 years to 74 years of age reported an activity limitation, whereas 50.2 percent of those 75 years and older reported a limitation. Seven years later, 25.5 percent of the younger group and 43.9 percent of the older cohort reported any disability (Centers for Disease Control and Prevention, 2006).

Income security remains another primary concern for many older adults in the United States. The Social Security Act of 1935 (P.L. 74-271) moved a substantial portion of older adults out of poverty, providing a permanent, inflation-protected benefit (Social Security Administration, 2003). Without the Social Security program, the poverty rate among older adults would increase to more than half (National Committee to Preserve Social Security and Medicare, 2008b).

Even with the safety net of social security, almost one in 10 adults age 65 and older lives in poverty (U.S. Census Bureau, 2007b); poverty rates are even higher for older adults who are black, Latino, American Indian, or Alaska Native (U.S. Census Bureau, 2007a, 2007b). Older women, on average, are nearly twice as likely as men to live in poverty (Administration on Aging, 2008); poverty rates among older black and Latina women are especially high (U.S. Census Bureau, 2005). Kinship care also increases the risk of poverty for both women and men: Nineteen percent of the 2.4 million grandparents raising grandchildren who live with them—of which 29 percent are 60 years and older—live in poverty (AARP Foundation et al., 2007).

Aging frequently presents other serious challenges to older women, who comprise almost 60 percent of the population age 65 years and older. Older women constitute about 75 percent of the nursing home population age 65 and older; are more than four times as likely as men to be widowed; and are more than twice as likely to live alone (Administration on Aging, 2006). Because adult women, as a whole, still comprise the majority (61 percent) of unpaid caregivers in the United States (National Alliance for Caregiving & AARP, 2004), they disproportionately experience the financial, physical, and emotional consequences of caregiving as they age.

The growing importance of gerontological social work manifests in increased foundation investments in gerontological social work education, training, and research. In its 2008 report on the future of the professional health care workforce for older adults, the Institute of Medicine (IOM) affirmed both the increasing need for gerontological social work and the profession's initiatives to address that shortage. Social workers are well positioned to support and advocate for older adults and their caregivers.

ISSUE STATEMENT

Health and Behavioral Health Care

Social workers interact with older adults across the continuum of health and behavioral health care. Chronic illness and functional disability severely affect the health and quality of life of older people. Access to health promotion activities and disease prevention services throughout a person's life span can prevent functional limitations and is essential to healthy aging (United Nations, 2003). The ability to participate actively in, and advocate for, one's own health care is key to health promotion and especially important for older adults, the majority of whom have multiple chronic conditions (Vogeli et al., 2007).

Though frequently overlooked by health care providers and older adults alike, behavioral health promotion and treatment are also crucial to the well-being of older people. Depression is the most common mental health condition among older adults (Administration on Aging, 2004). The suicide rate for adults 65 years and older, especially white men, remains the highest for any age cohort (Adamek & Slater, 2006; Centers for Disease Control and Prevention, 2007). The Substance Abuse and Mental Health Services Administration (SAMHSA) considers substance abuse—particularly the use of alcohol and prescription drugs among older adults—an invisible epidemic and one of the fastest growing health problems in the United States (SAMHSA, 1998). Gambling addiction is also growing among older adults (Administration on Aging, 2007). The Medicare Improvements for Patients and Providers Act of 2008 (P.L. 110-275) eliminates, over a six-year period, the discriminatory co-payment for outpatient mental health services. This legislation, long sought by NASW, eliminates a severe obstacle to mental health diagnosis and treatment for older adults.

The growing need for long-term services and supports presents another challenge to older adults' well-being and quality of life. The Centers for Medicare and Medicaid Services (2007) estimated that 12 million people will need long-term care services by 2020. Medicare, Medicaid, and other insurance systems have not adequately addressed the need for home, community-based, and nursing home care for older people and their caregivers, and will continue to be challenged to meet this burgeoning need.

Housing

Housing that is compatible with the abilities and needs of older people promotes positive health outcomes and well-being. Government funding for assistive technology and home repair, modification, and redesign, combined with coordinated health and social service programs, can help people age in place, thereby preventing unnecessary and unwanted institutionalization (Cox, 2005). Moreover, an increasing number of housing options are available or under development to meet the needs of older adults in the community and in congregate settings. These include naturally occurring retirement communities (NORCs), shared housing, independent and assisted-living residences, and continuing care retirement communities (Cox; Gonyea, 2006). This continuum of options, if truly affordable and accessible, can enable older adults to live independently as long as possible in their communities based on individual preferences (Gonyea). Within nursing facilities and other long-term care sectors, the culture change movement—of which the Green House Project is one example (Rabig, Thomas, Kane, Cutler, & McAlilly, 2006)—strives to create a social model of care centered on the strengths and preferences of individual residents (Krugh, 2003).

Economic Security, Work, and Retirement

Public policy, employer practices, and societal attitudes affect both employment and retirement opportunities and, subsequently, economic security for older adults (Hudson & Gonyea, 2007). Many older people want or need to continue working beyond the traditional retirement age, at least on a part-time basis; employer bias and social security income restric-

tions limit their participation and promotion in the workforce, however. At the same time, efforts to privatize social security—which constitutes over half the retirement income for two-thirds of older adults and the sole source of income for at least 20 percent (Social Security Administration, 2003)—persist (National Committee to Preserve Social Security and Medicare, 2008a).

Whether their contributions to society are paid or unpaid, older adults committed to civic engagement increasingly serve as vital resources to their communities and simultaneously experience enhanced well-being as a result of their efforts. Growing recognition of the individual and societal benefits of older adults' volunteerism, lifelong learning, and political advocacy is transforming the notion of old age and retirement as a period of disengagement (Hinterlong & Williamson, 2006).

Caregiving

Caregiving for family and friends—including physical care, financial assistance, and emotional support—is a major intergenerational role for adults of all ages and has become increasingly common for older adults in later life (Montgomery, Rowe, & Kosloski, 2007). Older adults, especially older women, frequently serve as the primary caregivers for aging parents, aging children with disabilities, adult relatives living with HIV/AIDS, the children of those relatives, and the children of incarcerated relatives (Hooyman, 1999; McCallion & Kolomer, 2003; Poindexter & Boyer, 2003). The pressures of caregiving affect the quality of life of older adults, who often struggle to care for themselves while caring for others (Kropf & Yoon, 2006; Roberts, Allen, & Blieszer, 1999). Although the National Family Caregiver Support Program and other programs provide valuable assistance, many older adults provide care at great cost to their own physical, emotional, and financial well-being.

Elder Abuse and Mistreatment

Mistreatment of older adults includes physical, sexual, and emotional or psychological abuse (National Center on Elder Abuse, 2007;

United Nations, 2003); neglect, abandonment, and self-neglect; and financial or material exploitation (National Center on Elder Abuse, 2007). Early studies suggested that elder mistreatment by family caregivers was due to caregiver stress (Steinmetz, 1988); however, later studies have suggested abuser characteristics are more likely to be predictors of abuse (Brownell, Berman, & Salamone, 1999; Reis, 2000).

National efforts to address elder abuse and mistreatment include public education, passage of reporting laws, development of intervention strategies and models (notably interdisciplinary teams), and criminal prosecution of abuses that rise to the level of a crime (Tomita, 2006).

Diversity

Commitment to cultural competence underlies gerontological social work and reflects the core values of both NASW and the Council on Social Work Education (Chadiha, 2006).

Policies and programs frequently do not reflect the cultures and languages of either older adults with a migration background (such as Asians and Latinos) or indigenous older people; consequently, these groups may underuse or fail to benefit from needed services (Barusch, 2006; Min & Moon, 2006). Black older adults, who represent diverse cultures and interests (Chadiha, Brown, & Aranda, 2006), also experience disparities in service access, usage, and outcomes (see, for example, Barton Smith et al., 2007).

Gerontological social work practice reflects growing sensitivity to and knowledge about spirituality and religion (Murdock, 2005). Similarly, social work literature increasingly incorporates the experiences, strengths, and needs of lesbian, gay, bisexual, and transgender older adults and their caregivers (Butler, 2004; Coon, 2007; Hunter, 2005; Schope, 2005).

Ethical Issues

Advances in medical treatment have increased the ability to sustain life, bringing to the forefront ethical concerns regarding quality of life, cultural values, and death with dignity (Galambos, 1998). Questions of self-determination, end-of-life autonomy, and competency have gained increasing prominence among geronto-logical social workers. Complex issues of autonomy and protection arise in social work practice with older adults receiving protective and guardianship services (Brownell, 2006; Crampton, 2004; Kosberg, Rothman, & Dunlop, 2006; Linzer, 2004).

Professional Training

The social work profession, with its strengths-based, person-in-environment perspective, enhances older adults' quality of life in unique ways. The National Institute on Aging (as cited in IOM, 2008) estimated in 1987 that between 60,000 and 70,000 social workers would be needed by 2010 to provide services to the aging population. Since that time, the profession has undertaken multiple initiatives to promote education, training, and competence in gerontological social work. Nonetheless, a national workforce study conducted by the National Association of Social Workers (Whitaker, Weismiller, & Clark, 2006) found that the social work profession faces significant obstacles in recruiting new social workers to serve older adults, and that training of additional gerontological social workers is needed—a conclusion affirmed by IOM's Committee on the Future Health Care Workforce for Older Americans (2008).

POLICY STATEMENT

NASW supports the following policy principles that promote the well-being of all older adults:

■ continued development and promotion of gerontological social work content and practicum opportunities at the bachelor's, master's, and doctoral levels; expansion and promotion of continuing education, competencies, frameworks, and credentialing in gerontological social work.

■ promotion of optimal physical, mental, emotional, social, spiritual, and functional well-being of people as they age.

■ advancement of policies, programs, and professional behavior that promote self-advocacy, lifelong learning, civic engagement, and intergenerational compatibility.

- advocacy for the preservation and integrity of social security; expansion of public, private, and commercial systems of economic security for older adults, with special attention to the needs of older women.

- promotion of wellness, prevention, early intervention, and outreach services in health, behavioral health, and social service programs for older adults and their caregivers.

- advocacy for a comprehensive health care system (including prescription drug coverage) for all older adults, regardless of ability to pay.

- advocacy for parity in reimbursement for behavioral health services; support for policies and programs that address depression and substance abuse and reduce the incidence of suicide among older adults.

- advocacy for a comprehensive and affordable system of long-term services and supports that enables older adults to maintain maximal independence in the setting of their choice.

- expanded recognition of and reimbursement for the social work role in meeting the biopsychosocial needs of older people and their caregivers, including advance care planning and comprehensive care management.

- elimination of biases and policies that contribute to poverty, unnecessary nursing home placements, employment discrimination, and health disparities among older adults.

- recognition of and respect for the role and expertise of caregivers; continued development and funding of psychosocial and financial support programs for caregivers, including respite services.

- strengthening of government oversight, requirements, and funding for the protection of vulnerable older people in the home, in communities, and in institutions; passage of a federal elder justice act and federal funding for state-based programs to prevent and address elder mistreatment.

- expansion of policies and programs that address the transportation, housing, and service access needs of older people in urban, suburban, rural, and frontier areas.

- support for programs that enable older adults to become formal or informal care providers for children, including financial support and legal guardianship.

- participation of older adults and caregivers in the design, implementation, and evaluation of programs, policies, and research related to aging; continued intergenerational exchanges between new and experienced or retired social workers within NASW.

- promotion of policies that support death with dignity.

- support for additional governmental and foundation funding for research, professional publications, and communication of best practices in gerontological social work; continued development and use of gerontological evidence-based assessments and interventions.

REFERENCES

AARP Foundation, The Brookdale Foundation Group, Casey Family Programs, Child Welfare League of America, Children's Defense Fund, & Generations United. (2007). *Grand-Facts: A state fact sheet for grandparents and other relatives raising children.* Retrieved July 2, 2008, from http://www.grandfactsheets.org/doc/National%202007%20New%20Template.pdf

Adamek, M. E., & Slater, G. Y. (2006). Older adults at risk of suicide. In B. Berkman & S. D'Ambruoso (Eds.), *Handbook of social work in health and aging* (pp. 149–161). New York: Oxford University Press.

Administration on Aging. (2004). *Promoting healthy lifestyles: Mental health.* Retrieved April 21, 2008, from http://www.aoa.gov/eldfam/Healthy_Lifestyles/Mental_Health/Mental_Health.asp

Administration on Aging. (2006). *A profile of older Americans: 2006.* Washington, DC: U.S. Department of Health and Human Services. Retrieved July 21, 2007, from http://www.aoa.gov/prof/Statistics/profile/2006/2006profile.pdf

Administration on Aging. (2007). *Gambling and older adults.* Retrieved April 18, 2008, from http://www.aoa.gov/prof/notes/Docs/Gambling_Older_Adults.pdf

Administration on Aging. (2008). *Snapshot: A statistical profile of older Americans aged 65+*. Retrieved May 1, 2008, from www.aoa.gov/press/fact/pdf/ss_stat_profile.pdf

Barton Smith, D., Feng, Z., Fennel, M. L., Zinn, J. S., & Mor, V. (2007). Separate and unequal: Racial segregation and disparities in quality across U.S. nursing homes. *Health Affairs, 26*, 1448–1458.

Barusch, A. (2006). Native American elders: Unique histories and special needs. In B. Berkman & S. D'Ambruoso (Eds.), *Handbook of social work in health and aging* (pp. 293–300). New York: Oxford University Press.

Brownell, P. (2006). Departments of public welfare or social services. In B. Berkman & S. D'Ambruoso (Eds.), *Handbook of social work in health and aging* (pp. 435–443). New York: Oxford University Press.

Brownell, P., Berman, J., & Salamone, A. (1999). Mental health and criminal justice issues among perpetrators of elder abuse. *Journal of Elder Abuse and Neglect, 11*(4), 81–94.

Butler, S. S. (2004). Gay, lesbian, bisexual, and transgender (GLBT) elders: The challenges and resilience of this marginalized group. *Journal of Human Behavior in the Social Environment, 9*(4), 25–44.

Centers for Disease Control and Prevention. (2006). *Health with chartbook on trends in the health of Americans*. Hyattsville, MD: National Center for Health Statistics. Retrieved July 21, 2007, from http://www.cdc.gov/nchs/data/hus/hus06.pdf

Centers for Disease Control and Prevention. (2007, Summer). *Suicide: Facts at a glance*. Retrieved April 16, 2008, from http://www.cdc.gov/ncipc/dvp/Suicide/SuicideDataSheet.pdf

Centers for Medicare and Medicaid Services. (2007). *Long term care*. Retrieved April 24, 2008, from http://www.medicare.gov/LongTermCare/Static/Home.asp

Chadiha, L. A. (2006). Section IV: Cultural diversity and social work practice with older adults—Overview. In B. Berkman & S. D'Ambruoso (Eds.), *Handbook of social work in health and aging* (pp. 245–246). New York: Oxford University Press.

Chadiha, L. A., Brown, E., & Aranda, M. P. (2006). Older African Americans and other black populations. In B. Berkman & S. D'Ambruoso (Eds.), *Handbook of social work in health and aging* (pp. 247–256). New York: Oxford University Press.

Coon, D. W. (2007). Exploring interventions for LGBT caregivers: Issues and examples. *Journal of Gay and Lesbian Social Services, 18*(3/4), 109–128.

Cox, C. B. (2005). *Community care for an aging society: Issues, policies, and services*. New York: Springer.

Crampton, A. (2004). The importance of adult guardianship for social work. *Journal of Gerontological Social Work, 43*(2/3), 117–129.

Ezzati, M., Friedman, A. B., Kulkarni, S. C., & Murray, C. J. L. (2008, April). The reversal of fortunes: Trends in county mortality and cross-county mortality disparities in the United States. *PLoS Medicine, 5*(4). Retrieved April 23, 2008, from http://medicine.plosjournals.org/perlserv/?request=get-document&doi=10.1371%2Fjournal.pmed.0050066

Federal Interagency Forum on Aging-Related Statistics. (2008). *Older Americans 2008: Key indicators of well-being*. Washington, DC: U.S. Government Printing Office.

Galambos, C. (1998). Preserving end-of-life autonomy: The Patient Self-Determination Act and the Uniform Health Care Decisions Act. *Health & Social Work, 23*, 275–281.

Gonyea, J. G. (2006). Housing, health, and quality of life. In B. Berkman & S. D'Ambruoso (Eds.), *Handbook of social work in health and aging* (pp. 559–567). New York: Oxford University Press.

Hinterlong, J. E., & Williamson, A. (2006). The effects of civic engagement of current and future cohorts of older adults. *Generations, 30*(4), 10–17.

Hooyman, N. (1999). Research on older women: Where is feminism? *Gerontologist, 39*, 115–118.

Hudson, R. B., & Gonyea, J. G. (2007). The evolving role of public policy in promoting work and retirement. *Generations, 31*(1), 68–75.

Hunter, S. (2005). *Midlife and older LGBT adults: Knowledge and affirmative practice for the social services*. New York: Haworth Press, Inc.

Institute of Medicine (IOM). (2008). *Retooling for an aging America: Building the health care workforce*. Washington, DC: National Academies Press.

Kosberg, J. I., Rothman, M. B., & Dunlop, B. D. (2006). Advocacy and protection of older adults. In B. Berkman & S. D'Ambruoso (Eds.), *Handbook of social work in health and aging* (pp. 551–558). New York: Oxford University Press.

Kropf, N. P., & Yoon, E. (2006). Grandparents raising grandchildren: Who are they? In B. Berkman & S. D'Ambruoso (Eds.), *Handbook of social work in health and aging* (pp. 355–362). New York: Oxford University Press.

Krugh, C. (2003, May). De-institutionalizing an institutionalized system. *Aging Section Connection*. Washington, DC: National Association of Social Workers.

Linzer, N. (2004). An ethical dilemma in elder abuse. *Journal of Gerontological Social Work, 43*(2/3), 165–173.

McCallion, P., & Kolomer, S. R. (2003). Aging persons with developmental disabilities and their caregivers. In L. K. Harootyan & B. Berkman (Eds.), *Social work and health care in an aging society: Education, policy, practice, and research* (pp. 201–225). New York: Springer.

Min, J. W., & Moon, A. (2006). Older Asian Americans. In B. Berkman & S. D'Ambruoso (Eds.), *Handbook of social work in health and aging* (pp. 257–271). New York: Oxford University Press.

Montgomery, R. J., Rowe, J. M., & Kosloski, K. (2007). Family caregiving. In J. A. Blackburn & C. N. Dulmus (Eds.), *Handbook of gerontology: Evidence-based approaches to theory, practice, and policy* (pp. 426–454). Hoboken, NJ: John Wiley & Sons.

Murdock, V. (2005). Guided by ethics: Religion and spirituality in gerontological social work practice. *Journal of Gerontological Social Work, 45*(1/2), 131–154.

National Alliance for Caregiving & AARP. (2004). *Caregiving in the U.S.* Retrieved July 2, 2008, from http://www.caregiving.org/data/04finalreport.pdf

National Center on Elder Abuse. (2007). *Major types of elder abuse*. Retrieved February 25, 2008, from http://www.ncea.aoa.gov/NCEA root/Main_Site/FAQ/Basics/Types_Of_Abuse.aspx

National Committee to Preserve Social Security and Medicare. (2008a). *Myths and realities about Social Security and privatization*. Retrieved April 22, 2008, from http://www.ncpssm.org/news/archive/myths/

National Committee to Preserve Social Security and Medicare. (2008b). *Social Security primer: History of the Social Security program*. Retrieved May 1, 2008, from http://www.ncpssm.org/ss_primer/

National Institute on Aging (National Institutes of Health, U.S. Department of Health and Human Services) and U.S. Department State. (2007). *Why population aging matters: A global perspective* (DHHS Publication No. 07-6134). Bethesda, MD: Author.

Poindexter, C. C., & Boyer, N. C. (2003). Strains and gains of grandmothers raising grandchildren in the HIV epidemic. In L. K. Harootyan & B. Berkman (Eds.), *Social work and health care in an aging society: Education, policy, practice, and research* (pp. 227–244). New York: Springer.

Rabig, J., Thomas, W., Kane, R. A., Cutler, L. J., & McAlilly, S. (2006). Radical redesign of nursing homes: Applying the Green House concept in Tupelo, Mississippi. *Gerontologist, 46*, 533–539.

Reis, M. (2000). The IOA screen: An abuse-alert measure that dispels myths. *Generations, 24*(11), 13–16.

Roberts, K. A., Allen, K. R., & Blieszer, R. (1999). Older women and their children and grandchildren: A feminist perspective on family relationships. In J. D. Garner (Ed.), *Fundamentals of feminist gerontology* (pp. 67–84). Binghamton, NY: Haworth Press.

Schope, R. D. (2005). Who's afraid of growing old? Gay and lesbian perceptions of aging. *Journal of Gerontological Social Work, 45*(4), 23–39.

Social Work Leadership Institute. (2007). *Looking for a long-term relationship: Integrating primary and long-term care delivery for older adults*. New York: New York Academy of Medicine.

Social Security Administration. (2003). *Income of the aged chartbook, 2001*. Retrieved May 1,

2008, from http://www.ssa.gov/policy/docs/chartbooks/income_aged/2001/

Steinmetz, S. (1988). *Duty bound: Elder abuse and family care.* Newbury Park, CA: Sage Publications.

Substance Abuse and Mental Health Services Administration. (1998). *TIP 26: Substance abuse among older adults* (DHHS Publication No. [SMA] 98-3179). Retrieved April 18, 2008, from http://ncadi.samhsa.gov/govpubs/BKD250/26d.aspx

Tomita, S. (2006). Mistreated and neglected elders. In B. Berkman & S. D'Ambruoso (Eds.), *Handbook of social work in health and aging* (pp. 219–230). New York: Oxford University Press.

United Nations. (2002). *World population ageing 1950–2050.* New York: UN Department of Economic and Social Affairs, Population Division.

United Nations. (2003). *Political declaration and Madrid international plan of action on ageing.* New York: UN Department of Public Information.

U.S. Census Bureau. (2001). *Census 2000 Summary File 1 (SF1) 100-Percent Data, Table PCT12.* Retrieved May 13, 2008, from http://factfinder.census.gov/servlet/DTTable?_bm=y&-geo_id=01000US&-ds_name=DEC_2000_SF1_U&-_lang=en&-_caller=geoselect&-state=dt&-format=&-mt_name=DEC_2000_SF1_U_PCT012

U.S. Census Bureau. (2005). *65+ in the United States: 2005.* Retrieved May 1, 2008, from http://www.census.gov/prod/2006pubs/p23–209.pdf

U.S. Census Bureau. (2007a). *The American community—American Indians and Alaska Natives: 2004.* Retrieved May 1, 2008, from http://www.census.gov/prod/2007pubs/acs-07.pdf

U.S. Census Bureau. (2007b). *Income, poverty, and health insurance coverage in the United States: 2006.* Retrieved May 1, 2008, from http://www.census.gov/prod/2007pubs/p60–233.pdf

U.S. Census Bureau. (n.d.). *General characteristics: Table 37—Age of the population of continental United States and of the population abroad, by sex: 1950.* Retrieved July 21, 2007, from http://www2.census.gov/prod2/decennial/documents/21983999v2p1ch3.pdf

Vogeli, C., Shields, A. E., Lee, T. A., Gibson, T. B., Marder, W. D., Weiss, K. B., & Blumenthal, D. (2007, December). Multiple chronic conditions: Prevalence, health consequences, and implications for quality, care management, and costs [Electronic version]. *Journal of General Internal Medicine, 22*(Suppl. 3), 391–395.

Wan, H., Sengupta, M., Velkoff, V. A., & DeBarros, K. A. (2005). *U.S. Census Bureau current population reports* (P23–209). Washington, DC: U.S. Government Printing Office.

Whitaker, T., Weismiller, T., & Clark, E. (2006). *Assuring the sufficiency of a frontline workforce: A national study of licensed social workers. Special Report: Social work services for older adults.* Washington, DC: National Association of Social Workers.

World Health Organization. (2002). *Healthy life expectancy (HALE) at birth (years).* Retrieved March 13, 2008, from http://www.who.int/whosis/indicators/2007HALE0/en/index.html

Policy statement approved by the NASW Delegate Assembly, August 2008. This policy statement supersedes the policy statement on Senior Health, Safety, and Vitality approved by the Delegate Assembly in 1999 and referred by the 2005 Delegate Assembly to the 2008 Delegate Assembly for revision, and the policy statement on Aging approved by the Delegate Assembly in 1990 and 1977. For further information, contact the National Association of Social Workers, 750 First Street, NE, Suite 700, Washington, DC 20002-4241. Telephone: 202-408-8600 or 800-638-8799; e-mail: press@naswdc.org

Affirmative Action

BACKGROUND

NASW's broad-based commitment to affirmative action incorporates diverse groups who have been historically or are currently oppressed, underserved and underrepresented, including people of color; people with disabilities; people who are gay, lesbian, bisexual, or transgendered; women; older people, and people who are disadvantaged or oppressed because of life circumstances. This list in no way, however, reflects all the groups who have been historically and are currently oppressed.

Mirroring society at large, NASW members have experienced a struggle regarding the support and acceptance of affirmative action, especially when we look at nominations and elections. Some members of the association believe that affirmative action has been successfully accomplished, and to this end, there is no need to continue addressing this issue. Other members, who are often in support of such inclusion policies, are still frustrated by the challenging process of meeting affirmative action guidelines.

At the federal government level, affirmative action originated in the 1930s. Affirmative action was not originally a civil rights effort. The 1935 National Labor Relations Act used the term "affirmative action" in a different context: ". . . an employer who was found to be discriminating against union members or union organizers would have to stop discriminating, and also take affirmative action to place those victims where they would have been without the discrimination" (Skrentny, p. 6).

President Roosevelt, responding to pressure from the prominent African American leader, A. Phillip Randolph, president of the Brotherhood of Sleeping Car Porters, as well the National Association for the Advancement of Colored People, issued Executive Order No. 8802 in June 1941 with the intent of fostering equal employment opportunities. That order created the Fair Employment Practices Commission to promote full participation in federal defense programs by all people regardless of race, creed, color, or national origin (Biermann, 2004). Since then, each president has continued some form of equal employment effort.

Affirmative action became a more widely used concept in the 1960s. Title VII of the Civil Rights Act of 1964 (P.L. 88-352) requires both public and private employers in traditionally segregated job categories to support the establishment of voluntary affirmative action plans. This law gives the courts the power to mandate affirmative action in cases of willful and intentional acts to deny equal opportunities. It also requires that the plans be flexible in application and temporary in duration. Employment issues have been further addressed through legislation, court interpretations, and additional executive orders. Notably, Presidents Kennedy and Johnson issued Executive Order No. 10925 (1961) and Executive Order No. 11246 (1965) respectively requiring government contractors to take affirmative action to ensure nondiscrimination and administratively strengthening compliance regulations through the creation of the Office of Federal Contract Compliance Programs (OFCCP) under the Department of Labor (Biermann, 2004). Presidents Nixon, Ford, and Carter continued enforcement of Executive Order No. 11246 and made significant changes with increased staff. The order specifically prohibits discrimination against workers on the basis of race, color, religion, sex, or national origin by government contractors receiving $10,000 or more in federal funds. Employers with 50 or more employees and who receive $50,000 or more in federal funds must have affirmative action plans, which are monitored by the OFCCP. The regulations implementing the order are found in 41 C.F.R. Chapter 60.

With Executive Order No. 12086 (1978), Carter consolidated enforcement of federal affirmative programs. Presidents Reagan, Bush, Clinton, and George W. Bush have continued enforcement of Executive Order No. 11246, but staff and budgets have been cut with each successive administration (Biermann).

Employment rules governing federal contractors and the Small Business Administration's Minority Enterprise Program have had some of the broadest impacts of any federal affirmative action program (Savage, 1995). An OFCCP study of 77,000 companies employing some 20 million people showed that minority employment increased by 20 percent and female employment by 15 percent after the implementation of affirmative action plans (National Council of La Raza, 1995). Some affirmative action programs in federal contracting have made initial attempts to resolve historic barriers toward advancement.

Executive Order No. 11063, issued in 1963 by President Kennedy addressed affirmative action in housing; it acknowledged that discriminatory practices in housing produce other forms of discrimination and segregation. The order directed all federal agencies to prevent discrimination based on race, color, creed, or national origin in the disposition of property, including sales, leasing, or rental, and in the lending practices of institutions with moneys insured or guaranteed by the federal government. The Fair Housing Act of 1968 (P.L. 90-284) and the Fair Housing Act Amendments of 1988 (P.L. 100-430) addressed housing discrimination and provided a basis for affirmative action policies in housing. The Housing and Community Development Act of 1974 (P L. 93-383), amended in 1981 (P.L. 97-35), required affirmative efforts by states and localities receiving community development block grants to strengthen fair housing practices. In January 1994, President Clinton issued Executive Order No. 12892, which retained the mandate to ensure fair housing and expanded President Kennedy's Executive Order No. 11063 to provide protection against discrimination in programs of federal insurance or guaranty to people with disabilities and to families with children.

Supreme Court cases *Grutter v. Bollinger* and *Gratz v. Bollinger*, decided in 2003, addressed affirmative action programs in university admissions, but their impact reaches beyond the educational arena. In *Grutter v. Bollinger*, the Supreme Court stated that race could be used as one factor for the University of Michigan's admissions, but in *Gratz v. Bollinger*, the Court indicated that points given to prospective students based solely on race were unconstitutional because this process violated the Equal Protection Clause. NASW participated in *amicus curiae* briefs supporting the University of Michigan's affirmative action principles.

NASW's rationale and position on affirmative action are well articulated in President Johnson's June 1965 speech at Howard University's commencement ceremony.

> Freedom is the right to share, share fully and equally, in American society—to vote, to hold a job, to enter a public place, to go to school. It is the right to be treated in every part of our national life as a person equal in dignity and promise to all others.
>
> But freedom is not enough. You do not wipe away the scars of centuries by saying: Now you are free to go where you want, and do as you desire, and choose the leaders you please.
>
> You do not take a person who, for years, has been hobbled by chains and liberate him, bring him up to the starting line of a race and then say, "You are free to compete with all the others," and still justly believe that you have been completely fair.
>
> Thus it is not enough just to open the gates of opportunity. All our citizens must have the ability to walk through those gates.
>
> This is the next and more profound stage of the battle for civil rights. We seek not just freedom but opportunity. We seek not just legal equity but human ability, not just equality as a right and a theory but equality as a fact and equality as a result. (Curry, 1996, pp. 17–18)

ISSUE STATEMENT

Despite equal protections that are supposed to be enforced under the U.S. Constitution, and regardless of laws and rhetoric, equal rights and just treatment have not been achieved in the United States. American history is filled with many examples of individual, organizational, institutional, and societal discrimination and disparities that adversely affected whole groups of people on the basis of their ancestral heritage, culture, ethnicity, skin color, primary language, age, class, gender, disability, sexual orientation, religion, spirituality, and other parts of their identity.

Persistent and ongoing discrimination and oppression early in our history has left an institutional base for inequality, and the residue continues to this day. Intended and unintended forms of discrimination abound, and without attention and corrective action, discrimination and the inequities that result from discrimination will continue. Affirmative action is one tool that our society has instituted to acknowledge past and current wrongs and to rectify actions.

Affirmative action is consistent with the social work profession's mission, which "is to enhance human well-being and help meet the basic human needs of all people, with particular attention to the needs and empowerment of people who are vulnerable, oppressed, and living in poverty. . . . Fundamental to social work is attention to the environmental forces that create, contribute to, and address problems in living."(NASW, 2000, p. 1)

NASW's *Code of Ethics* (2000) affirms the value of social justice:

> Social workers' social change efforts are focused primarily on issues of poverty, unemployment, discrimination, and other forms of social injustice. These activities seek to promote sensitivity to and knowledge about oppression and cultural and ethnic diversity. Social workers strive to ensure access to needed information, services, and resources; equality of opportunity; and meaningful participation in decision making for all people. (p. 5)

Opening access; promoting inclusive policies, programs, and practices; and working for equitable results are affirmative action components. Such focused affirmative action initiatives are needed to promote social work's equality and social justice agendas.

Affirmative action promotes mindfulness and action with regard to diversity. It has provided effective means for forcing changes in entrenched patterns of policy and practice, including those that were discriminatory and unjust. Furthermore, affirmative action programs have encouraged people to face and acknowledge factors related to unequal opportunities and access, including privilege, indifference, insensitivity, bias, and prejudice.

POLICY STATEMENT

Definition of Affirmative Action

NASW's definition of affirmative action is broad and inclusive. It reflects a firm commitment to actions leading to inclusive plans, processes, and results. Affirmative action seeks to address historical discrimination and the effects of such and to achieve substantially greater inclusion of and equity for diverse groups who have been historically or are currently oppressed, underserved, and underrepresented. These groups include people of color; people with disabilities; people who are gay, lesbian, or transgender; women; seniors; and people disadvantaged or oppressed because of life circumstances.

For the purpose of this NASW's policy statement, the following definition of affirmative action applies:

> *Affirmative action* is the mindful and deliberate steps taken to achieve an environment that values, respects, and reflects multicultural diversity. It includes efforts toward and achievements in:

- fair access
- equal opportunity
- just process
- equitable results.

NASW is firmly committed to affirmative action, and will vigorously pursue its development and implementation at all levels (organizational, local, state, and federal). Achieving an environment that values, respects, and reflects multicultural diversity will take deliberate and progressive actions.

Affirmative action is present-state oriented in that it is designed to address what is to transpire now and into the future. A policy cannot undo past wrongs, but it can acknowledge what happened and set into place proactive and preventive actions to ensure that unjust discriminatory practices are not repeated.

Affirmative action has been effective in a broad spectrum of domains, including, but not limited to, employment, education, housing, and government contracting. NASW strongly supports the inclusion of affirmative action principles and implementation of affirmative action programs in all arenas and contexts at all levels, including small groups, organizations, institutions, communities, societies, cities, and states, as well as implementation nationally. NASW supports affirmative action as a viable tool for upholding its ethical code to act to prevent and eliminate discrimination. NASW supports the following principles and actions:

■ Full endorsement of local, state, and federal policies and programs that give all people equal access to resources, services, and opportunities that they require—everyone should be given equal opportunity regardless of age, ancestral heritage, class, color, disability, gender, immigration status, language proficiency, national origin, race, religion, or sexual orientation.

■ Articulating recommendations and advocating for changes in local, state, and federal policies and programs to further open access and promote equality and social justice.

■ Supporting existing local, state, and federal policies and programs that open access and promote equality and social justice.

■ Joining forces with others to support affirmative action and social justice programs and counteract anti-affirmative action efforts or initiatives.

■ Creating, leading, and participating in coalitions for affirmative action and social justice.

■ Generating (or working with others in establishing) tactics and strategies for the passage of policies that strengthen affirmative action, civil rights, equity, and social justice.

■ Writing position statements, court briefs, and other documents in support of affirmative action, civil rights, equity, and social justice.

■ Publishing public information materials in support of affirmative action, civil rights, equity, and social justice agendas.

■ Conducting and supporting research about affirmative action and means to promote equity and social justice.

■ Identifying and supporting people running for public office who are proponents of affirmative action.

■ Being vigilant in upholding and promoting affirmative action and social justice initiatives.

■ Identifying measures to indicate what areas have been successfully or not successfully accomplished.

■ Supporting the development of policies that demonstrate accountability in working to achieve affirmative action in professional social work organizations.

■ Advocating for affirmative action practices within professional social work organizations to devise and implement plans to increase membership diversity reflective of the multicultural population demographics.

REFERENCES

Biermann, L. J. (2004). *Affirmative action basics: History of executive order program.* Denver, CO: National Employment Law Institute.

Civil Rights Act of 1964, Pub. L. No. 88-352, 78 Stat. 241.

Curry, G. E. (Ed.). (1996). *The affirmative action debate.* Reading, MA: Addison-Wesley.

Exec. Order No. 11063, 3 C.F.R., (1959–1963).

Exec. Order No. 12892, 59 C.F.R. 2939, (1994).

Fair Housing Act of 1968, Pub. L. 90-284, 82 Stat. 81.

Fair Housing Act Amendments of 1988, Pub. L. 100-430, 102 Stat. 1619.

Gratz v. Bollinger, 539 U.S. 244 (2003).

Grutter v. Bollinger, 539 U.S. 244 (2003).

Housing and Community Development Act of 1974, Pub. L. 93–383, 88 Stat. 633.

National Association of Social Workers. (2000). *Code of ethics of the National Association of Social Workers.* Washington, DC: Author.

National Council of La Raza. (1995). *Fact sheet on affirmative action and Latinos.* Washington, DC: Author.

Savage, D. (1995, April 2). Plan to boost firms owned by minorities is assailed. *Los Angeles Times,* pp. A14, A19.

Skrentny, J. D. (1996). *The ironies of affirmative action: Politics, culture, and justice in America.* Chicago: University of Chicago Press.

RESOURCES AND SUGGESTED READINGS

Web Sites

Affirmative Action Information Center
This site contains many articles, essays, and position statements related to affirmative action.
http://www.nationalcenter.org/AA.html

American Civil Liberties Union (ACLU)'s Supreme Court page
This section of the ACLU's site provides summaries of U.S. Supreme Court renderings, including discussions of affirmative action.
http://www.aclu.org/Court/CourtMain.cfm

American Association for Affirmative Action (AAAA)
This group addresses a range of issues in support of affirmative action.
http://www.affirmativeaction.org/and see http://www.affirmativeaction.org/resources/

Chronicle of Higher Education
This publication has an archive replete with current articles, books, and other resources on affirmation action.
http://chronicle.com

Coalition to Defend Affirmative Action, Integration, & Immigrant Rights and Fight for Equality By Any Means Necessary (BAMN)

This organization provides activist perspectives and information about student efforts for equity.
http://www.bamn.com/literature/lit-um-case.asp

Cornell University Legal Information Institute
Cornell's LII provides fast references to court cases, including those involving affirmative action.
http://supct.law.cornell.edu/supct/cases/topic.htm

In Motion Magazine
This online publication provides a great deal of diversity and multicultural content, including a dedicated section on affirmative action.
http://inmotionmagazine.com/pr.html

National Organization for Women
NOW offers resources about affirmative action and court cases (some are dated).
http://www.now.org/issues/affirm/

National Public Radio
NPR lists some interesting diverse positions are expressed in articles.
http://www.npr.org/news/specials/michigan/

The Pew Research Center for the People and the Press
A Pew Research Center national study revealed that 63 percent of Americans favor and 29 percent oppose affirmative action programs to overcome past discrimination. This site reports the full results of the survey.
http://people-press.org/reports/display.php3?ReportID=184

Washington Post
The newspaper has archived its affirmative action special report on its Web site.
http://www.washingtonpost.com/wp-dyn/education/specials/policy/affirmativeaction/

Court Cases and Public Laws

Adarand v. Pena, 16 F.3d 1537 (10th Cir. 1994), cert. granted, 115 S. Ct. 41 (1994).

Brown v. Board of Education I, 347 U.S. 483 (1954).

Brown v. Board of Education II, 349 U.S. 294 (1955).

City of Richmond v. J. A. Croson, 488 U.S. 469 (1989).

Civil Rights Act Amendments of 1988, Pub. L. 92-318, Title IX, 86 Stat. 375, 20 U.S.C. §§1681–1688.

Civil Rights Act of 1991, Pub. L. 102–166, 105 Stat. 1071.

Fullilove v. Klutznick, 448 U.S. 448 (1980).

Freedman's Bureau Bill, 13 Stat. 507 (1865).

Local 28, Sheet Metal Workers' International v. Equal Employment Opportunity Commission, 478 U.S. 421 (1986).

Plessy v. Ferguson, 163 U.S. 537 (1896).

Public Employment Works Act of 1977, Pub. L. 95-28, 9 Stat. 116 (codified as amended at 42 U.S.C. §§6701, 6705–6708, 6710 1988 & Supp. V 1993).

Regents of the University of California v. Bakke, 438 U.S. 265 (1978).

Rehabilitation Act of 1973, P.L. 93-112, 87 Stat. 355.

Small Business Investment Act of 1958, P.L. 85-699, 72 Stat. 689.

United States v. Paradise, 480 U.S. 149 (1987).

Books, Journals, Pamphlets, Newspapers, Reports

Anderson, T. H. (2004). *The pursuit of fairness: A history of affirmative action*. New York: Oxford University Press.

Bergmann, B. R. (1996). *In defense of affirmative action*. New York: Basic Books.

Cintron, D. (1995, Fall). Hispanics' housing conditions: Poor participation in federal housing programs. *Fair Housing Report*, p. 12.

Cohen, C., & Sterba, J. P. (2003). *Affirmative action and racial preference: A debate*. New York: Oxford University Press.

Excerpts from Clinton talk on affirmative action. (1995, July 20). *New York Times*, p. A9.

Ezorsky, G. (1991). *Racism and justice: The case for affirmative action*. Ithaca, NY: Cornell University Press.

Fiscus, R. J. (1992). *The constitutional logic of affirmative action*. Durham, NC: Duke University Press.

Graham, H. D. (2003). *Collision course: The strange convergence of affirmative action and immigration policy in America*. New York: Oxford University Press.

Holmes, S. A. (1995, March 19). Past support for affirmative action haunts Republicans. *San Francisco Examiner*, p. A19.

Lemann, N. (1995, June 11). Taking affirmative action apart. *New York Times Magazine*, pp. 36–43, 52, 54, 62, 66.

Mills, N. (Ed.). (1994). *Debating affirmative action: Race, gender, ethnicity, and the politics of inclusion*. New York: Dell.

Myers, S. L., Jr. (1995, July/August). Equity, fairness, and race relations. *Emerge*, pp. 6, 48–52.

National Association for the Advancement of Colored People Legal Defense and Education Fund. (1995). *Fact sheet on discrimination and affirmative action*. Washington, DC: Author.

National Association of Social Workers. (2001). *NASW Standards for Cultural Competence in Social Work Practice*. Washington, DC: Author.

National Organization for Women Legal Defense and Education Fund. (1995). *Legal basics on affirmative action*. New York: Author.

National Women's Law Center. (1995). *Affirmative action and what it means for women*. Washington, DC: Author.

Schrag, P. (1995, April 10). Nixon the quota king. *San Jose Mercury News*, p. 7B.

Scotch, R. K., Schriner, K., & Smith, R. A. (2004). *Americans with disabilities and political participation: A reference handbook*. Santa Barbara, CA: ABC-CLIO.

Steinberg, S. (1995). *Turning back: The retreat from racial justice in American thought and policy*. Boston: Beacon Press.

Stone, J. H. (Ed.). (2004). *Culture and disability: Providing culturally competent services*. Thousand Oaks, CA: Sage Publications.

Supreme Court ruling imperils U.S. programs of racial preference. (1995, June 13). *Wall Street Journal*, pp. A1, A10.

Swain, J., French, S., Barnes, C., & Thomas, C. (Eds.). (2004). *Disabling barriers—enabling environments*. Thousand Oaks, CA: Sage Publications.

U.S. Commission on Civil Rights. (1977). *Statement on affirmative action* (Clearinghouse Publication No. 54). Washington, DC: Author.

U.S. Commission on Civil Rights. (1981). *Affirmative action in the 1980s: Dismantling the process of discrimination* (Clearinghouse Publication No. 70). Washington, DC: Author.

U.S. Commission on Civil Rights. (1995). *The legislative, executive and judicial development* *of affirmative action*. Washington, DC: Office of the General Counsel.

Yzaguirre, R. (1995, June 13). *Statement of Raul Yzaguirre on* Adarand Constructors, Inc. v. Pena [News Release]. Washington, DC: National Council of La Raza.

Policy statement approved by the NASW Delegate Assembly, August 2005. This statement supersedes the statement on Affirmative Action approved by the 1996 Delegate Assembly and referred by the 2002 Delegate Assembly to the 2005 Delegate Assembly for revision. For further information, contact the National Association of Social Workers, 750 First Street, NE, Suite 700, Washington, DC 20002-4241; telephone 202-408-8600; e-mail: press@naswdc.org

Alcohol, Tobacco, and Other Drugs

BACKGROUND

The U.S. government uses a two-pronged approach to address alcohol, tobacco, and other drug (ATOD) problems. One prong focuses on supply, the other on demand.

Supply

Attempts to reduce the supply of illicit substances include interdiction and enforcement of laws that criminalize the sale and possession of certain substances. Other supply-side efforts include regulation of the production and sale of alcohol, tobacco products, prescription drugs, and over-the-counter drugs. The Office of National Drug Control Policy (ONDCP), headed by a cabinet-level official, dubbed the "drug czar," coordinates both the federal government's supply- and demand-side efforts. Some special initiatives, such as the High Intensity Drug Trafficking Area Program, fall under ONDCP.

The federal government spends billions each year to control illicit drug production and distribution in the United States and other countries. Trial judges may use judicial discretion in sentencing opportunities when defendants are found guilty of drug offenses. Whether the offense is major drug (cocaine) distribution or street distribution of less than a gram of marijuana, federal government statutes mandate sentencing of the offender. Many inner-city minority youths, males and female, are imprisoned for lengthy mandatory periods, instead of receiving penalties appropriate for their crimes.

Demand

Federal government attempts to address the demand for illicit drugs were first widely addressed in 1970 with the passage of Comprehensive Drug Abuse Prevention and Control Act (P.L. 91-513), popularly known as the Controlled Substances Act, which expanded the definition of a "drug dependent person" to enable more people to obtain treatment (National Institute on Drug Abuse [NIDA], 2003). That same year, Congress also passed the Comprehensive Alcohol Abuse and Alcoholism Prevention, Treatment, and Rehabilitation Act (P.L. 91-616), establishing the federal National Institute on Alcohol Abuse and Alcoholism (NIAAA). NIAAA along with NIDA, established in 1974, became leaders in the federal fight against substance use on several fronts. The missions of the organizations were to focus on research and education and help establish community-based treatment programs. Today NIAAA and NIDA are part of the National Institutes of Health and maintain a strong research focus.

The Substance Abuse and Mental Health Services Administration (SAMHSA), established in 1992, is another federal entity vitally concerned with reducing ATOD problems through applied research, prevention, and treatment. SAMHSA administers the Substance Abuse Prevention and Treatment Block Grant, which channels money for services to the states. Single state agencies distribute the funds to community- and faith-based programs that provide prevention and treatment services. Many of these programs serve individuals who would otherwise be unable to obtain services because they lack health care coverage. Other federal agencies also have a role in ATOD prevention and treatment, including the Department of Education, which operates and promotes programming to keep schools drug free and provides mental health services to students and their families; and the Department of Veterans Affairs, which operates the country's largest substance use treatment program for veterans.

The federal drug control budget has favored law enforcement and interdiction over prevention and treatment approaches, although treatment funding has increased (ONDCP, 2004). The federal government's policy role is important, but states carry most of the responsibility for ensuring that services are delivered to individuals and families experiencing ATOD problems.

The self-help or mutual help movement also plays a major role in addressing alcohol and other drug problems in the United States. Alcoholics Anonymous (AA), the first 12-Step program, was founded in 1935 and predated many attempts by professionals to assist individuals with alcohol problems. AA has had an important influence on the philosophy of treatment programs in the United States. Narcotics Anonymous began in the 1950s. Al-Anon, a mutual-help group for families and friends of those who have alcohol problems, and Nar-Anon for those with family members and friends who have drug problems also developed through the movement. Other self-help groups have emerged to assist people with alcohol and other drug problems.

Social workers, too, are vital to preventing and treating ATOD problems. Although only 2 percent of NASW members cite ATOD problems as their major practice area ("72 percent work," 2001), ATOD issues are pervasive problems encountered in social work practice. Practitioners address ATOD problems in child welfare, health care, criminal justice, schools, nursing homes, and many other settings. NASW, therefore, must maintain a comprehensive ATOD policy statement.

ISSUE STATEMENT

Prevalence and Consequences of ATOD Problems

Significant numbers of Americans are affected by ATOD problems. In 2002, approximately 22 million people (9.4 percent of the U.S. population age 12 and older) met criteria for substance abuse or dependence (SAMHSA, 2003). Most (14.9 million) met criteria for alcohol use disorders alone, 3.9 million met criteria for drug use disorders alone, and 3.2 million met criteria for both alcohol and drug use disorders.

Alcohol, tobacco, and other drug problems have severe consequences for all members of the family system, especially children (Huang, Cerbone, & Gfroerer, 1998; National Center on Addiction and Substance Abuse [CASA] at Columbia University, 2005). Children affected by parental alcohol and other drug problems in this country are largely overlooked. Approximately one in four American children (19 million) is exposed at some time before age 18 to familial alcohol dependence, alcohol abuse, or both. More than one in 10 children (9.2 million) live with a parent or other adult who uses illicit drugs (CASA; Grant, 2000). Very few children from these families ever receive help for the psychological consequences of growing up under these circumstances.

In the 1970s and 1980s, several comprehensive reviews of empirical findings documented a wide range of problems encountered by children of alcoholics (COAs), such as emotional problems and hyperactivity in childhood, emotional and conduct problems in adolescence, and alcoholism in adulthood (El-Guebaly & Offord, 1977; Russell, Henderson, & Blume, 1985). There is strong consensus in the scientific literature that alcoholism runs in families (Chassin, Jacob, Johnson, Shuckit, & Sher, 1997; Cotton, 1979; Goodwin, 1979), and that male COAs are four to 10 times more likely to develop alcoholism than children whose parents do not have an alcohol problem (Heath, 1995).

Although there have been some indications of decreased incidence and prevalence of ATOD problems among youths, significant prevailing risk factors still exist. In 2003, 28 percent of high school students reported episodic heavy drinking, and 22 percent indicated marijuana use (Grunbaum et al., 2004). Also, among youths ages 12 to 17 in 2000, 9.7 percent had used an illicit drug within a 30-day period before their interview, and nearly 10.7 million adolescents ages 12 to 20 were underage alcohol drinkers.

Among the youths who were reported heavy drinkers in 2000, 65.5 percent of them were also current illicit drug users. Among non-drinkers, only 4.2 percent were current illicit drug users. In addition, 71.5 million Americans age 12 and older reported use of a tobacco product. Among youths who smoked cigarettes, the rate of the past-month illicit drug use was 42.7 percent, compared with 4.6 percent for non-smokers. These facts underpin evidence of alcohol and tobacco being gateways to the use of illicit drugs. More than 40 percent of people who begin drinking alcohol before age 13 will develop alcohol dependence some time in their lives (SAMHSA, 2001). Likewise, the younger people are when they begin smoking cigarettes, the more likely they are to become addicted to nicotine (Centers for Disease Control and Prevention [CDC], 1994). Cigarette smoking is the addictive behavior most likely to become established during adolescence. Several studies have found nicotine to be additive in ways similar to heroin, cocaine, and alcohol (CDC, 1994).

Barriers to Treatment

Most people with alcohol and other drug problems do not receive treatment. Of those who needed treatment for an alcohol problem in 2002, only 8.3 percent received help from a specialty alcohol treatment program (SAMHSA, 2003). Of those who did not get treatment, only 4.5 percent felt they needed care. About 35 percent of the latter group said they tried but were not able to get help; 65 percent did not attempt to obtain treatment. Of the estimated 7.7 million who needed help for a drug problem in 2002, only 18.2 percent received help from a specialty drug treatment program (SAMHSA, 2003). Of those who did not get treatment, only 5.7 percent felt they needed care: 24.4 percent of this group said they tried but were not able to get help; 75.6 percent did not attempt to obtain treatment.

In addition, managed care has taken a toll on the ability to obtain alcohol and drug treatment services through private health plans (Hay Group, 2001). Publicly supported services wax and wane depending on state and local budgets. Thus, people in need do not receive care because they cannot find help, they do not seek treatment, or they do not recognize that they have a problem. They also may be painfully aware of the stigma attached to being an "addict" or "alcoholic" or even being a person who seeks out help, particularly mental health services.

The labels, too, have become a significant obstacle to people seeking resolution. The focus shifts from the problem to the fear of the label and its stigmatizing consequences. "Disease first" language, as opposed to "people first" language, obliterates individual differences and depersonalizes those to whom the label is applied. Such terms as "alcohol abuse," "drug abuse," and "substance abuse" can be perceived as springing from religious and moral conceptions of the roots of severe alcohol and other drug problems. Continued use of these terms with their emotional overtones, may serve only to perpetuate misguided public attitudes about drug-using behavior. To refer to people who are addicted as alcohol, drug, or substance abusers misstates the nature of their condition and calls for their social rejection and punishment.

Although the inclusion of the terms substance abuse and dependence in the DSM-IV has had the positive consequence of allowing these conditions to be recognized as mental disorders deserving of reimbursed treatment, social workers should endeavor to drop such objectifying labels as "substance abuser" and "addict" for more respectful and less stigmatizing people-first language. NASW supports the rejection of "labeling language" and embraces a people-first language. Terminology that is more respectful and less stigmatizing and suggests that if a person's alcohol or drug consumption is creating problems, then the person should do something about it. Such a stance might help to focus on a more concrete and verifiable question of whether alcohol and other drugs are creating problems in a person's life for which he or she might seek help (White, 2001).

In addition, many individuals with ATOD problems have co-occurring disabilities and often encounter increased difficulties in accessing appropriate treatment. In 2002, about 20 percent of adults who met criteria for substance abuse or dependence also had a serious mental illness (SMI) compared with a 7 percent rate of SMI for those without substance abuse and dependence (SAMHSA, 2003). Individuals with co-occurring ATOD problems and SMI may not receive services that are appropriately integrated to meet their needs (DiNitto & Webb, 2005; Mee-Lee, Shulman, Fishman, Gastfriend, & Griffiths, 2001). Many people who have a cognitive or physical disability (for example, intellectual disability, spinal cord injury, traumatic brain injury, or who are deaf, hard-of-hearing, blind, or visually impaired) and a co-occurring ATOD problem also experience substantial difficulties in obtaining treatment that appropriately accommodates their needs, despite requirements of the Americans with Disabilities Act ([ADA], [P.L. 101-336], de Miranda, 1999).

Criminal Justice and Social Welfare

Many people are arrested and incarcerated for alcohol or drug offenses, and many incarcerated individuals have ATOD problems. In 2002 there were an estimated 1.5 million arrests for drug law violations (more than 80 percent were for possession), 1.5 million arrests for driving under the influence, and 573,000 arrests for drunkenness in addition to 654,000 liquor law violations (Dorsey, Zawitz, & Middleton, 2003). Between 1990 and 1999, 61 percent of the growth in the federal prison population was due to drug offenses (U.S. Department of Justice, Bureau of Justice Statistics [BJS], 2001). In 2002, 20 percent of men and 30 percent of women in state prisons were serving time for drug offenses (BJS, 2003). In 1999, 53 percent of the women in state prisons were using alcohol and drugs at the time of the offense for which they were incarcerated, and one in three women had engaged in the crime to obtain money to get drugs (Greenfeld & Snell, 2000). Alcohol and drug treatment in prisons and jails has increased, but many individuals do not get services while incarcerated or after release.

The economic costs of ATOD problems are high. Costs of alcohol problems were estimated at $184.6 billion in 1998, with two-thirds due to losses in current and future earnings (Harwood, 2000). Costs of drug problems in 2000 were estimated at $160.7 billion (69 percent in productivity losses, 22 percent due to criminal justice and social welfare costs, and 9 percent in health care costs) (ONDCP, 2001). Medical costs of smoking are about $75 billion annually and productivity losses are about $80 billion (National Center for Chronic Disease Prevention and Health Promotion, 2004). The greatest toll of ATOD, however, comes in the form of human suffering.

Confounding Issues

There is lack of agreement about how to define, prevent, and treat ATOD problems. Professionals in the ATOD field view alcohol and drug dependence as a brain disease (Leshner, 2001) or a chronic medical illness with treatment compliance and relapse rates similar to other chronic medical illnesses (McLellan, Lewis, O'Brien, & Kleber, 2000). The ADA and other public policies treat ATOD problems differently from other mental and physical illnesses (DiNitto, 2002; McNeece & DiNitto, 2005). Alcohol or drug disorders alone are no longer sufficient to qualify for Supplemental Security Income (SSI) or Social Security Disability Insurance (SSDI). Those who use illicit drugs or are convicted of drug law violations may be denied access to public assistance programs such as Temporary Assistance for Needy Families (TANF), food stamps, publicly sponsored housing, and student loans. People with other chronic illnesses or criminal convictions are not treated in this manner.

Evidence indicates that every $1 spent on alcohol and drug treatment results in about $12 saved in crime, criminal justice, and health care costs (NIDA, 1999). Yet much of the national, state, and local drug control budgets go to law enforcement or interdiction, although there is little to suggest that such efforts reduce alcohol and drug abuse or dependence (McNeece & DiNitto, 2005). In fact, the so-called "war on drugs" has escalated violence in the United States and other countries as "drug lords" compete for the lucrative drug trade and poor people succumb or are forced to produce, transport, or sell drugs to survive.

Congress and state governments are loath to try harm reduction approaches that other countries have adopted to reduce the consequences of ATOD problems. For example, Congress has failed to approve needle exchange, even though the U.S. Department of Health and Human Services (HHS) has recognized that appropriately conducted needle exchange programs can reduce HIV transmission and do not encourage injection drug use (HHS, 1998). Decriminalization of drug use has largely been rejected, although approaches such as drug courts and Proposition 36 in California, which provides treatment instead of jail for certain convictions of nonviolent drug offenses, attempt to divert individuals to treatment in lieu of incarceration.

Furthermore, people of color are often disproportionately affected by ATOD problems and the drug war. African Americans in particular are overrepresented among inmates serving time for drug sentences. In 2001, 57 percent of drug offenders in state prisons were African American (BJS, 2003). Penalties under the Controlled Substances Act are much stiffer for crack cocaine, which can be purchased more cheaply than powdered cocaine. This stratifying of penalties disproportionately affects people who are poor and people of color.

Among male adults and adolescents in 2001, 43 percent of all AIDS cases among African Americans and the same percentage among Hispanic Americans were due to injecting drug use, having sex with men and injecting drugs, or having sex with a heterosexual injecting drug user. Just 18 percent of cases were similar among white men (Centers for Disease Control and Prevention, 2002). In 1997, the alcohol-related cirrhosis death rate for white Hispanic men was 12.6 per 100,000, compared with 7.3 for non-Hispanic African American men and 5.1 for non-Hispanic white men (Stinson, Grant, & Dufour, 2001). Cirrhosis mortality is 2.8 times higher among American Indian men than among non-Hispanic white men and 1.5 times higher among American Indian women than among non-Hispanic white women (Singh & Hoyert, 2000). From 1995 to 1997, across Alaska, Arizona, Colorado, and New York, the rate of fetal alcohol syndrome per 1,000 population for American Indian/Alaska Natives was 3.2 compared with 1.5 for the general population of those states (Miller et al., 2002).

To address and bridge the gap between research and treatment (see Lamb, Greenlick, & McCarty, 1998), NIDA established the Clinical Trials Network to increase knowledge exchange between researchers and practitioners. SAMHSA established Practice Research Collaboratives to increase communication among treatment providers, researchers, policymakers, consumers, and other stakeholders. SAMHSA also funds 13 regional Addiction Technology Transfer Centers (ATTCs) and a national ATTC office to increase practitioners' access to state-of-the-art research and education.

Professional Directives

Social workers also experience ATOD problems, although prevalence rates are not well established (Elpers, 1992; Fewell, King, & Weinstein, 1993; Siebert, 2005). There is no reason to believe that social workers experience rates lower than the general population, and because they perform work that often exposes them to the effects of secondary trauma, there is reason to believe that social workers may be at higher risk (Stamm, 1999). For those in the helping professions, the issue of impairment involves the potential for impinging on patient care in addition to personal consequences. NASW recognizes that social workers have an ethical duty to help colleagues who are experiencing ATOD problems and other physical and emotional impairments (NASW, 2000). Social workers, however, are frequently reluctant to approach a colleague with an ATOD problem (Fewell et al.). A survey of social workers at high risk of ATOD problems showed that only 24 percent sought help for their problems (Siebert). Only a small number of NASW chapters provide assistance to members with ATOD problems.

POLICY STATEMENT

To improve the response to ATOD problems, NASW's position is that

■ Social workers must advocate for an approach to ATOD problems that emphasizes prevention and treatment.

■ Social workers must advocate to eliminate objectifying and stigmatizing language and labels and promote a more respectful, nonstigmatizing strengths-based language.

- The ADA, SSI program, TANF, and other federal, state, and local legislation, policies, and programs must treat ATOD disorders in the same manner as other physical and mental disabilities.

- More efforts are needed to eliminate health disparities that accrue from ATOD problems and discriminatory practices from the criminal justice system.

- Individuals with ATOD problems need access to appropriate treatment. The risk of relapse or continued ATOD use is too great to do otherwise. To accomplish this goal, private and public health care plans need to offer treatment for ATOD problems in parity with other physical and mental health problems. Systems of care should be made available for those lacking insurance coverage, and public and private care should be of equally high quality.

- Providers of ATOD prevention and treatment services need to assess their approaches and use those with demonstrated effectiveness.

- All reasonable avenues to address ATOD problems must be considered, including psychosocial treatments, medications, alternatives to incarceration, and harm-reduction approaches.

- Treatment for individuals with ATOD problems and co-occurring mental, physical, and other disorders must be offered in an integrated manner, and treatment programs must be fully accessible.

- Treatment for ATOD problems must be comprehensive given that patients, clients, and consumers often present with additional problems (health, employment, family, housing, legal, and other problems) that may impede recovery.

- Social workers in all settings need knowledge of ATOD problems and the skills necessary to screen for ATOD problems, to educate at-risk drinkers and tobacco users about the options available for reducing or eliminating consumption, to refer those who need ATOD treatment to appropriate services, and to motivate patients, clients, and consumers to take appropriate action. Social workers also need to be capable of offering family members and friends services or referrals to appropriate services, including mutual-help groups.

- Social workers need to work with other groups and professional organizations to identify and support efforts that are evidence based, grounded in best practices, and improve treatment outcomes.

- Schools of social work need to be encouraged to incorporate more information about the knowledge and skills needed to intervene with ATOD problems in all areas of the curriculum. The training received toward the BSW and MSW degrees needs to be promoted as providing sufficient knowledge for intervening with ATOD problems.

- ATOD prevention and treatment strategies must address the characteristics and needs of individuals with regard to gender, sexual orientation, ethnicity, culture, religion and spiritual beliefs, socioeconomic status, disability, and other factors.

- NASW must assist and encourage chapters to provide services for all social workers who are personally affected by ATOD problems.

REFERENCES

Americans with Disabilities Act of 1990, Pub. L. 101-336, 42 USC 12101 et seq.

Centers for Disease Control and Prevention. (1994, March 11). Preventing tobacco use among young people: A report of the Surgeon General (Executive Summary). *MMWR Recommendations and Reports*, 43(RR-4), 1–10.

Centers for Disease Control and Prevention. (2002). U.S. HIV and AIDS cases reported through December 2001. *HIV/AIDS Surveillance Report*, 13(2). Retrieved May 26, 2004, from http://www.cdc.gov/hiv/stats/hasr1302.htm

Chassin, L., Jacob, T., Johnson, J. L., Shuckit, M. A., & Sher, K. J. (1997). A critical analysis of COA research. *Alcohol, Health & Research World*, 21, 258–264.

Comprehensive Alcohol Abuse and Alcoholism Prevention, Treatment, and Rehabilitation Act of 1970, Pub. L. 91-616, 84 Stat. 1848, 42 U.S.C. 4501 et seq.

Comprehensive Drug Abuse Prevention and Control Act of 1970, Pub. L. 91-513, 84 Stat. 1236, 21 U.S.C. 801 et seq.

Cotton, N. S. (1979). The familial incidence of alcoholism: A review. *Journal of Studies on Alcohol, 40*, 89–116.

de Miranda, J. (1999, May/June). Treatment services offer limited access for people with disabilities. *Counselor, 17*(3), 24–25.

DiNitto, D. M. (2002). War and peace: Social work and the state of chemical dependency treatment in the United States. In S.L.A. Straussner & L. Harrison (Eds.), *International aspects of social work practice in the addictions* (pp. 7–29). New York: Haworth Press.

DiNitto, D. M., & Webb, D. K. (2005). Substance use disorders and co-occurring disabilities. In C. A. McNeece & D. M. DiNitto (Eds.), *Chemical dependency: A systems approach* (3rd ed., pp. 423–483).

Dorsey, T. L., Zawitz, M. W., & Middleton, P. (2003, December). *Drugs and crime facts.* Washington, DC: U.S. Department of Justice, Bureau of Justice Statistics. Retrieved May 26, 2004, from http://www.ojp.usdoj .gov

El-Guebaly, N., & Offord, D. R. (1977). The offspring of alcoholics: A critical review. *American Journal of Psychiatry, 134*, 357–365.

Elpers, K. (1992). *Social work impairment: A statewide survey of the National Association of Social Workers.* Indianapolis: NASW Indiana Chapter.

Fewell, C. H., King, B. L., & Weinstein, D. L. (1993). Alcohol and other drug abuse among social work colleagues and their families: Impact on practice. *Social Work, 38*, 565–570.

Goodwin, D. W. (1979). Alcoholism and heredity: A review and hypothesis. *Archives of General Psychiatry, 36*, 57–61.

Grant, B. F. (2000). Estimates of U.S. children exposed to alcohol abuse and dependence in the family. *American Journal of Public Health, 90*, 112–115.

Greenfeld, L. A., & Snell, T. L. (2000). *Women offenders* [Bureau of Justice Statistics Special Report]. Washington, DC: U.S. Department of Justice, Bureau of Justice Statistics. Retrieved May 26, 2004, from http://www .ojp.usdoj.gov/bjs/abstract/wo.htm

Grunbaum, J. A., Kann, L., Kinchen, S., Ross J., Hawkins J., Lowry, R., Harris, W. A., McManus, T., Chyen, D., & Collins, J. (2004). Youth risk behavior surveillance-United States, 2003. *Morbidity and Mortality Weekly Report, 53*(SS-2): 1-95.

Harwood, H. (2000). *Updating estimates of the economic costs of alcohol abuse in the United States: Estimates, update methods, and data.* Washington, DC: National Institute on Alcohol Abuse and Alcoholism. Retrieved May 24, 2004, from http://www.niaaa.nih .gov/publications/economic-2000/printing .htm#top

Hay Group. (2001). *Employer health care dollars spent on addiction treatment.* Chevy Chase, MD: American Society of Addiction Medicine. Retrieved May 26, 2004, from http:// www.asam.org/pressrel/hay.htm

Heath, A. C. (1995). Genetic influences on drinking behavior in humans. In H. Begleiter & B. Kissin (Eds.), *The genetics of alcoholism* (Vol. I, pp. 82-121). New York: Oxford University Press.

Huang, L. X., Cerbone, F. G., & Gfroerer, J. C. (1998). *Children at risk because of parental substance abuse* [OAS Working Paper]. Rockville, MD: Substance Abuse and Mental Health Services Administration.

Lamb, S., Greenlick, M. R., & McCarty, D. (Eds.). (1998). *Bridging the gap between practice and research: Forging partnerships with community-based drug and alcohol treatment.* Washington, DC: Institute of Medicine, National Academies Press.

Leshner, A. I. (2001, Spring). Addiction is a brain disease. *Issues in Science and Technology.* Retrieved June 4, 2002, from http://www.nap.edu/issues/17.3/leshner .htm

McLellan, A. T., Lewis, D. C., O'Brien, C. P., & Kleber, H. D. (2000). Drug dependence, a chronic medical illness: Implications for treatment, insurance, and outcomes evaluation. *JAMA, 284*, 1689–1695.

McNeece, C. A., & DiNitto, D. M. (2005). *Chemical dependency: A systems approach* (3rd ed.). Boston: Allyn & Bacon.

Mee-Lee, D., Shulman, G. D., Fishman, M., Gastfriend, D. R., & Griffiths, J. H. (Eds.). (2001). *ASAM patient placement criteria for the treatment of substance-related disorders* (2nd ed.-rev., PPC-2R). Chevy Chase, MD: American Society of Addiction Medicine.

Miller, L., Tolliver, R., Druschel, C., Fox, D., Schoellhorn, J., Podvin, D., Merrick, S., Cunniff, C., Meaney, F. J., Pensak, M., Dominique, Y., Hymbaugh, K., Boyle, C., & Baio, J. (2002). Fetal alcohol syndrome-Alaska, Arizona, Colorado, and New York: 1995–1997. *Morbidity and Mortality Weekly Report, 51*(20), 433–435.

National Association of Social Workers. (2000). *Code of ethics of the National Association of Social Workers*. Washington, DC: Author.

National Center for Chronic Disease Prevention and Health Promotion. (2004). *Reducing tobacco use*. Atlanta: Centers for Disease Control and Prevention. Retrieved May 23, 2004, from http://www.cdc.gov/nccdphp/bb_tobacco

National Center on Addiction and Substance Abuse at Columbia University. (2005). *Family matters: Substance abuse and the American family*. New York: Author.

National Institute on Drug Abuse. (1999). *Principles of drug addiction treatment: A research-based guide*. Bethesda, MD: National Institutes of Health.

National Institute on Drug Abuse. (2003, April 11). *Congressional and legislative activities*. Retrieved May 25, 2004, from http://www.drugabuse.gov/about/legislation/Chronology/html

Office of National Drug Control Policy. (2001). *The economic costs of drug abuse in the United States, 1992–1998* (Publication No. NCJ-190636). Washington, DC: Executive Office of the President. Retrieved May 23, 2004, from http://www.whitehousedrugpolicy.gov

Office of National Drug Control Policy. (2004, March). *National drug control strategy, FY 2005 budget summary*. Washington, DC: Executive Office of the President. Retrieved May 25, 2004, from http://www.whitehousedrugpolicy.gov/publications/policy/budgetsum04/index.html

Proposition 36, Substance Abuse and Crime Prevention Act of 2000, California Penal Code 1210 et seq.

72 percent work for private organizations. (2001, January). *NASW News*, p. 8.

Russell, M., Henderson, C., & Blume, S. B. (1985). *Children of alcoholics: A review of the literature.* New York: Children of Alcoholics Foundation.

Siebert, D. C. (2005). Help seeking for AOD misuse among social workers: Patterns, barriers, and implications. *Social Work, 50*, 65–75.

Singh, G. K., & Hoyert, D. L. (2000). Social epidemiology of chronic liver disease and cirrhosis mortality in the United States, 1935–1977: Trends and differentials by ethnicity, socioeconomic status, and alcohol consumption. *Human Biology, 72*, 801–820.

Stamm, B. H. (Ed.). (1999). *Secondary traumatic stress: Self-care issues for clinicians, researchers, & educators* (2nd ed.). Baltimore, MD: Sidran Press.

Stinson, F. S., Grant, B. F., & Dufour, M. C. (2001). The critical dimension of ethnicity in liver cirrhosis mortality statistics. *Alcoholism: Clinical and Experimental Research, 25*, 1181–1187.

Substance Abuse and Mental Health Services Administration, Office of Applied Studies. (2001). *Summary of findings from the 2000 National Household Survey on Drug Abuse*. Rockville, MD: Author.

Substance Abuse and Mental Health Services Administration, Office of Applied Studies. (2003). *Overview of findings from the 2002 National Survey on Drug Use and Health*. Rockville, MD: Author.

U.S. Department of Health and Human Services. (1998, April 20). *Research shows needle exchange programs reduce HIV infections without increasing drug use*. Washington, DC: Author. Retrieved May 28, 2004, from http://www.hhs.gov/news/press/1998pres/980420a.html

U.S. Department of Justice, Bureau of Justice Statistics. (2001). *Prisoners in 2000*. Re-

trieved May 26, 2004, from http://www
.ojp.usdoj.gov/bjs/abstract/p02.htm

U.S. Department of Justice, Bureau of Justice
Statistics. (2003). *Prisoners in 2002*. Retrieved May 26, 2004, from http://www
.ojp.usdoj.gov/bjs/abstract/p00.htm

White, W. L. (2001). *The rhetoric of recovery advocacy: An essay on the power of language*. Peo-
ria, IL: Behavioral Health Management Project. Available at http://www.bhrm.org/
advocacy/rhetoric.pdf

*Policy statement approved by the NASW Delegate Assembly, August 2005. This statement supersedes the statement on Alcohol,
Tobacco, and Other Substance Abuse approved by the Delegate Assembly in 1996 and referred by the 2002 Delegate Assembly to the
2005 Delegate Assembly for revision. For further information, contact the National Association of Social Workers, 750 First Street,
NE, Suite 700, Washington, DC 20002-4241; telephone: 202-408-8600; e-mail press@naswdc.org*

Capital Punishment and the Death Penalty

BACKGROUND

Although more than two-thirds of the countries of the world have abolished the death penalty in law or practice since adoption of the Universal Declaration of Human Rights over 60 years ago, the practice of capital punishment persists in the United States. Although 16 states and the District of Columbia have abolished capital punishment (Death Penalty Information Center [DPIC], 2011), 34 states, the U.S. government, and the U.S. military continue to practice capital punishment.

According to the DPIC (2010a), 46 individuals were executed in the United States in 2010, representing a 12 percent decrease compared with 2009 and a 54 percent decrease since 2000. New death sentences were imposed on 114 individuals in 2010, compared with 234 in 2000.

Two Supreme Court decisions, *Ford v. Wainwright* (1986) and *Atkins v. Virginia* (2002), are believed to be significant factors in these declining numbers. *Ford v. Wainwright* established that it is unconstitutional to impose the death penalty on an individual deemed insane or incompetent to stand trial; that is, unable to understand the legal circumstances and participate in his or her defense as a result. In *Atkins v. Virginia*, the court ruled that execution of an individual with "mental retardation" (now referred to as *intellectual disability*) was a violation of the 8th Amendment ban on cruel and unusual punishment. Yet, while over two decades have passed since *Ford* and one since *Atkins*, mental health advocacy groups (that is, National Alliance on Mental Illness, Mental Health America) estimated that 5 percent to 10 percent of individuals on death row have a serious mental illness (American Civil Liberties Union [ACLU], 2009a; Mental Health America, 2011).

According to national polls, public support for the death penalty has shifted dramatically in recent years, with a growing number of people favoring penalties other than death, such as life without parole, restitution to victim families, and reallocation of limited funds to crime prevention initiatives (DPIC, 2010b). Concerns related to execution of innocents and doubts about the effectiveness of the death penalty in deterring crime are among the reasons cited for declining support. Even police chiefs have indicated that the death penalty is ineffective in reducing crime, placing the death penalty as a low priority in how limited funds for law enforcement should be allocated (Dieter, 2009).

Despite international calls to abolish the death penalty (United Nations Commission on Human Rights, 2005; United Nations General Assembly, 2007) and waning public support for capital punishment, it is significant to note that the United States remains the only country in the Americas to conduct executions. Between 1930 and 2009, 6,050 individuals have been executed in the United States, and more than 3,200 people currently on death row await execution (Amnesty International, 2010; DPIC, 2010a). Only China, Iran, Iraq, and Saudi Arabia execute more people than the United States (Amnesty International, 2010).

ISSUE STATEMENT

Several complex issues emerge in discussions of capital punishment and the death penalty. Given the complexity of the concerns related to capital punishment and the finality of an execution, the appropriateness of using the death penalty in the United States and other countries warrants consideration of several topics.

Equal application of the law and protection of the dignity of every human being are fundamental to a system that upholds social justice. Evidence that application of the death penalty is too arbitrary, too prone to error, and unfairly administered supports the argument that our current criminal justice system is not reliable enough to serve principles related to social justice ("National Coalition to Abolish," 2010). As noted by Amnesty International (2010), attorney competence, race, economics, local politics, geography, and the plea bargaining process are among the array of factors that affect prosecutorial decision making related to seeking the death penalty.

Considerable evidence exists that the U.S. criminal justice system has sentenced innocent people to death and that some have been executed (DPIC, 2011). Since 1973, 138 people have been exonerated and released from death row as a result of acquittal, dismissal of charges, or pardon. These individuals spent an average of 9.8 years incarcerated and awaiting execution prior to exoneration (DPIC, 2010b). Although it is impossible to determine with certainty how many innocent individuals have been executed, the DPIC (2011) has identified nine cases involving execution of individuals where strong evidence of innocence exists. In addition, four individuals have been issued posthumous pardons in Colorado, South Carolina, and Georgia, based on evidence of innocence.

Another aspect of social justice is the apparent racial disparity that exists in application of the death penalty at all levels—charging, sentencing, and executing. Of the nearly 3,300 inmates on death row today, 56 percent are people of color and 44 percent are black (DPIC, 2011). Race has been shown to be a factor in multiple ways, on both the defendant and victim sides of the equation. First, evidence exists that prosecutors are more likely to initiate the death penalty process in cases where the victim is white (Davis, 2007). Furthermore, according to the ACLU (2009b),

> studies consistently demonstrate that, everything else being equal, a defendant is approximately four times more likely to get the death penalty for killing a white person than for a black person. The racial configuration

by far the more likely to result in a death sentence is a black defendant and a white victim.

Over 75 percent of the murder victims in cases resulting in an execution were white, even though nationally only 50 percent of murder victims generally are white (National Association for the Advancement of Colored People, 2010). The issue of race also applies to racial composition of juries, with studies across various death penalty states demonstrating that in "black on white" murder cases juries with six or more white male jurors issue a death sentence 78.3 percent of the time (ACLU, 2009b). Finally, another level of racial disproportionality is reflected in executions. The U.S. Census Bureau (2010) estimated that 12.9 percent of the 2009 population was black. With 34 percent of inmates executed since 1976 being black, the racial disproportionality represented in executions is readily apparent.

According to Amnesty International (2009), approximately 90 percent of people facing the death penalty cannot afford their own attorneys, and many states continue to fail to meet standards developed by the American Bar Association for appointment, performance, and compensation of counsel for indigent prisoners. Amnesty International (2010) stated that poor legal representation is a persistent issue. The failure to provide adequate counsel to capital defendants and death row prisoners is a defining feature of the death penalty in the United States. The decision regarding whether a defendant will be sentenced to death typically depends more on the quality of the defense legal team than any other factor. Although some lawyers have provided outstanding representation to capital defendants, few defendants facing capital charges can afford to hire an attorney, so they are appointed attorneys who are frequently overworked, underpaid, and inexperienced in trying death penalty cases (Amnesty International, 2010). In some cases, lawyers representing defendants in capital trials have slept through parts of trial, shown up in court intoxicated, and failed to do any work at all in preparation for the sentencing phase (Amnesty International, 2010).

Although legal cases have established that individuals shown to meet the standard of mental retardation or incompetence at the time of trial should not be subject to the death penalty, other or lesser conditions of mental illness and neurological impairment as well as competence at the time of the crime have not been fully addressed judicially or legislatively. Therefore, individuals with such conditions are left to substantiate these issues during the guilt/innocence and penalty phases of trial, relying on effectiveness of counsel, affordability of experts, and understanding of jurists to weigh the mitigating evidence. The aforementioned issues related to effectiveness of legal counsel, impoverishment of capital defendants, and bias in jurist decision making raise serious questions about the degree to which mental illness and other brain impairments are adequately addressed during death penalty trials. With research evidence that nearly all death row inmates suffer from brain damage due to illness or trauma and that a vast number of them have experienced severe physical or sexual abuse, there is little doubt that the current system does not adequately account for and protect capital defendants suffering from mental illness, neurological impairments, and trauma histories that may have factored into a defendant's actions at the time of the crime (ACLU, 2009a; Beck, Britto, & Andrews, 2007).

Proponents of the death penalty point to deterrence of crime as a reason to uphold the death penalty. However, data released by the DPIC (2010c) reveal that states with the death penalty have had consistently higher murder rates over the past 20 years than those states without the death penalty. Furthermore, research has shown that "the murder rate in non–death penalty states has remained consistently lower than the rate in states with the death penalty, and the gap has grown since 1990" (DPIC, 2011). In addition, studies have shown that the United States continues to have a higher murder rate than other developed countries that do not use the death penalty (Amnesty International, 2010).

Although recognizing that deterrent sanctions may be a valid and necessary part of our system of criminal justice, statistics used to argue both sides fail to uphold the notion that the death penalty acts as a deterrent to homicide. In fact, Federal Bureau of Investigation reports show that, in general, homicide rates are lower in non–death penalty states. The South, which accounts for 80 percent of executions, repeatedly has the highest murder rate, and the Northeast, which accounts for less than 1 percent of executions, has the lowest murder rate (DPIC, 2011). Although these figures do not disprove that individuals may be deterred from committing murder by the existence of the death penalty, they do suggest that the death penalty is not likely to be a more effective deterrent than an alternative such as life imprisonment.

In a climate of concern about state and federal budgets, it is critical to consider fiscal issues in assessing application of the death penalty. Fiscal analysts have noted that the costs associated with the constitutionally required complex procedures in death penalty trials and subsequent appeals result in significantly higher costs in capital cases than in those involving life without parole (Death Penalty Focus, 2011). The ACLU has documented numerous incidences in which death penalty costs have presented significant budgetary challenges for jurisdictions, depleting funds that might otherwise be allocated to other priorities, such as job creation, public safety, and schools. The most comprehensive study found that the death penalty costs North Carolina $2.16 million more per execution than the cost of a non–death penalty murder case, with a sentence of imprisonment for life occurring at the trial level (DPIC, 2011). Thus, even with limits on appeals, the higher costs at the trial level would remain. A DPIC (2011) report suggested that since the reinstitution of the death penalty in 1976, the United States has spent $2.5 billion more than if the country used life imprisonment as the maximum punishment. In addition, data show that the costs for housing an inmate on death row in California is $90,000 per year greater than the housing costs associated with confinement of those serving life without possibility of parole (ACLU of North Carolina, 2008). The California Commission on Fair Administration of Justice (2008), in a study of the California criminal justice system, estimated that the state's current annual costs related to the death penalty approached $137 million annually. This compares with a system that would establish a maximum penalty of lifetime incarceration instead of the death penalty costing an estimated $11.5 million per year.

NASW's broad ethical principle that social workers respect the inherent dignity and worth of each person contraindicates support of the death penalty. Capital punishment represents an official, societally sanctioned act of killing as a way to deal with lethally violent behavior. Although homicide is unquestionably an act that diminishes the value and worth placed on human beings, the legitimization of killing through capital punishment also diminishes the value and worth of the perpetrator. Both forms of killing are thus a violation of individual dignity and worth.

Capital punishment and the death penalty undermine the ability of professional social workers working within the criminal justice system to enhance a defendant or convicted client's capacity and opportunity for ongoing change. Although murder is a reprehensible crime, infliction of the death penalty on people convicted of murder permanently forecloses their capacity for redemption and reform. Although returning individuals who have committed murder to the community may not serve the best interests of society, life terms served in prison create the potential for these incarcerated individuals to recognize and recover from the emotional wounds that fueled their addiction, violence, and criminal behavior. In addition, alternatives to capital punishment provide opportunities for the needs of offender families, victim families, and communities to be served (Beck et al., 2007). The very act of executing the condemned by capital punishment denies the inherent worth of the individual. Thus, capital punishment is antithetical to the theory of restorative justice and the view that rehabilitative restoration is valuable for the condemned and for society. Restorative justice has as its foundation the belief in the capacity of an individual to experience true remorse accompanied by a difference in mindset and behavior. Capital punishment completely eliminates any consideration of and possibility for a convict to change.

Finally, this ethical principle, and the corresponding standard in the *Code of Ethics* (NASW, 2008), urges social workers to be cognizant of their dual responsibility to clients and to the broader society and to seek to resolve conflicts between clients' interests and those of the broader society in a socially responsible manner consistent with the values, principles, and standards of the profession. Rather than being a deterrent to violent crime, capital punishment legitimizes and expands the cycle of violence in society at large by promoting violence as a solution to intractable human problems and behaviors. By opposing the death penalty, social workers seek socially responsible alternatives aimed at stopping the cycle of violence that is damaging and destroying human capacities and relationships in society and in the world.

Proponents of capital punishment often point to the penalty as a form of retribution for the families of victims. However, crime victims' families respond to the death penalty in a variety of ways. Whereas some argue for vengeance or atonement, others argue against the death penalty because it continues the cycle of violence. There are organizations aimed at assistance for crime victims that is congruent with social work values and ethics. For example, Murder Victims' Families for Reconciliation opposes the death penalty and supports the redirection of money currently spent on executions to victim-assistance programs. Restitution Incorporated helps death row inmates sell their artwork to support families of their victims or for crime prevention programs, and some groups seek actual reconciliation between murderers and victims' families (Murder Victims for Human Rights and National Alliance on Mental Illness, 2009).

POLICY STATEMENT

NASW supports

■ abolition of the death penalty and an immediate moratorium on executions for those already sentenced.

■ a system that encourages multi-stakeholder involvement in establishing opportunities for restorative justice rather than retributive justice.

■ a system that ensures that criminal defendants, especially in death penalty cases, receive thorough mental health, psychosocial, and trauma assessments.

- involvement of social workers as qualified professionals in the collection and assessment of mitigation evidence in guilt/innocence and penalty phases of capital trials.

- inclusion of social workers as qualified expert witnesses related to mental health and trauma history (such as domestic and community violence, trauma, substance use) issues in the backgrounds of capital defendants.

- allocation of limited budgetary resources to cost-effective sentencing and prevention initiatives.

- restorative justice programs that support the belief in the possibility for change and the option for rehabilitation and restoration.

REFERENCES

ACLU of Northern California. (2008). *The hidden death tax: The secret costs of seeking execution in California.* San Francisco: Author.

American Civil Liberties Union. (2009a). *Mental illness and the death penalty.* Retrieved from http://www.aclu.org/capital-punishment/mental-illness-and-death-penalty

American Civil Liberties Union. (2009b). *Race and death penalty links run deep and wide* Retrieved from http://www.aclu.org/2009/10/22/race-and-death-penalty-links-run-deep-and-wide

Amnesty International. (2009). *Death penalty and arbitrariness.* Retrieved from http://www.amnestyusa.org/death-penalty/death-penalty-facts/death-penalty-and-arbitrariness/page.do?id=1101083

Amnesty International. (2010). *The death penalty in 2009* [Online]. Retrieved from http://www.amnesty.org/en/death-penalty/death-sentences-and-executions-in-2009

Atkins v. Virginia, 536 U.S. 304 (2002).

Beck, E., Britto, S., & Andrews, A. (2007). *In the shadows of death: Restorative justice and death row families.* New York: Oxford University Press.

California Commission on the Fair Administration of Justice. (2008). *Final report.* Retrieved from http://www.ccfaj.org/documents/CCFAJFinalReport.pdf

Death Penalty Focus. (2011). *The high cost of the death penalty.* Retrieved from http://www.deathpenalty.org/article.php?id=42

Death Penalty Information Center. (2010a, December). *The death penalty in 2010: Year end report.* Retrieved from http://www.deathpenaltyinfo.org/documents/2010YearEnd-Final.pdf

Death Penalty Information Center. (2010b, October). *The innocence list.* Retrieved from http://www.deathpenaltyinfo.org/innocence-list-those-freed-death-row

Death Penalty Information Center. (2010c, October). *Size of death row by year: 1968 to present* Retrieved from http://www.deathpenaltyinfo.org/death-row-inmates-state-and-size-death-row-year#year

Death Penalty Information Center. (2011). *Facts about the death penalty.* Retrieved from http://www.deathpenaltyinfo.org/documents/FactSheet.pdf

Dieter, R. (2009). *Smart on crime: Reconsidering the death penalty in a time of economic crisis, National poll of police chiefs puts capital punishment at bottom of law enforcement priorities.* Washington, DC: Death Penalty Information Center.

Ford v. Wainwright, 477 U.S. 399 (1986).

Mental Health America. (2011, March). *Position Statement 54: Death penalty and people with mental illness.* Retrieved from http://www.mentalhealthamerica.net/go/position-statement/54)

Murder Victims for Human Rights (MVFHR) and National Alliance on Mental Illness. (2009, July). *Double tragedies: Victims speak out against the death penalty for people with severe mental illness.* Retrieved from http://www.mvfhr.org/sites/default/files/pdf/DoubleTragedies.pdf

National Association for the Advancement of Colored People. (2010). *Criminal justice advocacy toolkit—Smart and safe initiative.* Retrieved from http://naacp.3cdn.net/9202759105991f0377_lcm6iyyi2.pdf

National Association of Social Workers. (2008). *Code of ethics of the National Association of Social Workers.* Washington, DC: Author.

National Coalition to Abolish the Death Penalty. (2010, September 10). *Abolition Times.*

United Nations Commission on Human Rights. (2005, April 20). *Human rights resolution 2005/59*. Geneva: Author.

United Nations General Assembly. (2007, December 18). *Resolution 62/149—Moratorium on the use of the death penalty*. New York: Author.

U.S. Census Bureau. (2010). *State and county quickfacts*. Washington, DC: Author.

NASW Members with Primary Responsibility for Revision of This Policy

First Draft Revision:

Nathaniel Morley (PA)

Policy Panelists:

Zuline Gray Wilkinson (MA)
Virginia David (NYS)
Jackie Pray (GA)
Joe Harper (IL)
Wanda Whittlesey Jerome (NM)
Stacie Hiramoto (CA)
Joe Monahan (IL)

Policy statement approved by the NASW Delegate Assembly, August 2011. This statement supersedes the policy statement on Capital Punishment and the Death Penalty approved by the Delegate Assembly in August 2002. For further information, contact the National Association of Social Workers, 750 First Street, NE, Suite 700, Washington, DC 20002-4241. Telephone: 202-408-8600; e-mail: press@naswdc.org

Child Abuse and Neglect

BACKGROUND

Assessing the scope of child abuse and neglect in our nation is challenging. Accurate statistics can be gathered only from formal abuse reports to child protective service (CPS) units. The Children's Bureau of the U.S. Department of Health and Human Services, which maintains the National Child Abuse and Neglect Data System (NCANDS), reported in *Child Maltreatment 2001* that 3 million referrals on behalf of approximately 5 million children were made to CPS agencies throughout the United States (National Clearinghouse on Child Abuse and Neglect Information [NCCANI], 2003c; U.S. Department of Health and Human Services, 2003). One-third of these reports were screened out of the investigation and assessment process, but 28 percent of the investigated reports were substantiated (NCCANI, 20003c).

In 2001 more than 903,000 children suffered from abuse or neglect, representing a rate of 12.4 maltreated children for every 1,000 children in the general population. Almost one-third of these children were younger than three. An estimated 1,300 children died from child maltreatment in 2001; 41 percent of the deaths were children 12 months or younger, and 85 percent were six years old or younger (NCCANI, 2003c). Many researchers believe that 50 percent to 60 percent of childhood deaths result from abuse and neglect, but are not included in these abuse and neglect rates because of pervasive underreporting of child maltreatment (NCCANI, 2003b). The prevalence of child maltreatment tends to decrease as children get older (NCCANI, 2003c).

Clarity about the prevalence of child abuse is complicated also by the difficulty of assessing environmental risk factors. African Americans and Hispanics are overrepresented in the statistics. Research has suggested that poor and racial and ethnic minority children and their families are disproportionately reported, labeled, and routinely mandated into the child welfare system by professionals who are socially and culturally distant from their actual family contexts (Wells, 1995). Despite the difficulties of tracking the extent of the problem, statistics clearly reveal a national crisis.

Historical Trends

Child maltreatment can be explored in the context of anthropology and its foundations in the study of the development of cultures (Bakan, 2001; Tower, 1996). Check (1989) asserted: "During the medieval times, for instance, there was neither a definition of childhood nor a vocabulary to differentiate it from adulthood" (p. 21). The most consistent belief was that children were the property of the parents without rights of their own (Tower).

Organized efforts to protect children are evident as far back as the Elizabethan Poor Laws in England in the mid-1550s, which sought to provide care and support to impoverished children and families. Novels penned by Charles Dickens ignited some of the first social protests against societal neglect of abused, abandoned, and crippled children (Tower, 1996), and since then movements emerged across western Europe and the United States, joining activists in the cause to stop the maltreatment of children.

The history of organized protection of children in the United States began with the case of nine-year-old Mary Ellen Wilson in 1874. The child had been through successive placements after the death of her parents. When church worker Etta Wheeler inquired, a neighbor in her New York City tenement reported the cruelties perpetrated on the child that she had heard through the thin walls. Wheeler turned to Henry Bergh, then well known as the first president of the American Society for the Prevention of Cruelty to Animals. With the help of an attorney, Mary Ellen was removed from the home, and Mary Ellen's caregiver was sentenced to a year of hard labor in a penitentiary (Tower, 1996). These landmark actions resulted in the establishment of the Society for the Prevention of Cruelty to Children and catapulted child maltreatment from the shadows of oblivion.

From then, activists made much progress in protecting children in the first half of the 20th century. The National Child Labor Committee was organized in 1904, and with the help of Jane Addams and others, the committee began working to reform child labor laws. In 1962, Kempe and colleagues published "The Battered-Child Syndrome," an article in the *Journal of the American Medical Association* about a pioneering effort to protect children from physical, sexual, and emotional abuse and neglect. For the first time, medical professionals presented epidemiological data about the frequency of physical child maltreatment and ignited a social movement (Leventhal, 2003). Leventhal concluded: "The authors' point was to inform the reader that physical abuse was not a rarely occurring phenomenon, but rather a common problem that was already recognized . . . across the country" (p. 545).

Legislation and Policy Development

The increasing awareness of the need to protect children in this country led to the establishment of the federal Children's Bureau in 1912. The Child Welfare League of America (CWLA) had its start in 1915 in efforts to create standards for services and aid to children (Tower, 1996). The Social Security Act, passed in 1935 (P.L. 74-271) sustained efforts to protect children, particularly those living in poverty. Described by Tower, the law mandated "child welfare services for neglected dependent children and children in danger of becoming delinquent" (p. 11). Public agencies began to implement child welfare policies and laws. Bakan (2001) described the radical shift, stating: "By implication, legislation making the reporting of child abuse mandatory indicates the protection of children is not the restricted province of parents but rather the larger responsibility of the society as a whole, which is to take over when the parents fail either by willful injury or by neglect" (p. 162).

Despite these efforts, legislation designed to protect children was often ineffective because of the continuing paternalistic values, particularly the philosophy that children were the property of parents. Political and societal beliefs and norms did not support efforts to intervene in the private affairs of families.

In 1974 key federal legislation addressing child abuse and neglect was enacted (NCCANI, 2003a). The Child Abuse Prevention and Treatment Act (CAPTA) (P.L. 93-247) established minimum definitions that serve as a baseline for intervention. *Child abuse* and *neglect* were described as (1) "any recent act or failure to act on the part of a parent or caretaker which results in death, serious physical or emotional harm, sexual abuse or exploitation" or (2) "an act or failure to act which presents an imminent risk of serious harm" (NCCANI, 2002b).

CAPTA also provided funding for prevention, assessment, investigation, prosecution, and treatment activities. Congress reauthorized and amended CAPTA several times to include adoption reforms, at-risk infants with life-threatening congenital impairments, children born with HIV or other life-threatening illnesses, and children who have been perinatally exposed to dangerous drugs (NCCANI, 2003d).

Public policy has also focused on what happens to children whose abuse and neglect investigations have been substantiated and whose custody issues must be decided. In 1980 Congress enacted the Adoption Assistance and Child Welfare Act (P.L. 96-272) . This law requires a six-month review while a child is in care and a "permanent plan" for the child within 18 months. Permanency planning and family preservation concepts developed as a result of studies demonstrating the negative effects of remaining in the foster care system long-term (known as "foster care drift") (National Association of Foster Care Reviewers [NAFCR], no date). This law also introduced the concept that "reasonable efforts" should be made to keep families together. In 1997, with great bipartisan approval, Congress enacted the Adoption and Safe Families Act (AFSA) (P.L. 105-89). It established funding for family preservation and support and added funds for adoption services. The law established time limits for making permanency planning decisions and initiating proceedings to terminate parental rights. ASFA requires that child safety be the paramount concern in making service provision, placement, and permanency decisions. ASFA initiated other significant changes in child welfare practice, including:

- Shortening the deadline for holding permanency hearing from 18 to 12 months

- Encouraging concurrent planning for adoption in all foster care placements

- Requiring agencies to file a petition to terminate parental rights when a child has been in foster care in 15 of the past 22 months

- Providing adoption incentives to states that increase their number of adoptions of foster children over a base year

- Clarifying what constitutes reasonable efforts and conditions under which a state is not required to work toward family reunification

- Requiring states to report track statistics reflecting the implementation and results of ASFA.

Current Status of Child Welfare

Today, the stories of children lost by social services, abused and neglected in foster care settings, and killed while in the custody of social welfare agencies fill the national news. Pear (2004) reported that "federal investigators have found widespread problems in child welfare programs intended to protect children from abuse and neglect" (p. 1). In a Dear Col-

league letter drumming up support for increased funding for state CAPTA grants, Congressmen George Miller, from California, and Jim Greenwood, from Pennsylvania, ("Changes in the 2005 CAPTA," 2004) wrote: "The nation's child welfare system has long been stretched beyond capacity to handle the full scope of child maltreatment," and also pointed out that funding has been almost static for more than a decade.

ISSUE STATEMENT

Child maltreatment exists in a complex web of family interactions, and research has suggested serious, negative consequences for children that endure well into adulthood. According to NCCANI (2002a), "There is increasing awareness that child maltreatment and domestic violence co-exist in families" (p. 1). Brown and Bzostek (2003) reported that "recent research indicates that males exposed to domestic violence as children are more likely to engage in domestic violence as adults, and females are more likely to be victims as adults" (p. 4). Baldry (2003) demonstrated that a child witnessing violence is more likely to be involved in physical aggression, such as fighting, bullying, and threatening others, at school. Additional conflict arises when trying to protect women who are not only being abused by their partners, but also secondarily traumatized by having their children removed because of the dangerous home environment.

Furthermore, child welfare literature has suggested that "the link between substance abuse and child abuse has become stronger; parental substance abuse is highly correlated with child maltreatment and death" (Brissett-Chapman, 1995, p. 360). Some states take a highly punitive approach to parents who are substance abusers, and "this results in the substance-abusing mother not getting the treatment she needs for chemical dependency and inadequate medical care" (Alexander & McDougal, 2004, p. 5).

Childhood trauma has connections to heart disease, diabetes, obesity, unintended pregnancy, and alcoholism (Felitti, 2002). Childhood trauma can lead to significant mental health problems, such as posttraumatic stress disorder, depression, anxiety, and other disorders that impede an individual's ability to make healthy decisions concerning parenting, relationships, and health issues (Schnurr & Green, 2004). Hillis and colleagues (2000) found that being abused as a child may have long-term consequences for adult sexual behaviors that increase the risk of sexually transmitted diseases. Wyatt and colleagues (2002) warned that "the associations between child sexual abuse and HIV-related risks in adulthood have been well documented" (p. 661). The social costs of ignoring the effect of child maltreatment on physical health are enormous and impede our ability to break the cycle of family abuse.

While looking for the solutions in the United States, social workers also must advocate globally for coalitions designed to protect children around the world. More than 300,000 children worldwide are engaged as soldiers, abducted and forced to take up arms in bloody battles by political dissidents (Wadhams, 2004). Sexual exploitation of children occurs internationally with children being sold into prostitution and slavery. The United Nations Convention on the Rights of the Child (1989) is an important international child advocacy effort that "sets minimum international standards for the treatment of children to ensure their safety, survival and development" (Malcolm, 2000, p. 1). A total of 192 countries already have signed it. Somalia and the United States are the only member states that have not ratified this treaty.

Social workers have battled child maltreatment for more than 100 years, and to the battle they bring a unique body of knowledge. Concepts of working with people in their environments and of the primacy of the family help professionals understand that when dealing with child maltreatment, helping the child means working with the whole family and with other environmental factors in a culturally competent way. It means that they understand the devastating impact of poverty on children. Trained social workers understand the consequences of having natural and healthy developmental processes interrupted by traumatic events. As the United Nations Declaration on the Rights of the Child states, children "should grow up in a family environment, in an atmosphere of happiness, love and understanding."

Social workers are taught that prevention should be at the front end of all interventions. Prevention of child maltreatment is obviously a better strategy than dealing with the aftermath of child abuse and neglect. Miller and Greenwood (2004) pointed out that "if we could invest in proven prevention programs and strategies designed at the local level to meet individual, family and community needs, we could reduce the expenditure for costly back end crisis services."

POLICY STATEMENT

The National Association of Social Workers takes the following positions as an organization:

■ Children have the right to be treated with respect as individuals and to receive culturally sensitive services. Children have a right to express their opinions about their lives and have those opinions considered in all placement and judicial proceedings.

■ Immigrant children should have the same rights and protections as children who are citizens of this country.

■ Systems in place to protect children should be adequately staffed and fully funded, and they should provide service that reflects evidence-based or current best practices to address the problem of child abuse and neglect.

■ Communities, including extended family members, kinship networks, and neighborhoods must be involved in supporting children and caregivers to ensure a safe, secure, and consistently stable living environment.

■ All states must create and enforce laws that protect child witnesses of domestic violence and provide appropriate care for nonoffending parents and the children.

■ Authorities should leave nonoffending parents or guardians and their children in their own homes and remove the batterers to preserve the stability of children's caregiving and residence in domestic violence cases.

■ Child abuse and neglect investigations and substantiations are best conducted using a specially trained, multidisciplinary team, including social workers, law enforcement, and health and mental health professionals.

■ Policies and procedures should be developed in human services organizations to address and ensure the safety of social workers and other professionals working with abuse and neglect.

■ Staff with social work degrees should be employed in schools, mental health programs, hospitals, and other human services organizations that deal with children and their families. All comprehensive medical assessments should address abuse and neglect issues.

■ A bachelor's degree in social work is preferred for staff in child protective services. At the supervisory level, a master's degree in social work is recommended.

■ Child maltreatment issues should be part of the curricula of all programs that train health professionals.

■ Systematic changes are needed in child abuse reporting systems to ensure more standardized and effective intake assessments.

■ Standardized definitions of child abuse and neglect must include identification of emotional and psychological abuse and risks and harm to children exposed to violence, and they must state the responsibility to provide intervention for such conditions no matter the etiology.

■ Family-centered residential treatment programs for substance-abusing parents should be available to facilitate opportunities to help parents and children maintain the parent–child bond.

■ Public awareness, media, and educational campaigns are needed to highlight the significance of child abuse issues and the related legal requirements of reporting systems.

■ Sexual abuse and physical abuse prevention programs should be mandated in all schools from kindergarten to high school.

■ The United States should ratify the United Nations Convention on the Rights of the Child.

■ Funding should be dramatically increased for research, prevention, and services in all areas of child maltreatment.

■ To truly help protect children by preventing child maltreatment, social workers and other professionals must also help families by identifying and addressing the individual, familial, and community challenges they encounter (NASW, 2004).

■ Child maltreatment issues and concerns do not operate in isolation. To improve the service delivery in the area of child abuse and neglect, those systems that run parallel—mental health, substance abuse, domestic abuse, homelessness, and health care—need to be enhanced to effectively develop a service continuum directed at safety for children.

REFERENCES

Adoption Assistance and Child Welfare Act of 1980, Pub. L. 96-272, 94 Stat. 500.

Adoption and Safe Families Act of 1997, Pub. L. 105-89, 111 Stat. 2115.

Alexander, L., & McDougal, T. (2004). *Drug screening substance abusing parents.* Unpublished manuscript, University of North Carolina at Greensboro and North Carolina A&T University.

Baldry, A. C. (2003) Bullying in schools and exposure to domestic violence. *Child Abuse & Neglect, 27,* 713–732.

Bakan, D. (April, 2001). Slaughter of the innocents: A study of the battered child phenomenon. *Journal of Social Distress and the Homeless, 10,* 147–216.

Brissett-Chapman, S. (1995). Child abuse and neglect: Direct practice. In R. L. Edwards (Ed.-in-Chief), *Encyclopedia of social work* (19th ed., Vol. 1, pp. 353–366). Washington, DC: NASW Press.

Brown, B. V., & Bzostek, S. (2003). Violence in the lives of children [Child Trends Data-Bank Data Brief]. *CrossCurrents,* 1, 1–13. Child Trends. Available at http://www.childtrendsdatabank.org

Check, W. A. (1989). *The encyclopedia of health, psychological disorders and their treatment: Child abuse.* New York: Chelsea House.

Child Abuse Prevention and Treatment Act, Pub. L. 93-247, 88 Stat. 4 (1974).

Children's Defense Fund. (2000). Issue Basics, Adoption and Safe Families Act (ASFA). Retrieved October 10, 2004 from, http://www.cdfactioncouncil.org

Felitti, V. J. (2002). The relation between adverse childhood experiences and adult health: Turning gold into lead. *Permanente Journal, 6*(1), 44–47.

Hillis, S. D., Anda, R. F., Felitti, V. J., Nordenberg, D., & Marchbanks, P. A. (2000). Adverse childhood experiences and sexually transmitted diseases in men and women: A retrospective study. *Pediatrics, 106,* e11.

Kempe, C. H., Silverman, F. N., Steele, B. F., Droegemueller, W., & Silver, H. K. (1962). The battered-child syndrome. *JAMA, 181,* 17–24.

Leventhal, J. (2003). 'The Battered-Child Syndrome' 40 years later. *Clinical Child Psychology and Psychiatry, 8,* 543–545.

Malcolm, T. (2000, April 14). Advocates call for welcome for U.N. child rights document. Retrieved October 20, 2005, from http://natcath.org/NCR_Online/archives2/2000b/041400/041400l.htm

Miller, G., & Greenwood, J. (2004). Colleague letter in support of increased funding for fiscal year 2005 CAPTA appropriations. Washington, DC: 108th Congress.

National Association of Foster Care Reviewers. (n.d.). *Foster care review: past & present. Helping systems work for children.* Salt Lake City: Author. Available at http://www.nafcr.org./docs/foster_care_review.pdf

National Association of Social Workers. (2004, June). *"If you're right for the job, it's the best job in the world": The National Association of Social Workers' Child Welfare Specialty Practice Section members describe their experiences in child welfare.* Washington, DC: Author.

National Clearinghouse on Child Abuse and Neglect Information. (2002a). *Child abuse and neglect state statutes series, compendium of laws, child witness to domestic violence.* Washington, DC: U.S. Department of Health and Human Services.

National Clearinghouse on Child Abuse and Neglect Information. (2002b). *What is child maltreatment?* Washington, DC: U.S. Department of Health and Human Services.

National Clearinghouse on Child Abuse and Neglect Information. (2003a). *About the federal Child Abuse Prevention and Treatment Act.* Washington, DC: U.S. Department of Health and Human Services.

National Clearinghouse on Child Abuse and Neglect Information. (2003b). *Child abuse and neglect fatalities: Statistics and interventions.* Washington, DC: U.S. Department of Health and Human Services.

National Clearinghouse on Child Abuse and Neglect Information. (2003c). *Child maltreatment 2001: Summary of key findings.* Washington, DC: U.S. Department of Health and Human Services.

National Clearinghouse on Child Abuse and Neglect Information. (2003d). *Major federal legislation concerned with child protection, child welfare, and adoption.* Washington, DC: U.S. Department of Health and Human Services.

Pear, R. (2004, April 26). U.S. finds fault in all 50 states' child welfare programs. *New York Times,* p. A17.

Schnurr, P. P., & Green, B. L. (2004). *Trauma and health: Physical health consequences of exposure to extreme stress.* Washington, DC: American Psychological Association.

Social Security Act of 1935, Pub. L. 74–271, 49 Stat. 620.

Tower, C. C. (1996). *Understanding child abuse and neglect* (3rd ed.). Boston: Allyn & Bacon.

United Nations. (1989). Convention on the Rights of the Child (Resolution 44/25). New York: Author. Available at http://www.unicef.org/crc/fulltext.htm

U.S. Department of Health and Human Services, Administration for Children and Families. (2003). *Child maltreatment, 2001.* Washington, DC: U.S. Government Printing Office

Wadhams, N. (2004, January 20). United Nations seeks to end use of child soldiers. Retrieved October 20, 2005, from http://www.globalpolicy.org/security/issues/040120child.htm

Wells, S. J. (1995). Child abuse and neglect overview. In R. L. Edwards (Ed.-in-Chief),

Encyclopedia of social work (19th ed., Vol. 1, pp. 346–353). Washington, DC: NASW Press.

Wyatt, G. E., Myers, H. F., Williams, J. K., Kitchen, C. R., Loeb, T., Carmona, J. V.,

Wyatt, L. E., Chin, D., & Presley, N. (2002). Does a history of trauma contribute to HIV risk for women of color? Implications for prevention and policy. *American Journal of Public Health*, 92, 660–665.

Policy statement approved by the NASW Delegate Assembly, August 2005. This policy statement supersedes the statement on Child Abuse and Neglect approved by the Delegate Assembly in 1996 and referred by the 2002 Delegate Assembly to the 2005 Delegate Assembly for revision. For further information, contact the National Association of Social Workers, 750 First Street, NE, Suite 700, Washington, DC 20002-4241; telephone: 202-408-8600; e-mail: press@naswdc.org

Civil Liberties and Justice

BACKGROUND

Advancing social justice through the protection and preservation of individual civil liberties is a key tenet of the social work profession.

Beginning in the 1980s and into the 21st century, landmark, yet fragile, gains in civil liberties and social justice obtained by social movements of the 1950s, 1960s, and 1970s have been steadily eroded by executive order, legislation, voter referenda, and judicial decisions. Whereas the triumph of American freedom and democracy has been hailed by U.S. political leaders, it is ironic that in the United States the legal rights of women, people of color, people who are gay, lesbian, bisexual, and transgendered, and people with low incomes have been abrogated by federal cutback policies, judicial court decisions, and abridged by administrative neglect at all levels of government. Each of these groups is increasingly stigmatized as a means to distract attention from the socioeconomic and political issues that afflict the entire society. Under the guise of promoting family and cultural values, concerted political and ideological attacks have targeted immigrant groups, the changing roles of women in U.S. society, the growing acceptance of alternative sexual lifestyles, and the consequential evolution of diverse family constellations.

Simultaneously the civil liberties of many constituent populations—including people with AIDS or HIV-related illness, deinstitutionalized consumers of mental health services, recipients of public benefits, juvenile and adult offenders, union members, immigrants and refugees, pregnant women, terminally ill patients, and people with addictions—have been denied or severely limited by revisions of government policy or cutbacks in government programs. For example, the federal executive "gag" order issued in 1988 directed health care professionals in federally funded Title X family planning clinics to refrain from providing any abortion-related information to clients, including referrals for services, even when asked to do so by the client. If professionals failed to comply, their agency would lose Title X funding (Guttmacher Institute, 2000). The 1988 executive order not only denied women their reproductive rights, but also denied health and human services workers their right of free speech. The Supreme Court upheld the constitutionality of the rule in a 5-to-4 decision in *Rust v. Sullivan* in 1991. President Clinton suspended the rule in 1993, however formal repeal of the rule did not take effect until July 3, 2000.

■ The Constitution requires that habeas corpus shall not be suspended "unless when in cases of rebellion or invasion the public safety may require it" ("Brief Backs Habeas Corpus," 2007). Congress, the police, and the courts continue to abuse this constitutional check on abuses of power.

■ The purpose of the constitutional protection against self-incrimination is described in *Grunewald v. United States* (1957): "recent examination of the history and meaning of the Fifth Amendment has emphasized anew that one of the basic functions of the privilege is to protect *innocent* men" [italics added] (p. 353 U.S. 391).

■ There is no evidence that the death penalty serves as a deterrent to violent crime. In fact, an increase in homicides in the United States has occurred despite the reinstitution of capital punishment in most states. The abolition of the death penalty would bring the United States' penal system in line with other modern societies

In *Roper v. Simmons* (2005) the U.S. Supreme Court ended the death penalty for persons whose crimes were committed when they were juveniles. The Supreme Court cited the unique developmental forces at work, which affect the ability of juveniles to make judgments, solve problems, and control their behavior (Children's Defense Fund, 2005).

ISSUE STATEMENT

The profession vigorously pursues the attainment of the individual well-being of clients, and the achievement of the common good. Freedoms fundamental to the individual and society—freedom of speech, the press, and separation of church and state, the right to privacy, due process of the law, and freedom from self-incrimination and unreasonable search and seizures—are under attack at the local, state, and federal levels. A key question is how to balance the permissible exercise of government's executive power for the common good, with fundamental freedoms. Many political and religious leaders assert that the executive branch has authority to intervene to protect the safety interests of Americans, and may violate individual civil liberties and social justice goals to do so.

The assault on civil liberties also is demonstrated in the growing demands on censorship of books and other forms of cultural expression; restrictions on the rights of individuals to bring suit against the government and employers; persistent increases of police brutality, particularly in communities of color brought about, in part, by the absence of community oversight of law enforcement agencies; punishment of whistle blowers who expose government misconduct; and the criminalization of individual and social problems. These developments create a context conducive to the spread of harmful trends, as seen in racially or religiously motivated hate crimes, crimes against women, and restrictions on people's right to privacy. More than ever it is essential for social workers to take action to reverse these trends, in line with championing the cause of individual rights and social justice. If not, we risk losing the freedoms that social workers value and protect.

Although challenges to individual civil liberties and social justice are ever-present, the events of September 11, 2001, have spurred a significant imbalance in the concentration and abuse of government power, especially at the executive level. Those who criticize government policies are erroneously portrayed as "unpatriotic" or denigrating the "office of the presidency." Further, these events have led to concerted efforts to promote and protect the national safety through unconstitutional intrusions into the lives of persons in the United States. The far reaching powers of the Homeland Security Act (2002), the Patriot Act(s), and the myriad new "security measures" promoted by the executive branch of government are overly broad and in violation of civil liberty principles. For example, President George W. Bush authorized the National Security Agency "to eavesdrop without warrants on the international communications of Americans suspected of terrorist ties" (Lichtblau, 2008).

At minimum, setbacks to civil liberties and social justice continue in five major areas: (1) the criminal justice and penal systems; (2) access to justice, equal protection, and due process rights; (3) restrictions on First Amendment rights, particularly freedom of expression and the separation of church and state; (4) the right to privacy and its effects on social services; and (5) civil liberties and national security.

POLICY STATEMENT

NASW considers the protection of individual rights and the promotion of social justice essential to the preservation of our collective well-being as a society. Therefore, NASW urges social workers and other policymakers to focus on the following areas.

Criminal Justice and Civil Liberties

NASW supports

■ reduction of the disproportionate number of youth and adults of color within the criminal justice system;

■ expanding alternatives to detention and incarceration; and

- development of an accessible, community-based, network of resources that affords preventive services, mental health assessments, and early treatment for both juvenile and adult offenders.

NASW opposes

- the use of the death penalty as a method of punishment;

- any legislation and prosecutorial discretion that permit children to be charged and punished under adult standards;

- legislation that would permit no-knock entry by police into homes without a proper warrant, the use of preventive detention, or any other form of restraint that would erode constitutionally recognized Miranda rights against self-incrimination;

- the use of mandatory sentencing requirements, particularly for first-time offenders.

Access to Justice, Equal Protection, and Due Process

NASW supports

- the principle of habeas corpus, which safeguards people from unlawful imprisonment;

- the establishment of civilian review boards to monitor police conduct and practices and to investigate allegations of excessive use of force by police officers;

- restoration of full funding for comprehensive civil and criminal legal aid services;

- the appointment of judges who are committed to the maintenance of civil liberties as guaranteed by the Constitution;

- the appointment of judges who reflect the demographic diversity of the people of the United States, particularly women, people of color, people who are gay, lesbian, bisexual, and transgendered, and older adults;

- the unimpeded application of individuals' civil rights through the courts in such areas as sexual harassment, employment discrimination, and housing bias.

Alternately, with regard to access to justice, equal protection, and due process, NASW opposes

- threats to freedom of the press and due process;

- mandatory drug and HIV testing on employees, prospective employees, and criminal defendants for actions with no direct relation either to drug abuse or HIV status, and which puts persons at risk of criminal prosecution;

- any executive or legislative initiatives that would restrict the rights of individuals to file class action suits, either against the government or corporations.

First Amendment Rights

The right to dissent from prevailing opinions of the majority—in political and cultural arenas—is a fundamental principle of a democratic society. However, recent events have demonstrated that the existence of legislative or judicial rights does not guarantee their implementation by the executive branch of the government, particularly when the resistance of that branch is abetted by the judiciary. Therefore, NASW supports

- the full implementation of existing civil rights legislation and its application to women, people of color, gays, lesbians, bisexual, and transgendered people;

- the expansion of these rights to include immigrants and refugees, people who have mental illness (both hospitalized and in community settings), and recipients of public assistance and their families.

Furthermore, NASW supports

- the right of all individuals to exercise their right to dissent responsibly and with respect for the opinions of others;

- the right of all individuals arrested in the course of infraction of ordinary law to be fully informed of their rights;

- pretrial treatment, trial activities, and sentencing on the basis of the province of the judicial system, following the constitutional principle of due process;

- the constitutional principle of separation of church and state;

- the right of workers to organize, to engage in collective bargaining to improve their working conditions, and to strike to draw attention to their grievances.

Using the same fundamental principle, NASW opposes

- the denial of funds from federal or state agencies, or access to services to which an individual would be otherwise entitled, on the basis of his or her participation in lawful protest and dissent;

- the arrest of any individual for the lawful exercise of his or her First Amendment rights of free speech and free assembly;

- the use of undue force by law enforcement officers;

- the alteration of the status of individuals participating in any acts of dissent, particularly in regard to employment, access to services, and other legal entitlements;

- the use of sanctions that discourage or punish whistle-blowers;

- the suspension of work or eligibility status of individuals before the institution of formal legal charges;

- all executive, legislative, or judicial actions that restrict freedom of speech, assembly, or cultural expression;

- all attempts to limit artistic freedom through the withholding of government grants (for example, National Endowment for the Arts);

- the imposition of any form of censorship by local authorities in regard to museum exhibits, library holdings, or school reading lists;

- any government restrictions on the rights of individuals or groups to protest policies or actions to which they are opposed;

- any abrogation of these rights by administrative regulation, legislation, or judicial action;

- the use of medical screenings to deny workers access to health benefits, imposition of mandatory drug testing in the workplace, and

use of electronic or computer surveillance of employees to monitor job performance;

- all efforts to deny or retract these rights from any individuals or groups in the United States;

- the use of tax policy, administrative regulations, or distribution of government funds to support organized religion in any manner.

Right to Privacy and Effects on Social Services

NASW strongly supports the preservation of the constitutional right to privacy and entitlement to services, especially in health and human services settings, and strongly condemns the following:

- efforts by state legislatures, Congress, the executive branch of the federal government, or the courts to restrict access to information about abortion, contraception, or family planning, or to restrict access to any of these services; NASW specifically opposes the current ban on Medicaid funding for abortion and government efforts to erode and, ultimately, overturn the right of women to seek an abortion—established in *Roe v. Wade* (1973)—on the grounds that such actions constitute an unjustifiable invasion of privacy.

- mandatory HIV, DNA, or drug testing as a precondition for employment or the receipt of services for which an individual would be otherwise eligible.

- violation of the confidentiality of welfare case records of individuals who seek assistance because of drug or alcohol abuse or HIV-related illness.

- use of electronic information for purposes other than enhancement of services delivery to consumers.

- unannounced inspections of homes, made without warrants, at inappropriate times with the ostensible purpose of checking on continuing eligibility for public assistance or on the "desirability" of the home.

- use of degrading and humiliating methods to determine eligibility for public assistance or social services by investigators whose practices violate some of the basic principles of the profession.

- state legislation to sterilize welfare recipients or deny them benefits if the number of children in a family exceeds a specified limit.

- legislative or administrative actions that involve the imposition of punitive sanctions to deny the right of women on probation to become pregnant.

- eviction of tenants determined undesirable in low-income public housing, without providing such tenants with clear expectations of residency, and administrative or judicial due process.

Civil Liberties and National Security

- NASW supports government protection of the United States and its territories while upholding the constitutional rights of individuals, families, and communities.

- NASW opposes overly broad use of executive power and electronic surveillance without court authorization.

REFERENCES

Brief backs habeas corpus reviews for detainees. (2007, October). *NASW News*, p. 5.

Children's Defense Fund. (2005). *The state of America's children: Yearbook, 2005.* Retrieved January 23, 2008, from http://cdf.convio .net/site/DocServer/Greenbook_2005.pdf ?docID=1741

Grunewald v. United States, 353 U.S. 391 (1957).

Guttmacher Institute. (2000, August) Title X 'gag rule' is formally repealed. *The Guttmacher Report on Public Policy*, 3(4). Retrieved January 16, 2008, from http://www.gutt macher.org/pubs/tgr/03/4/gr030413.html

Homeland Security Act of 2002, P.L. 107-296, 116 Stat. 2135.

Lichtblau, E. (2008, January 23). Democrats try to delay eavesdropping vote. *The New York Times*, p. A20.

Roe v. Wade, 410 U.S. 113 (1973).

Roper v. Simmons, 543 U.S. 551 (2005).

Rust v. Sullivan, 500 U.S. 173 (1991).

Policy statement approved by the NASW Delegate Assembly, August 2008. This policy statement supersedes the policy statement on Civil Liberties and Justice reconfirmed by the Delegate Assembly in 1999 and approved in 1993, which superseded the policy statement on Civil Liberties and Justice approved in 1967 and revised in 1971. The Delegate Assembly in 1999 also voted not to combine this policy with the policy on Drug Testing in the Workplace. For further information, contact the National Association of Social Workers, 750 First Street, NE, Suite 700, Washington, DC 20002-4241. Telephone: 202-408-8600 or 800-638-8799; e-mail: press@naswdc.org

Community Development

BACKGROUND

The development of strong communities has long been a tenet of the social work profession (Shulman, 2009). Strong communities play a protective role in human development. Community development practice has defined and is often cited as the birth of the social work profession. It dates back to the 19th century, with the settlement house movement and social work leaders such as Jane Addams (Kirst-Ashman & Hull, 2009). This early work outlined the value of empowerment of people to direct their assets to improve social conditions. This general framework, which revolves around central democratic principles, has stood as a core value of community development to this day (Rubin & Rubin, 2008). Community development is focused on improvement in the lives of community members, with specific attention to those areas that form the bonds of membership (Butterfield & Chisanga, 2008). The social work profession's early community development efforts are notable for setting a practice agenda that called for a simultaneous focus on the interrelationship of the individual's and the community's development (Kirst-Ashman & Hull, 2009).

As society and the profession grew throughout the 20th century, community development, as a scope of practice, went through several developmental phases (Butterfield & Chisanga, 2008). The 1930s were a time of great expansion, with a large-scale federal response to address the compounded effects of the Great Depression (Kirst-Ashman & Hull, 2009). In the 1950s, the primary focus was on building an infrastructure of organizations that provided social services (Milligan, 2008). The 1960s saw the well-known emergence of social action campaigns to address community concerns. The results were far reaching in terms of both large-scale social policy reforms—such as the

Economic Opportunity Act of 1964 (P.L. 88-452), the Model Cities Program, and the Civil Rights Act of 1964 (P.L. 88-352)—and the growth of empowerment in communities of interest, such as women, African Americans, and gay communities. These efforts continued into the 1970s. Increasingly, though, the debate over the etiology of challenges faced by community members gained strength, with some advocating for an individual pathology understanding, whereas others favored a more holistic understanding of how the larger societal forces compounded to form challenges. The 1980s and 1990s saw the beginning of decreased federal funding to state and local governments, a decline in the overall strength of the national economy, and a growing call for personal responsibility. These societal changes had profound effects on the practice of community development. The cyclical nature of community development is often seen as a low watermark in the field (Fisher & Harding, 2008).

Communities have inherent strengths and resources and the capacity to positively address their own issues. The increasing complexity of U.S. society and the demands placed on the organizations, structures, and policies that affect communities present opportunities for democratic involvement. Community development work is directed at strengthening, empowering, and building community capacity in the face of the challenges presented by 21st century society (Gamble & Weil, 2008; Streeter, 2008). The viability of a community development approach draws on the assets of the diverse stakeholders who are involved in the community and how those assets are used to address the community challenges (Council on Accreditation of Services for Children and Families, 2008). Community development "establishes a process that promotes people working together for a common purpose in groups and organizations" (Milligan, 2008). With community members' participation, focused planning, and commitment, community development efforts work to increase the capacity of the community and its members in an increasingly complex and interdependent world. Community development work is thought of as both a process and as goal driven, with qualitative and quantitative goals as expected outcomes (Butterfield & Chisanga, 2008).

Effective community social work practice is integrative, comprehensive, collaborative, participatory, strengths and asset focused, founded on building capacity, sustainable, empowerment focused, focused on the present with an eye on the future, and inclusive (Mizrahi, 2009). Effective community development practice requires a multitude of skills sets (Shulman, 2009). Increasingly, these skills sets are seen as essential in the toolkit of all social workers. As an aspect of macro practice, the social work profession is seen as well positioned to play a major role in community development (Rothman, 2008).

The role of social work in community development varies. Some of the key roles that social work assumes are those of facilitator, enabler, mediator, broker, coordinator, and mobilizer (Kirst-Ashman & Hull, 2009). Each role can be seen as playing a part in supporting the linkages in the community and in supporting the process of building the capacity of the community to achieve its goals. The methods used by social workers to achieve the community's goals include, but are not limited to, facilitating and participating in the community's work to identify its core values, belief systems, rights, assets, resources, strengths, needs, and goals. Social workers engage with the community to create community-building strategies to meet the community's goals by collecting and analyzing data, studying alternatives, facilitating the community's selection of a course of action, facilitating and helping to implement this action, training and developing staff and community leadership, identifying and developing funding sources, and establishing ongoing evaluations and feedback mechanisms (Kirst-Ashman & Hull, 2009; Shulman, 2009). Com-

munity development social work is in the scope of practice that has direct connection to the profession's ethical responsibility to the broader society (NASW, 2008). Section 6 of the NASW *Code of Ethics* outlines responsibilities related to improving social welfare and promoting public participation and engagement in social and political action. In turn, community practice is supported by the Council on Social Work Education (2008) as a core competency of both undergraduate and graduate social work education.

In response to the increasing complexity of community life and challenges, social work has seen the rise of newer practice models—much of which is rooted in empowerment practice (Shulman, 2009)—that are well designed to meet the current challenges. Among these are consensus organizing (Ohmer & DeMasi, 2009), capacity development (Cnaan & Rothman, 2008), applications of the strengths perspective (Saleebey, 2009), community resiliency (Kulig, Edge, & Joyce, 2008), community empowerment (Miley, O'Melia, & DuBois, 2009), asset building in communities (Han, Grinstein-Weiss, & Sherraden, 2009), micro-enterprise and micro-credit (Yunus, 2006), and community capacity (Huebner, Mancini, Bowen, & Orthner, 2009). In addition, the community development social work literature has been increasingly augmented by international sources and practices (Cox & Pawar, 2006).

Twenty-first century social work practice has been marked by a return to the prominence of community development and attention given to macro social work practice (Kirst-Ashman & Hull, 2009). Spurred in part by the challenges outlined by Robert Putnam in the 1990s related to the state of community in the modern society, 21st century community development approaches have regained prominence as a critical field of practice (Netting, Kettner, & McMurtry, 2008).

ISSUE STATEMENT

The challenges present in the second decade of the 21st century include major global issues such as the worldwide economic downturn, large-scale environmental threats, civil unrest, wars and terrorism, and the resulting negative impacts that such challenges bring to communities. Determining the positive use of technology as a way to strengthen communities is a challenge to social work practice and policy, resulting in a need for meaningful community development in these areas (Mizrahi, 2009).

The concept of community is far-reaching and reflects the many different ways that human beings are linked, including natural disasters that have affected the global economic scene such as the earthquake and tsunami that occurred in Japan in 2011. Some of these linkages are physical linkages, such as a neighborhood community. Some are online communities or social networks. Communities may also be defined by the affinities of their members, such as people living with certain physical, emotional, financial, cultural, intellectual, and developmental challenges. Regardless of the type of community, the linkages and sense of belonging are seen as central constructs (Rubin & Rubin, 2008). The communities of the 21st century are increasingly affected by the significant social, economic, political, and cultural changes that affect these vital linkages and, thereby, create needs and opportunities for social work services. A rapidly changing society requires ongoing attention to the manner in which social work considers community, understands community, engages community, and ultimately works to make change in the community.

The effects of societal changes, in combination with changing societal structures, pose challenges to the supports that community membership can provide. Factors that affect community life include, but are not limited to, inadequate programs and resources that supports self-determination to empower individual and community successes; changing demographics in physical communities; the ever-changing political climate; the effects of globalization; income disparities and health disparities; deterioration of neighborhoods; lack of affordable housing and related services; homelessness; social disorganization; violence, institutionalization and deinstitutionalization of varied communities; underachievement in educational settings, including low graduation rates; domestic violence; divorce rates; unplanned and teen-age pregnancies; infant mortality rates; racial, class, and political tensions; and disenfranchisement and discrimination against diverse groups (which may include, but are not limited to, people of color; those considered undocumented; the lesbian, gay, bisexual, and transgender community; people who are aging; returning military/veterans and their families; and women). These factors and others increasingly present a challenge to the ability of communities to foster social well-being, protection, and an enhanced quality of life (Hill & Blanck 2009; Rotabi, Gammonley, Gamble, & Weil, 2007; Tett, 2006).

POLICY STATEMENT

NASW recognizes the wide range of compounding issues and forces that affect the variety of community life in the 21st century. As such, NASW endorses the following policy and practice principles:

■ The right of a community and its individual members to reach their full potential

■ Communities gaining access to information and resources, developing participatory organizational mechanisms, and helping members make socially responsible decisions and contributions

■ Community-identified goals and concerns being in the forefront of all community development activities

■ Community development practice including continuous reflection on the intersection and role of diversity and pluralism within the community exchange

■ Social work curriculums related to community development being continually revised and integrated to ensure that the ever-changing field of community development policy and practice remains current and viable

■ Social work students being knowledgeable about the ways in which communities and populations can become more involved and competent in drawing on their strengths and assets to solve problems and enhance the quality of their lives

- The development of community leaders who can address the needs of community and participate in the coordination of the multidisciplinary efforts of a variety of community groups

- Initiatives that support state and local community development

- Federal, state, and private funding procurement to assure community development successes

- Legislation supporting the self-identified needs of communities and strategies that directly engage community residents in leadership and service provision.

REFERENCES

Butterfield, A. K., & Chisanga, B. (2008). Community development. In T. Mizrahi & L. E. Davis (Eds.-in-Chief), *Encyclopedia of social work* (20th ed., Vol. 1, pp. 375–381). Washington, DC, and New York: NASW Press & Oxford University Press.

Civil Rights Act of 1964, P.L. 88-352, 78 Stat. 241 (1964).

Cnaan, R., & Rothman, J. (2008). Capacity development and the building of community. In J. Rothman, J. Erlich, & J. Tropman (Eds.), *Strategies of community intervention* (7th ed., pp. 243–262). Peosta, IA: Eddie Bower.

Council on Accreditation of Services for Children and Families. (2008). *Standards and self-study manual* (8th ed., version 1.0). New York: Author.

Council on Social Work Education. (2008). *Educational policy and accreditation standards.* Alexandria, VA: Author.

Cox, D., & Pawar, M. (2006). *International social work: Issues, strategies and programs.* Thousand Oaks, CA: Sage Publications.

Economic Opportunity Act of 1964, P.L. 88-452, 78 Stat. 508 (1964).

Fisher, R., & Harding, S. (2008). Political life and public life: The context for community organizing. In J. Rothman, J. Erlich, & J. Tropman (Eds.), *Strategies of community intervention* (7th ed., pp. 5–26). Peosta, IA: Eddie Bower.

Gamble, D. N., & Weil, M. (2008). Community: Practice interventions. In T. Mizrahi & L. E. Davis (Eds.-in-Chief), *Encyclopedia of social work* (20th ed., Vol. 1, pp. 355–368). Washington, DC, and New York: NASW Press & Oxford University Press.

Han, C.-K., Grinstein-Weiss M., & Sherraden, M. (2009). Assets beyond savings in individual development accounts. *Social Service Review, 83,* 221–244.

Hill, E., & Blanck, P. (2009). Future of disability rights advocacy and "the right to live in the world." *Texas Journal on Civil Liberties & Civil Rights, 15*(1), 1+. Retrieved from http://www.questia.com/PM.qst?a=o&d =5044785678

Huebner, A. J., Mancini, J. A., Bowen, G. L., & Orthner, D. K. (2009). Shadowed by war: Building community capacity to support military families. *Family Relations, 58,* 216–228.

Kirst-Ashman, K., & Hull, G., Jr. (2009). *Generalist practice with organizations and communities* (2nd ed.). Belmont, CA: Wadsworth.

Kulig, J., Edge, S., & Joyce, B. (2008). Community resiliency as a measure of collective health status. *Canadian Journal of Nursing Research, 40,* 92–110.

Miley, K., O'Melia, M., & DuBois, B. (2009). *Generalist social work practice: An empowering approach* (6th ed.). Boston: Pearson.

Milligan, S. (2008). Community building. In T. Mizrahi & L. E. Davis (Eds.-in-Chief), *Encyclopedia of social work* (20th ed., Vol. 1, pp. 371–375). Washington, DC, and New York: NASW Press & Oxford University Press.

Mizrahi, T. (2009). Community organizing principles and practice guidelines. In A. Roberts (Ed.), *Social workers' desk reference* (2nd ed., pp. 872–881). New York: Oxford University Press.

National Association of Social Workers. (2008). *Code of ethics of the National Association of Social Workers.* Washington, DC: Author.

Netting, F. E., Kettner, P., & McMurtry, S. (2008). *Social work macro practice* (4th ed.). Boston: Pearson.

Ohmer, M., & DeMasi, K. (2009). *Consensus organizing: A community development workbook.* Thousand Oaks: Sage Publications.

Rotabi, K. S., Gammonley, D., Gamble, D. N., & Weil, M. O. (2007). Integrating globalization into the social work curriculum. *Journal of Sociology & Social Welfare, 34,* 165. Retrieved from http://www.questia.com/PM.qst?a=o&d=5024109510

Rothman, J. (2008). Multi modes of community intervention. In J. Rothman, J. Erlich, & J. Tropman (Eds.), *Strategies of community intervention* (7th ed., pp. 141–170). Peosta, IA: Eddie Bower.

Rubin, H., & Rubin, I. (2008). *Community organizing and development* (4th ed.). Boston: Pearson.

Saleebey, D. (2009). *The strengths perspective in social work practice* (5th ed.). Boston: Pearson.

Shulman, L. (2009). *The skills of helping individuals, families, groups, and Communities* (6th ed.). Belmont, CA: Brooks/Cole.

Streeter, C. (2008). Community: Overview. In T. Mizrahi & L. E. Davis (Eds.-in-Chief), *Encyclopedia of social work* (20th ed., Vol. 1, pp. 347–355). Washington, DC, and New York: NASW Press & Oxford University Press.

Tett, L. (Ed.). (2006). *Community education, lifelong learning and social inclusion* (2nd ed.). Edinburgh, Scotland: Dunedin Academic Press. Retrieved from http://www.questia.com/PM.qst?a=o&d=113445710

Yunus, M. (2006). The Nobel Peace Prize 2006: Nobel lecture. *Law and Business Review of the Americas, 13.* Retrieved from http://heinonline.org/HOL/Page?handle=hein.journals/lbramrca13&div=24&g_sent=1&collection=journals

NASW Members with Primary Responsibility for Revision of This Policy

First Draft Revision:

Jed Metzger (NYS)

Policy Panelists:

Joanne Iurato (CT)
Leah Lazzaro (NJ)
Tanya Roberts (NC)
Myke Selha (IA)
Mary Bishop (TX)
Rick Collins (CA)
Anna Scheyett (NC)

Policy statement approved by the NASW Delegate Assembly, August 2011. This policy statement supersedes the policy statement on Community Development approved by the Delegate Assembly in 2002. For further information, contact the National Association of Social Workers, 750 First Street, NE, Suite 700, Washington, DC 20002-4241. Telephone: 202-408-8600; e-mail: press@naswdc.org

Confidentiality and Information Utilization

BACKGROUND

The confidential nature of communications between social workers and their clients has been a cardinal principle of the social work profession from its earliest years. Legislative protection for social work information in adoption and juvenile court records dates back half a century. The Social Security Act of 1935 (P.L. 74-271), as amended in 1939, required state public assistance plans to "provide safeguards which restrict the use or disclosure of information concerning applicants and recipients to purposes directly connected with the administration of [the program]" [Title IV, section 502(a) (8)]. The Office of Vocational Rehabilitation issued regulations during the 1940s requiring similar safeguards. There are specific federal statutes related to confidentiality of alcohol and drug treatment records (42 U.S.C. §§ 290dd-2; 42 C.F.R. pt. 2). In 1975, when special education became a federal mandate under the Education for All Handicapped Children Act of 1975 (P.L. 94-142), the first federal requirements concerning students with special needs and pupil records, including confidentiality and parental consent, were codified. These mandates were expanded under the Individuals with Disabilities Education Act (P.L. 90-247) and were reauthorized under the Individuals with Disabilities Education Act Amendments of 1997 (P.L. 105-17). With the advent of the HIV/AIDS epidemic, many states have enacted statutes protecting the confidentiality of an individual's HIV/AIDS records and providing civil and criminal penalties for unlawful release of information (see, for example, N.J. Stat. 26: 5C-7, et seq., 2011). The Health Insurance Portability and Accountability Act of 1996 (P.L.104-191) (HIPAA) was enacted by the U.S. Congress, and it included administrative simplification provisions for streamlining the payment processes for health care services. These included the creation of national minimum standards to secure confidentiality in the utilization of health care information. State and federal legislation, regulations, and guidelines dealing with a broad array of health, welfare, and educational programs in varying degrees have recognized the need for limiting and safeguarding the collection and use of personal data.

Social workers have access to clients' personal information that is both confidential and privileged. Social workers are duty bound to protect all client information, regardless of the means by which it was conveyed. Issues of confidentiality and privacy are even more important now that the patient's or client's record—which once consisted of writing on pieces of paper—may consist of thousands of electronic bits of information that include written, audio, and visual records and links to other files within an agency or to other locations and may also include personal, medical, financial, and other types of data. Social workers are now using technology for documentation, electronic billing, communication, supervision, and client-based counseling. The NASW (2008) *Code of Ethics* provides strict guidelines for protection of confidentiality, informed consent, and maintenance and security of records [see 1.07, 1.03, 1.08, 2.02, and 3.04(c, d)].

Furthermore, there is an increasing amount of interdisciplinary communication within social work practice. Collaboration can, however, raise direct or indirect confidentiality dilemmas. Problems involved in the use or misuse of individually identifiable information, privacy, confidentiality, and privileged communications have commanded increased attention in both the public and private sectors of U.S. society in recent years.

In *Jaffee v. Redmond* (1996), the U.S. Supreme Court recognized a social worker–client privilege in the federal court system, protecting the confidentiality of patient and client communications with licensed therapists. Some federal legislation specifies confidentiality requirements for federal programs (such as Veterans Administration facilities), other legislation contains requirements for programs that receive federal funding (such as substance abuse and education programs), and still other federal legislation specifies confidentiality requirements that states must include in their programs as a condition of receiving federal grants.

HIPAA had a compliance date for its privacy rule in 2003, with detailed regulations about confidentiality and informed consent for an individual's health information (Centers for Medicare and Medicaid Services [CMS], 2010). HIPAA has standards for several areas that are pertinent to social work practice. These include using HIPAA-compliant computer billing software, ensuring the encryption of individually identifiable patient information that is electronically stored or transmitted, using secure passwords for protection of electronic data and electronic firewalls and physical safeguards for data backup in case of emergencies or natural disasters, maintaining an audit trail of access to electronic clinical information, and providing written notice to a client about privacy rights and how his or her information may be used (Morgan, Carvino, Polowy, & Kraft, 2007).

The Health Information Technology for Economic and Clinical Health Act (P.L. 111-5) (HITECH) was signed into law in 2009. This act promotes the use of electronic health records with the goal of making an electronic health record available for each person in the United States by 2014 (HITECH, 2009). HITECH also provides for increased privacy protection for personal health information and expands the scope of HIPAA to ensure that business associates providing services on behalf of health plans and health care providers are now directly subject to HIPAA regulations (Morgan & Polowy, 2009). HIPAA applies to clinical social workers, and it is important to note that the NASW *Code of Ethics* remains applicable as well in the area of electronic communications (Reamer, 2008).

In schools, hospitals, and agencies in which there is a team approach to treatment, disclosure of information frequently is critical to treatment planning and individualized educational programs. Insurance carriers and managed care firms often demand detailed diagnostic and other personal data in the name of accountability. Private practitioners and agency social workers are often subpoenaed to testify and reveal clients' confidences in divorce and custody proceedings and in other domestic lawsuits, and law enforcement agencies occasionally seek information from case records. In both public and private settings, social workers and other human services professionals must deal with the question of when legal protections of privacy—including statutory requirements for privileged communications—must yield to other legal requirements, such as protecting children from abuse or third parties from intended harm. When working collaboratively, social workers should ensure that colleagues understand social workers' obligations to respect confidentiality and any exceptions to it.

ISSUE STATEMENT

Over the past decade, the nation has seen the implementation of HIPAA and its expansion under the HITECH amendments, both of which have implications for social workers to uphold high standards for information use and release, data security and data storage, and how clients are informed about how personal data are being used (CMS, 2010; HITECH, 2009). With the increasing use of electronic communication and media of all formats in social work practice, these laws point to the importance of social workers maintaining the most current electronic security software to advance client confidentiality. These laws also discuss the importance of data destruction. Data destruction is an important area as the "complete" destruction of data takes specific intent; otherwise, data will remain on a system or electronic server, open to potential breach (Nelson, Phillips, & Steuart, 2010). Social workers need to be reminded of this technological fact to increase awareness about necessary steps to completely remove electronic data from computers, networks, and other systems, including backup systems, to ensure client confidentiality.

Technological advances that have created the need for new regulations have also brought new ways to interact in virtual worlds and through social networking, with online chatting, Facebook, Skype, and even online counseling and virtual support groups. However, it is important to note that these platforms are not as secure and confidential as one might hope (Jones & Soltren, 2005). In fact, it has been reported that "over 40 percent of an individual's [online] social 'footprint' can be reconstructed by using a single pseudonym" (Irani, Webb, Li, & Pu, 2009). Therefore, carefully setting passwords, restricting access to only authorized individuals, and thoughtfully posting online material helps to maintain client confidentiality as it helps to maintain professional boundaries for the social worker, much in the way that having an unlisted telephone number might have helped in the past.

The emergence and rapid expansion of information and communication technology have made the development of a strong information policy a primary concern for social workers. The social worker's central role as the recipient and custodian of personal information places a particularly heavy responsibility on the social work profession and on individual practitioners to maintain current knowledge of legal requisites and then to weigh consequences, balance equities, and assume responsibility for actions taken. Social workers also bear a responsibility to understand the technologies used and to optimize the potential value of technology to serve clients effectively and efficiently while safeguarding against exposure of confidential information.

The profession also must reassess its policies and ethical base regarding privacy issues. It must consider the need to assume a more vigorous and active posture in this area, including the assumption of new advocacy roles. In addition, social workers must be aware of protections and constraints on patient or client confidentiality, which may be legally imposed. Every state has extended the protection of psychotherapist–patient privilege to communications with mental health professionals (*Jaffee v. Redmond*, 1996), although what communications are protected and how professions are included varies (Polowy, Morgan, Bailey, & Gorenberg, 2008). Privilege may be waived by a patient or client, as the legally recognized holder of the privilege, or may be legally required to be breached, as in cases of child abuse or when it could prevent harm to a foreseeable victim. Privacy laws vary by state, and it is critical for social workers to be aware of these laws and changes in them. Some laws apply to the federal government—such as the Privacy Act of 1974 (P.L. 93-579), which makes unauthorized release a federal offense—and some federal laws apply to records in specific settings—such as the Family Educational Rights and Privacy Act of 1974 (P.L. 93-380), which protects the confidentiality of student records in schools and colleges that receive federal funding. The confidentiality of other records maintained by state and local governments may be protected by other statutes and regulations in specific locales.

In addition, social workers are constrained to some degree by privileged communication. Whereas confidentiality is a professional mandate, privileged communication is a legal issue in which a client's right to privacy is protected by state or federal law. Many courts have held that the right belongs to the client and that only the client can waive the protection (NASW Legal Defense Fund, 2011; Polowy et al., 2008).

POLICY STATEMENT

NASW supports the following:

■ Legislation, regulations, or policies that ensure adherence to the NASW *Code of Ethics* regarding confidentiality

■ An individual's right of access to personal information that is maintained about him or her and the right to decide how it is used

■ An individual's right to correct or amend a record of his or her identifiable information

■ The profession becoming proficient in the technological tools and skills required for competent and ethical practice and staying current with emerging technology

■ Information system technology that prevents unauthorized access to client information and *complete* record destruction in compliance with *NASW & ASWB* [Association of Social Work Boards] *Standards for Technology and Social Work Practice* (NASW & ASWB, 2005)

■ Policies and practices that promote respect for confidential information exchanged by colleagues in the course of their professional relationships and transactions when collaboration is required and appropriate

■ Social workers being fully knowledgeable about and compliant with federal and state regulations regarding confidentiality and information utilization.

REFERENCES

Centers for Medicare and Medicaid Services. (2010). *HIPAA general information*. Retrieved from http://www.cms.gov/HIPAAGenInfo/

Education for All Handicapped Children Act of 1975, P.L. 94-142, 89 Stat. 773 (1975).

Family Educational Rights and Privacy Act of 1974, P.L. 93-380, 88 Stat. 571 (1974).

Health Information Technology for Economic and Clinical Health Act, P.L. 111-5, 123 Stat. 226, 467 (2009).

Health Insurance Portability and Accountability Act of 1996, P.L. 104-191, 110 Stat. 1936 (1996).

Individuals with Disabilities Education Act, P.L. 90-247, 81 Stat. 804 (1968).

Individuals with Disabilities Education Act Amendments of 1997, P.L. 105-17, 111 Stat. 37 (1997).

Irani, D., Webb, S., Li, K., & Pu, C. (2009). Large online social footprints—An emerging threat. In Proceedings of the 2009 International Conference on Computational Science and Engineering (pp. 271–276). Washington, DC: IEEE Computer Society.

Jaffee v. Redmond, 518 U.S. 1, 116 S. Ct. 1923, 135 L.Ed.2d 337 (1996).

Jones, H., & Soltren, J. H. (2005). Facebook: Threats to privacy. Retrieved from http://ocw.mit.edu/courses/electrical-engineering-and-computer-science/6-805-ethics-and-the-law-on-the-electronic-frontier-fall-2005/projects/facebook.pdf

Morgan, S., Carvino, L., Polowy, C. I., & Kraft, E. G. (2007). *The social worker and protection of privacy*. Washington, DC: NASW Legal Defense Fund.

Morgan, S., & Polowy, C. I. (2009). *HITECH HIPAA for social workers*. Retrieved from https://www.socialworkers.org/ldf/legal_issue/2009/200903.asp

NASW Legal Defense Fund. (2011). *Client confidentiality and privileged communications*. Washington, DC: NASW Press.

National Association of Social Workers. (2008). *Code of ethics of the National Association of Social Workers*. Retrieved from http://www.socialworkers.org/pubs/code

National Association of Social Workers & Association of Social Work Boards. (2005). *NASW & ASWB standards for technology and social work practice*. Retrieved from http://www.socialworkers.org/practice/standards/NASWTechnologyStandards.pdf

Nelson, B., Phillips, A., & Steuart, C. (2010). *Guide to computer forensics and investigations*. Boston: Course Technology PTR.

Polowy, C. I., Morgan, S., Bailey, W. D., & Gorenberg, C. (2008). Confidentiality and privileged communication. In T. Mizrahi & L. E. Davis (Eds.), *Encyclopedia of social work* (20th ed., Vol. 1, pp. 408–414). Washington, DC, and New York: NASW Press & Oxford University Press.

Privacy Act of 1974, P.L. 93-579, 88 Stat. 1896 (1974).

Reamer, F. (2008). The challenge of electronic communication. *Social Work Today, 8*. Retrieved from http://www.socialworktoday.com/archive/EoEMayJun08.shtml

Social Security Act of 1935, P.L. 74-271, 49 Stat. 620 (1935).

NASW Members with Primary Responsibility for Revision of This Policy

First Draft Revision:

Raelene Freitag (WI)

Policy Panelists:

Brenda Pitmon (MA)
Patricia Findley (NJ)
Bettye Bradshaw (FL)
Elena Delavega (TX)
Kimiko Kuroda (CA)
Diana Stroud (IL)

Policy statement approved by the NASW Delegate Assembly, August 2011. This policy statement supersedes the policy statement on Confidentiality and Information Utilization approved by the Delegate Assembly in 2002. For further information, contact the National Association of Social Workers, 750 First Street, NE, Suite 700, Washington, DC 20002-4241. Telephone: 202-408-8600; e-mail: press@naswdc.org.

Crime Victim Assistance

BACKGROUND

During the 1970s, the harmful effects of crime and the often insensitive treatment of crime victims by police, prosecutors, and judges were brought to public attention by individual crime victims, research studies, and advocacy groups (Cassell, 2007). In 1982, the President's Task Force on Victims of Crime pointed out that victims also were being mistreated by many other entities, including hospitals, faith communities, schools, and businesses (Cassell, 2007). Crime victimization studies identified a large gap between the number of crimes reported to police and the number of self-identified crime victims (U.S. Department of Justice, Office for Victims of Crime, Office of Justice Programs, 2011). Fear of involvement with the criminal justice system was found to be a common reason for not reporting crime. Victims, survivors, and those affected by homicide, domestic violence, sexual assault, hate-based attacks, and other personal crimes often described their encounters with the criminal justice system as a "revictimization" (Cassell, 2005).

The crime victims' rights movement developed in the 1970s because of the absence of victims from criminal processes and the view of advocates that the criminal justice system was preoccupied with defendants' rights to the exclusion of the legitimate interests of crime victims (Cassell, 2007). Victims were either ignored or viewed as "tools" to use to identify and punish offenders, and all too often, victims suffered additional hardship as a result of contact with the criminal justice system (U.S. Department of Justice, Office of Justice Programs, Office for Victims of Crime, 2005). Advocates have focused on legislation at both the state and federal level to protect victims' rights and fund services for victims (Cassell, 2007).

The first piece of federal legislation introduced in the U.S. Congress was the Victim and Witness Protection Act of 1982, which established the provision of services to victims, legal protections, and training for law enforcement and others (U.S. Department of Justice, Office of Justice Programs, Office for Victims of Crime, 2005). Since then, Congress has passed several bills that further protect victims' rights and other federal statutes to deal with specialized victim situations, such as child victims and witnesses (Cassell, 2005).

In 1984, Congress passed the Victims of Crime Act (P.L. 98-473), which established strong federal leadership in victim assistance. The act funded qualified victim assistance and state compensation programs in all 50 states and the District of Columbia.

In 1994, the Violence Against Women Act (P.L. 103-322) (VAWA) provided federal funding for programs to combat domestic violence and sexual assault. In 2004, the Justice for All Act (P.L. 108-405) authorized efforts to encourage compliance with victims' rights, and in 2005, VAWA was reauthorized to include dating violence and stalking. Although varying from state to state, every state has passed a "Victims' Bills of Rights," and 32 states have enacted constitutional amendments requiring certain services for crime victims (National Center for Victims of Crime, 2011).

The Office for Victims of Crime in the U.S. Department of Justice administers the nation's two major formula grant programs (noncompetitive awards given out on the basis of predetermined formulas): Crime Victims Compensation and Victims of Crime Assistance (VOCA) (U.S. Department of Justice, Office for Victims of Crime, Office of Justice Programs, 2011). VOCA funds grants to programs that provide services to crime victims.

Numerous innovative programs have sprung from the traditional victim assistance programs. One of the more empirically grounded, yet controversial, victim services is victim–offender mediation, or, as it is more commonly known now, victim–offender mediation/dialogue (VOM/D). VOM/D is an expression of restorative justice, a process that is initiated by victims who choose to participate, that elevates the role of crime victims in the justice process, and that holds offenders directly accountable to both the victims and the communities they have violated. VOM/D also designs opportunities for offenders to repair some of the harm they have caused and to engage the community in these processes (Umbreit, 2001).

ISSUE STATEMENT

The social work profession has long been concerned with issues surrounding crime and violence. Social workers' efforts commonly have targeted crime prevention and rehabilitation of offenders, but, more recently, the profession has expanded its focus to include the consequences of crime for victims, their families, and their communities.

The number of people affected by crime each year is significant. Over the past decade, the rate for violent and property crimes has averaged 4 percent of the population each year (4,000 per every 100,000) (U.S. Department of Justice, Federal Bureau of Investigation, 2010). The number of crime victims rises when one considers that only about half (49 percent) of all violent crimes and about 40 percent of all property crimes are reported to police (Bureau of Justice Statistics, 2009).

Research shows that the shock waves from victimization touch not only the victim, but also the victim's immediate family and relatives, neighbors, and acquaintances. Along with individuals, communities and organizations can be victimized, leading to their deterioration over time as confidence ebbs, fear increases, and the economic burden of victimization becomes insupportable (United Nations Office for Drug Control and Crime Prevention [ODCCP], 1999). Victims of crimes can suffer serious biopsychosocial, economic, and spiri-

tual injuries that may continue long after the crime has occurred (Boccellari et al., 2007; Germain, Shear, Hall, & Buysse, 2007; McCollister, French, & Fang, 2010; Vincent, 2009). In their quest to transform themselves from crime victims to crime survivors, individuals may need a variety of social and mental health provisions, along with advocacy. The most comprehensive comorbidity study to date showed that lifetime prevalence of other psychological disorders in male and female crime victims with posttraumatic stress disorder (PTSD) is 88 percent and 79 percent, respectively. The most common comorbid disorders are depression, substance abuse, and phobias (Young, 1993). Social workers identify and assist victims in many community settings, including human service agencies, child welfare and adult protective service agencies, mental health clinics, and hospitals and medical clinics (Danis, 2006). Therefore, the likelihood of victims having contact with professional social workers is extremely high, whatever the practice setting.

Victims' reactions to crimes may vary by individual characteristics such as preexisting physical and mental health, racial and ethnic background, age, gender, sexual orientation, immigration status, and disability; the type of crime committed; the crime scene; and the perpetrator and his or her relationship to the victim. The effects of victimization strike particularly hard at vulnerable individuals, including those living in poverty, those with a disability, and those who are socially isolated. Research shows that those already affected by victimization are particularly susceptible to subsequent victimization by the same or other forms of crime (ODCCP, 1999).

Social workers who practice extensively with victims may be at risk for secondary traumatic stress (STS): work-related, secondary exposure to people who have experienced extremely or traumatically stressful events. The negative effects of STS may include fear, sleep difficulties, intrusive images, and avoiding reminders of the person's traumatic experiences. STS is related to vicarious trauma, having many similar characteristics. Listening to the stories of traumatized clients can cause vicarious trauma symptoms and compassion fatigue (Stamm, 2010), which may lead to burnout, high agency turnover rates, and inconsistent services to clients. Opportunities for ongoing education and skill development that strengthen and enhance the resiliency of service providers can benefit those working with this complex population.

Federal statistics document a wide variety of crimes—including homicide, assault, sexual violence, domestic violence, workplace violence, hate crimes, stalking, and terrorism—and their impact on victims, including PTSD, depression, substance abuse, and other mental and physical disorders (Bureau of Justice Statistics, 2009; Logan & Cole, 2007; National Center for Posttraumatic Stress Disorder, n.d.). In recent years, there has been increasing attention to the crimes against the elderly, cybercrime, identity theft, and human trafficking and the difficulties faced by victims in obtaining services (Allison, Schuck, & Lersch, 2005; Kritzinger & von Solms, 2010; Powell, 2006; Reid, 2010).

POLICY STATEMENT

NASW supports the following:

■ Universal screening of clients of all ages to determine whether they have been or are currently being victimized in order to provide the best services and support culturally competent practice when working with victims of crime

■ Policy advocacy at the local, state, and national levels to promote assistance for victims of crime and to facilitate their safety and recovery from criminal victimization

■ Advocacy for individual victims of crime to help them overcome obstacles, barriers, and loopholes that may impede or prevent them from obtaining needed services

■ Increased funding to assist crime victims, particularly services for underserved populations and oppressed groups that may be more vulnerable targets of crime

■ Curriculum development in schools of social work and continuing education to identify victims of crime, to understand the biopsychosocial effects of victimization, and to

acquire knowledge of services available to crime victims along with the development of field placements in victim services agencies so that students can gain experience in this area

■ Research on the effects of crime on victims, including psychological and financial consequences, and the effects on secondary victims such as family, friends, communities, and service providers as well as research on the effectiveness of services, interventions, and treatment modalities to help victims heal from their trauma

■ Research-informed practice and practice-informed research within the profession of social work and the field of crime victim services

■ Self-determination of victims of crime in all situations, acknowledging the right of victims to define the harm done to them and the services that would be most helpful to them, regardless of the goals of the service program

■ Opportunities for victims to share the impact of the crimes they suffered in the courts and in the community

■ Restorative justice through VOM/D only if initiated by the victim but strongly discourages routine use of this process in domestic violence cases

■ Agency policies and procedures, supervisory strategies, and training programs that are sensitive to the risk of secondary trauma for social workers and other advocates who work with victims of crime

■ Efforts to gain recognition for all same-sex and heterosexual domestic partners by providing access to compensation and other assistance programs for all such partners who are crime victims.

REFERENCES

Allison, S.F.H., Schuck, A. M., & Lersch, K. M. (2005). Exploring the crime of identity theft: Prevalence, clearance rates, and victim/offender characteristics. *Journal of Criminal Justice, 33,* 19–29.

Boccellari, A., Alvidrez, J., Shumway, M., Kelly, V., Merrill, G., Gelb, M., et al. (2007). Characteristics and psychosocial needs of victims of violent crime identified at a public-sector hospital: Data from a large clinical trial. *General Hospital Psychiatry, 29,* 236–242.

Bureau of Justice Statistics. (2009). *Criminal victimization.* Washington, DC: U.S. Department of Justice.

Cassell, P. G. (2005). Recognizing victims in the federal rules of criminal procedure: Proposed amendments in light of the Crime Victims' Rights Act. *Brigham Young University Law Review, 2005,* 835–925.

Cassell, P. G. (2007). Treating crime victims fairly: Integrating victims into the federal rules of criminal procedure. *Utah Law Review, 2007*(4), 861–970.

Danis, F. (2006, March). The victim assistance field and the profession of social work. *OVC Bulletin.* Retrieved from http://www.ovc.gov/publications/bulletins/NASW victimassistance/ncj210592.pdf

Germain, A., Shear, M. K., Hall, M., & Buysse, D. J. (2007). Effects of a brief behavioral treatment for PTSD-related sleep disturbances: A pilot study. *Behaviour Research and Therapy, 45,* 627–632.

Justice for All Act of 2004, P.L. 108-405, 118 Stat. 2260 (2004).

Kritzinger, E., & von Solms, S.H. (2010). Cyber security for home users: A new way of protection through awareness enforcement. *Computers and Security, 29,* 840–847.

Logan, T., & Cole, J. (2007). The impact of partner stalking on mental health and protective order outcomes over time. *Violence and Victims, 22,* 546–562.

McCollister, K. E., French, M. T., & Fang, H. (2010). The cost of crime to society: New crime-specific estimates for policy and program evaluation. *Drug and Alcohol Dependence, 108,* 98–109.

National Center for Posttraumatic Stress Disorder. (n.d.). *Types of trauma.* Retrieved from http://www.ptsd.va.gov/professional/pages/types-of-trauma.asp

National Center for Victims of Crime. (2011). *Issues: Victims' bill of rights.* Retrieved from http://www.ncvc.org/ncvc/main.aspx?dbName=DocumentViewer&DocumentID=32697

Powell, M. E. (2006). Effects of dependency on compliance rates among elder abuse victims at the New York Department for the Aging, Elderly Crime Victim's Unit. *Journal of Gerontological Social Work, 46,* 229–247.

Reid, J. A. (2010). Doors wide shut: Barriers to the successful delivery of victim services for domestically trafficked minors in a southern U.S. metropolitan area. *Women & Criminal Justice, 20,* 147–166.

Stamm, B. H. (2010). *The concise ProQOL manual* (2nd ed.). Pocatello, ID: ProQOL.org.

Umbreit, M. S. (2001). *The handbook of victim–offender mediation: A guide for practice and research.* San Francisco: Jossey-Bass.

United Nations Office for Drug Control and Crime Prevention. (1999). *Handbook on justice for victims.* Retrieved from http://www.uncjin.org/Standards/9857854.pdf

U.S. Department of Justice, Federal Bureau of Investigation. (2010, September). *Crime in the United States, 2009.* Retrieved from http://www.fbi.gov/ucr/09cius.htm

U.S. Department of Justice, Office of Justice Programs, Office for Victims of Crime. (2005, May). *Attorney General guidelines for victim and witness assistance.* Retrieved from http://www.justice.gov/olp/pdf/ag_guidelines.pdf

U.S. Department of Justice, Office for Victims of Crime, Office of Justice Programs. (2011). *2011 National Crime Victims' Rights Week resource guide.* Retrieved from http://ovc.ncjrs.gov/ncvrw2011/index.html

Victims of Crime Act of 1984, P.L. 98-473, 98 Stat. 4792 (1984).

Vincent, N. J. (2009). Exposure to community violence and the family: Disruptions in functioning and relationships. *Families in Society, 90,* 137–143.

Violence Against Women Act of 1994, P.L. 103-322, 108 Stat. 1902 (1994).

Young, M. (1993). *Victim assistance: frontiers and fundamentals.* Dubuque, IA: Kendall/Hunt.

NASW Members with Primary Responsibility for Revision of This Policy

First Draft Revision:

Marti Anderson (IA)
Melissa Atwood (TX)
Stephanie Books (TX)
Janice Harris Lord (TX)
Derrelyn Perryman (TX)

Policy Panelists:

Jennifer Markens (MA)
Dorothy Gaboda (PA)
Kim Kuhn (VA)
Kelli Soyer (IA)
Mary Bahney (NE)
Kimberly Harper (WY)

Policy statement approved by the NASW Delegate Assembly, August 2011. This policy statement supersedes the policy statement on Crime Victim Assistance approved by the Delegate Assembly in 2002. For further information, contact the National Association of Social Workers, 750 First Street, NE, Suite 700, Washington, DC 20002-4241. Telephone: 202-408-8600; e-mail: press@naswdc.org

Cultural and Linguistic Competence in the Social Work Profession

BACKGROUND

Elements of cultural competence have received wide and far-ranging attention in social work literature. The discussion places major emphasis on the effective use of knowledge and skill application within an ecological context and transactional dimensions of motivation, skill, and empowerment (Breton, 1994). Cultural competence implies a heightened consciousness and analytical grasp of racism, sexism, ethnocentrism, class conflict, and cross-cultural and intracultural diversity. Furthermore, cultural competence contributes to efforts to address racial and ethnic disparities in health and mental health status and the disproportionate confinement in restrictive settings in the child welfare, juvenile justice, and criminal justice systems.

American society is constantly undergoing major demographic changes that heighten the diversity issues confronting social workers. The 2000 Census reported that the largest single ethnic minority group is the Hispanic population, who comprise 13 percent of the U.S. population (U.S. Census Bureau, 2001). Continued immigration and current birth rates are the factors propelling this growth and change in America's racial and ethnic makeup. Immigration to the United States by peoples from Asia, Eastern Europe, Russia, Africa, and Latin America can be expected to intensify the diversity social workers will witness in their practice settings. By 2050, population projections estimate that only 50 percent of the U.S. population will be "white alone, not Hispanic" (U.S. Census Bureau, 2004).

One dimension of cultural competence is the capacity to communicate. In the United States, the number of people for whom English is not the primary language has grown. The 2000 Census documented more than 380 language groups spoken in this country. More significantly, more than 18 percent of all families speak a language other than English in their households. Although many of these individuals are also fluent in English, 11.9 million people are linguistically isolated, meaning they do not speak English well or not at all (U.S. Census Bureau, 2003). As the country becomes more linguistically diverse, linguistic competence within the social work profession becomes more critical for effective service delivery. *Linguistic competence* is "the capacity of an organization and its personnel to communicate effectively, and convey information in a manner that is easily understood by diverse audiences including persons of limited English proficiency, those who have low literacy skills or are not literate, and individuals with disabilities" (Goode & Jones, 2003, p. 1). Individual practitioners and organizations are challenged to develop the capacity to use the verbal, written, and multimedia communications in a manner that supports effective practice.

Culture is not just an attribute of racial and ethnic groups. Cultural differences are often made manifest by belief systems founded in religions. The values, beliefs, and practices of particular faith groups can be the primary source of cultural identity and create a specific worldview that affects every component of a person's life. In addition, people who identify with a sexual orientation different from the dominant society also represent distinct cultural groups. Gay, lesbian, bisexual, *omnisexual* (people having or open to many forms of sexual expression), transgender, queer and questioning women, men, and youths have established their own cultural identity and demand fair treatment and inclusion in all aspects of American life. Social workers of all sexual orientations must be prepared to bridge the crosscultural experiences of people of different sexual orientations.

Another example includes people with disabilities who have established a cultural identity that demands more than empathy and accommodation. They wish to be recognized as bicultural people with the right to seek inclusion in both mainstream and their own cultures.

Professional interest in cultural competence among social workers is predated by a rich and varied history on the subject and many decades of discourse regarding the profession's response or lack of response to the service needs of diverse clients. The settlement house movement in the early history of the profession is an example of efforts to serve immigrants, many of whom were culturally different from the dominant population at the time. In retrospect, the practice at the time was designed to facilitate acculturation of immigrants into the dominant society. The Civil Rights movement of the 1960s marked the beginning of a shift in focus from promotion of acculturation and advocacy against the barriers to acculturation to greater affirmation of differences and recognition of the need to offer services attuned to the client's view of his or her life circumstances shaped by his or her cultural worldview.

In the 1960s, the Council on Social Work Education (CSWE) began to address the issues of racial and ethnic diversity in the recruitment and training of social work students and faculty, as well as in the content of social work curriculums. Schools emphasized the "dual perspective," or the concept that all people are part of at least two systems: the larger societal system and their immediate environment (Norton, 1978). Solomon (1976) defined *empowerment* as facilitating clients' connection with their own power, and in turn, being empowered by the very act of reaching across cultural barriers. Gallegos (1982) provided one of the first conceptualizations of racial and ethnic competence as "a set of procedures and activities to be used in acquiring culturally relevant insights into the problems of diverse clients and the means of applying such insights to the development of intervention strategies that are culturally appropriate for these clients" (p. 4).

Green (1995) identified some culturally competent qualities and procedures: (1) clarification of the worker's personal values concerning "minority" people; (2) articulation of personal and professional values and ways they might conflict with or accommodate the needs of clients of color; (3) development of interviewing skills that reflect the worker's understanding of the role of language in racially and ethnically distinct communities; (4) the ability to relate to professionals of color in ways that enhance effectiveness with clients; (5) the capacity to use resources on behalf of communities of color; (6) the mastery of techniques for learning the history, traditions, and values of a racial or ethnic group; (7) the ability to communicate information on the cultural characteristics of a given group to other professionals; and (8) the knowledge of the effect of social policies and services on clients of color.

The concept of cultural competence has moved through a progression of ideas and theoretical constructs favoring cultural pluralism, cultural sensitivity, multiculturalism, and a transcultural orientation to social work practice (Gould, 1995). A brief review of the social work literature in the past few years reveals a range of content areas present in cultural competence, including racial identity formation; the interrelationship among race, gender, class, and ethnicity; HIV/AIDS among Hispanics and African Americans; work with poor families; work with poor African American or Puerto Rican families; sexual identity and sexual orientation; gay adolescents; acculturation and immigration; spirituality and religious diversity; biculturalism and multiculturalism; crossracial practice considerations; work with people with disabilities; outreach to American Indian and Asian American clients; empowerment; interracial marriage; racially mixed clients; biracial children; mental health services for Chinese, Cuban, Indochinese, and West Indian clients; sociocultural models of practice; and training of culturally sensitive practitioners.

Social workers must consider that cultural distinctions lie in many areas of life and even in abstraction. Cultural differences are evident in language; family lifestyle; roles of children;

treatment of and relations with elderly people, spouses, men, and women; religious beliefs and practices; orientation toward work; attitudes regarding justice and authority; social status; problem-solving methods; privacy; and attitudes toward the dominant group. Social workers need to consider the relationship among their own values, beliefs, and practices; the values, beliefs, and practices that guide the philosophy and administrative decisions of the organization that provides the auspice of their work, and the values, beliefs, and practices of the service population. This analysis may yield many areas of incongruence that must be resolved to achieve effective service delivery.

Diverse groups have differential experiences in American society. The differential treatment is a function of the dynamic interaction with the dominant culture of U.S. society, which in turns contributes to the values, beliefs, and practices adopted by the group. Social workers need sophisticated skills and abilities to advocate for clients against the underlying devaluation of cultural experiences based on difference and oppression. This mandate is addressed to social workers of all cultures, not just those who are members of historically and currently underserved, underrepresented, and oppressed groups. All social workers need to master culturally competent knowledge and skills because the pluralistic society is a social reality (Gould, 1995).

Cultural competence requires awareness. The quest for authentic cultural competence is a process of becoming more attuned to how clients experience their uniqueness, deal with their differences and similarities, and cope with a sociopolitical environment that is often unconcerned with the welfare of their people, however diverse their needs may be. Culturally competent social work practice starts with the driving assumption of individual uniqueness connected to humanness, and the individual experience of culture through which reality is seen and meaning is interpreted (Congress, 1994). Social workers' self-awareness of their own cultures is as fundamental to culturally competent practice as the informed assumptions about clients' cultural background and experiences. Just as the advocacy agenda is applicable to social workers of dominant groups, the need to develop crosscultural skills is requisite for all social workers, including those from historically oppressed, underserved, and underrepresented populations. This expectation is important because of intragroup variability and the recognition that any given individual is a member of multiple cultures.

Although the discussion of culture often isolates people by virtue of race, ethnicity, religion, nationality, gender, class, sexual orientation, physical ability, and other attributes, in reality people represent intersections of these various cultural groups. Cultural competence requires the capacity to recognize the interaction of these multiple identities at the individual, family, group, neighborhood, and community levels and discern the salient cultural issues within any given helping relationship. Cultural competence requires a heightened consciousness of how clients experience their uniqueness and deal with their differences and similarities within a larger social context (NASW, 2001).

ISSUE STATEMENT

The complexities associated with cultural diversity in the United States affect all aspects of professional social work practice, requiring social workers to deliver culturally competent services to a broad range of clients. Cultural and linguistic competence requires knowledge, skills, and attitudes that promote and support respectful and effective crosscultural communication and practice. To that end, efforts are required at the micro-, mso-, and macropractice levels to affect direct practice and supervision, program administration, and social policy to achieve meaningful outcomes as defined by consumers, families, and communities.

Social workers using a person-in-environment framework for assessment need to include to varying degrees important cultural factors that have meaning for clients and reflect the culture of the world around them. Although in U.S. social work cultural diversity historically has been associated primarily with race and ethnicity, social workers are also aware of the need to develop culturally competent skills, knowledge, and values when working with people of a different gender, social class, religion or spiritual belief, sexual orientation, age, and disability. This kind of sophisticated cultural competence does not come naturally to any social worker and requires a high level of professionalism. This policy statement speaks to the need for definition, support, and encouragement of a heightened level of social work practice that encourages cultural competence among all social workers so that they can respond effectively, knowledgeably, and sensitively to the diversity inherent in the agencies they work in and with the clients and communities they serve.

Cultural competence is a vital link with the theoretical and practice knowledge base that defines social work expertise. Increasing cultural competence within the profession requires efforts to recruit and retain as diverse a group of social workers as possible, many of whom bring some "indigenous" cultural competence to the profession. In addition, cultural competence requires efforts to increase avenues for the acquisition of culturally competent skills by all social workers. Indigenous cultural competence is a result of absorbing positive and negative cultural memories through lifelong experiences, which can be an advantage as well as an obstacle when the workers confront the subjective qualities of sharing the same cultural experiences as their clients.

Cultural competence should not be equated with cultural identity or consciousness. For example, a Latino social worker is not inherently culturally competent when working with Latino clients; that is, it is not the social worker's ethnicity that makes him or her effective when dealing with clients of similar heritage. Rather, it is the combination of the worker's cultural history that is mediated through his or her social work training that makes for effective social work practice. This training emphasizes focus on the client context of socioeconomic status, race, gender, sexual orientation, religion, age, and abilities—all of which may vary among clients who share an ethnic heritage. When social workers have little contact with people who are culturally different, they must acquire cultural competence through cognitive methods to achieve affective insight. The profession needs to enhance culturally competent social work practice by

addressing the needs of both indigenous workers and those from different cultures struggling to acquire competence.

Cultural competence builds on the profession's stance on self-determination and individual dignity and worth, adding inclusion, tolerance, and respect for diversity in all its forms. Social workers know the importance of developing practices that are sensitive to different races, nationalities, language proficiencies, and immigration or migration experiences. Social workers are keenly aware of the deleterious effects of racism, sexism, ageism, anti-Semitism, homophobia, and xenophobia on clients' lives and the need for social advocacy and action to better empower diverse clients and communities. This policy statement reinforces this awareness but moves the discussion toward the development of clearer guidelines, goals, and objectives for the future of social work practice in which cultural diversity will increase in complexity.

POLICY STATEMENT

NASW seeks to promote cultural and linguistic competence in all areas of social work education, research, and practice. Social workers must honor the ethical responsibility to be culturally competent practitioners, as the NASW *Code of Ethics* (NASW, 2000) instructs. This policy statement adopts the definition of *cultural competence* proffered by Cross and colleagues (1989) as "a set of congruent behaviors, attitudes, and policies that come together in a system or agency or among professionals and enables the system, agency, or professionals to work effectively in cross-cultural situations" (p. 13). The word "culture" is used because it implies the integrated pattern of human behavior that includes thoughts, communications, actions, customs, beliefs, values, and institutions of a racial, ethnic, religious, or social group. The word "competence" is used because it implies having the capacity to function effectively. A culturally competent system of care acknowledges and incorporates at all levels the importance of culture, the assessment of crosscultural relations, vigilance toward the dynamics that result from cultural differences, the expansion of cultural knowledge, and the adaptation of services to meet culturally unique needs (Cross, Bazron, Dennis, & Isaacs, 1989; NASW, 2001).

NASW promotes and supports the implementation of cultural and linguistic competence at three intersecting levels: the individual, institutional, and societal. Cultural competence requires social workers to examine their own cultural backgrounds and identities while seeking out the necessary knowledge, skills, and values that can enhance the delivery of services to people with varying cultural experiences associated with their race, ethnicity, gender, class, sexual orientation, religion, age, or disability. Culturally competent practice is a critical component of professional social work expertise in all practice settings that include but are not limited to direct practice, community organizing, supervision, consultation, administration, advocacy, social and political action, policy development and implementation, education, and research and evaluation. Culturally competent practice is required in all geographic communities, whether urban, suburban, rural or frontier.

Culturally competent social work practice cannot occur within a vacuum. It requires an institutional and professional infrastructure that supports the efforts of individual practitioners to conduct themselves in a culturally competent manner. This means that the organization must have policies, procedures, and financial allocations that support and reward the growth and development of the staff. Furthermore, organizations must have the appropriate philosophy, policies, and procedures to ensure that the appropriate structures and practices are designed, funded, staffed, implemented, and evaluated to achieve the most effective and acceptable services to meet the unique needs and perspectives of a culturally and linguistically diverse service population. It is only through partnership with consumers, families, and cultural communities that social work institutions can successfully design the appropriate services.

It is the position of NASW that social policy be developed at the local, state, and national levels to promote cultural and linguistic competence. Such policies should assert the expectation of cultural and linguistic competence,

institute the structures and financing to facilitate cultural and linguistic competence, and demand accountability of institutions and practitioners for cultural and linguistic competence. Such policies must address human resources and program factors that promote the recruitment and retention of a culturally diverse workforce, require appropriate educational preparation and continued professional development in cultural and linguistic competence of the workforce, and establish strategies to monitor and evaluate service outcomes for people of diverse cultures. Not only are these social policies needed to address the requirements of cultural and linguistic competence, but also such policies are needed to continue to work against the continued expression of racism, prejudice, and discrimination in this country.

NASW recognizes that the expertise required for the development of appropriate and effective interventions for diverse populations resides within that population. It is the position of NASW that collaboration with consumers, families, and cultural communities is a precondition for creation of culturally and linguistically competent services, reasonable accommodations, interventions, programs, and policies.

It is the position of NASW that practitioners and their host organizations ensure that services are offered in the language preferred by the consumers and families receiving service. In addition, NASW supports tending to the linguistic needs of social work's diverse workforce. Linguistic competence requires the growth in capacity to use the preferred language of the consumer and also to develop the skills to use appropriate strategies for interpretation and translation. Several strategies that organizations can pursue include modifications in staffing and operations, such as the inclusion of bilingual and bicultural staff; foreign language interpretation services; use of cultural brokers; provision of materials in alternative formats such as audiotape, Braille, enlarged print; and print materials in easy-to-read, low-literacy, picture, and symbol formats (Goode & Jones, 2003).

NASW recognizes that a policy statement alone cannot fully define the values, knowledge, and skills required for culturally and linguistically competent practice. Cultural competence is an important ingredient of professional competence, as important as any other component that forms the basis of the theoretical and clinical knowledge that defines social work expertise. This policy statement supports and encourages promulgation and adherence to the *NASW Standards for Cultural Competence in Social Work Practice* (2001).

NASW supports the advancement of practice models that have relevance for the range of needs and services represented by diverse client populations. It promotes the application of practices for which there is evidence of effectiveness for the relevant cultural group and the development of a knowledge base that emanates for the practice within and on behalf of cultural communities. As advocates for the providers and consumers of social work services, social workers need to promote cultural competence by supporting the evaluation of delivery models that are offered as culturally competent. Monitoring cultural competence among social workers should include establishing mechanisms for obtaining direct feedback from clients.

The social work profession is encouraged to take proactive measures to ensure cultural competence as an integral part of initial and continuing social work education and practice and to increase research and scholarship among its professionals. The social work profession should ensure cultural competence is an integral part of organizational practice and social policy.

REFERENCES

Breton, M. (1994). Relating competence: Promotion and empowerment. *Journal of Progressive Human Services, 5*(1), 27–44.

Congress, E. P. (1994). The use of culturagrams to assess and empower culturally diverse families. *Families in Society, 75,* 531–540.

Cross, T. L., Bazron, B. J., Dennis, K. W., & Isaacs, M. R. (1989). *Towards a culturally competent system of care: A Monograph on effective services for minority children who are severely emotionally disturbed,* Volume I. Washington, DC: Georgetown University Child Development Center, Child and Adolescent Services Program Technical Assistance Center.

Gallegos, J. S. (1982). The ethnic competence model for social work education. In B. W. White (Ed.), *Color in a white society* (pp. 1–9). Silver Spring, MD: National Association of Social Workers.

Goode, T., & Jones, W. (2003). *A definition of linguistic competence.* Washington, DC: Georgetown University Center for Child and Human Development, National Center for Cultural Competence.

Gould, K. H. (1995). The misconstruing of multiculturalism: The Stanford debate and social work. *Social Work, 40,* 198–205.

Green, J. W. (1995). *Cultural awareness in the human services: A multi-ethnic approach* (2nd ed.). Boston: Allyn & Bacon.

National Association of Social Workers. (2000). *Code of ethics of the National Association of Social Workers.* Washington, DC: Author.

National Association of Social Workers. (2001). *NASW standards for cultural competence in social work practice.* Washington, DC: Author.

Norton, D. G. (1978). *The dual perspective: Inclusion of ethnic minority content in the social work curriculum.* New York: Council on Social Work Education.

Solomon, B. B. (1976). *Black empowerment: Social work in oppressed communities.* New York: Columbia University Press.

U.S. Census Bureau. (2001). *Overview of race and Hispanic origin 2000.* Retrieved May 14, 2004, from http://www.census.gov

U.S. Census Bureau. (2003). *Language use and English-speaking ability: 2000.* Retrieved May 14, 2004, from http://www.census .gov

U. S. Census Bureau. (2004). *Projected population of the United States, by race and Hispanic origin: 2000 to 2050.* Washington, DC: Author. Available at http://www.census .gov/ipc/www/usinterimproj/

SUGGESTED READINGS

Child Welfare League of America. (2002). *Cultural competence agency self-assessment instrument* (rev. ed.). Washington, DC: CWLA Press.

Hogan-Garcia, M. (2003). *The four skills of cultural diversity competence: A process for understanding and practice* (2nd ed.). Pacific Grove, CA: Brooks/Cole—Thomson Learning.

Jackson, V., & Lopez, L. (Eds.). (1999). *Cultural competence in managed behavioral healthcare.* Providence, RI: Manisses Communications Group.

Lum, D. (2003). *Culturally competent practice: A framework for understanding diverse groups and justice issues* (2nd ed.). Pacific Grove, CA: Brooks/Cole—Thomson Learning.

Morales, A. T., & Sheafor, B. W. (2002). *The many faces of social work clients.* Boston: Allyn & Bacon.

U. S. Department of Health and Human Services, Substance Abuse and Mental Health Services Administration, Center for Mental Health Services. (2000). *Cultural competence standards in managed care mental health care services: Four underserved/underrepresented racial/ethnic groups.* Rockville, MD: Author.

Policy statement approved by the NASW Delegate Assembly, August 2005. This statement supersedes the statement on Cultural Competence in the Social Work Profession approved by the Delegate Assembly in 1996 and referred by the 2002 Delegate Assembly to the 2005 Delegate Assembly for revision. For additional information, contact the National Association of Social Workers, 750 First Street, NE, Suite 700, Washington, DC 20002-4241; telephone 202-408-8600; e-mail: press@naswdc.org

Deprofessionalization and Reclassification

BACKGROUND

Beginning with Abraham Flexner's paper presented in 1915, "Is social work a profession?" the issue of professionalism has been a prominent point of discussion. Some of the factors contributing to this question included the status of the earliest practitioners: upper class, women volunteers; and a lack of a professional code of ethics, professional schools of study, and research focused on social work issues. At the time of Flexner and Jane Addams, women rarely worked for pay. The only acceptable areas of "women's work" were caregiving and helping jobs such as teaching and nursing. Social work became part of this. Because women were not seen as equal in vocational arenas, work they did was rarely considered "professional."

Things changed after World War I for social work when there was a shift from apprenticeship training to university-based education and when there was more of a need for services. Although social work is still predominately a "women's profession" (NASW [2006] reports that 81 percent of all members are women), many concurrent trends have led social work to a clearer professional status. Some of the important trends include the national public service expansions in the 1930s and the 1960s, licensing, privatization of social services, the diversification of practitioners, and the growth of managed care. NASW and Council on Social Work Education (CSWE) now both define *professional social workers* as "individuals who have graduated from an educational program accredited by the Council on Social Work Education with at least a bachelors degree in social work" (NASW, 2006, p. 6). Unfortunately, once the answer to Flexner's question was "yes," then the stage was set for the current trend toward deprofessionalization and reclassification.

In 1983, Carol Meyer cautioned, "in every field of practice, on every level of government, and in the voluntary sector, the declassification of professional social work positions has become a dismal reality" (p. 419).

Gibelman and Schervish (1996) have documented similar phenomena where the public sector agencies have a great deal of difficulty attracting social workers. They identify causes for this as large caseloads, decrease in quality of service, insufficient personnel, and negative views of this area of social work practice.

With privatization often comes a decrease in accountability and regulation. As part of this shift, there is more of a separation between funders and practitioners, which in turn affects professional standards. As this shift occurred, agencies were left without accreditation, leaving them open for possible legal challenges. To protect themselves, agencies sought out accreditation from groups that "require agencies to use research and business models to analyze and improve policies and practices." (California Association of Deans and Directors, 2004). In addition, agencies that were once sure of funding now needed to raise their own capital. A by-product of these shifts included the hiring of non–social work executive directors. People trained in finance, business, and law are now frequently found in positions previously held by social workers (Healy & Meagher, 2004). They were also in a position to evaluate the services and the staff at these agencies.

Kahn (1981) described deprofessionalization as a trend that results in "reduction in educational requirements for entry-level jobs, assumption of interchangeability of bachelors degrees, reorganization of jobs to reduce educational requirements, nonrecognition of the exclusivity of bachelors (BSW) or master's of social work (MSW) skills, and equating education with experience" (p. 3). Healy and Meager (2004) saw the causes of deprofessionalization as "fragmentation and routinization of social work roles and tasks, a decline in professional categories of social work employment, and underemployment of social workers in paraprofessional positions" (p. 244).

At times, under various deprofessionalization and reclassification schemes, public and private agencies have created generic job classifications, such as clinical case manager, case management specialist, and social services worker that eliminated the title of social worker. The combined effect of the deprofessionalization and reclassification movement has been civil service systems that permit hiring of unqualified and uncredentialed individuals for social work positions.

Another consequence has been the eradication of chief social worker positions and functions in major agencies and departments. In addition, public and private agencies will often substitute in-service training for formal professional training. Several investigative reports support the position that social work education provides the beginning level practice knowledge and skills necessary for entry-level positions, and that experience alone is an unreliable indicator of job performance. A more recent NASW study concluded that graduate social work education is the best predictor of performance (NASW, 2006). Although the importance of social work education has been denigrated by the change in requirements for specific social service jobs, job performance requirements—such as psychosocial assessment, treatment planning, and discharge planning—have remained unchanged. Paraprofessionals, counselors, or human services personnel often are considered as trained "social workers" and are, at times, sanctioned to function under the title "social worker." As such, these noncredentialed personnel are held responsible for delivering social services although they lack the social work knowledge base, skills, and values necessary to perform such tasks.

Deprofessionalization and reclassification must focus on factors both external and internal to the social work profession, as well as on the value of social work education. Some external factors include relaxation of social services standards, at both the state and federal levels; reduction in federal and state funding for social services programs; radical changes in personnel policies; the diminished number of social workers in administrative and policy-making positions; and the changes in the insurance industry's payment for social services. Increasingly, people from other human services disciplines are competing with individuals who have BSWs and MSWs for jobs that once exclusively required social work education. Internal factors of the profession include the redefinition of tasks and responsibilities by specialty groups and a preference by social workers for employment in private agencies.

Trends in social work education indicate that students interested in social policy, social research, or social services administration choose other professional degrees, and workers with MSWs often must enroll in doctoral programs to specialize. As a result, non-social workers occupy decision-making and supervisory positions and make policies that affect the status of social workers and social work practice.

Since 1981, NASW has enhanced its capabilities to address deprofessionalization and reclassification. First, NASW has intensified legislative capabilities and lobbying activities at state and federal levels, resulting in the achievement of landmark legislative goals with the inclusion of social workers as payees under Part B and other sections of Medicare and the establishment of standards for social services staffing in nursing facilities. In addition, NASW has blocked legislation in some states that would have required social workers to obtain other professional licenses and certifications to practice in areas traditionally within their scope, such as family therapy.

Important research done in 2004 and published in 2006 through the Center For Workforce Study in collaboration with the University of Albany gives us a great deal of information regarding licensed social workers in terms of areas of concentration, gender, age, and pay among other characteristics. It enables the profession to better define itself and to work toward increasing awareness of and perceived perception of social workers by the public. This in turn helps further underscore professionalization in social work.

In 2001, NASW established the NASW Foundation, with the following goals:

■ to identify, develop and respond to social work policy and practice issues;

■ to assist with rapid response to social crises;

■ to support practice-based research, so that practice and research are directly linked;

■ to raise the visibility of social work and enhance public esteem for the profession;

■ to support the development of cutting edge continuing education that addresses critical issues;

■ to promote the appropriate application of new technology to the practice of social work.

As part of the Foundation's work, in 2004 NASW created "Help Starts Here," a public education campaign geared toward changing the public perceptions of social work and to improve the profession.

Finally, NASW increasingly has demonstrated its effectiveness in promoting the social work profession by assuming a leadership role in the social policy and political arena. In addition, NASW has supported national-level projects to increase the number of trained staff in child welfare, student loan forgiveness, and research and resources for major reinvestment initiatives. Since NASW designated social work licensing a high-priority action, all states have established some form of licensing or regulation. As insurance for high-quality social work services and maintenance of professionalism, it is necessary to evaluate our current licensing efforts and refine them accordingly. The focus now can move to providing stronger title protection and clearer, more universal licensing requirements for all social workers at all education levels.

ISSUE STATEMENT

Many legislators have failed to recognize the social work profession as a major contributor to effective social services and as an advocate for social welfare policies and programs in the United States. Systematically, social workers are being eliminated from direct services, supervision, policy making, and administrative positions. This elimination is being accomplished by deprofessionalizing and reclassifying traditional social work positions in the public and private sectors. Increasingly, public and private employers are hiring staff members who are uncredentialed as social workers and as such they are, inadequately trained, and not qualified to fill social work positions (Healy & Meagher, 2004). To help eradicate the issue, it is important to develop uniform national standards on all levels to define and regulate social work practice. NASW reports the number of practicing social workers to be 840,000, whereas only 310,000 hold state licenses (NASW, 2006). According to a 2007 survey of licensure boards conducted by NASW, all states regulate MSW social workers (NASW, 2007). Only 24 states refer to those with BSWs as licensed, though a limited number of other states certify them. Forty-nine states have advanced licensing requiring post master's supervised hours. In some of these states, only advanced practice is licensed. A handful of states have licenses for nonclinical social workers. This hodgepodge of licensing requirements only adds to the confusion over professionalism and leaves the door open for further deprofessionalization and declassification (NASW, 2007).

This trend is a result of the sociopolitical climate of downsizing; devolution of the role of government; cost containment in health and mental health services through managed care; and competition with allied professions for direct services, as well as supervisory and administrative positions. Many of these individuals, hired as a result of deprofessionalization and reclassification, lack social work practice knowledge, values, and skills, yet are required to perform such complex tasks as biopsychosocial assessment, treatment planning, interviewing, and acting as change agents. In addition, in many public sector agencies, work is being contracted out, again eliminating the assurance that these jobs will be filled with social workers with appropriate training and licensing. One way to change this trend is to make sure that title protection is in place not only in licensing professionals but also in job descriptions at the agency level. The term *social worker* should not be used unless the person in the position has had at least a minimal social work education and is licensed at that level. The California Master plan (California Association of Deans & Directors, 2004) includes a "Ladder of Learning" that comprises seven levels ranging from high school certificate, followed by an associate degree, and ending with the doctoral degree. This can be used as a national example. Through the use of this or some other such schema on a national level, the standards of professionalism through uniform requirements at multiple levels of licensing can be ensured. In addition to deprofessionalization, declassification remains an issue for social workers. Contributing factors to this include the following:

■ Because there are insufficient numbers of people with BSW or MSW degrees (currently 30,000 MSWs and BSWs graduate nationwide each year, with an overall ratio of 101 licensed social workers per 100,000 people) (NASW, 2006) or because of a lack of interest in employing these individuals in public services agencies, vacancies are filled by untrained staff with undifferentiated undergraduate degrees, causing agencies to emphasize on-the-job training.

■ Carework in this culture is generally assumed to be women's work, and it is implied women do not need an independent living wage. There is a discrepancy of 14 percent between the mean wages of men and women who are licensed social workers.

■ State employee unions have emphasized promotion on the basis of experience and do not support professional education.

■ Legislation and administrative rules have allowed other educational degrees and work experience to serve as the equivalent of social work education.

■ Fewer resources and budget cuts have led to a justification to lower social work standards and to fill jobs with less-qualified personnel who fit lower salary standards.

POLICY STATEMENT

Professional social workers possess the specialized knowledge necessary for an effective social services delivery system. Social work education provides a unique combination of knowledge, values, skills, and professional ethics that cannot be obtained through other degree programs or by on-the-job training.

Therefore, NASW supports

■ promotional opportunities for all social workers, including policy-making and administrative positions based on levels of social work education, experience, and competence.

■ service delivery that adheres to NASW's *Code of Ethics* (2000).

■ clients' rights to expect and to receive high standards of professional services. Under the equal protection law, clients served by both public and private organizations have the right to receive the same quality care provided by trained social workers.

■ the increased recruitment of high school students and early college students to the social work major in order to ensure an adequate number of social workers filling professional social work jobs.

■ efforts at the state level to implement regulations for the entire profession, including title protection, certification, and/or licensure.

■ organizational and public policies that promote the hiring of CSWE degreed social work practitioners and halt the general trend to hire less-qualified staff.

■ the promotion of social work as a distinctly different profession from other human services disciplines (such as counseling, clinical psychology, nursing, marriage and family therapy, and so forth) as it focuses on the intra- and interpersonal aspects of clients' lives.

■ the expertise, knowledge, and skills demonstrated by social workers with BSWs, MSWs and doctoral degrees should be actively communicated to clients, colleagues, and others at all times.

■ the identification of tangible social work skills gained through social work education such as bio-psychosocial assessment, treatment planning, interviewing, discharge planning, and so forth that are essential to the social services delivery system.

- the education of social workers in accredited programs with courses designed and taught by social work educators that will promote the culture, knowledge, and values and ethics of the profession.

- research and outcome studies that demonstrate the effectiveness and cost–benefit of hiring trained social workers. This research promotes the relevance of social work education to the tasks performed in public and private organizations.

- title and practice protection through regulation for social work in all practice settings on all practice levels.

- efforts to oppose legislation and policies that allow for the practice of social work by individuals without social work education, experience, and competencies.

- title protection in job descriptions so that the title "social worker" can be used only to refer to professionally prepared social workers.

REFERENCES

California Association of Deans and Directors of Schools of Social Work. (2004). *Master plan for social work education in the state of California*. Berkeley, CA: Author.

Flexner, A. (1915). *Is social work a profession?* Presentation to the National Conference on Charities and Corrections.

Gibleman, M., & Schervish, P. (1996). Social work and public services practice: A status report. *Families in Society, 77,* 117–124.

Healy, K., & Meagher, G. (2004). The reprofessionalization of social work: Collaborative approaches for achieving professional recognition. *British Journal of Social Work, 34,* 243–260.

Kahn, T. (1981). *Chapter action guide on declassification*. Lansing: National Association of Social Workers, Michigan Chapter.

Meyer, C. M. (1983). Declassification: Assault on social workers and social services [Editorial]. *Social Work, 28,* 419.

National Association of Social Workers. (1991). NASW: Relationships with other social work organizations and other human services disciplines. In *Social work speaks: NASW policy statements* (2nd ed., pp. 204–206). Silver Spring, MD: Author.

National Association of Social Workers. (2000). *Code of ethics of the National Association of Social Workers*. Washington, DC: Author.

National Association of Social Workers. (2007). Cross-state data. Retrieved March 12, 2008, from http://www.socialworkreinvestment.org/State/

Scheffler, R., & Kirby, P. (2003). The occupational transformation of the mental health system. *Health Affairs, 23,* 177–188.

Whitaker, T., Weismiller, T., & Clark, E. (2006). *Assuring the sufficiency of a frontline workforce: A national study of licensed social workers*. Washington, DC: National Association of Social Workers.

Policy statement approved by the NASW Delegate Assembly, August 2008. This policy statement supersedes the policy statement on Deprofesionalization and Reclassification approved by the Delegate Assembly in August 1999 and referred by the 2005 Delegate Assembly to the 2008 Delegate Assembly for revision, and the policy statement on Declassification approved by the Assembly in 1993 and 1981. For further information, contact the National Association of Social Workers, 750 First Street, NE, Suite 700, Washington, DC 20002-4241. Telephone: 202-408-8600 or 800-638-8799; e-mail: press@naswdc.org

Disasters

BACKGROUND

Disasters are collective, community-wide traumatic events that cause extensive destruction, death or injury, and widespread social and personal disruption (Freedy, Resnick, & Kilpatrick, 1992). The steadily changing global, political, and environmental climate has led to an increase in terrorism, random acts of violence, and catastrophic occurrences of nature. Federal laws, in particular the Disaster Relief Act of 1970 (P.L. 91-606), the Disaster Relief Act Amendments of 1980 (P.L. 96-568), and the Robert T. Stafford Disaster Relief and Emergency Assistance Act (P.L. 93-288), address disaster-related concerns.

A local emergency is declared when the governance of a city or county deems conditions to pose an extreme threat to the safety of people and property within that jurisdiction. When the disaster conditions threaten the safety of people and property within a state, the governor may proclaim a state of emergency, making mutual aid assistance mandatory from other cities, counties, and state authorities. When damage exceeds the resources of local and state governments, the president may declare a disaster, which activates federal assistance as provided for in the Stafford Act. Individual assistance may include low-interest loans, individual and family grants, temporary housing, assistance with basic needs, and crisis counseling.

In addition to Federal Emergency Management Agency (FEMA) and state and local governments, several volunteer agencies assume defined roles and responsibilities in disaster situations. Among these are the American Red Cross, Volunteer Organizations Active in Disasters (VOAD), and the Salvation Army. Other key organizations are involved in disaster response, including Volunteers of America, the United Methodist Church, the Southern Baptist Convention, the National Catholic Conference and Catholic Charities, the Mennonite Disaster Services, and the Christian Reformed World Belief (Myers, 1994).

NASW entered into the first of a succession of professional agreements with the American Red Cross in 1990 to facilitate social work participation in the planning, training, and provision of mental health services to disaster victims. In 1993, the California Chapter of NASW, Los Angeles County regions, developed a statement of understanding with the American Red Cross (NASW & American Red Cross, 1993). In 1994, after the Northridge earthquake, NASW, the California Chapter, and the American Red Cross' California Chapter formed a statewide statement of understanding. And in 2005 in response to the crisis caused by Hurricane Katrina, NASW engaged with the Red Cross to maintain a database—the Disaster Services Human Resources System—as a registry of trained disaster mental health professionals. The development of agreements with volunteer organizations and the delivery of disaster-related services continue to evolve. In the process, there is a need to understand the roles of the various organizations, to continue collaboration, and to have regular meetings to enhance cooperative service delivery and ensure comprehensive disaster management. In collaboration with the state mental health authority, social workers are among the professionals who make up the roster of volunteers being readied in New Jersey to be called in the event of a disaster. The phases of disaster management articulated by FEMA are (1) mitigation, (2) preparedness, (3) response, and (4) recovery. It is important to consider the commitment required in each of the phases of disaster in service delivery. Nearly three years after the events of September 11, 2001, local, state, federal, and international agencies continue with mitigation and preparedness activities. FEMA's (1996) *State and Local Guide 101: Guide for All-Hazards Emergency Operations Planning* assigns responsibility to carry out actions in emergencies and is the basis for government response to any disaster. Mental health planning is based on recommendations in the *Mental Health All-Hazards Disaster Plan Guidance* manual developed by Substance Abuse and Mental Health Services Administration (SAMHSA) (SAMHSA 2003). This manual helps state mental health program directors assess the status of mental health disaster plans throughout the country and provide guidance in the planning process.

In a community affected by disaster, in addition to people directly affected, several special populations can be identified. Among these groups of disaster survivors and victims are subpopulations historically of concern to social work: older adults, people with low incomes, people with preexisting mental illness, children, immigrants, refugees, people with disabilities, and people who are isolated, institutionalized, or otherwise at social or physical risk. These populations are among the most vulnerable disaster survivors and require special attention during preparedness, immediate relief, and recovery. People who have a history of trauma are also a group at risk. Virtually no one experiences or responds to disasters unscathed. Rescue workers and military personnel, witnesses to the event, first responders, people who are physically injured, mental health professionals, and the skilled workers on the scene all constitute at-risk populations. The makeup of the at-risk population group is determined by the nature of the disaster.

Whole communities warrant assistance, particularly in light of the constant stream of media coverage. Television also broadens the scope of the disaster. On one hand, covering a disaster is a public service, commanding the attention of the world to the needs of the people affected. On the other hand, the coverage deepens the wounds and intensifies the anxiety of people affected because of the constant repetition of the stories, the misinformation that breaking news is often fraught with, and the response of people and government as a result of the media coverage. Furthermore, media workers also constitute a population at risk because of their extended involvement in the areas affected.

Social workers from all fields of practice must have knowledge and understanding about disasters and the course of recovery. Effective interventions must be tailored to phases of recovery. There is a range of reactions to stress—reactions that are universal, normal for the situation, widely shared, and that abate naturally (Cohen & Ahearn, 1980; Weaver, 1995). The DSM-IV-TR states that "community-based studies reveal a lifetime prevalence for Posttraumatic Stress Disorder of approximately 8% of the adult population in the United States" (American Psychiatric Association, 2000, p. 466). Interventions models must be based on resilience and strengths rather than pathology and deficit.

Because of the chaos that ensues after a disaster, a well-ordered and coordinated mass response system is needed for effective disaster management. NASW has adopted a disaster policy at the national level for four primary reasons:

1. Disasters are large-scale catastrophes that affect whole communities or multiple communities in geophysical, social, and psychological ways.

2. The trauma and deprivation resulting from disasters often are magnified for those with few resources and reduced opportunities to rebuild homes and replace losses. As such, vulnerable populations are likely to be among those especially affected by disasters.

3. Social workers are well suited to interpret the disaster context, to advocate for effective services, and to provide leadership in essential collaborations among institutions and organizations. Furthermore, compatible with social work epistemology, disaster assistance must be construed holistically, encompassing the physical, developmental, psychological, emotional, social, cultural, and spiritual needs of individuals and systems. Finally, respected disaster response modalities readily translate

to the language of empowerment and classic, generalist social work practice.

4. Social workers continue to respond quickly and effectively to need in the immediate aftermath of disasters. The importance of the potential contribution and role of social work warrants more than ad hoc, intuitive, spontaneous responses on a disaster-by-disaster basis. Effective disaster leadership and a proactive presence on the part of the profession require preparation, direction, training, and practice.

ISSUE STATEMENT

According to the Robert T. Stafford Disaster Relief and Emergency Assistance Act, as amended by the Disaster Mitigation Act of 2000 (P. L. 106-390) "major disaster means any natural catastrophe (including any hurricane, tornado, storm, high water, wind driven water, tidal wave, tsunami, earthquake, volcanic eruption, landslide, mudslide, snowstorm, or drought), or, regardless of cause, any fire, flood, or explosion, in any part of the United States, which in the determination of the President causes damage of sufficient severity and magnitude to warrant major disaster assistance under this Act to supplement the efforts and available resources of States, local governments, and disaster relief organizations in alleviating the damage, loss, hardship, or suffering caused thereby." (Title I, §§ 102, 5122).

Not all disasters meet the requirements for "major disaster," yet every disaster causes extensive destruction, death, or injury and produces widespread community disruption and individual trauma (Hartsough & Myers, 1987). Disasters occur from natural causes, human error, equipment or technological failure, and intentional human actions.

Inherent in social work policy is the recognition of individual as well as systems considerations. Incidents that affect individuals, such as rape or other violent crime, a serious home fire, or a tragic accident, may affect the family system and certain community members. These incidents are not "declared" disasters, but they create upheaval in communities. The financial resources to address them may

not be available. At times disasters are sudden, unexpected events; at other times they are slow, insidious occurrences allowing some degree of predictability.

A common language is essential to effective communication, policy, and planning. Quarantelli (1985) used the term "collective stress situation" to refer to a circumstance in which a social system fails to provide expected life conditions for its members. These extreme stress situations are divided into disasters and conflicts. Conflicts include war, riots, and terrorist attacks. Emergency services personnel experience the impact of an event through their response to the call for service as well as their membership in their family and community. Use of the term "critical incident stress" has proliferated. It is not uncommon to hear this phrase used to describe civilian stress responses. Traumatic stress differs from posttraumatic stress disorder. "Most people recover fully from even moderate stress reactions within 6 to 16 months" according to the *Disaster Mental Health Response Handbook* (New South Wales Institute of Psychiatry, 2000, p. 27). SAMHSA's service model calls for providing crisis counseling, including psychoeducation about reactions to disaster, in an attempt to prevent the onset of serious mental illness (SAMHSA, 2003).

The broad range of social work practice allows social workers to provide services in a variety of settings. Of necessity, social workers will follow the lead of the disaster response organizations in providing these services. Because of the increasing number and scope of disasters worldwide, multidisciplinary partnerships, training, research, and coordination of response efforts are needed.

POLICY STATEMENT

NASW supports participation in and advocates for programs and policies that serve individuals and communities in preparation for, during, and in the wake of disaster. NASW supports:

■ prevention or mitigation of the adverse consequences of disaster and effective preparation for disaster by individuals, families, social networks, neighborhoods, schools, organizations, and communities, especially where vulnerable populations are concentrated

■ enhancement of the efficiency, effectiveness, orchestration, and responsiveness of disaster relief and recovery efforts to prevent exacerbation of problems related to the disaster

■ policies and procedures that provide access to disaster relief services and resources to all (including relationship rights for gay, lesbian, bisexual and transgender people and undocumented immigrants

■ provision of behavioral health and social services to survivors in a context of normalization and empowerment, with sensitivity to the phases of disaster recovery and with understanding of the unique cultural characteristics of the affected community and its populations

■ attention to the long-term recovery phase of disasters

■ attention to the special training needs, stress management techniques, and support needs of first responders and other disaster workers

■ education of social workers and social work students in the specialized knowledge and methods of trauma response

■ continued research on the impact of disasters, effective interventions, and disaster management strategies

■ development of a cadre of well-trained, culturally competent disaster professionals committed to effective interdisciplinary and interorganizational collaboration in disaster planning and disaster response

■ provision of accurate and effective public information on the normal phases of disaster reaction, functional coping methods, and strategies for accessing and successfully using the disaster assistance systems.

REFERENCES

American Psychiatric Association. (2000). *Diagnostic and statistical manual of mental disorders* (4th ed., Text Rev.). Washington, DC: Author.

Cohen, R. E., & Ahearn, F. L. (1980). *Handbook for mental health care of disaster victims.* Baltimore: Johns Hopkins University Press.

Disaster Mitigation Act of 2000, Pub. L. 106-390, 114 Stat. 1552.

Disaster Relief Act of 1970, Pub. L. 91-606, 84 Stat. 1744.

Disaster Relief Act Amendments of 1980, Pub. L. 96-568, 94 Stat. 3334.

Federal Emergency Management Agency. (1996). *State and local guide 101: Guide for all-hazards emergency operations planning.* Washington, DC: Author.

Freedy, J. R., Resnick, H. S., & Kilpatrick, D. G. (1992). Conceptual framework for evaluating disaster impact: Implications for clinical intervention. In J. H. Gold (Series Ed.) & L. S. Austin (Vol. Ed.), *Clinical practice: Volume 24. Responding to disaster* (pp. 3–23). Washington, DC: American Psychiatric Press.

Hartsough, D. M., & Myers, D. G. (1987). *Disaster work and mental health: Prevention and control of stress among workers* (DHHS Publication No. ADM 87-1422). Washington, DC: U.S. Government Printing Office.

Myers, D. (1994). *Disaster response and recovery: A handbook for mental health professionals* (DHHS Publication No. SMA 94-3010). Washington, DC: U.S. Government Printing Office.

National Association of Social Workers, & American Red Cross. (1990). *Statement of understanding between National Association of Social Workers and the American Red Cross.* Washington, DC: Authors.

National Association of Social Workers, & American Red Cross. (1993). *Statement of understanding between the California chapter of the National Association of Social Workers, Los Angeles County regions and the American Red Cross.* Los Angeles: Authors.

New South Wales Institute of Psychiatry and Centre for Mental Health. (2000). *Disaster mental health response handbook.* North Sydney, Australia: Author.

Quarantelli, E. L. (1985). An assessment of conflicting views on mental health: The consequences of traumatic events. In C. R. Figley (Ed.), *Trauma and its wake: The study and treatment of post-traumatic stress disorder* (pp. 173–215). New York: Brunner/Mazel.

Robert T. Stafford Disaster Relief and Emergency Assistance Act, Pub. L. 93-288, 88 Stat. 143.

Substance Abuse and Mental Health Services Administration, Center for Mental Health Services. (2003). *Mental health all-hazards disaster plan guidance* (DHHS Publication No. SMA 3829). Rockville, MD: U.S. Department of Health and Human Services.

Weaver, J. (1995). *Disasters: Mental health interventions*. Sarasota, FL: Professional Resource Press.

SUGGESTED READINGS

American Red Cross. (1992). *Disaster mental health services I: Glossary of terms* (ARC Publication No. 3077-1A). Washington, DC: Author.

Austin, L. (Ed.). (1992). *Clinical practice: Responding to disaster*. Washington, DC: American Psychiatric Press.

Ayalon, O., Lahad, M., & Cohen, A. (Eds.). (1998). *Community stress prevention. Volume 3*. Upper Galilee, Israel: Tel Hai Academic College, Community Stress Prevention Centre.

Ayalon, O., Lahad, M., & Cohen, A. (Eds.). (1999). *Community stress prevention. Volume 4*. Upper Galilee, Israel: Tel Hai Academic College, Community Stress Prevention Centre.

Coarsey, C. (2004). *Handbook for human services response*. Blairsville, GA: Higher Resources.

Cohen Silver, R., Holman, E. A., McIntosh, D., Poulin, M., & Gil-Rivas, V. (2002). Nationwide longitudinal study of psychological responses to September 11. *JAMA, 288,* 1235–1244.

Farberow, N. L., & Gordon, N. S. (1986). *Manual for child health workers in major disasters* (DHHS Publication No. ADM 86-1070). Washington, DC: U.S. Government Printing Office.

Green, B. L. (1993). *Mental health and disaster: Research review* (Report to NIMH, Requisition 91MF175040). Washington, DC: Georgetown University Medical Center, Department of Psychiatry.

Green, B., Grace, M., Lindy, J., Gleser, G., Leonard, A., & Kramer, T. (1990). Buffalo Creek survivors in the second decade: Comparison with unexposed and nonlitigant groups. *Journal of Applied Social Psychology, 20,* 1033–1050.

Green, B., Grace, M., Lindy, J., Titchener, J., & Lindy, J. (1983). Levels of functional impairment following a civilian disaster: The Beverly Hills Supper Club fire. *Journal of Consulting and Clinical Psychology, 51,* 573–580.

Herman, J. (1992). *Trauma and recovery*. New York: Basic Books.

Holen, A. (1991). A longitudinal study of the occurrence and persistence of post-traumatic health problems in disaster survivors. *Stress Medicine, 7,* 11–17.

LeDoux, J. (2002). *Synaptic self*. New York: Viking.

Lima, B., Pai, S., Lozano, J., & Santacruz, H. (1990). The stability of emotional symptoms among disaster victims in a developing country. *Journal of Traumatic Stress, 3,* 497–505.

National Institute of Mental Health. (2002). *Mental health and mass violence: Evidence-based early psychological intervention for victims/survivors of mass violence. A workshop to reach consensus on best practices* (NIH Publication No. 02-5138). Washington DC: U.S. Government Printing Office.

North, C. S., Smith, E. M., & Spitznagel, E. L. (1994). Post-traumatic stress disorder in survivors of a mass shooting episode. *American Journal of Psychiatry, 151,* 82–88.

Pearlman, L. (1995). *Trauma and the therapist*. New York: W. W. Norton.

Phifer, J., & Norris, F. (1989). Psychological symptoms in older adults following natural disaster: Nature, timing, duration, and course. *Journal of Gerontology: Social Sciences, 44,* S207–S217.

Shore, J., Tatum, E., & Vollmer, W. (1986). Psychiatric reactions to disaster: The Mount St. Helens experience. *American Journal of Psychiatry, 143,* 590–595.

Stith Butler, A., Panzer, A. M., & Goldfrank, L. (Eds.). (2003). *Preparing for the psychological consequences of terrorism: A public health strategy*. Washington, DC: Institute of Medicine, National Academies Press.

U.S. Department of Veterans Affairs, National Center for Post-Traumatic Stress Disorder (n.d.). *Effects of traumatic stress in a disaster situation*. Washington, DC: Author.

Ursano, R. J., Fullerton, C. S., & Norwood, A. E. (Eds.). (2003). *Trauma and disaster responses and management* (Review of Psychiatry Series, Vol. 22, No. 1). Arlington, VA: American Psychiatric Publishing.

Policy statement approved by the NASW Delegate Assembly, August 2005. This policy statement supersedes the statement on Disasters approved by the Delegate Assembly in 1996 and referred by the 2002 Delegate Assembly to the 2005 Delegate Assembly for revision. For additional information, contact the National Association of Social Workers, 750 First Street, NE, Suite 700, Washington, DC 20002-4241; telephone: 202-408-8600; e-mail: press@naswdc.org

Drug Testing in the Workplace

BACKGROUND

The testing of employees for the presence of alcohol and illicit drugs is an area of concern for employers and employees, to the legal and social environment, and to professional practice. Increasingly, the idea of drug testing demands that social workers make professional, ethical, and even personal decisions. The abuse of alcohol and illicit drugs is common in our society.

Section 504 of the Rehabilitation Act of 1973 (P.L. 93-112) and the Drug-Free Workplace Act of 1986 (Federal Register, 1986) are federal laws. The former protects qualified individuals from discrimination on the basis of their disability. Examples of impairments include alcoholism and drug addiction. The latter applies specifically to workplaces that are a recipient of federal funds. To be certified as a drug-free workplace, a drug-free policy must be published and a drug-free awareness program must be in place.

The NASW *Code of Ethics* (2000) states that "the social worker should respect clients' rights to privacy. . . . Social workers should protect the confidentiality of all information obtained in the course of professional service, except for compelling professional reasons" (Section 1.07c). Recognizing the stigma associated with substance abuse, the social worker needs to be aware of the federal confidentiality regulations (42 CFR Part 2) (HHS 2004) in which, confidentiality has been the practice for substance abuse treatment programs across the country. Similar privacy rules also apply with the Health Insurance Portability and Accountability Act of 1996 (P.L. 104-191) standard.

Federal laws and the NASW *Code of Ethics* (2000) affect the profession's response to drug and alcohol policies in the workplace, directly and indirectly. Since the inception of the industrial–occupational social work field of practice, practitioners have been concerned about the lives of workers, their conditions of employment, the structures and cultures of their workplaces, and the relationships among these elements.

ISSUE STATEMENT

The social worker's response to workplace issues raised by drug-testing policies neither resolve nor explore all of the social, legal, scientific, and or ethical issues posed by drug testing in the workplace. As in all areas of professional work, the social worker facing drug-testing policies are guided by the NASW *Code of Ethics* (2000), in addition to reason and the law, while balancing the interests of the employer, the employees, and the public. Although the social worker is expected to observe the law, this expectation in itself does not mean that an employer's legal rights coincide with social work ethics. The social worker evaluates each situation and makes informed decisions on whether to promote drug-testing policies, acquiesce to them, challenge them, or even withdraw from the organization in protest.

Employers may be justified in implementing drug-testing policies to protect their organizations, their customers, other employees, or society. The profession is concerned with helping individuals who abuse alcohol and other drugs (AOD) to find successful treatment and preservation of employment consistent with the Rehabilitation Act of 1973 (P.L. 93-112) and other employee protection regulations.

Employers are entitled to maintain safe and healthy workplaces and to take steps to ensure that their products and services are not affected by employees' substance abuse. Drug testing is not required under the Drug-Free Workplace Act of 1986. Employees are entitled to expect AOD-abusing coworkers to be appropriately treated when it is probable that the person abusing substances will injure other employees or their interests. The public is entitled to expect protection from issues and problems that may result from substance abuse. Each situation compels the social worker to formulate his or her own ethical evaluation, abiding by the *NASW Code of Ethics* (2000). For example, Section 1.01 provides that "[t]he social worker's primary responsibility is to promote the well being of clients." However, Section 3.09 requires that "social workers generally should adhere to commitments made to employers and employing organizations."

A drug-testing policy that appears to promote the general well-being also may discriminate against substance-abusing individuals or vulnerable populations for whom services must be an ethical focus. The *NASW Code of Ethics* (2000) mandates that social workers "should not practice, condone, facilitate, or collaborate with any form of discrimination on the basis of race, ethnicity, national origin, color, sex, sexual orientation, age, marital status, political belief, religion, or mental or physical disability" (Section 4.02). When a drug-testing policy is the sole approach to substance abuse, the employer strongly risks punishing individual workers without helping them to obtain treatment. A health and wellness program that includes education, assessment, and employee assistance incorporated within a drug-testing policy may be more effective. Providing access to treatment is in accord with the *NASW Code of Ethics* (2000), which states that "social workers should engage in social and political action that seeks to ensure that all people have equal access to the resources, employment, services, and opportunities they require to meet their basic human needs and to develop fully"(Section 6.04a). Whenever possible, referral to an Employee Assistance Program (EAP) should be encouraged.

Drug-testing policies are considered punitive in workplaces where companies do not clearly communicate the rationale, procedures, laboratory methods, and consequences of a negative test. Positive results of drug tests have too often led to automatic dismissal or refusal to consider employment.

False positives are relatively uncommon if the laboratory is using the federal guidelines of the U.S. Department of Health and Human Services (DHHS) (2004). Although the potential of persons who do not abuse substances being stigmatized by the false positive is low, the consequences can be disastrous. The biggest source of inaccurate results is an interruption of the chain of custody, faulty protections, or contamination at specimen collection sites (DHHS, 2004). The employee should be given an opportunity for retesting following a positive test result.

Policies and practices should link the positive results of tests to assessment and referral to company EAPs or to treatment and other resources, when appropriate. AOD abuse is not restricted to any one group of employees but afflicts people at all levels of the organization. Any drug-testing policy should be bias-free to preclude resentment, morale problems, and discrimination.

POLICY STATEMENT

NASW supports

■ comprehensive and ethical approaches to the problem of AOD abuse at the work place, preferably as a cooperative labor–management initiative.

■ consideration of alternatives to drug testing, such as hand–eye coordination and response time performance tests.

■ an approach that includes education, prevention strategies, and treatment options for those who have been identified as abusing AOD.

■ confidential referrals to an EAP and encouragement of self-referrals. Sharing information with management must be consistent with federal laws and HIPAA on confidentiality.

■ health and wellness programs that include education, assessment, and employee assistance incorporated within a drug testing policy.

■ advocacy for clients' access to comprehensive treatment and insurance coverage.

- community treatment programs that anticipate obstacles to treatment, such as lack of child care for mothers, who are less likely than other groups to be treated for AOD abuse.

- the promotion of clearly defined policies and testing procedures that are consistent and fair to all employees, following the federal guidelines for workplace drug testing.

- education of all social workers on the issues of drug testing, including its effect on civil rights, etiology of AOD abuse, its course, and its effect on individuals and family systems.

- monitoring and publication of research, law, and practice on drug-testing issues.

- appropriate political action to challenge and change inadequate or inappropriate existing laws.

- the development of comprehensive curriculums on AOD abuse in schools of social work that include relevant theory, practice, and policy issues.

- the education of society at large about the nature of AOD abuse, its far-reaching effects, the importance of treatment, and the best ways to link clients with treatment.

- vigorous advocacy for improved AOD services for all socioeconomic groups.

REFERENCES

Federal Register. (1986). Drug-free federal workplace (Executive order 12564). Available at http://www.archives.gov/federal-register/codification/executive-order/12564.html

Health Insurance Portability and Accountability Act of 1996 (HIPAA), P.L. 104-191, Aug. 21, 1996, 110 Stat. 1936.

National Association of Social Workers. (2000). *Code of ethics of the National Association of Social Workers*. Washington, DC: NASW Press.

Rehabilitation Act of 1973, P.L. 93-112, Sept. 26, 1973, 87 Stat. 355.

U.S. Department of Health and Human Services. (2004). *Mandatory guidelines and proposed revisions to mandatory guidelines for federal workplace drug testing programs*. Washington, DC: U.S. Government Printing Office.

Policy statement approved by the NASW Delegate Assembly, August 2008. This policy statement supersedes the policy statement on Drug Testing in the Workplace approved by the Delegate Assembly in 1999 and referred by the 2005 Delegate Assembly to the 2008 Delegate Assembly for revision. The 1999 Delegate Assembly also voted to not combine this statement with the policy on Civil Liberties and Justice. This policy statement also supersedes the policy statement approved in 1990. For further information, contact the National Association of Social Workers, 750 First Street, NE, Suite 700, Washington, DC 20002-4241. Telephone: 202-408-8600 or 800-638-8799; e-mail: press@naswdc.org

Early Childhood Care and Services

BACKGROUND

Early childhood is a diverse field that is unified by a common core of knowledge: Children from birth through eight years of age require special attention to begin the developmental process in an optimal fashion. The growing awareness of the critical nature of experiences during these years requires the social work profession to be involved in setting policies that ensure the well-being of young children and their families. The United States remains the only technologically developed nation that lacks a national policy regarding the early childhood years.

Early and extensive enrollment in nonparental child care is the norm in the United States. In 1999, the National Household Education Survey (National Center for Education Statistics, 1999), which questions families about nonparental child care arrangements regardless of the employment status of the mother, reported that 61 percent of children younger than four were in regularly scheduled child care arrangements, including 44 percent of infants, 53 percent of one-year-olds, and 57 percent of two-year-olds. Although parents and relatives continue to provide vast amounts of early child care, reliance on child care centers outside the home has increased. An estimated 12 million children age six and younger spend some or all of their day being cared for by someone other than their parents (U.S. Department of Education, National Center for Education Statistics, 2002). According to Capizzano and Adams (2004), 73 percent of children age five and younger with working mothers are regularly in child care; 46 percent of children ages three and four from high-income families are in center-based care compared with 36 percent of children from low-income families.

Economic necessity often demands dual-earner families in the United States, and with the rate of marital disruption and single child-bearing, many women have no choice but to work. According to the Whirlpool Foundation (1995), the majority (55 percent) of working women in the United States bring home half or more of the family's earnings. According to the Children's Defense Fund (2003), 6 million young children are living in single-parent families where working is necessary if these families are not to be dependent on welfare. The proportion of children age three and younger who are in child care centers, preschools, Head Start programs, and other early childhood education programs tripled between 1977 and 1994, from 8 percent to 24 percent of children with employed mothers (U.S. Census Bureau, 1982, 1997).

As many recipients of Temporary Assistance for Needy Families are entering the workforce to comply with federal and state work requirements, the demand for child care is growing. These families deserve access to the same quality of early childhood education and child care that higher-income families receive, and most need some form of child care assistance. Welfare reform must focus not only on getting parents to enter the workforce, but also on equity of access to high-quality child care for children living in poverty to have the optimal environment for learning and development.

It is important for children to have quality child care. High-quality early childhood programs provide important educational and nurturing experiences to young children. Findings from a study of by Peisner-Feinberg and colleagues (1999) revealed that children in high-quality child care demonstrated greater mathematical ability, greater thinking and attention skills, and fewer behavioral problems; these findings were particularly significant for at-risk children. However, many families experience difficulty finding quality and affordable child care. Parents pay most of child care costs—60 percent; the federal, state, and local governments pay 39 percent; and private financing covers less than 1 percent (Mitchell, Stoney, & Dichter, 2001).

ISSUE STATEMENT

The National Association for the Education of Young Children (NAEYC) advocates for high-quality early childhood education and child care and provides accreditation to child care facilities that meet certain standards. NAEYC (2000) offers six statements that define its vision for excellence:

(1) that all young children deserve excellent early care and education;

(2) that high quality early experiences make a difference in children's lifelong academic and social success;

(3) that programs must be accessible to all families;

(4) that early childhood professionals must have excellent preparation, ongoing professional development, and compensation commensurate with their qualifications and experience;

(5) that effective early education must be both challenging and appropriate to young children's ages, individual needs, and culture and;

(6) that everyone needs to work together to build a successful future for our youngest children. (pp. 2–3)

The development of knowledgeable, competent, and culturally sensitive professionals to work with young children and their families is a continuous process. The revised NAEYC *Standards for Preparation of Early Childhood Professionals* (2001) requires closer partnerships among institutions of higher education and education settings in the community. These guidelines require enhanced emphasis on linguistics and cultural diversity, inclusion, subject matter, and the communities in which children live. In addition, the standards call for attention to the complexity of assessment issues in today's educational settings, a "continuum of teaching strategies" and developmentally effective approaches, and field experiences for future educators. The revised standards emphasize that professionals in early childhood work in many diverse settings.

Early childhood care and services should be designed to incorporate the principles of infant mental health, which concern the optimal development of infants and toddlers within the context of secure and stable relationships with caregivers. For example:

Infant mental health is the developing capacity of the child from birth to age 3 to experience, regulate, and express emotions, form close and secure interpersonal relationships; and explore the environment and learn—all in the context of family, community, and cultural expectations for young children. Infant mental health is synonymous with healthy social and emotional development. (Zero to Three Infant Mental Health Task Force, 2002, p. 1)

A healthy parent–infant relationship is necessary for the competent physical, cognitive, social and emotional development of the infant. All early development takes place within the framework of interaction between the infant and adults partners. The parent's capacity to nurture the infant depends upon the extent to which she herself is supported and nurtured as well as her abilities to use the support that is available to her. (Weatherston & Tableman, 2002)

The quality of care is most important in child development. Young children who receive high-quality child care, including good verbal and cognitive stimulation, sensitive and responsive interaction with caregivers, and large amounts of attention and support, are more advanced in all areas of development compared with children who fail to receive these important facets of care (Lamb, 1998; Smith, 1998). These findings are applicable to infants, toddlers, and preschoolers and to all forms of child care, ranging from family to center-based programs (National Institute of Child Health and Human Development [NICHD] Early Child Care Research Network, 1998, 2000). Parental involvement and support are crucial factors in any good early childhood program. Parents must always be supported in their role as the primary educators and caregivers for their children. Parents provide the stimulation; emotional, social, and financial support; structure; safety; and interactions and learning experiences on a constant basis for their children. Family-centered care is an integral part of any high-quality early childhood and child care program. In essence, the basic elements of high-quality child care are similar to those of good parenting, and both promote positive developmental outcomes.

Social work is a critical component of a community system of early childhood care and services. A comprehensive system of care must incorporate a multi-disciplinary approach in which collaboration and coordination of care are essential components. Social workers bring a unique understanding of coordinated care and collaboration and are especially trained in identifying and addressing the special emotional and developmental needs of young children who have been exposed to environmental stressors, including neglect, social isolation, violence, substance abuse, and mental illness of primary caregivers.

POLICY STATEMENT

Early childhood is recognized as including a broad range of experiences from birth through 8 years (NAEYC, 2001). NASW supports effective early childhood programs and services that:

■ are offered in diverse settings: families' homes, public and private schools, family day care homes, and group child care centers. Programs should be designed to include children from various racial, ethnic, cultural, and socioeconomic backgrounds.

■ are integrated and include perinatal services, family support services, health and mental health services, educational services, day care (full- and part-time), respite care, culturally sensitive parenting education, and before- and after-school care.

■ include comprehensive prevention, intervention, and support services that are provided for infants and young children, with and without special needs, and their families.

■ are built on the belief that families, as the constant in their children's lives, should be supported in actively participating in the development and implementation of services and programs affecting their children.

■ are built on the belief that families, as the constant in their children's lives, should be supported in actively participating in the development and implementation of family-centered, multidisciplinary services and programs affecting their children, and social workers should be members of that team.

■ use the services of appropriately trained and culturally competent providers who receive ongoing training to ensure continuous learning and professional development.

Furthermore, NASW supports:

■ national, state, and local policies that use the principles of child development and early childhood education to meet the physical, social, emotional, and educational needs of young children and their families.

■ equal access to high-quality, culturally and developmentally appropriate, affordable early childhood services and programs.

■ programs and services that reflect the needs of a variety of family structures and have as their basis sound principles of child development.

■ parents as the first and primary educator and caregiver for young children, and the belief that all children benefit from a sustained primary relationship that is nurturing, supportive, and protective.

■ the co-location of early childhood services including health, education, and child welfare services.

- continuing implementation of existing legislation to ensure appropriate early childhood programs and services for all infants and young children, including children with special needs and their families.

- programs and services that conduct regular, periodic developmental assessments of children in care, provide universal parent education components, and address factors that place children at risk, including health and nutrition, environmental, psychosocial, economic, racial, ethnic, cultural, and linguistic factors.

- high-quality standards with adequate safeguards for very young children and their families in all settings.

- a living wage and adequate benefits for providers of early childhood care and services.

- efforts to ensure continuity for infants and young children receiving services.

- universal access to early childhood services and care including evidence-based home-visiting and preschool programs.

- family leave policies that are equitable, affordable, and universal.

- child care subsidy policies to ensure that all families who need it have access to assistance.

- a variety of equitable child care choices for all families. Those choices should be comparable in terms of quality, accessibility, and availability, and include other family support services such as health, education, and transportation services.

REFERENCES

Capizzano, J., & Adams, G. (2004). *Children in low-income families are less likely to be in center-based child care.* Washington, DC: Urban Institute.

Children's Defense Fund. (2003). *Quality child care helps parents work and learn.* Washington, DC: Author.

Lamb, M. (1998). Nonparental child care: Context, quality, correlates. In W. Damon, I. Sige, & K. Renninger (Eds.), *Handbook of child psychology* (5th ed., pp. 73–134). New York: John Wiley & Sons.

Mitchell, A., Stoney, L., & Dichter, H. (2001). *Financing child care in the United States: An expanded catalog of current strategies.* Kansas, MO: Ewing Marion Kauffman Foundation.

National Association for the Education of Young Children. (2000). *A call for excellence in early childhood education.* Washington, DC: Author.

National Association for the Education of Young Children. (2001). *Standards for preparation of early childhood professionals.* Washington, DC: Author.

National Center for Education Statistics. (1999). *National Household Education Survey, 1999.* Washington, DC: U.S. Department of Education.

National Institute of Child Health and Human Development Early Child Care Research Network. (1998). *Chronicity of maternal depressive symptoms, maternal behavior, and child functioning at 36 months: Results from the NICHD study for early child care.* Washington, DC: U.S. Department of Health and Human Services, National Institutes of Health.

National Institute of Child Health and Human Development Early Child Care Research Network. (2000). The NICHD study of early child care: Contexts of development and developmental outcomes over the first seven years of life. In J. Brooks-Gunn & L. J. Berlin (Eds.), *Young children's education, health, and development: Profile and synthesis project report.* Washington, DC: U.S. Department of Education.

Peisner-Feinberg, E. S., Burchinal, M. R., Clifford, R. M., Culkin, M. L., Howes, C., Kagan, S. L., Yazejian, N., Byler, P., Rustici, J., & Zelazo, J. (1999). *The children of the Cost, Quality, and Outcomes Study go to school.* Chapel Hill, NC: University of North Carolina Frank Porter Graham Child Development Center.

Smith, S. (1998, April). *The past decade's research on child care quality and children's development: What we are learning, directions for the future.* Paper prepared for the Child Care in the New Policy Context meeting of the Office of the Assistant Secretary for Planning and Evaluation, U.S. Department of Health and Human Services, Bethesda, MD.

U.S. Census Bureau. (1982). Trends in child care arrangements of working mothers. In *Current population reports*. Washington, DC: U.S. Government Printing Office.

U.S. Census Bureau. (1997). *Who's minding our preschoolers? Fall 1994* (Update). Washington, DC: U.S. Government Printing Office.

U.S. Department of Education, National Center for Education Statistics. (2002). *America's children: Key national indicators of well-being, 2002*. Washington, DC: U.S. Government Printing Office.

Weatherston, D., & Tableman, B. (2002). *Infant mental health services: Supporting competencies/reducing risks* (2nd ed.). Southgate, MI: Michigan Association for Infant Mental Health.

Whirlpool Foundation. (1995). *Women: The new providers*. New York: Families and Work Institute.

Zero to Three Infant Mental Health Task Force. *What is infant mental health?* Washington, DC: Zero to Three.

SUGGESTED READINGS

Brandon, P. (2000). Child care utilization among working mothers raising children with disabilities. *Journal of Family and Economic Issues, 21*, 343–364.

Children's Defense Fund. (2002). *Low–income families bear the burden of state child care cutbacks*. Washington, DC: Author.

Children's Defense Fund. (2002). *State developments in child care, early education, and school-age care 2001*. Washington, DC: Author.

Children's Defense Fund. (2003). *Quality child care helps parents work and children learn*. Washington, DC: Author.

Donahue, E. H., & Campbell, N. D. (2002). *Making care less taxing: Improving state child care and dependent care tax provisions*. Washington, DC: National Women's Law Center.

Gnezda, M. T. (1996). Public policy report. Welfare reform: Personal responsibilities and opportunities for early childhood advocates. *Young Children, 52*(1), 55–58.

Shonkoff, J. P., & Phillips, D. A. (2000). *From neurons to neighborhoods: The science of early childhood development*. Washington, DC: National Academies Press.

Policy statement approved by the NASW Delegate Assembly, August 2005. This policy statement supersedes the statement on Early Childhood Care and Services approved by the Delegate Assembly in 1996 and referred by the 2002 Delegate Assembly to the 2005 Delegate Assembly for revision. For additional information, contact the National Association of Social Workers, 750 First Street, NE, Suite 700, Washington, DC 20002-4241; telephone: 202-408-8600; e-mail: press@naswdc.org

Education of Children and Youths

BACKGROUND

Federal Legislation

The War on Poverty launched during the administration of President Lyndon B. Johnson arguably set the pattern for the significant involvement of the federal government in public education that we observe today. The original Elementary and Secondary Education Act of 1965 (ESEA) (P.L. 89-10) set standards for students, teachers, and most important, formulas for block grants to states. The landmark legislation was hailed as one of the most important components of the War on Poverty because it instituted large-scale resources to educationally deprived students, including those from low-income neighborhoods, those who were nonnative English speakers, and those with disabilities.

The passage of the Education for All Handicapped Children Act of 1975 (P.L. 94-142) brought a major shift in responsibility for educating people with disabilities. This landmark legislation guaranteed all children a free and appropriate public education (FAPE), the right to due process, and individualization of instruction according to need. Subsequent reenactments of this legislation have broadened the coverage to include the educational needs of children ages three to 21 years, additional conditions that qualify people with disabilities for coverage, and greater encouragement for the implementation of local programs for children from birth to three years.

At first, this legislation ironically resulted in the segregation of children with disabilities from the regular education classrooms for some or all of the school day to receive specialized instruction and therapy. The Regular Education Initiative (McDonald, 1996) sought to rectify this situation by emphasizing "inclusion" for people with developmental disabilities. Schools are now encouraged to deliver services in the regular classroom with classmates who are not identified as students with special needs. Inclusion also refers to students with other problems, who can benefit from personalized instruction in small groups or with specialized co-instructors assigned to the regular classroom to support their specialized learning needs (McDonald, 1996). It remains essential, however, that accommodation of students with severe disabilities in pull-out programs continue to be available when their individualized education plan (IEP) identifies the need. This approach was mandated and reinforced with passage of the Individuals with Disabilities Education Act (IDEA) (P.L. 101-476), which mandated specific changes in IEPs to include measurable goals and clear intervention strategies.

Perhaps the most dramatic and far-reaching federal legislation affecting primary and secondary education has been the passage of the No Child Left Behind Act (P.L. 107-110). This act mandates specific testing of students on their proficiency in basic skills at various intervals. Because of this and other issues, the law has become a lightening rod of controversy with opponents questioning the reliability of standardized tests. Says Disability Rights Advocates (2001):

> It is a basic principle of test validity that a test must actually measure what the test is intended to measure. A test is not valid in itself, but is valid only for a particular purpose. A test that is valid for one purpose may not be valid for another. As noted in a recent

report by the National Research Council of the National Academy of Sciences, "tests that are valid for influencing classroom practice "leading" the curriculum, or holding schools accountable are not appropriate for making high-stakes decisions about individual student mastery unless the curriculum, the teaching, and the tests are aligned." (p. 14)

No Child Left Behind mandates teacher accountability on an unprecedented scale. Although supported by most parents, teacher unions continue to be increasingly disturbed by this legislation.

The No Child Left Behind Act, as well as many other educational issues, became highly politicized in the presidential campaign of 2004. Some of the issues included proposals for proficiency tests in math and reading for high school graduates, increased funding of private schools through vouchers for low-income families, increased funding for charter schools, Pell grants for regular course work assistance for high school students, and strengthened partnerships between employers and college students. The 2004 Individuals with Disabilities Education Improvement Act (P.L. 108-446), a revision of IDEA, calls on educational institutions to demonstrate improved outcomes for all students.

Federal and State Funding

Since 1980, most federal funds were disbursed to states through block grants and earmarked for mandated categorical programs. Over the years, this method has significantly changed in favor of unrestricted funding to individual states for disbursement. This change allows individual states to determine how this money is spent. As a result there has been a progressive decline in funds appropriated for educational services. Also, although many states have opted to pay for education through property taxes, this has shifted an unequal burden onto homeowners. Increased income taxes are proving to be unpopular, so many states are looking at sales taxes or gambling revenues to pay for increased school funding.

High-Risk Students

There is an urgent need to better identify and provide services to vulnerable student groups, such as children with disabilities, poor rural youths, children of migrant laborers, other economically disadvantaged children, children of color, pregnant adolescents, children of adolescent single parents, new immigrants, abused and neglected children, truant children, drug-dependent children, latchkey children, and children who move frequently. For example, children who have limited language skills have a four times greater chance of graduating from high school if they participate in bilingual programs, yet these programs are threatened constantly with cutbacks (Committee on Education and Labor, 1986). Specific legislation that mandates continuous services to transient or homeless students was established in 1987 by the Stewart B. McKinney Homeless Assistance Act (P.L. 100-77), which has been amended and later became known as the McKinney-Vento Act.

Many of the reforms of the 1960s and 1970s, such as the War on Poverty's attempts to raise family incomes and to provide school breakfasts and health programs, were based on the recognition that students who are hungry, sick, or worried about their families could not achieve as well in school as students who were free of these cares. These reforms have been continuously threatened by budget cuts. A movement to develop a full-ranging curriculum focused on children's health and mental health issues to be offered from kindergarten through high school is widely supported, but such a curriculum is hollow without the provision of concrete services, such as school breakfast and lunch programs and counseling for anxiety-producing problems in students' lives.

Potential dropouts and push-outs represent another significant high-risk group in the educational system. In too many cases, discipline involves suspensions or expulsions that deny access to school or placement in supervised atmospheres. Given that these students have already shown that their ability to maintain self-control and anticipate consequences is limited, their exclusion from school increases the risk of negative behaviors, such as crime and misuse of alcohol and other drugs.

Furthermore, students from racial and ethnic minority groups experience a disproportionately high incidence of suspensions and expulsions. Various alternatives to out-of-school suspension are being implemented in many districts around the country, but the results of these experiences have not been evaluated (Gay, 1989). In addition, children and youths who have been incarcerated must not lose their right to an equal education.

Safe, Positive, and Secure Schools

Fortunately, the use of corporal punishment has been declining in U.S. schools. Decreased public acceptance, increased litigation against school boards and educators, and legislative actions such as child abuse laws have contributed to this decline. Regretfully, however, many states continue to use corporal punishment as a disciplinary measure, even though research and experience prove it counterproductive and harmful in the long term (Strauss, 1991). As many studies have shown, showing expectations of success have a positive effect on how well students do. Students can be provided with a safe, positive, and secure school environment by valuing all students for the contributions they make, promoting the cultural sensitivity and competence of faculty and staff by ensuring a nondiscriminatory educational climate, establishing rational and humane disciplinary policies and alternatives to suspension and expulsion, and eliminating corporal punishment, intimidation, and scapegoating from public school education.

Alternative Education

Millions of youths are underserved or not served at all by the public educational system. About 30 percent of children who start first grade do not finish high school. Of those who complete 12th grade, many do not have the requisite skills and behaviors to enter the labor market successfully. Many become marginal participants in society and heavy users of public health, welfare, rehabilitation, and penal resources (Children's Defense Fund, 1990; Hare & Sullivan, 1996). Any reform in public educa-

tion must include alternative routes to becoming educated and finding successful roles as adults. These alternatives, however, must not isolate "undesirable" students from the mainstream, but rather offer them sufficient support to meet their unique behavioral and situation needs.

The widespread availability of the computer, and the Internet in particular, has had a revolutionary impact in the classroom, and more significantly, on educational formats for learning at home. The 1999 Parent Survey of the National Household Education Surveys indicated that 850,000 parents are home schooling their children (Bielick, Chandler, & Broughman, 1999). No doubt, parents who are home schooling are sincere in their efforts and are providing an education that allows their children to be competitive in a rapidly changing and highly technical world. Home schooling arrangements, however, lack reasonable oversight by qualified school personnel to ensure that all children have access to the highest level of their educational ability.

Relationship of School to Home and Community

Parents and school personnel often have mistaken perceptions of each other because of problems in negotiating the bureaucratic maze of public school education and because of the blame and antagonism over students' problems. Effective communication among school personnel, families, and communities is vital to reach the goals set for each student. Coordination of services is critical to the efficient and effective use of resources and the attainment of goals. Making school buildings available for use as community centers and early childhood education sites is key to building schools' relationships with families and communities. Providing services to parents after school and at night gives the school a position in the community as not just a caretaker and educator of students. Most school buildings are underused during summer seasons and can be available for educational purposes.

Sex Education

Although more young people are sexually active at an earlier age than in the past, in general they lack adequate knowledge and motivation to protect themselves from the hazards of premature sexuality, including pregnancy and disease. Sexually active adolescents and preadolescents who are experimenting with drugs are particularly vulnerable. Although education in this area may be crucial, this topic is characteristically downplayed for fear of offending some constituent group.

In 1986, Surgeon General C. Everett Koop called for AIDS education to be included in sex education curriculums beginning in elementary schools (Koop, 1986). At the time, NASW commended Koop for this brave stand. The need still exists. Public schools have been loath to comply with Koop's call because of public dissent. A few exceptions have braved the path, but much still needs to be done to support young people dealing with their emerging sexuality.

Social Workers in Public Schools

School social workers are one of the few resources in schools for addressing personal and social problems that inhibit students' ability to learn. They constitute a stable and growing force within the field of education. Approximately 9,300 school social workers serve students in 37 education jurisdictions across the country (Torres, 1996). Sadly, the distribution of social workers is uneven and inequitable; school social workers tend to be clustered in greater proportions in industrial states and in school districts with greater resources. The skills and competencies of school social workers enable schools to carry out their primary functions of educating all pupils more effectively, by:

■ assessing and intervening in the social and emotional needs of students in relation to learning;

■ understanding, evaluating, and improving the total environment of pupils and thus contributing to a positive school climate;

■ strengthening the connections among families, schools, and communities by identifying and linking these components to create the best learning environment for the student and making education relevant to all constituents;

■ building mutual communication and support among all participants in the school system, including other professionals, parents, students, staff, and the community;

■ developing preventive and remedial intervention programs for systemic problems

■ providing meaningful and relevant consultation and in-service programs to teachers and school administrators concerning student needs and counterproductive school policies;

■ providing group and individual counseling for students and when necessary, for the family;

■ ensuring that students with disabilities receive appropriate educational services; and

■ providing training and support for conflict resolution programs and other student support programs, such as drug use prevention, sex education, alternative suspension programs, and parent education programs.

ISSUE STATEMENT

The education of our nation's children continues to be a top priority of NASW. NASW has been very active in advancing legislation to promote the role of school social workers, and many NASW publications have highlighted the role of school social workers in education. In addition, in 1995 NASW established the first Specialty Practice Section for School Social Work. School social workers continue to collaborate closely with school psychologists and other professionals in the school system. In fact, many policies identified and incorporated in this statement were collaboratively developed with other agencies and organizations.

Public education is a primary institution that shares with the family the responsibility for raising and training children and youths. Furthermore, public education is a vital socializing force that, with the family, promotes the total development of the child—intellectually, socially, and physically. To nurture the full potential of children and youths, our nation's public schools are an excellent forum to ensure equal opportunity and preparation. NASW believes that schools must pursue excellence and provide for the physical and emotional safety and growth, in addition to the education, of children. Schools must identify students with disabilities and disadvantages early and provide support to such students in accordance with federal legislation, such as the Individuals with Disabilities Education Improvement Act of 2004. Educational environments promote transitional learning in the areas of work, community living, and civic responsibility. Students with excessive truancy and who are at risk of dropping out must receive outreach services, and factual health information for students regarding sexuality, relationships, and sexually transmitted diseases must be provided within the context of a comprehensive health and family life education course.

POLICY STATEMENT

Components of Education

Education is a continuing maturation process that promotes the intellectual, physical, and social development of students in their environments. It is the position of NASW that the educational system has a responsibility to provide all students with free, appropriate, and high quality education. Through quality education, students should be able to attain full vocational and career skills and concomitant behaviors conducive to success and lifelong learning. In addition, students need educational opportunities that foster increased self-awareness and self-actualization, empathy for others, understanding and acceptance of differences in race, culture, ethnicity, and sexual orientation, and understanding of the personal realities of individuals with disabilities and how to help them to participate more fully in normal daily

activities. Finally, educators should facilitate an awareness that health-compromising behaviors, particularly sexual ones, substance abuse, and violence, can have lifelong and life-threatening consequences. The following are steps school districts can take toward achieving these goals.

- **Pupil Services Teams.** The policy of NASW is that the model of collaboration used by multidisciplinary teams, including school social workers, psychologists, pupil services personnel, teachers, administrators, and families, in the identification and evaluation of students for special services is optimal for the delivery of services to all students. The school social worker provides expertise in coordinating home, school, and community resources to enhance learning objectives, in assessing students' adaptive behaviors, and in describing cultural history. The multidisciplinary team can also implement intervention and prevention strategies for at-risk students before a special education referral is made as a result of the diagnostic assessment team process.

- **Least-restrictive Environment.** Every student has the right to a free, appropriate public education in the least-restrictive environment. NASW supports the least-restrictive environment concept as it is determined individually for each student. The school social worker on the multidisciplinary team plays a key role in determining the least-restrictive setting for each student and in helping parents and students become involved in the decision making process. NASW supports the regular education environment as the first placement consideration, and NASW strongly supports placement of students in the setting that best meets the student's needs, with the appropriate continuum of services, staffing, and assistive devices, and re-placement in a more restrictive setting if so determined by student need.

- **Alternative Testing and Performance.** All students do not learn in the same fashion. Divergent learners may test poorly on standardized tests. This does not mean the student is not learning, rather the particular testing used may not adequately tap the student's knowledge. Therefore, alternate ways to measure academic growth is essential, especially among the learning disabled population of students and other educationally disadvantaged pupils in American public schools. There is a risk that educationally disadvantaged students held to the same standards as other students will be "responsible" for low test scores that districts receive and therefore will place school districts on various watch lists. This combination of circumstances can often result in discrimination toward the educationally disadvantaged population if the standards of achievement are not changed to reflect growth among divergent leaders.

■ **Family, School, and Community Linkages.** Strengthening the relationship among the families, schools, and communities is a fundamental principle of any educational policy. NASW encourages linking the school to community resources as sound public policy and encourages further policy development focused on bringing schools, families, and communities together for mutual support and problem solving as well as for cultural and celebratory events. School–community centers, which facilitate the participation of families and the wider community in school activities, allow opportunities for community-based social workers to collaborate with school social workers in working with teachers and families.

■ **Early Childhood Education.** It is the policy of NASW that early childhood education should continue to be expanded and made available to all children through federal and state support (Bishop, 1996; see also NASW policy statement on *Early Childhood Care and Services*). Significant research supports the position that early intervention for children with disabilities of all types benefits their later ability to succeed educationally. In addition, such programs promote total learning for all children through their emphasis on early stimulation of children within the home, recognition and use of parenting skills, provisions for adequate nutrition and medical care, and the introduction of important social skills needed for later school success.

■ **Career and Vocational Education.** NASW affirms that the primary function of education is to prepare students for life tasks, specifically the world of work. Preparation should include instilling the attitudes and behaviors that ensure successful entry into the labor market. American children must be prepared to compete in a global society that offers opportunities for all nations to share the resources of the world. It is the policy of NASW that transitional experiences and entry structures should be available throughout the educational ladder. To accomplish this, schools, postsecondary educational institutions, communities, and businesses should continue to form linkages that provide opportunities for entry into the labor market. Career and vocational programs should have the same economic and academic investment from school facilities and administrations as college preparatory programs have (see NASW policy statement on *School Dropout Prevention*). High schools should assist all students who are preparing for post-secondary education, and all students should be graduating with a high school diploma.

■ **Comprehensive Health and Mental Health Education.** It is the policy of NASW that educating students about their health and physical needs and about optimal health practices, including sexual conduct and HIV/AIDS education, is a necessary and appropriate function of public schools. Such programs should be developed by multidisciplinary teams that include, but are not restricted to, social workers, health care providers, educators, and parents. The programs should be evidence-based and use best practices. They should be offered in early childhood programs or kindergarten and should continue throughout students' formal public education. Naturally, such programs should be age and developmentally appropriate and provide information that enables students to make responsible choices about their bodies, behavior, relationships, and emotions. To make responsible choices, students need access to basic facts about human physiology and psychology, including information on reproduction, family planning, pregnancy prevention, responsible parenting, HIV/AIDS and sexually transmitted diseases, substance use, healthy eating, exercise, stress management, anger management, and general lifestyle decisions.

A comprehensive life education program should involve parents and should promote open communication among parents, students, and schools. With increasing attention to children suffering physical and sexual abuse, it is imperative that students are protected from violence and abuse. Social work services must be made available for the education and counseling of affected students. Prevention programs that build self-esteem, teach conflict mediation and bully prevention skills, promote positive decision making and help students develop protective behaviors to guard against victimization should be provided in schools.

■ **Nondiscriminatory and Integrated Education**. The right to equal educational opportunity requires a nonsegregated, nonsexist environment and a curriculum that reflects a pluralistic society. NASW views the optimal goal of integration as a requisite for a positive, pluralistic educational experience. Integration should provide for and facilitate interaction among students and faculty of diverse racial, cultural, religious, spiritual, and ethnic backgrounds. An integrated environment promotes understanding, knowledge, and acceptance of diversity in family composition (for example sexual orientation and same-sex families). To ensure nondiscriminatory education for all races, a policy prohibiting the use of discriminatory or stereotyping labels, for example by sports teams and mascots, should be established. Bilingual education programs promote greater understanding of the educational process of those experiencing language and cultural barriers.

■ **Discipline.** It is the policy of NASW that disciplinary practices in schools, including detention, suspension, and expulsion, must reflect the desire to shape students' behavior toward productive participation in schools and society. Many such policies are clearly punitive in intent and thus do not reflect the school's concern for retaining and successfully graduating

students involved in their disciplinary system. The focus of school discipline should be to help students accept responsibility for their own behavior, rather than punishment, through a shared problem-solving process with parents and guardians. NASW subscribes to the following recommendations as policy initiatives related to disciplinary actions:

1.   Students should be guaranteed due process in serious disciplinary actions;

2.   Social workers should be used as advocates in promoting the best interests of the students and schools;

3.   Alternative education programs should be developed based on students' unique educational needs; and

4.   The use of corporal punishment in schools should be abolished in the remaining states that still approve of such practices, and social work services should be made available to train teachers to teach children conflict resolution techniques, including improved interpersonal communication skills.

■ **Full Funding for Education.** All legally mandated educational programs must be funded at a level that ensures their effective implementation. Such programs include IDEA; the Education of the Handicapped Act Amendments of 1986, including Part H; the Rehabilitation Act of 1973 (P.L. 93-112), especially section 504; the Americans with Disabilities Act of 1991; the No Child Left Behind Act; and Title IV, VI, and VII of the Civil Rights Acts of 1957 and 1964. Programs must not be weakened by changing or eliminating key rules and regulations because of politically shortsighted initiatives or economic recession. The rights of students and families should not be eliminated or reduced to foster a more controlling, and in some cases, more oppressive environment. Mandating educational programs without allocating the full cost of implementing such programs is not good public policy. Full funding for education should include safe and fully functioning educational facilities in addition to appropriate programming.

■ **Evaluation and Research.** Evaluation of school social work services is critical in documenting effectiveness. Federal, state, and local education agencies as well as school social workers should conduct research related to the effectiveness of social work services in the schools. Research that examines both the short-term and long-term effectiveness of innovative prevention programs must be supported.

■ **Role of School Social Workers.** NASW encourages legislation and funding at the federal and state levels to substantially increase the number of social workers available in schools to serve both students with identified disabilities and students in the general school population. Because of the inequitable distribution of social workers both nationally and within individual states, NASW recommends that pupil services teams in every state include school social workers on the elementary and secondary levels who graduated from a Council on Social Work Education–accredited program. Furthermore, school social workers are qualified to implement interagency agreements between school districts and human services agencies, both public and private, to promote collaboration in the provision of services to all pupils. Human services agencies include protective services, juvenile courts, mental health facilities, family services agencies, and rehabilitative resources. School social workers are the professionals who help ensure that students have access to necessary components of education. These components enable students to acquire the academic skills and the ability to function in and contribute to a multicultural society.

REFERENCES

Americans with Disabilities Act, Pub. L. 101-336, 104 Stat. 327 (1990).

Bielick, S., Chandler, K., & Broughman, S. P. (1999). Homeschooling in the United States: 1999. *Education Statistics Quarterly, 3*(3).

Bishop, K. (1996). Part H of the Individuals with Disabilities Education Act: Analysis and implications for social workers. In R. Constable, J. Flynn, & S. McDonald (Eds.), *School social work: Practice and research perspectives* (3rd ed., pp. 116–131). Chicago: Lyceum Press.

Children's Defense Fund. (1990). *Children, 1990: A report card, briefing book and action primer.* Washington, DC: Author.

Civil Rights Act of 1957, Pub. L. 86-387, Title IV, Sec. 401, 73 Stat. 724.

Civil Rights Act of 1964, Pub. L. 88-352, 78 Stat. 241.

Committee on Education and Labor, House of Representatives. (1986). *The report on bilingual education of the 99th Congress, 2d session.* Washington, DC: U.S. Government Printing Office.

Disability Rights Advocates. (2001). *Do no harm—High stakes testing and students with learning disabilities.* Retrieved March 12, 2005 from, http://www.dralegal.org/publications/do_no_harm.pdf

Education for All Handicapped Children Act of 1975, Pub. L. 94-142, 89 Stat. 773.

Education of the Handicapped Act Amendments of 1986, Pub. L. 99-457, 100 Stat. 1145.

Elementary and Secondary Education Act of 1965, Pub. L. 89-10, 79 Stat. 27.

Gay, G. (1989). Ethnic minorities and educational equality. In J. A. Banks & C. A. Banks (Eds.), *Multicultural education: Issues and perspectives.* Boston: Allyn & Bacon.

Hare, I., & Sullivan, K. (1996). The economic, political and social world of school social work. In R. Constable, J. Flynn, & S. McDonald (Eds.), *School social work: Practice and research perspectives* (3rd ed., pp. 66–84). Chicago: Lyceum Press.

Individuals with Disabilities Education Act, Pub. L. 101-476, 104 Stat. 1142 (1990).

Individuals with Disabilities Education Improvement Act, Pub. L. 108-446, 118 Stat. 2647 (2004).

Koop, C. E. (1986). *The Surgeon General's report on Acquired Immune Deficiency Syndrome.* Washington, DC: U.S. Government Printing Office.

McDonald, S. (1996). The trend toward inclusion. In R. Constable, J. Flynn, & S. McDonald (Eds.), *School social work: Practice and research perspectives* (3rd ed., pp. 147–155). Chicago: Lyceum Press.

No Child Left Behind Act of 2001, Pub. L. 107-110, 15 Stat. 1425.

Rehabilitation Act of 1973, Pub. L. 93-112, 87 Stat. 355.

Strauss, M. A. (1991). *Beating the devil out of them*. New York: Lexington Books.

Torres, S. (1996). The status of school social workers in America. *Social Work in Education, 18,* 8–18.

Policy statement approved by the NASW Delegate Assembly, August 2005. This policy statement supersedes the policy on Education of Children and Youths approved by the NASW Delegate Assembly, August 1996 and referred by the 2002 Delegate Assembly to the 2005 Delegate Assembly for revision, which superseded the statement on Preschool, Elementary, and Secondary Education, approved by the Delegate Assembly in 1987. The original policy statement was approved by the NASW National Board of Directors in June 1985 following recommendations by the Delegate Assembly in 1984. For additional information, contact the National Association of Social Workers, 750 First Street, NE, Suite 700, Washington, DC 20002-4241; telephone: 202-408-8600; e-mail: press@naswdc.org

Electoral Politics

BACKGROUND

Social workers have always participated vigorously in political processes. The social work profession grew out of the political activism of its founders, from Jane Addams and Jeanette Rankin in the early 1900s to Frances Perkins, Harry Hopkins, and Molly Dewson in the New Deal era, to current political office holders. Social workers now hold many prominent political offices, and, in recent decades, have moved toward greater participation in political activity (Weismiller & Rome, 1995).

In most representative democracies around the world, the electoral political system is the determining vehicle for expressing human values and for the provision of resources. As experts in the areas of human needs and services delivery, social workers' role in the political process is axiomatic. Since the early part of the 20th century, social workers have participated in national, state, and local political party campaigns and elections, and they have lobbied the legislative and executive branches of government, advancing policy recommendations and implementing new programs.

Beginning with Theodore Roosevelt's Progressive Party in 1912, social workers have been active in presidential campaigns, including those of Franklin Roosevelt, Lyndon Johnson, and Bill Clinton. NASW has been active in partisan federal and state elections since 1976. Social workers show a growing willingness to enter the political arena in all capacities—as voters, party officials, political professionals, candidates, and officeholders.

Two studies fortify the perception that social workers are active in campaigns and elections and that they vote at much higher rates than the general public. One conducted in 1984 replicated a 1968 survey designed to assess the level of activism by social workers (Reeser & Epstein, 1990). Among measures of electoral participation, this study found increases in specific behaviors, such as giving money to campaigns, volunteering for candidates, and encouraging political activity among clients. Reeser and Epstein's historical comparison of social workers' political behavior in the original survey and their own demonstrated fundamental increases in the profession's political activism profile.

The second study examined social workers' electoral participation in the 1988 presidential campaign (Sherradan & Parker, 1991). More than 92 percent of the 222 social workers who responded reported voting in that election, a turnout rate 1.62 times that of the general public. In the same study, social workers reported making campaign contributions, going to meetings and rallies, and working for candidates or political parties at a rate twice that of the general public. The authors concluded that these high participation levels provide a foundation from which the profession can exert increased political influence.

Throughout its 50-year history, NASW has promoted the broad concept of electoral political action in various ways. Political activity is encouraged in the *Code of Ethics* (NASW, 2000), and successive Delegate Assemblies have encouraged social worker involvement. On the practice level, valuable program initiatives have included:

- operating federal and state political action committees (PACs)

- organizing national, regional, and chapter training programs

- establishing a check-off system on annual membership renewal forms to enhance voluntary candidate contributions

- mobilizing Association support for political candidates whose stance on issues advances NASW's professional and program agenda

- encouraging social workers to seek public office

- promoting voter registration.

Furthermore, by supporting practitioners who spent decades securing legal and commercial recognition of the profession through licensing and vendorship campaigns in state legislatures, NASW steadily built elements of electoral political activity into its program.

Some social work educators and practitioners, however, have been more equivocal and cautious in their approach to electoral politics (Salcido & Seck, 1992; Weismiller & Dempsey, 1993). Educators' ambivalence is reflected in social work education programs with a dearth of either electoral political field placements or specific curriculum material about campaigns, elections, political parties, or other important electoral institutions and processes (Wolk, Weismiller, Dempsey, & Pray, 1994).

Electoral Political Institutions and Processes

Electoral politics are the formal and informal systems by which citizens and groups in a democracy contest for the power to run government (Plano & Greenberg, 1989). Primary electoral political institutions include political parties, interest groups and coalitions, candidate campaign organizations, PACs, the campaign industry (that is, businesses that provide management, polling, fundraising, and communication services to candidates), and the media. Electoral political processes encompass candidate nominations, party conventions, primaries, caucuses, campaigns, elections (including primary, general, and special), voter registration, voting (including absentee and special voting programs), ballot measures, and transitions. Some aspects of electoral politics, including political parties, PACs, transitions, and political education require special attention by NASW. Participation in these processes often amplifies the political influence of a group.

Political parties are voluntary groups of voters with shared ideology, who organize to try to win elections, control government, and influence public policy. Political party activity increases organizational electoral power. A person who holds firmly to a party or its cause is a *partisan*, hence the term "partisan politics." Partisan politics are about working with, or within, major political parties to achieve desired public policy goals. Whatever partisan choices an individual or organization makes, it is still possible and often necessary to have civil and constructive relationships with partisans of other political parties.

Confusion often occurs about the terms "bipartisan" and "nonpartisan." *Bipartisan* means relating to, or involving, members of two parties. Republicans and Democrats presenting a united front in the face of a serious foreign threat to the country is a bipartisan action. *Nonpartisan* usually refers to elections in which candidates have no party designations, and political parties are prohibited from entering candidates.

Federal election law refers to a corporate political committee as a separate, segregated fund (SSF), although it is more commonly called a PAC. As the name implies, money contributed to an SSF is held in a separate bank account from the general corporate treasury. These accounts hold money voluntarily contributed by Association members, and can be used legally for candidate contributions (Plano & Greenberg, 1989). NASW maintains such an account, called Political Action for Candidate Election (PACE), in accordance with federal election law. Authority to make decisions about candidate endorsements and disbursements from the PACE fund has been delegated by the NASW National Board of Directors to the National PACE Board of Trustees.

Transition refers to the time between election to an office and the assumption of the office. Successful candidates use transition time to prepare to hold office. This presents an opportunity for organizations and campaign activists to shape the development of a new administration.

Political education is how an organization develops a sense of the framework in which its political activity will take place. It involves educating members about specific policy issues, candidates, parties, and electoral processes, and how these relate to the economic, political, and social situations in local, state, and national elections (Kahn, 1991). Political education also includes helping members develop an understanding of the relationship between politics and economics that they can explain easily to others. In asking rhetorically, "What makes politics so important?" Jesse Jackson answered: "The political order is the distribution system for the economic order. Politics determines who gets what, when, where, and how" (National Rainbow Coalition, 1994, p. 1).

NASW Involvement in Electoral Politics

Current tax and campaign election laws permit corporations such as NASW to use dues-generated funds to support all electoral activity of their members, except for direct contributions to candidates. Although these laws make much activity legally permissible, the availability of funds limits what is organizationally feasible. NASW has numerous demands on its resources and must balance many needs in its program planning and budgeting process.

National Level. Elections provide a vehicle for accomplishing diverse Association agendas. NASW has focused on electing progressive candidates to public offices for three decades. Since 1984, NASW and PACE have made it a priority to support the candidacies of women and people of color seeking election to federal offices whose agendas are aligned with those of the Association on the most significant issues. The composition of Congress shows some increased diversity, and social workers can be proud of the role NASW has played in that change.

Elections can also be used to gain power for the profession. The 1993 Delegate Assembly made support of social worker candidates for public offices a priority. Between 1991 and 1995 the Association published three editions of the directory, *Social Workers Serving in Elective Offices* (NASW, 1995).

State Level. NASW electoral activity in states originated primarily from chapter legislative initiatives on professional issues such as licensing and vendorship. Acquiring the means to support or oppose legislators spurred the creation of chapter PACs. Once they were in the electoral arena, chapters quickly realized the value of trying to influence the outcome of statewide office races, particularly the governor's office and capitalized on opportunities to do so.

Ballot measures are also an increasingly used electoral tool that chapters are using to spread their sphere of influence. NASW's interest in state ballot measures is mounting. These measures include the *initiative*, a mechanism by which citizens can propose legislation or constitutional amendments; the *referendum*, a mechanism by which voters can veto a bill passed by their legislature; and the *recall*, a procedure enabling voters to remove an elected official from office before his or her term has expired (Plano & Greenberg, 1989).

Recent election cycles have seen important referenda on abortion in Maryland (in 1992) and on public school financing in Michigan (in 1994). Initiatives on welfare reform in California, anti-gay and lesbian rights proposals in Oregon and Colorado, and tax limitations in Washington state went before voters in 1992. In the 1994 election cycle, several states authorized anti-gay and lesbian proposals, and California presented restrictive immigration legislation, an initiative on a single-payer health care system, and a recall vote on a state senator who supported gun control restrictions (Priest, 1994). Ballot measures present major threats and opportunities in the electoral arena (Pear, 1994).

Issues Raised by Electoral Political Participation

Candidate Endorsements. A candidate endorsement is a public statement of support and commitment to provide resources and mobilize members to promote, work, and vote for the candidate. NASW has authorized PACE to make such endorsements on behalf of the Association. Endorsement decisions are based on established process and criteria, including thorough research on the potential endorsees and their opponents and deliberations between NASW, PACE, and chapters (NASW, 1994).

Candidate Contributions. Through PACE, NASW provides financial support to endorsed candidates. Current federal law and state laws require that money given to candidates by corporations such as NASW come only from monies voluntarily contributed by members and disbursed by PACs. NASW may also make other campaign support available to candidates such as recruiting volunteers; mailing information to members; publicizing a candidate's record on policy issues; and using an endorsement by NASW, photo opportunities, letters of support, and assistance with position papers and issue development.

Fairness. The social work professional value of fairness requires that the Association maintain procedures for candidate endorsements that are open and even-handed. To maintain credibility with candidates and its own members, NASW and PACE follow a clearly defined endorsement process, with criteria that are applied fairly to all candidates who wish to go through the process.

NASW can promote inclusion of members in its political activities by respecting the diversity of political positions they hold. PACE is committed to endorsing political candidates only on the basis of their support for NASW policy positions, not on the basis of political party affiliation. It is PACE's responsibility during its endorsement deliberations to give fair consideration to all candidates (Kendall, 1994).

Communication with Power versus Exercise of Power. Having readily available communication with a public official is often confused with having power to influence that official. Having readily available communication with a decision maker is not synonymous with power. Social workers frequently view a friendly political relationship as a successful relationship, regardless of whether it advances the agenda of the profession or of that professional. The goal of NASW is to build political relationships with elected leaders that will result in a favorable action on its policy priorities (Kendall, 1994).

ISSUE STATEMENT

Social work is inextricably linked to electoral politics in a variety of ways. The political authority of decision makers confers ability to determine access to, and distribution of, vital resources. Political power sets, limits, and defines quality of life for all citizens, affecting almost every aspect of their daily lives.

Social workers possess a continuum of knowledge about human needs and behavior, services delivery, systems that affect individuals and groups, and the effects of public policy. Therefore, they are in a unique position to participate in electoral politics, to advocate for candidates, laws, and policies that promote NASW's agenda. As a profession, it is imperative that social workers become informed about, and involved in, all levels of electoral politics.

Social workers frequently approach electoral politics with great caution because of its potential for divisiveness. The major cause for division occurs around the concepts of partisanship and political parties. Some members of the profession believe that NASW should be nonpartisan in terms of candidates for office or that NASW should take positions only on issues, not candidates. Other members think that NASW should be aligned with only one of the major parties, and still others favor a bipartisan or multi-partisan approach.

There are two practical difficulties with NASW adopting a nonpartisan approach to candidates or taking positions on issues instead of candidates. For most political offices in this country, partisanship is unavoidable. Only a few offices, such as those on school boards and some municipal and judicial positions, are contested on a nonpartisan basis. Virtually all other elective offices involve partisan contests. If an individual or group wants to be able to influence electoral outcomes, it has to make partisan choices. Campaigns and elections in the U.S. political system are, by and large, about choices among candidates, not issues. Social workers must be involved in the election of candidates who support NASW values and issues to advance the profession.

POLICY STATEMENT

1. NASW reaffirms that participation in electoral politics is consistent with fundamental social work values, such as self-determination, empowerment, democratic decision making, equal opportunity, inclusion, and the promotion of social justice.

2. NASW's ability to achieve public policy goals and other political objectives depends on participation in the full spectrum of legitimate electoral activities; these activities should be thoroughly integrated into other Association programs.

3. NASW's primary organizational strength lies in the involvement and mobilization of its members in all aspects of electoral politics, with particular emphasis on campaigns and elections, electoral coalitions, fundraising, and the seeking of public office.

4. NASW reaffirms that members seeking or serving in appointive and elective public offices are rendering community service consistent with the profession's *Code of Ethics*.

5. NASW encourages its members to participate in all facets of electoral political activity and recognizes the right of individual members to make their own choices about electoral participation and candidate support.

6. NASW seeks to work collaboratively with the Council on Social Work Education and social work education programs to develop appropriate curriculum material on, and field placements in, electoral politics, and to expand opportunities for political social work practice.

7. NASW cautions that members' vigorous participation in electoral politics and advocacy for NASW positions are bounded by

avoidance of conflicts of interest that would take unfair advantage of any professional relationship or exploitation of others to further their personal, religious, political, or business interests (NASW, 2000).

REFERENCES

Kahn, S. (1991). *Organizing: A guide for grassroots leaders*. Silver Spring, MD: NASW Press.

Kendall, J. (1994). *Report and recommendations: Midwest PACE project meeting and focus group*. Washington, DC: National Association of Social Workers.

National Association of Social Workers. (1994). *Candidate endorsements* (PACE Tip Sheet Series No. 4). Washington, DC: Author.

National Association of Social Workers. (1995). *Social workers serving in elective offices* (3rd ed.). Washington, DC: Author.

National Association of Social Workers. (2000). *Code of ethics of the National Association of Social Workers*. Washington, DC: Author.

National Rainbow Coalition. (1994, June 10). *Jax Fax*, 2(23).

Pear, R. (1994, November 7). Debate on whose voice is heard on initiatives. *The New York Times*, p. B11.

Plano, J. C., & Greenberg, M. (1989). *The American political dictionary* (8th ed.). Fort Worth, TX: Holt, Rinehart & Winston.

Priest, D. (1994, November 2). Ballot names may yield to ballot measures. *Washington Post*, p. A9.

Reeser, L. C., & Epstein, I. (1990). *Professionalization and activism in social work: The sixties, the eighties, and the future*. New York: Columbia University Press.

Salcido, R. M., & Seck, E. T. (1992). Political participation among social work chapters. *Social Work, 37*, 563–564.

Sherradan, M., & Parker, M. D. (1991). Electoral participation of social workers. *New England Journal of Human Services, 11*(23), 23–28.

Weismiller, T., & Dempsey, D. (1993). NASW becoming a dynamic political force [Letter]. *Social Work, 38*, 645–646.

Weismiller, T., & Rome, S. H. (1995). Social workers in politics. In R. L. Edwards (Ed.-in-Chief), *Encyclopedia of social work* (19th ed., Vol. 3, pp. 2305–2313). Washington, DC: NASW Press.

Wolk, J. L., Weismiller, T., Dempsey, D., & Pray, J. L. (1994, November 12). *Political practicums: Educating social workers for policy making*. Paper presented at the Baccalaureate Program Directors Meeting, San Francisco.

Policy statement approved by the NASW Delegate Assembly, August 2005. This policy statement supersedes the policy statement on Electoral Politics approved by the Delegate Assembly in 1996 and referred by the 2002 Delegate Assembly to the 2005 Delegate Assembly for revision. For additional information, contact the National Association of Social Workers, 750 First Street, NE, Suite 700, Washington, DC 2002-4241; telephone 202-408-8600; e-mail press@naswdc.org

Employee Assistance

BACKGROUND

One of social work's primary missions is to support individuals, families, and communities as they strive to achieve and sustain basic needs. For many families, continuous and full employment of one or more members is vital to providing for these needs, including food, clothing, and shelter. Social workers in the workplace support employees in meeting those needs, for themselves and for their families (Akabas & Kurzman, 2005). Employee assistance (EA) is a multidisciplinary field with a strong value placed on collaborative work relationships with other professionals and paraprofessionals within the workplace (Employee Assistance Professionals Association [EAPA], 2009). Through employee assistance programs (EAPs), social workers provide organizational consultation and frontline social support, mental health care, and wellness services for the many working adults in the Unites States and their family members, especially in large companies and institutions (Akabas, 2008).

Established in the United States during the 1940s, EAPs were originally referred to as occupational alcohol programs (OAPs) and focused on identification of and early intervention for alcohol problems among employees. The federal Comprehensive Alcohol Abuse and Alcoholism Treatment and Rehabilitation Act of 1970 (P.L. 91-616) mandated that OAPs be made freely available to all federal employees. In addition, this legislation established the National Institute on Alcohol Abuse and Alcoholism (NIAAA), whose mission included the promotion of EAPs throughout the nation. To accomplish this daunting task, NIAAA funded two occupational program consultants in each state who worked collaboratively with labor representatives to educate private industry about the need for alcohol programs. Together, the consultants and labor organizations formed the Association of Labor–Management Administrators and Consultants on Alcoholism (ALMACA), a nonprofit organization and the precursor of the present-day EAPA.

During the 1980s, OAPs expanded their scope of services, covering a wider array of personal and work-related problems and were renamed EAPs. Passage of the Drug-Free Workplace Act of 1988, as amended by HR 1107 (2011), and its subsequent amendments spurred further growth of EAPs.

Throughout the 1990s, EAPs partnered with larger managed behavioral care (MBC) companies to provide continuous and seamless behavioral health care. EAPs continued their focus on initial assessment to identify underlying personal problems that might negatively affect the workplace and to assist employees in accessing appropriate care within their benefit plan or the community. Within the MBC environment, EA professionals often advocated on behalf of employee clients for effective and timely services. EAPs gained acceptance among public and private workplaces and succeeded in offering "broad brush" services (Akabas, 2008) to employees, family members, and managers. Currently, EAPs offer diverse services related to trauma and crisis intervention; assessment and grief therapy; work–life balance; elder and child care; legal and adoption referrals; workplace and interpersonal violence; and support during organizational changes, such as mergers and downsizing.

Compared with other fields of practice, EA is relatively new, yet it already has standards and practice guidelines developed by social workers and other EA professionals (Council on Accreditation, 2008; EAPA, 2010b). Social workers make up a significant percentage of professionals providing a broad range of workplace and EA services (Jacobson & Hosford-Lamb, 2008; Zastrow, 2008, 2009). The social work field is well-positioned to offer or expand undergraduate and graduate education that will result in increasing numbers of formally trained EA professionals able to fill a wide range of EA positions, including program managers, clinical roles requiring licensure, management consultants, work–life specialists, account managers, researchers, and policy experts (Kurzman, 2008; Pompe & Sharar, 2008).

Social workers excel in EA practice, in part because of their professional training in systems theory and their application of the person-in-environment, or person-in-work-environment, perspective within an ecological framework (Zastrow, 2009). Social workers in EAPs serve employees and family members on a micro practice level; train managers, organizational leaders, and other employees on a mezzo practice level; and promote integration of community, society, and legislative policy on a macro practice level (Jacobson & Hosford-Lamb, 2008). Viewed from a public health perspective (Federal Occupational Health, Leadership Today, 2007), EA professionals have a unique opportunity to apply primary prevention and early intervention services that frequently eliminate the need for additional and often costly health care. EA professionals attend to the needs of the working poor and other potentially vulnerable adults and family members by providing outreach, education, and early intervention to working populations including, but not limited to, racial, ethnic, and religious groups or minorities; older adults; people with disabilities; and employees of all genders and sexual orientations.

The EAPA defines *EA* as the "work organization's resource that utilizes specific core technologies to enhance employee and workplace effectiveness through prevention, identification and resolution of personal and productivity issues" (2010c). This definition originates from research conducted by Roman and Blum (1985, 1988), resulting in EAP (EAPA, 2010a) core technology, the unique characteristics common to all EAPs, which were recently confirmed as still relevant to the field through survey research (Bennett & Attridge, 2008). The certified employee assistance professional cre-

dential is recognized internationally as the knowledge standard for individuals who provide EA services.

Although EAPs address a diverse array of personnel problems through outreach, education, and early identification of and intervention for employees in need, they have demonstrated success in helping businesses reduce costs associated with employee personal, mental health, and substance abuse concerns (Christie & Harlow, 2007; Greenwood, DeWeese, & Inscoe, 2005; Hargrave & Hiatt, 2005; Hargrave, Hiatt, Alexander, & Shaffer, 2008; Wang, Simon, & Kessler, 2008). With the economic downturn starting in 2008, EAPs have expanded their roles to help businesses with organizational development goals, employee termination, supervisory consultations, and management and leadership training.

ISSUE STATEMENT

Two of the most prevalent and costly problems addressed by EAPs are alcohol abuse and depression (National Institute of Mental Health, 2008); employers rank mental illness as the health issue they believe has the most effect on their indirect health costs, ahead of high blood pressure, heart disease, asthma and allergies, diabetes, cancer, smoking, substance abuse, and back problems (Employer Benefit News, 2007). Depression alone is estimated to cost businesses over $44 billion per year and is predicted by the World Health Organization (WHO) to become the second leading source of disability globally by 2020 (Marlowe, 2002; WHO, 2009). In addition to medical-related indirect costs, there are many work-related indirect costs associated with mental illness and substance abuse, such as absenteeism and turnover (Bernstein, 2011).

The Society for Human Resource Management (SHRM) (2009) reported that over 75 percent of U.S. businesses provided EA services; similar results were reported by Mercer (2008) for large U.S. employers. Availability of EA services appears to be somewhat dependent on the size of the workplace, with larger employers being more likely to offer EA services (SHRM, 2009). According to the U.S. Department of Labor, Bureau of Labor Statistics (2008), more than 75 percent of people employed by state and local government have access to EA services. Conversely, EAPs are not available to most people in the workforce, including those who work for small businesses or are self-employed. In addition, women and ethnic or racial minorities are not as attracted to the EAP model as are white men, possibly due to issues involved in supervisory referrals for such services (Akabas, 2008).

Future trends in EA include the adoption of evidence-based screening protocols, such as alcohol screening and brief intervention with referral to treatment, which have been shown in initial tests to reduce at-risk drinking behavior and have a positive return on investment (Substance Abuse and Mental Health Services Administration, 2008). In today's economic environment, services such as management consultation and organizational programs are increasingly considered more important to both employers and EAPs as they may be the best types of services that reach the most troubled employees and, when handled appropriately, provide the best return on investment. EAPs are becoming more decentralized by offering services at multiple locations, using contracted providers, distance counseling, and triage. With the expanding use of technology, online evidence-based self-assessment tools, online wellness information, Webinars, and blogs for employees may reach many more workers and offer effective resources for problem solving (Jacobson & Attridge, 2010; Jacobson & Hosford-Lamb, 2008). Additional activities for EAPs include supporting the global and diverse workplace; providing services from a health promotion, wellness, or work–life balance paradigm; and integrating technology into traditional EA service-delivery systems (Jacobson & Attridge, 2010). EA professionals have made significant strides to eliminate stigma and other barriers to health and mental health care within the workplace through benefit plan consultation and design, education through workshops and health fairs, and case-finding initiatives such as depression and substance abuse screening. EAPs also provide services in a manner that ethically balances dual relationships and sometimes opposing goals of various clients and stakeholders (Mizrahi & Davis, 2008). Services to managers and supervisors include, but are not limited to, consultation and organizational services regarding troubled employees, policy development, and crisis intervention. By influencing workplace policies, benefit plan design, and service selection, EAPs translate social work ideals into business terms and develop them into tangible policies and programs that can improve productivity, workplace safety, and overall employee and organizational health and wellness.

POLICY STATEMENT

NASW supports and advocates for the following:

■ the accessibility and availability of EAP services to all employees in all types and sizes of work settings.

■ the application of *both* the NASW (2008) *Code of Ethics* and EA professional standards and ethics when social workers are providing EA services.

■ the inclusion of EA in social work higher education curriculums and research as well as professional continuing education, including content related to business management and financial knowledge and skills.

■ legislation and public policy designed to improve the employment and well-being of working adults, their families, and communities. Some examples are mental health parity legislation; health care reform; workplace safety provisions; labor relations; and legislation designed to improve federal, state, and global workplaces.

■ expansion of specialized certifications or credentials for social workers as EA professionals.

REFERENCES

Akabas, S. H. (2008). Employee assistance programs. In T. Mizrahi & L. E. Davis (Eds.-in-Chief), *Encyclopedia of social work* (20th ed., Vol. 2, pp. 115–118). Washington, DC, and New York: NASW Press & Oxford University Press.

Akabas, S. H., & Kurzman, P. A. (2005). *Work and the workplace: A resource for innovative policy and practice.* New York: Columbia University Press.

Bennett, J. B., & Attridge, M. (2008). Adding prevention to the EAP core technology. *Journal of Employee Assistance, 38*(4), 3–6.

Bernstein, C. A. (2011, February 4). Advancing mental health by partnering with employers. *Psychiatric News, 46,* 7.

Christie, J., & Harlow, K. (2007). Presenting the business case. *Journal of Employee Assistance, 37*(3), 21–23.

Comprehensive Alcohol Abuse and Alcoholism Treatment and Rehabilitation Act of 1970, P.L. 91-616, 84 Stat. 1848 (1970).

Council on Accreditation. (2008). *Employee assistance program services.* Retrieved from http://www.coastandards.org/standards.php?navView=private&section_id=115

Drug-Free Workplace Act of 1988, § 701, 41 U.S.C. 701 (1996), as amended by Public Contracts, HR 1107, 111th Cong., 2nd Sess. (2011).

Employee Assistance Professionals Association. (2009). *EAPA code of ethics.* Retrieved from http://www.eapassn.org/i4a/pages/index.cfm?pageid=3307

Employee Assistance Professionals Association. (2010a). *The core technology of EAP.* Retrieved from http://www.eapassn.org/i4a/pages/index.cfm?pageid=521

Employee Assistance Professionals Association. (2010b). *EAPA standards and professional guidelines for employee assistance programs.* Retrieved from http://www.eapassn.org/i4a/pages/index.cfm?pageid=804

Employee Assistance Professionals Association. (2010c). *What is an employee assistance program (EAP)?* Retrieved from http://www.eapassn.org/i4a/pages/index.cfm?pageid=869

Employer Benefit News. (2007, May). *21*(6).

Federal Occupational Health, Leadership Today. (2007).

Greenwood, K. L., DeWeese, P., & Inscoe, P. S. (2005). Demonstrating the value of EAP services: A focus on clinical outcomes. *Journal of Workplace Behavioral Health, 21*(1), 1–10.

Hargrave, G. E., & Hiatt, D. (2005). The EAP treatment of depressed employees: Implications for return on investment. *Journal of Employee Assistance and Workplace Behavioral Health, 18*(4), 39–49.

Hargrave, G. E., Hiatt, D., Alexander, R., & Shaffer, I. A. (2008). EAP treatment impact on presenteeism and absenteeism: Implications for return on investment. *Journal of Workplace Behavioral Health, 23,* 283–293.

Jacobson, J. M., & Attridge, M. (2010, July). Employee assistance programs (EAPs): An allied profession for work/life. *Sloan Work and Family Encyclopedia.* Retrieved from http://wfnetwork.bc.edu/encyclopedia_entry.php?id=17296&area=All

Jacobson, J. M., & Hosford-Lamb, J. (2008). Working it out: Social workers in employee assistance. *Social Work Today, 8*(2), 18–23.

Kurzman, P. A. (2008). Occupational social work. In T. Mizrahi & L. E. Davis (Eds.-in-Chief), *Encyclopedia of social work* (20th ed., Vol. 3, pp. 311–319). Washington, DC, and New York: NASW Press & Oxford University Press.

Marlowe, J. F. (2002, March). Depression's surprising toll on employee productivity. *Employee Benefits Journal,* 16–20.

Mercer. (2008). *Mercer 2007 national survey of employer-sponsored health plans.* Retrieved from http://www.mercer.com/custom benchmarkpurchase

Mizrahi, T., & Davis L. E. (Eds.-in-Chief). (2008). *Encyclopedia of social work* (20th ed., Vols. 1–4). Washington, DC, and New York: NASW Press & Oxford University Press.

National Association of Social Workers. (2008). *Code of ethics of the National Association of Social Workers.* Washington, DC: Author.

National Institute of Mental Health. (2008). *The numbers count: Mental disorders in America.* Retrieved from http://www.nimh.nih.gov/health/publications/the-numbers-count-mental-disorders-in-america/index.shtml

Pompe, J. C., & Sharar, D. (2008). Preparing for the challenges of research. *Journal of Employee Assistance, 38*(2), 7–9.

Roman, P. M., & Blum, T. C. (1985). The core technology of employee assistance programs. *ALMACAN, 15*(3), 8–9, 16–19.

Roman, P. M., & Blum, T. C. (1988). Reaffirmation of the core technology of employee assistance programs. *ALMACAN, 19*(8), 17–22.

Society for Human Resources Management. (2009). *2008 employee benefits*. Retrieved from http://www.shrm.org/Research/SurveyFindings/Documents/08-0335_BenefitsSR_FINAL_pdf

Substance Abuse and Mental Health Services Administration. (2008, March/April). Screening works: Update from the field. *SAMHSA News, 16*(4). Retrieved from http://www.samhsa.gov/samhsa_news/VolumeXVI_2/article2.htm

U.S. Department of Labor, Bureau of Labor Statistics. (2008). *National compensation survey: Employee benefits in the United States*. Retrieved from http://www.bls.gov/ncs/

Wang, P. S., Simon, G. E., & Kessler, R. C. (2008). Making the business case for enhanced depression care: The National Institute of Mental Health–Harvard Work Outcomes Research and Cost-Effectiveness Study. *Journal of Occupational & Environmental Medicine, 50*, 468–475.

World Health Organization. (2009). *Depression*. Retrieved from http://www.who.int/mental_health/management/depression/definition/en/

Zastrow, C. (2008). *Social work with groups: A comprehensive workbook*. Belmont, CA: Brooks/Cole.

Zastrow, C. (2009). *Introduction to social work and social welfare: Empowering people* (10th ed.). Belmont, CA: Brooks/Cole.

NASW Members with Primary Responsibility for Revision of This Policy

First Draft Revision:

Jeffrey Christie (TX)
Jodi Jacobson (MD)
Jan Price (VA)
Pam Ruster (IN)
David Worster (NH)

Policy Panelists:

Jennifer Coplon (MA)
Carrie Moore (NJ)
Alisa Lear (LA)
Victoria Marion (OH)

Policy statement approved by the NASW Delegate Assembly, August 2011. This policy statement supersedes the policy statement on Employee Assistance approved by the Delegate Assembly in 2002. For further information, contact the National Association of Social Workers, 750 First Street, NE, Suite 700, Washington, DC 20002-4241. Telephone: 202-408-8600; e-mail: press@naswdc.org

End-of-Life Care

BACKGROUND

Advances in health care technology have given physicians the ability to prolong life in ways that would have seemed impossible only a few years ago. Often, however, the psychosocial consequences of prolongation of life are not considered as an important part of end-of-life decision making and care. Advances in critical care medicine enhance physicians' and clients' opportunities to avoid discussions about death, quality of life, and suffering.

Decisions regarding end-of-life care should be considered at numerous junctures over the course of one's life, not just when diagnosed with a terminal illness or faced with an acute, life-ending event. End-of-life decisions encompass a broad range of medical, spiritual, and psychosocial determinations that each individual should make before the end of her or his life. A person may choose to delegate end-of-life decisions, with or without an advance directive, depending on an individual's capacity to do so. Ideally, individuals decide to address such decisions through advance care planning. In emergencies, when care consideration is not possible, difficult decisions may need to be made by family members and friends, who are often ill-prepared to decide what their loved ones might have wanted. Such decisions can include where a person plans to spend the final months before death and the degree of self-sufficiency and technological intervention she or he wishes during that time. The use of personal, family, and social resources to carry out these decisions may change, depending on the course of the particular illness, and are among some of the most important decisions individuals and their loved ones face (NASW, 2004).

Definitions

For the purpose of this position statement, the following are common terms and definitions associated with end-of-life care. It should be noted that many of these terms are interpreted differently, based on state laws and regulations, across the United States. Here, for the sake of clarity, we describe our specific use of the terms.

Advance Care Planning. Advance care planning encompasses all aspects of an individual's desires for end-of-life care, including living will, health care proxy, "do not resuscitate" orders, and funeral planning.

Health Care Directives. These are written statements that instruct family, friends, medical professionals, and others how an individual wishes to be treated at the end of life, including medical care preferences (resuscitation orders, surgeries, artificial feeding, and organ donation, for example) and how his or her affairs are to be settled. Advance directives include the Durable Power Of Attorney for Health Care and Living Will (also known as Directive to Physician) documents (see definitions below). The appointment only takes effect when individuals are no longer able to make decisions for themselves. It is a Medicare requirement that each client, on admission to a hospital, nursing home, or end-stage renal disease (ESRD) treatment facility be asked if she or he wishes to assign a health care power of attorney, or if she or he has an advance care directive or health care proxy (Patient Self Determination Act, P.L. 101-508).

Minors. Most states will not recognize a formal advance directive signed by a minor, even if he or she is living independently. In most situations, parents and legal guardians retain legal authority to make decisions about medical treatments for a child (Institute of Medicine, 2003).

Decisional Capacity. Decisional capacity is the ability of an individual to understand his or her medical condition, to participate in treatment planning in and out of hospital care, to understand the consequences of his or her decisions, and to meet all other criteria as defined by law (Last Acts, 2001). Decisional capacity can be determined by a psychiatrist or any other physician. The legal definition may vary based on state laws and regulations.

Do Not Resuscitate (DNR) or Do Not Attempt Resuscitation (DNAR). A DNR is an order written by a physician indicating that cardiopulmonary resuscitation is not to be performed. This may also include removal of medications that artificially maintain a blood pressure and the discontinuation of artificial nutrition (New York State and Missouri are exceptions on nutrition). A DNR or DNAR option is discussed with a client or health care agent or family member, but the recommendation not to resuscitate is a medical decision, thereby alleviating a client or family member from making this decision.

Double Effect. This term is related to the ethical principle of "the rule of double effect," which refers to medical treatment that can both produce a desired effect, such as pain relief, but also cause secondary adverse effects, including death. The logic, in effect, is that if the treatment is given only for the desired effect, to relieve pain, the treatment is ethical, even if one could reasonably expect the client to die from the treatment (Last Acts, 2001). Many experts cite morphine given in hospice care as an example. It has powerful pain-relieving properties, but also depresses respiration, which can lead to death.

Durable Power of Attorney for Medical Decision Making (Health Care Proxy). A durable power of attorney for health care decisions is a way to give another individual legal power to make medical decisions when the individual no longer can. The written form used to designate the proxy is also called a durable power of attorney for decision making in health care matters (Lynn & Harrold, 1999). Different states have different versions of this form.

Euthanasia. Euthanasia is the intentional act of ending the life of an individual who would otherwise suffer terribly from a terminal condition. This act is illegal in the United States and also referred to as "mercy killing" (Lynn & Harrold, 1999). It is not to be confused with physician-assisted suicide, described later in this statement.

Family. Anyone the client defines as her or his family, including spouses, partners, parents, siblings, and friends falls into this category. Friends and partners may not have legal status to make decisions for clients unless they are designated as such by a durable power of attorney for health care decisions, but their input should be sought and noted.

Medical Futility. Treatments and procedures provided near the end of life that offer little or no benefit are called medically futile (Bartlow, 2000). The underlying idea of futile care is that if an individual or family member wants life-sustaining treatment, but the physician does not believe the quality of the individual's life justifies the physical burdens of care on the patient, the doctor has the right to withhold any such treatments other than comfort care (Smith, 2002).

Hospice Care. Hospice care is care provided under eligibility guidelines, including diagnosis and prognosis, that focuses on caring, not curing, and in most cases, is provided in the client's home. The focus is on ameliorating physical, psychosocial, and existential suffering (National Hospice and Palliative Care Organization, 2003).

Incompetent. This is a legal term that can only be applied and decided by a judge. This term is often confused with diminished or lack of decisional capacity.

Life-Sustaining Treatment. Life-sustaining treatments are expected to extend life. In the context of end-of-life care, these may also be considered to be futile or death avoidant.

Living Will (Directive to Physician). A living will is a legal document that declares an individual's wish to die a natural death. The document informs the physician that, in the event of a terminal or irreversible condition, she or he does not wish to have her or his life prolonged by artificial or extraordinary means. These documents are not legally binding in all states.

Pain. Pain is the physical sensation resulting from physical illness or conditions that cause discomfort for a client. There are varieties of verbal and nonverbal methods to assess pain. Severity of pain is whatever the client tells the health care provider. Pain should be assessed for clients with and without consciousness (Joint Commission on Accreditation of Healthcare Organizations [JCAHO], 1999).

Palliative Care. Palliative care is an approach that improves quality of life for clients and families facing life-threatening illness (NASW, 2004). This approach is applicable early in the course of illness in conjunction with other therapies that are intended to prolong life and includes those investigations needed to better understand and manage distressing clinical complications (World Health Organization, 2003).

Palliative Sedation. This treatment involves the monitored use of drugs and other procedures intended to induce varying degrees of relief of unmanageable, intractable, and intolerable symptoms in imminently dying clients (Hospice and Palliative Nurses Association, 2003).

Physician-Assisted Suicide. In physician-assisted suicide, a client ends her or his life with the prescription requested of and provided by a physician for that purpose. As of 2005, the state of Oregon was the only state where this act is legally permissible. In all cases, the client must have decisional capacity and meet other criteria as defined by law (Oregon Department of Human Services, 1997).

Suffering. Although suffering can be both physical and psychological in nature, it can extend itself in the dying trajectory to the existentialist level. Depression or existential suffering refers to the feelings of misery, fear, and immobilization, as well as the search for meaning an individual may feel at the end of life. As soon as an individual begins the difficult work of grieving, including "struggling with," and through depression, the road to resolution, acceptance, and healing has started (Bartlow, 2000; Peck, 1997).

Terminal and Irreversible Condition. This phrase defines a condition with no reasonable chance of recovery or a condition caused by injury, disease, or illness, which, within reasonable medical judgment, would produce death within a short time, and for which the application of life-sustaining procedures would serve only to postpone the moment of death or be futile.

Withdrawal or Withholding of Treatment. These are acts that eliminate interventions that prolong death or that create further pain and suffering. Action is followed at the direction of the client or his or her health care agent. Withdrawal of treatment may include the following: removal of medicines that artificially maintain blood pressure, and extubation and withdrawal of ventilatory support. Withdrawal comes with assurances that the physician will provide enough sedating medication to avoid patient and family suffering.

Legislation

In recent years, a proliferation of state legislation has been introduced concerning assisted suicide, most notably Oregon's 1997 implementation of physician-assisted suicide. However, state legislatures across the country are debating similar "death with dignity" bills, many of which would authorize physician-assisted suicide. Legislatures and state ballot initiatives that recently have discussed death with dignity bills include those in Arizona, Florida, Hawaii, Maine, Wisconsin, Wyoming, and Vermont. In 2001 U.S. Attorney General John Ashcroft filed suit against Oregon to overturn the Death with Dignity Act and stop its proliferation to other states. In 2004 a federal appeals court ruled against the Attorney General and upheld the Oregon statute.

Political and social leaders are also attempting to influence personal choice and clinical practice in this area. State legislatures have become involved in such high profile cases as the Terri Schiavo case in Florida and the illegal Jack Kevorkian practice, in which he euthanized several patients. In 2004, the Vatican released an opinion that feeding tubes are medical therapy and cannot be withheld from a permanently unconscious person (Smith, 2004). It is not clear what impact the Pope's statement will have on the nation's Catholic hospitals or health care providers and clients.

The 1990 Patient Self-Determination Act mandated the requirement that hospitals, skilled nursing facilities, ESRD facilities, home health agencies, hospice programs, and HMOs maintain written policies and procedures guaranteeing that every adult receiving medical care is given written information concerning living wills, durable powers of attorney for health care, or advance directives.

A groundswell of new policies and practices in end-of-life care has been positive in recent years. The positive changes include state policies on pain and symptom management, the JCAHO's requirements for pain assessments, reconsideration of state-mandated advance directives, the use of out-of-hospital DNRs, and the increased practice of palliative care.

ISSUE STATEMENT

Social work practice settings addressing end-of-life care include health and mental health agencies, schools, courts, child welfare and family service agencies, correctional systems, agencies serving immigrants and refugees, military service agencies, substance abuse programs, and employee assistance programs. Social work is a broadly based profession that can meet the needs of individuals and families affected by end-of-life situations. Social workers require guidelines that are compatible with professional and personal ethics, legal parameters, and respect for client self-determination. Furthermore, other professionals may look to social work for guidelines on these complex issues.

Using the expertise in working with populations from varying cultures, ages, socioeconomic statuses, and traditional and nontraditional families, social workers help clients and families across the life span cope with loss, trauma, suicide, dying, death, and bereavement; they must be prepared to assess such needs and to intervene appropriately.

In acknowledging and affirming social work's commitment to respecting diverse value systems in a pluralistic society, we recognize that end-of-life issues as complex because they reflect the varied value systems of different groups. Consequently, NASW does not take a position regarding the myriad moral and value-laden questions associated with end-of-life decisions, but affirms the right of individuals to direct their end-of-life care.

We also recognized that de facto rationing of health care based on age, sexual orientation, religion, socioeconomic status, race, ability to pay, provider biases, and government policy differentially affect people's rights to choose among viable service alternatives and diminishes their ability to give truly informed consent. Social workers should advocate to minimize the effect of these factors when determining the care options available to individuals.

In examining the social work role with clients concerning end-of-life decisions, the following issues must be addressed:

■ potential conflict of social work values with those of the clients, clients' families, other health care professionals, or agency settings

■ limits of confidentiality, social work licensing laws, and state and federal laws and regulations

- emerging pressures for cost control and rationing of health care (for example, using health care institutions and insurers to encourage use of end-of-life practices to control costs)

- the possibility that individuals would feel the need to hasten their deaths and the social work role of exploring such feelings and discussion with clients

- the necessity to define, defend, and advocate for safeguards that protect individuals and society in the implementation of end-of-life practices

- lack of access to end-of-life care options for all persons.

POLICY STATEMENT

NASW's position concerning end-of-life decisions is based on the principle of client self-determination. Choice should be intrinsic to all aspects of life and death. Social workers have an important role in helping individuals identify the end-of life options available to them. This role must be performed with full knowledge of and compliance with the law and in accordance with the *NASW Code of Ethics* (NASW, 2000) and *NASW Standards for Social Work Practice in Palliative & End of Life Care* (NASW, 2004).

Often, social workers meet with clients who express a desire to talk about their thoughts and feelings about dying and death. Social workers play an important role in assessing desire-to-die statements; in providing appropriate knowledge, compassion, and skill; and intervening to ameliorate pain and suffering. Social workers can explore and assess all these issues with clients and can educate and direct them to appropriate resources such as pain management, palliative care, or hospice care.

The position of the National Association of Social Workers on end-of-life care provides several areas of consideration and specific action steps for social workers and other providers dealing with this issue.

Practice

- Facilitate client and family understanding of all aspects and options in end-of-life care.

- Provide emotional, psychological, social, and spiritual care and services along the end-of-life continuum.

- Be aware of cultural diversity in end-of-life care practices and beliefs so that culturally sensitive practices in end-of-life care can be used with clients and families.

- Provide access to information to facilitate informed consent for decision making.

- Be aware of client diagnoses and trajectories of illness to best prepare for future health care needs and decisions.

- Discuss and encourage advance care planning if appropriate.

- Be present (if the social worker is comfortable with being present) with the client and family at the very end of life (whatever the site) as appropriate, and when requested by the client or family.

- Be present (if social worker is comfortable with presence) with a client or family in assisted-suicide situations in states where this practice is legal and requested by the client.

- Strive to facilitate continuity of care across all care settings.

- Assess mental health functioning to include assisting in decisional capacity determinations, depression, anxiety, suicidal ideation, and facilitate or provide interventions or referrals for care.

- Be knowledgeable about institutional policies on capacity, advance directives, pain management, futile care, and DNR orders.

- Be knowledgeable about state specific policies on end-of-life care.

- Recognize the importance of an initial and ongoing assessment to provide the appropriate intervention(s) along the continuum of care.

- Be competent in assessing pain and other symptoms.

■ Be able to differentiate between pain and existential suffering.

■ Act as a liaison with other health care professionals to communicate clients' and families' concerns to the health care team to improve the quality of end-of-life care.

■ Provide mentoring and consultation to other health care professionals and social work colleagues and students in the field of end-of-life care.

■ Be self-aware of personal values and feelings about dying and death and obtain assistance for the best interests of client, as well as to meet one's own personal needs to resolve issues.

■ Refer the client or family to another social worker if your own value system conflicts with your client's decisions.

■ Prevent abandonment by care providers of the client or family facing an end-of-life situation.

■ Obtain competent supervision when working in end-of-life care.

■ Be knowledgeable about hospice care for cancer and non-cancer diagnoses, such as congestive heart failure, diabetes, and ESRD.

■ Keep abreast of changes in end-of-life care by participating in continuing education and research activities.

Advocacy

■ Advocate for adequate pain control and symptom management in institutional and agency committees and in state and national legislative and regulatory forums.

■ Promote access to care for all people facing end-of-life situations.

■ Participate in local, state, and national committees, activities, and task forces concerning client self-determination and end-of-life decisions.

■ Include education and research on these complex topics in social work curricula.

■ Support initiatives, both public and private, that seek to expand the hospice benefit.

REFERENCES

Bartlow. B. (2000). *Medical care of the soul.* Boulder, CO: Johnson Printing.

Hospice and Palliative Nurses Association. (2003). *Palliative sedation.* Retrieved May 11, 2004, from http://www.hpna.org/position_PalliativeSedation.asp

Institute of Medicine. (2003). *When children die: Improving palliative and end of life care for children and their families* (Summary). Washington, DC: Author.

Joint Commission on Accreditation of Hospitals. (1999). *Pain: Current understanding of assessment, management and treatment.* Retrieved May 11, 2004, from http://www.jcaho.org/news+room/health+care+issues/pain+mono_npc.pdf

Last Acts. (2001). *What does it mean? Common terms used in talking about end of life care.* Retrieved May 11, 2004, from http://www.lastacts.org/files/misc/glossary.pdf

Lynn, J., & Harrold. J. (1999). *Handbook for mortals: Guidance for people facing serious illness.* New York: Oxford University Press.

National Association of Social Workers. (2000). *Code of ethics of the National Association of Social Workers.* Washington, DC: Author.

National Association of Social Workers. (2003). Client self-determination in end-of-life decisions. *Social work speaks: National Association of Social Workers policy statements, 2003–006* (6th ed., pp. 46–49). Washington, DC: NASW Press.

National Association of Social Workers. (2004). *NASW standards for social work practice in palliative & end of life care.* Washington, DC: Author.

National Hospice and Palliative Care Organization. (2003). *What is hospice care.* Retrieved May 11, 2004, from http://www.nhpco.org/i4a/pages/index.cfm?pageid=3281

Oregon Department of Human Services. (1997). *Oregon's death with dignity act.* Retrieved May 11, 2004, from http://www.dhs.state.or.us/publichealth/chs/pas/pas.cfm

Patient Self-Determination Act (PSDA), Pub. L. 101-508, 104 Stat. 1388 (1990).

Peck, F. S. (1997). *Denial of the soul: Spiritual and medical perspectives on euthanasia.* New York: Harmony Books.

Smith, V. A. (2004) Pope's feeding-tube declaration pits religion, medicine. *Philadelphia Inquirer.* Retrieved November 17, 2004, from http://www.philly.com/mld/philly/

Smith, W. J. (2002). *Doctors deny some patients hospital care.* Detroit News. Retrieved June 1, 2004, from http://www.detnews.com/2002/editorial/0201/13/a13-389247.htm

World Health Organization. (2003). *Palliative care.* Retrieved May 11, 2004, from http://www.who.int/cancer/palliative/definition/en/

Policy statement approved by the NASW Delegate Assembly, August 2005. This statement supersedes the policy statement on Client Self-Determination in End-of-Life Decisions approved by the Delegate Assembly in 1993 and reconfirmed in 1999. For further information, contact the National Association of Social Workers, 750 First Street, NE, Suite 700, Washington, DC 20002-4241; telephone: 202-408-8600; e-mail: press@naswdc.org

Environment Policy

BACKGROUND

Evidence suggests that all elements of the global ecosystem are under attack and threatened in ways that may be reaching the point of irreversibility. The threats to the natural environment include damage to the ozone layer; unplanned, not "smart growth" land use that is based on private property and profit motives rather than any sense of collective good; the escalating use of nonrenewable natural resources; and the rapid extinction of whole species of plants and animals, along with the invasion of nonnative species; and an increasingly scarce and contaminated water supply (Shiva, 2002). For most of human history, estimated to be between 500,000 years and 1.5 million years, the effect of human activity on the biosphere has been negligible. In the final decades of the 20th century, and into the 21st, the human race in all areas of the globe has created technologies and lifestyles that threaten to alter irrevocably the habitability of the biosphere for all life forms (Berger & Kelly, 1993; Gore, 2006; Pruss-Ustun & Corvalan, 2006). Although human population growth is in and of itself a significant factor, those of us who live in highly developed regions on the planet have contributed disproportionately to environmental pollution and degradation.

The environmental crisis cuts across political, economic, cultural, and social boundaries. It will affect all countries, races, ethnicities and nationalities, classes of people, political parties, and economic interests (United Nations, 2007). In the early 2000s, considerable focus was put on global warming as a major environmental challenge. Former Vice President Al Gore took a major and effective leadership role in educating the citizens of the world about the "inconvenient truth" of climate change (Gore, 2006). His essential argument, one that is well grounded in scientific data, is that the activities of human beings contribute to global warming such that the viability of the planet is now in danger. He presents information that demonstrates that global warming is a clear and present danger but that there is still time to take action to protect, restore, and save the environment. Data documenting global warming were first published in 1957, when Roger Revelle and chemist Hans Suess published an article in the journal *Tellius*. Five years later, Rachel Carson (1962) sounded a broader environmental alarm about the natural environment with her book *Silent Spring*. Colburn and colleagues' (1997) book *Stolen Future*, described by some as the *Silent Spring* of the 1990s, provided research on how human-made chemicals disrupt endocrine systems.

In the first decade of the 21st century, increasingly sophisticated methods are producing a rigorously examined, disturbing body of scientific documentation with regard to human exposure to and harmful health effects associated with industrial, commercial, agricultural, and household chemical use (Beyond Pesticides, n.d.; Centers for Disease Control and Prevention, 2005; Poppell, 2003). Techniques such as integrated pest management are identifying best practices in reducing and balancing human health risks from pests and pesticides (United States Environmental Protection Agency, 2007). The precautionary principle, as an alternative to traditional risk assessment methods, is used increasingly to apply research knowledge while protecting the most vulnerable citizens (Myers & Raffensperger, 2005).

Neighborhoods, communities, and countries that are poor, especially those that are populated by people of color, are at greater risk of environmental pollution and its effects (Morello-Frosch & Jesdale, 2006). Citing findings from various research studies, Rogge and Combs-Orme (2003) reported evidence that ethnic minority groups and rural communities in the United States and internationally are disproportionately exposed to the dangers associated with environmental degradation. Whether it is the location of a toxic waste dump, the locations of storage facilities for nonbiodegradable toxic substances, the exportation of banned pesticides, or the location of dangerous chemical manufacturing plants (for example, the Dow Chemical plant in Bhopal, India), people of color and poor people are often exposed to many more environmental hazards than the rest of the population. Often, residents feel they have no power to resist either having dangerous sources of contamination in their communities or accept the argument put forth by corporate and governmental agents that these sources attract desperately needed economic development (Bullard, Mohai, Saha, & Wright, 2007).

The inextricable links among poverty, environmental degradation, and risk to human well-being cannot be denied. Children have a particular risk. Developing cells are more susceptible to damage, and toxins concentrate more rapidly in smaller bodies. Pesticides may concentrate in sources of nutrition, including breast milk. Hand-to-mouth activity of children increases the likelihood of ingesting toxins. Pesticides and other toxins concentrate in or near the ground, where children play, particularly in developing countries (Healthy Schools Network, 2007; United Nations Environment Programme, 2002). The relationships and subsequent health disparities are clear in polluted inner city neighborhoods, where children of color suffer from high rates of asthma; in crop lands, where poor migrant workers carry agriculture pesticides home to their families on their work clothes; in low-income Louisiana parishes along the industrial "Cancer Alley" stretch of the Mississippi River; and in the unsanitary, crowded, and hastily and poorly constructed maquiladoras that house

Mexican plant workers along the U.S.–Mexico border. Air pollution is linked to asthma among U.S. children, which increased 118 percent from 1980 to 1993. Despite earlier legislation that reduced lead in the air by an estimated 98 percent, 35 percent of African American children living in inner cities are still estimated to have elevated blood lead levels (Children's Environmental Health Network, n.d.; Gorey, 1995; Rogge & Combs-Orme, 2003). Although most research examining the effects of toxic exposure on children occurs in industrialized countries, children's risk, exposure, and harm are global phenomena.

As Hoff and McNutt (1994) illustrated in the first edited volume on social work practice and the environmental crisis, all forms of social work practice are affected by environmental degradation. Park (1996) stated that "the violent threat to the Earth requires an emphatic response from social workers" (p. 320).

Social work is unique among the helping professions in its emphasis on the person-in-environment perspective. Until recently, much of our professional attention to the environment emphasized its social, cultural, and economic components, oftentimes to the exclusion of the natural or physical environment. Beginning in the latter two decades of the 20th century, a few social work scholars began to consider the implications of this exclusion by focusing attention on the natural environment as a critical component of the social work person-in-environment perspective.

The "ecological paradigm" and "life model" developed by Germain and Gitterman (1980) have been widely embraced by social workers as a practice perspective and strategy that encompasses the person and environment configuration. This model drew heavily from ecological thinking and opened the door for the profession to understand and consider the environment to both the social and natural realms. The use of the ecological metaphor for understanding the environment gave social workers the tool necessary to go beyond its traditional concentration on the social environment.

Berger and Kelly (1993) explored the idea that social workers at all levels and in all forms of practice have a role to play in the developing environmental crisis. In 1994, Hoff and McNutt published an edited book that laid out the reasons why the environmental crisis was an important issue for social welfare and social workers. Later, Berger (1995) argued that social workers needed to face up to and act on their awareness of the out of control "habitat destruction." Hoff and Rogge (1996) argued for the compelling need for the social work profession to develop and implement responses to the environmental crisis, particularly the omnipresent "environmental injustice."

ISSUE STATEMENT

Environmental justice is a concept that has gained currency in the public arena and has particular relevance for the social work person-in-environment perspective (Rogge, 2008). *Environmental justice* is defined as "fair treatment and meaningful involvement of all people regardless of race, ethnicity, income, national origin, or educational level with respect to the development, implementation, and enforcement of environmental laws, regulations, and policies" (p. 136). Fair treatment means that no population, because of policy or economic disempowerment, is forced to bear a disproportionate burden of the negative human health or environmental effects of pollution or other environmental consequences resulted from industrial, municipal, and commercial operations or the execution of federal, state, local, and tribal programs and policies" (U.S. Environmental Protection Agency, Office of Federal Activities, 1998, p. 2). Environmental justice is a fundamental principle embedded in the idea of sustainable development and is consistent with the principles of social work. Shorthand definitions of this complex construct often note the importance of attending simultaneously to the "three Es" of equity (social justice), economy, and environment to manage world resources for current and future generations (Rogge, 2000). For social workers, more fully integrating environmental, social, and economic justice means applying familiar social work knowledge, skills, and methods to new substantive areas and learning new applications for substantive expertise.

Social workers have a special concern for and responsibility to oppressed populations who suffer disproportionately with dangerous environmental conditions. Social workers have fought against "environmental racism." *Environmental racism* is defined in the *Social Work Dictionary* (5th ed.) as "The practice of operating hazardous businesses or storing toxic waste products in or near areas inhabited primarily by racial and ethnic minorities groups" (Barker, 2003, p. 145). Poor communities often are similarly affected disproportionately. For example, many landfills located in inner city areas are filled with refuse from wealthier suburban communities. Some poor communities have agreed to store hazardous materials as a source of much needed economic activity.

Although the social work profession has been gaining understanding of the importance of the natural environment and how this affects all populations, and particularly those who are already vulnerable, the environmental crisis has worsened. Thus, it can be argued that the more economically developed world carries a greater responsibility for facing up to and addressing the crisis that has resulted. For example, climate change created by global warming stems from the size of our individual and collective "carbon and ecological footprints," which are much greater for those of us in the developed world (Hoff, 2002; Natural Resources Defense Council, 2007). Social work, with its focus on political advocacy, can be an important force in addressing this problem.

It is estimated by some that we have a mere two decades to address global warming in a significant way or the damage to the earth's atmosphere will be irreparable (Gore, 2006). Current attitudes, practices, and lifestyles in developed countries that are based on the misguided notion that there is an endless supply of fresh water and other natural resources that can be exploited at will still predominate. In developing countries, growing populations who seek the industrial, commercial, and economic benefits of the Western world produce another potentially unprecedented strain on diminishing and nonrenewable natural resources. Our collective refusal to acknowledge and act on the perilous reality we face, in light of mounting evidence, is the result of more than collective ignorance. True understanding requires some sophisticated knowledge about the physical and biological working of the biosphere, yet requires knowledge of social and psychological dynamics as well.

Facing up to the needs of the natural environment requires change in how society organizes and sets priorities about community capital and means of production. It requires that we all alter, at least in some way, our current lifestyles, provoking great resistance among those who are happy with their lifestyles as well as those who aspire to become like those of us who have comfortable lifestyles. As a result, it is easier, with some notable exceptions, to collectively numb ourselves and otherwise ignore the needs of the environment while pretending that our collective destruction of it is not likely. Social workers and those we serve will benefit by the profession's increasing awareness of the reality of our current environmental situation as we educate ourselves and others to gain further understanding and to take action. Action in support of the environment should be included in all of the profession's public and private activities.

POLICY STATEMENT

Social workers need an environmentally responsible credo to which we can subscribe and that will influence our individual and collective actions. Social workers must become dedicated protectors of the environment. Together, we can model environmental awareness for those who come in contact with us in our personal and professional lives.

NASW supports and advocates for

■ policies that reduce environmental risks to poor, minority, and disadvantaged communities who have been disproportionately affected.

■ more rigorous and effective testing, regulation, and labeling of chemicals and products that contain them.

■ the elimination of fossil fuels, where feasible, to be replaced with clean energy, such as solar, wind, and water.

■ secure and affordable food systems that are free of toxic chemicals and pesticides.

■ the reduction of children's exposure to pesticides and other chemicals through approaches such as the precautionary principle and integrated pest management.

■ the protection of individuals who work in hazardous jobs by strict national and international environmental standards, including effective enforcement mechanisms.

■ interdisciplinary research, policy practice, and community-based actions to promote environmental health and justice.

■ strategies that will reduce our individual and collective "carbon and ecological footprints."

■ adequate funding of such agencies as the U.S. Environmental Protection Agency. State and local counterparts must have the necessary resources and authority to establish and enforce environmental protection in accordance with generally acceptable scientific standards and data.

■ the development and funding of environmental governing agencies throughout the world, with enforcement by the appropriate offices within the United Nations and other appropriate entities.

■ the reduction or elimination of all forms of environmental racism and injustice.

■ social work education at all levels, incorporating discussions of the natural environment, ideas of habitat destruction, chemical contamination, environmental racism, environmental justice, and sustainability.

■ social work practice methods and techniques broadened to consider the natural environment.

■ comprehensive training and development of social workers' skills in identifying difficult-to-detect workplace and environmental hazards to physical and mental health.

■ programs that enable social workers to achieve a deeper awareness and understanding of environmental dangers through the study of traditional perspectives and theories held by indigenous peoples in the United States and other countries.

■ community organizing, coalition building, social and economic development planning, case advocacy, and political action to improve the person–natural environment interface.

■ the inclusion of the natural environment as a routine part of the assessment and treatment planning activities of social workers in all settings with all clients, especially those clients who are most likely to be victimized by unsound and unsafe environmental practices.

■ social services agencies and organizations, including NASW, recognizing the need to protect the environment and acting accordingly.

In addition, NASW advocates against

■ policies that allow toxic waste to be relocated or exported from wealthy industrialized areas and nations to less economically favored areas and nations

■ government and corporate policies which further environmental injustice.

REFERENCES

Barker, R. L. (2003). *The social work dictionary* (5th ed.). Washington, DC: NASW Press.

Berger, R. M. (1995). Habitat destruction syndrome. *Social Work, 40,* 441–443.

Berger, R. M., & Kelly, J. J. (1993). Social work in the ecological crisis. *Social Work, 38,* 521–526.

Beyond Pesticides. (n.d.). Retrieved October 8, 2007, from http://www.beyondpesticides.org/

Bullard, R. D., Mohai, P., Saha, R., & Wright, B. (2007). *Toxic wastes and race at twenty: 1987–2007: Grassroots struggles to dismantle environmental racism in the United States.* Retrieved July 11, 2007, from http://www.snre.umich.edu/news/newsdocs/Toxic%20Wastes%20and%20Race%20at%20Twenty%20Rpt%20(2).pdf

Carson, R. (1962). *Silent spring.* Boston: Houghton Mifflin.

Centers for Disease Control and Prevention. (2005). *Third national report on human exposure to environmental chemicals.* Retrieved September 17, 2007, from www.cdc.gov/exposurereport

Children's Environmental Health Network. (n.d.). Retrieved October 8, 2007, from http://www.cehn.org

Colburn, T., Dumanoski, D., & Myers, J. P. (1997). *Stolen future: Are we threatening our fertility, intelligence, and survival?—A scientific detective story.* New York: Plume.

Germain, C. B., & Gitterman, A. (1980). *The life model of social work practice.* New York: Columbia University Press.

Gore, A. (2006). *An inconvenient truth* [Documentary]. Retrieved October 8, 2007, from http://www.climatecrisis.net/aboutthefilm/

Gorey, K. M. (1995). Environmental health: Race and socioeconomic factors. In R. L. Edwards (Ed.), *Encyclopedia of social work* (19th ed., Vol. 1, pp. 868–872). Washington, DC: NASW Press.

Healthy Schools Network. (2007). *Healthy schools network.* Retrieved October 8, 2007, from http://www.healthyschools.org/

Hoff, M. D. (2002). Effects of global warming on human cultural diversity. In *Encyclopedia of life support systems* (Chapter 3a). Retrieved November 3, 2007, from http://www.eolss.net/E1-04-toc.aspx

Hoff, M. D., & McNutt, J. G. (Eds.). (1994). *The global environmental crisis: Implications for social welfare and social work.* Brookfield, UK: Avebury/Gower House.

Hoff, M. D., & Rogge, M. E. (1996). Everything that rises must converge: Developing a social work response to environmental injustice. *Journal of Progressive Human Services, 7,* 41–57.

Morello-Frosch, R., & Jesdale, B. M. (2006). Separate and unequal: Residential segregation and estimated cancer risks associated with ambient air toxics in U.S. metropolitan areas. *Environmental Health Perspectives, 114,* 386–393.

Myers, N. J., & Raffensperger, C. (2005). *Precautionary tools for reshaping environmental policy.* Cumberland, RI: MIT Press.

Natural Resources Defense Council. (2007). *Global warming.* Retrieved October 8, 2007, from http://www.nrdc.org/globalWarming/gsteps.asp

Park, K. M. (1996). The personal is ecological: Environmentalism of social work [Commentary]. *Social Work, 41,* 320–323.

Poppell, C. (2003). *Bearing the burden: Health implications of environmental pollutants in our bodies*. Washington, DC: Physicians for Social Responsibility.

Pruss-Ustun, A., & Corvalan, C. (2006). *Preventing disease through healthy environments: Toward an estimate of the environmental burden of disease*. Retrieved October 8, 2007, from http://www.who.int/quantifying_ehim pacts/publications/preventingdisease/en/index.html

Rogge, M. E. (2000). Social development and the ecological traditions. *Social Development Issues, 22*(1), 32–41.

Rogge, M. E. (2008). Environmental justice. In T. Mizrahi & L. Davis (Eds.-in-Chief). *Encyclopedia of social work* (20th ed., pp. 136–139). Washington, DC and New York: NASW Press/Oxford University Press.

Rogge, M. E., & Combs-Orme, T. (2003). Protecting children from chemical exposure: Social work and U.S. social welfare policy. *Social Work, 48*, 439–450.

Shiva, V. (2002). *Water wars: Privatization, pollution, and profit*. London: Pluto Press.

United Nations. (2007). *The millennium development goals report 2007*. New York: United Nations. Retrieved October 8, 2007, from http://www.un.org/millenniumgoals/pdf/mdg2007.pdf

United Nations Environment Programme, United Nation's Children's Fund, & World Health Organization. (2002). *Children in the new millennium: Environmental impact on health*. Retrieved October 8, 2007, from http://www.unep.org

United States Environmental Protection Agency. (2007). *Integrated pest management (IPM) in schools*. Retrieved October 8, 2007, from http://www.epa.gov/pesticides/ipm/

United States Environmental Protection Agency, Office of Federal Activities. (1998). *Final guidance for incorporating environmental justice concerns in EPA's NEPA compliance analyses*. Washington, DC: U.S. Government Printing Office.

Policy statement approved by the NASW Delegate Assembly, August 2008. This policy statement supersedes the policy statement on Environmental Policy approved by the Delegate Assembly in 1999 and referred by the 2005 Delegate Assembly to the 2008 Delegate Assembly for revision. For further information, contact the National Association of Social Workers, 750 First Street, NE, Suite 700, Washington, DC 20002-4241. Telephone: 202-408-8600 or 800-638-8799; e-mail: press@naswdc.org

Family Planning and Reproductive Choice

BACKGROUND

The modern history of family planning in the United States began in 1916 when Margaret Sanger, a public health nurse in New York City, opened the first birth control clinic. She and two of her associates were arrested and sent to jail for violating New York's obscenity laws by discussing contraception and distributing contraceptives. Ms. Sanger argued that birth control must be legalized.

Government support of family planning in the United States began in the 1960s when President Kennedy endorsed contraceptive research and the use of modern birth control methods as a way to address the world's population growth. It was under President Johnson and the War on Poverty that family planning services became more widely available. The rate of unwanted childbearing among people living in poverty was twice as high as it was among the more affluent population. This difference was attributed to the lack of available family planning services for women living in poverty.

By 1965, with bipartisan support, federal funds were made available to support family planning services for low-income women.

Title X of the Public Health Service Act of 1970 provided the majority of public funding for family planning services until 1985. Because of fiscal pressures and political factors, such as the growing power and influence of the religious right (mobilized in opposition to the 1973 Supreme Court decision legalizing abortion), Congress has not formally reauthorized Title X since 1985. Appropriations have continued, but inflation-adjusted funding for Title X services decreased by 58 percent from 1980

over the next two decades. More recently, other federal sources—including Medicaid, social services, and maternal and child health block grants; state children's health insurance programs; and Temporary Assistance for Needy Families—as well as state and local funds—have become available to subsidize family planning. Nonetheless, Title X remains central to the national effort (Gold, 2001).

As a result of Title X funding, contraceptive use among American women increased considerably between the early 1980s and the mid-1990s, and the country's unintended pregnancy rate—and the abortion rate—declined. But as Title X funding decreased, the decline in the number of unintended pregnancies slowed sharply. According to research by the Guttmacher Institute in 2006, this progress has ground to a halt:

> The newest data paint a disturbing picture of two very different Americas—one in which middle- and upper-class women are continuing decades of progress in reducing unplanned pregnancy and abortion, and the other in which poor women are facing more unplanned pregnancies and growing rates of abortion. (Gold, 2006, p. 3)

Although progress on universally accessible family planning in the United States has stalled, international family planning efforts are also challenged. The World Health Organization (WHO) defines *family planning* as "the ability of individuals and couples to anticipate and attain their desired number of children and the spacing and timing of their births. It is achieved through use of contraceptive methods and the treatment of involuntary infertility" (WHO, 2007b, p. 1). WHO estimated that more than 120 million couples worldwide do not use contraception, despite wanting to space or limit their childbearing.

There are numerous economic and social benefits to good public family planning policies. In the United States, public funding for family planning prevents more than a million pregnancies each year. It has been estimated that each federal and state tax dollar spent on family planning saves three dollars in Medicaid costs for pregnancy-related and newborn care (Gold, 2001). Women who use family planning services are more likely to use prenatal services and thus have reduced infant mortality and fewer low-birth weight babies, in addition to reducing their own risk of death or health problems. Family planning also reduces infant deaths by helping women space pregnancies. The infant mortality rate is two times higher for a child born within two years of a sibling, a rate that is constant throughout the world (Pichler, 2007).

Emergency Contraception

The "morning after pill," or emergency contraception (EC), is a form of contraception that can be used shortly after sexual intercourse to prevent unintended pregnancy. Offered as a "second chance" for individuals who did not use contraception before intercourse, EC is equally valuable as a safeguard against method failure. EC pills are estimated to reduce the risk of pregnancy by up to 89 percent (Rodrigues, Grou, & Joly, 2002). When offered in a timely manner to victims of sexual assault, EC almost eliminates the fear of pregnancy resulting from this criminal act, helping to restore a sense of control to the victim.

Although this form of fertility control is safe, inexpensive, and easy to use, EC generates opposition by groups who oppose all forms of birth control or believe that it is an abortifacient. These arguments among policymakers threaten the accessibility of emergency contraception to those who might benefit from its protection.

Abortion

Research indicates that half of all pregnancies of American women are unintended and that four in 10 of these end in abortion (Guttmacher Institute, 2008). The correlation between high levels of unintended pregnancy and abortion cannot be discounted. As stated by Sharon Camp of the Guttmacher Institute (2006), "behind almost every abortion in the United States is an unplanned and unwanted pregnancy . . . [Abortion] . . . is a last resort for a woman who is faced with a crisis pregnancy" (p. 1). The United States has one of the highest abortion rates in the developed world, and it is estimated that 35 percent of women will have an abortion by 45 years of age. Although women of all backgrounds have abortions, abortion in the United States is increasingly likely to occur among single women, racial or ethnic minority women, low-income women, and women who have had at least one child (Boonstra, Gold, Richards, & Finer, 2006).

Abortion is a controversial medical procedure, but it has been performed over an average of a million times each year since 1973. The right of American women to terminate their pregnancy is founded on the Supreme Court decision in *Roe v. Wade* (1973) that has been under assault since the ruling was pronounced. A July 2007 national poll affirms, however, that a small majority of Americans, despite their ambivalence, still support the legal status of abortion. Looking at polls spanning the decade before, the percentages for all abortion questions have only fluctuated a few points over these 10 years, perpetuating an uneasy, but relatively stable tension (Polling Report, 2008).

Abortion rhetoric has always been highly charged, but only a tiny fraction of opponents have dedicated their lives to fight abortion on every level—from political activism to physical violence against abortion providers and patients. During the 1980s and 1990s, violence and physical, emotional, and social harassment forced many providers to abandon their practices. In addition, restrictions and regulations at every level of government have made it harder for women who need abortion services to access them. Consequently, one-third of

American women live in counties with no source of abortion services (Guttmacher Institute, 2003).

Men and Contraception

The primary methods of birth control before the 1960s were abstinence, withdrawal, and condoms, methods that depended on the cooperation of men. After the pill revolution, men have been largely left out of the area of reproductive choices (Ndong & Finger, 1998). However, men are important to reproductive health (Population Reports, 1998). The only effective ways to prevent sexually transmitted infections (STIs) are abstinence or condom use, both involving the cooperation of men. As research continues on male methods of contraception, fertility control and reproductive health are coming to be viewed through the wider lens of gender equality and shared responsibility.

Violence and Reproductive Health

Physical consequences of sexually violent acts may include STIs, HIV/AIDS, unwanted pregnancy, miscarriage, gynecological problems, sexual dysfunction, and injury. These wreak havoc on the victim's reproductive and emotional health (WHO, 1998).

ISSUE STATEMENT

Although contraceptive coverage in private insurance plans has improved in recent years, many women still lack coverage or have plans that do not cover the specific contraceptive they would like or face a prohibitive co-pay for their method of choice. As of 2004, only 20 states had comprehensive contraceptive coverage mandates, and employer self-insurance plans are generally not covered by these mandates (Moore, Finer, & Darroch, 2003).

The NASW *Code of Ethics* (2000) states that "social workers promote clients' socially responsible self-determination" (p. 5). Self-determination related to reproductive health means that without government interference, people can make their own decisions about sexuality and reproduction. As social workers, we sup-

port the right of individuals to decide for themselves, without duress and according to their own personal beliefs and convictions, whether they want to become parents, how many children they are willing and able to nurture, the opportune time for them to have children, and with whom they may choose to parent. Caring for children presents challenges for all parents, but for unwilling or unprepared parents, the economic, social, physical, or emotional challenges may be too great. Conversely, the right to parent should not be denied to capable people, regardless of gender or gender identity and expression.

Decisions about parenthood are crucial for individuals, their families, and their local communities, and multitudes of individual decisions even bear significant implications for the global community. Resolving personal issues of such importance should not be undertaken without access to reproductive health services that are based on the most current science and address the needs of a diverse population.

To support self-determination, these reproductive health services, including abortion services, must be legally, economically, and geographically accessible to all who need them. Medical research has advanced the prevention and treatment of HIV/AIDS and other STIs, the development of effective male contraceptives, wider choices of female contraceptive methods, and safer childbirth practices. Denying people with low income access to the full range of contraceptive methods, abortion, and sterilization services, and the educational programs that explain them, perpetuate poverty and the dependence on welfare programs and support the status quo of class stratification.

The United Nations' Fourth World Conference on Women adopted a platform statement in 1995 recognizing the importance of women's sexual and reproductive health (United Nations, 1995). The International Federation of Social Workers (IFSW) has adopted a policy statement on women's health issues, including sexual and reproductive health, and has identified this as an area of critical concern to social work (IFSW, 1999). WHO confirms that, despite tremendous advances in the development and accessibility of family planning services, there are still millions of individuals around the world who are unable to plan their families as they wish. In addition to lack of access, poor quality of services, and technological issues, the utilization of family planning practices is hampered by power imbalances within couples and families and broader social, cultural, and religious issues (WHO, 2007a).

In 1979, the United Nations Commission for Human Rights stated that unimpeded access to family planning and reproductive health services, including abortion services, is a fundamental human right that contributes to the advancement of women worldwide (United Nations, 1979). Women who defer childbearing have the chance to further their education, develop work skills, acquire broader life experiences, have fewer children, provide better for the children they do have, and improve the well-being of their families. Family planning and access to a full range of reproductive health services are basic to meeting family needs, as well as allowing individual self-determination in reproduction and sexuality to be realized. Adequate financing through a continuing partnership between the private and the public sectors is necessary to make family planning programs and professional services available to all, regardless of the ability to pay. Government policies and medical programs, as well as medical programs under private auspices, should ensure that individuals have full access to the technical knowledge and resources that will enable them to exercise their right of choice about whether and when to have children.

As part of the professional team operating these programs, social workers must realize their professional duty to promote self determination and assist clients in obtaining whatever help and information they need for effective family planning and for maintaining their reproductive health. Social workers also have a professional obligation to work in local, state, national, and international arenas to establish, secure funding for, and safeguard family planning and reproductive health programs, including abortion services and HIV/AIDS prevention and treatment, to ensure that these services remain legal, increasingly more effective, and available to all who need them.

POLICY STATEMENT

The NASW position concerning family planning, abortion, and other reproductive health services is based on the bedrock principles of self-determination, human rights, and social justice:

■ Every individual, within the context of her or his value system, must have access to family planning, abortion, and other reproductive health services.

■ The use of all reproductive health services, including abortion and sterilization services, must be voluntary and preserve the individual's right to privacy.

■ Women (in particular women of color, women in institutions, and women from other vulnerable groups) should not be unethically used in the testing and development of new reproductive techniques and technologies.

■ The nature of the reproductive health services that a client receives should be a matter of client self-determination in consultation with the qualified health care provider furnishing them.

■ Public policies and legislation, nationally and internationally, must support a woman's authority over her sexual life and reproductive capacity, free from coercion, violence, and discrimination.

■ Lesbians, gay men, and both male-to-female and female-to-male transgender people, as well as those who feel more comfortable living androgynously, are as capable as any other people of being good parents and should have equal access to parenting support services.

■ Social workers who choose to restrict their services to clients and the community in a way that deprives their clients or community of a comprehensive consideration of all legal reproductive health options have a responsibility to disclose the limited scope of their services and to assist clients in obtaining comprehensive services elsewhere.

Availability of and Access to Services

NASW supports

■ the fundamental right of each individual throughout the world to manage his or her fertility and to have access to a full range of effective family planning and reproductive health services, regardless of the individual's income, marital status, age, race, ethnicity, gender, sexual orientation, national origin, or residence; these services include, but are not limited to, contraception; and emergency contraception; fertility enhancement; prevention and treatment of HIV/AIDS, STIs, and the human papillomavirus (HPV); prenatal, birthing, and postpartum care; sterilization, abortion services, and adoption rights.

■ a woman's right to obtain an abortion, performed according to accepted medical standards and in an environment free of harassment or threat for both patients and providers.

■ reproductive health services, including abortion services, that are confidential, available at a reasonable cost, and covered in public and private health insurance plans on a par with other kinds of health services (contraceptive equity).

■ improved access to the full range of reproductive health services, including abortion services, for groups currently underserved in the United States, including people with low income and those who rely on Medicaid to pay for their health care, adolescents, individual challenges and needs, sex workers, single people, lesbians, people of color and those from nondominant ethnic and cultural groups, those in rural areas, and those in the many counties and municipalities that currently do not have providers of such services.

■ public and private adoption services that better address the needs of birth parents and that invite women and men, regardless of sexual orientation or gender expression, to consider adoption as a genuine alternative to abortion or parenting, contributing to a broader range of options.

■ national, state, and local public awareness campaigns and educational programs relating to reproductive health and choice.

Legislation

Recent years have seen many initiatives at the state and federal levels to challenge and thereby overrule or undermine the rights granted by the Supreme Court's *Roe v. Wade* (1973) decision and subsequent high court decisions. Federal and state legislative bodies have sought to restrict funding for abortion and other reproductive health care services and research and impose restrictions to impede the use of services, while Congress has restricted or eliminated funding to developing countries.

Therefore, NASW

■ supports legislation to facilitate a woman's access to contraceptives and emergency contraception.

■ supports legislation to ensure that women who have been sexually assaulted have access to emergency contraception.

■ supports legislation that ensures privately and publicly funded health insurance coverage includes access to all forms of reproductive health technologies, contraceptives, vaccinations, and medication equally for men and women.

■ supports legislation to permit women and couples to donate human tissue and frozen, living, or deceased embryos to legitimate research projects.

■ opposes government restrictions designed to limit access to reproductive health services, including abortion services.

■ opposes government restrictions on financing reproductive health services, including abortion services, in health insurance and foreign aid programs.

■ opposes any special conditions and requirements imposed on reproductive health care providers, such as the prescribed warning of unsubstantiated health risks resulting from abortion or mandatory waiting periods, which are not based on medical standards.

- opposes legislative or funding restrictions on medically approved forms of contraceptives and emergency contraception.

- opposes limits and restrictions on adolescents' access to confidential reproductive health services, including contraceptive and abortion services, and the imposition of parental notification and consent procedures.

- opposes legislative restrictions limiting access to parenting for lesbian, gay, bisexual, and transgender individuals.

Education and Research

For people to exercise self-determination in making choices related to sexuality and reproductive health care for themselves and their families, NASW supports

- public and private funding for research to develop and disseminate medically safe and effective methods of preventing, postponing, or promoting conception (including antiretroviral therapy), appropriate for women and men;

- academic and clinical education for students in the medical and health professions relating to the physical and psychological consequences of pregnancy and pregnancy loss and education for appropriate specialties on pregnancy termination techniques, postabortion care, contraceptive methods, and appropriate contraception counseling;

- school-based age-appropriate, culturally informed sexuality and reproductive health education programs that include information about the role of personal beliefs, culture, and values in individual and family decision making on these issues; prevention of STIs; range of reproductive health services and contraceptive methods; and introduction to skills for making healthy personal choices about sexuality and reproduction;

- funding for the development of sexuality education curriculums, as described earlier;

- development and funding of education and research programs to prevent the spread of STIs, to prevent unwanted pregnancies, and to reduce all forms of sexual violence and coercion from which many unwanted pregnancies result; education that informs students, social workers, or others, about the normally occurring diversity of sexuality and of gender identity and expression, including the equal ability of all people to have their family planning and reproductive health care needs met.

REFERENCES

Boonstra, H., Gold, R. B., Richards, C., & Finer, L. B. (2006). *Abortion in women's lives.* Retrieved May 15, 2008, from http://www.guttmacher.org/pubs/2006/05/04/AiWL.pdf

Gold, R. B. (2001). *Title X: Three decades of accomplishment.* Retrieved September 27, 2007, from http://www.guttmacher.org/pubs/tgr/04/1/gr040105.html

Gold, R. B. (2006). *Rekindling efforts to prevent unplanned pregnancy: A matter of 'equity and common sense.'* Retrieved May 15, 2008, from http://www.guttmacher.org/pubs/gpr/09/3/gpr090302.html

Guttmacher Institute. (2003, January 15). *After three decades of legal abortion, new research documents declines in rates, numbers and access to abortion services* [Press Release]. Retrieved September 20, 2007, from http://www.guttmacher.org/media/nr/2003/01/15/nr_011003.html

Guttmacher Institute. (2006, May 6). *A tale of two Americas for women* [Press Release]. Retrieved September 15, 2007, from http://www.guttmacher.org/media/nr/2006/05/05/index.html

Guttmacher Institute. (2008, January). *Facts on induced abortion in the United States.* Retrieved February 1, 2008, from http://www.guttmacher.org/pubs/fb_induced_abortion.html

International Federation of Social Workers. (1999). *International policy on women.* Oslo, Norway: Author.

Moore, K., Finer, L., & Darroch, J. (Eds.). (2003, October). *The unfinished revolution in contraception: Convenience, consumer access and choice.* Retrieved September 12, 2007, from http://www.guttmacher.org/pubs/2004/09/20/UnfinRevInContra.pdf

National Association of Social Workers. (2000). *Code of ethics of the National Association of Social Workers*. Washington, DC: NASW Press.

Ndong, I., & Finger., W. (1998). *Introduction: Male responsibility for reproductive health*. Retrieved May 30, 2008, from http://www.reproline.jhu.edu/english/6read/6issues/6network/v18-3/v18-3.htm

Pichler, S. (2007). *Griswold v. Connecticut—The impact of legal birth control and the challenges that remain*. Retrieved May 30, 2008, from http://www.plannedparenthood.org/files/PPFA/fact-griswold.pdf

Polling Report. (2008). *Abortion and birth control*. Retrieved May 30, 2008, from http://www.pollingreport.com/abortion.htm

Population Reports. (1998). *Reproductive health: New perspectives on men's participation*. Baltimore: Johns Hopkins School of Public Health, Population Information Program.

Rodrigues, I., Grou, F., & Joly, J. (2002). Effectiveness of emergency contraceptive pills between 72 and 120 hours after unprotected sexual intercourse. *American Journal of Obstetrics/Gynecology, 186*(1), 167–168.

Roe v. Wade, 410 U.S. 113 (1973).

United Nations. (1995). *Platform for action summary: Obstacles, strategies, actions*. New York: Author.

United Nations Commission for Human Rights. (1979). *Convention on the elimination of all forms of discrimination against women*. New York: Author.

World Health Organization. (1998). *Gender and health: Technical paper*. Retrieved October 19, 2007, from http://www.who.int/reproductive-health/publications/WHD_98_16_gender_and_health_technical_paper/WHD_98_16.chapter3.en.html

World Health Organization. (2007a). *Family planning: Promoting family planning*. Retrieved October 18, 2007, from http://www.who.int/reproductive-health/family_planning/index.html

World Health Organization. (2007b). *Working definition used by department of reproductive health and research*. Retrieved September 20, 2007, from http://www.who.int/topics/family_planning/en/

Policy statement approved by the NASW Delegate Assembly, August 2008. This policy statement supersedes the policy statement on Family Planning and Reproductive Choice approved by the Assembly in 1999 and referred by the 2005 Delegate Assembly to the 2008 Delegate Assembly for revision, the policy statement on Family Planning approved by the Assembly in 1967 and reconfirmed in August 1990, and the policy statement on Abortion approved by the Assembly in 1975 and reconfirmed by the Assembly in 1990. For further information, contact the National Association of Social Workers, 750 First Street, NE, Suite 700, Washington, DC 20002-4241. Telephone: 202-408-8600 or 800-638-8799; e-mail: press@naswdc.org

Family Policy

BACKGROUND

Strengthening families and providing family support are priorities of the social work profession. The family is the primary socializing agent and the primary economic unit in our culture. Families in the United States have undergone tremendous changes in composition, structure, and roles in the 20th century (Ooms, 1995). They have fewer children, and people are living longer. An increasing number of women, including women with young children, are in the workforce. In addition, families have been highly mobile, moving away from parents and other natural support systems. New immigrants and refugee families help expand the cultural, religious, and ethnic diversity on which this nation was built. Economic and political conditions around the world, particularly in developing countries, profoundly affect the conditions in which families in the United States live.

Contemporary American families are an amalgam of many different lifestyles and many different structures. Policy cannot be primarily based on the traditional nuclear family. Families can include a mixture of race, culture, religion, ethnicity, and sexual orientations. Family composition may cover a range of constellations, including traditional married parents with biological children; divorced, separated, or unmarried parents who have individual, separate, or shared responsibility for the care of children; intergenerational arrangements for child or elder care; gay and lesbian couples with or without the care of children; couples in which one or both partners is transgendered; and adoptive parents and foster families (U.S. Household and Family Structure, 2008).

The makeup of families is shifting in other ways. An elderly population provides new challenges and opportunities. Changing the dynamics of retirement and the concepts of extended family, baby boomers will soon become a significant part of the aging population. Baby boomers will inevitably "reinvent" aging, along with the types of care needed for older adults, and affect families' perceptions of aging. Grandparents are now raising grandchildren and facing many challenges as parents abdicate responsibility of their children. Often the grandparents are required to step in because of incarceration, economic hardship, teenage pregnancy, death, HIV/AIDS, unemployment, mental illness, domestic violence, divorce, substance abuse, and other issues. These grandparents provide a safety net for vulnerable children.

Elder abuse looms as a major issue for the 21st century (U.S. Department of Health and Human Services, 2008). The most common category of investigated reports involves self-neglect. Caregiver neglect, financial neglect, and financial exploitation follow. These issues will have a significant effect on how families perceive themselves in the later years and the policies that can affect a better outcome for the accommodation of those changes.

Baby boomers (people born between 1946 and 1960) have assumed leadership roles during their lives. They often find themselves as caregivers, squeezed in between caring for younger loved ones such as children and their elderly parents or other elderly family members. In 2005, 71 percent of baby boomers, then aged 41 to 59, had at least one living parent

(Pew Research Center, 2005). They now seek to influence ideas about retirement or semiretirement in a way older adults of past generations never thought possible. Their voices dominate public debate and make demands for changes to public policy. "Phased retirement" has become the watchword for baby boomers who seek to affirm family life yet still make contributions to the workforce. Such a lifestyle affects the various roles in the family.

Family social policy needs to recognize and respect a variety of family compositions and their respective specific needs. *Family* is defined in its broadest sense to include two or more people who consider themselves "family" and who assume obligations and responsibilities that are generally considered essential to family life. Families are first-line providers of such services as health care, counseling, education, dependent care, long-term care, and income support. Whereas, in general, families strive for financial and social independence, some families must depend on external support systems, such as social services or social insurance entitlements. Many, however, have no guarantee that they will receive assistance when it is needed. When families are unable to perform the roles expected of them, they may incur great stress and deep stigma before they can get the help they need. When help is received, it may be too little and not appropriate to address the families' needs.

ISSUE STATEMENT
Stress of the Caregiving and Provider Roles

Profound changes in family structure have been brought about by the increase in longevity, which has resulted in many four- and five-generation families. According to the U.S. Census Bureau (2000), 2.4 million of the nation's families consisted of grandparents raising their grandchildren. This represents a 19 percent increase over 1990 data. Adult family caregivers, usually women, may experience five or more episodic or continuous caregiving phases: caring for children, parents, grandparents, spouses, and siblings. Family caregiving has not been compensated in this society

except for families receiving Temporary Assistance for Needy Families, which provides income below the federal poverty level and is severely restricted and time limited. The caregiving role can be financially precarious, as well as emotionally stressful and physically straining. As women increase their participation in the workforce, and increasingly all two-parent families (whether gay, lesbian, or heterosexual) have both parents working, prioritizing and balancing home and work responsibilities become more challenging, especially for parents also caring for elders. Welfare legislation, which forces a parent to obtain employment without providing adequate quality child care, places additional hardship on the family.

Grandchildren in need of care by their grandparents pose other challenges for the family. According to the American Association of Retired Persons (2007), more than 6 million children—approximately one in 12—are living in households headed by grandparents (4.5 million children) or other relatives (1.5 million children). Nationally, 2.4 million grandparents are responsible for the basic needs of their grandchildren. These needs include child care, schools, child development, health, mental health, safety, and education, among others. These needs are being thrust on grandparents to respond to with little or no support from the parents. Some grandparents are the custodial grandparents with legal custody of their grandchildren. Other grandparents provide daily care for their grandchildren but do not have legal custody. A number of grandparents simply focus on helping the child's parent provide better care of the grandchild. Though the elderly and the disabled are protected in the United States, children and their families do not have the same universal social insurance entitlements or health care. Changes in the local, national, and world economies have brought about major shifts in livelihoods. Kammerman and Doverman (2007) utilize Census and Labor Department data to profile U.S. families (The Clearinghouse on International Developments in Child, Youth and Family Policies at Columbia University, 2007). The authors note the changing ethnic, racial, and gender landscape of the workforce that is due to immigration largely from Asian and Hispanic countries and female labor force participation. These families may encounter multiple job changes and the lack of financial security. The loss of jobs, underemployment, lack of health benefits, inability to obtain a job because of one's racial or ethnic identity, primary fluency in a language other than English, and sexual orientation are critical factors in many contemporary families. These factors may threaten the survival of a family unit. The lack of resources also threatens the fundamental biopsychosocial development of family members. Kammerman and Doverman (2007) also observe that the U.S. compares unfavorably to Europe in the development of family social policies. The lack of paid family and medical leave may create stress in the workplace and at home for U.S. families. Lack of comprehensive prenatal care is linked to low birthweight, developmental delays, and health problems. The lack of early childhood education or day care is linked to poor social development and poor performance in school. The lack of financial support for home-based care may leave a medically fragile child or adult unattended.

Family Violence

Family violence is growing in frequency and intensity in our society. Elimination of family violence is not dependent merely on better services, punitive judicial actions, and other protective approaches. Family violence must be seen in the context of root causes of violence in our society, including poverty, racism, sexism, unmet needs, and insufficient supports for child and elder care. Van Soest and Bryant's (1995) study supports this view, concluding that social workers have overlooked institutional and structural–cultural explanations for violence and have focused instead on interpersonal family concerns.

Culturally Diverse Families

The meaning of cultural diversity is changing in the United States. Hispanic and Asian American populations in the United States are expected to triple by 2050, making white peo-

ple only a slight majority. Black families have myriad within-group differences, with historically diasporic roots from Africa and the Caribbean. Today, communities are rich with people and families from all racial and ethnic groups and increasingly with people from around the world. Many families are now multicultural in composition, and this blending will undoubtedly characterize families of the future. This growing diversity in race and ethnicity brings strength to our communities and potential understanding, although it challenges the skills of social workers. Many families with members who are relatively recent immigrants face the effects of discriminatory legislation and policies.

Families with Gay and Lesbian Members

Families with gay and lesbian members face a multitude of challenges (Hunter, cited in Jordan & Franklin, 2003). They face discrimination that includes loss of employment, absence of domestic partnership rights, and lack of support from law enforcement agencies and the courts concerning civil rights. They are also the targets for residential discrimination, personal violence, and family prejudices in matters of child custody, foster care, or adoption decisions. Some human services organizations that provide enrichment programs for youths openly discriminate by prohibiting the participation of gay or lesbian young people in their programs and as staff members. Positive gains are beginning to be seen, for example, the United States Court of Appeals for the Fifth Circuit upheld an employer's job termination of a counselor who refused to counsel a lesbian client on relationship issues, stating that homosexuality conflicted with the counselor's religious beliefs (2001). In June, 2003, the U.S. Supreme Court ruled that homosexual sodomy laws are unconstitutional in the 50 states, Puerto Rico, and Washington, DC. The right to marry is gradually being afforded to gay and lesbian couples, though it promises to remain a state-by-state battle for many years to come.

Family- and System-Focused Services and Practice

Increases in substance abuse, school dropouts, teenage out-of-wedlock pregnancies, suicide attempts, family violence, and stress-related health disorders are as rooted in societal failures as in family dysfunction. Multi-problem families experiencing more than one stressful event need multi-level assessment (Jordan & Franklin, 2003). However, solutions often focus on single symptoms and families may have multiple service providers, each addressing a different facet of their family functioning. The fragmentation of services and symptom-focused practice cannot be eliminated unless service providers reframe the presenting problems as family- and community-systems issues.

Moreover, practice that focuses on the individual in isolation from his or her family and primary support network may be limited in scope and effectiveness. Thus, as in child welfare and care for the elderly population, the very protection of the child and elderly person depends on effective, evidence-based services with family members (Janzen, Harris, Jordan, & Franklin, 2006). In addition, individual problems must be understood in the socioeconomic context. Family-focused practice requires community mobilization to parallel the support network. Many times, change in the family system or community institution, such as the workplace, is a precondition for the growth and development of individuals or families.

Economic and Social Services Infrastructure

Families juggle numerous economic responsibilities. Supports to families should encompass a comprehensive array of economic and social services entitlements to enhance family functioning. Gaps in social services and economic resources are often the root of homelessness or family violence. Although the nation has developed a patchwork of services, according to Kammerman and Doverman (2007), no comprehensive family support system exists (The Clearinghouse on International Developments in Child, Youth and Family Policies at Columbia University, 2007). Adequate dependent care, flexible work schedules, and other family supports are essential. Companies and corporations need to be much more responsible in responding to the requirements of the families of their employees. Wages that allow families to live above the poverty line and benefits that include health care options, retirement plans, and paid family leaves will reduce family stresses.

Inequitable pay for women is another serious problem for families, because so many women are the sole supporters of their families. About 71 percent of women participated in the labor force in 2005, whereas 60 percent of married women with children and 75 percent of single mothers work (Kammerman & Doverman, 2007). Equal pay for equal work will allow women to support their families. Workplace policies and practices historically have been overlooked in debates about family policy despite their critical role in promoting or undermining family stability and functioning. Employee policies, wages, and work roles are critical to the stability of families and to the development and protection of both children and adults. Therefore, the role of private-sector policies in promoting family support policies in the United States warrants attention.

POLICY STATEMENT

NASW advocates a full range of comprehensive services to families from primary prevention to rehabilitation across the life cycle. Strengthening families also necessitates the creation of policies that recognize the family as an intergenerational system that includes biological, social, and psychological ties. Understanding what happens in families in terms of the flow of life over the generations, the impact of gender on family life, the family life cycle, and cultural variations in life cycle patterns is essential. Governmental programs and policies must recognize and support the family unit. Social workers can effectively develop a comprehensive national family policy by working together with other advocates, including other providers of human services and health care, law enforcement officials, criminal justice personnel, educators, and community groups. Social workers who, by virtue of their values and education, view strengths and problems in a family and larger systems context should take a leadership role in this effort. Social work professionals in the United States need to consult and collaborate with social work professionals in other countries to benefit from and build on the policy and practice experience of colleagues around the world.

NASW recommends that a comprehensive family support policy be built on the following principles:

■ Families are given a strong voice in all aspects of decision making that affect their lives.

■ Families are provided support that is flexible and targeted to meet the unique, diverse needs of family members.

■ Families are provided available and accessible services within communities and at flexible hours.

■ Support to families encompasses a comprehensive infrastructure of economic and social entitlements, including health care; income supports; family allowance; and access to employment, education, dependent care, housing, and social services.

■ Welfare policies that enable families to achieve self-sufficiency and contain national standards that ensure education and training opportunities, including school-based options for young parents to attain high-level skills; sufficient choices of high-quality day care for parents and other primary caregivers who are entering the workforce or undertaking training and educational programs; provision of transitional health and day care services; and adequate family income supports.

■ Opposition to profit-oriented ownership of the essential safety net services for families, such as welfare supports, job assistance, and schools.

■ Education of policymakers on the development of family policy legislation that includes cultural competency and the diversity of today's families.

■ Assistance to grandparents raising grandchildren.

■ Encouragement by the media of positive messages about families and sensitivity to the level of violence portrayed and its effect on families.

■ Affirmation of cultural diversity; elimination of biases by institutions or practitioners.

■ Services to families that are delivered by adequately trained professionals, including training on working with culturally diverse families.

■ Diverse families are supported in relation to their ability to function biculturally.

To support these principles, it is important that the social work profession advocates policies that will provide support to families. These policies include the following:

■ full and equitable employment, including initiatives that promote permanent part-time jobs with adequate wages and benefits for adults and youths.

■ early childhood and family life education addressing all aspects of caregiving, couple relationships, and problem solving throughout the life span.

■ affordable, accessible, and high-quality dependent care in a variety of settings to meet the needs of all families.

■ affordable, accessible, and high-quality housing available in all urban, suburban, and rural areas so that families may experience a high quality of life.

■ paid family and medical leave to provide time off from work for the birth, adoption, or illness of a child or the illness of a spouse or older or disabled relative.

■ comprehensive and available health, mental health, and family planning services, including strategies focused on prenatal and perinatal care for high-risk mothers.

■ comprehensive services that are designed to keep family units together and to preserve the quality of life, especially when families are faced with chronic and life-threatening illnesses, such as HIV or AIDS.

- gender-equitable income supports or credits for people whose family caregiving demands impede their continuous participation in the labor force.

- supportive programs in the workplace that provide education, flexible working hours, day care facilities, counseling, and assistance to working family members.

- a comprehensive range of supportive and protective services that meet the needs of family members who are abused or neglected and also include corrective intervention services for the perpetrator.

- policies that assist the public in understanding family violence, encourage citizens' involvement, and use multidisciplinary teams to find a solution.

- same-sex marriage and second-parent adoption for gay- and lesbian-headed families.

In working with families, social workers need to be constantly aware of the social justice mission of the social work profession and of the empowerment goal in practice at all levels. This suggests that social workers become allies with families in their struggles for adequate resources and environmental supports, prerequisites for quality of life. As a profession, we know that taking significant initiatives will strengthen families and communities and will add vitality and meaning to the lives of people and to society. We must work to identify significant indicators that will demonstrate to the profession and to society that working to achieve the mission of supporting and strengthening families does produce significant results.

REFERENCES

American Association of Retired Persons. (2007). *State fact sheets for grandparents and other relatives raising children*. Retrieved December 18, 2007, from http://www.grandfactsheets.org/state_fact_sheets.cfm

Janzen, C., Harris, O., Jordan, C., & Franklin, C. (2006). *Family treatment: Evidence-based practice with populations at risk* (4th ed.). Belmont, CA: Brooks/Cole.

Jordan, C., & Franklin, C. (2003). *Clinical assessment for social workers: Quantitative and qualitative methods*. Chicago: Lyceum Books.

Kammerman, S., & Doverman, E. (2007). *The Clearinghouse on International Developments in Child, Youth and Family Policies at Columbia University*. Retrieved from http://www.childpolicyintl.org/countries/us.html

Ooms, T. (1995). *Taking families seriously: Family impact analysis as an essential policy tool*. Washington, DC: Federal Family Impact Seminar Reports.

Pew Research Center. (2005). *Baby boomers approach 60: From the age of Aquarius to the age of responsibility*. Washington, DC: Author.

U.S. Census Bureau. (2000). *Grandparents living with grandchildren: 2000*. Retrieved December 18, 2007, from http://www.census.gov/prod/2003pubs/c2kbr-31.pdf

U.S. Department of Health and Human Services, Administration on Aging. (2008). *Elders & families*. Retrieved February 8, 2008, from http://www.aoa.gov/eldfam/eldfam.aspx

U.S. Household and Family Structure. (2008). *Census 2000 analysis by the Social Science Data Analysis Network*. Retrieved February 8, 2008, from http://www.censuscope.org/us

Van Soest, D., & Bryant, S. (1995). Violence reconceptualized for social work: The urban dilemma. *Social Work, 40*, 549–557.

Policy statement approved by the NASW Delegate Assembly, August 2008. This policy statement supersedes the policy statement on Family Policy approved by the Delegate Assembly in 1999, 1990, and 1981. For further information, contact the National Association of Social Workers, 750 First Street, NE, Suite 700, Washington, DC 20002-4241. Telephone: 202-408-8600 or 800-638-8799; e-mail: press@naswdc.org

Family Violence

BACKGROUND

The term "family violence" is used with a range of terms, including intimate partner violence, child abuse and neglect, teenage dating violence, elder and differently abled abuse/neglect/exploitation, and sibling abuse. Intimate partner violence is harm committed by a current or former partner or spouse and is a serious, preventable public health problem that affects millions of Americans. The violence takes the form of physical, sexual, or psychological harm. Child abuse includes physical, sexual, and psychological harm by a parent or responsible caretaker. Elder abuse can be physical, sexual, and psychological harm by an intimate partner, child, or close caregiving individual and also may include financial exploitation (see http://www.cdc.gov/). Animal abuse in families also has been connected to the dynamics and trauma of family violence (Siebert, 2010).

Family violence has become an increasing concern in recent times in the United States as deaths resulting from homicides and suicides, combined with other violence in intimate and family relationships, have drawn the attention of the Centers for Disease Control and Prevention (CDC). All too often, research on family violence has been presented as a "one size fits all" approach. This is inadequate to address the experiences and needs of diverse groups of family members who are abused.

Mainstream feminist theory argues that socially constructed gender inequality has limited and compromised our understanding of family violence. However, the intersectional or multicultural family violence approach challenges gender inequality as the primary factor explaining family violence. Gender inequality is neither the most important nor the only factor that must be considered to understand family violence as it occurs in the lives of women. Gender inequality is only part of women's marginalized and oppressed status. In fact, it is argued that gender inequality is modified by its intersection with other systems of power and inequality, including economic and political privilege, that affect the lives of battered women. One's experience as a battered woman is realized in relation to the intersectionalities in society of race, ethnicity, class, socioeconomic status, sexual orientation, immigration, and disability status (Murphy, Hunt, Zajicek, Norris, & Hamilton, 2009).

The scope of family violence has come to public attention over the past 30 to 40 years. In 1979, the U.S. surgeon general declared that violence is a significant public health problem and that it is preventable. Through this designation, violence reduction as a public health goal included priority objectives to reduce the number of types of violence—including sexual violence, intimate partner violence, and child maltreatment—along with objectives to reduce homicides and suicides (Dahlberg & Mercy, 2009). Child abuse was brought to the attention of the public in the 1960s and 1970s through the work of the medical profession (Kempe & Kempe, 1978). Elder abuse was identified as a problem in the late 1970s (Gelles, 1997).

Gender-based violence prevention and intervention has evolved from grassroots feminist efforts of the 1970s as women worked in communities to advocate for women's rights and safety. Passage of the 1984 Family Violence Prevention and Services Act (FVPSA) provided federal funding to deliver family violence services (Goodman & Epstein, 2008). This was a turning point in the move from local advocacy efforts to government partnerships for developing solutions to address family violence. Since then, nonprofit, for-profit, and government agencies have advocated for and gained legal remedies for family violence in all

50 states. At the federal level, advocacy efforts have secured legislation and funding to support communities to offer families and children options for protection. The legislation, originally enacted and revised in states, provides for reporting, social services investigation of abuse and neglect, and provision of services for child and adult protection. With the reauthorization of the Violence Against Women Act (VAWA) in 2005, the federal government affirmed its commitment to ensuring the safety of victims of domestic and sexual violence and their families. The VAWA addresses the cycle of violence through prevention and early intervention programs with children who have witnessed family violence, assists families at risk for violence, and targets interventions with men and youths. Along with FVPSA funding for family violence services, the VAWA includes provisions for families and children to be protected by strengthened confidentiality requirements, which is a critical factor in protection from perpetrators. The needs of immigrants and others in relation to family violence are also addressed. The Affordable Care Act of 2010 supports those experiencing family violence as it provides for the meeting of health care needs for those without the ability to purchase insurance. Dependence on an abuser for health insurance is one of the most difficult challenges for many families and children who experience violence and injuries at the hands of their abusers (U.S. Department of Health and Human Services, 2010).

Advocates, agencies, and communities have developed expertise and programs to provide for the legal, social, and physical protection for individuals and families. At the same time, advocates have lobbied for laws to protect the abused. As the professionalization and standardization of the field of family violence have developed, the challenges for communities have continued to grow. The evolving and unique needs of those seeking services, and more structured delivery of services, may not always allow for prevention and interventions that are culturally sensitive and flexible enough to meet individual or community needs. Other groups that have not traditionally been identified as needing, or asking for, services and who may not have knowledge of community resources include teenagers; immi-grant groups; some communities of color; and lesbian, gay, bisexual, and transgender communities. There are growing numbers of elders in the population who may be experiencing isolation in addition to violence or exploitation. Other groups such as veterans and indigenous peoples have been "hidden" from the larger systems and service providers, and are becoming more visible (Aravanis, 2008; CDC, 2010; Runner, Yoshihama, & Novick, 2009).

Inadequate local, state, and federal funds are not sufficient for provision of quality, culturally competent, and sensitive services for outreach and detection; for mental health and social services agencies to offer more than mandated services; for court systems to handle workloads; and for communities to develop the unique services to best meet needs. Furthermore, funding is limited for developing and expanding successful model programs to reach both victims and perpetrators and to pursue research to determine evidence-based and user-flexible programs geared to the unique needs of individuals and communities.

ISSUE STATEMENT

Factors that contribute to family violence include poverty and economic conditions, lack of education and skills to handle conflicts and solve problems, role expectations, power differences, family traditions, and substance abuse. A culture of violence in communities, the world, the media, and in recreation and in entertainment, also can contribute to family violence (CDC, 2010).

Culturally competent services are needed to eliminate family violence, its causes, and consequences. This can be possible through conducting of research, sharing of models that are found to be successful, and building on early family violence service approaches that focus on the individual experiencing violence (Goodman & Epstein, 2008). Neighborhood and community building that engage neighbors and networks to take bystander responsibility for the protection and well-being of themselves and others is needed in addition to standardized professional programs and services (McKnight & Block 2010). However, efforts focused on affecting individual victims or perpetrators of family violence are insufficient as a solution to the problem. Solutions must address risk and protective factors across all levels of the social ecology and include comprehensive primary prevention as well as intervention strategies at the peer/relationship, community, and societal levels (World Health Organization [WHO], 2005). Family violence does not occur in a vacuum, nor does it affect individuals alone. Thus, there is a need to challenge social and cultural norms that support violent behavior of individuals, peer support for violent behavior, and social norms that continue to limit the freedom of women and children, such as sexism and ageism (WHO, 2009).

Unfortunately, family violence is often unrecognized and untreated due to shame, tolerance of violence, self-blame and victim blaming, and lack of knowledge about victim's rights and resources. Furthermore, family violence is just beginning to be recognized as an issue of importance to men. Outreach to responsible fatherhood initiatives and men's groups as allies to women is in its infancy.

CDC surveys have found that women experience an estimated 4.8 million physical assaults and rapes each year, and men are victims of about 2.9 million partner-related assaults each year. Child abuse data reported in *Child Maltreatment 2008*, collected by National Child Abuse and Neglect Data Center in 2006, showed 1,530 fatalities, a rate of 2.04 children per 100,000 (U.S. Department of Health and Human Services, Administration for Children and Families, Administration on Children, Youth and Families, Children's Bureau, 2010). The same report estimated 772,000 cases of child maltreatment for federal fiscal year 2008. This rate was 10.3 per 1,000 children. In an economic impact study dated September 2007, the estimated cost of child abuse and neglect in the United States was $103.8 billion of direct and indirect costs in 2007 value. A 2006 report of data collected from all 50 states, the District of Columbia, and Guam found that of adults 60 years of age and older, 191,908 Adult Protective Services (APS) referrals were substantiated in 2004. This represented an increase of 15.6 percent over the APS 2000 survey (Teaster et al., 2006).

The impact of electronic technology has brought about new concerns for youths and adults, with the practices of sexting, Internet pornography, stalking, and other harassing and violent behaviors toward intimate partners on the rise. There is increasing concern about the violence in the media—which includes movies, television, the Internet, newspapers and other print media—violence demonstrated in recreation, the emphasis on self-protection with guns, and the use of violence to solve problems. In 2008, an average of just under five women were murdered each day by an intimate male partner, and 52 percent of those homicides were committed with firearms (Violence Policy Center, 2010).

It is essential for governments, neighborhoods, communities, and advocacy groups—including survivors—to coordinate efforts to eliminate family violence and ensure that civil and human rights are protected for all individuals and families. NASW is the largest professional body of social workers in the world and is in a key position to provide leadership to advocate for the elimination of family violence.

POLICY STATEMENT

The position of NASW is that family violence is an issue of human and civil rights that affects social, psychological, economic, and public health outcomes for many segments of the population. NASW is concerned that the physical, emotional, and economic harm of family violence to children, adults, and elders results in negative repercussions for the health and mental health, healthy relationships, and productive functioning of individuals, families, and communities.

The growing need for services requires creative efforts among professionals, advocates, and communities to explore opportunities, challenges, and solutions to eliminate all forms of violence. Specifically, NASW supports elimination of social and institutional barriers that perpetuate family violence, demonstrated through all forms of gender-based exploitation and structural inequities.

NASW supports the following:

■ coordinated efforts with schools of social work and universities, government bodies, private and public sectors, and voluntary groups to ensure adequate funding for research programs and services focused on the goal of eliminating family violence and its causes.

■ professional social work education, including ongoing continuing education, to prepare students to deliver family violence services within the matrix of power, privilege, and oppression.

■ strengths-based, community-centered models that include personal safety for victims.

■ curriculums and field learning experiences that help students gain current knowledge and skills to provide culturally sensitive program planning and services and to function effectively as members of teams and community groups. In addition, social work education should include recognition and identification of risk factors, early warning signs, and known patterns of domestic violence.

■ a focus of social work education and practice on capacity building for primary prevention of family violence that moves solutions away from an individual victim onus and toward comprehensive strategies that engage multiple levels of the social ecology.

■ prevention education in schools, neighborhoods, and communities directed toward promoting awareness, skills in advocacy, bystander intervention skills, and programs to teach children, youths, and adults about their right to live a violence-free life.

■ engagement of men and boys to end violence against women and children and research to further examine the relationship between animal abuse and family violence, child abuse, and childhood trauma.

■ research and grants to address all forms of family violence to improve assessment procedures, causality and connectivity among causes, intervention, treatment, and prevention approaches, including publication of research findings.

■ legislative and practice-based research efforts to identify and strengthen evidence-based solutions while focusing on unique needs of individuals and communities.

■ policies, programs, and leadership at the federal and state government levels that promote healthy relationships and violence prevention.

■ adequate funding at the federal and state levels to provide services for perpetrators as well as victims of family violence.

■ efforts to raise awareness about the intersections of gun violence and family violence and promotion of adherence to federal guidelines related to seizure of weapons in family violence cases.

■ protection of children, adults, and elders from exposure to firearms and any violence-producing conditions.

■ emergency shelters and support services that are culturally sensitive yet do not excuse violence for all individuals, families, and communities in need. In addition, social workers who work in batterers' intervention programs should work closely with domestic violence survivors and their advocates to include quality of life of survivors and their children as one measure of successful outcome.

■ flexible and culturally sensitive services and settings that allow for time frames that meet the requirements of those using services rather than the institutions providing the services.

■ child welfare system efforts to assist, rather than punish, nonoffending custodial parents for "failure to protect" when children have witnessed domestic violence, including differential response and alternative response models that include best practices training for all child welfare staff about how to work with nonoffending parents and hold offenders accountable.

■ use of technological advances to reach out, educate, and increase access to information and services to all segments of society.

■ innovative and confidential approaches to provide prevention and intervention services and technology that allows seamless, culturally sensitive service delivery systems and appropriate reporting and referrals among public and private/nonprofit partners.

■ coordinated, interdisciplinary community efforts to promote the bridging of philosophical gaps among disciplines and agencies that serve diverse groups, including children, elders, women, parents and teenagers, differently-abled people, people with different sexual orientations, immigrants and refugees, indigenous groups, and military families and veterans.

■ a focus on universal screening for those experiencing domestic violence to identify the effects of cyclical family trauma.

■ universal prevention education for all clients to promote healthy relationships.

■ appropriate resources, safety planning, and other family violence services. Systems to capture societal trends that result during and after natural and human-induced disasters—economic changes, crime patterns, changing workplaces and work opportunities, increasing aging populations with unique needs, underserved indigenous groups, immigrant and refugee groups, mobile families and changing family structures, wars, hazardous spills, major storms, and other stress-inducing conditions that may lead to family violence.

■ efforts by the media—including television, video, cable, and the Internet—to provide programming that minimizes youth exposure to violence.

■ self-disclosure by battered employees and employers about how to interact with orders of protection for battered employees, thereby increasing safety for all employed parties. NASW recommends that employers have safety policies and plans to address domestic violence incidents, including crisis debriefing postincident.

■ elimination of sexism, racism, classism and elitism, ageism, homophobia, ableism, religious oppression, militarism and other oppressions within the social work profession, culture, and institutions.

REFERENCES

Aravanis, S. (2008). *Late life domestic violence: What the aging network needs to know.* Washington, DC: National Center for Elder Abuse.

Centers for Disease Control and Prevention. (2010, September 20). *Intimate partner violence: Risk and protective factors.* Retrieved from http://www.cdc.gov/Violence Prevention/intimatepartnerviolence/risk protectivefactors.html

Dahlberg, L. L., & Mercy, J. A. (2009). History of violence as a public health issue. *AMA Virtual Mentor, 11*(2), 167–172. Retrieved from http://virtualmentor.ama-assn.org/2009/02/mhstl-0902.html

Gelles, R. J. (1997). *Intimate violence in families* (3rd ed.). Thousand Oaks, CA: Sage Publications.

Goodman, L. A., & Epstein, D. (2008). *Listening to battered women.* Washington, DC: American Psychological Association.

Kempe, R., & Kempe, H. (1978). *Child abuse.* Cambridge, MA: Harvard University Press.

McKnight, J., & Block, P. (2010). *The abundant community: Awakening the power of families and neighborhoods.* San Francisco: Berrett-Koehler.

Murphy, Y., Hunt, V., Zajicek, A. M., Norris, A.N., & Hamilton, L. (2009). *Incorporating intersectionality in social work practice, research, policy, and education.* Washington, DC: NASW Press.

Runner, M., Yoshihama, M., & Novick, S. (2009). *Intimate partner violence in immigrant and refugee communities: Challenges, promising practices and recommendations.* Retrieved from http://www.rwjf.org/vulnerablepopulations/product.jsp?id=41231

Siebert, C. (2010, June 7). The animal-cruelty syndrome. *New York Times Magazine.* Retrieved from http://www.nytimes.com/2010/06/13/magazine/13dogfighting-t.html?_r=1andpagewanted=p

Teaster, P. B., Dugar, T. A., Mendiondo, M. S., Abner, E. L., Cecil, K. A., & Otto, J. M. (2006). *The 2004 survey of state adult protective services: Abuse of adults 60 years of age and older.* Retrieved from http://www.nsvrc.org/publications/reports/2004-survey-state-adult-protective-services-abuse-adults-60-years-age-and-older

U.S. Department of Health and Human Services. (2010). *Factsheet: The affordable care act's new patient's rights.* Retrieved from http://www.healthreform.gov/newsroom/new_patients_bill_of_rights.html

U.S. Department of Health and Human Services, Administration for Children and Families, Administration on Children, Youth and Families, Children's Bureau. (2010). *Child maltreatment 2008.* Retrieved from http://www.acf.hhs.gov/programs/cb/stats_research/index.htm#can

Violence Policy Center. (2010). *When men murder women: An analysis of 2008 homicide data.* Retrieved from http://www.vpc.org/studies/wmmw2010.pdf

World Health Organization. (2005). *WHO multi-country study on women's health and domestic violence against women: Summary report of initial results on prevalence, health outcomes, and women's responses.* Geneva: Author.

World Health Organization. (2009). *Violence prevention, the evidence: Changing culture and social norms that support violence.* Retrieved from http://whglibdoc.who.int/publications/2009/9789241598330_eng.pdf

NASW Members with Primary Responsibility for Revision of This Policy

First Draft Revision:

Dana N. Courtney (NC)

Policy Panelists:

Allison Scobie Carroll (MA)
Rhea Almeida (NJ)
Vikki Peay (LA)
Rebecca Cline (OH)
Elena Delavega (TX)
Joe Torres (CA)
Nelly Rojas Schwan (CT)

Policy statement approved by the NASW Delegate Assembly, August 2011. This policy statement supersedes the policy statement on Family Violence approved by the Delegate Assembly in 2002. For further information, contact the National Association of Social Workers, 750 First Street, NE, Suite 700, Washington, DC 20002-4241. Telephone: 202-408-8600; e-mail: press@naswdc.org

Foster Care and Adoption

BACKGROUND

Foster care and adoption have long served as society's approach to providing alternative care for children who, on either a temporary or a permanent basis and for a number of reasons, cannot live with their families of origin. Although child placement institutions have aimed to provide the necessary assistance for these vulnerable children, a lack of resources has limited their potential to effectively address these children's needs.

During the past several decades, social services systems have significantly evolved. The focus on reunification began in earnest in 1980; however, it continues. In 2009, reunification was listed as the primary goal for 49 percent of all foster children (U.S. Department of Health and Human Services [HHS], 2010a, 2010b). Over the years, the number of children in foster care placements has decreased from 552,000 children in 2000 (Child Welfare Gateway, 2010) to a low of 423,773 children in 2009 (HHS, 2010a, 2010b). The two most common placements for children in the United States today are kinship placements (48 percent) and foster care placements (24 percent) (HHS, 2010a, 2010b). Adoptions from public child-placing agencies have also risen, reaching 57,466 in 2009; however, 114,556 children were still waiting for a permanent home (HHS, 2010a, 2010b). In addition, there has been an increase in the number of youths who age out of foster care; 22,432 exited care in 2003 (HHS, 2006), whereas 29,471 transitioned out of foster care in 2009 (HHS, 2010a, 2010b). Data also reveal that children of color are disproportionately represented in foster care in comparison with white children (Harris & Hackett, 2008; U.S. Government Accountability Office, 2007; Washington State Racial Disproportionality Advisory Committee, 2008). In fact, 58 percent of children in foster care are children of color, including 30 percent black, 20 percent Hispanic (of any race), 2 percent Alaskan Native/American Indian, and 5 percent two or more races; the race/ethnicity of 2 percent of the children in foster care was unknown or could not be determined (HHS, 2010a, 2010b). Despite the efforts of states and local governments to reduce the disproportionate numbers of children of color in care (national percentage of black and Hispanic children in care decreased 7 percent over seven years), poor children and children of color still enter care in greater numbers and leave in smaller numbers than do white and middle and upper class children (HHS, 2010a, 2010b). More American Indian children remain in the system, partly due to a lack of access to Title IV-E funding for administrative support and for foster care and adoptive subsidies.

Significant Legislations

Federal legislation has had a profound effect on all aspects of foster care and adoption. Beginning with the passage of the Child Abuse Prevention and Treatment Act (CAPTA) (P.L. 93-247) in 1974, a number of laws have significantly affected child welfare systems. CAPTA was the first major piece of legislation addressing child abuse and neglect. Four years later, the Indian Child Welfare Act of 1978 (P.L. 95-608) focused on establishing standards to ensure reasonable efforts prior to the removal of Indian children from their families, whereas the Adoption Assistance and Child Welfare Act of 1980 (P.L. 96-272) prioritized family preservation and permanency as major goals of child welfare. The latter law helped to decrease the number of children in the foster care system. The significance of permanence for a child or youth has become an increasingly important point in practice and in law. The Family Preservation and Support Services Program Act of 1993 (P.L. 103-66) authorized funding for family preservation and support services, aiming to keep families together and to assist in family reunification.

The Multiethnic Placement Act (MEPA) of 1994 (P.L. 103-382) intended to prevent discrimination on the basis of race, color, and national origin in the making of foster and adoptive placements. The Interethnic Adoption Provisions of the Small Business Jobs Protection Act of 1996 (P.L. 104-188) later clarified the intent of MEPA to eliminate placement searches to match by race or culture, decrease the length of time in care, facilitate the recruitment and retention of foster parents, and establish specific financial penalties for noncompliance with MEPA. With passage of the 1997 Adoption and Safe Families Act (P.L. 105-89) (ASFA), state child welfare agencies were mandated to improve their foster care systems. ASFA emphasized the safety of children as a priority and established time lines relating to permanency and termination of parental rights after the first 15 months that a child is in placement. In addition, ASFA mandated state child and family services reviews and program improvement plans for states that failed the federal review process.

Older youths in care also require critical services to help to prepare them for adulthood. The Foster Care Independence Act of 1999 (P.L. 106-169) expanded existing independent living programs to include services for youths preparing to transition to adulthood and former foster youths up to age 21 years. The Promoting Safe and Stable Families (PSSF) Amendments of 2001 (P.L. 107-133) extended the PSSF program and also created a state grant program to provide educational and training vouchers for youths aging out of foster care. They also created a program for children with incarcerated parents.

Another change in the last quarter-century in foster care is the growing awareness of the need to have trained professionals who have the passion and skills to work with the foster care and adoption populations. The Child and Family Services Improvement Act of 2006 (P.L.

109-288) reserved funds to develop programs to improve caseworker retention, recruitment, and training.

Two pieces of legislation intended to improve the child welfare systems have recently been signed into law. The Fostering Connections to Success and Increasing Adoptions Act of 2008 (P.L. 110-351) is the most significant child welfare reform legislation in more than a decade. The result of this legislation has been improved outcomes for children and youths who have spent time in foster care as well as for those at risk of child welfare involvement. The provisions of this law will help more children who cannot return to their parents to exit the foster care system more quickly and safely and enter the care of permanent families, which can include relatives or adoptive parents. The law also provides support for young people at age 18 and older as they begin the transition from foster care to adulthood. In addition, Native American tribes will have the opportunity to receive federal resources to strengthen services that address child welfare needs in their communities (Fostering Connections Resource Center, n.d.). Finally, the CAPTA Reauthorization of 2010 (P.L. 111-320) aimed to improve data collection; improve systems for training and supporting individuals who identify, prevent, and respond to reports of child maltreatment; and strengthen coordination among service providers focused on challenges associated with child maltreatment (American Humane Association, 2010). Child welfare legislations have underscored the importance of safety, family reunification, and child well-being.

Fifty-four percent of children in foster care were adopted by foster parents, while 32 percent were adopted by relatives (HHS, 2010a, 2010b). Traditionally, postadoption services were not provided to families by the child welfare agencies. Budget constraints have limited response to this need (Coakley & Berrick, 2008; Gibbs, Barth, & Houts, 2005). Federal legislation has been active in encouraging and supporting adoption of children who cannot return to their original homes. Adoption subsidies established to support the financial burdens taken on by adoptive parents were originally focused on children with special needs (for example, P.L. 95-266) but have been expanded as experts have explained that all children in foster care have experienced difficulties and trauma (for example, P.L. 96-272; P.L. 99-509; P.L. 101-508; P.L. 104-191; P.L. 106-310). In 1993, access to family leave was broadened to include a new family member through adoption (P.L. 103-03). Since then, legislation at the federal level has changed tax codes to assist adoptive parents (P.L. 104-188), expanded medical insurance coverage definitions to include adopted people (P.L. 104-188), and clarified citizenship issues in international adoptions (P.L. 106-398).

ISSUE STATEMENT

Many of the most vulnerable children, youths, and families are touched by foster care and adoption programs across the country. The children, from infants to older youths, who are involved with the child welfare system come from diverse racial, ethnic, and economic backgrounds. They often have special needs and require resources and supports to address their physical, developmental, educational, and emotional challenges. Compared with their peers, maltreated children are more likely to experience depression, posttraumatic stress disorder, chemical dependency, and poor physical health, and they are more likely to engage in criminal activity (Paxson & Haskins, 2009). Generally, the families that come to the attention of child welfare have experienced a range of risk factors that can include a lack of child care, unstable or unsafe housing, disadvantaged neighborhoods, limited support networks, and financial hardships. Domestic violence in the home and behavioral issues can also put children at risk of child welfare involvement. Another growing population is children of incarcerated parents. Children with incarcerated mothers are four times more likely than others to continue to be in foster care. They are also more likely to age out of foster care and less likely to be reunified with their parents, get adopted, enter into a subsidized guardianship, or go into independent living (Casey Family Programs, n.d.).

By the time children, youths, and families come to the attention of child welfare systems, they have already experienced multiple stressors. In some instances, families have been investigated and provided the necessary resources (for example, housing, child care, and so forth) to keep the family intact. However, in cases in which safety is a concern, children are removed from their family's care and placed in foster care while their family is stabilized. Although the placement of children in out-of-home care is generally avoided unless it is the only way to keep them safe, there are some cases in which removal is necessary. After removal from their parent's care, children go into a kinship care or adoption placement.

Across the country, social workers in child welfare systems work diligently to serve some of the most vulnerable children, youths, and families with limited resources, high caseloads, and stressful working conditions that can include inadequate salaries, numerous administrative burdens, and limited supervision training and supports (NASW, 2010). In addition, social workers are at risk of experiencing safety issues while on the job. All of these factors can influence the recruitment and retention of qualified social workers in child welfare systems. To help reduce some of these stressors, an increasing amount of child welfare agencies have used technology to track data, clients, and outcomes. Over the past 10 years, federal, state, and local agencies have spent more than 2.8 billion dollars on child welfare technologies (Bissell & Miller, 2007).

In addition to complex work environments, funding of child welfare services is affected by economic downturns, which affect budgets and force many agencies to reduce capacity. Some agencies cut programs, decrease foster care subsidies, and furlough or lay off qualified staff. Another growing trend in the child welfare arena is privatization and the use of managed care. Although this approach may help to reduce costs, it is difficult for public agencies to monitor areas such as staffing, quality of service, and caseloads (American Federation of State, County and Municipal Employees, n.d.), all of which can influence child, youth, and family outcomes.

Another emerging population for child welfare is immigrant families and youths. Immigrant raids, limited supports and resources, and cultural differences—including parenting styles and language barriers—can lead many immigrants to the attention of child welfare systems. Unfortunately, social workers face several challenges in addressing the complex needs of immigrants. A shortage of bilingual or bicultural staff and limited translation services are among some of the biggest challenges in serving immigrants. In many instances, a lack of culturally relevant services can affect permanency goals, leaving children in out-of-home placements.

Current laws and policies can also make it difficult for social workers to deliver effective services to immigrants. State and local child welfare systems are forced to rely on scarce local funding streams to fund child welfare services, translation services, and immigration counsel because of the lack of federal reimbursement of child welfare services for undocumented immigrant children (Lincroft & Resner, 2006). In addition to families, social workers also face challenges in serving undocumented, unaccompanied youths. Undocumented youths cannot transition into adulthood successfully without a legal status. However, the Trafficking Victims Protection and Reauthorization Act of 2008 (P.L. 110-457) grants a special immigrant juvenile status to youths who are under the care of child welfare as a result of abuse, neglect, or abandonment. To effectively serve this population, agencies and social workers have to seek out appropriate resources, including training and technical assistance to address such immigrant relief options.

In addition to the immigrant youths in care, social workers continue to support other youths aging out of foster care. Despite previous changes in legislation providing supports and resources to older youths in care, they continue to face challenges after they exit foster care. Former foster youths face a range of hardships, including inadequate educational preparation, unstable finances, and limited access to employment and housing opportunities. Many former foster youths experience negative outcomes once they transition into adulthood. In fact, 74 percent completed high school, 3 percent to 11 percent completed a bachelor's degree; 52 percent were employed at age 21, 22 percent experienced homelessness, and 25 percent report suffering from posttraumatic stress disorder (Casey Family Programs, 2010).

Currently, greater numbers of self-identified parents and children who are lesbian, gay, bisexual, and transgender (LGBT) are found in the foster care and adoptive arena, both as children in need of care and adults willing to parent. McRoy and Madden (2009) found that more gay men and lesbian women are interested in becoming foster and adoptive parents, sometimes placing agencies, social workers, and local governments in positions at variance with societal preferences. The NASW (2008) *Code of Ethics* is clear about the ethical responsibilities of a professional in this area.

The complex issues of families involved with the child welfare system require professionals who have proper education and training, supervision, and resources. As policies and practice evolve to support child welfare–involved families, states have also developed relationships with schools of social work to provide specialized certificates, courses, and workshops to improve social work skills for professionals who work with the child welfare population. A strong workforce is critical to effectively address the needs of child welfare–involved children, youths, and families.

POLICY STATEMENT

NASW supports the following:

■   a child welfare policy designed to provide the best care for all children in need of foster care and adoption services.

■   the prioritization of child safety; permanency for children involved in the child welfare system; and respect for the civil rights of parents and children, regardless of their race, ethnicity, language, capabilities, religion, sexual orientation, gender identity, geographic location, or socioeconomic status.

■   concurrent planning for family reunification or preparation for adoption through termination of parental rights when a child enters the foster care system.

■ a transparent system in which all parties involved have timely access to all relevant information involving the indexed case.

■ all efforts to keep siblings together in placement. Siblings should be separated only for the purpose of child safety.

■ all efforts to ensure that children of immigrant families, regardless of citizenship status, are subject to the same societal protection and foster care and adoption services as children from nonimmigrant families.

■ efforts to maintain a child's identity and his or her ethnic heritage in all services and placement actions.

■ the removal of barriers that prevent children from being placed in permanent homes, including barriers that are unsupported by tested experience such as resistance to using single parents, foster parents (for adoption), and nontraditional family patterns (including LGBT parents) as potential foster care and adoption resources.

■ the employment of social workers with professional social work education to provide child welfare services.

■ recruitment of qualified foster and adoptive parents, including gay and lesbian and racially diverse individuals.

■ required comprehensive and specialized training of foster parents as a precondition of licensure of foster homes and in-service trainings as a condition of continuing licensure.

■ rigorous training and ongoing services of adoptive parents as needed and in the best interests of the child.

■ the provision of publicly funded subsidies in all cases in which the cost of a child's permanent care becomes a barrier to appropriate adoptive placement.

■ the needs and rights of adult adoptees to have access to legally available information regarding their birth and family medical history.

■ legislation legitimizing second-parent adoptions in same-sex households.

■ competitive compensation for all professionals, especially social workers, employed in the field of child welfare.

■ the funding of foster care and adoption services to guarantee high-quality needed services to all children, youths, and families.

■ additional recruitment alternatives for LGBT adolescents for whom existing resources are not accepting or are inadequate, such as family foster care using LGBT adults as foster parents and group homes designed specifically for LGBT adolescents.

■ reasonable caseload limits, in accord with nationally established standards, to allow child welfare workers to provide competent and effective services.

■ the involvement of relatives and grandparents through policies that give them standing when it is in the child's best interests. Accordingly, this would include support for the financial, educational, and emotional support of children in foster care and of those who would care for them permanently.

REFERENCES

Adoption and Safe Families Act of 1997, P.L. 105-89, 111 Stat. 2115 (1997).

Adoption Assistance and Child Welfare Act of 1980, P.L. 96-272, 94 Stat. 500 (1980).

American Federation of State, County and Municipal Employees. (n.d.). *Child welfare and privatization: Trends and considerations.* Retrieved from http://www.afscme.org/issues/1506.cfm

American Humane Association. (2010). *CAPTA Reauthorization Act of 2010.* Retrieved from http://www.americanhumane.org/assets/docs/advocacy/capta-reauthorization-act-of-2010.pdf

Bissell, M., & Miller, J. (2007). *Child welfare and technology.* Retrieved from http://www.cwla.org/voice/0707technology.htm

Casey Family Programs. (2010). *Foster care by the numbers.* Retrieved from http://www.

casey.org/Press/MediaKit/pdf/Foster
CareByTheNumbers.pdf

Casey Family Programs. (n.d.). *Children of incarcerated parents fact sheet.* Retrieved from http://www.fcnetwork.org/AECF Children%20of%20Incarcerated%20Parents %20Factsheet.pdf

Child Abuse Prevention and Treatment Act, P.L. 93-247, 88 Stat. 4 (1974).

Child Abuse Prevention and Treatment Act Reauthorization of 2010, P.L. 111-320, 124 Stat. 3459 (2010).

Child and Family Services Improvement Act of 2006, P.L. 109-288, 120 Stat. 1233 (2006).

Child Welfare Gateway. (2010). *Numbers and trends.* Retrieved from http://www.child welfare.gov/pubs/factsheets/foster.cfm

Coakley, J. F., & Berrick, J. D. (2008). Research review: In a rush to permanency: Preventing adoption disruption. *Child & Family Social Work, 13,* 101–112.

Family Preservation and Support Services Program Act of 1993, P.L. 103-66, 107 Stat. 312 (1993).

Foster Care Independence Act of 1999, P.L. 106-169, 113 Stat. 1822 (1999).

Fostering Connections Resource Center. (n.d.). *Description of the law.* Retrieved from http:// www.fosteringconnections.org/about_ the_law?id=0001

Fostering Connections to Success and Increasing Adoptions Act of 2008, P.L. 110-351, 122 Stat. 3949 (2008).

Gibbs, D., Barth, R. P., & Houts, R. (2005). Family characteristics and dynamics among families receiving postadoption services. *Families in Society, 86,* 520–532.

Harris, M. S., & Hackett, W. (2008). Decision points in child welfare: An action research model to address disproportionality. *Children and Youth Services Review, 30,* 199–215.

Indian Child Welfare Act of 1978, P.L. 95-608, 92 Stat. 3069 (1978).

Lincroft, Y., & Resner, J. (2006). *Undercounted, underserved: Immigrant and refugee families in the child welfare system.* Retrieved from http:// www.caseyfoundation.org/upload/ publicationfiles/ir3622.pdf

McRoy, R., & Madden, E. (2009). Youth permanence through adoption. In B. Kerman, M. Freundlich, & A. Maluccio (Eds.), *Achieving permanence for older children and youth in foster care* (pp. 244–265). New York: Columbia University Press.

Multiethnic Placement Act of 1994, P.L. 103-382, 108 Stat. 3518 (1994).

National Association of Social Workers. (2008). *Code of ethics of the National Association of Social Workers.* Washington, DC: Author.

National Association of Social Workers. (2010). *Supporting the child welfare workforce to reduce child maltreatment.* Washington, DC: Author.

Paxson, C., & Haskins, R. (2009). Introducing the issue. *Preventing Child Maltreatment, 19*(2), 3–17.

Promoting Safe and Stable Families Amendments of 2001, P.L. 107-133, 115 Stat. 2413 (2001).

Small Business Jobs Protection Act of 1996, P.L. 104-188, 110 Stat. 1755 (1996).

U.S. Department of Health and Human Services. (2006). *The AFCARS report.* Retrieved from http://www.acf.hhs.gov/ programs/cb/stats_research/afcars/tar/ report10.htm

U.S. Department of Health and Human Services. (2010a). *Adoption and foster care analysis and report (AFCARS).* Retrieved from http://www.acf.hhs.gov/programs/cb/ stats_research/afcars/tar/report17.htm

U.S. Department of Health and Human Services. (2010b). *Trends in foster care and adoption: FY 2002–2009.* Retrieved from http://www.acf.hhs/gov/programs/cb/ stats_research/afcars/trends.htm

U.S. Government Accountability Office. (2007). *African American children in foster care: Additional HHS assistance needed to help states reduce the proportion in care.* Washington, DC: Author.

Washington State Racial Disproportionality Advisory Committee. (2008). *Racial disproportionality in Washington state* (2nd ed.). Olympia, WA: Author.

NASW Members with Primary Responsibility for Revision of This Policy

First Draft Revision:

Joanne Caye (NC)

Policy Panelists:

Allison Scobie Carroll (MA)
Isabel Rose (NYS)
Jackie Pray (GA)
Yolanda Jordan (IL)
Mary Bahney (NE)
Marian Harris (WA)
Robin Russel (ME)

Policy statement approved by the NASW Delegate Assembly, August 2011. This policy statement supersedes the policy statement on Foster Care and Adoption approved by the Delegate Assembly in 2002. For further information, contact the National Association of Social Workers, 750 First Street, NE, Suite 700, Washington, DC 20002-4241. Telephone: 202-408-8600; e-mail: pressnaswdc.org.

Gender-, Ethnic-, and Race-Based Workplace Discrimination

BACKGROUND

Discrimination is defined as treating one person unfairly over another according to factors unrelated to their ability or potential, such as age, disability, sex, gender, or national origin (http://www.legal-definitions.com/discrimination.htm). Discrimination based on age, disability, gender, gender identity, national origin, race, religion, and sexual orientation continues to affect a variety of employable citizens in the workplace. New forms of discrimination such as genetics, size and body image, and discrimination based on credit are on the increase in the workplace. These practices occur at every stage of the employment process, from interviewing, hiring, training and promotion, through retention and times of lay off. Ethnic slurs, graffiti, and other forms of offensive conduct have become more pervasive in the workplace and can make the employment arena a hostile and abusive place to be. Most analyses of wage discrimination and other workplace-related issues analyze either gender or race and ethnicity separately. However, because patterns of employment discrimination by gender, race, and ethnicity intersect and reinforce each other, it is useful to consider them together. Doing so should not obscure the fact that African Americans, Native Americans, and Americans in each of the Spanish-speaking and Asian ethnic and cultural groups have their own unique histories of employment in the United States and have faced oppression and discrimination at different times in the history of this nation (Amott & Matthei, 1991; Glenn, 1985).

Men and women in each of these groups not only have shared many experiences of oppression but also have had experiences of oppression that have been unique. In employment, gender has affected patterns of work and employment-related discrimination in each of these groups. Most analysts agree that race, ethnicity, class, and gender together powerfully shape social and economic life in America (Amott & Matthei, 1991; Glenn, 1985; Rothenberg, 1995). "Differences in race, class and gender are very costly for some and very profitable for others" (Rothenberg, p. 117).

The civil rights protests of the 1960s brought to the forefront of America the injustices perpetrated on segments of U.S. society through racial segregation and discrimination. During the height of the civil rights protests and demonstrations, President John F. Kennedy went on television on June 11, 1963, to address the nation. He said, "We are confronted primarily with a moral issue. It is as old as the scriptures and it is as clear as the American Constitution. The heart of the question is whether all Americans are afforded equal rights and equal opportunities, whether we are going to treat our fellow Americans as we want to be treated."

Since the 1960s, several pieces of federal legislation addressed discrimination in the workplace: Equal Pay Act of 1963 (EPA) (P.L. 88-38), Title VII of the Civil Rights Act of 1964, Age Discrimination in Employment Act of 1967 (ADEA) (P.L. 90-202), and the American's with Disabilities Act of 1990 (ADA). Title VII of the Civil Rights Act of 1964 (P.L. 88-352) prohibits discrimination based on race, color, national origin, sex, and religion and prohibits retaliation. The Equal Pay Act of 1963 prohibits discrimination on the basis of sex in the payment of wages or benefits, where men and women perform work of similar skill, effort, and responsibility for the same employer under similar working conditions. The ADEA prohibits employment discrimination against people

40 years of age and older. The ADA prohibits employment discrimination against people with disabilities and requires employers to make reasonable accommodations for people with disabilities. There are also federal protections from discrimination on other bases, including status as a parent, marital status, political affiliation, and conduct that does not adversely affect the performance of the employee (U.S. Equal Employment Opportunity Commission [EEOC], 1964).

The EEOC, created in 1964, enforces statutes that make it illegal to discriminate against employees or applicants for employment on the basis of race, color, religion, sex, national origin, disability, or age. Despite more than four decades of legislation calling for nondiscrimination in employment, in 2004 the EEOC received more than 100,000 complaints of discrimination (EEOC, n.d.) and recovered more than $352 million in monetary benefits for complainants (EEOC, n.d.). In 2004, charges of discrimination based on race accounted for about 27 percent of all complaints filed with EEOC, followed by charges of discrimination based on gender (24 percent), age (17 percent), and disability (15 percent) (EEOC, n.d.).

Discrimination can occur at every stage of employment, from recruitment, application process, hiring, and remuneration to separation. Discrimination based on race is deeply entrenched in the workplace and remains pervasive. Forms of occupational segregation, subjugation, subordination, and violence are still with us. Although the extent to which earnings differentials by gender and race and ethnicity result from discrimination is disputed widely, research has repeatedly shown that the earnings gap between white American men and both white American women and men and women of all other racial and ethnic groups cannot be explained fully by training, education, work experience, or attachment to the labor force (Freeman, 1991). Discrimination alone accounts for a significant proportion of the wage gap between white women and men and women of color compared with white men (Freeman; National Committee on Pay Equity, 1995).

The wage gap is a statistical indicator often used as an index of the status of women's earnings relative to men's. It is also used to compare earnings of other races and ethnicities to those of white men, a group generally not subject to race or sex-based discrimination. The wage gap varies from 73 percent to 77 percent between men and women. These figures are based on the 2000 median annual earnings for year-round, full-time workers (see National Committee on Pay Equity, Q&A, (http://www .pay-equity.org/info.html). The wage gap exists, in part, because many women and people of color are still segregated into a few low-paying occupations. More than half of all women workers hold sales, clerical, nurses, teachers, and service jobs. Studies show that an occupation pays less when women or people of color dominate it (National Committee on Pay Equity, 1995).

Women still earn 73 cents to every dollar that men earned in 2000. African American women make only 63 cents and Latinas a mere 56 cents to every dollar earned by white men. Because of the lower earnings of women, families maintained solely by women are disadvantaged economically. Thus, the low earnings of white, African American, Latino, and Native American women have major effects on children; low wages for women are a major cause of child poverty. Even without children, being female and being a member of one of these racial and ethnic groups contributes to the chances of being poor: Poverty rates are approximately one in 10 for white men and women, one in three for white female heads of households, one in three for Hispanic men and women, one in two for Hispanic female heads of households, one in three for African American men and women, and one in two for African American female heads of households, demonstrating that race and gender each have a powerful influence on poverty in the United States (Mantsios, 1995). Pay equity by gender and by race and ethnicity is essential if the suffering of children in poverty is to be eliminated. If working women earned the same as men (those who work the same number of hours; have the same education, age, and union status; and live in the same region of the country), their annual family incomes would rise by $4,000 and poverty rates would be cut in half (National Women's Law Center, 2005).

Occupational segregation results in the "crowding" of women and people of color into a narrow range of professions and occupations. A relatively high percentage of white and Asian men are employed in managerial and professional occupations, whereas African American, Hispanic, and American Indian men tend to be concentrated in the "lower skilled," lower paid occupations of operators, fabricators, and laborers. Women of all groups are most likely to be employed in technical sales and administrative support occupations. A high percentage of white and Asian women are also employed in managerial and professional occupations, and a high percentage of African American, Hispanic, and American Indian women are also employed in service (Cotter, Hermsen, & Vanniman, 2003).

One characteristic of the occupational groups in which women who are employed are concentrated, and especially women from different racial and ethnic groups, is that many of them are involved with domestic work or service work that replaces the household work of others. Historically, social practice and social policy have rewarded and protected the unpaid family work of white middle- and upper-class women; programs such as Aid to Families with Dependent Children were originally started so that white widows would be able to rear their dependent children without having to resort to paid employment (Miller, 1992); however, the household and child-rearing work of women from different racial and ethnic groups in relation to their own dependent children has not been so protected (Abramovitz, 1988; Glenn, 1985). The ways in which this phenomenon has played out differed for each racial and ethnic group, depending on its immigration history. The forms of oppression the group as a whole has encountered in the United States, and the content of the dominant stereotypes of each group, has also varied (Amott & Matthei, 1991; Glenn). In fact, some groups of women, such as African American, some Asian and Pacific Islander, and some Hispanic women, have been employed to do the child-rearing and household work of affluent white women, and both men and women of color are often employed in the secondary labor market and the service sectors of the economy in devalued and poorly paid "dirty work" (Gilkes, 1990). Thus, what Abramovitz (1988) has termed "the family ethic" has been applied differently to rationalize the work of men and women and that of white Americans compared with people from different racial and ethnic groups.

African Americans, Hispanics, and American Indians are more likely than non-Hispanic white people or Asians to work in lower-paying, semi-skilled jobs as service workers. They are less likely to hold white-collar jobs, which range from managerial and professional to clerical positions. African Americans, Hispanics, and American Indians who hold these white-collar jobs are more likely than white people or Asians to work as typist, clerks, or salespeople rather than as higher-earning managers or professionals. Although the share of U.S. workers in farming, fishing, or forestry is small, it is greatest among Hispanics, reflecting the large number of Hispanics who work in agriculture (Population Reference Bureau, Racial Inequalities in Managerial & Professional Jobs, 2004).

An important consequence of the lower earnings and different jobs held by women and by men from different racial and ethnic groups is the effect of these patterns of employment on work-related benefits. The U.S. economy is organized in such a way that access to many economic resources in addition to income is determined by paid employment. Access to and levels of benefits from such publicly supported federal social insurance programs as unemployment insurance and Old Age and Survivors Disability Insurance for workers who are older and disabled and their dependents, as well as from state-controlled systems such as workers' compensation, are determined by a person's (or their spouse's) level of compensation and tenure on the job.

White American male workers have traditionally received higher levels of benefits from these programs than others because they are less likely to be underemployed or more likely to be employed in jobs with greater stability or with higher levels of compensation (Ozawa, 1989). The same is true of access to such privately funded job-related benefits as pension plans and affordable health insurance. The pattern of distribution of these noncash benefits mirrors and reinforces the pattern of earnings differences in which white American men tend to get more than women and more than men from other racial and ethnic groups. These differences in employment-related benefits affect these workers and their families not only during their years of employment, but also during retirement, because retirement income programs, both public and private, are involved. Thus, these employment-related differences contribute substantially to the higher rates of poverty that white women, especially those living alone, and men and women of color suffer in old age (Crawley, 1994). For example, the median income for all older African Americans was 59.6 percent of older white Americans, and the median income of older African American women was only 67.6 percent of that for older white women (Crawley).

Even in occupations and professions in which women predominate numerically, the glass ceiling has a major effect (Mason, 1992). This situation unfortunately pertains to the social work profession as well; recent studies have shown that women are paid less compared with men and are less likely than men to advance in the profession (Gibelman & Schervish, 1993, 1996). In the field of social work as a whole, women from different racial and ethnic groups are disproportionately found in the lowest level or paraprofessional positions (Martin & Chernesky, 1989). Although the earnings and advancement gaps in social work may be less than in other professions (Sokoloff, 1988), given the profession's commitment to ending discrimination in all forms and to developing diversity within the profession that will mirror the diversity in U.S. society, any gender-, ethnic-, or race-based discrimination in the profession is cause for concern.

ISSUES STATEMENT

NASW and the social work profession have long been concerned with working to eliminate discrimination in all forms. This commitment is embodied in the *Code of Ethics of the National Association of Social Workers* (NASW, 2000) and determines the major policies that NASW supports. Unfortunately, discrimination based on race, ethnicity, age, ability, sexual orientation, and gender continues to be pervasive in modern American life. Discrimination has an enormous and pernicious impact on the lives of the diverse clients that the social work profession and NASW members serve. It also affects NASW members who are women (the majority of members), people of color, people with disabilities, sexual minorities, older people, and people of diverse religions. U.S. society and social policy are organized in such a way that employment is the major means for distributing income and most other essential material social benefits, such as health insurance, public and private retirement plans, and disability insurance, as well as many nonmaterial benefits, such as status and prestige. The 1993 Delegate Assembly voted to retain both a general statement on women's issues and a more specific statement on workplace discrimination. For these reasons, it is essential that NASW continue to have a strong and up-to-date policy statement addressing discrimination in the workplace to guide the association and its members in practice, advocacy, and policy development activities.

Discriminatory workplace policies and practices, such as those affecting advancement, training, and the working environment, limit opportunities for advancement and for participation in organizational decision making. These other forms of discrimination interact with wage discrimination to affect earnings, benefits, occupations, and personal and household income. Despite federal and state civil rights legislation, affirmative action programs, and other legislative and policy efforts to reduce these differences in the past several decades, workplace discrimination has not disappeared.

POLICY STATEMENT

Given the persistence and pervasiveness of workplace discrimination, pay and employment equity must remain a major policy issue for the social work profession and for the nation. The many aspects of the problem require that the solutions pursued also be multifaceted (Davis, 1994; Miller, 1992). NASW supports a number of principles and strategies for change in legislative, administrative, and educational areas.

There is evidence that men and women of all racial and ethnic groups benefit from unionization (Institute for Women's Policy Research, 1993). Unions with a high proportion of women in their membership have also broadened the scope of their negotiations to include such issues as affirmative action, family leave, and the elimination of sexual harassment on the job (Institute for Women's Policy Research). Therefore, worker's efforts to organize should be supported, including those that incorporate diverse membership, to promote progressive employment policies and address employment discrimination.

Affirmative action is another powerful tool that can be used to reduce inequities in the employment of all women and of men from different racial and ethnic groups. Affirmative action policies aim to open hiring systems and procedures and career development and advancement on the job to those who have historically been discriminated against. Affirmative action can be a powerful tool for helping men and women from different racial and ethnic groups gain access to higher paying jobs from which they have traditionally been excluded. It can also help eliminate the glass ceiling that prevents many white women and workers from different racial and ethnic groups from attaining the levels of advancement in their chosen fields that they are qualified to achieve. Affirmative action is one of the few methods identified for reducing the underrepresentation of white women and workers from different racial and ethnic groups in the highest levels of employment in America. NASW reaffirms its commitment to affirmative action in the public and private sectors and will publicize the nature and benefits of well-designed affirmative action programs. Affirmative action should also be a consideration as employers restructure and downsize.

NASW therefore reaffirms its commitment to its own program of affirmative action within the association, which has succeeded in identifying people from historically oppressed groups as leaders in the profession. All social work employers, associations of social workers, and social and human services agencies should develop and implement similar affirmative action programs.

Policies to end employment discrimination include the following:

■ federal and state legislative measures that aim to eliminate discrimination in employment, training, compensation, and job-related benefits

■ enforcement of all laws and regulations that forbid discrimination in the workplace, including adequate funding for the federal and state agencies charged with the enforcement of civil rights and antidiscrimination laws and regulations

■ public and private affirmative action programs that aim to ensure that people from historically oppressed populations have access to employment, opportunities for advancement, nondiscriminatory working conditions, and fair compensation

■ legislative, training, and educational programs that help people from historically oppressed populations qualify for and enter occupations and fields from which they have traditionally been excluded

■ adequate funding for social, health, and human services agencies and services so that inequities in employment and compensation that exist in social work and social work agencies can be eliminated

■ elimination of all federal and state measures that unfairly limit employment and otherwise have a negative impact on immigrants and undocumented workers

■ human and civil rights measures to protect all Americans, including lesbian, gay, bisexual transgender, and intersex

■ adoption of federal and state measures that prohibit discrimination based on sexual orientation and gender identity

■ promotion of quality child care to remove barriers to employment.

REFERENCES

Abramovitz, M. (1988). *Regulating the lives of women: Social welfare policy from colonial times to the present.* Boston: South End Press.

Age Discrimination in Employment Act of 1967 (ADEA). P.L. 90-202, 81 Stat. 602

Amott, T. L., & Matthei, J. A. (1991). Race, gender, and work: A multicultural economic history of women in the United States. Boston: South End Press.

Civil Rights Act of 1964, P.L. 88-352, 78 Stat. 241.

Cotter, D. A., Hermsen, J. A., & Vanniman, R. S. (2003). Segregation across race. *Sociological Quarterly, 44,* 1.

Crawley, B. (1994). Older women: Public policy issues for the twenty-first century. In L. V. Davis (Ed.), *Building on women's strengths: A social work agenda for the twenty-first century* (pp. 159–178). New York: Haworth Press.

Davis, L. V. (1994). Why we still need a women's agenda for social work. In L. V. Davis (Ed.), *Building on women's strengths: A social work agenda for the twenty-first century* (pp. 1–26). New York: Haworth Press.

Equal Pay Act of 1963, P.L. 88-38, 77 Stat. 56 (29 sect. 206).

Freeman, M. L. (1991). Pay equity and social work. *Affilia, 6,* 7–19.

Gibelman, M., & Schervish, P. H. (1993). The glass ceiling in social work: Is it shatterproof? *Affilia, 8,* 442–455.

Gibelman, M., & Schervish, P. H. (1996). *Who we are: A second look.* Washington, DC: NASW Press.

Gilkes, C. T. (1990). Liberated to work like dogs!: Labeling black women and their work. In H. Y. Grossman & N. L. Chester (Eds.), *The experience and meaning of work in women's lives* (pp. 165–188). Hillsdale, NJ: Lawrence Erlbaum.

Glenn, E. N. (1985). Racial ethnic women's labor: The intersection of race, gender and class oppression. *Review of Radical Political Economics, 17*(3), 86–108.

Mantsios, G. (1995). Class in America: Myths and realities. In P. S. Rothenberg (Ed.), *Race, class, and gender in the United States: An integrated study* (3rd ed., pp. 131–143). New York: St. Martin's Press.

Martin, P. Y., & Chernesky, R. H. (1989). Women's prospects for leadership in social welfare: A political economy perspective. *Administration in Social Work, 13*(3/4), 117–143.

Mason, M. A. (1992). Standing still in the workplace: Women in social work and other female-dominated occupations. *Affilia, 7,* 23–43.

Miller, D. C. (1992). *Women and social welfare: A feminist analysis.* New York: Praeger.

National Association of Social Workers. (2000). *Code of ethics of the National Association of Social Workers.* Washington, DC: Author.

National Committee on Pay Equity. (1995). In P. S. Rothenberg (Ed.), *Race, class, and gender in the United States: An integrated study* (3rd ed., pp. 144–151). New York: St. Martin's Press.

National Women's Law Center. (2005). *The wage gap.* Retrieved from http://www.inforplease.com/ipa/A0763170.html

Ozawa, M. N. (Ed.). (1989). *Women's life cycle and economic insecurity: Problems and proposals.* Westport, CT: Praeger.

Rothenberg, P. S. (1995). *Race, class, and gender in the United States: An integrated study* (3rd ed.). New York: St. Martin's Press.

Sokoloff, N. J. (1988). Evaluating gains and losses by black and white women and men in the professions, 1960–1980. *Social Problems, 35,* 336–340.

U.S. Equal Employment Opportunity Commission. (n.d.). *U. S. Equal Employment Opportunity Commission.* Retrieved on May 2, 2005, from http://www.eeoc.gov/

U.S. Equal Employment Opportunity Commission. (1964). *Furthering the protections against workplace discrimination and harassment.* Retrieved from www.eeoc.gov/about eeoc/35th/1990s/furthering.html

U.S. Equal Employment Opportunity Commission. (2003). *Pre 1965: Events leading to the creation of EEOC.* Retrieved from www.eeoc.gov/about eeoc/35th/pre1965/

SUGGESTED READINGS

American Association of University Women Educational Foundation. (1992). *How schools shortchange girls: A study of major findings on girls and education.* Washington, DC: Author.

American Civil Liberties Union. (1998) *Workplace rights: Lifestyle discrimination in the* workplace: Your right to privacy under attack. Retrieved from www.aclu.org/workplacerights/gen/13384res19981231.html

Furchtgott-Roth, D., Stolba, C. (1999). *Women's figures: An illustrated guide to the economic progress of women in America.* Washington, DC: American Enterprise Institute Press.

Hochschild, A. (1989). *The second shift: Working parents and the revolution at home.* New York: Viking Press.

Huffman, M. L., & Cohen, P. N. (2004). Occupational segregation and the gender gap in workplace authority: National versus local labor markets. *Sociological Focus, 19*(1), 121–147.

Immigration Reform and Control Act of 1986, P.L. 99-603, 100 Stat. 3359.

Institute for Women's Policy Research. (1993). *What do unions do for women?* Washington, DC: Author.

Lopez, J. A. (1995). Women face glass walls as well as glass ceilings. In P. S. Rothenberg (Ed.), *Race, class, and gender in the United States: An integrated study* (3rd ed., pp. 241–242). New York: St. Martin's Press.

McElroy, W., (2001). *Unlocking the potential of America's "pink collar" workers.* Retrieved July 24, 2001, from http://www.foxnews.com/story/0,2933,30307,00.html

Population Reference Bureau. (2001). *Record numbers of women in the U. S. labor force, and occupational segregation.* Retrieved from Template.cfm?Section=RaceandEthnicity&template=/Content

U.S. Department of Commerce. (1993). *Statistical abstract of the United States* (113th ed.). Lanham, MD: Bernan Press.

U.S. Department of Labor. (1991). *Report on the glass ceiling initiative.* Washington, DC: U.S. Government Printing Office.

Weinstein, D. (2003, Fall). Got religion? Accommodating America's diverse religious beliefs and practices in the workplace. *The Philadelphia Lawyer.*

Policy statement approved by the NASW Delegate Assembly, August 2005. This policy supersedes the policy statement on Gender-, Ethnic-, and Race-Based Workplace Discrimination approved by the Delegate Assembly in 1996 and referred by the 2002 Delegate Assembly to the 2005 Delegate Assembly for revision. For further information, contact the National Association of Social Workers, 750 First Street, NE, Suite 700, Washington, DC 20002-4241. Telephone: 202-408-8600 or 800-638-8799; e-mail: press@naswdc.org

Genetics

BACKGROUND

With the completion of the human genome sequence in 2003, it is thought that all disease, with the possible exception of trauma, is a result of the interaction of one's genes and the environment. Emerging advances in the science of *genetics* (the study of single genes and their effects) and *genomics* (the study of the functions and interaction of all the genes in the human body) not only identify thousands of rare disorders, but also define genetic components of common diseases such as Alzheimer's, cancer, mental illness, diabetes, heart disease, and autism (Guttmacher & Collins, 2002). As predictive genetic testing becomes more available for some of these common diseases, it is imperative that social workers begin incorporating genetic thinking and genetic principles in their practices. Understanding the psychosocial and ethical implications of genetic testing is important for all social workers, no matter where they are practicing. Social workers can take an active part in ensuring that clients are protected against genetic discrimination by insurance companies, employers, schools, adoption agencies, and the government.

As social workers, we must respect genetic diversity and the uniqueness of the individual, regardless of his or her genetic makeup (Weiss, 2004), including the ability to recognize the difference between components of genetic make-up and learned traits. It is important that social workers recognize how vital their role is in helping clients come to terms with being at risk of a genetic condition or facing the uncertainty of a genetic diagnosis in the family.

Genetic research studies each individual's unique combination of approximately 30,000 genes located on the 23 pairs of chromosomes found in each human cell. Each gene or combi-nation of genes in interaction with the environment is responsible for an individual's particular traits and disorders. For example, one's hair color, gender, and eye color are determined by genes. Genes also play an important role in health, mental health, and to a yet unknown degree, behavior. One interesting finding of the Human Genome Project was that all individuals are 99.9 percent the same with respect to their DNA sequence. Pharmacogenomics is a recent development of tailoring of drugs for patients on an individual basis. The National Human Genome Research Institute (1997) supports the dissemination of genome information to the public and health professionals.

Genetics is not a new science; Gregor Mendel discovered the laws of heredity in the 1800s (Bishop & Waldholz, 1990). Neither is genetics a new field for social workers; for the past 40 years, social workers have been providing genetic services and writing about the effect of genetic diagnoses on families (Schild, 1966; Schultz, 1966; Weiss, 1976). In recent years, the social work profession has taken a more active role in the arena of genetics and genomics. The Human Genome Education Model (HuGEM) project, funded by the National Institutes of Health and co-chaired by two social workers, offered workshops and training programs in genetics for social workers and other disciplines across the country from 1997 to 2001 (Lapham, Kozma, Weiss, Benkendorf, & Wilson, 2000). The National Coalition of Health Professional Education in Genetics (NCHPEG) was formed in 1996 and included two social workers representing both NASW and the Council on Social Work Education on its steering committee. NASW developed *Standards for Integrating Genetics in*

Social Work Practice in 2003 and an online continuing education course titled "Understanding Genetics: The Social Worker's Role" in 2007. What is new is the genetic information now available and its effect on both clients and practitioners. An array of issues related to genetics arises at all levels of social work practice—from clinical practice to family practice to policy making. Clients face both benefits and risks now and in the future as a result of genetic research.

Genetics is an expanding field of practice for social workers. Science and technology are quickly moving toward a time in which most human maladies can be identified and, once identified, treated, cured, or even prevented. Yet this seemingly liberating possibility for knowledge is fraught with potential for harm to the people social workers serve. Issues of informed consent and confidentiality arise, as do those of discrimination, self-determination, and the immediate benefits of genetic test results.

Unfortunately, in most cases, results of genetic tests are not clear-cut. One-to-one gene-disorder relationships are rare. In fact, most disorders are the combination of more than one gene and environmental factors. Predictive or presymptomatic tests can identify individuals at risk of getting a disease, such as certain types of cancer, before the onset of symptoms. However, although a particular gene combination may be identified with certainty, these tests cannot predict whether the disorder will ever be manifested, with the possible exception of identifying a late-onset condition, such as Huntington disease. For example, the genes linked to breast cancer, BRCA1 and BRCA2, can be identified by a predictive test. These genes are found in only 5 percent of the population, and even if the gene is found, 20 percent of individuals with a positive test will never get that type of breast cancer. On the other hand, even though the gene is not present, one in nine women (11 percent) will have breast cancer in their lifetime (Geller et al., 1997). Although genetic testing is becoming an integral part of health care, often the availability of the test is not followed by developed treatments. Advantages of genetic testing, such as facilitating choices about family planning, pre-

ventive lifestyle measures, or increased surveillance must be balanced against the risk of genetic discrimination. The advent of genetic testing, now available for about 1,000 diseases, raises many questions about how an individual's genetic information can be used, and the threat of discrimination hinders both genetic research and clinical practice (Williams, 2006). Direct-to-consumer marketing of genetic testing increases the risk that violations of genetic privacy will follow and eliminates face-to-face counseling (Roche & Annas, 2006).

To make an informed decision to have a genetic test, a client has to have access to current, accurate information regarding benefits and risks of genetic testing to the client and to family members. Information includes limits of protection of confidentiality under federal and state law; strengths and limitations of the test itself; availability of prevention, treatment, and cure; and potential risks of stigmatization, discrimination, and psychological distress, including risk to intrafamily relationships. Social workers may make referrals to other professionals, such as genetic counselors, to maximize the amount of knowledge available to the client for purposes of deciding whether to be tested.

People seek genetic testing usually for one of four reasons: (1) for diagnosis—to determine whether they currently have a particular disorder; (2) for asymptomatic testing—to determine whether they have a particular genetic disorder that will manifest itself in the future; (3) for prenatal planning—to determine whether they carry the gene or genes for a particular disorder that may affect future generations; or (4) for susceptibility testing—to determine whether they are susceptible to a particular disorder that could manifest itself in the future. The results of these tests carry unique psychological implications for individuals and their families (Fanos, 1997; Fanos & Johnson, 1995).

Once educated about whether treatment for a particular disease exists, each person must weigh the options on the basis of individual benefits and risks. In cases in which a treatment or cure is possible, the options seem clear. However, if the test can only establish susceptibility, if there is no treatment or cure, or both, then for some the risks of discrimination and psychological stress may outweigh the benefits. Social workers should ensure that the client has access to all of the information necessary to make the decision to be tested and that the decision reflects the self-determination of the client.

Minors often do not have the opportunity to make decisions for themselves about whether to be tested. The Task Force on Genetic Testing, the advisory committee of the National Human Genetic Research Institute (1997) stated the following: "Genetic testing of children for adult onset disease should not be undertaken unless direct medical benefit will accrue to the child and this benefit would be lost by waiting until the child has reached adulthood" (chapter 1). Many of the issues regarding children are still formative, including those relevant to testing minors for decisions to be made by adoptive parents, adopted children having the right to know their biological parents' genetic makeup, and children conceived by a gamete donor having a right to their donor's genetic test (Fanos, 1997; Wertz, Fanos, & Reilly, 1994). Research is continuing with regard to genetic determinants for psychiatric disorders, addictions, and social behavior, and some progress has been made. However, this raises the question of potential treatment when needed versus labeling and incarceration.

ISSUE STATEMENT

Fear of genetic discrimination could limit participation in research, willingness to have genetic testing, and genetic screening (Hall et al., 2005). At least three possibilities for discrimination arise regarding genetic testing. One is societal: People may be stigmatized or labeled if they are found to be susceptible, for example, to cancer or have a potential disability. Another is financial: An employer could turn down a person for employment because the person may cost the company too much money in insurance costs related to his or her genetic test results, or the person could be denied insurance coverage for the treatment of the disease. A third is access to potentially helpful genetic testing for members of minority

groups and poor people (Hudson, Rothenberg, Andrews, Kahn, & Collins, 1995; Rothenberg et al., 1997, Wertz, 1998). Although many states have laws that provide protections from using genetic information in a discriminatory manner, the need for federal legislation has not been met (Smith, 2004).

Social work practice in the context of genetic testing is guided by the *NASW Code of Ethics* (2000) and the *NASW Standards for Integrating Genetics in Social Work Practice* (2003). Although several ethical standards apply to genetic practice, three are especially relevant: informed consent, confidentiality, and protection from discrimination. Ability to gain knowledge of one's genetic makeup or a family member's genetic makeup carries significant risks. A genetic test may alert people about the prevention, treatment, and cure of some disorders, but currently the ability to test for a genetic disorder often exceeds science's ability to prevent, treat, and cure genetic disease (Taylor-Brown & Johnson, 1998). In most cases, people are tested for diseases for which there is no known treatment or cure. Clients thus face significant psychological risks when learning of traits or disorders as a result of genetic testing (Lapham, Kozma, & Weiss, 1996). They also risk potential discrimination by insurance companies, employers, and society for traits or disorders. In addition, there are financial incentives for private companies to patent and sell genetic tests, even though their use is of limited benefit to some clients. Consequently, the requirement for comprehensive informed consent cannot be overstated.

To protect clients, social workers must know of the limitations of confidentiality to genetic test information. There are enormous financial incentives for insurance companies, employers, the criminal justice system, and other government agencies to have access to people's genetic information, and never before have these groups had the ability to know the potential for future health problems (Andrews, Fullarton, Holtzman, & Motulsky, 1994). Although most states have some protections against the discriminatory use of genetic information by health insurers and employers, the laws differ widely and there is no national standard at present. Current federal and state policies do not protect the use of genetic tests for purposes of discrimination in underwriting and employment (Hudson, 2007). Of particular concern to social workers is the potential for labeling individuals and withholding services for people with mental health, mental retardation, and behavioral disorders such as alcoholism, drug use, and even anger. Testing of minors is also a relevant issue here. The right to confidentiality extends to both the decision to be tested and the decision of who is allowed access to the test results. Ethical Standard 1.07(d), Privacy and Confidentiality, is applicable: "Social workers should inform clients, to the extent possible, about the disclosure of confidential information and the potential consequences, when feasible before the disclosure is made" (NASW, 2000, p. 10). Applied to genetic testing, this means that social workers should inform clients of the potential limitations to confidential test results and the consequences.

Two other significant issues involve competence in providing services alone and in teams and advocacy. If social workers are to provide services related to genetic testing, they must be competent in the content and services they provide, and they must remain competent as the field emerges (Ethical Standards 1.04, Competence, and 1.05, Cultural Competence). In light of the plethora of issues, the decision to be tested must be the client's, without coercion from insurance companies or family members and based on informed consent (Ethical Standard 1.02, Self-Determination). Because of the complexity of providing genetics services, social workers often practice with multidisciplinary teams. Ethical Standard 2.03, Interdisciplinary Collaboration, defines the social worker's role and ethical responsibilities to the client in relation to interdisciplinary collaboration. Finally, for social workers to help protect clients' and society's interest in the benefits of genetic testing, social workers' advocacy role in public policy is essential (Ethical Standard 6.04, Social and Political Action). The role of social workers as advocates in the field of genetics is defined in the *NASW Standards for Integrating Genetics in Social Work Practice*. Standard 9 discusses the need to advocate on behalf of clients to ensure fair social policies and access to quality genetic services (NASW,

2003). As more attention is paid to benefits and risks of stem cell research, reproductive technology, tissue cloning, and gene therapy, social workers will be called on to develop and confront emerging policies related to genetic testing and treatment.

POLICY STATEMENT

The Profession

■ NASW maintains a commitment to continue work to establish the social work profession as a leader in the field of genetics.

■ NASW encourages social workers to educate themselves through formal and informal educational opportunities as well as through reading professional journals and chapter materials regarding current issues in genetics.

■ NASW recommends that social workers become familiar with the *Standards of Integrating Genetics in Social Work Practice*.

■ NASW supports the development of programs, training, and information that provide social workers with current genetics information for use with clients.

State and Federal Policies

■ NASW opposes genetics policies that interfere with an individual's right to choose whether or not to be tested.

■ NASW opposes genetics testing policies that are discriminatory in terms of access to genetics services.

■ NASW opposes policies that coerce clients into reproductive decisions as a result of genetics test results that they would not otherwise make.

■ NASW opposes the use of genetic research to alter populations of people and to remove certain traits deemed by society as "unfit."

■ NASW opposes patenting naturally occurring human genetic structure.

- NASW supports policies that protect the client's ownership of his or her own genetic information and that protect the confidentiality of, access to, and use of an individual's genetic tests.

- NASW supports policies that provide protection for clients from discrimination in employment and by insurance companies or protection from efforts to limit freedom of education or other civil rights on the basis of a genetic test.

- NASW advocates for client-focused public policy for genetic testing, so that all clients may receive the benefits of genetic testing.

- NASW supports policies that protect the rights of minors to be tested only when there is a present and current benefit to the child that would be lost if the test is not done until the child becomes an adult.

- NASW supports responsible stem cell research.

Practice

- NASW encourages interdisciplinary research between social work and other disciplines to determine the effect of genetic testing on clients.

- NASW encourages ongoing collaborative research between social work practitioners and educators to determine the effect of genetic testing on clients.

- NASW supports the development of psychosocial support services for clients with genetic disorders.

- NASW encourages all social workers to take families histories that include medical intergenerational information whenever possible.

- NASW supports client self-determination regarding genetic testing decisions and encourages social workers to educate clients about the benefits and risks of genetic testing and to provide such education in a value-free, nondirective way.

REFERENCES

Andrews, L., Fullarton, J., Holtzman, N., & Motulsky, A. (Eds.). (1994). *Assessing genetic risks: Implications for health and social policy.* Washington, DC: National Academies Press.

Bishop, J., & Waldholz, M. (1990). *Genome.* New York: Simon & Schuster.

Fanos, J. (1997). Developmental tasks of childhood and adolescence: Implications for genetic testing. *American Journal of Medical Genetics, 71,* 22–28.

Fanos, J., & Johnson, J. (1995). Perception of carrier status by cystic fibrosis siblings. *American Journal of Human Genetics, 57,* 431–438.

Geller, G., Botkin, J., Green, M., Press, N., Biesecker, B., Wilfond, B., Grana, G., Daly, M., Schneider, K., & Kahn, M. (1997). Genetic testing for susceptibility to adult-onset cancer: The process and content of informed consent. *JAMA, 277,* 1467–1474.

Guttmacher, A., & Collins, F. S. (2002). Genomic medicine: A primer. *New England Journal of Medicine, 347,* 1512–1513.

Hall, M. A., McEwen, J. E., Barton, J. C., Walker, A. P., Howe, E. G., Reiss, J. A., Power, T. E, Ellis, S. D., Tucker, D. C., Harrison, B. W., McLaren, G. D., Ruggiero, A., & Thomson, E. J. (2005). Concerns in a primary care population about genetic discrimination by insurers. *Genetics in Medicine, 7,* 311–316.

Hudson, K. (2007). Prohibiting genetic discrimination. *New England Journal of Medicine, 356,* 2021–2023.

Hudson, K., Rothenberg, K., Andrews, L., Kahn, M., & Collins, F. (1995, October 20). Genetic discrimination and health insurance: An urgent need for reform [Policy Forum]. *Science, 270,* 391.

Lapham, V., Kozma, C., & Weiss, J. (1996, October 25). Genetic discrimination perspectives of consumers. *Science, 274,* 621–624.

Lapham, E. V., Kozma, C., Weiss, J. O., Benkendorf, J. L., & Wilson, M. A. (2000). The gap between practice and genetics education of health professionals: HuGEM survey results. *Genetics in Medicine, 2,* 226–231.

National Association of Social Workers. (2000). *Code of ethics of the National Association of Social Workers*. Washington, DC: NASW Press.

National Association of Social Workers. (2003). *NASW standards for integrating genetics in social work practice*. Washington, DC: NASW Press.

National Human Genome Research Institute. (1997). *Promoting safe and effective genetic testing in the United States. Executive summary: Testing of children*. Retrieved April 6, 2006, from http://www.genome.gov/1000 2393

Roche, P. A., & Annas, G. J. (2006). DNA testing, banking, and genetic privacy. *New England Journal of Medicine, 355*, 545–546.

Rothenberg, K., Fuller, B. Rothstein, M., Duster, T., Kahn, M., Cunningham, R., Fine, B., Hudson, K., King, M., Murphy, P., Swergold, G., & Collins, F. (1997, March 21). Genetic information and the workplace. *Science, 275*, 1755–1757.

Schild, S. (1966). The challenging opportunity for social workers in genetics. *Social Work, 11*(2), 22–28.

Schultz, A. L. (1966). The impact of genetic disorders. *Social Work, 11*(2), 29–34.

Smith, M.J.W. (2004, October). Genetics and genetic testing: Policy implications. *Inter-sections in practice* (Vol. 3, pp. 11–13). (Available from NASW, Specialty Practice Section, 750 First Street, NE, Suite 700, Washington, DC 20002-4241)

Taylor-Brown, S., & Johnson, A. (1998). *Clinical practice update: Social workers' role in genetic services*. Retrieved June 1, 1998, from http://www.socialworkers.org/practice/health/genetics.asp

Weiss, J. O. (1976). Social work and genetic counseling. *Social Work in Health Care, 2*, 5–12.

Weiss, J. O. (2004, October). What social workers need to know about genetics. In *Intersections in practice* (Vol. 3, pp. 1, 17–20). (Available from NASW, Specialty Practice Section, 750 First Street, NE, Suite 700, Washington, DC 20002-4241)

Wertz, D. (1998). State laws on employer use of genetic information. *The gene letter* [Online Series]. Retrieved June 30, 1998, from http:/www.geneletter.org/0398/state.htm

Wertz, D. C., Fanos, J. H., & Reilly, P. R. (1994). Genetic testing for children and adolescents: Who decides? *JAMA, 272*, 875–881.

Williams, S. (2006, October 24). The impact of genetic discrimination [Issue Briefs]. Available from http://www.dnapolicy.org/policy.issue.php?action=detail&issue brief_id=37

Policy statement approved by the NASW Delegate Assembly, August 2008. This policy statement supersedes the policy statement on Genetics approved by the Delegate Assembly in 1999 and referred by the 2005 Delegate Assembly to the 2008 Delegate Assembly for revision. For further information, contact the National Association of Social Workers, 750 First Street, NE, Suite 700, Washington, DC 20002-4241. Telephone: 202-408-8600 or 800-638-8799; e-mail: press@naswdc.org

Health Care Policy

BACKGROUND

The past decade has seen an increasing awareness of the importance of promoting health throughout the U.S. population, as demonstrated in the goals and objectives set out in the Healthy People 2010 initiative (U.S. Department of Health and Human Services, 2000). Healthy People 2010 has two overarching goals: (1) to increase the quality and years of healthy life and (2) to eliminate health disparities within the U.S. population. Achieving these goals depends on both a health system that reaches all ages and all people in the United States and the integration of personal health care and population-based public health care. The vision of building healthy communities involves broad-based efforts to prevent common health problems by moving beyond health care settings such as hospitals, clinics, and physician's office into neighborhoods, schools, and workplaces within the community. Eliminating disparities in Healthy People 2010 focus areas such as prevention of health problems, tobacco and substance abuse, and injury and violence prevention requires coordination between clinical and public health disciplines, as well as strong community involvement.

Research on health care access has found that barriers to equitable health care for all segments of the population can arise at the public policy, community, organizational, and provider levels (Andersen, 1995; Institute of Medicine, 2002). A key barrier is lack of health care coverage. Individuals without health coverage use fewer health care services and are less healthy than those with coverage (Ayanian, Ginsburg, Schneider, Weismann, & Zaslavsky, 2000; Ku & Broaddus, 2006). The Institute of Medicine (2004) found that uninsured children and adults suffer worse health and die sooner than those with insurance. Delaying or not receiving treatment can lead to more serious illnesses and avoidable health problems. People without insurance are less likely to receive preventive care than those with insurance and more likely to be hospitalized for conditions that could have been avoided. Charitable care and the safety net of community clinics and public hospitals do not fully substitute for health insurance. State and local government ability to finance health care for uninsured people is most limited during economic downturns, when the need is the greatest.

Financing and Delivery of Health Care

Equitable access to health care services is complicated by the fragmented nature of health coverage in the United States. The two major methods of coverage are private insurance, whether employer-based or individually contracted, and public programs, such as Medicare, Medicaid, the State Children's Health Insurance Program, and military coverage. Individual states have provided coverage through Medicaid waiver programs for portions of their population not covered by basic Medicaid. However, these types of coverage leave substantial numbers of the population without health insurance coverage. In 2006, the Census Bureau reported that 59.7 percent of the U.S. population was covered by employment-based insurance, 9.1 percent was covered by directly purchased insurance, 13.6 percent was covered by Medicare, 12.9 percent was covered by Medicaid, and another 3.6 percent by military coverage (DeNavas-Walt, Proctor, & Smith, 2007).

Regardless of the financing, the delivery of health care has moved from fee for service to managed care such as health maintenance organizations and preferred provider organizations. A single payer system has been proposed as a way to provide universal health care in the U.S. However, the trend has been to revise the current multipayer system. The health care systems have become more complex and this causes barriers and challenges for individuals who need to access and navigate their own health care benefits.

ISSUE STATEMENT

In 2006, 47 million people were uninsured, an increase of 2.2 million from the previous year, largely because of a decline in employer-sponsored insurance. Since 2004, census data indicate that employer coverage has declined but public coverage has not increased, resulting in sharp increases in the number of uninsured adults and children. The increase in loss of insurance was highest among Hispanics compared with Asian, African American, and non-Hispanic white people. Uninsurance rates across states varied from 8.5 percent to 24.1 percent as a result of differences in state economies, patterns of employer coverage, the share of families with low incomes, and the scope of state Medicaid programs. Almost 80 percent of the uninsured are citizens (Kaiser Family Foundation, 2007).

Disparities in Health Care

Minority and poor populations are disproportionately uninsured. U.S. families with incomes below 200 percent of the federal poverty level run the highest risk of being uninsured. More than 80 percent of the uninsured people are in working families. Low-wage workers, those in small businesses, service workers, and part-time workers run a greater risk of being uninsured. African Amer-

icans and Hispanics are disproportionately likely to be uninsured compared with Asian and non-Hispanic white Americans (Kaiser Family Foundation, 2007). In addition, even among those with health coverage, racial and ethnic minority groups are more likely than are white people to be enrolled in "lower end" health plans characterized by lower reimbursement levels and stricter limits on covered services, leading to potential differences in provider behavior (Phillips, Mayer, & Aday, 2000).

The lack of insurance coverage for minority and poor populations exacerbates other barriers to access within the health care system that prevent vulnerable individuals from receiving appropriate health care. Stigmatizing practices in health care delivery, a lack of racial and ethnic diversity and cultural competence among health care providers, differences in health literacy between groups, and the failure to include minority populations in medical research produce a lower quality of health services for racial and ethnic minority groups even after adjustment for socioeconomic characteristics and other access-related factors (Institute of Medicine, 2002; Kressin & Petersen, 2001). This lower quality of care may be manifested through a failure to provide recommended care or the substitution of less desirable procedures. These disparities exist across a variety of conditions, including cancer, cardiovascular disease, HIV/AIDS, maternal and child health care, diabetes, and mental illness; they are found in treatment for serious disease and also in routine treatments for common health problems (Allison, Kiefe, Centor, Box, & Farmer, 1996; Barker-Cummings, McClellan, Soucie, & Kirshner, 1995; Cunningham, Mosen, & Morales, 2000; Johnson, Lee, Cook, Rouan, & Goldman, 1993). Preventive measures such as breast, cervical, and prostate cancer screenings are not always provided as recommended to minority individuals (Brownstein, 1992). More research is needed to fully understand how patient race or ethnicity, disease status, sexual orientation, and other characteristics may influence physician decision making and the experience of minority groups during health care encounters.

Trends in Health Care Social Work Services

Every state has deregulated their health care system and lifted regulated rate-setting mandates on hospitals. The subsequent restructuring resulted in a move away from professionally defined structures, such as departments of social work. Social work roles and responsibilities are changing to include case management, discharge planning, and working collaboratively on interdisciplinary teams. However, social workers are also experiencing an increase in workload and a decrease in the psychosocial or clinical component of social work practice (Mizrahi & Berger, 2001).

As part of deregulation, several proposals by the Centers for Medicare & Medicaid Services (which administers Medicaid and Medicare) have been made to lessen the regulations governing providers, including social workers who are reimbursed by Medicare and Medicaid (known as *conditions of participation*). These include actual downgrading or efforts to downgrade the definitions and qualifications for social workers who provide services through Medicare's home health, hospice, skilled nursing facilities, and end-stage renal disease programs. There is now a countervailing trend for increasing social work services in regulatory mandates that is still ahead of the reality of providing qualified health care social work services (Department of Health and Humans Services, 2007; Institute of Medicine, 2008).

POLICY STATEMENT

NASW supports

■ a national health care policy that ensures the right to universal access to a continuum of health and mental health care throughout all stages of the life cycle. The goal of such a policy is to promote wellness, maintain optimal health, prevent illness and disability, treat health conditions, ameliorate the effects of unavoidable incapacities, and provide supportive long-term and end-of-life care. This policy should result in the equitable delivery of services for all people in the United States, regardless of financial status, race, ethnicity, disability, religion, age, gender, sexual orientation, or geographic location.

■ efforts to increase health care coverage to uninsured and underinsured people until universal health and mental health coverage is achieved.

■ an equal right to continuous, high-quality care that is effective, efficient, safe, timely, and patient-centered.

■ ongoing dialogue and research about the best practices to finance health system.

■ efforts to eliminate racial, ethnic, and economic disparities in health service access, provision, utilization, and outcomes.

■ the coordination of NASW chapter efforts to influence state and federal health care policy.

■ policies and practices requiring that mandated medical social work services be provided by qualified social workers in all health care settings.

■ active participation of social workers on public and private health care policy and planning bodies.

■ efforts to provide comprehensive education in health care social work, working with the Council on Social Work Education.

■ policies and practices that promote and protect social work and social workers in all health and mental health settings.

■ improved access, choice, quality, and comprehensiveness of health and mental health services, including parity of mental health care with medical care.

■ policies and practices that ensure that patients receive necessary and appropriate care and guarantee patient rights protections.

■ workforce development to meet the needs of burgeoning and existing special populations (such as geriatrics, pediatrics, people with disabilities, and so forth).

■ active and organized consumer participation in the planning, implementation, evaluation, and maintenance and governance of health and mental health services.

REFERENCES

Allison, J. J., Kiefe, C. I., Centor, R. M., Box, J. B., & Farmer, R. M. (1996). Racial differences in the treatment of elderly Medicare patients with acute myocardial infarction. *Journal of General Internal Medicine, 11*, 736–743.

Andersen, A. M. (1995). Revisiting the behavioral model and access to health care: Does it matter? *Journal of Health and Social Behavior, 36*(1), 1–10.

Ayanian, J. Z., Ginsburg, J. A., Schneider, E. C., Weismann, J. S., & Zaslavsky, A. M. (2000). Unmet health needs of uninsured adults in the United States. *JAMA, 284*, 1260–1269.

Barker-Cummings, C., McClellan, W., Soucie, J. M., & Krishner, J. (1995). Ethnic differences in the use of peritoneal dialysis as initial treatment for end-stage renal disease. *JAMA, 279*, 1858–1862.

Brownstein, J. N. (1992). Breast and cervical cancer in minority populations: A model for using lay health educators. *Journal of Cancer Education, 7*, 321–326.

Cunningham, W. E., Mosen, D. M., & Morales, L. S. (2000). Ethnic and racial differences in long-term survival from hospitalization with HIV infection, *Journal of Health Care for the Poor and Underserved, 11*(2), 163–178.

DeNavas-Walt, C., Proctor, B. D., & Smith, J. (2007). *Income, poverty, and health insurance coverage in the United States: 2006* (Current Population Reports, P60-233). Washington, DC: U.S. Government Printing Office.

Department of Health and Humans Services. (March 2007). *Medicare program; hospital conditions of participation: requirements for approval and re-approval of transplant centers to perform organ transplants; final rule.* Retrieved March 11, 2008, from http://www.cms.hhs.gov/CFCsAndCoPs/downloads/trancenterreg2007.pdf

Institute of Medicine. (2002). *Unequal treatment: Confronting racial and ethnic disparities in health care.* Washington, DC: National Academies Press.

Institute of Medicine. (2004). *Insuring America's health: Principles and recommendations.* Washington, DC: National Academies Press.

Institute of Medicine. (2008). *Committee on Psychosocial Services to Cancer Patients/Families in a Community Setting. Cancer care for the whole patient: Meeting psychosocial health needs.* Washington, DC: National Academies Press.

Johnson, P. A., Lee, T. H., Cook, E. F., Rouan, G. W., & Goldman, L. (1993). Effects of race on the presentation and management of patients with acute chest pain. *Annals of Internal Medicine, 118*, 593–601.

Kaiser Family Foundation. (2007). *The uninsured: A primer.* Retrieved October 20, 2007, from http://www.kff.org/uninsured/upload/7451-03.pdf

Kressin, N. R., & Petersen, L. A. (2001). Racial differences in the use of invasive cardiovascular procedures: Review of the literature and prescription for future research. *Annals of Internal Medicine, 135*, 352–366.

Ku, L., & Broaddus, M. (2006). *Coverage of parents helps children, too.* Retrieved October 20, 2007, from http://www.cbpp.org/10-20-06health.htm

Mizrahi T., & Berger, C. S. (2001). Effect of a changing health care environment on social work leaders: Obstacles and opportunities in hospital social work. *Social Work, 46*, 170–182.

Phillips, K. A., Mayer, M. L., & Aday, L. A. (2000). Barriers to care of racial/ethnic groups under managed care. *Health Affairs, 19*(4), 65–75.

U.S. Department of Health and Human Services. (2000). *Healthy People 2010 midcourse review.* Retrieved October 20, 2007, from http://www.healthypeople.gov/data/midcourse/default.htm#pubs

Policy statement approved by the NASW Delegate Assembly, August 2008. This policy statement supersedes the policy statement on Health Care approved by the Delegate Assembly in August 1999 and referred by the 2005 Delegate Assembly to the 2008 Delegate Assembly for revision. The 1999 policy statement combined with and superseded the policy statement on Health Care Financing approved by the Assembly in 1990, the policy statement on the Role of Social Work in Health Maintenance Organizations approved by the Assembly in 1981 and reconfirmed by the Assembly in 1990, the policy statement on Social Work in Home Health Care approved by the Assembly in 1990 (that policy statement superseded the policy statement on Social Work in Home Health Care approved in 1981), and the policy statement on Social Work Practice in the Health Care Field approved by the Assembly in 1990 (that policy statement superseded the policy statement on Social Work Practice in the Health Care Field approved by the Assembly in 1984). For further information, contact the National Association of Social Workers, 750 First Street, NE, Suite 700, Washington, DC 20002-4241. Telephone: 202-408-8600 or 800-638-8799; e-mail: press@naswdc.org

HIV and AIDS

BACKGROUND

HIV and AIDS are serious global public health concerns with biological social and economic ramifications. Throughout the world, HIV and AIDS disproportionately affects marginalized and disempowered populations throughout the world. Today one in three people infected with HIV do not know they are living with HIV or AIDS (American Association for World Health [AAWH], 2001). The key areas of concern are prevention, testing, treatment, and the effect of HIV on individuals, families, and communities.

In the United States HIV and AIDS prevention and treatment services available today are the result of significant biomedical and social advocacy efforts by many groups over a long period of time (Wheeler, 2007). However, effectiveness of some prevention programs has been hindered by racism, sexism, heterosexism, and homophobia (Ferrales, 2003).

Limited government response resulted in the establishment of many community-based AIDS service organizations (ASO), and many are still in existence today. The design of AIDS prevention strategies largely occurred on a small scale because of limited funding options. Not only has there been a failure to develop effective programs, there has been a governmental and societal hindrance to the development of effective programs, such as needle exchange programs or sex education for young adults.

Testing

Testing is an important component of HIV prevention. Research has shown that people who are aware of being HIV-infected may be more likely to take steps to prevent transmitting the virus to others. In addition, when a positive test result is obtained, appropriate medical treatment can be initiated to slow the disease process (Zúñiga et al., 2007). The availability of testing on an anonymous or confidential basis is thought to maximize the number of people who choose to get tested. To protect confidentiality of HIV status, all states apply confidentiality laws to HIV test results. Throughout the pandemic, there have been many struggles over federal and state policies on imposing mandatory testing or mandatory reporting of test results for certain populations, including prisoners, pregnant women, and child care workers. In addition, a number of states have criminalized the potential transmission of HIV through sex, needle sharing, breast-feeding, or organ donation by a person who is HIV-positive or diagnosed with AIDS (American Civil Liberties Union, 2000). Unlike HIV serostatus, all diagnoses of AIDS must be reported to state public health departments.

The Centers for Disease Control and Prevention (CDC) Revised Recommendations for HIV Testing in Health Care Settings recommends that HIV testing be voluntary and recommended for patients in all health care settings after the patient is notified that testing will be performed unless the patient declines (or opts out of screening) (CDC, 2006). This recommendation replaces the practice of informed, written consent. These recommendations notwithstanding, many people obtain HIV tests without pre- or posttest counseling, especially when they test in a physician's office or in their own homes.

Treatment

The emergence of antiretroviral therapies (ART), and increased access through private insurance, Medicare, and AIDS Drug Assistance Programs (ADAPs), has resulted in a positive, dramatic change for many people living with HIV/AIDS (PLWH/As). For many, living with HIV or AIDS has transitioned to living with a lifelong, chronic illness, often with a renewed sense of hope and challenges (Tomaszewski, 2001). For others, however, the complexities of a strict medication regimen cannot be sustained over extended periods of time, because adherence is not as simple as taking medications. An increasing number of people living with AIDS are unable to tolerate the toxicity and severe side effects that are common with the medications (ART and prophylaxis treatments); others experience unexpected and unexplained health deterioration, or the drugs simply "fail the patient."

Economic issues continue to affect access to care. Few people can afford the drugs unless they are enrolled in a private health insurance plan with prescription drug benefits or state-administered Medicaid or ADAPs for those who are underinsured and uninsured. Although ADAP funding is available nationwide, some state ADAP programs limit coverage of certain medications, resulting in access and adherence problems, or have waitlisted or capped enrollment (National Alliance of State and Territorial AIDS Directors [NASTAD], 2007).

Effects of HIV/AIDS on Individuals, Families, and Communities

HIV/AIDS can have devastating consequences on affected individuals and members of their families and support systems. HIV and AIDS are highly stigmatized conditions (Fullilove & Fullilove, 1999), and people living with HIV/AIDS are likely to experience stigmatization and discrimination (Diaz & Ayala, 2001) in areas such as education, employment, housing, insurance, and health care. Although the Americans with Disabilities Act of 1990 (P.L. 101-336) has provided legal protection for such people, its scope has been reduced by subsequent court rulings. In addition, state laws regarding HIV/AIDS discrimination vary con-

siderably, with some states allowing certain forms of discrimination (Gostin, Feldblum, & Webber, 1999). In too many cases, PLWH/As continue to be denied basic civil and human rights. They may face discrimination in employment, military service, housing, child care, access to health care services, and social and community support programs.

ISSUE STATEMENT

Social workers increasingly encounter HIV/AIDS, either directly or indirectly, regardless of their area of practice, geographic location, or practice setting. Because of its ecological perspective and commitment to social justice, social work is particularly well suited for addressing the complex problems associated with the epidemic, including those experienced by PLWH/As, their friends, and their families. Globally, HIV/AIDS continues to have catastrophic effects on communities, particularly those in resource poor countries where people cannot afford medications or access treatments.

Heterosexism and homophobia contribute to the spread of HIV in other populations as well. For example, HIV prevention and care programs for gay men that include explicit sexual information or language continue to be threatened periodically with loss of federal funding (Erickson, 2001). Also, the increase in HIV infection among African American men who have sex with men (MSM) may be due in part to these attitudes among African American communities and the continuing belief that AIDS is a "gay disease" (Fullilove & Fullilove, 1999). In addition, women may often contract HIV because their male sexual partners cannot admit that they also engage in high-risk sex with other men.

Racism contributes to the spread of HIV. For example, MSM of color might not benefit from prevention resources distributed within predominantly white gay and lesbian communities because of actual and perceived racism within them (Diaz & Ayala, 2001). Also, many of the strategies that have effectively prevented the spread of HIV in the white gay community are not effective among men of color because these programs lack in cultural context. In addition, racism is an important link to disempowerment and the lack of financial and other resources among communities of color, which prevents such communities from responding to the epidemic as effectively as the predominantly white gay community. Sexism contributes to the spread of HIV. For many years, virtually no attention was given to women's risks or needs with respect to prevention or treatment of HIV/AIDS. Consequently, knowledge about the specific ways in which HIV affected women, and the best ways to treat it, lagged far behind such knowledge in relation to men. Women may not feel empowered in relationships to insist that their sexual partners use condoms, or they may engage in sexual practices (such as anal sex) that are considered high-risk for HIV transmission in efforts to prevent pregnancy. Also, women who are impoverished are more likely to prioritize daily survival issues over safer sex (Kline, Kline, & Oken, 1992). Educational, occupational, and economic discrimination may lead some women into high-risk sex work and IV drug use. Finally, the lack of funding for female-specific microbicides is rooted in the historical lack of recognition for women's sexuality, reproductive health of women and girls, and the right to control one's body.

Discrimination against transgender people may lead to at-risk behaviors that increase risk for HIV and other STDs. Factors such as mental health concerns, physical abuse, social isolation, economic marginalization, and unmet transgender-specific healthcare needs can potentially lead to increased HIV risk (Herbst et al., 2008). In addition, the inability to obtain or pay for hormone therapy drives some transgender people to seek hormones illegally and to inject them with shared needles (Clements-Nolle, Marx, Guzman, & Katz, 2001).

Discrimination toward people who use street drugs also contributes to the spread of HIV. Federal policy continues to oppose clean needle exchanges (National Minority AIDS Council, 2002). Although research shows that needle exchange programs can reduce the transmission of HIV, federal policies and laws in many states and localities prevent the access of IV drug users to sterile syringes (Vertefeuille et al., 2000).

Prevention efforts continue to be underfunded and excessively influenced by moralistic politics instead of empirical research. Limitations created by federal and state policies, and funding levels and regulations, hamper the efforts of community-based organizations to reduce HIV/AIDS incidence in populations at high risk.

The CDC Revised Recommendations for HIV Testing in Health Care Settings (2006) recommends that HIV testing be voluntary and recommended for patients in all health care settings after the patient is notified that testing will be performed, unless the patient declines (opt-out screening). These recommendations remove the requirement for pretest and posttest counseling, a critical step in helping individuals prepare for a positive test result and providing the context for exploring behavioral risk regardless of test results. HIV antibody testing also provides an important opportunity for health professionals to elicit important information about partners of the person being tested. Such information can be used to help patients communicate to partners their risk for HIV infection. Partner notification laws, however, limit the confidentiality of testing results in some states.

HIV testing and counseling are important components of a comprehensive public health approach to reducing the devastation of HIV and AIDS, however, services for infected persons, and treatments for comorbidities (for example, other sexually transmitted diseases and substance abuse) must be available to persons after they receive their HIV testing results.

The advent of highly active antiretroviral therapy has greatly changed the quality of life for many people living with HIV/AIDS. Yet there is evidence that the effectiveness of HIV medications may cause some people to believe that HIV is no longer a threat, leading to an increase in risky sexual or drug-taking behaviors (Halkitis & Wilton, 1999). In addition to the high cost of medications, other medical care for people living with HIV/AIDS is exorbitant and unevenly available. Coverage for emergency room visits, hospital stays, diagnostic tests, physicians' fees, and nursing care may be inadequate for many people. Those enrolled in public health plans are unlikely to be able to obtain the same quality of care available to those with private insurance. The quality of HIV/AIDS-related medical care may depend on where people are living, given that specialized HIV/AIDS services are not universally available, especially in rural areas.

POLICY STATEMENT

Across fields of practice, social workers provide services to HIV-positive clients, their families, and clients who are at risk of becoming infected with HIV. Given the high incidence of HIV/AIDS and the rapid spread of the pandemic over the last two decades, the social work profession should take an active stand to mitigate the overwhelming psychological and social effects, including the inequality of access to health and mental health care and the lack of education and prevention in the United States and internationally.

NASW supports the following:

Prevention and Education

■ professional cooperation with existing HIV and AIDS educational, treatment, and research organizations to develop and implement programs that include educational and prevention strategies that meet the needs of all segments of our society.

■ prevention programs designed and implemented to ensure that they are tailored to the specific needs and risks of diverse populations. Programs must be culturally appropriate, taking into account the language, culture, ethnicity, sexual orientation, gender and gender identity, religion, and age of the target population.

■ the implementation of prevention strategies that focuses on harm reduction.

■ evidence-based prevention efforts that target children and adolescents in both public and private school systems and comprehensive sexuality education programs for youths and adults.

■ the establishment of both publicly and privately funded needle exchange programs and efforts to increase the quantity and quality of drug abuse treatment, to reduce HIV incidence among IV drug users.

Social Work Education

■ the education of all social workers so they are knowledgeable about behavioral strategies to prevent the transmission of HIV, including safer sex and harm reduction. Use of assessment tools that assess all clients for HIV risk and that educate clients about ways to reduce their risk.

■ social workers taking responsibility to continuously update their knowledge about all aspects of HIV disease, including new prevention strategies, treatment models, medication regimens, and policies.

■ social work education programs that include curriculums that examine the ramifications of HIV/AIDS from the perspective of the profession's core values. Content should cover the range of health and mental health issues of PLWH/As and their families, support systems, and communities and interventions at all levels of practice.

Testing

■ the education of all practitioners about both the availability and the accessibility aspects of HIV antibody testing and referrals related to living with HIV and AIDS.

■ voluntary and confidential testing which is available on an anonymous basis, and includes prior informed consent.

■ pre- and posttest counseling programs, provided by trained caregivers.

■ rapid testing conducted only by people trained and certified to do so and implemented only when consent is granted by the client or patient.

■ access to competent professional counseling by phone for people using home-testing kits at no additional charge and referral to a formal HIV testing site.

■ informed consent of pregnant and birthing mothers prior to mandatory HIV testing of themselves and their newborn child or children.

■ prior consent for release of clients' test results. Social workers with HIV-positive clients who have not informed sexual or needle-sharing partners about their sero status should use their clinical skills to encourage them to do so.

Service Delivery, Care, and Treatment

■ the right of people living with HIV/AIDS to receive the highest quality care, including those confined in correctional institutions.

■ a comprehensive services delivery system based on a quality case management model that includes access to suitable and affordable housing, mental and health care services, adult and child foster care, home health care, nursing home care, legal services, and transportation.

■ readily available comprehensive bio-psycho-social-spiritual support for people with HIV/AIDS and those affected. Service programs should be culturally competent, linguistically appropriate, and client and patient centered.

■ elimination of the inequities or obstacles in access to medication, clinical trials, and HIV care specialists; or services that ensure psychological, social, cultural, and economic well-being.

■ policies that facilitate access to affordable pharmaceuticals worldwide. Clients should have sufficient supports to help them maintain difficult medication regimens.

■ the right to confidentiality relating to HIV/AIDS status. Clients should be informed of the limits of confidentiality, including the existence of partner notification and record keeping. Social workers should be familiar with applicable state laws, regulations, and federal guidelines.

Political Action and Advocacy

■ continued public and private funding and advocacy for health and mental health care provider programs that address HIV/AIDS and related health and mental health issues, including state, local, national, and international HIV/AIDS prevention and treatment programs;

■ domestic and international initiatives that address structural factors such as poverty, community disinvestment, and interpersonal violence to curtail the HIV/AIDS epidemic;

■ leadership in advocacy efforts at the local, state, and federal levels to improve the quality of life of all PLWH/As and to protect their civil liberties, including maximum access to confidential testing, diagnosis, and treatment;

■ advocacy for adequate funding of research on all aspects of HIV/AIDS, including prevention, clinical interventions, and vaccine development.

Research

■ research, including epidemiological, clinical, and comprehensive, biopsychosocial–spiritual studies, funded at appropriate levels by the federal government.

■ research protocols that address the unique biomedical needs of women, children and adolescents, and the psycho–social–spiritual needs of all people affected by HIV/AIDS.

■ funding for research to accurately assess the effectiveness of primary and secondary prevention and educational strategies, service delivery models, and the effect of related policies. Research protocols must include the bio-psycho-social-spiritual issues of people living with and affected by HIV/AIDS; the unique needs of women, children, and adolescents; and the needs of all people affected by HIV/AIDS.

REFERENCES

American Association for World Health (AAWH). (2001). World AIDS Day resource booklet. *Factsheet on treatment information.* Washington, DC: Author.

American Civil Liberties Union. (2000). *State criminal statutes on HIV transmission.* Washington, DC: Author.

Americans with Disabilities Act of 1990, P.L. 101-336, 104 Stat. 327.

Centers for Disease Control and Prevention. (2006). *Revised recommendations for HIV testing of adults, adolescents, and pregnant women in health-care settings. Morbidity and Mortality Weekly Report, 55* (RR14), 1–17. Retrieved November 13, 2007, from http://www.cdc.gov/hiv/topics/testing/guideline.htm

Clements-Nolle, K., Marx, R., Guzman, R., & Katz, M. (2001). HIV prevalence, risk behaviors, health care use, and mental health status of transgender persons: Implications for public health intervention. *American Journal of Public Health, 91*, 915–921.

Diaz, R. M., & Ayala, G. (2001). *Social discrimination and health: The case of Latino gay men and HIV risk.* New York: Policy Institute of the National Gay and Lesbian Task Force.

Erickson, E. (2001, November 30). Audit calls into question funding for sexually explicit AIDS prevention programs for gays. *New York Blade News,* p. 7.

Ferrales, D. (2003). *The development of HIV/AIDS policy: An international policy analysis.* Austin: University of Texas at Austin, School of Social Work.

Fullilove, M. T., & Fullilove, R. E. (1999). Stigma as an obstacle to AIDS action: The case of the African American community. *American Behavioral Scientist, 42*, 1117–1129.

Gostin, L. O., Feldblum, C., & Webber, D. W. (1999). Disability discrimination in America: HIV/AIDS and other health conditions. *JAMA, 281*, 745–752.

Halkitis, P. N., & Wilton, L. (1999). Beyond complacency: The effects of treatment on HIV transmission. *Focus: A guide to AIDS research and counseling, 14*(5), 1–4.

Herbst, J., Jacobs, E., Finlayson, T., McKleroy,V., Neumann, M., & Crepaz, N. (2008). Estimating HIV prevalence and risk behaviors of transgender persons in the United States: A systematic review. Retrieved June 30, 2008, from http://www.medscape.com/viewarticle/571708

Kline, A., Kline, E., & Oken, E. (1992). Minority women and sexual choice in the age of AIDS. *Social Science and Medicine, 31*, 447–457.

National Alliance of State and Territorial AIDS Directors (NASTAD). (2007). *June 2007 ADAP watch.* Retrieved November 7, 2007, from http://www.nastad.org/Publications/adapwatch.aspx?Area=Publications

National Minority AIDS Council. (2002). *Bush administration HIV/AIDS report card.* Washington, DC: Author.

Tomaszewski, E. (Ed.). (2001). *Mental health and HIV/AIDS: Social work practice issues* [Trainer Manual]. Washington, DC: National Association of Social Workers.

Vertefeuille, J., Marx, M. A., Tun, W., Huettner, S., Strathdee, S. A., & Vlahov, D. (2000). Decline in self-reported high-risk injection-related behaviors among HIV-seropositive participants in the Baltimore needle exchange program. *AIDS and Behavior, 4*, 381–388.

Wheeler, D. P. (2007). HIV and AIDS today: Where is social work going? [National Health Line]. *Health & Social Work, 32*, 155–157.

Zúñiga, M. A., Baldwin, H., Uhler, D., Brennan, J., Olshefsky, A. M., Oliver, E., & Matthews, W. C. (2007). Supporting positive living and sexual health (SPLASH): A clinician and behavioral counselor risk-reduction intervention in a university-based HIV clinic. *AIDS Behavior, 11*, S58–S71.

Policy statement approved by the NASW Delegate Assembly, August 2008. This policy statement supersedes the policy statement on HIV and AIDS approved by the Delegate Assembly in August 2002 and the statement on AIDS/HIV approved by the Assembly in 1987 and reconfirmed by the Delegate Assembly in 1990, 1993, 1996, and 1999. For further information, contact the National Association of Social Workers, 750 First Street, NE, Suite 700, Washington, DC 20002-4241. Telephone: 202-408-8600 or 800-638-8799; e-mail: press@naswdc.org

Homelessness

BACKGROUND

The plight of children, women, men, and families who are without residence continues to befuddle social workers in their recent efforts, reaching back nearly three decades, to both serve people who are homeless and to find policy solutions. Indeed, scholars working in this area have suggested that the persistence of homelessness in the richest country in the world at the beginning of the 21st century is a consequence of massive policy failure (Stretch, 2004). Although sources disagree as to the exact strategies for determining the extent of the problem (Dworsky & Piliavin, 2002), on any given night, point prevalence estimates indicate that as many as 800,000 people are without shelter and are homeless in the United States. Furthermore, period prevalence estimates of the number of people who are homeless over a given year have been as high as 3.5 million (National Alliance to End Homelessness, 1999).

Considerable literature has accumulated in social work and related professions covering a myriad of strategies for both better understanding and better serving people who are homeless (First, Rife, & Toomey, 1999). Homelessness has been addressed broadly as a housing policy problem of largely political and economic origins, and more narrowly it has been discussed as a mental health issue often related to deinstitutionalization. It has been studied as a domestic violence concern, a veterans issue, a disability issue, a welfare reform dilemma, a teenage runway or "throwaway" problem, and a transitional or temporary housing situation. It has been investigated as a migrant and immigrant problem, and a concern for people with communicable diseases. The problem for the consumer of this literature has been to decide exactly how a particular contribution fits into this vast pool of data, dimensions of practice, and policy recommendations. Fortunately, a variety of summary resources has recently become available, both in the traditional published record (see for example, Levinson, 2004) and from more diffuse electronic sources (Table 1).

No matter what the practice, policy or theoretical orientation of practitioners, researchers, and policy advocates, it is routinely recognized that the persistence of homelessness is evidence that poverty and the lack of affordable housing in the United States still persist and are likely to remain critical policy issues for this next century. Homelessness is a complex problem that cannot be ameliorated until the shortcomings of past policies are recognized and the causes and consequences of persistent poverty combined with a lack of affordable housing are a matter of public record. The plight of people who are homeless must be better understood from the perspectives of those who suffer, and it can be seen in

1. people with psychiatric disorders who lack the social networks, health care, and other program supports to live independently in the community (North, Eyrich, Pollio, & Spitznagel, 2004; Wong, 2002);

2. individuals with physical disabilities, whose mobility limitations compound service inaccessibility (Pardeck & Rollinson, 2002);

3. women and children who are victims of domestic violence fleeing abusive domiciles (Bufkin & Bray, 1998; Danis, 2003);

4. asthmatic children in shelters who are not receiving adequate medical attention (Holden, Wade, Mitchell, Ewart, & Islam, 1998; McLean et al., 2004; Stretch & Kreuger, 1990);

Table 1. Sources of Information on Homelessness in the United States

Site	URL
National Coalition for the Homeless	www.nationalhomeless.org
National Alliance to End Homelessness	www.endhomelessness.org
National Law Center on Homelessness & Poverty	www.nlchp.org/
National Health Care for the Homeless Council	www.nhchc.org/
National Coalition for Homeless Veterans	www.nchv.org/
National Low Income Housing Coalition	www.nlihc.org
National Resource Center on Homelessness and Mental Illness	www.nrchmi.samhsa.gov/
HUD Homelessness Website	www.hud.gov/homeless/

5. individuals currently employed either full- or part-time, with too little income to afford adequate housing (Hutchison, Searight, & Stretch, 1986; Johnson, 1999), or food (Biggerstaff, Morris, & Nichols-Casebolt, 2002);

6. single mothers unable to work because of child care responsibilities or the lack of skills to meet the demands of a rapidly changing economy (Fogel, 1997; Johnson & Kreuger, 1989; North & Smith, 1993; Rivera, 2003);

7. runaway youths who are without access to adequate services (Baker, McKay, Lynn, Schlange, & Auville, 2003; Thompson, Safyer, & Pollio, 2001);

8. rural families who have been forced to abandon family farms or small towns due to economic crises in regional, national, and global markets (Goodfellow, 1999);

9. men, many of whom are veterans, who have only the life of the street for economic and social supports (Benda, 2002);

10. people with chemical dependencies, who are unable to maintain a stable residence (Bride & Real, 2003);

11. refugees, asylees, and migrants who have no place to turn to (Kohli, 2003);

12. individuals and families excluded because of their criminal history (Center for Law and Policy, 2003)

13. those displaced by disasters, whether natural, human-made or both (Zakour, 2000).

Past and Prologue

Throughout U.S. history policy on homelessness has tended to mirror societal responses to the conditions of the poorest of the poor population. At the beginning of the 20th century, policy focused on either homeless men or dependent children in need of care. Men were often immigrants and lived in boarding houses during the winter months until seasonal jobs resumed. Those who were classified as transients were given aid through such practices as "passing on," the forerunner to the "bus therapy" of today (Menzies & Webster, 1987). Interventions by the Charity Organization Society, the settlement house movement, and faith-based groups focused on encouraging moral treatment for worthy poor people and work for unworthy poor people.

During the Great Depression, policy focused on families with children standing in soup lines and newly caught in the web of abject poverty. These new poor populations joined together with the transients and older beggars of the 1930s. Policy efforts were numerous and focused on structural causes rather than the personal deficits of poor people.

In the 1950s the focus shifted to skid row, downtown areas populated by single adult men in cheap single room hotels. Policymaking focused on the housing crisis through new construction and loan programs; however, after urban renewal, residents were displaced and when they could no longer pay rent, they turned to the only available temporary services provided by organizations such as the Salvation Army.

From the mid-1960s to the early 1970s, the War on Poverty and the Great Society began to illuminate what had been a private problem and helped the nation to see that it required a public response. Welfare programs provided economic opportunity for poor people, but federal policy initiatives failed to give adequate attention to extreme poverty and the growing crisis in low-income housing (Blasi, 1994). The scope of the crisis in affordable housing was not well recognized or completely understood. It was generally assumed that homelessness had diminished or could be eliminated through other reform efforts.

The Past 25 Years

Beginning in the early 1980s, homelessness exploded as a social issue providing a sharp contrast to the values of opportunity for all. Before the public rediscovery of homelessness in the 1980s (Segal & Baumohl, 1980), it was widely assumed that homelessness was a social problem found either in Third World countries (now more accurately described as "dedeveloped nations," Crotty [2001]), or in an earlier and less enlightened era in the United States. However, by the mid-1980s, rising housing costs, changes in labor markets, deinstitutionalization of people with psychological or developmental disabilities (Bachrach, 1996; Fisk, Rowe, Laub, Calvocoressi, & DeMino, 2000; Segal & Baumohl, 1985), inadequate response to the needs of veterans, and related social forces cried out for greater response in the form of public policy. As this population grew, the estimated number of shelter accommodations rose from 275,000 beds in 1988 to almost 608,000 in 1996 (Blau & Abramovitz, 2004).

As U.S. communities began to face the challenge of increasing numbers of people who were homeless in shelters or living in public spaces in the 1980s, research efforts in social work and related disciplines began to better document the nature and scope of the problem. Charitable organizations such as the Robert Wood Johnson Foundation funded health care for the homeless coalitions around the nation. Fundraising for these new public–private part-

nerships and media focus increased national attention to homelessness as an ever-present problem. Debates about the numbers, characteristics, causes, and consequences revolved around the definition of the problem as a personal crisis in the lives of individuals and families who were unable to afford housing or to benefit from job opportunities in the emerging postindustrial economy. Media coverage focused on the plight of people who were homeless, and old myths about personal responsibility, worthy and unworthy poor people, and work continued to be perpetuated by conservative policy shapers and others as a part of the public debate. Advocacy groups were formed and focused on the need for affordable housing. Faith-based organizations set up community kitchens and other services; missions, public shelters, and local action groups grew in numbers and zeal.

After passage of the Stewart B. McKinney Homeless Assistance Act of 1987 (P.L. 100-77), initiatives and grant-in-aid structures began to emerge. In addition to emergency shelter care, local efforts in service delivery began to include transitional housing, outreach, and case management, particularly to people with mental disabilities who were homeless. However, the crisis of homelessness continued to grow, particularly among people of color (Kreuger & Stretch, 1987), women with children; people living in overcrowded and poorly maintained housing, people with psychiatric disabilities (Segal, Silverman, & Temkin, 1995), and other families who were unable to close the gap between affordable housing and total family income (Stretch & Kreuger, 1989).

Scholars such as Jahiel (1992) have identified a number of reasons for the growth of shelter-based services during the 1980s and 1990s, including their obvious preferable value to sleeping in harsh or dangerous conditions under bridges or in cardboard shacks. Shelters have been seen as providing emergency living quarters for low-income families who suffer from loss of residence as a result of random and unpredictable events such as fires and natural or human-made disasters. Critics have pointed out that shelters also developed partially in response to more predictable political or economic pressures (Kreuger & Stretch, 1995). For example, condemnations that arose from the demolition of low-cost housing because of gentrification also contributed to the growth of shelters. All too often, affordable housing was replaced by shopping malls and entertainment complexes. Shelters offer safe haven for victims of domestic and street violence, and they provide security as stopping off points for transients who otherwise would be stranded. Shelters have been seen as a mechanism for obtaining access to improved housing through residential placement networks and public subsidies such as vouchers for Section 8 assistance. Finally, shelters may provide alternative support for law enforcement officers who respond to requests from sometimes hostile city audiences to arrest people who are homeless. Shelters provide care for people who realistically need a place to live rather than more extreme alternatives such as hospitalization or punitive incarceration. Evaluation studies have assessed both shorter-term outcomes (Glisson, Thyer, & Fischer, 2001) and longer-term effectiveness (Stretch & Kreuger, 1993) of shelter services, with mixed conclusions.

In 1994 the federal government published the first federal plan to break the cycle of homelessness, entitled Priority: Home! (U.S. Department of Housing and Urban Development [HUD], 1994). The plan stated that "for the most part, homelessness relief efforts remain locked in an 'emergency register'" (p. 18). Homelessness is divided into two broad categories of problems: crisis poverty and chronic disability. The plan called for efforts to "reinvent the approach" because the "current approach is plainly not working and must be changed" (HUD, p. 4). A number of factors place people at risk of homelessness, including alcoholism; drug abuse; low education and illiteracy; sexual exploitation; chronic mental disability, developmental disabilities, or mild mental retardation; and HIV/AIDS. Our society systematically and traditionally viewed those labeled as "worthy" poor people in these situations as "unworthy" poor people.

On August 22, 1996, President Clinton ended "welfare as we know it" by signing the Personal Responsibility and Work Opportunity Reconciliation Act. This act ended the existing income maintenance system known as Aid to Families with Dependent Children, the Job Opportunities and Basic Skill Training Program, and Emergency Assistance. These programs were replaced by the new federal block grant program known as Temporary Assistance for Needy Families (TANF). Analysis by Sard (2001) of these changes in welfare spending indicates that some progress has been made in accommodating homelessness in TANF administration. However, consistent cuts in public expenditures for housing have been noted in the fact that HUD's budget has decreased from approximately $85 billion in 1978 to just $29.4 billion in 2002, in inflation-adjusted terms (Blau & Abramovitz, 2004).

Lessons from the Past

After a century of shifting definitions of the problem, political denial, and policy neglect, the core of the homelessness problem clearly is extreme poverty and lack of affordable housing. Policies on homelessness, with only a few exceptions, have emphasized the alleviation of individual need and have underestimated the influence of systemic factors that would be significant in reversing or preventing the underlying conditions of homelessness (Jones & Crook, 2001). Past policy failures (Johnson, Kreuger, & Stretch, 1989) together with reductions in public assistance, housing, health care, economic opportunity, education, nutrition, and affirmative action do not offer much hope that society is capable of learning from either past mistakes or accomplishments.

Too often policy-making processes at the federal, state, and local levels have been limited to local emergency measures, such as various health care for the homeless coalitions that began in the 1980s, rather than addressing the long-term structural and preventive dimensions of severe poverty and homelessness. Recurring themes of individual rather than communal responsibility and labels such as "bag ladies," "panhandlers," "handouts," "hobos," and "transients" have been the focus of public attention. Somewhat analogous to blaming each individual drop of rain for causing one to get wet, rather than responding to the larger weather system (structural foundations), policymakers have tended to rely on compartmentalized solutions. Critics have pointed out that too often people who are homeless are substance dependent, illegal immigrants, or psychiatric outpatients, whose conditions would seem to justify narrower problem-focused solutions. But according to Blau and Abramovitz (2004), when homelessness is seen through the lens of an inadequate supply of affordable housing, who other than people in extreme situations are likely to be left after competition for scarce low-cost housing has run its course?

However, valuable lessons are there to be learned. First, the scope of emergency measures during the Depression Era had a measurable effect in alleviating suffering and extreme poverty. Second, long-term structural measures such as social security and the indexing of these benefits, Medicare, and services to elderly citizens have been effective in protecting some low-income older Americans from the risks of homelessness. Third, the failure to adequately respond to the needs of individuals who were homeless in the 1980s and 1990s led to an even greater crisis in the 21st century. The new chronic homelessness is recognized as a more multifaceted and entrenched problem than in earlier decades, one exacerbated by new at-risk populations, including those with communicable diseases. And far too often, communities have responded with more punitive efforts to criminalize homelessness, rather than to work to prevent it ("Illegal to be homeless," 2003).

ISSUE STATEMENT

After three decades of disjointed efforts to address the crisis of homelessness in the United States, it remains a significant issue. The reasons for this are primarily systemic, and homelessness and poverty are inextricably linked. Being poor means living on the verge of being an accident, an illness, a paycheck, a violent event, or a condemnation away from living on the streets. Being poor means having limited resources to cover the necessities of housing, nutrition, child care, health care, and education. Affordable housing, which absorbs a large proportion of income for people who are poor, is too often abandoned when economic resources are insufficient to meet basic needs. The cost

and difficulty of trying to find low-income housing once a domicile has been lost can present tremendous obstacles, and cogent policies not supported by adequate resources exacerbate this problem. Studies indicate that whereas there were 6.5 million low-cost housing units for 6.2 million renters in 1970, by 1995 there were only 6.1 million low-cost units for 10.5 million renters (Blau & Abramovitz, 2004).

Policy making in relation to the problem of homelessness illustrates a drastic reshaping of the federal social welfare agenda in the United States during the past 25 years, but no single legislative answer has solved or significantly reduced homelessness (Burt, 2000). The dilemma of how to achieve this goal in a time of massive federal budget deficits, narrowly focused policy agendas, and the recent trend toward criminalization of people who are homeless, merits our attention. In keeping with an empowerment perspective, social workers can and must join with people who are homeless to make significant changes in their lives and in the social structures that surround them.

POLICY STATEMENT

To adequately address the problem of both shorter duration and chronic homelessness in the United States, policies should range from strengthening the capacities of the many people who are homeless who are system victims, to changing social and economic conditions that foster extreme poverty and increase the risk of homelessness. NASW advocates the following as supportive and long-term solutions to the problem of homelessness:

1. The goal of an affordable and adequate home and a suitable living environment for everyone in the United States (Housing Act of 1949) should be vigorously pursued (HUD, 2004).

2. Social workers need to be actively involved side by side with people who are homeless (see, for example, Busch-Geertsema, 2002) in national, state, and local coalitions to network with and create advocacy groups; to identify significant problems in localities and create linkages to address and alleviate these

problems; and to encourage state and local communities to use mainstream programs in building a continuum of care that integrates housing, income maintenance, and supportive services.

3. Federal, state, and local housing subsidies should be available as an entitlement for all households with new emphasis on advocacy for McKinney-Vento Homeless Assistance Programs; HOPWA (Housing Opportunities for Persons with AIDS); Section 811 for Persons with Disabilities; and programs for the Education for Homeless Children and Youth (EHCY).

4. The complex patchwork of housing assistance programs (Mulroy & Ewalt, 1996) for low-income families should be organized into a more efficient and coordinated system that targets very poor people and households at highest risk of homelessness.

5. Efforts to encourage state and local communities to use mainstream programs in building a continuum of care that integrates housing, income maintenance, and supportive services should be strengthened.

6. Education, job training, and related support services should be expanded to serve as key elements in the prevention of homelessness. Studies show that only 11 percent of people who are homeless receive SSI benefits, whereas almost 40 percent experience mental health problems, and 46 percent report having at least one chronic health condition (Interagency Council on Homelessness, 1999).

7. Homeless children need to be identified as a special population. They require proper nutrition, adequate clothing and hygiene, and continuous, appropriate education (including a space to study). Services to homeless children should be provided with an overall goal of stopping the cycle of homelessness.

8. Treatment and supportive services for special populations should be expanded and be focused on innovative approaches.

9. Federal, state, and local proposals to cut expenditures and restructure social welfare programs should be studied to determine their impact on homelessness.

10. The lack of bipartisan effort and consensus on policy goals to end mass homelessness continues and is a major stumbling block to federal leadership in agenda setting and appropriations. Political action strategies are needed to reverse this trend.

11. Support for a living wage to help prevent homelessness should be widespread.

Short-term program and policy changes are needed to cope with fiscal crises and the disjointed community system of emergency services for individuals and families who are homeless. Fiscal and programmatic recommendations contained in new ventures, including the development of a National Housing Trust Fund and the Bringing America Home Act (www. bringingamericahome.org), merit our attention. State and local communities as well as nonprofit and public agencies should rethink the place of shelter care within a larger continuum of services for special at-risk populations faced with crisis poverty and homelessness. Shelters have become an institutional response, but their presence should not be viewed as a policy solution (Kreuger, Stretch, Hodges, & Word, 2002). Social workers should be actively involved, in the company of people who are homeless, in the development of continuity of services for children and families. School social workers should work as advocates for the needs of children who are members of families who are homeless (Markward & Biros, 2001).

Excessive rent and other housing burdens on poor people in urban and rural communities must be alleviated. State and local resources, including voluntary efforts, must be mobilized to develop creative solutions and stopgap measures for protecting people who are precariously housed. Misconceptions about the causes of homelessness and severe poverty have contributed to the lack of public support for efforts to alleviate homelessness. Social workers in partnership with elected officials and others must lead the fight in the interests of people who are homeless. The impact of homelessness on women and people of color in U.S. society is an important national issue and for the social work profession that must be translated into more effective efforts at coalition building.

Although more demands are being placed on shelters and emergency services to help people who are homeless, mainstream programs for housing assistance, public assistance, and health care have been drastically cut to fund other political priorities. As programs are paralyzed by too many funding reductions, poverty becomes more severe and homelessness emerges as a growing and chronic reality for the poorest population.

After three decades of disjointed efforts to address the crisis of homelessness in the United States, gaps in federal and state policies and inadequate funding are producing more homeless individuals. The impact of homelessness necessitates immediate action on the part of the social work profession.

REFERENCES

Bachrach, L. (1996). Deinstitutionalization: Promises, problems and prospects. In J. Knudsen & G. Thornicrotf (Eds.), *Mental health service evaluation* (pp. 3–18). New York: Cambridge University Press.

Baker, A., McKay, M., Lynn, C., Schlange, H., & Auville, A. (2003). Recidivism at a shelter for adolescents: First-time versus repeat runaways. *Social Work Research, 27,* 84–93.

Benda, B. (2002). Test of a structural equation model of comorbidity among homeless and domiciled military veterans. *Journal of Social Service Research, 29*(1), 1–35.

Biggerstaff, M., Morris, P., & Nichols-Casebolt, A. (2002). Living on the edge: Examination of people attending food pantries and soup kitchens. *Social Work, 47,* 267–277.

Blasi, G. (1994). Ideological and political barriers to understanding homelessness. *American Behavioral Scientist, 37,* 563–586.

Blau, J., & Abramovitz, M. (2004). *The dynamics of social welfare policy.* New York: Oxford University Press.

Bride, B., & Real, E. (2003). Project Assist: A modified therapeutic community for homeless women living with HIV/AIDS and chemical dependency. *Health & Social Work, 28,* 166–168.

The Bringing America Home Act, H.R. 2897, 108 Cong., 1st Sess. (2004). Retrieved July 20, 2004, from www.bringingamericahome.org

Bufkin, J., & Bray, J. (1998). Domestic violence, criminal justice responses and homelessness: Finding the connection and addressing the problem. *Journal of Social Distress and the Homeless, 7,* 227–240.

Burt, M. (2000). *What will it take to end homelessness?* Retrieved April 11, 2004, from www.urban.org/url.cfm?ID=310305

Busch-Geertsema, V. (2002). When homeless people are allowed to decide by themselves. Rehousing homeless people in Germany. *European Journal of Social Work, 5*(1), 5–19.

Center for Law and Policy. (2003). *One strike and you're out: Low-income families barred from housing because of criminal records* (fact sheet). Washington, DC: Center for Law and Policy.

Crotty, R. (2001). *When histories collide: The development and impact of individualistic capitalism.* Walnut Creek, CA: AltaMira Press.

Danis, F. (2003). The criminalization of domestic violence: What social workers need to know. *Social Work, 48,* 237–246.

Dworsky, A., & Piliavin, I. (2002). Homeless spell exits and returns: Substantive and methodological elaborations on recent studies. *Social Service Review, 74,* 193–213.

First, R. J., Rife, J. C., & Toomey, B. G. (1999). Homeless families. In R. L. Edwards (Ed.-in-Chief), *Encyclopedia of social work* (19th ed., Vol. 2, pp. 1330–1337). Washington, DC: NASW Press.

Fisk, D., Rowe, M., Laub, D., Calvocoressi, L., & DeMino, K. (2000). Homeless persons with mental illness and their families: Emerging issues from clinical work. *Families in Society, 81,* 351–359.

Fogel, S. (1997). Moving along: An exploratory study of homeless women with children using a transitional housing program. *Journal of Sociology and Social Welfare, 24*(3), 113–133.

Glisson, G., Thyer, B., & Fischer, R. (2001). Serving the homeless: Evaluating the effectiveness of homeless shelter services. *Journal of Sociology and Social Welfare, 27*(4), 89–97.

Goodfellow, M. (1999). Rural homeless shelters: A comparative analysis. *Journal of Social Distress and the Homeless, 8*(1), 21–35.

Holden, B., Wade, S. L., Mitchell, H., Ewart, C., & Islam, S. (1998). Caretaker expectations and the management of pediatric asthma in the inner city: A scale development study. *Social Work Research, 22,* 51–59.

Hutchison, W. J., Searight, P., & Stretch, J. J. (1986). Multidimensional networking: A response to the needs of homeless families. *Social Work, 31,* 427–430.

Illegal to be homeless: The criminalization of homelessness in the United States. (2003, August). Washington, DC: National Coalition for the Homeless and the National Law Center for Homelessness and Poverty.

Interagency Council on Homelessness. (1999). *Homelessness: Programs and the people they serve—Findings from a National Survey of Homeless Providers and Clients.* Washington, DC: National Law Center for Homelessness and Poverty.

Jahiel, R. (Ed.). (1992). *Homelessness: A prevention-oriented approach.* Baltimore: Johns Hopkins University Press.

Johnson, A. (1999). Working and nonworking women: Onset of homelessness within the context of their lives. *Affilia, 14,* 42–77.

Johnson, A., & Kreuger, L. (1989). Toward a better understanding of homeless women [Briefly Stated]. *Social Work, 34,* 537–540.

Johnson, A., Kreuger, L., & Stretch. J. (1989). A court-ordered consent decree for the homeless: Process, conflict and control. *Journal of Sociology and Social Welfare, 16*(3), 29–42.

Jones, J., & Crook, W. (2001). Homelessness and the social welfare system: The Briar Patch revisited? *Journal of Family Social Work, 6*(3), 35–51.

Kohli, R. (2003). Child and family social work with asylum seekers and refugees. *Child and Family Social Work, 8*(3).

Kreuger, L., & Stretch, J. (1987, June 7). *Ethnic differentials among homeless families seeking shelter.* Paper presented at the Minority Issues Conference of the National Association of Social Workers, Washington, DC.

Kreuger, L., & Stretch, J. (1995, April). *Preventing homelessness: An empirical study of why shelter services don't work.* Paper presented at the annual meeting of the Society for Social Work and Research, Washington, DC.

Kreuger, L., Stretch, J., Hodges, J., & Word, D. (2002). Are governmental policies solving the problem of homelessness? In C. Breme, H. Karger, & J. Midgley (Eds.), *Controversial issues in social policy* (Vol. 2, pp. 57–64). Boston: Allyn & Bacon.

Levinson, D. (2004). *Encyclopedia of homelessness* (Vol. 2). Newbury Park, CA: Sage Publications.

Markward, M., & Biros, E. (2001). McKinney revisited: Implications for school social work. *Children & Schools, 23,* 182–187.

McLean, D., Bowen, S., Drezner, K., Rowe, R., Sherman, P., Schroeder, S., Redlener, K., & Redlener, I. (2004). Undercounting and undertreating the underserved. *Archives of Pediatric Adolescent Medicine, 158,* 244–249.

Menzies, R., & Webster, C. (1987). Where they go and what they do: The longitudinal careers of forensic patients in the medicolegal complex. *Canadian Journal of Criminology, 29,* 275–293.

Mulroy, E. A., & Ewalt, P. L. (1996). Affordable housing: A basic need and a social issue [Editorial]. *Social Work, 41,* 245–249.

National Alliance to End Homelessness. (1999). *Homelessness: Programs and the people they serve—Findings of the National Survey of Homeless Assistance Providers and Clients* [Highlights]. Washington, DC: Interagency Council on the Homeless.

North, C., Eyrich, K., Pollio, D., & Spitznagel, E. (2004). Are rates of psychiatric disorders in the homeless population changing? *American Journal of Public Health, 94,* 103–108.

North, C. S., & Smith, E. M. (1993). A comparison of homeless men and women: Different populations, different needs. *Community Mental Health Journal, 29,* 423–431.

Pardeck, J., & Rollinson, P. (2002). An exploration of violence among homeless women with emotional disabilities: Implications for practice and policy. *Journal of Social Work in Disability and Rehabilitation, 1*(4), 63–73.

Rivera, L. (2003). Changing women: An ethnographic study of homeless mothers and popular education. *Journal of Sociology and Social Welfare, 30*(2), 31–51.

Sard, B. (2001, April). *Using TANF funds for housing-related benefits to prevent homeless-*

ness. Center on Budget and Policy Priorities. Retrieved April 23, 2004, from http://www.cbpp.org/4-3-01TANF.htm

Segal, S. P., & Baumohl, J. (1980). Engaging the disengaged: Proposals on madness and vagrancy. *Social Work*, 25, 358–365.

Segal, S., & Baumohl, J. (1985). The community living room. *Social Casework*, 66, 111–116.

Segal, S., Silverman, C., & Temkin, T. (1995). Characteristics and service use of long-term members of self-help agencies for mental health clients. *Psychiatric Services*, 46, 269–274.

Stewart B. McKinley Homeless Assistance Act of 1987, P.L. 100-77, 101 Stat. 482.

Stretch, J. (2004, April). Opening plenary. Missouri Association for Social Welfare Conference on Homelessness, Jefferson City.

Stretch, J., & Kreuger, L. (1989, August). *Impact study on outcomes of services to homeless families: The results of a public-private partnership.* Paper presented to the National Association for Welfare Research and Statistics, Kalispell, MT.

Stretch, J., & Kreuger, L. (1990). The twig is bent: An empirical study of homeless children. *Health Progress*, 1(2), 14–19.

Stretch, J., & Kreuger, L. (1993). Five-year cohort study of homeless families: A joint policy research venture. *Journal of Sociology and Social Welfare*, 19(1), 73–88.

Thompson, S. J., Safyer, A. W., & Pollio., D. E. (2001). Differences and predictors of family reunification among subgroups of runaway youths using shelter services. *Social Work Research*, 25, 163–172.

U.S. Department of Housing and Urban Development. (1994). *Priority home!* (HUD-1454-CPD[1]). Washington, DC: Author.

Wong, Y. I. (2002). Tracking change in psychological distress among homeless adults: An examination of the effect of housing status. *Health & Social Work*, 27, 262–273.

Zakour, M. J. (Ed.). (2000). *Disaster and traumatic stress research and intervention: Tulane studies in social welfare.* New Orleans: Tulane University Press.

Policy statement approved by the NASW Delegate Assembly, August 2005. This policy supersedes the policy statement on Homelessness approved by the Delegate Assembly in 1996 and referred by the 2002 Delegate Assembly to the 2005 Delegate Assembly for revision. For further information, contact the National Association of Social Workers, 750 First Street, NE, Suite 700, Washington, DC 20002-4241. Telephone: 202-408-8600 or 800-638-8799; e-mail: press@naswdc.org

Hospice Care

BACKGROUND

The dramatic attention accorded hospice care in the United States in recent decades reflects not only the variety of interests and needs identified by the U.S. General Accounting Office in its 1979 landmark report to Congress, but also recent shifts in health care trends and practice approaches (Bern-Klug, 2010; Csikai & Chaitin, 2006; Gwyther et al., 2005). Multiple factors related to death and dying have given impetus to the hospice movement: the effects of life-limiting illness on individuals and families, medical advances that enable life to be prolonged in the face of degenerative diseases and impending death, renewed attention to home care and other alternatives to hospitalization, scarcity of financial resources, a growing emphasis on holistic health, and increasing recognition of the rights of people who are dying.

Individual and societal attitudes toward death and dying have historically affected the treatment of people who are dying and their loved ones. The 20th century marked a shift in outlook toward people who were dying and a growing focus on self-determination as integral to end-of-life care. In the early part of the 20th century, families and physicians routinely cared for dying people at home. However, care progressively shifted to hospitals, where diagnosis, treatment, and cure were emphasized and the focus was on the physical condition of the dying person. Social and emotional needs were largely ignored. The trauma of dying and death for both the individual and his or her family was inadequately understood and poorly handled. It was not until Dame Cicely Saunders—who trained as a nurse, social worker, and physician (Clark, n.d.)—traveled to the United States in the early 1960s that people began to explore the idea of specialized care for people with life-limiting illness. Recognition of the need for expert knowledge and skills grew. Gradually, the institutionally oriented, medically dominated health care system began to recognize and respond to that need.

Hospice was the first statutorily created, home-based, per diem–reimbursed approach to end-of-life care (Feeg & Elebiary, 2005). The term "hospice" derives from a Latin term for way station or inn, a place of succor and rest for weary travelers in the middle ages (Hospice Foundation of America, n.d.). Since the 1960s, hospice has come to be understood as an interdisciplinary model of care designed to maximize the quality of life—physical, psychosocial, and spiritual—of people with life-limiting illness and their families (*family* is defined by each individual and may include spouses or domestic partners, children, family of origin, extended family, and other people who provide support at the end of life). Hospice care is palliative in nature; rather than seeking to cure disease or prolong life, it alleviates pain and other symptoms so that the dying person and loved ones experience dignity at the end of life. Each individual's and family's goals, strengths, and needs guide hospice care. In accordance with that philosophy, care may be provided in the individual's home or other setting of choice and generally remains available when individuals transition to other settings.

Hospice programs serve all people at the end of life (usually defined as a life expectancy of no more than six months) regardless of the etiology of their disease or their age, religion, race, or illness. People age 65 years and older remain the primary users of hospice services, however (National Hospice and Palliative Care Organization [NHPCO], 2010).

Since the 1982 advent of the Medicare hospice benefit, federal law has stipulated that Medicare-certified hospice programs include an interdisciplinary team consisting of at least one physician, one registered nurse, one social worker, and one pastoral or other counselor (Social Security Act, Title XVIII, § 1861dd, 2008). The law also requires Medicare-certified hospice programs to provide a number of other services, including (but not limited to) spiritual support, home health aide services, volunteer services, and bereavement support. A Medicaid Hospice Benefit also exists, though—as of 2011—it was not yet available in every state (NHPCO, n.d.). Furthermore, the federal benefit package for veterans includes hospice care (U.S. Department of Veterans Affairs, 2010). Private insurance coverage for hospice care varies widely. Similarly, hospice programs that are not Medicare or Medicaid certified may not offer all the services required by federal law and regulation for Medicare and Medicaid certified hospices.

The 21st century has given rise to a broader discussion about hospice as only one model of end-of-life care (U.S. Government Accountability Office, 2007). In recent decades, advances in medical technologies have changed both the trajectory of illness and how people die. Consequently, people with life-threatening illnesses may have a limited understanding of end-of-life care that promotes *palliation* (symptom relief and biopsychosocial and spiritual support) rather than cure. The debate about hospice as a hallmark of optimal care at the end of life can be understood through both its congruence with social work values and its relevance to individuals and families affected by life-limiting illness.

The NHPCO has noted shifting trends in the use of hospice services in the United States. For example, the proportion of deaths served by hospice is increasing; in other words, more people are using hospice services at the end of their lives (NHPCO, 2010). In part, this is because hospice programs care for people with an increasingly broad range of illnesses. In the 1970s, most people using hospice care had cancer diagnoses. By 2010, however, more than half the people admitted to hospice had other illnesses, such as heart disease, dementia, or lung disease (NHPCO, 2010).

During the early 1980s and thereafter, many hospice programs were pioneers in caring for people with HIV/AIDS. Thanks to highly active antiretroviral therapies, the rise of HIV specialty care in high-prevalence areas, and Ryan White government funding (which increased access to care and treatment for people living with HIV/AIDS), HIV is now regarded as a chronic illness. In fact, less than 1 percent of people admitted to hospice in 2009 had a primary diagnosis of HIV/AIDS (NHPCO, 2010). Nonetheless, HIV/AIDS is a primary cause of death in some communities (Centers for Disease Control and Prevention, 2010), and it is unclear how many people with end-stage AIDS die without hospice care. Consequently, hospice remains an integral service for individuals and families affected by HIV/AIDS.

Just as use of hospice care has changed over time, so too has the provision of hospice care. The number of hospice programs grew 37 percent between 2004 and 2010 (NHPCO, 2009b, 2010). An increasing number of hospice programs are freestanding, independent programs, with fewer hospital-based systems of hospice care (NHPCO, 2010). Furthermore, the number of for-profit hospice programs—which formerly composed a small minority of hospices—has steadily increased since 2002, now constituting almost half of all hospice programs (NHPCO, 2010).

Given the high national priority on controlling health care costs, the cost-effectiveness of hospice services is noteworthy. Between 1999 and 2009, the average cost of one day of hospice care for Medicare beneficiaries remained exponentially lower than one day of either hospital inpatient or skilled-nursing facility care (Hospice Association of America, 2010). Research has documented that use of hospice services decreased Medicare costs by an average of $2,309 per beneficiary (Taylor, Osterman, Van Houtven, Tulsky, & Steinhauser, 2007). Even more compelling than its cost-effectiveness, however, is that hospice provides high-quality, compassionate care to individuals and families affected by life-limiting illness.

ISSUE STATEMENT
Reimbursement for Hospice Services

Reimbursement rates for hospice care have not kept up with the increasing cost of providing care. Rapidly increasing pharmaceutical costs contribute to this problem. Many hospice programs provide care regardless of clients' ability to pay, adding to the financial struggle. Moreover, multiple cuts in Medicare hospice reimbursement rates are scheduled through fiscal year 2019 (NHPCO, 2011), which is estimated to put almost 90 percent of hospice programs—many of them in rural areas—at risk of operating with negative margins (Moran Company, 2011). Amid these financial stressors, services at particular risk of being diminished include social work, pastoral counseling, and bereavement support.

Length of Service

Although the number of individuals receiving hospice care continues to increase and the median length of service remained fairly steady between 2006 and 2009, a growing percentage of hospice participants are dying or discharged within two weeks or even seven days of hospice enrollment (NHPCO, 2009b, 2010). Several factors may contribute to this trend: the increasing availability of advanced medical technologies designed to cure illness or prolong life, societal denial of dying and death, and a lack of education about hospice care among consumers and health care providers. Whatever the cause, individuals and families who use hospice for two weeks or less may not benefit from the full range of services and support available in hospice care (Medicare Payment Advisory Commission, 2010; NHPCO, 2009a). At the same time, fewer people are using hospice for more than 180 days, or one Medicare benefit period (NHPCO, 2009b, 2010). Political pressure to reduce health care spending, scrutiny of hospice reimbursement rates, and provider fears about lack of reimbursement for long lengths of service may contribute to this trend.

Underserved Populations

People of color are underrepresented among hospice participants in the United States. Studies have identified several barriers to hospice access and use by African Americans: distrust of the health care system, low awareness regarding hospice services, economic factors, lack of racial diversity among health care staff, and differences in African American and European American values regarding medical care and spiritual beliefs (Bullock, 2011; Bullock, McGraw, Blank, & Bradley, 2005; Crawley, 2005). Barriers to hospice care for Hispanics/Latinos may include geographic distance, immigration status, lack of health care coverage, low English proficiency and literacy, concerns about discrimination, and cultural values held within families (Smith, Sudore, & Perez-Stable, 2009). People who are uninsured or underinsured may constitute another population that is underserved by hospice. Although the Patient Protection and Affordable Care Act (P.L. 111-148) is expected to reduce the number of uninsured people in the United States, a significant portion of the population remains at risk of not accessing hospice care.

Support of Self-Determination

The cornerstone of hospice is the right to self-determination—each individual's right to choose the types of care and services she or he wants (or does not want) at the end of life. This philosophy mirrors that of the NASW (2008) *Code of Ethics*, which directs social workers to promote the right of clients to self-determination. Hospice programs encourage advance care planning—which can include, but is not limited to, appointment of a health care agent, completion of a living will, and enactment of physician orders for life-sustaining treatment—to ensure that each person's goals for end-of-life care are honored.

Caregiver Availability

Many people enrolled in hospice require a full-time caregiver to assist them when hospice staff is not present in the home. Geographic mobility, changes in family composition, employment obligations, and financial limitations present difficulties to some families in providing round-the-clock care. Expanded funding for and access to home- and community-based services are essential to enable hospice participants to die in their setting of choice.

Professional Training

With its strengths-based, person-in-environment perspective; collaborative approach; and expertise in psychosocial assessment and intervention, the social work profession has long played a critical role in supporting individuals and families in dealing with the biopsychosocial complexities of dying, death, and grief. The 1983 Medicare Conditions of Participation (CoP) mandated that hospices hire individuals with bachelor's or master's degrees in social work to provide social work services (as cited in Social Work Policy Institute, 2010). In contrast, the 2008 CoP (Medicare and Medicaid Programs: Hospice Conditions of Participation) weakened social work personnel qualifications to include people with bachelor's degrees in psychology, sociology, or other fields related to social work, provided such individuals also have one year of social work experience in a health care setting. Furthermore, the CoP now require all bachelor's-level employees—with the exception of BSWs who were already employed by hospices before the CoP took effect in late 2008—to be supervised by an MSW.

These changes have presented grave challenges to the social work profession, limiting job opportunities for both BSWs and MSWs. Even more important, social service workers who lack social work education and training may also lack the competence to provide the psychosocial care individuals and families need and deserve at the end of life (Social Work Policy Institute, 2010).

POLICY STATEMENT

NASW supports policies, regulations, legislation, and programs that promote access to high-quality hospice care, based on the following principles:

■ Promotion of optimal physical, mental, emotional, social, spiritual, and functional quality of life for individuals facing life-limiting illness

■ Promotion of self-determination in end-of-life choices; individualized, person-centered hospice care; and death with dignity

■ Availability of hospice services to individuals and families affected by life-limiting illness, without respect to race, ethnicity, or national origin; migration background and documentation status; biological sex, gender identity, and gender expression; sexual orientation and marital or partnership status; spiritual, religious, and political belief or affiliation; mental and cognitive ability; and ability to pay

■ Promotion of cultural and linguistic competence in the delivery of hospice services

■ Elimination of disparities in access to and utilization of hospice care

■ Enhanced consumer and professional education about hospice care as an alternative to life-prolonging medical interventions

■ Availability of hospice care across health, home, and community-based settings and expansion of social service programs to enable people to die in their setting of choice

■ Comprehensive utilization of hospice services, including early access to hospice care and access to multiple hospice benefit periods for individuals with life-limiting conditions

■ Preservation and integrity of hospice benefits for Medicare and Medicaid beneficiaries and veterans

■ Expansion of governmental and private funding for hospice services

■ Restoration and maintenance of sustainable reimbursement rates for hospice programs

■ Expansion of specialized pediatric hospice care programs

■ Recognition of and respect for each individual's unique definition of *family* and for the role and expertise of family caregivers in hospice care

■ Continued development and funding of hospice services that support family caregivers, including inpatient respite services

■ Availability of bereavement services (including services tailored for children, adolescents, and adults) for at least one year following the death of a hospice patient

■ Participation of individuals with life-limiting illness and their families in the design, implementation, and evaluation of programs, policies, and research related to hospice care

■ Promotion of interdisciplinary collaboration as essential to hospice care delivery and professional sustainability

■ Expansion of medical and psychosocial treatments to ease pain and other symptoms associated with life-limiting illness and dying

■ Preservation of social work and other psychosocial support services (including, but not limited to, spiritual support, bereavement support, and volunteer services) within hospice care programs and reimbursement structures

■ Professional social work education and training (specifically, a bachelor's, master's, or doctoral degree in social work) as a prerequisite for hospice social work

■ Continued development and promotion of social work content and practicum opportunities in hospice and end-of-life care at the bachelor's, master's, and doctoral levels

■ Expansion and promotion of continuing education, competencies, frameworks, and credentialing in hospice social work.

REFERENCES

Bern-Klug, M. (2010). *Transforming palliative care in nursing homes: The social work role.* New York: Columbia University Press.

Bullock, K. (2011). The influence of culture on end-of-life decision making. *Journal of Social Work in End-of-Life & Palliative Care, 7,* 83–98.

Bullock, K., McGraw, S. A., Blank, K., & Bradley, E. H. (2005). What matters to older African Americans facing end-of-life decisions? A focus group study. *Journal of Social Work in End-of-Life & Palliative Care, 1,* 3–19.

Centers for Disease Control and Prevention. (2010). *HIV in the United States: An overview.* Retrieved from http://www.cdc.gov/hiv/topics/surveillance/resources/fact sheets/pdf/us_overview.pdf

Clark, D. (n.d.). *Dame Cicely biography.* Retrieved from http://www.cicelysaundersfoundation.org/about-us/dame-cicely-biography

Crawley, L. M. (2005). Racial, cultural, and ethnic factors influencing end-of-life care. *Journal of Palliative Medicine, 8*(Suppl. 1), S58–S69.

Csikai, E., & Chaitin, E. (2006). *Ethics in end-of-life decisions of social work practice.* Chicago: Lyceum Books.

Feeg, V. D., & Elebiary, H. (2005). Exploratory study of end-of-life issues: Barriers to palliative care and advance directives. *American Journal of Hospice & Palliative Medicine, 22,* 119–124.

Gwyther, L. P., Altilio, T., Blacker, S., Christ, G., Csikai, E. L., Hooyman, N., et al. (2005). Social work competencies in palliative and end-of-life care. *Journal of Social Work in End-of-Life & Palliative Care, 1,* 87–120.

Hospice Association of America. (2010). *Hospice facts & statistics.* Retrieved from http://www.nahc.org/facts/HospiceStats10.pdf

Hospice Foundation of America. (n.d.). *What is hospice?* Retrieved from http://www.hospicefoundation.org/pages/page.asp?page_id=47055

Medicare and Medicaid Programs: Hospice Conditions of Participation, 42 C.F.R. § 418 (2008).

Medicare Payment Advisory Commission. (2010). Hospice (Chapter 2E). In *Report to the Congress: Medicare payment policy.* Retrieved from http://www.medpac.gov/document_TOC.cfm?id=602

Moran Company. (2011, March 4). *Summary of profit margin analysis for rural and urban hospices, 2009–2019* [Memorandum to the National Hospice and Palliative Care Organization]. Retrieved from http://www.nhpco.org/files/public/public_policy/Profit-Margin-Summary.pdf

National Association of Social Workers. (2008). *Code of ethics of the National Association of Social Workers.* Retrieved from http://www.socialworkers.org/pubs/code

National Hospice and Palliative Care Organization. (2009a). *NHPCO cites concern over growing short length of service in new facts and* figures on hospice care in the U.S. [Press release]. Retrieved from http://www.nhpco.org/i4a/pages/index.cfm?pageID=6120

National Hospice and Palliative Care Organization. (2009b). *NHPCO facts and figures: Hospice care in America* (2009 edition). Retrieved from http://www.nhpco.org/files/public/Statistics_Research/NHPCO_facts_and_figures.pdf

National Hospice and Palliative Care Organization. (2010). *NHPCO facts and figures: Hospice care in America* (2010 edition). Retrieved from http://www.nhpco.org/files/public/Statistics_Research/Hospice_Facts_Figures_Oct-2010.pdf

National Hospice and Palliative Care Organization. (2011). *Board education template on hospice rates.* Retrieved from http://www.nhpco.org/i4a/pages/Index.cfm?pageID=5579

National Hospice and Palliative Care Organization. (n.d.). *Does my loved one have hospice benefits?* Retrieved from http://www.caringinfo.org/i4a/pages/index.cfm?pageid=3298

Patient Protection and Affordable Care Act, P.L. 111-148, 119–124 Stat. 1025 (2010).

Smith, A. K., Sudore, R. L., & Perez-Stable, E. J. (2009). Palliative care for Latino patients and their families. *JAMA, 301,* 1047–1057.

Social Work Policy Institute. (2010). *Hospice social work: Linking policy, practice, and research. A report from the March 25, 2010 symposium.* Retrieved from http://www.socialworkpolicy.org/wp-content/uploads/2010/09/SWPIHospice-Report-FINAL.pdf

Social Security Act, Title XVIII, § 1861dd (2008).

Taylor, D. H., Jr., Osterman, J., Van Houtven, C. H., Tulsky, J. A., & Steinhauser, K. (2007). What length of hospice use maximizes reduction in medical expenditures near death in the U.S. Medicare program? *Social Science & Medicine, 5,* 1466–1478.

U.S. Department of Veterans Affairs. (2010). *Federal benefits for veterans, dependents and survivors: 2010 edition.* Retrieved from http://www.va.gov/opa/publications/benefits_book.asp

U.S. General Accounting Office. (1979). *Hospice care—A growing concept in the United States. Report to the Congress by the Comptroller General of the United States* (HRD-79-50). Retrieved from http://archive.gao.gov/f0302/108711.pdf

U.S. Government Accountability Office. (2007). *End-of-life care: Key components in four states. Report to the Honorable Ron Wyden, U.S. Senate* (GAO-08-66). Retrieved from http://www.gao.gov/new.items/d0866.pdf

NASW Members with Primary Responsibility for Revision of This Policy

First Draft Revision:

Karen Bullock (CT)

Policy Panelists:

Sherry Ostrout (CT)
Penny Schwartz (NYC)
Charlene Turner (GA)
Roberta Hanus (WI)
Sarah Schulz (OK)
Bobbie Moodie (AZ)
Esther Langston (NV)

Policy statement approved by the NASW Delegate Assembly, August 2011. This policy statement supersedes the policy statement on Hospice Care approved by the Delegate Assembly in 2002. For further information, contact the National Association of Social Workers, 750 First Street, NE, Suite 700, Washington, DC 20002-4241. Telephone: 202-408-8600; e-mail: press@naswdc.org.

Housing

BACKGROUND

Housing and community environments that meet the universal need for shelter, privacy, and positive social relationships are essential for stable family life, personal development, and health and safety. Deteriorating housing results in a four-way loss to (1) the health and welfare of the population, (2) property values and economic vitality, (3) community morale, and (4) housing stock. Thus, decisions regarding housing cannot be left wholly to the interplay of the supply and demand of the marketplace. The private real estate market cannot be expected to meet the needs of many groups adequately, particularly those with low incomes. Policy choices, along with market forces, drive housing and community development, and it is up to public policy, primarily at the federal level, to take the lead in developing affordable housing within livable communities (Dreier, Mollenkopf, & Swanstrom, 2001). Historically, federal housing policy development has occurred within the context of varying political agendas and reflects wide differences in ideology that shift with political forces. These philosophical variations have resulted in waves of disconnected housing policies at best (Marcuse & Keating, 2006). National policy has evolved slowly, in a patchwork manner, leaving many gaps and discrepancies that often work to the disadvantage of those who most need assistance and protection. In 1949, Congress set forth a national housing goal—not a policy—of "a decent home and suitable living environment for every American family." For 30 years, progress toward this goal was measured in the statistics of dollars allocated, units planned, and housing starts rather than in the quality of housing or improvements in communities. Still missing is a national policy on housing that ensures equity within regional, economic, and racial differences and that emanates not from concepts of property values but from concepts of human need and healthy communities (Dreier et al., 2001).

National policy has eroded financing and the efficacy of the housing programs that emerged as well as related fair housing and financial enforcement (for example, anti-redlining) (Bryson, 2006). Housing should be a national priority and a right as a basic human need. Housing affects other services and clearly illustrates the concept of mutuality. Foster care, shelters, mental and physical health, and education are affected by housing programs. When decent housing is available, the benefit in financial and human terms is well documented.

The foremost federal policy, the Fair Housing Act (P.L. 90-284), was passed by Congress in 1968 (Title VIII of the Civil Rights Act of 1968). The U.S. Department of Housing and Urban Development (HUD) is the agency with statutory authority to administer and enforce the act, through HUD's Office of Fair Housing and Equal Opportunity (FHEO). FHEO administers federal laws and establishes national policies that ensure all Americans have equal access to the housing of their choice and prohibits discrimination in housing on the basis of race, color, religion, sex, national origin, age, disability, and familial status.

ISSUE STATEMENT

Adequate, affordable housing is a basic right that is critical for the flourishing of individuals and families (Keyes, 2007).

Housing Supply and Affordability

In the 1949 Housing Act, Congress declared "a decent home and a suitable living environment for every American family" to be our national housing goal. Today, little more than half a century later, upwards of 100 million people in the United States live in housing that is physically inadequate, unsafe, overcrowded, or unaffordable (Bratt, Stone, & Hartman, 2006). The supply of suitable and affordable housing to meet the diverse needs of individuals and families in the United States continues to be inadequate (Atlas & Drier, 2007). Housing has become more expensive and has not kept up with wages, and the key to housing affordability is that it must meet the needs of the people who provide the services everyone depends on—teachers, police officers, nurses, firefighters, and other public servants, as well as millions of Americans in the services and retail industries (National Association of Home Builders, 2008).

The real cause of affordable housing shortages is a shortage of overall housing caused by government restriction on supply (Powell & Stringham, 2004). Inclusionary zoning has two major effects on local economies; The costs in the housing market drain wealth out of the local economy and the zoning leads to losses in state and local government revenue (Powell & Stringham, 2004).

Populations with Special Needs

For those who are poor, there are few housing options that meet their needs. With the expansion of community-based support services, many older adults and people with disabilities remain in their communities and are able to live reasonably independently. Many youths whose needs are not met by the child welfare system, and an increasing number of individuals who are returning to the community from institutions, have few or no suitable housing options. These groups, along with others with special housing needs—immigrants, people in "isolated and depressed communities," and large families who have lost their homes and are deprived socially and economically—now are swelling the ranks of the home-less population. A greater awareness of populations with special needs and the crisis of homelessness are forcing new approaches to housing (Segal, 1995).

Relationship of Housing and Social Services

The interface of housing and supportive services has received increased attention, which is in part due to federal emphasis on the Housing First model and is beginning to be understood by planners and policymakers (U.S. Department of Housing and Urban Development 2008). However, the allocation of resources that could tie together the delivery of housing with the delivery of services remains minimal and haphazard. Supportive services must be an integral part of a housing program (Cohen, Phillips, Mendez, & Ordonez, 2000).

Housing and the Community Infrastructure

In the past there was little integrated planning for housing and the community infrastructure of facilities and services, such as transportation, schools, public services, and civic and neighborhood organizations. Such planning must be encouraged now and in the future. The current cost of energy, which circumscribes the area within which families can live suitably and meet their economic and social needs, demands the integrated planning of housing and urban or rural development (Naparstek & Dooley, 1997).

Housing and Employment

The cause-and-effect relationship between housing and jobs has been acknowledged belatedly in the aftermath of the suburban expansion of the past three decades, resulting in urban sprawl and economic segregation. Lack of federal policy and conservative market forces have caused distinct disparities in job opportunities and income levels (Dreier et al., 2001); low- and moderate-income families have been unable to take advantage of employment opportunities because without an adequate income they are unable to meet the cost of housing in areas where new job opportunities have become available. Unemployed people, particularly, are locked in, unable to meet their housing costs and unable to relocate.

POLICY STATEMENT

NASW supports

■ the right of all individuals and families to have affordable housing that meets their basic needs for shelter and provides for a rewarding community life.

■ a national housing policy that views housing as a social utility and a basic human need for all income groups that includes programs of government-sponsored or nonprofit rental housing, cooperative housing, the rehabilitation of housing, and homeownership.

■ housing policies that ensure the availability of accessible housing that meets diverse needs and that are distributed geographically.

■ the adoption of policies at all levels of government that stimulate and support the rehabilitation, construction, and maintenance of rented and owned dwellings to meet the needs of all populations.

■ programs to revitalize deteriorated public housing structured in such a manner as to ensure that there is no reduction in the number of affordable housing units in the community and that maximum possible efforts are undertaken to preserve existing neighborhoods and communities.

■ federal, state, and local government programs, including housing trust funds and land trusts, which provide the maximum possible funding to assist with the production, operation, and maintenance of affordable housing, through both homeownership and rental assistance programs. Such funding should be available to both public and private, including commercial and nonprofit, organizations.

■ varied public and private sector efforts to meet the housing needs of Americans with low incomes. These options should include shared or accessory housing, single-room occupancy housing and congregate-living arrangements.

■ citizen participation and community involvement in development of housing policy.

■ inclusive decision making about housing planning and operation by consumers, tenants, landlords, real estate and building interests, and community groups.

■ new housing development or existing housing rehabilitation linked to employment opportunities and community services.

■ enforcement of fair housing and financing laws.

■ enforcement and expansion of the Community Reinforcement Act of 1977.

■ the recognition of housing programs as integral to national economic growth and stability.

■ income tax codes, property assessments, and monetary policies that address the needs of low-income people.

■ further research to determine the most effective types of housing assistance programs and best practices in housing policy and program implementation.

REFERENCES

Atlas, J., & Drier, P. (2007). *The conservative origins of the sub-prime mortgage crisis.* Retrieved April 4, 2008, from http://www .prospect.org/cs/articles?article=the_ conservative_origins_of_the_subprime_ mortgage_crisis

Bratt, R. G., Stone, M. E., & Hartman, C. (Eds.). (2006). *A right to housing: Foundation for a new social agenda.* Philadelphia: Temple University Press.

Bryson, D. (2006). *The role of the courts and a right to housing.* In M. E. Stone & C. Hartman (Eds.), *A right to housing: Foundation for a new social agenda* (pp. 193–212). Philadelphia: Temple University Press.

Burt, M., Aron, L. Y., Lee, E., & Valente, J. (2001). *Helping America's homeless: Emergency shelter or affordable housing.* Washington, DC: Urban Institute Press.

Cohen, C. S., Phillips, M. H., Mendez, M. A., & Ordonez, R. (2000). Sustaining strong communities in a world of devolution: Empowerment-based social services in housing settings. In R. Perez-Koenig & B. D. Rock (Eds.), *Social work in the era of devolution: Toward a just practice.* New York: Fordham University Press.

Community Reinvestment Act of 1977, P.L. 95-128, Title VIII, Oct. 12, 1977, 91 Stat. 1147.

Dreier, P., Mollenkopf, J., & Swanstrom. T. (2001). *Place matters: Metropolitics for the twenty-first century.* Lawrence: University Press of Kansas.

Fair Housing Act, P.L. 90-284, Title VIII, Apr. 11, 1968, 82 Stat. 81.

Housing Act of 1949, 63 Stat. 413.

Keyes, C. (2007). Towards a mentally flourishing society: mental health promotion, not cure [Guest Editorial]. *Journal of Public Mental Health.* Available at http://www.pavpub.com/pavpub/journals/JPMH/showjournal.asp?Title=Journal+of+Public+Mental+Health

Marcuse, P., & Keating, W. D. (2006). The permanent housing crisis: The failures of conservatism and the limitations of liberalism. In M. E. Stone & C. Hartman (Eds.), *A right to housing: Foundation for a new social agenda* (pp. 139–162). Philadelphia: Temple University Press.

Naparstek, A. J., & Dooley, D. (1997). Community building. In R. L. Edwards (Ed.-in-Chief), *Encyclopedia of social work* (19th ed., 1997 Suppl., pp. 77–89). Washington, DC: NASW Press.

National Association of Home Builders. (2008). *Regulatory barriers to housing affordability.* Retrieved from http://www.nahb.org/page.aspx/category/sectionID=1016

Powell, B., & Stringham, E. (2004). *Housing supply and affordability: Do affordable housing mandates work?* Retrieved from http://www.reasons.org/ps318polsum.pdf

Segal, S. P. (1995). Deinstitutionalization. In R. L. Edwards (Ed.-in-Chief), *Encyclopedia of social work* (19th ed., Vol. 1, pp. 704–712). Washington, DC: NASW Press.

U.S. Department of Housing and Urban Development. (2008). Washington, DC: Author.

Policy statement approved by the NASW Delegate Assembly, August 2008. This policy statement supersedes the policy statement on Housing approved by the Delegate Assembly in 1999 and referred by the 2005 Delegate Assembly to the 2008 Delegate Assembly for revision. The 1999 Assembly also voted to not combine this policy statement with the policy statement on Homelessness. This policy statement also supersedes the policy statement on Housing approved by the Delegate Assembly in 1984 and reconfirmed by the Assembly in 1990. For further information, contact the National Association of Social Workers, 750 First Street, NE, Suite 700, Washington, DC 20002-4241. Telephone: 202-408-8600 or 800-638-8799; e-mail: press@naswdc.org

Immigrants and Refugees

BACKGROUND

International migration is substantially changing the demographic profile of many communities across the United States. Immigration increased rapidly in the 1990s, when more than 13 million people moved to the United States. Throughout our national history, policies on immigrants and refugees have been influenced by the competing values and themes of humanitarian response, human rights, national security, and economics. At different points, one or more of these themes have gained ascendancy and brought about changes in immigration laws, affecting the lives of those within and outside U.S. borders.

Current Migration Statistics

As of 2006, approximately 31 million residents in the United States were foreign-born. Of these, most were either lawful permanent residents or naturalized citizens (60 percent); refugees and asylees made up another 7 percent; however, an estimated 29 percent were undocumented (U.S. Census Bureau, 2006). Representation by foreign-born individuals in the U.S. population—11 percent in 2006—is expected to increase.

The demographic picture shows that noncitizen households are far more likely to contain children (55 percent compared with 35 percent) and that 85 percent of immigrant families with children are so-called "mixed-status" families—a situation whereby members of the same family may include various combinations of citizens and noncitizens; for example, undocumented parents, citizen children, and undocumented siblings (Fix & Zimmerman, 1999). These families present distinct challenges for

human services providers in the face of recent federal, state, and local legislation that has sought to restrict substantially the legal and social rights of immigrants ("Problems facing immigrant families," 2002). Many immigrant populations remain invisible or marginally recognized.

History of Immigration Policy in the United States

In 1965 the Immigration and Nationality Act Amendments (P.L. 89-236) provided a sweeping change in immigration law. The national origins system was abolished and a new set of priorities for admitting immigrants was adopted. Priority was given to family members of U.S. citizens and permanent residents and to those with skills needed by the U.S. labor market (Drachman, 1995). Race and country of origin were removed as criteria for admission, which provided the foundation for an increase in immigration. Laws passed in the 1980s and 1990s largely reflected concern with the economic impact of immigration and led to the Immigrant Reform and Control Act of 1986 (P.L. 99-603), that introduced employer sanctions for hiring undocumented individuals. However, the act also provided for legalization of several million undocumented immigrants.

Of special concern to social workers in the child welfare system and those who work with victims of family violence, the Immigration Act of 1990 (P.L. 101-649) allowed eligible immigrant children and youths in long-term foster care to adjust their immigration status and become permanent residents. This immigration relief process is known as Special Immigrant

Juvenile Status and must be undertaken before the child turns 21 or ages out of care. Likewise, the Violence Against Women Act of 1990 allows certain eligible immigrant spouses and their children who are victims of domestic violence to apply for legal permanent residency.

Although legislative changes at the federal level in 1996 instituted immigration status as a category determining eligibility for certain types of benefits and services, the Illegal Immigration Reform and Immigrant Responsibility Act of 1996 (P.L. 104-208) and the Antiterrorism and Effective Death Penalty Act of 1996 (P.L. 104-132) both contain deportation provisions that can have devastating effects nationally and internationally at both the family and societal levels. These laws redefined deportable offenses and retroactively reclassified minor offenses as felonies. Deportable offenses include convictions for domestic violence and child abuse or neglect (Medina, 1997). The laws also removed the right to judicial review in many deportation cases and authorized "expedited removal" of people who arrive at the U.S. border without proper documents.

The terrorist attacks of September 11, 2001, ignited national security concerns, and the Uniting and Strengthening America by Providing Appropriate Tools Required to Intercept and Obstruct Terrorism Act of 2001 (USA PATRIOT ACT) (P.L. 107-56) allowed the government to "impose guilt by association on immigrants; authorize the indefinite lock up of aliens on mere suspicion . . . and the use of secret evidence in immigration proceedings that aliens cannot confront or rebut" (p. 620). Young Muslim men and those who appeared to be of Middle Eastern origin were particularly targeted with special registration requirements. The Immigration and Naturalization Service was reorganized as the U.S. Citizenship and Immigration Services under the newly created Department of Homeland Security (Snyder, May, Zulcic, & Gabbard, 2005).

Admissions of Refugees and Asylum Seekers

A *refugee* is defined as a person with a "well-founded fear of persecution on the basis of race, religion, nationality, membership in a particular social group or political opinion" (Capps, 2006). Historically, U.S. policy has favored involvement in conflicts in Europe over those in Africa and other developing parts of the world. Refugee policy reflects both important humanitarian efforts and foreign policy priorities. This has been particularly played out in the contrast between treatment of Cubans and Haitians; whereas the former have been welcomed as refugees, Haitians, labeled "economic refugees," are not official refugees under U.S. law, are interdicted at sea, and quickly returned to Haiti (Newland & Grieco, 2004).

In March 2002 the Division of Unaccompanied Children's Services (DUCS) program was brought under the auspices of the Office of Refugee Resettlement. The Unaccompanied Refugee Minors Program provides specialized resettlement and foster care services for refugee minors who either have no living relative overseas or whose family situation breaks down soon after arrival. The DUCS program may also receive minors under the age of 18 who enter the United States alone and are undocumented, are victims of trafficking, or fit some other categories of eligibility for reclassification as refugee minors.

Immigrant Policy

Immigrant policy consists of laws, regulations, and programs that affect immigrants' access to health and human services (Siegel & Kappaz, 2002). Since the passage of the Personal Responsibility and Work Opportunity Reconciliation Act of 1996 (P.L. 104-193), only a categorical group of qualified immigrants has been entitled to receive assistance from federal benefits programs. Furthermore, all new legal immigrants were barred, for a period of five years, from accessing federal means-tested benefits, including TANF, Medicaid, and the Child Health Insurance Program, while states were given the option to define to what extent they wished to pursue these categorical distinctions for immigrants to access state aid programs. The unintended consequence of this policy is that many immigrant families have not accessed services to which they are legally entitled (Fix & Zimmerman, 1999). As a result, immigrant families and their children are disproportionately poor and lack adequate health care, food, and shelter (Capps et al., 2002).

ISSUE STATEMENT

"Migration is an important, complex and multi-dimensional issue" (Global Migration Group, 2006). The Universal Declaration of Human Rights (United Nations, 1948) and subsequent treaties recognize the right to leave one's country as a basic human right when stating, "Everyone has the right to leave any country, including his own, and to return to his country." However, there is no corresponding principle of a right to enter. Isbister (1996) referred to immigration policies as "inherently immoral" because they require choices between competing goods or competing evils and often involve the protection of privilege. Deciding whether priority should be given to refugees fleeing oppression, reuniting a long-separated immigrant family, or whether amnesty should be granted to undocumented people rather than increasing entry for those who obey the laws are moral and ethical policy dilemmas.

Often, social workers' capacity to assist clients is constrained by immigration policies, especially policies that limit family visitation and family reunification. Immigration policies intervene in social work practice when family offenses become grounds for deportation and thereby impede willingness to report. The impact on families can be devastating; marital partners have been separated and parents have been deported, leaving their U.S.-born citizen children without support or parental supervision (Segal & Mayadas, 2005). Furthermore, although security concerns dictate restrictive procedures for entry into this country, the challenge is to determine the reasonable balance between security and human rights. The United Nations Declaration on the Human Rights of Individuals Who Are Not Nationals of the Country in which They Live (Office of the United Nations High Commissioner for Human Rights, 1985), specifically

states that aliens shall enjoy "the right to life and security of person; no alien shall be subjected to arbitrary arrest or detention" (Article 5:1). Procedures to protect security should be within the guidelines of basic human rights protections.

Throughout U.S. history, conflicting views about the economic effects of immigration have shaped immigration policies. One view defines immigrants as a drain on the economy and users of public benefits who take needed jobs away from Americans; the opposing view sees immigrants as enhancing the economy through payment of taxes, investment in small businesses, and reinvigoration of the rapidly aging U.S. native-born population (Capps, Passel, Perez-Lopez, & Fix, 2003). Although studies show a positive economic effect, and some credit relatively high immigration with strengthening the U.S. economic position vis-à-vis western Europe and Japan ("U.S. Immigration," 2001), Isbister (1996) cautioned that high rates of immigration may harm low-income Americans.

Current debates about possible guest worker programs or provisions to legalize segments of the undocumented population raise additional policy questions. Policies must be developed that address the situation of long-term resident undocumented families, many of whom have U.S. citizen children. At the same time precautions must be taken to address the fairness implications for those who "played by the rules" and entered the United States through legal channels. Special care must be taken in the design of guest worker programs not to tie immigrants to potentially abusive or exploitative employers.

Social workers will undoubtedly encounter immigrants and their children in schools, health and mental health care, child welfare, and other human service-related settings (Earner & Rivera, 2005; Matthews & Ewen, 2006; Reardon-Anderson, Capps, & Fix, 2002). Social workers not only need to be aware of the special needs of this population, but also need to understand the dynamics of migration and the interface between immigration and immigrant policies (Drachman, 1995; Padilla, 1997).

POLICY STATEMENT

NASW supports federal, state, and local policies and procedures that

■ provide support for victims of the African slave trade, internally displaced people, and victims of trafficking.

■ expand research on the dynamics of migration, especially as it relates to social work practice.

■ fairly and equally apply the definition of migration to all populations, including those caught up by armed conflict.

■ uphold and support equity and human rights for immigrants and refugees, while at the same time protecting national security.

■ promote social justice and avoid racism and discrimination or profiling on the basis of race, religion, country of origin, gender, sexual orientation, or other grounds.

■ ensure due process for all individuals, including immigrants.

■ guarantee the human service and education needs of all children are met regardless of their or their parent's legal status.

■ promote training of social workers and other human services providers on the effect of immigration status on access to human services.

■ ensure access to language-appropriate services in the form of interpreters, translated documents, and other resources as needed.

■ provide for the alleviation of economic and political conditions that force people to flee their homes and ensure that victims of human conflict in the poorest, least strategically important countries of the world do not continue to be ignored.

■ replace the current patchwork of immigration laws and procedures with a fair, equitable, and comprehensive national plan.

■ support restoration of federal and state entitlements for legal immigrants.

■ ensure access to emergency health and mental health care for all immigrants.

■ ensure appropriate immigration-related services to undocumented minors in foster care and, if they are eligible, adjustment of their status before they leave foster care.

■ ensure access to higher education for the children of immigrants.

■ provide for efforts to remove penalties on the children of undocumented immigrants for their parents' actions.

■ promote knowledge of immigration and immigrant issues as a factor in culturally competent service provision.

■ protect all immigrants from family violence, including the undocumented, with provisions to protect women from gender-specific forms of violence.

■ ensure fair treatment and due process in accordance with international human rights for all asylum seekers.

■ remove offenses of domestic violence, child abuse and neglect, and child abandonment from the category of automatically deportable offenses, to ensure reporting, protection, and safeguarding the long-term family preservation rights of children.

■ continue guarantee of citizenship for those born in the United States.

■ ensure and affirm English-access legislation.

■ oppose mandatory reporting of immigration status by health, mental health, social service, education, police, and other public service providers.

■ ensure procedures and policies do not target immigrants solely on the basis of country of origin, religion, or race.

■ support the human rights of day laborers.

■ support immunity from deportation for those who report substantiated incidents of severe employment abuses or criminal activities.

■ support humanitarian measures to protect victims of and enforcement to prevent human trafficking.

■ eliminate backlogs and lengthy delays in processing of immigration status and related applications.

- provide reasonable student, temporary, and transit visa regulations and processes that welcome and encourage international intellectual exchange.

- provide adequate U.S. contributions to refugee assistance globally through support of the UNHCR budget and other aid programs.

- provide fair refugee admissions policies and priorities that respond to human emergencies, including review of policies such as interdiction at sea that violate international human rights law.

- provide refugee resettlement programs adequate in length and substance to include English language training, trauma and mental health counseling, and job readiness and placement.

- restore the right to judicial review and modification of expedited removal provisions, especially for those claiming the right to asylum.

Although daunting, the challenges of working toward fair and just immigration and refugee policies are appropriate for the profession of social work. Social workers must promote greater education and awareness of the dynamics of global migration and of the impact of U.S. and other countries' immigration and foreign policies on human well-being and world peace and stability.

REFERENCES

Antiterrorism and Effective Death Penalty Act of 1996, P.L. 104-132, 110 Stat. 1214.

Capps, R. (2006, July 24–26). *The demography of U.S. children of immigrants.* Presentation at Migration and Child Welfare Roundtable, American Humane Association; Loyola University, Chicago.

Capps, R., Ku, L., Fix, M. E., Furgiuele, C., Passel, J. S., Ramchand, R., McNiven, S., & Perez-Lopez, D. (2002). *How are immigrants faring after welfare reform? Preliminary evidence from Los Angeles and New York City—Final report.* Washington, DC: Urban Institute.

Capps, R., Passel, J. S., Perez-Lopez, D., & Fix, M. (2003). *The new neighbors: A user's guide to data on immigrants in U.S. communities.* Washington, DC: Urban Institute.

Drachman, D. (1995). Immigration statuses and their influence on service provision, access, and use. *Social Work, 40,* 188–197.

Earner, I., & Rivera, H. (2005). Special edition: Immigrants and refugees in child welfare. *Journal of Child Welfare, 84,* 531–536.

Fix, M. E., & Zimmerman, W. (1999). *All under one roof: Mixed-status families in an era of reform.* Washington, DC: Urban Institute.

Global Migration Group. (2006). *Global migration group.* Retrieved September 18, 2007, from http://www.un.int/iom/GMGFlyer.pdf

Illegal Immigration Reform and Immigrant Responsibility Act of 1996, P.L. 104-208, 110 Stat. 3009-546.

Immigration Act of 1990, P.L. 101-649, 104 Stat. 4978.

Immigration and Nationality Act Amendments, P.L. 89-236, 79 Stat. 911 to 920 (1965).

Immigration Reform and Control Act of 1986, P.L. 99-603, 100 Stat. 3359.

Isbister, J. (1996). *The immigration debate: Remaking America.* West Hartford, CT: Kumarian Press.

Matthews, H., & Ewen, D. (2006). *Reaching all children? Understanding early care and education participation among immigrant families.* Washington, DC: Center for Law and Social Policy.

Medina, I. (1997). Judicial review—A nice thing? Article III, separation of powers and the Illegal Immigration Reform and Immigrant Responsibility Act of 1996. *Connecticut Law Review, 29,* 1525–1563.

Newland, K., & Grieco, E. (2004). *Haiti and the United States: Connected by crisis. A migration information source spotlight.* Retrieved September 18, 2007, from http://www.migrationpolicy.org/news/2004_04_05.php

Office of the United Nations High Commissioner for Human Rights. (1985). *Declaration on the human rights of individuals who are not nationals of the country in which they live.* Retrieved September 18, 2007, from http://www.ohchr.org/english/law/individual.htm

Padilla, Y. C. (1997). Immigrant policy: Issues for social work practice. *Social Work, 42,* 595–606.

Personal Responsibility and Work Opportunity Reconciliation Act of 1996, P.L. 104-193, 110 Stat. 2105.

Problems facing immigrant families in the child welfare system: Hearing before the New York State Assembly Standing Committee on Children and Families and New York State Assembly Legislative Task Force on New Americans (2002, July 11). (Testimony of Jennifer Baum and Barrie L. Goldstein, The Legal Aid Society).

Reardon-Anderson, J., Capps, R., & Fix, M. E. (2002). *The health and well-being of children in immigrant families.* Washington, DC: Urban Institute.

Segal, U. A., & Mayadas, N. S. (2005). Assessment of issues facing immigrant and refugee families. *Journal of Child Welfare, 84,* 563–583.

Siegel, W. L., & Kappaz, C. M. (2002). *Strengthening Illinois' immigrant policy: Improving health and human services for immigrants and refugees* [Project report of the Health and Human Services Immigrant Policy Working Group]. Chicago: Illinois Immigrant Policy.

Snyder, C. S., May, J. D., Zulcic, N. H., & Gabbard, W. J. (2005). Social work with Bosnian Muslim refugee children and families: A review of the literature. *Child Welfare, 74,* 607–630.

United Nations. (1948). *Universal declaration of human rights.* Retrieved September 18, 2007, from http://www.un.org/Overview/rights.html

Uniting and Strengthening America by Providing Appropriate Tools Required to Intercept and Obstruct Terrorism Act of 2001 (USA PATRIOT Act), P.L. 107-56, 115 Stat. 272.

U.S. Census Bureau. (2006). *The foreign-born population in 2004.* Retrieved September 18, 2007, from http://www.census.gov/population/pop-profile/dynamic/ForeignBorn.pdf

U.S. immigration at the beginning of the 21st century: Testimony before the Subcommittee on Immigration of the U.S. House of Representatives and Claims Hearing on "The U.S. Population and Immigration" Committee on the Judiciary U.S. House of Representatives (2001, August 2) (testimony of Michael E. Fix and Jeffrey S. Passel, the Urban Institute). Retrieved November 19, 2007, from http://www.urban.org/publications/900417.html

Policy statement approved by the NASW Delegate Assembly, August 2008. This policy statement supersedes the policy statement on Immigrants and Refugees approved by the Delegate Assembly in 2005 and 1996 and referred by the 2002 Delegate Assembly to the 2005 Delegate Assembly for revision. For further information, contact the National Association of Social Workers, 750 First Street, NE, Suite 700, Washington, DC 20002-4241. Telephone: 202-408-8600 or 800-638-8799; e-mail: press@naswdc.org

International Policy on Human Rights

BACKGROUND

History of Human Rights

From the Babylonian *Code of Hammurabi* (1750 B.C.E.) to the present, there is written evidence of humanity's struggle to protect the rights of vulnerable people from exploitation by more powerful individuals, groups, or the state itself. Social justice concepts appeared in the writings of Confucius (551–479 B.C.E.) and the ancient Greeks (4th century B.C.E.). The Romans recognized the need to protect individuals from the potential abuses of political authority; from its origins in the 7th century, Islam valued the sanctity of human life and the right to seek justice. Closer to our roots in the Western world, the Hebrew and Christian scriptures spoke of the inherent dignity and worth of the person and equality under the law. Great Britain's *Magna Carta* (1215) referred to the values of human dignity and justice, while affirming the notion that a ruler has an obligation to serve society. The 17th and 18th centuries gave birth to notions of natural rights, the social contract, the limitations of state powers, and the rights of people to rebel if their rights were trampled (Falk, 2005; Laqueur & Rubin, 1979; Lauren, 1998; McKinney & Park-Cunningham, 1997; Wronka, 1995, 1998).

The U.S. *Declaration of Independence* [1776], and *Bill of Rights* [1791], and the French *Declaration of the Rights of Man and the Citizen* [1936] clearly articulated a set of political rights, including the rights to life, liberty, and the pursuit of happiness; freedom of speech, the press, and religion; property rights; and the right to a trial by jury. During the 19th century, women's rights and the rights of ethnic and cultural minority groups were developed (Laqueur &

Rubin, 1979). The human rights perspective thus has roots in the religious, political, and intellectual traditions of many cultures. Crossing cultural boundaries, human rights identify the essential qualities of life for all people everywhere that must be valued and protected.

In response to the horrors of the Holocaust, under the leadership of Eleanor Roosevelt, representatives of the nations of the world came together to find a way to prevent such an event from ever happening again. The first step was the *Universal Declaration of Human Rights*, which was presented in 1948 to the U.N. General Assembly and the world as a foundation document upon which an edifice of protections for human rights could be built. This document has become the standard reference for all subsequent United Nations human rights efforts. It has heralded the inherent dignity and equal and inalienable rights of both male and female adults and children as members of the human family. Human rights were defined from the start to include the universal right to a standard of living that is adequate for the health and well-being of individuals and their families. The document spells out the essential resources to meet such a standard—food, clothing, housing, and medical care. It calls for the right to security in the event of unemployment, sickness, disability, widowhood, old age, or other circumstances beyond one's control. And it calls for "necessary social services" (United Nations, 1948, Article 25, 1).

The *Declaration* is distinctive in that it gave the world, for the first time in history, the right to ask of sovereign nations questions that were previously considered to be their internal affairs. By 1990 the document had become customary international law. Now even nonmember nations, however reluctantly, recognize that the world should not turn its back on social and humanitarian concerns within their borders (Wetzel, 1993, 1998).

Since the Universal Declaration of Human Rights was developed in 1948, more than 100 U.N. human rights instruments have been ratified, providing an even stronger legal mandate to protect human rights and fulfill human needs (Office of the United Nations High Commissioner for Human Rights, 2007). The most fundamental and general U.N. human rights instruments include the following:

■ the Charter of the United Nations (1945)

■ the Universal Declaration of Human Rights (1948)

■ the two Covenants on Human Rights (1966)

> 1. International Covenant on Civil and Political Rights (the right to life, liberty, and security; the right not to be subjected to cruel, inhuman, or degrading treatment, or punishment; prohibition of slavery; and the right not to be detained arbitrarily)

> 2. International Covenant on Economic, Social and Cultural Rights (the right to work, right to social security, right to protection of the family, and the right to an adequate standard of living).

■ There are also a number of U.N. human rights instruments (United Nations, 1994) that address the needs of specific groups, among them: the International Convention on the Elimination of All Forms of Racial Discrimination (1965); the Convention on the Elimination of All Forms of Discrimination against Women (1981); the Convention against Torture and Other Cruel, Inhuman and Degrading Treatment or Punishment (1984); the Convention on the Rights of the Child (1996); and the International Convention on the Protection of the Rights of All Migrant Workers and Members of Their Families (1990).

The United States ratified the Covenant on Civil and Political Rights in 1966, but it has never ratified the Covenant on Economic, Social and Cultural Rights, a fact that explains much about the absence of support for social legislation in this country. For example, education, housing, health care, income maintenance, and child care are not considered human rights in the United States. Neither has the United States ratified the Convention on the Elimination of All Forms of Discrimination against Women or the Convention on the Rights of the Child, two documents that call into question the most recent erosion of economic support and social services. These documents are essential to the human development and quality of life of people in the United States, as well as in other nations.

Link with Social Work

When the Universal Declaration of Human Rights was ratified, human rights concerns had been the bedrock of the social work profession in the United States for more than 50 years. Discrimination and social exclusion based on racial and religious intolerance; gender inequality and violence; denial of the rights of women and ·children, refugees, and older people—all are social justice issues that long have concerned social work (Wetzel, 1993, 1998; Wronka, 1995, 1998). Social workers know that civil and political rights must be supplemented by economic, social, and cultural rights. Social work, with its person-in-environment perspective, is vividly aware of the deleterious effects of human rights violations on the development of individuals, families, and communities. Social workers, on whatever level they practice, advocate for people's rights to have paid employment, adequate food, education, shelter, health care, as well as the right to freedom from violence and freedom to pursue their dreams (Hokenstad & Midgley, 1997; United Nations, 1995; Wetzel, 1993).

But the realization of social work's professional social justice goals and aspirations, like the United Nation's, is in evolution. NASW (1981), the Council on Social Work Education (2002), the International Federation of Social Workers (IFSW, 1996), the International Association of Schools of Social Work (1996), and United Nations (1993), have all acknowledged the importance of a global human rights perspective, the fact is, the profession does not fully use human rights as a criterion with which to evaluate social work policies, practice, research, and program priorities (Ife, 2001).

According to the Preamble to the NASW *Code of Ethics* (NASW, 2000), "the primary mission of the social work profession is to enhance human well-being and help meet the basic human needs of all people, with particular attention to the needs and empowerment of people who are vulnerable, oppressed, and living in poverty" (p. 1).

ISSUE STATEMENT

Human rights violations are prevalent throughout the world, including the United States. Civilians are injured, maimed, and killed in times of conflict, far outnumbering military personnel. Refugees and immigrants are fleeing their countries in record numbers. Women everywhere continue to be treated as second-class citizens and subjected to violence in epidemic proportions. The social situation of children and elderly people alike is of grave concern the world over and appears to be deteriorating. There has been a resurgence of violence and oppression against ethnic and racial minority groups, and against lesbian, gay, bisexual, and transgender people in many regions of our globe, and poverty is endemic, fueling the fires of unrest and making a sham of the very concept of human rights. The U.S. government's repeated insistence from 2001 through 2008 (Amnesty USA AI Index: AMR 2008) on redefining torture to allow practices disallowed by the Geneva Convention is an example of eroding human rights values (U.S. Department of Justice, 2002). Because the United States is the most powerful nation on earth, our policies and practices influence and affect not only our own people, but also those in developed and developing countries. The National Association of Social Workers is the most influential professional social work body in the world. Its effectiveness in the 21st century will depend on the extension of its social justice values within the context of global human rights.

The events of the 20th and 21st centuries demonstrate that the struggle for human rights goes on. For example,

■ events such as wars, genocide, and ethnic cleansing; discrimination and social exclusion based on race, ethnicity, caste, or religious identity; gender inequality, battering, rape, and the sale of women; child abuse; sweatshops, child labor, and slavery

■ suppression of the rights of ethnic and cultural minority groups, migrants, refugees, asylum seekers, indigenous peoples, older people, and people with mental and physical disabilities; and terrorism

■ denial of access to clean water, adequate nutrition, shelter, and health care; and environmental degradation

■ recognizing that the death penalty has not been found to be a deterrent to violent crime and that it provides inhumane and degrading punishment, as well as an irreversible act regardless of proven innocence at a later date.

Common Values and Mission

"Human rights condenses into two words the struggle for dignity and fundamental freedoms which allow the full development of human potential" (IFSW, 1996). The human rights value base, which has been articulated throughout history in religious texts and legal documents, in political writings and those of philosophers and social activists, parallels the values put forth in NASW's *Code of Ethics* (NASW, 2000) (especially, social justice and dignity and worth of the person) and the ethical principles that flow from those values. The *Code's* Ethical Standard 6.01 states that "social workers should promote the general welfare of society, from local to global levels, and the development of people, their communities, and their environments" (p. 26). Furthermore, social workers are urged to act to prevent and eliminate domination, exploitation, and discrimination.

The aim of the human rights edifice created during the past half century, which includes United Nations' declarations and treaties; UN administrative bodies; and regional, governmental, and nongovernmental organizations, is to root out oppression and to establish conditions in which human beings can meet their needs, develop their humanity, and flourish. This aim is closely akin to social work's mission.

Social work can be proud of its heritage. It is the only profession imbued with social justice as its fundamental value and concern. But social justice is a fairness doctrine that provides civil and political leeway in deciding what is just and unjust. Human rights, on the other hand, encompasses social justice, but transcends civil and political customs. It takes into consideration the basic life-sustaining needs of all human beings, without distinction.

Common Roles in Society

The human rights movement was formally recognized by the global community to identify barriers to the protection of human rights and to set up policies and procedures to abolish such barriers and thereby guarantee that human dignity and essential freedoms are protected for every person. Similarly, social work is expected by society to address the needs of people who are vulnerable to the vicissitudes of social life, while working toward establishing a more just society. The United Nations declarations, conventions, and treaties provide a human rights template. Social work can provide a biopsychosocial, body of knowledge gleaned from more than 100 years of experience to bring life to such a plan, grounding human rights in the everyday lives of the people (Wetzel, 1998).

POLICY STATEMENT

As social work practitioners and advocates of human rights, NASW's position is

■ to endorse the principle that the rights of people take precedence over social customs when those customs infringe on human rights. Ritual female genital mutilation, a practice that persists internationally despite governmental sanctions, is a case in point.

■ to promote U.S. ratification of the Universal Declaration of Human Rights; critical UN treaties, such as the Covenant on Economic, Social and Cultural Rights (1966); the Convention on the Elimination of All Forms of Discrimination Against Women (1981); and the Convention on the Rights of the Child (1996).

■ to be especially vigilant about human rights violations related to children's rights and exploitation such as child labor, child prostitution, and other crimes of abuse and to take leadership in developing public and professional awareness regarding the issues.

■ to endorse the UN resolution that women's rights are human rights, no longer simply to be considered civil and political rights.

■ to advocate for the rights of vulnerable people and to condemn policies, practices, and attitudes of bigotry, intolerance, and hate that put any person's human rights in grave jeopardy. The violation of human rights on the basis of race, ethnicity, gender, gender identity or expression, sexual orientation, age, disability, immigration status, or religion are examples.

■ the support of the right to a standard of living that is adequate for the health and well-being of all people and their families, without exception, and the essential resources to meet such a standard; adequate housing; basic health care; education; security in the event of unemployment, sickness, disability, widowhood, old age, or other lack of livelihood beyond one's control; and necessary social services.

■ to support the right not to be subjected to dehumanizing treatment and punishment.

■ to advocate the elimination of the death penalty.

■ to work in collaboration with nongovernmental organizations and community groups when entitlements are nonexistent or inadequately implemented and to become a leading force for the health and welfare of all people, including the world's most vulnerable.

■ to continue our work with the United Nations in advancing human development and human rights, including economic human rights and closing the economic gap.

- to work for the eradication of modern-day slavery and growing incidence of human trafficking.

- to advocate for the elimination of the practice of torture.

- to advocate for policies within the U.S. government in its methods of providing homeland security and combating terrorism that are consistent with human rights values and ethics.

The struggle for human rights remains a vital priority for the social work profession in the 21st century.

REFERENCES

Amnesty USA. (2008, June 13). *USA: Time for real change as Supreme Court rules on Guantanamo detentions.* Retrieved from www.amnestyusa.org/document.php?id= ENGAMR510612008&lang=e

Council on Social Work Education. (2002). *Educational policy and accreditation standards.* Alexandria, VA: Author.

Falk, D. S. (2005). *Human rights in global perspective.* Course outline and website. In R. J. Link, and L. M. Healy (Eds.), *Teaching international content: Curriculum resources for social work education* (pp. 103–109). Alexandria, VA: Council on Social Work Education.

Hokenstad, M. C., & Midgley, J. (Eds.). (1997). *Issues in international social work: Global challenges for a new century.* Washington, DC: NASW Press.

Ife, J. (2001). *Human rights and social work: Towards rights-based practice.* Cambridge, England: Cambridge University Press.

International Association of Schools of Social Work & International Federation of Social Workers. (1994). *Human rights and social work: A manual for schools of social work and the social work professions.* Professional training series. United Nations Centre for Human Rights: Geneva and New York.

International Federation of Social Workers. (1996). *International policy on human rights.* Retrieved October 20, 2007, from http://www.ifsw.org/en/p38000212.html

Laqueur, W., & Rubin, B. (Eds.). (1979). *The human rights reader.* Philadelphia: Temple University Press.

Lauren, P. G. (1998). *The evolution of international human rights: Visions seen.* Philadelphia: University of Pennsylvania Press.

McKinney, C. M., & Park-Cunningham, R. (1997, Spring). Evolution of the social work profession: An historical review of the U.S. and selected countries, 1995. In *Proceedings: 28th Annual Conference, New York State Social Work Education Association* (pp. 3–9). Syracuse: New York State Social Work Education Association.

National Association of Social Workers. (1981). *International policy on human rights.* [NASW Delegate Assembly Proceedings]. Washington, DC: Author.

National Association of Social Workers. (2000). *Code of ethics of the National Association of Social Workers.* Washington, DC: NASW Press.

Office of the United Nations High Commissioner for Human Rights. (2007). *International law.* Retrieved June 22, 2007, from http://www.ohchr.org/english/law/

United Nations. (1948). *Universal declaration of human rights.* New York: Author.

United Nations. (1993). *Declaration on the elimination of violence against women.* New York: Author.

United Nations. (1994). *Human rights and social work: A manual for schools of social work and the social work profession* (Professional Training Series No. 4). New York and Geneva: Author.

United Nations. (1995). *The United Nations and human rights: 1945–1995.* New York: U.N. Department of Public Information.

U.S. Department of Justice, Office of Legal Counsel. (2002). Memorandum for Alberto R. Gonzales Counsel to the President Re: Standards of conduct for interrogation under 18 U.S.C. 2340-2340A. Retrieved June 22, 2007, from http://www.washingtonpost.com/wp-srv/nation/documents/dojinterrogationmemo20020801.pdf

Wetzel, J. W. (1993). *The world of women: In pursuit of human rights.* London: Macmillan.

Wetzel, J. W. (1998). *Human rights values: An international challenge to social work.* Paper presented at the 15th Annual Social Work Day at the United Nations, New York, March 25; at the International Association of Schools of Social Work symposium, Council of Social Work Education Annual Program Meeting, Orlando, FL, March 8; at the University of Texas "Celebrate International Social Work," Austin, March 27.

Wronka, J. (1995). Human rights. In R. L. Edwards (Ed.-in-Chief), *Encyclopedia of social work* (19th ed., Vol. 1, pp. 1405–1418). Washington, DC: NASW Press.

Wronka, J. (1998). *Human rights and social policy in the 21st century: A history of the idea of human rights and comparison of the United Nations Universal Declaration of Human Rights with United States federal and state constitutions* (rev. ed.). Lanham, MD: University Press of America.

SUGGESTED READINGS

Reichert, E. (2003). *Social work and human rights: A foundation for policy and practice.* New York: Columbia University Press.

Reichert, E. (2006). *Understanding human rights: An exercise book.* Thousand Oaks, CA: Sage Publications.

Reichert, E. (Ed.). (2007). *Challenges in human rights: A social work perspective.* New York: Columbia University Press.

Tessitore, J., & Woolfson, S. (Eds.). (1997). *A global agenda: Issues before the 52nd General Assembly of the United Nations.* New York: Rowman & Littlefield.

Wetzel, J. W. (2001). Human rights in the 20th century: Weren't gays and lesbians human? In M. E. Swigonski & R. Mama (Eds.), *From hate crimes to human rights: Resources for lesbian, gay & bisexual empowerment & social action—A tribute to Matthew Shepard* (pp. 15–31). Binghamton, NY: Haworth Press.

Policy statement approved by the NASW Delegate Assembly, August 2008. This policy statement supersedes the policy statement on International Policy on Human Rights approved by the Delegate Assembly in 1999 and referred by the 2005 Delegate Assembly to the 2008 Delegate Assembly for revision. For further information, contact the National Association of Social Workers, 750 First Street, NE, Suite 700, Washington, DC 20002-4241. Telephone: 202-408-8600 or 800-638-8799; e-mail: press@naswdc.org

Juvenile Justice and Delinquency Prevention

BACKGROUND

Juvenile justice is a relatively recent and ever-evolving system for dealing with young people who violate social standards of behavior and laws, ranging from school truancy to murder. The current juvenile justice system has evolved from several important events.

In 1967, the Gault decision by the Supreme Court affirmed the necessity of requiring juvenile courts to respect due process of juveniles during their proceedings. The ruling was the result of an evaluation of Arizona's decision to confine Gerald Francis Gault. Gault, at the age of 15, had been placed in detention for making an obscene call to a neighbor while under probation. The Supreme Court decision emphasized that youths had a right to receive fair treatment under the law and pointed out the following rights of minors:

■ The right to receive notice of charges

■ The right to obtain legal counsel

■ The right to "confrontation and cross-examination"

■ The "privilege against self-incrimination"

■ The right to receive a "transcript of the proceedings," and

■ The right to "appellate review"

In 1968, Congress passed the Juvenile Delinquency Prevention and Control Act (P.L. 90-445). The act was designed to encourage states to develop plans and programs that would work on a community level to discourage juvenile delinquency. By 1974 the United States had developed a strong momentum toward preventing juvenile delinquency, deinstitutionaliz-

ing youths already in the system, and keeping juvenile offenders separate from adult offenders. The Juvenile Justice and Delinquency Prevention Act (JJDPA) (P.L. 93-145) was passed in 1974. It established the "separation requirement of juveniles from adults, the deinstitutionalization of status offenders (DOS) requirement and created the Formula Grants Program," which are noncompetitive grant awards based on a predetermined formula (Office of Juvenile Justice and Delinquency Prevention (OJJDP, 2010). Also included in juvenile policy in the 1970s were community-based programs and diversion from juvenile justice involvement (OJJDP, 2006).

Beginning in the 1980s and continuing into the 1990s, the juvenile crime rate reportedly increased, with the highest rates being between 1989 and 1995. In response, many states passed more punitive laws for juveniles, including transferring juveniles to adult court and lowering the age of responsibility (OJJDP, 2006).

In 2002, the JJDPA was reauthorized. It included "four custody-related requirements: (1) the same deinstitutionalization of status offenders and non-offenders as 1974, (2) sight and sound separation, (3) jail and lockup removal, and (4) disproportionate minority confinement changed to minority disproportionate contact (MDC)" (p. 11).

A steep rise in juvenile crime occurred between the late 1980s and mid-1990s. The increase in crime hit a peak in 1994 and then began to gradually decline. In response to a fear that juvenile crime would continue to rise at the rate seen between 1987 and 1994, legislatures enacted measures designed to "get tough on crime." The 1974 JJDPA was amended to include provisions that would allow states to try juveniles as adults for some violent crimes and weapons violations. Minimum detention standards were also put into place in some states (OJJDP, 2002). Collectively, this legislative and policy evolution has shaped the current juvenile justice system. Operationally, the juvenile justice system is a federal and state government collaboration. State governments are responsible for moving youths through their continuum of juvenile justice processes. The federal government provides policy guidelines and national standards for how young people are managed once they are arrested and adjudicated (Campaign for Youth and Justice, 2009).

Over recent years, there has been a slowing of the rate of juvenile crime and detention (Sentencing Project, 2011). However, there continues to be a significant number of young people who are arrested in the United States. The data presented next highlights the extent of the problem.

Juveniles accounted for 16 percent of all violent crime arrests and 26 percent of all property crime arrests in 2008. Between 1999 and 2008, juvenile arrests for aggravated assault decreased more for male than for female youths (22 percent compared with 17 percent). During the same time, the number of male arrests for simple assault declined 6 percent and female arrests increased by 12 percent (OJJDP, 2010).

In 2008, although black youths accounted for just 16 percent of the youth population ages 10 to 17, they were involved in 52 percent of juvenile violent crime index arrests and 33 percent of juvenile property crime index arrests. In 2008, female youths accounted for 30 percent of juvenile arrests. During the same year, 629,800 of the juvenile arrests were of girls younger than 18 years of age (see http://www.ojjdp.gov/ojstatbb/default.asp).

The Juvenile Justice System comprises a number of key stakeholders with a vested interest in preventing delinquent and criminal behaviors among young people and improving the correctional system once a juvenile is adjudicated. The major stakeholders include federal and state juvenile justice policymakers, including

- juvenile court
- probation agencies
- child welfare agencies
- public school systems
- national youth advocacy groups and service provider groups, and
- law enforcement agencies.

Under certain vague definitions with the family court act, the social services, and the penal law, children who are denominated by the state as "incorrigible," "ungovernable," "habitually disobedient," or "beyond the control of parents" are deemed "persons in need of supervision" and are subject to the jurisdiction of the court system, even though they have committed no crime. There is now ample evidence that coercive court intervention and detention of children who have committed no crimes increases the likelihood of subsequent crime behavior (American Civil Liberties Union [ACLU], n.d.). The reality is that Persons in Need of Supervision proceedings are not rehabilitative. If anything, the process has shown to have a deleterious effect (ACLU, n.d.). The social work profession has a significant stake in advocating for an effective system for dealing with problem juvenile behaviors and makes up a significant part of the workforce that provides services to at-risk youths.

Recent research has produced results that indicate a relationship between childhood trauma and the onset of antisocial or criminal behavior during adolescence. Of particular interest is the research on the long-term impact of childhood abuse and neglect and witnessing acts of violence such as in-family domestic violence or "street" violence on their social development. It is widely known that children experiencing such physical and emotional trauma tend to exhibit behaviors associated with posttraumatic stress disorders during childhood and into adolescence (Giardino, n.d.). It has been further documented that exposure to domestic violence during preadolescence can have significantly negative consequences (Volpe, 1996).

Social workers who work with juveniles are positioned to recognize the signs of posttraumatic stress and predelinquent behaviors. As a result, the profession plays a role in preventing children's progression in the juvenile justice system during adolescence.

ISSUE STATEMENT

Nationally, the OJJDP is addressing a range of concerns, including gang involvement, serious crimes, commercial sexual exploitation, underage drinking, bullying, school dropout, and other issues. There remain many critical issues facing all professionals who deal with children, youths, and their families, including prevention, rehabilitation, confinement, alternatives to incarceration, and aftercare or reentry into society. Social workers, in particular, must be knowledgeable and resourceful to effectively work with children, youths, and families.

Youths in the child welfare system often end up in the juvenile justice system, and many jurisdictions lack the resources to adequately address the history of abuse and neglect that may have led these youths to juvenile delinquency. A study from the National Institute of Justice found that abused and neglected children were 11 times more likely to be arrested for criminal behavior as juveniles and 2.7 times more likely to be arrested for violent and criminal behaviors as adults (Federal Advisory Committee on Juvenile Justice [FACJJ], 2010). These youths often have negative outcomes in education, substance abuse, mental health, and employment (Wiig & Tuell, 2004). Youth-serving agencies must better coordinate and integrate their services to reduce maltreatment and delinquency when dealing with dual adjudicated or "crossover" youths (youths known to both child welfare and juvenile justice systems).

A disproportionate number of crossover youths, and youths arrested in the United States, are minorities, which often begins a cycle of disproportionality throughout the juvenile justice system (FACJJ, 2010). As communities and jurisdictions create multiple disproportionate minority contact (DMC) reduction interventions and enhance existing services for minority youths, a broad base of culturally diverse stakeholders, including social workers, have focused on these issues.

Diversion programs, which offer juveniles alternative programs to juvenile court, including teen courts, victim restitution, and mediation, are cost-effective for handling first-time offenders, increase youth and parent communication, and produce positive behavior and relationship changes among participants (FACJJ, 2010).

The DMC requirement of the JJDPA requires states to assess and address the disproportionate contact of youths of color at key decision points in the juvenile justice system. In 2002, the DMC requirement was broadened from disproportionate confinement of minority youths to disproportionate contact, such as disproportionate representation throughout the juvenile justice system. The work on this issue should be driven by informed and data-driven strategies (W. Haywood Burns Institute for Juvenile Justice and Fairness and Equality, n.d.). As an example, Latino youths are incarcerated in local detention and state correctional facilities nearly two times more frequently than white youths (Sickmund, Sladky, & Kang, 2008). Also, African American youths represent 16 percent of the adolescents in this country (Puzzanchera, Finnegan, & Kang, 2007) but are 40 percent of the youths incarcerated in local detention and state correctional facilities (Sickmund et al., 2008). These youths would greatly benefit from cross-system collaboration. Coordination of these systems is noted to be slow as a result of policy obstacles, volume of data that needs to be shared, funding challenges, and privacy concerns (Siegel & Lord, 2004).

Youths involved in the juvenile justice system often face significant barriers to academic achievement. Detained or committed youths are displaced from their normal school environment and face difficulties reentering school after they exit the system. Educational experiences across institutions vary significantly, ranging from facilities offering only minimal instruction for a few hours to those providing nearly full-day academic programming. In addition, many children within the juvenile justice system have educational disabilities that either are ignored or go unnoticed. These youths are at a greater risk for academic failure than their peers. *Suspended Education: Urban Middle Schools in Crisis*, published by the Southern Poverty Law Center in September 2010, revealed significant racial gaps in suspension rates among middle school students. Education researchers Daniel J. Losen and Russell J. Skiba conducted the study, which found that 28 percent of African Americans male students were suspended at least once during a school year in a national sample of over 9,000 middle schools, which is nearly three times the 10 percent rate for white male students. That disparity was even more significant in a subsample of 18 urban school districts.

Agencies and social workers must take a proactive role to improve educational outcomes for children in the juvenile justice system by fostering communication in the local school districts and among school social workers relative to developing strategies focused on reducing suspensions and improving services to youths with educational disabilities. In collaboration with other parallel systems, the work should focus on helping at-risk youths achieve their educational potential.

POLICY STATEMENT

NASW supports

■ continuation of the movement toward assisting children and youths who enter the juvenile justice system in a manner commensurate with their age, developmental level, and ability to differentiate between right and wrong.

■ fair and equal treatment of youths regardless of socioeconomic status, race/ethnicity, gender, or sexual preference.

■ interdisciplinary collaborations and communication with key stakeholders in the juvenile justice systems to focus on a child's educational needs and stability.

■ evidence-based policies and practices, ongoing research and evaluation, with input from families and stakeholders, to be used by service providers in the juvenile justice system.

■ the importance of ethnic and cultural sensitivity.

■ encouragement of the child welfare system and the juvenile justice system to develop strategies and policies that will provide for greater levels of collaboration, screening, data sharing, assessment, case management and supervision, and interagency collaboration.

■ the hiring of professional social work practitioners who have skills in case management, counseling, intake, interviewing, and cultural competency and expertise in youths to effectively handle individuals and their families who are involved in the juvenile justice system.

■ interdisciplinary services that exemplify social work practice and values and provide effective and efficient services to youths and their families; age-appropriate treatment that continues to be delivered with a mind toward age-appropriate handling and management regardless of placement setting; support for the move toward replacement of state correctional systems by local systems of community-based care that is necessary for effective rehabilitation and change; alternate options, such as small correctional and treatment facilities, located around the state to promote person-in-environment treatment, which includes postrelease or discharge planning and aftercare programming.

■ overall system improvement that results in periodic screenings of children in various care setting; use of evidence of tools that can identify the mental health/emotional impact of early childhood trauma (such as child abuse and neglect, exposure to domestic violence) and physical trauma (such as traumatic brain injury); use of coordination of service concepts/models to provide oversight to ensure adherence to relevant national standards and guidelines and that services are culturally competent, are data driven, minimize duplication of services, incorporate a continuous quality improvement component, encourage the use of evidence-based and informed interventions.

■ elimination of the death penalty for juveniles under the age of 18 years.

- elimination of the imposition of life sentences without the possibility of parole for juveniles convicted of a capital offense in an adult court.

- due process and proper representation for all juveniles.

- education of the public continuously against executing children younger than 18 years of age.

REFERENCES

American Civil Liberties Union. (n.d.). *Legislative memo: Persons in need of supervision.* Retrieved from http://www.nyclu.org/content/legislative-memo-persons-need-of-supervision

Campaign for Youth and Justice. (2009). *Former justice officials recognize critical federal role in juvenile justice: Call on Congress to support Juvenile Justice & Delinquency Prevention Act* Retrieved from http://www.prweb.com/releases/OJJDPLetter/2009/prweb3312574.htm

Federal Advisory Committee on Juvenile Justice. (2010). *2010 Annual report.* Washington, DC: Author.

Giardino A. (n.d.). *Posttraumatic stress disorder due to child abuse and neglect.* Retrieved from http://emedicine.medscape.com/article/916007-overview

Juvenile Justice and Delinquency Prevention Act of 1974, P.L. 93–415, U.S.C. 5601 et seq.

Juvenile Delinquency and Prevention Control Act of 1968, P.L. 90-445, 82 Stat. 462 (1968).

Losen, D. J., & Skiba, R. J. (2010). *Suspended education: Urban middle schools in crisis.* Montgomery, AL: Southern Poverty Law Center.

Office of Juvenile Justice and Delinquency Prevention. (2004). *The causes and correlates of studies: Findings and policy implications.* Retrieved from http://www.ncjrs.gov/html/ojjdp/203555/jj2.html

Office of Juvenile Delinquency and Prevention. (2006). *Juvenile offenders and victims: 2006 national report.* Washington, DC: U.S. Department of Justice.

Office of Juvenile Justice and Delinquency Prevention. (2010). *OJJDP fact sheet: Delinquency cases waived to criminal court, 2007.* Washington, DC: U.S. Department of Justice.

Puzzanchera, C., Finnegan, T., & Kang, W. (2007). *Easy access to juvenile population* Retrieved from http://www.ojjdp.ncjrs.gov/ojstatbb/ezpop/

Sentencing Project. (2011). *Recommendations for juvenile justice reform.* Washington, DC: Author.

Sickmund, M., Sladky, T. J., & Kang, W. (2008) *Census of juvenile in residential placement databook.* Retrieved from http://www.ojjdp.ncjrs.gov/ojstatbb/cjrp

Siegel, G., & Lord, R. (2004). *When systems collide: Improving court practices and programs in dual jurisdiction cases.* Pittsburgh: National Center for Juvenile Justice.

Volpe, J. (1996). Effects of domestic violence on children and adolescents: An overview. Retrieved from the American Academy of Experts in Traumatic Stress Web site: http://www.aaets.org/arts/art8.htm

W. Haywood Burns Institute for Juvenile Justice and Fairness Equality. (n.d.). *Working locally to reduce disproportionality.* Retrieved from http://www.burnsinstitute.org

Wiig, J. K., & Tuell, J. A. (2004). *Guidebook to juvenile justice and child welfare system coordination and integration.* Washington, DC: Child Welfare League of America.

NASW Members with Primary Responsibility for Revision of This Policy

First Draft Revision:

Camielle Call (AK)

Policy Panelists:

Denise Lavallee (MA)
Diane Morales (NYC)
Carmen Weisner (LA)
Wendy Volz Daniels (WI)
Greg Tangari (KS)
Pat Berckman (UT)
Guadalupé Lara (MI)

Policy statement approved by the NASW Delegate Assembly, August 2011. This statement supersedes the policy statement on Juvenile Justice and Delinquency Prevention approved by the Delegate Assembly in 2002 and the statement on Juvenile Justice and Adult Crime approved by the Delegate Assembly in 1977, which incorporated portions of the policy statement on Juvenile Delinquency and Adult Crime (approved in 1969) and Prisons and Jails (approved in 1971) and reconfirmed in 1993. For further information, contact the National Association of Social Workers, 750 First Street, NE, Suite 700, Washington, DC 20002-4241. Telephone: 202-408-8600; e-mail: press@naswdc.org

Language and Cultural Diversity in the United States

BACKGROUND

Cultural diversity encompasses the cultural differences that exist between people, such as language, dress and traditions, and the way societies organize themselves, their conception of morality and religion, and the way they interact with the environment (Wikipedia, 2008).

"[E]very human language is an exquisitely complex intellectual masterpiece" (Wilkinson, 2005, p. 361) that expresses the culture that created it. Culture can often influence language, identity, dress, music, and food, as well as problem solving and coping with various life circumstances, and goes far beyond race and ethnicity. Culture can be applied to geographic areas of the country, professions, developmental stages of life, socioeconomic status, sexual orientation, religion and spirituality, and institutions and can even be issue oriented, such as drug or gang cultures (Lopez, 2007).

Different languages represent different ways of thinking about our surroundings and ourselves. "Every language offers a unique insight into the nature of speech and thought" (Vaux, cited in Lewis, 1998, p. A14). As a result of past government policy, many American Indian languages and Alaskan Native languages have become extinct (Native American Languages Act Amendments, 2000). Linguists report that the extinction of a language is a significant loss of knowledge about human achievement and thought (Lewis, 1998). The history of the United States has shown the significant contributions to the development of this country by the African Americans, American Indians, Asian Americans and Pacific Islanders, and Hispanic/Latino peoples. One example of this was the use of Navajo and other tribal code talkers in World War II. They were greatly responsible for shortening the war and for winning the Pacific by using a language code that could not be broken. There are more than 6,900 languages spoken in the world today, but 90 percent of them are spoken by fewer than 100,000 people, and some languages are even rarer—46 are known to have just one native speaker. "There are 357 languages with under 50 speakers," said Professor Bill Sutherland, a population biologist at the University of East Anglia in Norwich (Connor, 2003). Indigenous cultures and immigration have deeply transformed the racial and ethnic composition of the United States. Ethnic minorities currently compose approximately one-third of the population of the United States (Russell Searight & Gafford, 2005).

The growth of the Latino population has been the fastest rate of any major racial category, and in 2006 the Latino population made up nearly 4 percent of the U.S. population (U.S. Census Bureau, 2006). In 2006, the total population of the United States surpassed the 300 million mark (Lelchuck, 2006) and the percentage of people who speak a language other than English at home has increased to 17.9 percent (U.S. Census Bureau, 2000). Similarly, in 2003 the percentage of people five years and older who speak English less than very well was 8.4 percent of the total census population (U.S. Census Bureau, 2003).These demographic shifts have affected the care and services provided by health and human services providers.

The past several years have been rife with proposed English-only legislation—especially after the events of September 11, 2001. The ultimate goal of the English-only movement, which emerged in the 1980s was to amend the U.S. Constitution to declare English the official language of this nation. This also occurred in the early part of the 20th century in reaction against speakers of the German language. It is a resurgence reflecting economic and political tensions. The decade of the 1990s and the first years of the 21st century have brought continuing hostility and violence toward populations of ethnic minority groups, racism, and xenophobia, of which the attack on bilingual education is but one example (Edwards & Curiel, 1989; Macedo, 2000). Supporters of the movement have worked energetically and have succeeded in obtaining passage of legislation. To date, 30 states have made English the official language of the state. In 2007–2008, bills were introduced in 20 states that would make English the official language or strengthen existing official English laws (U.S. English, 2008). In practice, implementation has meant that government institutions only provide services and information in English. Use of other languages has been prohibited. Some of the states that have enacted English-only legislation are among the largest and most populous in the country with extremely diverse cultural populations (Crawford, 2000).

In terms of social work and mental health services, according to national data on Latino and Asian American cultures (Alegria, Mulvaney-Day, Torres, Gao, & Oddo, 2006), cultural factors such as nativity, language, age at immigration, year of residence in the United States, and generational status affect the use of mental health services. English proficiency not only affects treatment for adults, but also can affect the care of children. Yu and colleagues (2006) compared children in English-speaking households and non-English-speaking households and found that children in non-English-speaking households are less likely to have access to health insurance and physician care and are more likely to go to other countries for their health care.

Recent developments in the immigration debate have sparked interest in the issues of diversity in the United States. The systematic issues of discrimination and social justice should be addressed to develop a system that is equitable to the growing immigrant population in the United States. "As society evolves, we encounter more diversity in our workplaces, in our neighborhoods, and in every other facet of our lives. Our entire country depends on individuals obtaining a greater understanding of the similarities and differences among ethnic, racial, and cultural groups" (Daniel K. Inouye, U.S. Senator, Hawaii, January 1996).

ISSUE STATEMENT

The essence of the social work profession is to promote social justice and eliminate discrimination. Language and cultural diversity are recognized as issues that are intrinsic to the profession's mission and commitment to advocacy of access to services, to quality of care, and ultimately to outcomes. According to Title VI of the Civil Rights Act of 1964, no persons on the grounds of race, color, or national origin should be denied services (U.S. Department of Health and Human Services, 2000). Agencies and service providers receiving federal financial assistance are obligated to not discriminate or have methods of administering services that may subject an individual to discrimination. The ramifications of discrimination are far reaching and affect clients in all fields and settings in which social workers practice.

In 2001, the *NASW Standards for Cultural Competence in Social Work Practice* affirmed the importance of cultural diversity and linguistic access in Standard 9, Language Diversity: "Social workers shall seek to provide and advocate for the provision of information, referrals, and services in the language appropriate to the client, which may include the use of interpreters" (p. 27) and translators.

NASW past—President Craig de Silva pointed out that "immigration weaves the frayed threads of poverty and racism with strings of fear." She also credited social workers as being "instrumental in helping newcomers make the transition into American society and helping communities embrace increased diversity" (Craig de Silva, 2006, p. 3). The social work literature on cultural competency helps shape our profession to improve the quality of social work services and work toward eliminating racial and ethnic disparities in services (Garcia & Van Soest, 2006; National Association of Social Workers, 2001).

Assessing a client's cultural background and values may be challenging for the social worker because individuals might belong to several cultures (Lopez, 2007).

POLICY STATEMENT

As social workers, we understand that language is a source and extension of personal identity and culture, and, therefore, is one way individuals interact with others in their families and communities and across different cultural groups. To limit or deny language as an extension of culture is to reject that aspect of human beings that helps to define them. NASW embraces the view that language access to services is a right and people's native language should be celebrated and encouraged as an example of diversity. NASW considers the use of various languages as a right and a resource that is closely aligned with the ethical principles of service and social justice.

Therefore, NASW

■ supports the continuity and preservation of native indigenous languages such as the languages of Native Alaskan, American Indian, and Native Hawaiian peoples. NASW rejects any hostility toward foreign-born or foreign-language-speaking individuals. NASW rejects such racially and culturally biased xenophobia.

■ believes that human service programs should have written limited-English-proficiency policies that include the following elements: assessment of language needs and capabilities, recruitment and hiring of bilingual and bicultural staff of major groups in the program's service area, training on how best to meet language needs of clients, use of interpreters and translators, and translation of documents (Barnett, 2004).

■ advocates for the provision of information, referrals, and services in the language and culture appropriate to the client.

■ supports research on culture and linguistic diversity that enhances the lives of all people.

■ supports educational programs that accept the importance of other languages within the mainstream culture, such as bilingual education and multicultural programs.

■ encourages schools of social work to recruit culturally and linguistically diverse students and faculty. The curriculum should also teach the skills necessary for culturally competent practice, which might include use of interpreters.

■ opposes any legislation that promotes English-only agendas.

REFERENCES

Alegria, M., Mulvaney-Day, N., Torres, M., Gao, S., & Oddo, V. (2006). Correlates of past-year mental health services among Latinos: Results from the national Latino and Asian American study. *American Journal of Public Health, 97*, 76–83.

Barnett, H. (2004). *Services to clients with limited English proficiency* (Program letter 04-2). Retrieved June 8, 2007, from www.lri.lsc.gov

Connor, S. (2003, May 13). Alarm raised on world's disappearing languages. *The Independent/UK.* Retrieved May 30, 2008, from http://www.commondreams.org/headlines03/0515-05.htm

Craig de Silva, E. (2006, August). Weaving the fabrics of diversity. *NASW News, 51*, p. 3.

Crawford, J. (2000). *Anatomy of the English-only movement.* Retrieved May 30, 2008, from http://ourworld.compuserve.com/homepages/jWCRAWFORD/anatomy.htm

Edwards, R. L., & Curiel, H. (1989). Effects of the English-only movement on bilingual education. *Social Work in Education, 12,* 53–66. Retrieved May 30, 2008, from socialwork.rutgers.edu/oldssw/documents/cvedwards106.doc

Garcia, B., & Van Soest, D. (2006). *Social work practice for social justice: Cultural competence in action.* Alexandria, VA: Council on Social Work Education.

Native American Languages Act Amendments Act of 2000: Hearing before the Senate Committee on Indian Affairs, 106th Cong., 648 (2000) (statement of Michael E. Krauss). Retrieved May 20, 2008, from http://indian.senate.gov/2000hrgs/nala_0720/krauss.pdf

Lelchuck, I. (2006). *The changing face of America.* Retrieved June 8, 2007, from http://www .sfgate.com/cgi-bin/article.cgi?fil.../a/ 2006/10/15/MNGA4LPT7H1.DTL& type=printable

Lewis, P. (1998, August 15). Too late to say 'extinct' in Ubykh, Eyak or Ona; Thousands of languages are endangered. *New York Times*, p. A14. Retrieved May 30, 2008, from http://www.uwm.edu/~vaux/ubykh.htm

Lopez, S. (2007, November/December). *Honoring cultural diversity at the end of life. Social Work Today*, 7(6), 36. Retrieved May 30, 2008, from http://www.socialworktoday.com/ archive/novdec2007p36.shtml

Macedo, S. (2000). *Diversity and distrust: Civic education in a multicultural democracy.* Cambridge, MA: Harvard University Press. Retrieved May 30, 2008, from http://edrev .asu.edu/reviews/rev171.htm

National Association of Social Workers. (2001). *NASW standards for cultural competence in social work practice.* Washington, DC: NASW Press.

Russell Searight, H., & Gafford, J. (2005). *Cultural diversity at the end of life: Issues and guidelines for family physicians.* Retrieved May 30, 2008, from http://www.aafp.org/ afp/20050201/515.html

U.S. Census Bureau. (2000). *Quickfacts: Current population reports.* Washington, DC: U.S. Government Printing Office. Retrieved June 8, 2007, from http://quickfacts.census.gov

U.S. Census Bureau. (2003). *Factfinder: Current population reports.* Washington, DC: U.S. Government Printing Office. Retrieved June 8, 2007, from http://www.factfinder.census .gov

U.S. Census Bureau. (2006). *Quickfacts: Current population reports.* Washington, DC: U.S. Government Printing Office. Retrieved June 8, 2007, from http://quickfacts.census.gov

U.S. Department of Health and Human Services. (2000). *HHS guidelines on Title V of the Civil Rights Act of 1964.* Retrieved June 8, 2007, from www.hhs.gov/ocr/lep

U.S. English. (2008). *Legislation introduced to make English the official language of Texas.* Retrieved November 17, 2008, from http://www .usenglish.org/view/518

Wikipedia. (2008). Cultural diversity. Retrieved May 30, 2008, from http://en.wikipedia .org/wiki/Cultural_diversity

Wilkinson, C. (2005). *Blood struggle. The rise of modern Indian nations.* Retrieved May 30, 2008, from http://books.google.com/books ?id=moDHKMJXfKwC&pg=PA361&dq= %22Every+human+language+is+an+exq uisitely+complex+intellectual+master piece%22&sig=ACfU3U1c94i_sgE9WJzOm H3c2xT0KtzeSA

Yu, S., Huang, J., Schwalberg, R., & Nyman, R. (2006). Parenting English proficiency and children's health service access. *American Journal of Public Health, 96,* 1449–1455.

Policy statement approved by the NASW Delegate Assembly, August 2008. This policy statement supersedes the policy statement on Linguistic/Cultural Diversity in the United States approved by the Delegate Assembly in 1999. The 1999 Delegate Assembly also voted to not combine this statement with the policy statements on Affirmative Action or Immigrants and Refugees. This policy statement also supersedes the policy statement on Cultural and Linguistic Diversity in the United States approved by the Assembly in 1990. For further information, contact the National Association of Social Workers, 750 First Street, NE, Suite 700, Washington, DC 20002-4241. Telephone: 202-408-8600; e-mail: press@naswdc.org

Lesbian, Gay, and Bisexual Issues

BACKGROUND

In U.S. society, lesbian, gay, bisexual, transgender, and intersex people are still considered by some to be immoral, unnatural, and/or dysfunctional. Until 1973, homosexuality was defined as a mental illness by the American Psychiatric Association's (APA) Diagnostic and Statistical Manual (DSM) (APA, 1952). Lesbian, gay, bisexual, transgender, and intersex (LGBTI) people do not have civil and statutory protection under the law (Title VII of the Civil Rights Act) (Herek & Berrill, 1992). In fact, the government takes a leading role in the subjugation of lesbians and gay men by denying legal recognition of same-sex marriage. There is much violence and social injustice that must be overcome before sexual minority people are able to enjoy the full benefits of our society (Sloan & Gustavsson, 1998). It is important that NASW take a strong stance on behalf of LGBTI people and work to end the prejudice, oppression, and discrimination that confront LGBTI people on a daily basis. Although LGBTI people share many of the same discrimination and concerns, NASW has a separate policy statement on transgender and gender identity issues, therefore, this policy primarily addresses lesbian, gay, and bisexual people (LGB).

Discrimination against LGB people has a long history in the United States. Following World War II, President Eisenhower banned gay men and lesbians from all federal jobs; many state and local governments and private companies followed suit (Garraty & Foner, 1991). Until 1961, sodomy and homosexuality were illegal in all 50 states. Sodomy laws were used in many states to deny lesbians and gay men custody of their children, employment, and the opportunity to foster or adopt children in state care (National Gay and Lesbian Task Force [NGLTF], 2004c). Throughout the 1950s and 1960s, police frequently raided gay bars, arresting employees and patrons.

By the late 1950s, the gay rights movement was beginning to grow and reject the discrimination faced by LGB people. On June 27, 1969, when New York City police raided a Greenwich Village gay bar, the LGB community was ready to fight back. As police arrested employees and patrons of the Stonewall Inn, a fight ensued and soon hundreds of people were protesting and rioting. Over the next three days, the crowd of protesters grew to over 1,000. Although not the beginning of the gay rights movement, the Stonewall riots were an important milestone in the gay rights movement. Over the next decades, changes would spread across the country. In 1973, APA removed homosexuality from its list of mental disorders. By 1975, the federal government had lifted the employment ban on lesbians and gay men (in most jobs) (Garraty & Foner, 1991). On June 26, 2003, the Supreme Court ruled sodomy laws unconstitutional (*Lawrence v. State of Texas*, 2003). Later in 2003, the Massachusetts Supreme Court ruled that banning lesbians and gay men from marrying was a violation of the state's constitution, opening the way for same-sex couples to legally marry in the state.

Internationally, other countries were also beginning to fight against discrimination of LGB people. In 1994, the United Nations ruled that discrimination based on sexual orientation violates the International Covenant on Civil and Political Rights. In 1996, post-apartheid South Africa became the first country to include nondiscrimination based on sexual orientation in its constitution (Human Rights Watch [HRW], 2004). From 1981 to 2003, the European Court of Human Rights overturned sodomy, recognized gay and lesbian partnerships, condemned discriminatory age-of-consent laws (that is, differing age of consent to engage in sex for heterosexual versus LGB youths), and gave transgender people the right to legally change their identity and to marry (HRW). In 1998, Denmark legalized same-sex partnerships; within two years, Norway, Sweden, Iceland, and France followed. In 2001, the Netherlands legalized same-sex marriages, followed in 2003 by Belgium and the Canadian provinces of Ontario and British Columbia. In 2004, Quebec, the Yukon, Manitoba, Nova Scotia, and Saskatchewan legalized same-sex marriage.

ISSUE STATEMENT

Despite the successes of the gay rights movement, there continues to be discrimination against LGB people. Thirty-five states do not protect LGB people from discrimination in employment, education, credit, housing, and other public accommodation. Six states do not allow lesbians or gay men to adopt (Florida and Mississippi), or foster children (North Dakota, Utah, Arkansas, and Oklahoma) (NGLTF, 2004a). Thirteen states passed state constitutional amendments that prohibit same-sex marriage (although the courts in Louisiana struck down their amendment). Alabama, Arizona, Mississippi, South Carolina, and Texas prohibit any discussion of homosexuality in school or "mandate that any references to homosexuality be exclusively negative" (NGLTF, 2004b, p. 1).

The federal government has also failed to support nondiscrimination against LGB people. The 1994 Employment Non-Discrimination Act (ENDA), which would protect LGB people from workplace discrimination, has failed to pass Congress. In 1996, the federal government passed the Defense of Marriage Act (DOMA), allowing states to not recognize gay marriages sanctioned in other states or countries. Currently, President Bush proposed a constitutional amendment to define marriage as between one man and one woman.

The impact of discrimination, homophobia, heterosexism, and biphobia have a serious impact on LGB people. Homophobia and heterosexism inhibit effective and appropriate service delivery for sexual minority people. Hate crimes based on sexual orientation account for 16 percent of all hate crimes reported to law enforcement (FBI, 2004). Research suggests that harassment and hatred of LGB people is related to higher rates of depression, suicide, high school drop out, and teen homelessness (HRW, 2001). Gay men earn 20 percent less than heterosexual men, and due to the inequity in women's salaries compared with men, lesbian couples earn less than heterosexual couples (Badgett, 1998).

Discrimination within the LGB community must be acknowledged. LGB people represent all of the diversity of our society—people of color, people who are disabled, people who are elderly, people who are immigrants and refugees, and people of all religious and political beliefs. LGB people facing multiple forms of oppression also face discrimination from LGB people. In addition, bisexual identity is often dismissed by lesbians and gay men as a means to avoid the full brunt of homophobia, and not a true sexual orientation. Bisexuals are frequently told that bisexuality is just a phase, and they will either eventually identify as heterosexual or homosexual. The complexities of multiple forms of oppression cannot be ignored.

Homophobic or heterosexist views also reduce the effectiveness of support services and treatment social workers offer to gay and lesbian clients. Homophobia and/or heterosexism may cause social workers to minimize or exaggerate the importance of sexual orientation in the gay, lesbian, or bisexual individual's life, perpetuating self-hatred experienced by some gay and lesbian clients (Brown, 1996; McHenry & Johnson, 1993; Peterson, 1996). Taken to the extreme, homophobia in social workers and other practitioners can lead to the use of conversion or reparative therapies, which are explicitly condemned by NASW, the American Psychological Association, the American Counseling Association, and the American Psychiatric Association (American Academy of Pediatrics et al., n.d.; American Psychiatric Association, 1998; NASW, 2000).

POLICY STATEMENT

It is the position of the NASW that same-gender sexual orientation should be afforded the same respect and rights as other-gender orientation. Discrimination and prejudice directed against any group is damaging to the social, emotional, and economic well-being of the affected group and of society as a whole. NASW is committed to advancing policies and practices that will improve the status and well-being of all lesbian, gay, and bisexual people. NASW reaffirms its support of the Transgender and Gender Identity Issues policy statement, recognizing the intersection of oppression among lesbian, gay, bisexual, transgender, and intersex people.

Nondiscrimination

- NASW supports all social agencies, universities, professional associations, and funding organizations in their efforts to broaden statements of nondiscrimination to include sexual orientation.

- NASW supports the adoption of local, state, federal, and international policies/legislation that ban all forms of discrimination based on sexual orientation. LGB people must be granted all rights, privileges, and responsibilities that are granted to heterosexual people, including but not limited to inheritance rights, insurance, marriage, child custody, employment, credit, and immigration.

- NASW supports the adoption of local, state, federal, and international policies/legislation that protect the rights and well-being of the children of lesbian, gay, and bisexual people.

- NASW supports efforts to end discrimination and harassment of lesbian, gay, and bisexual youths in public schools. NASW also supports the rights of LGB youths and allies to organize and operate in schools.

- NASW is committed to working toward the elimination of prejudice, social injustice, violence, and discrimination of LGB people in all aspects of society.

Social Work Profession and Education

- NASW encourages curriculum policies in schools of social work that eliminate discrimination against lesbian, gay, and bisexual people. Schools of social work are expected to articulate the NASW position in curriculum policy and standards; to require content on lesbian, gay, and bisexual people throughout the curriculum, in field instruction, and in continuing education programs and through the selection of textbooks; and to provide training for classroom instructors, field supervisors, and field advisers regarding lesbian, gay, and bisexual issues.

- NASW encourages social workers to increase their awareness of oppression, heterosexism, homophobia, and the intersection of multiple forms of oppression.

- NASW encourages all social work organizations and associations to use inclusive, gender-neutral language, non-homophobic, non-heterosexist language in all materials.

- NASW encourages licensing bodies to include questions specific to lesbian, gay, and bisexual sex issues.

- NASW strives for full representation and establishment of means to affirm the presence of lesbian, gay, and bisexual people at all levels of leadership and employment in social work and in NASW and its chapters.

Education and Public Awareness

- NASW encourages the development of programs, training, and information regarding the specific health, mental health, and development needs of lesbian, gay, and bisexual youths and their families.

- NASW encourages the development of programs to increase public awareness of the violence and social injustice experienced by lesbian, gay, and bisexual people. Public awareness and education in schools should include information on the contributions made to society by lesbian, gay, and bisexual people.

- NASW encourages the development of programs, training, and information that promote proactive efforts to end the violence and stereotypes perpetrated against lesbian, gay, and bisexual people.

- NASW applauds organizations that fund, develop, and provide programming that portrays the lesbian, gay, and bisexual communities compassionately and accurately.

Health and Mental Health Services

- NASW supports the right of the individual to self-disclose, or to not disclose, sexual orientation and encourages the development of supportive practice environments for lesbian, gay, and bisexual clients and colleagues.

- NASW reaffirms its stance against reparative therapies and treatments designed to change sexual orientation or to refer clients to practitioners or programs that claim to do so (NASW, 2000).

- NASW strongly advocates for the availability of culturally appropriate comprehensive health and mental health services for LGB people across the life span, including HIV prevention and treatment; substance abuse treatment; psychological stress and dysfunction prevention and treatment; and suicide prevention.

- NASW recognizes the increasing number of lesbian, gay, and bisexual people who are making reproductive choices and encourages the establishment of legal, medical, and psychological supports for these families.

Political Action

It is important for NASW and its chapters to develop and participate in coalition with other human rights, social action, and professional associations to lobby for the rights of lesbian, gay, and bisexual people; to defeat efforts to limit the rights of lesbian, gay, and bisexual people; to advocate for increased funding for programs designed to eliminate hate crimes and antigay violence; to advocate for increased funding for programs designed to provide education, health and mental health services; and to advocate for increased funding for research that increases our understanding of issues affecting lesbian, gay, and bisexual people.

REFERENCES

American Academy of Pediatrics. (n.d.). *Just the facts about sexual orientation and youth: A primer for principals, educators, and school personnel.* Retrieved January 26, 2004, from http://www.apa.org/pi/lgbc/facts.pdf

American Psychiatric Association. (1952). *Diagnostic and statistical manual: Mental disorders.* Washington, DC: Author.

American Psychiatric Association. (1998). *Lesbian, gay and bisexual issues fact sheet: APA fact sheet pertinent to gay and lesbian issues.* Retrieved January 26, 2004, from http://www.psych.org/public_info/gaylesbian-bisexualissues22701.pdf

Badgett, M. V. (1998). *Income inflation: The myth of affluence among gay men, lesbians, and bisexuals.* New York: Policy Institute of the National Gay and Lesbian Task Force and Institute for Gay and Lesbian Strategic Studies.

Brown, L. S. (1996). Preventing heterosexism and bias in psychotherapy and counseling. In E. Rothblum & L. Bond (Eds.), *Preventing heterosexism and homophobia* (pp. 36–58). Thousand Oaks, CA: Sage Publications.

Defense of Marriage Act, P.L. 104-199, 110 Stat, 2419.

Federal Bureau of Investigation. (2004). *Hate crimes 2003.* Washington, DC: Author [Available from author, U. S. Department of Justice, Washington, DC 20535].

Garraty, J., & Foner, E. (Eds.). (1991). *A reader's companion to American history.* New York: Houghton Mifflin.

Herek, G. M., & Berrill, K. T. (1992). *Hate crimes: Confronting violence against lesbians and gay men.* Newbury Park, CA: Sage Publications.

Human Rights Watch. (2001). *Hatred in the hallways: Violence and discrimination against lesbian, gay, bisexual and transgender students in U.S. schools.* New York: Author.

Human Rights Watch. (2004). *Lesbian and gay rights: Resource library for international jurisprudence on sexual orientation and gender identity.* Retrieved March 25, 2005, from http://hrw.org/lgbt/jurisprudence.htm

Lawrence v. State of Texas, 123 S.Ct. 2472 (2003).

McHenry, S. S., & Johnson, J. W. (1993). Homophobia in the therapist and gay or lesbian client: Conscious and unconscious collusions in self-hate. *Psychotherapy, 30,* 141–151.

National Association of Social Workers. (2000). *Position statement: "Reparative" and "conversion" therapies for lesbians and gay men.* Retrieved April 18, 2004, from http://www.naswdc.org/diversity/lgb/reparative.asp

National Gay and Lesbian Task Force. (2004a). *Anti-gay parenting laws in the U.S.* Retrieved March 24, 2005, from http://www.thetaskforce.org/downloads/adoptionmap.pdf

National Gay and Lesbian Task Force. (2004b). *Youth.* Retrieved March 24, 2005, from http://www.thetaskforce.org/theissues/issue.cfm?issueID=13

National Gay and Lesbian Task Force. (2004c). *Sodomy.* Retrieved March 24, 2005, from http://www.thetaskforce.org/theissues/issue.cfm?issueID=11

Peterson, K. J. (1996). Preface: Developing the context: The impact of homophobia and heterosexism on the health care of gay and lesbian people. In K. J. Peterson (Ed.), *Health care for lesbians and gay men: Confronting homophobia and sexism* (pp. xx). Binghamton, NY: Harrington Park Press.

Sloan, L. M., & Gustavsson, N. (1998). *Violence and social injustice against lesbian, gay and bisexual people.* New York: Haworth Press.

United Nations. (1994). Toonen v Australia. *Human Rights Committee Communication No. 488/1992.* Retrieved March 25, 2005, from http://www.hrw.org/lgbt/pdf/toonen.pdf

SUGGESTED READINGS

Davies, D. (1996). Towards a model of gay affirmative therapy. In D. Davies & C. Neal (Eds.), *Pink therapy: A guide for counselors and therapists working with lesbian, gay and bisexual clients* (pp. 24–40). Philadelphia: Open University.

National Gay and Lesbian Task Force. (2003). *National Gay and Lesbian Task Force welcomes Supreme Court sodomy decision—Calls opinion a major advance for individual liberty.* Retrieved April 17, 2004, from http://www.thetaskforce.org/news/release.cfm?releaseID=551

National Gay and Lesbian Task Force. (2005). *Second parent adoption in the U.S.* Retrieved March 24, 2005, from http://www.thetaskforce.org/downloads/secondparentadoptionmap.pdf

Policy statement approved by the NASW Delegate Assembly, August 2005. This policy supersedes the policy statement on Lesbian, Gay, and Bisexual Issues approved by the Delegate Assembly in 1996 and referred by the 2002 Delegate Assembly to the 2005 Delegate Assembly for revision. For further information, contact the National Association of Social Workers, 750 First Street, NE, Suite 700, Washington, DC 20002-4241. Telephone: 202-408-8600 or 800-638-8799; e-mail: press@naswdc.org

Long-Term Care

BACKGROUND

According to Barker (2003), *long-term care* (LTC) is "a system of providing social, personal, and health care services over a sustained period to people who in some way suffer from functional impairment, including a limited ability to perform activities of daily living. LTC services are required mostly by older people, adults with developmental disabilities, people who are mentally ill, and people with disabling and prolonged chronic illness. It is provided by professionals, family members, and volunteers under public or private auspices in nursing homes, boarding houses, assisted-living facilities, adult day care centers and home community-based facilities. In addition to health care and case management services, LTC services can include transportation, escort, homemaker services, night sitting, recreation, home health services, home meals, and ombudsperson services" (p. 253).

The U.S. Senate Special Committee on Aging (2000) stated that the goal of LTC is to allow an individual to attain and maintain an optimal level of functioning. This makes LTC distinct from acute health care, which is primarily designed to cure illness. LTC includes diagnostic, preventive, supportive, rehabilitative, maintenance, and personal care services provided by informal caregivers, such as family or friends, or formal caregivers, such as specially trained or licensed professionals. Care may be provided in a nursing facility or in a less restrictive environment, such as a person's home, or assisted-living facilities. Support for living in a less restrictive environment is complemented by community-based programs, such as home health care, respite care, and adult day care.

There has been substantial growth in the numbers of people needing LTC as a result of a growing aging population, a higher prevalence of chronic illness and disability, and an increasing number of people with chronic, infectious diseases such as HIV, and dementias such as Alzheimer's disease. In 2001 about 7 million men and women over age 65 needed LTC. The number is projected to increase to 12 million people by the year 2020. Family and friends provide care for 70 percent of the older adults (American Association of Retired Persons, 2004). The demand for formal LTC will continue to grow as a result of changes in family dynamics—that is, the stress of the psychosocial aspect of LTC on family caregivers, spousal impoverishment, and the changing role of women who have provided the majority of informal LTC services.

Consumers are demanding more home- and community-based services, a movement that gained support from the Olmstead decision (Centers for Medicare and Medicaid Services, 2004), which indicated support for encouraging aging and disabled populations to live in the least restrictive settings as long as possible. The ideal formal LTC system would offer a full continuum of care, including acute medical services (for example, rehabilitative care, skilled care at home), LTC services (for example, nursing home care, adult day care, home-delivered meals, personal care attendants), social services (for example, assistance with Medicare and Medicaid forms, socialization opportunities), and housing services (for example, assisted living, subsidized housing) (Branch, 2001). Such a system also needs to include client choice, and financial and emotional support to clients and caregivers, especially in home-based situations. As a result of the Olmstead decision, new providers and new services have developed, often in an uncoordinated manner. The present system of LTC is characterized as fragmented, inappropriate, and inadequate. Home- and community-based services (for example, mental health, transportation, and adult day care) have various, fragmented funding sources and auspices. Service availability differs from state to state; even in communities there are gaps in the continuum of care (Branch, 2001). There is tremendous need for reform to create an integrated, cohesive, and comprehensive system of services and better funding (U.S. Senate Special Committee on Aging, 2002).

Currently, services are funded primarily by state and federal programs with Medicaid as the primary payer of LTC. During fiscal year 2000, Medicaid paid for 45 percent of the $137 billion that the United States spent on LTC. Despite the allocation of state and federal monies to long-term care, older adults and their families either pay out-of-pocket for much of the LTC services rendered or receive care provided by informal (unpaid) support systems such as family, neighbors, and friends (Branch, 2001; U.S. Senate Special Committee on Aging, 2002). Clearly, caregiving of this type needs to be supported, especially financially, or replaced.

Medicaid has allowed for great variability in benefits for optional services such as case management, psychosocial rehabilitation, and clinical services entailing outpatient therapy, partial hospitalization, and home-based personal care by nonphysician providers. Availability of these services is limited, inequitable, and in some states, unavailable. There has been great variability in Medicaid services for older people with chronic, severe physical disabilities, mental illness, or dementia, and it had provided few additional services. Lack of services or overuse of physical restraints and psychotropic drugs has been the response of many nursing homes to people with chronic mental illness, mental retardation or developmental disabilities, and those who exhibit behavioral symptoms of dementia. Legislation has sought to eliminate this ineffective, custodial-oriented response ("Medicare and Medicaid: Requirements," 1989). Nursing home regulations have sought to correct abusive situations by providing adequate safeguards for promoting maximization of independence, discharge planning,

and resident rights through ombudsman programs and efforts to enhance the quality of life of residents.

There is a lack of services available to older adults who are developmentally disabled and are either residents in nursing homes or being cared for at home by their families. Nursing home employees are not adequately trained to meet the specialized mental and emotional needs of this population. In addition, most professionals working in LTC, including social workers, have a lack of educational opportunities and lack of continuing education in gerontology (Council on Social Work Education, 2001; Health Resources & Services Administration, 1995). There is a continued need for increased field practicum opportunities in home- and community-based LTC services and a continued need to integrate aging and LTC content into the curriculum of all bachelor's and master's degree programs in social work (Scharlach, Damron-Rodriguez, Robinson, & Feldman, 2000). This should also include attitude changes and reduction of ageism.

Financial pressures on the health care system have resulted in the promotion of managed care programs for health services. The growth of managed care has had an effect on older people and others with chronic mental and physical illnesses who are eligible for Medicare and Medicaid. A growing number of retirees are enrolled in Medicare managed care plans. In addition, many states have opted to seek Medicaid waivers of federal regulatory requirements to experiment with providing cost-effective services to recipients, including managed care models (Cauchi, 1999).

Although managed care organizations have made respectable attempts to provide cost-effective, quality services for people with chronic illnesses (Cauchi, 1999), the philosophy of managed care is not easily adapted to optimum delivery of LTC services. Managed care methods of intervention, although effective for many patients, are not the most effective for providing services to isolated, frail people (Knight & Kaskie, 1995). Also, the managed care approach generally has not promoted outreach services to vulnerable clients, LTC research, and training, including field instruction. Managed care has tended to exacerbate the fragmentation problem of LTC services delivery and has not promoted the development of a continuum of care approach (Greene, 1995).

As a result of the development of managed care and the increased growth in the numbers of vulnerable, frail, and disabled people, there is a need for heightened attention to ethical and legal considerations in LTC. Some of the areas that warrant attention are

- fairness and adequacy of care

- client and professional input in decision making and rationing of care decisions

- supportive, client-oriented services in making end-of-life decisions

- flexible and humane policies related to guardianship

- accountability and protection regarding use of client and client records

- government responsibility for protecting vulnerable people and providing services to the economically poor people (Fahey, 1995; Kane, 1996).

The involvement of the National Association of Social Workers (NASW) in LTC includes both advocacy efforts and the development of standards for the field. NASW supports national health care reform and has taken the position that there is a need to regulate the managed care industry (NASW, 1998). NASW was instrumental in recommending revisions to the Omnibus Reconciliation Act (OBRA) nursing home regulations and actively participated in the 1995 White House Conference on Aging. The development of professional standards includes participation in the formation of LTC accreditation standards for the Joint Commission on Accreditation of Healthcare Organizations. In addition, NASW is a participating member of the Quality Improvement Organization's Public Advisory Panel, which is composed of allied health and mental health organizations and advocates who are interested in discussing ways to improve the quality of care in skilled-nursing facilities (Yagoda, 2004). NASW has created *Standards for Social Work Services in Long-Term Care Facilities* (NASW,

2003), *Clinical Indicators for Social Work and Psychosocial Services in Nursing Homes* (NASW, 1993), and *Standards for Social Work Practice in Palliative and End-of-Life Care* (NASW, 2004).

ISSUE STATEMENT

Long-term care services are characterized by deficit focus, stereotypical medical models on aging, an inadequate funding system, and a lack of continuity and coordination between insufficient use of a continuum of acute and chronic care to promote maximum self-determination of clients in the least restrictive setting. The government at all levels and the private sector have had little success in integrating or coordinating the growing array of available services into a viable system to meet individual and functional needs of clients, caregivers, and families. There is no comprehensive policy that includes guiding principles as a focus for ongoing planning, policy development, and change. The increasing societal need for LTC must be a catalyst for the health care system to re-examine and improve its low emphasis on prevention and client satisfaction and high emphasis on cost-effectiveness of services. Major problem areas within the LTC system include access to care (that is, urban versus rural), eligibility for and availability of services, the provision of quality care, the need for guiding principles for policy development, definition of ethical underpinnings, and the financing of LTC services.

In response to the changes occurring in LTC, the social work profession must examine its role and function throughout the continuum of care. Social work practice approaches, such as strength-based case management, family intervention, psychosocial assessment, interdisciplinary teamwork, and practice-based evaluation, can provide effective and efficient integration of services in LTC. Social workers also need to be active and take a leadership role in advocacy and policy making related to LTC.

The important social work role of advocacy for appropriate, culturally competent quality care and quality of life for clients and caregivers is critical in meeting the needs for consumer protection and consumer involvement. Careful consideration must be given to an ethical review that includes redefinition of roles, changes in legal perspective, and much more emphasis on self-determination and autonomy. The changing LTC environment presents both a challenge and an opportunity for the profession.

POLICY STATEMENT

NASW advocates for the continued reform of the LTC system with emphasis on strengthening the social work role in a continuum of care services delivery model. NASW supports inclusion of the following principles in LTC reform:

Access, Eligibility, and Availability of Services

■ access to a variety of physical and mental health and support services, based on individual needs to enable individuals to attain and maintain their optimal level of functioning in the least restrictive environment

■ access to LTC services for all who need them, regardless of age, income, disability, race, national origin, gender, sexual orientation, ethnicity, or geographic location

■ access to qualified, professional social work services at all levels of care to facilitate the integration of services in LTC to meet individual needs

■ promotion of the integration of competency-based gerontological content in BSW and MSW curriculum

■ eligibility for LTC services based on individual, functional need and economic and social support not solely on medical necessity

■ inclusion of social workers in managed care planning teams to ensure equitable use of resources in care and treatment

■ availability of services on a continuum that links all levels of LTC and addresses the physical, social, mental, cultural, and spiritual needs of the individual, family, and caregivers

■ availability of social work services based on individual functional need that is not solely related to medical diagnosis or dependent on the involvement of another health or mental health discipline

■ availability of specialized care for individuals with cognitive and functional impairments

■ social work services that address the needs of informal caregivers for people who are chronically ill, so that both the caregiver and the receiver of care enjoy a good quality of life.

Quality of Life and Quality of Care

■ emphasis on the quality of life for each client and quality care in services across the continuum of LTC

■ promotion and support of client self-determination in making choices and client participation in decisions that affect the delivery and provision of LTC services, including initiatives that encourage people to use advance directives in planning health care

■ participation of client-designated family members, and other client-designated caregivers, to ensure choice and quality at all levels of care

■ assurance of confidentiality and ethical considerations in all areas of decision making

■ ongoing expansion of education, staff development, training, and continuing education programs, including learning and understanding about the impact of the societal ageism and ableism on LTC policies for all levels of social workers employed along the LTC continuum

■ use of standards for gerontological social work that enhances the proficiency of social work practitioners in our aging society

■ adherence to regulatory requirements that recognize both quality-of-care and quality-of-life issues

■ dignified, humane, effective, and client-based services that are consistent with professional social work values

■ promotion of practice-based research on social, mental health, and substance abuse issues in LTC, with a focus on racial, cultural, ethnic, ability, and gender perspectives

- program evaluation, including client satisfaction surveys, focus groups, professional performance appraisals, evaluation and assessment of client goals, and service/treatment plans with full participation of clients and their families.

Financing

- development of an adequate financing system for LTC that preserves, increases, and redistributes revenue to increase access and provide coverage based on the client's need

- solvency of social security, Medicare, and Medicaid programs as well as the pursuit of alternative sources for LTC funding

- federal and state funding for cost-effective community-based alternatives to nursing home care, including assisted living, adult day care, shared housing, home health care, home-delivered meals, transportation, and hospice care

- initiatives that encourage all people to plan for health care needs and retirement

- continuation of the provision of consumer protection guidelines for LTC insurance, even for those who have established chronic disabilities, so cost of coverage is reasonable.

REFERENCES

American Association of Retired Persons. (2004). *Home and community-based long-term care.* Retrieved May 31, 2004, from http://research.aarp.org/health/hcb_ltc.html

Barker, R. L. (2003). *The social work dictionary* (5th ed.). Washington, DC: NASW Press.

Branch, L. G. (2001). Community long-term care services: What works and what doesn't? *Gerontologist, 41,* 307–308.

Cauchi, R. (1999, March). Managed care: Where do we go from here? In *State legislatures.* Retrieved May 31, 2004, from http://www.ncsl.org/programs/pubs/399mancare.htm#facts

Centers for Medicare and Medicaid Services. (2004, September). Americans with Disabil-ities Act/Olmstead Decision. Retrieved December 13, 2004, from http://www.cms.hhs.gov/olmstead

Council on Social Work Education. (March 2001). *A blueprint for the new millennium.* Alexandria, VA: Author.

Fahey, C. (1995). The ethical underpinnings of long-term care reform. *Care Lines, 2*(4), 1.

Greene, R. (1995). Family involvement in mental health care for older adults: From caregiving to advocacy and empowerment. In M. Gatz (Ed.), *Emerging issues in mental health and aging* (pp. 210–230). Washington, DC: American Psychological Association.

Health Resources and Services Administration, Bureau of Health Professions. (1995). *A national agenda for geriatric education: White papers.* Washington, DC: Author.

Kane, R. (1996). The ethics of health care delivery to elders in a managed care environment. *Managed Care & Aging, 3*(1), 1.

Knight, B., & Kaskie, B. (1995). Models for mental health service delivery to older adults: Implications for reform. In M. Gatz (Ed.), *Emerging issues in mental health and aging* (pp. 231–255). Washington, DC: American Psychological Association.

Medicare and Medicaid: Requirements for Long Term Care Facilities. (1989, February 2). *Federal Register, 54,* 5333, 5335.

National Association of Social Workers. (1993). *NASW clinical indicators for social work and psychosocial services in nursing homes.* Washington, DC: Author.

National Association of Social Workers. (1998). NASW position paper on managed care. Retrieved May 31, 2004, from http://www.socialworkers.org/archives/advocacy/positions/mngdcare.asp

National Association of Social Workers. (2003). *NASW standards for social work services in long-term care facilities.* Washington, DC: Author.

National Association of Social Workers. (2004). *NASW standards for social work practice in palliative and end-of-life care.* Washington, DC: Author.

Scharlach, A., Damron-Rodriguez, J., Robinson, B., & Feldman, R. (2000). Educating social workers for an aging society: A vision for the 21st century. *Journal of Social Work Education, 36,* 521–538.

U.S. Senate Special Committee on Aging. (2000). *Developments in aging: 1997 and 1998* (Report 106-229). Washington, DC: U.S. Government Printing Office.

U.S. Senate Special Committee on Aging. (2002). *Long-term care report* (Report 107-74).

Washington, DC: U.S. Government Printing Office.

Yagoda, L. (2004). *Aging highlights*. Retrieved May 31, 2004, from http://www.social-workers.org/practice/aging/021304notes.asp

Policy statement approved by the NASW Delegate Assembly, August 2005. This policy supersedes the policy statement on Long-Term Care approved by the Delegate Assembly in 1996, 1993, and 1979 and referred by the 2002 Delegate Assembly to the 2005 Delegate Assembly for revision. For further information, contact the National Association of Social Workers, 750 First Street, NE, Suite 700, Washington, DC 20002-4241. Telephone: 202-408-8600 or 800-638-8799; e-mail: press@naswdc.org

Mental Health

BACKGROUND

The social work profession has provided leadership in the provision of mental health services. Social workers develop and implement multilevel interventions that target the individual, family, community, and larger psychosocial systems.

Psychiatric conditions are common in the United States, with a lifetime prevalence rate of 46.4 percent (Kessler, Berglund, et al., 2005) and a 12-month prevalence rate of 26.2 percent for any diagnosis (Kessler, Chiu, Demler, & Walters, 2005). The costs pertaining to mental health conditions are staggering and are illustrated through statistics, role disability, financial burden of disease, and the face of human suffering and disability (Heller & Gitterman, 2010). Social workers are the largest group of clinically trained mental health providers in the United States (Newhill & Korr, 2004; Substance Abuse and Mental Health Services Administration [SAMHSA], 2006). By the nature of the profession's dual focus on enhancing the well-being of individuals and working toward social and economic justice, social workers are well-positioned to intervene, on both individual and systemic levels, with people affected by the challenges of mental health conditions. Recent legislation (the Patient Protection and Affordable Care Act of 2010 [111-148]; the Paul Wellstone and Pete Domenici Mental Health Parity and Addiction Equity Act of 2008 [P.L. 110-343]) has promised significant changes in access to both insurance and services to a broader range of the American population, but current political and economic forces make the eventual realization of these efforts uncertain.

The history of treatment for mental illness in the United States is marked by shifting assumptions about the etiology of mental illness, from theories of moral depravity, maternal failures, brain disease, and social construction to philosophies, levels of care, and legislation regarding access to care (Mechanic, 2008).

Legislative and policy decisions that demonstrate the country's developing beliefs about definitions of mental illness, the settings in which care should occur, and the degree to which society should make available both access and funding for the provision of services to people with mental illness include the following:

- the National Mental Health Act of 1946 (P.L. 79-487), which emerged from the controversial screenings for recruits for military service and resulted in the establishment of National Institute of Mental Health.

- the Mental Health Study Act of 1955 (P.L. 84-182), which led to the Joint Commission on Mental Illness and Health's report *Action for Mental Health* in 1961.

- the Mental Retardation Facilities and Community Mental Health Centers Construction Act of 1963 (P.L. 88-164) and its amendments (1965, 1975), which authorized funding for professional training for community mental health centers for outpatient, inpatient and partial hospitalization, emergency care, and education for community caretakers.

- the Health Maintenance Act of 1973, outlining patient protection obligations.

- the Education for All Handicapped Children Act of 1975 (P.L. 94-142).

- the Mental Health Systems Act of 1980, providing improved services to people with mental illness.

- the Omnibus Budget Reconciliation Act of 1981 (P.L. 97-35), which repealed the Mental Health Services Act and withdrew the federal government's involvement in service provision by the Alcohol, Drug Abuse, and Mental Health Administration's consolidation of funding into single block grants to each state.

- the State Comprehensive Mental Health Services Plan Act of 1986 (P.L. 99-660), with its focus on people with severe mental illness, particularly the homeless.

- the 1987 Omnibus Budget Reconciliation Act of 1987 (P.L. 100-203), which aimed to see that people were treated in the least restrictive setting.

- the Stewart B. McKinney Homeless Assistance Act of 1987 (P.L. 100-77).

- the Americans with Disabilities Act of 1990 (P.L. 101-336), covering people with both physical and psychiatric conditions.

- the development of SAMHSA in 1992, which made available community mental health services block grants that included a focus on children and adolescents with mental health issues and, subsequently, specialized programs targeting women, older adults, and various other age groups and ethnic populations.

- the Mental Health Parity Act of 1996 (P.L. 104-204), which prohibited disparate annual or lifetime limits on coverage for mental health and general health care.

- In 1997 the insurance industry's regulatory body, the National Committee on Quality Assurance (NCQA), began to require compliance with postpsychiatric discharge follow-up standards.

- the Paul Wellstone and Pete Domenici Mental Health Parity and Addiction Equity Act of 2008 (P.L. 110-343), which extends parity to health and mental health diagnoses in the *International Classification of Diseases, Ninth Revision, Clinical Modification*.

- the Patient Protection and Affordable Care Act of 2010 (P.L. 111-148), which aims, among other things, to make health insurance available to more individuals and expands Medicaid's eligibility requirements for mental health treatment.

One of the explicit objectives of managed care was seamless patient transition between levels of care, including institutional, residential, hospital, partial hospital, intensive outpatient, and outpatient. Although such a seamless transition is a natural conceptual extension of the "one-stop-shopping" afforded by health maintenance organizations, especially those sponsored by hospitals, vertical integration proved to be challenging. In response, 1997 saw the industry's primary regulatory body, the NCQA, begin to require compliance with postpsychiatric discharge follow-up standards. The data do show improvement; however, the outcomes still fall short of the goals of seamlessness and vertical integration. Such is the case in community mental health care as well.

Linkages across types of systems are even more fractured. Although there are higher rates of mental illness in incarcerated populations than in the general population (Rouse, 1995), there continue to be low rates of follow-up for mental health services after release from correctional facilities.

Compared with involuntary inpatient hospitalization, compulsory outpatient treatment is a relatively new phenomenon. An individual must be assessed to be unlikely to live safely without supervision. In addition, he or she must have a history of treatment noncompliance related to psychiatric hospitalization or incarceration or have committed serious acts— or threats—of violence to self or others. Forty-four states have enacted legislation related to involuntary treatment over the last decade.

There have been three empirical studies of the effectiveness of Kendra's Law, a 1999 New York state piece of legislation addressing court-ordered, outpatient treatment. The conclusions of the New York State Office of Mental Health's 2005 study were that Kendra's Law resulted in dramatically lower rates of homelessness, psychiatric hospitalization, and arrest and incarceration. Costs varied directly with these reductions. Moreover, rates of substance abuse, victimization, and harm to self, other, or property all plummeted, whereas illness-related psychosocial functioning improved.

ISSUE STATEMENT

Mental illness is a common health problem in the United States affecting millions of people each year in all age groups. More than 26 percent of the nation's adult population experiences mental illness, and 6 percent of this population experiences a severe mental illness (see http://www.nimh.nih.gov/statistics/index.shtml). However, because many people with mental illness never receive treatment, it is difficult to determine the actual prevalence of mental illness. With the stigma of mental illness decreasing, more Americans are seeking mental health services. From 1996 to 2006, the number of Americans paying for mental health services increased 87 percent (Agency for Healthcare Research Quality, n.d.). Yet there continue to be key barriers to treatment, including cultural disparities, access to care, stigma, and reimbursement challenges (President's New Freedom Commission on Mental Health, 2003).

The burden of mental illness is concentrated on those who experience a serious mental illness resulting in functional impairment that interferes or limits one or more major life activities. Comorbid conditions complicate mental illness, and populations with comorbid conditions usually seek help, whereas others with single disorders may not. In the United States, depression leads individual diseases and disorders that contribute to total number of years lost to illness, disability, or premature death. Suicide has increased over the past 10 years and in 2007 was the fourth leading cause of death in the United States for people ages 18 to 65 years (Centers for Disease Control and Prevention, 2007).

Over 20 percent of children and adolescents in the United States have experienced a severe mental illness. Attention-deficit hyperactivity disorder and mood and conduct disorders are most common among youths ages eight to 15, and gender does not appear to be a statistical factor (see http://www.nimh.nih.gov/statistics/index.shtml).

Adolescents and adults in the mental health system often have histories of early trauma, abuse, and neglect. Inadequate prenatal care, lack of appropriate nutrition, difficult birth, and high levels of stress in the mother affect the developing fetus, creating neurochemical vulnerabilities within the child as it develops through infancy and into adulthood (Purvis, Cross, & Sunshine, 2007).

In infancy, a child's beliefs about self and others are taking form through the attachment process with his or her primary caregivers. Impaired attachment in childhood can, and often does, affect the ability of the individual to develop healthy relationships in adulthood, leading to mental health concerns, damaged interpersonal relationships, and an impaired ability to care for and value self and others (Schechter & Willheim, 2009). The availability and use of professional support for parents in preparing for the birth of a child, and through the early years of the child's development, can have a significant positive impact on the outcomes for the child and the family (Purvis et al., 2007).

Mental health is the fourth highest ranking rural health concern (Gamm, Stone, & Pittman, 2003). Yet, in many rural communities, mental health services are not available (Gustafson, Preston, & Hudson, 2009) due to chronic shortages of clinical social workers and mental health clinicians (Gale, Loux, Shaw, & Hartley, 2010; Gustafson et al., 2009). Data show that residents of the most rural areas receive less mental health treatment than people residing in metropolitan areas (Hauenstein et al., 2007). Furthermore, there is evidence of higher suicide rates, a standard indicator of mental illness, in rural areas (D'Mello, 2010). Higher suicide rates correspond to regions in the United States that have the least number of mental health providers (D'Mello, 2010). Despite the need for mental health services in rural communities, availability and accessibility are major barriers that prevent rural Americans from receiving the care they need (Gustafson et al., 2009). Military personnel and veterans encounter stress through being at war, multiple and extended deployments, and separation from loved ones. These factors contribute to the development of mental health issues such as posttraumatic stress disorder, depression, substance use, and anxiety. Mental health problems experienced by this population have an effect on military personnel's families while they are serving as well as when they return home.

A related development is the growing impact of the recovery movement on the ways in which mental health care is conceptualized and delivered. "The concept of recovery is consistent with the values of social work" (Garrison, Ackerson, & Forrest, 2010) and is widely embraced by the social work profession. A pioneer in recovery, William Anthony (1993), defined *recovery* as

> a deeply personal, unique process of changing one's attitudes, values, feelings, goals, skills and/or roles. It is a way of living a satisfying, hopeful, and contributing life even with limitations caused by the illness. Recovery involves the development of new meaning and purpose in one's life as one grows beyond the catastrophic effects of mental illness.

Social work has been at the forefront of the development and implementation of this model. The recovery movement/model allows for and supports the integration of consumers in their own treatment, allowing them to guide their own treatment as they move toward improved health and recovery.

POLICY STATEMENT

NASW maintains its commitment to enhancing the well-being of people living with mental health conditions and working toward increased access to appropriate services and interventions. NASW is committed to improving mental health services and advocates for legislative action to improve the quality of care, access, reimbursement, research, and education in mental health.

To further the advances that have been made in the prevention, diagnosis, assessment, and treatment of mental illness, NASW supports the following:

Prevention and Education

■ Prevention and outreach programs—including education, consultation, and early intervention—should be fully funded and provided to the public to

- promote an understanding of the effects of prenatal and early childhood issues on the subsequent development of mental illness

- destigmatize and maximize early identification and treatment of mental illness

- promote individual and family wellness programming

- foster resilience in people experiencing mental illness and in those who care for them.

Access to Services

■ Fully integrated, comprehensive services should be made available for all who experience mental illness, particularly those with chronic and severe illness.

■ Culturally responsive interventions in the consumers' native languages should be included in the provision of effective mental health care.

■ Family members and significant others should be included in the process of assessment, treatment planning and intervention and should have access to supportive services to help them address the problems posed by the mental illness of a loved one.

■ Mental health parity is important and should be defined consistently among health plans.

■ The process of, and opportunities for, appealing adverse treatment decisions should be enhanced.

■ A broad range of housing and vocational services should be available to people who have severe mental illness so as to strengthen their independent living skills, support their efforts to build stable and supportive relationships, and improve their quality of life.

■ Productive work should not result in sanctions affecting social insurance, public assistance, or access to other programs.

Intervention and Treatment

■ Behavioral health care plans should rely on the best judgment of mental health clinicians when making service determinations, including the type, level, and duration of services.

■ Consumers should be given choices of service options that meet their needs, with services provided in the most therapeutic and least restrictive environments possible.

■ Evidence based-practice paired with clinical judgment should be considered in making clinical decisions.

■ Involuntary hospitalization or outpatient treatment should balance consumers' rights to self-determination with the safety of family members and the community.

■ Comorbid substance use disorders should not be given undue weight in the assessment of functional capacity or in eligibility determination for social insurance, public assistance, and social services.

■ The mental health challenges faced by veterans and their families should be addressed in a comprehensive and readily accessible manner. Education and early intervention for returning service personnel and their families should be provided as an integral part of that care.

■ Incarcerated individuals should be provided full access to mental health services, including screening, assessment, medication, counseling, and discharge planning.

■ To strengthen best practices, social workers should pursue research funding to test mental health treatment methodologies and outcomes. Underserved populations should be included in the design of research projects whenever possible.

REFERENCES

Agency for Healthcare Research Quality. (n.d.). *Medical expenditure panel survey 2007.* Retrieved from http://www.meps.ahrq.gov/mepsweb

Americans with Disabilities Act of 1990, P.L. 101-336, 104 Stat. 327 (1990).

Anthony, W. A. (1993). Recovery from mental illness: The guiding vision of the mental health service system in the 1990s. *Psychosocial Rehabilitation Journal, 16*(4), 11–23.

Centers for Disease Control and Prevention, National Vital Statistics System. (2007). *Leading causes of death ages 18–65 in the United States.* Retrieved from http://www.nimh.nih.gov/statistics/3AGES1865.shtml

D'Mello, D. (2010, May). *Rurality, suicide and the availability of mental health providers.* Poster session presented at the 163rd Annual Meeting of the American Psychiatric Association, New Orleans.

Education for All Handicapped Children Act of 1975, P.L. 94-142, 89 Stat. 773 (1975).

Gale, J., Loux, S., Shaw, B., & Hartley, D. (2010). *Encouraging rural health clinics to provide mental health services: What are the options?* Retrieved from http://muskie.usm.maine.edu/ihp/ruralhealth

Gamm, L. G., Stone, S., & Pittman, S. (2003). *Mental health and mental disorders—A rural challenge: A literature review.* Retrieved from http://www.srphtambsc.edu/centers/rhp2010/08Volume2mentalhealth.pdf

Garrison, M. E., Ackerson, B. J., & Forrest, J. (2010). Consumers as providers: What inhibits the success of this practice? *Best Practices in Mental Health: An International Journal, 6*(2), 1–2.

Gustafson, D. T., Preston, K., & Hudson, J. (2009). *Mental health: Overlooked and disregarded in rural America.* Retrieved from http://www.cfra.org

Hauenstein, E. J., Petterson, S., Rovnyak, V., Merwin, E., Heise, B., & Wagner, D. (2007). Rurality and mental health treatment. *Administration and Policy in Mental Health, 34,* 255–267.

Heller, N., & Gitterman, A. (2010). *Mental health and social problems.* New York: Routledge.

Joint Commission on Mental Illness and Health. (1961). *Action for mental health: Final report of the Joint Commission on Mental Illness and Health.* New York: Basic Books.

Kessler, R. C., Berglund, P., Demler, O., Jin, R., Merikangas, K. R., & Walters, E. E. (2005). Lifetime prevalence and age-of-onset distributions of *DSM–IV* disorders in the National Comorbidity Survey Replication. *Archives of General Psychiatry, 62,* 593–602.

Kessler, R. C., Chiu, W., Demler, O., & Walters, E. E. (2005). Prevalence, severity, and comorbidity of 12-month *DSM–IV* disorders in the National Comorbidity Survey Replication. *Archives of General Psychiatry, 62,* 617–627.

Mechanic, D. (2008). *Mental health and social policy: Beyond managed care* (5th ed.). Boston: Pearson/Allyn & Bacon.

Mental Health Parity Act of 1996, P.L. 104-204, 110 Stat. 2944 (1996).

Mental Health Study Act of 1955, P.L. 84-182, 69 Stat. 381 (1955).

Mental Retardation Facilities and Community Mental Health Centers Construction Act of 1963, P.L. 88-164, 77 Stat. 282 (1963).

National Mental Health Act of 1946, P.L. 79-487, 60 Stat. 421 (1946).

Newhill, C. E., & Korr, W. S. (2004). Practice with persons with severe mental illness: Rewards, challenges, and burdens. *Health & Social Work, 29,* 297–305.

New York State Office of Mental Health. (2005). *Kendra's Law: Final report on the status of assisted outpatient treatment.* Albany, NY: Author.

Omnibus Budget Reconciliation Act of 1981, P.L. 97-35, 95 Stat. 357 (1981).

Omnibus Budget Reconciliation Act of 1987, P.L. 100-203, 101 Stat. 1330 (1987).

Patient Protection and Affordable Care Act, P.L. 111-148, 119–124 Stat. 1025 (2010).

Paul Wellstone and Pete Domenici Mental Health Parity and Addiction Equity Act of 2008, P.L. 110-343 (2008).

President's New Freedom Commission on Mental Health. (2003). *Achieving the promise: Transforming mental health care in America.* Washington, DC: U.S. Government Printing Office.

Purvis, K. S., Cross, D. R., & Sunshine, W. L. (2007). *The connected child.* New York: McGraw-Hill.

Rouse, B. A. (Ed.). (1995). *Substance abuse and mental illness sourcebook* (DHHS Publication No. SMA 95-3064). Washington, DC: U.S. Government Printing Office.

Schechter, D. S., & Willhelm, E. (2009). Disturbances of attachment and parental psychopathology in early childhood. *Child and Adolescent Psychiatric Clinics of North America, 18,* 665–687.

State Comprehensive Mental Health Services Plan Act of 1986, P.L. 99-660, 100 Stat. 482 (1986).

Stewart B. McKinney Homeless Assistance Act of 1987, P.L. 100-77, 101 Stat. 482 (1987).

Substance Abuse and Mental Health Service Administration. (2006). *Mental health, United States, 2004* (DHHS Publication No. SMA 06-4195). Rockville, MD: Author.

NASW Members with Primary Responsibility for Revision of This Policy

First Draft Revision:

Daniel M. Potter (IL)

Policy Panelists:

Nina Heller (CT)
Charles Greco (NYS)
Robin Lennon Dearing (TN)
Mary Garrison (IL)
Susan Eldredge (TX)
Renée Rivera (CO)

Policy statement approved by the NASW Delegate Assembly, August 2011. This policy statement supersedes the policy statement on Mental Health approved by the 2002 Delegate Assembly. For further information, contact the National Association of Social Workers, 750 First Street, NE, Suite 700, Washington, DC 20002-4241. Telephone: 202-408-8600; e-mail: press@naswdc.org.

Parental Kidnapping

BACKGROUND

Parental kidnapping, or abduction of children, is linked with major social changes that have affected U.S. families during the past 30 years. These changes include the rise in single parenthood and divorce, shifts in gender roles within families that affect child care and custody, and increased visibility of family violence. The number of children under 18 years of age living with a single parent increased from fewer than 6 million in 1960 to more than 19 million by 1996, and the total has since ranged from 19 to 21 million (U.S. Census Bureau, 2009). In addition to children who have a noncustodial parent, children with quarreling or violent parents who are married or who share joint custody are also potential targets for parental abduction. The pool of children at risk is linked to the legal definitions of parental kidnapping, which vary among state, national, and international jurisdictions. Some legal definitions include any parent whose actions deprive the other parent of custody or access to the child, whether the couple is married, separated, or divorced. At the other end of the continuum, some states have laws that define abduction only in terms of violating a custody order.

Studies that have defined parental abduction broadly identify men and women as the abductors in roughly equal proportions (Hegar & Greif, 1991; Janvier, McCormick, & Donaldson, 1990; Sagatun & Barrett, 1990). Earlier studies that considered only abductions by noncustodial parents reported a much higher proportion of male perpetrators (Agopian, 1984). Boys and girls were abducted in almost equal numbers in all of the studies reviewed, and the studies indicated that toddlers and preschoolers may be at greatest risk of abduction. Children who have been abducted encounter a range of experiences, from dislocation and confusion to child abuse and the trauma of repeated snatchings (Greif, 2009). The effect of parental abduction is often devastating for the parents and other family members left behind (Greif, 2007, 2009; Greif & Hegar, 1993; Sagatun & Barrett, 1990).

Although public awareness of parental kidnapping has grown because of coverage in the print and broadcast media, it is a long-standing problem that has been recognized in federal and state policies for decades. For example, for almost 50 years, parents who kidnapped their children were specifically exempt from criminal prosecution under the federal Kidnapping Act. Because of the differences in state laws and practices regarding child custody during this period, some parents who failed to receive custody in one state kidnapped their children and sought custody in another state (Sagatun & Barrett, 1990).

The problem of recovering abducted children who are taken out of the country has been particularly acute because, until the 1980s, there was no major treaty that addressed the return of internationally abducted children. As of 2009, there were approximately 10,000 parental abductions involving U.S. children held in foreign countries by a parent of a different nationality (Slota, 2009).

Significant policy developments at the state, federal, and international levels have been initiated in the past three decades. To date, most efforts to combat parental kidnapping have emphasized primarily one approach: preventing abducting parents from going to another jurisdiction to obtain a custody order in their favor. To that end, all states have adopted some version of the model Uniform Child Custody

Jurisdiction Act, and most have passed additional legislation aimed at reducing parental kidnapping.

At the federal level, the National Center for Missing and Exploited Children was founded in 1984, and the Parental Kidnapping Prevention Act (P.L. 96-611) (PKPA) was enacted in 1980. However, enforcement of the act depends in part on state criminal law, because its Unlawful Flight to Avoid Prosecution provisions apply only if a state felony has been committed. The act encourages cooperation among the states and provides for Federal Bureau of Investigation (FBI) assistance in locating and returning kidnapped children (Chiancone, 2008; Cracchiolo, 2007).

The U.S. Supreme Court in 1988 interpreted parts of the PKPA in *Thompson v. Thompson*, in which the court established that parents are generally unable to resort to the federal courts to resolve conflicting awards of custody in state courts as a result of noncompliance with the PKPA. State courts also cite the PKPA in resolving disputes that arise under state law (for example, "Child Abduction," 2008; *In Re Axel Michael Sigmar*, 2008). Civil suits (torts) arising out of loss of physical custody are also possible in many states, and some have made or proposed statutory provisions for civil suits in parental kidnapping cases (Berger, 2000, Stern & Oehme, 2003).

In 1980, participants from 29 countries, including the United States, drafted the Hague Convention on the Civil Aspects of International Child Abduction. The Hague Convention provides for children under the age of 16 years to be returned to the country in which they were habitually resident immediately before a breach of custody or access rights. As of 2010, more than 80 nations have adopted the Hague Convention by ratification or accession (Hague Conference on Private International Law, 2010). However, there remain patterns of noncompliance with the provisions of the convention.

Enforcement of the convention has been hampered by a number of factors. For example, the United States signed the convention in 1981 and ratified it in 1986, but its provisions were not implemented until July 1988, when the International Child Abduction Remedies Act (P.L. 100-300) took effect. That law provides specific mechanisms for the United States to comply with the convention and makes the U.S. Department of State the agency in charge of enforcement (Estin, 2010; Pfund, 1997). Subsequently, the United States enacted the International Parental Kidnapping Crime Act, which has overcome various legal challenges (for example, Alanen, 2008; "Child Abduction," 2002, 2004; Weiner, 2008).

Despite these policy developments on state, national, and international levels, there is evidence that U.S. state laws remain uneven in their provisions and judicial interpretations (Freeman, 2000; Maxwell, 2005).

ISSUE STATEMENT

Social workers encounter families who are at risk of or who have experienced abduction in practice settings. These settings may include counseling and therapy; school social work; child protection and foster care; battered women's programs and shelters; social media networks; electronic communication; and forensic settings such as police departments, prosecutors' and public defenders' offices, and prisons.

Kidnapping or abduction of children by their parents is a complex social and legal problem that has received sporadic public and professional attention. Much of the social work literature addressing parental abductions dates from the 1990s, when both relevant research and policy changes were prevalent. However, many of the issues that underlie this form of family disruption continue to require interventions in multiple social service and legal arenas. Among the problems interwoven with parental abduction are the acrimony of many child custody disputes (Elrod, 2001), dissatisfaction with custody and visitation rights within many separated and divorced families, high rates of domestic violence and the special difficulties of parents who take their children and flee abuse (Jaffee, Johnston, & Crooks, 2008), and the need for specialized services of all types to prevent and resolve abductions and to help the families who experience them (Spilman, 2006; Zawis, 2008).

POLICY STATEMENT

To address and ameliorate the problem of parental kidnapping, NASW supports the following:

■ developing social services, such as supervised visitation that is fair and affordable, to provide both parents equal opportunity to visit with their children in an effort to prevent child abduction.

■ providing postkidnapping counseling and mediation services to minimize the effects of kidnapping and diminish the likelihood of recurrence.

■ promoting consensual models, such as parental coordination and facilitation; coparent education; and collaborative legal efforts to work out divorce and postdivorce conflicts regarding child custody, except in families experiencing domestic violence, the threat of violence, child abuse and neglect, or sexual exploitation.

■ collaborating with other professions, particularly those within the legal system, to curb and resolve parental abductions of children.

■ educating social workers in schools, workplaces and through continuing education to become more knowledgeable about the problem of parental kidnapping and its causes.

■ participating in shaping public policies at all levels that will prevent or reduce the occurrence of parental kidnapping.

■ adopting statutes in each state that include custody arrangements, such as joint custody, that reinforce the continued involvement of both parents in the important decisions about their children's welfare and upbringing, except in the potentially dangerous situations noted earlier.

■ establishing public awareness programs about the problems associated with parental kidnapping and using print, broadcast, and social media to educate the public and to locate abducted children.

■ establishing professional education programs to inform practitioners about the causes, dynamics, and laws regarding parental abduction.

■ strengthening policies of agencies in which children usually are present, particularly schools and child care facilities, to reduce the likelihood that those agencies will become sites of parental kidnapping.

■ strengthening state and federal laws concerning parental kidnapping, particularly toward achieving uniform definitions of abduction and uniform compliance with child custody and enforcement across state borders.

■ encouraging interdisciplinary cooperation to ensure the availability of comprehensive services.

■ ensuring availability of services to help both victims and perpetrators of parental kidnapping.

■ working toward a coordinated national network for the reunion of abducted children and their families and encouraging the full assistance of law enforcement agencies, particularly the FBI, in locating abducted children, with increased efforts to eliminate all discriminatory barriers that affect the definition of parental kidnapping and efforts to locate children of color.

■ working through international professional organizations to encourage adoption by more countries of the Hague Convention on the Civil Aspects of International Child Abduction and to advocate for compliance with the convention by signatory countries.

■ advocating for state criminal statutes that allow distinction among abductions on the basis of circumstances, such as the use of force, harm done to the child, length of absence, and whether the child was concealed from the searching parent. Statutes should include a defense against the charge of parental abduction if the abductor acted to prevent or avoid harm to the child.

REFERENCES

Agopian, M. W. (1984). The impact on children of abduction by parents. *Child Welfare, 63,* 511–519.

Alanen, J. (2008). When human rights conflict: Mediating international parental kidnapping disputes involving the domestic violence defense. *University of Miami Inter-American Law Review, 40,* 49–108.

Berger, L. L. (2000). Lies between mommy and daddy: The case for recognizing spousal emotional distress claims based on domestic deceit that interferes with parent–child relationships. *Loyola of Los Angeles Law Review, 33,* 449–532.

Chiancone, J. (2008). *Parental abduction: A review of literature.* Washington, DC: U.S. Department of Justice, Office of Juvenile Justice and Delinquency Prevention.

Child abduction. (2002). *International Law Update, 8,* 34–35.

Child abduction. (2004, February). *International Law Update, 10,* 19–20.

Child abduction. (2008, October). *International Law Update, 14,* 158–159.

Cracchiolo, F. (2007). Parental Kidnapping Prevention Act. *Journal of Contemporary Legal Issues, 16,* 299–303.

Elrod, L.D.H. (2001). Reforming the system to protect children in high conflict custody cases. *William Mitchell Law Review, 29,* 495–551.

Estin, A. L. (2010). Families across borders: The Hague Children's Conventions and the case for international family law in the United States. *Florida Law Review, 62,* 47–108.

Freeman, M. (2000). Rights of custody and access under the Hague Child Abduction Convention—"A questionable result?" *California Western International Law Journal, 31,* 39–51.

Greif, G. L. (2007). Unresolved loss: Issues in working with adults whose siblings were kidnapped years ago. *American Journal of Family Therapy, 35,* 203–215.

Greif, G. L. (2009). The long-term aftermath of child abduction: Two case studies and implications for family therapy. *American Journal of Family Therapy, 37,* 273–286.

Greif, G. L., & Hegar, R. L. (1993). *When parents kidnap: The families behind the headlines.* New York: Free Press.

Hague Conference on Private International Law. (2010). *Convention of 25 October 1980 on the civil aspects of international child abduction—status on: 1 November 2010.* Retrieved from http://www.hcch.net/upload/abduct overview_e.pdf

Hegar, R. L., & Greif, G. L. (1991). Abduction of children by parents: A survey of the problem. *Social Work, 36,* 421–426.

In Re Axel Michael Sigmar, No. 10-08-00328-CV (Court of Appeals of Texas, Tenth Dist., 2008).

International Child Abduction Remedies Act (ICARA), P.L. 100-300, 102 Stat. 437 (1988).

Jaffe, P. G., Johnston, J. R., & Crooks, C. V. (2008). Custody disputes involving allegations of domestic violence: Toward a differentiated approach to parenting plans. *Family Court Review, 46,* 500–522.

Janvier, R. F., McCormick, K., & Donaldson, R. (1990). Parental kidnapping: A survey of left-behind parents. *Juvenile & Family Court Journal, 41,* 1–8.

Maxwell, L. (2005). The disparity in treatment of international custody disputes in American courts: A post-September 11th analysis. *Pace International Law Review, 17,* 105–130.

Parental Kidnapping Prevention Act of 1980, P.L. 96-611, §§ 6–10, 94 Stat. 3568, 3569 (1980).

Pfund, P. H. (1997). The developing jurisprudence of the rights of the child: Contributions of the Hague Conference on International Law. *ILSA Journal of International and Comparative Law, 3,* 665.

Sagatun, I. J., & Barrett, L. (1990). Parental child abduction: The law, family dynamics, and legal system responses. *Journal of Criminal Justice, 18,* 433–442.

Slota, H. J. (2009). Preventing and responding to international child abduction. *American Journal of Family Law, 23,* 73–78.

Spilman, S. K. (2006). Child abduction, parents' distress, and social support. *Violence and Victims, 21,* 149–165.

Stern, N., & Oehme, K. (2003). Toward a coherent approach to tort immunity in judicially mandated family court services. *Kentucky Law Journal, 92,* 373–438.

Thompson v. Thompson, 108 S.Ct. 513 (1988).

U.S. Census Bureau. (2009). *Children under 18 years living with mother only, 1960 to present.* Retrieved from http://www.census.gov/population/www/socdemo/hh-fam.html#ht

Weiner, M. H. (2008). Half-truths, mistakes, and embarrassments: The United States goes to the fifth meeting of the special commission to review the operation of the convention on the civil aspects of international child abduction. *Utah Law Review, 2008*, 221–313.

Zawis, J. (2008). Practical and ethical implications of mediating international child abduction cases: A new frontier for mediators. *University of Miami Inter-American Law Review, 40*, 1–47.

NASW Members with Primary Responsibility for Revision of This Policy

First Draft Revision:

Rebecca L. Hegar (TX)

Policy Panelists:

Phyllis King (MA)
Marlene Huff (KY)
Pam Patton (OH)
Deneece Ferrales (TX)
Edward Davila (CA)

Policy statement approved by the NASW Delegate Assembly, August 2011. This policy statement supersedes the policy statement on Parental Kidnapping approved by the 2002 Delegate Assembly. For further information, contact the National Association of Social Workers, 750 First Street, NE, Suite 700, Washington, DC 20002-4241. Telephone: 202-408-8600; e-mail: press@naswdc.org.

Peace and Social Justice

BACKGROUND

The social work profession in the United States has its roots in the principles of peace and social justice. Jane Addams, winner of the Nobel Peace Prize in 1931 ("The Nobel Peace Prize 1932"), is likely the most notable of pacifist social work pioneers and is also known to be among the first in the United States to speak out against strengthening military might (Sullivan, 1993). Sullivan also noted that the first call to action by the public was made by social workers. At the beginning of the World War I, meetings focused on protesting war were held by social workers at the Henry Street Settlement House in New York. It was here and in other settlement houses and meeting places that Addams, Florence Kelly, and other social reformers of the time worked toward the creation of several peace and justice organizations, some of which still exist today, including the Women's International League for Peace and Freedom (formerly known as the Women's Peace Party) (see http://wilpf.org/US_WILPF).

Although the global trend is toward demilitarization (Grebe, 2011), we still live in a world where armed conflict exists and peaceful solutions to disagreements and social inequities can be preempted by militaristic solutions. Full participation with organizations such as the United Nations and international allies are critical steps in finding constructive, collaborative means to deal with international conflicts. The United States has a long history of supporting United Nations human rights mechanisms. Former First Lady Eleanor Roosevelt, who is well known for her support of social reforms for the poor, led the effort to develop the Universal Declaration of Human Rights (UDHR), adopted by the United Nations General Assembly in 1948. The UDHR recognizes that "the inherent dignity and the equal and inalienable rights of all members of the human family is the foundation of freedom, justice and peace in the world" (UDHR, 1948, p. 1). In 2009, the United States joined the United Nations Human Rights Council. Their participation on the council has helped to identify constructive mechanisms to fight discrimination and increase scrutiny of serious human rights violations around the world (Fassihian, 2011). However, the United States continues to fall too short in promoting social justice around the world. The United States is one of a small number of countries that have not ratified the Convention on the Elimination of All Forms of Discrimination Against Women and the Convention on the Rights of the Child.

Moreover, the gap in human standards of living continues to widen on a global and national level Kreutzmann, 2008). In the United States the gap between wealthy and poor people continues to widen (Sherman & Stone, 2010) as it does worldwide. As social justice takes a backseat in our national and world economies and social institutions, tensions grow and conflicts erupt. Ironically, those whose lives are most vulnerable and over whom these conflicts often are instigated are the very people who suffer the most damage from war—physically, emotionally, and economically. Poor people, especially children, are the primary casualties of conflict, whether that conflict be in the form of street violence, or civil or international war (Office of the Special Representative of the Secretary-General for Children and Armed Conflict, n.d.). Social workers are united by their *Code of Ethics* (NASW, 2008) in which the promotion and well-being of humans regardless of location or nationality and advocacy for attainment of basic human needs and the actualization of social justice for all are among their professional obligations.

Full participation with organizations such as the United Nations and international allies are critical steps in finding constructive, collaborative means to deal with international conflicts.

ISSUE STATEMENT

"Peace is not merely a distant goal that we seek, but . . . a means by which we arrive at that goal."—Martin Luther King, Jr. (1967). According to the *Social Work Dictionary* (Barker, 2003), *social justice* is "an ideal condition in which all members of a society have the same basic rights, protection[s], opportunities, obligations, and social benefits" (pp. 404–405). The important factors that affect peace and social justice are as follows:

■ Poverty as a result of weakening the power of organized labor, reduction in government social expenditures, and abandoning of full employment as a standard (Cornia, 2004; Lynch, Smith, Kaplan, & House, 2000; Putnam, 2000; Rank, 2008; Sapolsky, 2005; Schoen, Collins, Kriss, & Doty, 2008).

■ Economic disparities within geographic societies, with recognition that groups with lower economic status include disadvantaged populations such as immigrants, the poorly educated, those who are victims of bigotry based on race, gender, religion, age, or sexual orientation (Anderson, & Atkinson, 2007; Benabou, 2000; Bergensen & Bata, 2002; Himmelstein, Thorne, Warren, & Woolhandler, 2009; Pickett, Kelly, Brunner, Lobstein, & Wilkinson, 2005; Wilkinson & Pickett, 2006, 2010).

■ Limited and or unequal parity to health including morbidity and mortality, infant–mother mortality rates, obesity, drugs, teenage birth rates, and mental illness (Gold, Kawachi, Kennedy, Lynch, & Connell, 2001; Gold, Kennedy, Connell, & Kawachi, 2002; Health Development Agency, 2003; Hudson, 2005; McMunn, Bartley, Hardy, & Kuh, 2006; Pickett, James, & Wilkinson, 2006; Pickett, Mookherjee, & Wilkinson, 2005; Putsch & Pololi, 2004;

Ritsher, Warner, Johnson, & Dohrenwend, 2001; Tunstall, Shaw, & Dorling, 2004).

■ The quality of social relationships measured through the level of trust, competitiveness, the lack of commitment to civic duties, reduction of hostility, discrimination, and homicide rates (Chong, 2009; Lobmayer & Wilkinson, 2002; McMunn et al., 2006; Uslander, 2002; Wilkinson, 2005).

■ The level of educational performance in math and literacy for all children and the rate of secondary school dropouts that are contributing factors to social instability (Claussen, Smits, Naess, & Davey Smith, 2005; U.S. Department of Education, National Center for Education Statistics, 2004; Wilkinson & Pickett, 2010).

■ The death penalty and imprisonment rates which relate more to sentencing patterns than to actual crime rates (Marsh, 2003; Mauer, 2001; Sen, 2008; United Nations Crime and Justice Information Network, 2000; Uslander, 2002).

■ Carbon emissions, waste production, and use of the earth's resources in a way that contributes to stagnation and economic instability. The development of sustainable economic systems requires rapid innovation and change, much of which must be resource and energy saving (International Federation of Social Workers, 2007; Johnson, 2005; Kawachi, 2002; Lundy & van Wormer, 2007; Mackenbach, 2006; Wilper et al., 2009; World Health Organization, 2000).

■ The lack of social mobility or the ability to improve on income between generations (Bladen, Gregg, & Machin, 2005; Claussen et al., 2005; Ritsher et al., 2001).

POLICY STATEMENT

NASW supports

■ advocacy for peace initiatives at the local, state, and national levels and with international organizations and public leaders to achieve social change consistent with social work values.

■ efforts to address and redress violations of peace and economic and social justice by emphasizing nonviolent and peaceful solutions and remedies.

- inclusion of formalized coursework in peace and social justice studies as part of the undergraduate and graduate generalist curriculums.

- federal funding of social programs that ensure progress toward social and economic justice.

- a U.S. foreign policy approach that includes all of the tools of diplomacy and development, including mediation and reconciliation, and recognizes the urgency and importance of development assistance.

- the promotion of U.S. ratification of critical United Nations treaties and conventions that support human rights and social justice, such as the Convention on the Elimination of All Forms of Discrimination Against Women and the Convention on the Rights of the Child.

REFERENCES

Anderson, A., & Atkinson, M. (2007). Introduction. In *The NASW peace toolkit* (p. 1). Washington, DC: National Association of Social Workers.

Benabou, R. (2000). Unequal societies: Income distribution and the social contract. *American Economic Review, 90,* 96–129.

Bergensen, A. J., & Bata, M. (2002). Global and national inequality: Are they connected? *Journal of World-Systems Research, 3*(1), 130–144.

Bladen, J., Gregg, P., & Machin, S. (2005). Intergenerational mobility in Europe and North America. London: Centre for Economic Performance, London School of Economics.

Chong, D.P.L. (2009). Five challenges to legalizing economic and social rights. *Human Rights Review, 10,* 183–204.

Claussen, B., Smits, J., Naess, O., & Davey Smith, G. (2005). Intergenerational mobility and mortality in Oslo: Social selection versus social causation. *Social Science and Medicine, 61,* 2513–2520.

Cornia, G. A. (2004). Inequality, growth and poverty: An overview of changes over the last two decades. In G. A. Cornia (Ed.), *Inequality, growth and poverty in the era of liberalization and globalization* (pp. 3–25). Oxford, England: Oxford University Press.

Fassihian, D. (2011, March 25). Is the U.S. prepared to win at the UN Human Rights Council? *Huff Post World.* Retrieved from http://www.huffingtonpost.com/dokhi-fassihian/is-the-us-prepared-to-win_b_840760.html

Gold, R., Kawachi, I., Kennedy, B. P., Lynch, J. W., & Connell, F. A. (2001). Ecological analysis of teen birth rates: Association with community income and income inequality. *Maternal and Child Health Journal, 5,* 161–167.

Gold, R., Kennedy, B., Connell, F., & Kawachi, I. (2002). Teen births, income inequality and social capital: Developing an understanding of causal pathway. *Health & Place, 8,* 77–83.

Grebe, J. (2011). *The Global Militarization Index—Use of the GMI for evaluating the development orientation of states and regional militarization.* Bonn International Center for Conversion. Retrieved from http://www.bicc.de/uploads/pdf/publications/papers/occ_paper_07/occasional_paper_VII_02_11_eng.pdf

Health Development Agency. (2003). *Teenage pregnancy and parenthood: A review of reviews—Evidence briefing.* London: Health Development Agency, National Health Service.

Himmelstein, D. U., Thorne, D., Warren, E., & Woolhandler, S. (2009, August). Medical bankruptcy in the United States, 2007: Results of a national study. *American Journal of Medicine, 122,* 741–746.

Hudson, C. G. (2005). Socioeconomic status and mental illness: Tests of the social causation and selection hypothesis. *American Journal of Orthopsychiatry, 75,* 3–18.

International Federation of Social Workers. (2007). IFSW statement on peace and social justice. In *The NASW peace toolkit* (pp. 98–100). Washington, DC: National Association of Social Workers.

Johnson, H. F. (2005). Poverty and global justice: Some challenges ahead. In A. Follesdal & T. Pogge (Eds.), *Real world justice* (pp. 21–26). Netherlands: Springer.

Kawachi, I. (2002). Income inequality and economic residential segregation. *Journal of Epidemology & Community Health, 56,* 165–166.

King, M. L., Jr. (1967). *A Christmas sermon.* Retrieved from http://mlk-kpp01.stanford.edu/index.php/resources/article/king_quotes_on_war_and_peace/

Kreutzmann, H. (2008). Dividing the world: Conflict and inequality in the context of growing global tension. *Third World Quarterly, 29,* 675–689.

Lobmayer, P., & Wilkinson, R. G. (2002). Inequality, residential segregation by income and mortality in US cities. *Journal of Epidemiological and Community Health, 56,* 183–187.

Lundy, C., & van Wormer, K. (2007). Social and economic justice, human rights and peace: The challenge for social work in Canada and the USA. *International Social Work, 50,* 727–739.

Lynch, J. W., Smith, G. D., Kaplan, G. A., & House, J. S. (2000). Income inequality and mortality: Importance to health of individual income, psychosocial environment, or material conditions. *British Medical Journal, 320,* 1200–1204.

Mackenbach, J. P. (2006). *Health inequalities: Europe in profile* [Report for "Tackling Health Inequalities Governing for Health"]. London: Central Office of Information.

Marsh, J. C. (2003). The social work response to violence [Editorial]. *Social Work, 48,* 437–438.

Mauer, M. (2001). The causes and consequences of prison growth in the United States. *Punishment and Society, 3,* 9–20.

McMunn, A., Bartley, M., Hardy, R., & Kuh, D. (2006). Life course social roles and women's healthy in mid-life: Causation or selection? *Journal of Epidemiology & Community Health, 60,* 484–489.

National Association of Social Workers. (2008). *Code of ethics of the National Association of Social Workers.* Washington, DC: Author.

The Nobel Peace Prize 1932-Jane Addams Biography. (n.d.). Retrieved from http://www.nobelprize.org/nobel_prizes/peace/laureates/1931/addams-bio.html

Office of the Special Representative of the Secretary-General for Children and Armed Conflict. (n.d.). *Changing characteristics of armed conflict and consequences for children.* Retrieved from http://www.un.org/children/conflict/english/changing-characteristics-and-consequences.html

Pickett, K. E., James, O. W., & Wilkinson, R. G. (2006). Income inequality and the prevalence of mental illness: A preliminary international analysis. *Journal of Epidemiology & Community Health, 60,* 646–647.

Pickett, K. E., Kelly, S., Brunner, E., Lobstein, T., & Wilkinson, R. G. (2005). Wider income gaps, wider waistbands? An ecological study of obesity and income inequality. *Journal of Epidemiology & Community Health, 59,* 670–674.

Pickett, K. E., Mookherjee, J., & Wilkinson, R. G. (2005). Adolescent birth rates, total homicides, and income inequality in rich countries. *American Journal of Public Health, 95,* 1181–1183.

Putnam, R. D. (2000). *Bowling alone: The collapse and revival of American community.* New York: Simon & Schuster.

Putsch, R. W., & Pololi, L. (2004). Distributive justice in American healthcare: Institutions, power and equitable care of patients [Special issue]. *American Journal of Managed Care, 10,* 45–51.

Rank, M. R. (2008). Poverty. In T. Mizrahi & L. E. Davis (Eds.-in-Chief), *Encyclopedia of social work* (20th ed., Vol. 3, pp. 387–395). Washington, DC and New York: NASW Press and Oxford University Press.

Ritsher, J. E., Warner, V., Johnson, J. G., & Dohrenwend, B. P. (2001). Intergenerational longitudinal study of social class and depression: A test of social causation and social selection models. *British Journal of Psychiatry, 40*(Suppl.), s80–s90.

Sapolsky, R. (2005). Sick of poverty. *Scientific America, 293*(6), 92–99.

Schoen, C., Collins, S. R., Kriss, J. L., & Doty, M. M. (2008, June). How many are underinsured? Trends among U.S. adults, 2003 and 2007. *Health Affairs* Web Exclusive, w298–w309. Retrieved from http://www.commonwealthfund.org/Content/Publications/In-the-Literature/2...

Sen, A. (2008). Violence, identity and poverty. *Journal for Peace Research, 45,* 5–15.

Sherman, A., & Stone, C. (2010). *Income gaps between very rich and everyone else more than tripled in last three decades, new data show.* Retrieved from http://webcache.google usercontent.com/search?q=cache:4v4o6-NSXdkJ:www.cbpp.org/cms/%3Ffa%3Dvi ew%26id%3D3220+Sherman+and+Stone, +peace+2010&cd=1&hl=en&ct=clnk&gl =us&source=www.google.com

Social justice. (2003). In *The social work dictionary* (5th ed., pp. 404–405). Washington, DC: NASW Press.

Sullivan, M. (1993). Social work's legacy of peace: Echoes from the early 20th century. *Social Work, 38,* 513–520.

Tunstall, H. V., Shaw, M., & Dorling, D. (2004). Places and health. *Journal of Epidemiology & Community Health, 58,* 6–10.

United Nations. (1948). *Universal declaration of human rights.* New York: Author.

United Nations Crime and Justice Information Network. (2000). Survey on crime trends and the operations of criminal justice systems (5th, 6th, 7th). New York: Author.

U.S. Department of Education, National Center for Education Statistics. (2004). *The nation's report card: Reading highlights 2003.* Washington, DC: Author.

Uslander, E (2002). *The moral foundations of trust.* Cambridge, England: Cambridge University Press.

Wilkinson, R. G. (2005). *The impact of inequality.* New York: New Press.

Wilkinson, R. G., & Pickett, K. E. (2006). Income inequality and population health: A review and explanation of the evidence. *Social Science & Medicine, 62,* 1768–1784.

Wilkinson, R. G., & Pickett, K. E. (2010). *The spirit level.* New York: Bloomsbury Press.

Wilper, A. P., Woolhandler, S., Lasser, K. E., McCormick, D., Bor, D. H., & Himmelstein, D. U. (2009). Health insurance and mortality in US adults. *American Journal of Public Health, 99,* 2289–2295.

World Health Organization. (2000). *The world health report* (Statistical Annex Table 7, p. 189). Retrieved from http://www.who.int/whr/ 2000/en/whr00_annex_en.pdf

NASW Members with Primary Responsibility for Revision of This Policy

First Draft Revision:

Teri Cardwell (IN)

Policy Panelists:

Gail Wright (ME)
Isabel Rose (NYS)
Patricia Randich-Dumas (AL)
Nancy Udolph (OH)
Daryl Handlin (KS)
Tiko Hardy (CO)
Robin Mama (NJ)

Policy statement approved by the NASW Delegate Assembly, August 2011. This statement supersedes the policy statement on Peace and Social Justice approved by the Delegate Assembly in 2002 and 1990 and reconfirmed by the Delegate Assembly in 1993. For further information, contact the National Association of Social Workers, 750 First Street, NE, Suite 700, Washington, DC 20002-4241. Telephone: 202-408-8600; e-mail: press@naswdc.org

People with Disabilities

BACKGROUND

In 2001, the U.S. Census Bureau reported that 52.6 million (nearly 20 percent of the population) people have some level of disability and 33 million (nearly 4 percent of the population) have severe disability. With medical advances and an aging population, that number grows daily. A study by the Population Reference Bureau states that "due to better trauma care . . . severe brain injuries and spinal cord injuries account for an estimated 80,000 new disabilities a year" (Fujiura, 2001). The disability community consists of a wide array of individuals from all races, ages, and genders with a tremendous variety of backgrounds and life experiences. The term "disability" itself is difficult to define; people with disabilities vary widely and experience physical, sensory, and cognitive impairments, as well as mental, physical, and chronic illness. Disabilities can be acquired, congenital, physical, cognitive, or a combination of multiple conditions. The experience of disability may be different for each person. Disabilities may be visible; in some instances disabilities are invisible and are not readily apparent to others. Functional limitations from disabilities range from none to profound. Many disabilities are temporary; however, once acquired, most are lifelong. Numerous polls and studies have documented that people with disabilities, as a group, are relegated to an inferior status in our society and are severely disadvantaged socially, vocationally, economically, and educationally (Americans with Disabilities Act of 1990 [ADA] [P.L. 101-336]). What is considered a disability at a certain point in time derives from informal and formal societal processes whereby subjective definitions of disability become objective and socially accepted. For example, much of the general public think of disability as the person's type of physical impairment or functional limitation before the reference to the person, such as a "blind man," "paralyzed woman," or "mental patient," all of which are derogatory. In the past socially acceptable labels used to describe people with disabilities were even more demeaning, with terms like "invalid," "cripple," "moron," or "crazy."

During the past 40 years, social attitudes and policies in the United States have slowly begun to recognize the civil rights of people with disabilities. Since the late 1960s, Congress has passed more than a dozen laws addressing issues related to people with disabilities. These laws include the Architectural Barriers Act of 1968 as amended (P.L. 42 U.S.C. §§ 4151 *et seq.*) Title VII of the Civil Rights Act of 1968 (P.L. 90-284) and the Fair Housing Amendment Act of 1988 (P.L. 42 U.S.C. §§ 4151 *et seq.*) which addressed fair housing issues, and the Mental Health Bill of Rights Act of 1985, which expanded state protection and advocacy systems to cover mental illness, and the Americans with Disabilities Act of 1992. Yet these laws continue to afford only limited protection to people with disabilities. For example, the Rehabilitation Act of 1973 (P.L. 93-112) prohibited discrimination and mandated affirmative action in employment and education for people with disabilities in the federal government and with any organizations or entities receiving federal assistance or contracts. In 1975 the Education for All Handicapped Children Act (P.L. 94-142) provided federal funds to states that provided appropriate and free public education to children with disabilities. In 1986 amendments to the Education for All Handicapped Children Act expanded educational services, from birth, to all children with disabilities. Numerous reauthorizations have expanded this law, such as the Individuals with Disabilities Education Act (IDEA) (P.L. 90-247). The Developmentally Disabled Assistance and Bill of Rights Act (P.L. 94-103) further enhanced treatment and care for people with developmental disabilities.

Although these laws worked to address the inequities affecting people with disabilities, a common limitation was that they offered protection only in activities and programs involving the government. In recent decades, people with disabilities have become an active political force in the United States (De Jong, 1979). Simultaneously, direct consumer involvement saw the disability rights movement grow with the development of the independent living (IL) movement in the early 1970s. IL applied this model to the political process of gaining civil rights for people with disabilities (Berkowitz, 1987). Whereas traditional culture and traditional models of professional treatment focused on individual pathology of people with disabilities, IL focused on discrimination of an oppressed minority group and societal responses as the root of their problems. The disability rights movement and the IL movement, specifically, were founded on the belief that people with disabilities have the right to participate fully both in society and in the development and implementation of social policies affecting people with disabilities. The advocacy efforts of people with disabilities, joined by people without disabilities, created a sociopolitical force that resulted in the passage of the ADA (P.L. 101-336). With enactment of the ADA, people with disabilities for the first time were afforded rights in all segments of society. The content of the legislation is clearly addressed in the purpose of the act:

■ to provide a clear and comprehensive national mandate for the elimination of discrimination against individuals with disabilities

■ to provide clear, strong, consistent, enforceable standards addressing discrimination against individual disability

■ to ensure that the federal government plays a central role in enforcing the standards established in the act on behalf of individuals with disabilities

■ to invoke the sweep of congressional authority, including the power to enforce the fourteenth amendment and to regulate commerce, in order to address the major areas of discrimination faced day-to-day by people with disabilities. (ADA, 2, 204)

The evolution of the disability rights movement continues today. The Rehabilitation Act Amendments of 1992 established the purpose of Title VII (P.L. 94-1442) as mandating the "creation of statewide networks of Centers for Independent Living," with the goal of ensuring greater involvement and authority of people with disabilities in services delivery and program management. The New Freedom Initiative is a comprehensive program to promote the full participation of people with disabilities in all areas of society. The aim of the initiative is to increase access to assistive and universal design technology, expand educational and employment opportunities, promote home ownership, integrate Americans with disabilities into the workforce, expand transportation options, and promote increased access into daily community life (http://www.whitehouse.gov/infocus/newfreedom/).

ISSUE STATEMENT

A common experience that the vast majority of people with disabilities share is that of social and economic injustice. People with disabilities often have difficulty with social and economic issues, including employment, income, health care, housing, and full participation in their communities. Although there are tens of millions of people with disabilities—actually having a disability can be a very solitary experience. Negative attitudes regarding people with disabilities (for example, that they are needy, less productive, dangerous, frightening, or distasteful to others), continue to facilitate discrimination and segregation. Other challenges may be created by the devaluation and discrimination of people who are perceived to have a disability, such as people who are HIV-positive, people who have a mental illness, or people who have survived cancer. Services are often interrupted and do not comprehensively continue throughout their lifetime. Many people with psychiatric diagnoses are inappropriately or forcibly treated (National Council on Disability, 2000).

Although it is certainly true that social and economic justice issues are intrinsically connected to race and gender, those same issues are just as relevant to disability. Many adults and children with disabilities are denied or cut off from benefits and live in serious income inadequacy and poverty (Axin & Levin, 1992) with inadequate health care, food, and shelter. The U.S. Census Bureau 2001 noted that the presence of a disability lowers income and increases the likelihood of poverty. The poverty rate for people with disabilities is 28 percent compared with 8.3 percent of the general population. According to the National Organization on Disability, 2002, people with disabilities are more likely to put off or postpone medical care because of cost (28 percent compared with 12 percent) even though they may be insured; since 1994 this differential has increased 13 percent.

Social workers have worked with the disability rights movement throughout their struggle in a variety of roles, including self-advocacy. Historically, however, professionals and helpers have abrogated decision making by people with disabilities and denied them self-determination (Salsgiver & Mackelprang, 1993). The traditional model emphasizes pathology, deficit, and malfunctioning and relies on the medical model, according to which disability is a chronic disease requiring various forms of treatment (Roth, 1987). Although this definition no longer is used exclusively, it still has an overwhelming effect on disability issues and on people with disabilities by inappropriately viewing them as passive, dependent, and deficient. More progressive models used to identify and work with people with disabilities view the person as participating in and contributing to society ("Communication," 1991).

A core social work value is that of self-determination. Accordingly, this principle is a model in which social workers work with clients, rather than providing services for them. This approach encompasses a continuum that ranges from involving the client in the decision making about the treatment plan to having people with disabilities define the goals of such a plan. People with disabilities may define program objectives in organizations where they are themselves employed as decision makers, only using professionals for their specialized expertise and for access to resources. People with disabilities may become these experts, assisting others as well.

Contemporary views of disability have moved beyond focusing on the disability to focusing first on the person. One example is the use of people first language—placing the individual first rather than the disability (for example, people who have a mental illness rather than the mentally ill). By identifying people with disabilities as "people first," we make the presence of a disability a characteristic, not the individual's sole identity while honoring their right to self-determination. Social workers, along with people with disabilities, must affirm the practice of self-determination and use of appropriate language that places people first in all areas of social work practice and the community at large. Although people with disabilities may be handicapped by environmental or individual or societal attitudes, they are not "disabled" or "handicapped" people.

POLICY STATEMENT

NASW supports

■ a national policy that ensures the right of people with disabilities to participate fully and equitably in society. This participation includes the freedom, to the fullest extent possible, to live independently, to exercise self-determination, to make decisions about their living conditions and treatment plans, to obtain an education, to be employed, and to participate as citizens.

■ state and federal funding to allow people with disabilities to participate fully and equitably in society with appropriate supports to meet individual needs.

- the right of people with disabilities to have public access to goods and services available to others, including transportation and reasonable accommodations to provide ready access to buildings throughout the community. Physical access includes internal and external building access (for example, ramps, doors, rest rooms, drinking fountains, and elevators), telecommunications, and alternate means of communication (for example, Braille, sign-language interpreters).

- the right of people with disabilities to a basic level of income that allows all people with disabilities to have the necessities of life and to participate in the community.

- the right of people with disabilities to pursue vocational and occupational opportunities in accessible environments with reasonable accommodations, in accordance with laws that ensure nondiscriminatory access to employment.

- the right of individuals with disabilities to affordable, accessible, and comprehensive health care.

- the right of individuals with disabilities to have early and continued access to individualized appropriate education and vocational opportunities that are accessible in the least restrictive environment possible.

- the development of social workers' expertise in partnering with people with disabilities, by the study of disability history, culture, research, best practices, and civil rights in the curriculums of schools of social work and in continuing education.

- the inclusion of social workers with disabilities in all areas of the professional organization, including policy-making boards, staff and administrative positions, and the board of directors.

- advocacy in collaboration with people with disabilities and their families to reduce discrimination, stigma, and restriction of rights based on inaccurate perceptions of individuals with disabilities in their communities and in society.

REFERENCES

Americans with Disabilities Act of 1990, P.L. 101-336, 104 Stat. 327.

Architectural Barriers Act of 1968, P.L. 90-480, 82 Stat. 718 (Aug. 12, 1968), codified at 42 U.S.C. § 4151 *et seq.*

Axin, J., & Levin, H. (1992). *Social welfare: A history of the American response to need* (3rd ed.). New York: Longman.

Berkowitz, E. D. (1987). *Disabled policy: America's programs for the handicapped.* London: Cambridge University Press.

Civil Rights Act of 1968, P.L. 90-284, 82 Stat. 73 (Apr. 11, 1968).

Communication about disability. (1991). *RehabBrief, 13*(12), 2.

De Jong, G. (1979). *The movement for independent living: Origins, ideology, and implications for disability research.* East Lansing: Michigan State University, University Center for International Rehabilitation.

Developmentally Disabled Assistance and Bill of Rights Act, P.L. 94-103, 89 Stat. 486 to 506 (Oct. 4, 1975).

Developmental Disabilities Assistance and Bill of Rights Act of 2000, P.L. 106-402, 104 Stat. 1191 (Oct. 31, 1990).

Education for All Handicapped Children Act of 1975, P.L. 94-142, 89 Stat. 773 (Nov. 29, 1975).

Fair Housing Amendment Act of 1988, P.L. 42 U.S.C. 3601 (1988) *seq.*

Fujiura, G. (2001). *Emerging trends in disability.* Retrieved November 12, 2004, from Population Today Web site: http://www.prb.org

Freire, P. (2004). *Pedagogy of the oppressed.* New York: Continuum.

Halantic, F., & Berg, G. (1995). Perceptions of disabilities among Kel Tamasheq of Northern Mali. In B. Ingstad & S. R. Whyte (Eds.), *Disability in a cross-cultural perspective* (Working Paper No. 4). Oslo: University of Oslo, Department of Social Anthropology.

Individuals with Disabilities Education Act (IDEA), P.L. 90-247, Title 1, § 154, 81 Stat. 804 (Jan. 2, 1968).

Longmore, P. K. (1987). Elizabeth Bovia, assisted suicide and social prejudice. *Issues in Law and Medicine, 3,* 141–168.

National Association of Social Workers. (2000). *Code of ethics of the National Association of Social Workers*. Washington, DC: NASW Press.

National Council on Disability. (2000). *From privileges to rights: People labled with psychiatric disabilities speak for themselves*. Washington, DC: Author.

Nerney, T., & Shumway, D. (1998, July). *The importance of income* [Monograph sponsored by the Robert Wood Johnson Foundation]. Durham: University of New Hampshire, Institute of Disability Research.

Rehabilitation Act of 1973, P.L. 93-112, 87 Stat. 355 (Sept. 26, 1974).

Rehabilitation Act Amendments of 1992, P.L. 94-1442 (1977).

Roth, W. (1987). Disabilities: Physical. In A. Minahan (Ed.-in-Chief), *Encyclopedia of social work* (18th ed., Vol. 1, pp. 434–438).

Silver Spring, MD: National Association of Social Workers.

Salsgiver, R., & Mackelprang, R. (1993, February). *Persons with disabilities and social work practice: Historical and contemporary issues*. Paper presented at the Annual Program Meeting of the Council on Social Work Education, New York.

Sargent, C. F. (1982). *The cultural context of therapeutic choice: Obstetrical care decisions among the Bariba of Benin*. Boston: D. Reidel.

Tuvim, M. B. (1991). *Reasonable accommodation v. undue hardship: The ADA on trial*. Unpublished law review article, University of California, Los Angeles.

Vachon, R. A. (1989–1990). Employing the disabled. *Issues in Science and Technology, 6*(2), 44–50. Retrieved from http://cdrc.ohsu.edu/oodh/publications/DisabilityandPublicHealthCurriculumOutline.htm

Policy statement approved by the NASW Delegate Assembly, August 2008. This policy statement supersedes the policy statement on People with Disabilities approved by the Delegate Assembly in 1999 and 1993, the policy statement on Handicapped Persons: Rehabilitation approved in 1967, and the policy statement on Handicapped Persons: Rights and Needs approved in 1977. For further information, contact the National Association of Social Workers, 750 First Street, NE, Suite 700, Washington, DC 20002-4241. Telephone: 202-408-8600 or 800-638-8799; e-mail: press@naswdc.org

Physical Punishment of Children

BACKGROUND

Discipline of children has always been a controversial issue. "Not only in the home but in the classroom, corporal punishment was a means to mold children into moral, God-fearing, respectful human beings" (Crosson-Tower, 1999, p. 3). *Physical punishment* and *corporal punishment* are interchangeable terms; both mean the intentional infliction of physical pain or discomfort on the body of a child as a penalty for behavior disapproved of by the punisher or as a method of modifying negative behavior. When punishment occurs in the home with the parent or caregiver as punisher, it is often described as physical punishment. This policy statement pertains to punishment in the home, schools, and custodial settings. The term *physical punishment* is used in this policy statement because of the commonality of issues in any setting. Physical punishment does not include physical restraint to prevent a child from harming himself or herself or others or to protect property, nor does it include self-defense by an adult.

Several countries have policies or laws that prohibit parents from using corporal punishment as a means of discipline (Austria, Croatia, Cyprus, Denmark, Finland, Germany, Israel, Italy, Latvia, Norway, and Sweden) (Bitensky, 1998, EPOCH-USA, 2000), yet, corporal punishment is strongly supported and used in the United States. According to Straus and Stewart (1999), 94 percent of American parents spank their children by the time they are three or four years old. There is much controversy regarding the benefits and harm of corporal punishment. Some studies have revealed that corporal punishment is effective and desirable (Baumrind, 1996a, 1996b, 1997; Larzelere, 1996, 2000). Other studies, however, have demonstrated

that corporal punishment is related to short- and long-term negative effects on children: increased antisocial behavior (Giles-Sims, Straus, & Sugarman, 1995); higher levels of psychological distress and depression (Straus, 1994; Turner & Finkelhor, 1996); lower IQ scores (Smith & Brooks-Gunn, 1997); and increased likelihood of suicidal ideation, physically abusing one's children, alcohol abuse, engaging in masochistic sex, and lower income (Straus, 1994).

According to Davidson (1997), legal statutes in 48 states and the District of Columbia specify what constitutes corporal punishment in their definition of child abuse. Corporal punishment encompasses the use of "reasonable" force in 29 states; some states add that corporal punishment must be "appropriate" (Alabama, Arkansas, Arizona, California, Colorado), "moderate" (Arkansas, Delaware, South Carolina, South Dakota), or "necessary" (Montana, New Hampshire, New York, Oregon, Texas, Wisconsin); and corporal punishment is limited to "nondeadly force" in Arkansas, New York, and Texas. Corporal punishment has been investigated as a form of abuse. Some states include the term "excessive corporal punishment" in their definitions of child maltreatment (Davidson, 1997). Corporal punishment also is included in some state laws as physical abuse.

It is important to consider social and cultural systems when examining physical punishment of children. Customs and practices in some cultures would be considered abusive by child protective services. For example, some Vietnamese families engage in the ritual of *cao gio* (rubbing their children with a very hot coin that leaves burn marks); the purpose of this ritual is to cure several ills. Child-rearing patterns are determined by parenting beliefs, goals, and expectations inherent in the culture's model of parent–child relations (Greenfield & Suzuki, 1998); this is often referred to as cultural capital (Xu, Tung, & Dunaway, 2000). When physical punishment is the accepted and expected norm in a culture, some parents may feel justified in using it as a means of discipline. The acceptance of physical punishment as normative and beneficial by children largely depends on whether this disciplinary measure is acceptable or unacceptable in the larger cultural context (Deater-Decker & Dodge, 1997).

Studies of physical punishment and parents' ethnicity have been inconclusive. Some studies found that African American parents used corporal punishment more often than did European American parents (Day, Peterson, & McCracken, 1998; Giles-Sims et al., 1995; Loeber et al., 2000; Pinderhughes, Dodge, Bates, Pettit, & Zelli, 2000; Straus & Stewart, 1999). Other studies have shown that European Americans spank their children the most (Escovar & Escovar, 1985; Straus, 1994), and that Latino/a Americans or Asian Americans were least likely to spank their children (Hashima & Amato, 1994; Wissow, 2001). Findings from other studies have shown no differences in frequency between ethnic groups (Ellison, Thompson, & Segal, 1995; Hemenway, Solnick, & Carter, 1994).

Social workers in the field of child abuse observe that, in some instances, what starts out as physical punishment may become abuse when the adult goes too far and injures the child or places the child at risk of injury. Children age three and younger are most often the victims of child fatalities; this population is the most vulnerable because of their dependency, small size, and inability to defend themselves. According to the U.S. Administration for Children and Families (ACF), 30 percent of the reported child fatalities were the result of physical abuse; the rate of child abuse and neglect fatalities increased from 1.84 per 100,000 children in 2000 to 1.96 in 2001 and 1.98 in 2002 (U.S. Department of Health and Human Services, 2004). In 2003, a Child Abuse Prevention Initiative was launched by the ACF, Children's Bureau, Office of Child Abuse and Neglect. The purpose of this initiative was to raise awareness of the issue in communities throughout the United States as a way to keep children safe and provide support for families to stay together and raise children and youths to be happy, secure, and stable adults.

ISSUE STATEMENT

Physical punishment in institutions, foster care (including kinship care, residential settings, and institutions), and day care settings is no longer tolerated by most licensing authorities. Having a humane, effective, and consistent philosophy of discipline in schools, custodial settings, and homes is thought to be highly desirable by adults who are responsible for the care of children in these settings and by society in general. It is not congruent to oppose physical punishment in schools and custodial settings as being inhumane and ineffective without recognizing that the same concerns exist when physical punishment is inflicted on children by their parents. Many parents who use physical punishment are adamantly opposed to and do not engage in abusive physical punishment. Conversely, punishment that does not involve physical contact, such as denigrating statements and excessive timeouts, can also be abusive.

It is important to support actions and conditions that facilitate the healthy emotional, physical, and mental development of children. Discipline is necessary for children to become social, productive, and responsible adults. Physical punishment is one form of discipline. The weight of the evidence has repeatedly shown that physical punishment of children is not as effective as other means of behavior management. There are many effective types of discipline that promote socially acceptable behavior in constructive, nonphysical ways. Physical punishment has been banned in several states and school districts. Legislation is pending in other states and school districts. The National Mental Health Association, a leader in advocacy and social action on behalf of the mental health of children and adolescents, supports the elimination of corporal punishment from all schools in our nation. The National Parent Teachers Association, American Academy of Pediatrics, American Academy of Child and Adolescent Psychiatry, National Congress of Parents and Teachers, National Education Association, and American Bar Association also support the abolishment of corporal punishment in schools in this country.

In 2001, the Global Initiative to End All Corporal Punishment of Children (2001) was launched to

■ form a strong alliance of human rights agencies, key individuals, and nongovernmental organizations against corporal punishment

■ make corporal punishment of children visible by building a global map of its prevalence and legality, ensuring that children's views are heard, and charting progress to end it

■ lobby state governments to ban all forms of corporal punishment and develop public education programs

■ provide detailed technical assistance to support states with these reforms.

The Committee on the Rights of the Child, which monitors implementation of the Convention on the Rights of the Child, has always maintained that legal and social acceptance of physical punishment of children in the home and in institutions is not compatible with the Convention. Since 1993 the Committee has recommended prohibition of physical punishment in the family and institutions. It has also recommended campaigns to encourage positive, nonviolent child rearing and education. In September 2000 the Committee on the Rights of the Child held the first of two General Discussion days on violence against children and recommended

that States parties review all relevant legislation to ensure that all forms of violence against children, however light, are prohibited, including the use of torture, or cruel, inhuman or degrading treatment (such as flogging, corporal punishment or other violent measures) for punishment or disciplining within the child justice system, or any other context. The Committee recommends that such legislation incorporate appropriate

sanctions for violations and the provision of rehabilitation for victims. The committee urges the launching of public information campaigns to raise awareness and sensitize the public about the severity of human rights violations in this domain and their harmful impact on children, and to address cultural acceptance of violence against children promoting instead "zero-tolerance" of violence. (Committee on the Rights of the Child, 2004, p. 4)

Social workers encourage parents and caregivers to use other discipline methods, such as time-out and negative reinforcement when disciplining their children. Social workers and much of the general public increasingly advocate nonviolence and peace in the family as well as in the social, political, educational, and economic environments.

POLICY STATEMENT

The National Association of Social Workers (NASW) believes in the right of every child to have a safe and nurturing environment, including home and educational experiences that promote every child's optimal growth and development. The use of physical force against people, especially children, is antithetical to the best values of a democratic society and of the social work profession. Thus, NASW opposes the use of physical punishment in homes, schools, and all other institutions, both public and private, where children are cared for and educated.

NASW affirms that all children need parental guidance and discipline and that most parents want to be able to discipline in a way that works and is helpful to children. Therefore, NASW will support

■ parenting programs and evidence-based practices that provide parents with access to training and support for learning and using nonviolent disciplinary techniques, such as positive reinforcement, time-out, and verbal problem solving

- professional social work practice, social programs, and social policies that allow children to have their basic needs met so that parents have the energy and emotional resources to use nonviolent disciplinary procedures with their children

- a media-supported public and professional education campaign to abolish physical punishment

- legislation that prohibits the use of physical punishment in schools, other child-care facilities, and institutions

- programs to help prepare administrators, teachers, school personnel, child care workers, and parents to use nonviolent forms of discipline

- research about alternative forms of discipline that are effective in changing behavior.

In adopting this policy, NASW is proud to support the movement to promote the nonviolent discipline and care of children in the United States.

REFERENCES

Baumrind, D. (1996a). A blanket injunction against disciplinary use of spanking is not warranted by the data. *Pediatrics, 98,* 828–831.

Baumrind, D. (1996b). The discipline controversy revisited. *Family Relations, 45,* 405–415.

Baumrind, D. (1997). Necessary distinctions. *Psychological Inquiry, 8,* 176–182.

Bitensky, S. H. (1998). Spare the rod, embrace our humanity: Toward a new legal regime prohibiting corporal punishment of children. *University of Michigan Journal of Law Reform, 31,* 353–474.

Committee on the Rights of the Child. (2004). The committee's general discussion days on violence against children. Retrieved June 1, 2004, from http://www.endcorpalpunishment.org/pages/hrlaw/crc_session.html

Crosson-Tower, C. (1999). The maltreatment of children from a historical perspective. In C. Crosson-Tower (Ed.), *Understanding child abuse and neglect* (4th ed., pp. 1–20). Boston: Allyn & Bacon.

Davidson, H. (1997). The legal aspects of corporal punishment in the home: When does physical discipline cross the line to become child abuse? *Children's Legal Rights Journal, 17,* 18–29.

Day, R. D., Peterson, G. W., & McCraken, C. (1998). Predicting spanking of younger and older children by their mothers and fathers. *Journal of Marriage and the Family, 60,* 79–94.

Deater-Deckard, K., & Dodge, K. A. (1997). Externalizing behavior problems and discipline revisited: Nonlinear effects and variation by culture, context, and gender. *Psychological Inquiry, 8,* 161–175.

Ellison, C. G., Thompson, T. E., & Segal, M. L. (1995). *Race differences in the parental use of corporal punishment.* Unpublished manuscript, University of Texas at Austin.

EPOCH-USA. (2000). *Legal reforms: Corporal punishment of children in the family.* Retrieved June 2, 2004, from http://www.stophitting.com/legalReform.php

Escovar, L. A., & Escovar, P. L. (1985). Retrospective parental child-rearing practices in three culturally different college groups. *International Journal of Intercultural Relations, 9,* 31–49.

Giles-Sims, J., Straus, M. A., & Sugarman, D. B. (1995). Child, maternal, and family characteristics associated with spanking. *Family Relations, 44,* 170–176.

Global Initiative to End All Corporal Punishment of Children. (2001). *End all corporal punishment of children.* Retrieved June 1, 2004, from http://www.endcorporalpunishment.org/

Greenfield, P. M., & Suzuki, L. K. (1998). Culture and human development: Implications for parenting, education, pediatrics, and mental health. In W. Damon, I. E. Siegel, & K. A. Renninger (Eds.), *Handbook of child psychology: Vol 4. Child psychology in practice* (5th ed., pp. 1059–1109). New York: John G. Wiley & Sons.

Hashima, P. Y., & Amato, P. R. (1994). Poverty, social support, and parental behavior. *Child Development, 65,* 394–403.

Hemenway, D., Solnick, S., & Carter, J. (1994). Child-rearing violence. *Child Abuse & Neglect*, *18*, 1011–1020.

Larzelere, R. E. (1996). A review of the outcomes of parental use of nonabusive or customary physical punishment. *Pediatrics*, *98*(4, Pt. 2), 824–828.

Larzelere, R. E. (2000). *Child outcomes of nonabusive and customary physical punishment by parents: An updated literature review.* Unpublished manuscript, University of Nebraska Medical Center, Omaha, and Father Flanagan's Boys Home, Boys Town, NE.

Loeber, R., Drinkwater, M., Yin, Y., Anderson, S. J., Schmidt, L. C., & Crawford, A. (2000). Stability of family interaction from ages 6 to 18. *Journal of Abnormal Child Psychology*, *28*, 353–369.

Pinderhighes, E. E., Dodge, K. A., Bates, J. E., Pettit, G. S., & Zelli, A. (2000). Discipline responses: Influences of parents socioeconomic status, ethnicity, beliefs about parenting, stress, and cognitive–emotional processes. *Journal of Family Psychology*, *14*, 380–400.

Smith, J. R., & Brooks-Gunn, J. (1997). Correlates and consequences of harsh discipline for young children. *Archives of Pediatric and Adolescent Medicine*, *151*, 777–786.

Straus, M. A. (1994). *Beating the devil out of them: Corporal punishment in American families.* New York: Lexington Books.

Straus, M. A., & Stewart, J. H. (1999). Corporal punishment by American parents: National data on prevalence, chronicity, severity, and duration, in relation to child and family characteristics. *Clinical Child and Family Psychology Review*, *2*, 55–70.

Turner, H. A., & Finkelhor, D. (1996). Corporal punishment as a stressor among youth. *Journal of Marriage and the Family*, *58*, 155–166.

U.S. Department of Health and Human Services. (2004). *Child abuse and neglect fatalities: Statistics and interventions.* Retrieved June 6, 2004, from http://nccanch.acf.hhs.gov/pubs/factsheets/fatility.cfm

Wissow, L. S. (2001). Ethnicity, income, and parenting contexts of physical punishment in a national sample of families with young children. *Child Maltreatment*, *6*, 118–129.

Xu, X., Tung, Y., & Dunaway, R. G. (2000). Cultural, human, and social capital as determinants of corporal punishment: Toward an integrated theoretical model. *Journal of Interpersonal Violence*, *15*, 603–630.

SUGGESTED READINGS

Ashton, V. (2001). The relationship between attitudes toward corporal punishment and the perception and reporting of child maltreatment. *Child Abuse & Neglect*, *25*, 389–399.

Kanoy, K., Ulku-Steiner, B., Cox, B., & Burchinal, M. (2003). Marital relationship and individual psychological characteristics that predict physical punishment of children. *Journal of Family Psychology*, *17*(1), 20–28.

Mahoney, A., Donnelly, W. O., Lewis, T., & Maynard, C. (2000). Mother and father self-reports of corporal punishment and severe physical aggression toward clinic-referred youth. *Journal of Clinical Child Psychology*, *29*, 266–281.

National Maternal and Child Health Center for Child Death Review: Web site: www.childdeathreview.org

O'Neil, C. (2001). Avoiding saying too much: The complexity of relationships between permanent parents and social workers. *Children Australia*, *26*(2), 19–25.

Thompson, J. (2000). Smacking children: Attitudes and alternatives. *Social Work Now*, *15*, 39–44.

Trocme, N., & Durant, J. (2003). Physical punishment and the response of the Canadian child welfare system: Implications for legislative reform. *Journal of Social Welfare and Family Law*, *25*(1), 39–56.

U.S. Department of Health and Human Services. (2001). *Child maltreatment 1999: Reports from the states to the national child abuse and neglect data system.* Washington, DC: U.S. Government Printing Office.

U.S. Department of Health and Human Services. (2004). *Child maltreatment 2002: Reports from the states to the national child abuse and neglect data system*. Washington, DC: U.S. Government Printing Office.

Whaley, A. L. (2000). Sociocultural differences in the developmental differences in the developmental consequences of the use of physical discipline during childhood for African Americans. *Cultural Diversity and Ethnic Minority Psychology, 6*, 5–12.

Policy statement approved by the NASW Delegate Assembly, August 2005. This policy supersedes the policy statement on Physical Punishment of Children approved by the Delegate Assembly in 1990 and referred by the 2002 Delegate Assembly to the 2005 Delegate Assembly for revision and the statement on Corporal Punishment of Children in Schools and Custodial Settings approved by the Delegate Assembly in 1984. The 1999 Delegate Assembly voted not to combine this policy statement with Child Abuse and Neglect. For further information, contact the National Association of Social Workers, 750 First Street, NE, Suite 700, Washington, DC 20002-4241. Telephone: 202-408-8600 or 800-638-8799; e-mail: press@naswdc.org

Poverty and Economic Justice

BACKGROUND

A just society not only ensures that basic human needs are met, but also invests in the social well-being of all of its members, especially those who are unable to provide for themselves. Historically, the social work profession has advocated for socially just income and employment policies. The profession has fought to protect the most vulnerable and the most oppressed: children, single parents, older adults, and, in particular individuals, families, and communities who are in economic distress.

A just society not only ensures that basic human needs are met, but also invests in the social well-being of all of its members, especially those who are unable to provide for themselves.

As the social work profession moves into in the 21st century, iteration of critical economic policy priorities is essential. These priorities include promoting just policies that build a universal system of support, promote financial security, and provide an adequate safety net for those in need.

Moreover, economic systems, institutions, and practices influence how well individuals and groups fulfill their needs and achieve optimum development. People's health and general well-being depend on how well their intrinsic needs are fulfilled. Consistent frustration of these needs tends to cause physical, emotional, and social problems, and correcting these problems at their root is critical.

In 2006, the Census Bureau estimated that 36.5 million Americans or 12.3 percent of the population, lived in poverty, and over 15.4 million of the poor population lived in severe poverty, defined as annual income below 50 percent of the poverty threshold (DeNavas-Walt, Proctor, & Smith, 2007). Over 5.5 million children under 18 years of age lived in severe poverty in 2006.

America's "new economy" is a tale of skewed wealth and income (Ozawa, Kim, & Joo, 2006). The new economy generates extraordinary riches for the few, but creates declining wages, rising debt, and the risk of deep and persistent poverty for many.

In the State of Working America 2006/2007, researchers at the Economic Policy Institute examined America's new economy and the relationship of poverty and the job market (Mishel, Bernstein, & Allegretto, 2007). In 2004, the top 1 percent of wealthy families received almost 17 percent of all income, and more than 42 percent of net assets. Wealth in the United States (defined as net worth, which is the value of assets minus debts) is concentrated at the very top of the economic ladder. One-one-hundredth percent of U.S. families, or about 15,000 families, control 5 percent of the nation's income (Uchitelle, 2007).

U.S. workers are dividing a shrinking share of the economic pie (Aron-Dine & Shapiro, 2007). Danziger (2005) analyzed trend from 1964 to 2004, affecting weekly earnings of U.S. private sector, nonfarm, and nonsupervisory production workers. Danziger concluded that, by 2004, when adjusted for inflation, weekly earnings averaged $529 per week, and "were still about 19 percent below the 1973 level" (p. 4). Furthermore, a large part of the U.S. workforce, approximately one-fourth of the U.S. labor force, works at "poverty-level" wages (Mishel et al., 2007).

Another residual problem is the manner in which the U.S. Census Bureau determines income thresholds for establishing who is in poverty. Administratively, the U.S. Census Bureau continues to use a set of income thresholds, which vary by the number of adults or children in a family, to ascertain poverty levels. Indeed, selected government assistance programs are not required to use the official poverty thresholds as eligibility criteria, and many programs use different measures. Mollie Orshansky, an analyst at the Social Security Administration, developed the formula for calculating the poverty thresholds in 1964. The thresholds do not vary geographically or include actual living expenses or noncash benefits such as food stamps. The Census Bureau updates the thresholds annually and makes adjustments for inflation; however, Orshansky's basic formula for calculating who is poor is unchanged. Other industrialized countries use "relative measures" of poverty, typically set at about 50 percent of the nation's median income. The median household income in the United States in 2006 was $48,200 (DeNavas-Walt et al., 2007).

To calculate who is poor in the United States, the Census Bureau compares a family's annual, pretax, income to their poverty threshold. If the income falls below the threshold, the family is considered poor. In 2006, the weighted average poverty threshold for four people was set at $20,614; for three people, $16,079; for two people, $13,167; and for one person, $10,294 (U.S. Census Bureau, 2007).

Following the passage of welfare reform legislation in 1996, welfare caseloads plunged, by about half, between 1996 and 2000 (Urban Institute, 2006). In 1997, the portion of welfare recipients working in the prior 12 months was 31 percent; by 1999 this portion rose to 44 percent, and by 2002 it began to drop to 39 percent. Many parents who left welfare, especially single mothers, found low-wage jobs and their annual wages, according to the calculations of Urban Institute, left them at a poverty level income—a poverty-level wage. Although many of these families continue to need some level of support, researchers have identified the components of welfare reform programs that are successful in moving families from welfare to work.

ISSUE STATEMENT

Each day, in their work with individuals, families, and communities, social workers see firsthand the devastating costs and consequences of poverty and unemployment. Joblessness and economic insecurity contribute to the incidence of mental illness, family violence, suicide, substance abuse, crime, and diminished capacity for healthy family and community functioning. Effective provision of traditional social work services, including individual and family therapy, group work, vocational counseling, or community organization is compromised when provided in the context of economic insecurity. It is this knowledge and experience that gives the social work profession a special responsibility to advocate for income, employment, and social support policies that promote the economic justice and social well-being of all members of society.

Disparities in Wealth

Analysts found "vast" differences between the economic status of black families and white families when examining their respective median and average financial wealth (Mishel et al., 2007). The data on median wealth indicated that the disparities were extreme; in 2004, the median wealth of black families was $300 and the median wealth for white families was more than $36,000, a black–white ratio of less than 1 percent. The data on average wealth was no less extreme, in 2004; black families had an average wealth of $61,500 and white families had an average wealth of $402,500, a black–white ratio of 15 percent. A full 17 percent of all U.S. households had zero or negative net worth in 2004 (Mishel et al., 2007).

A Rise in Debt

To make ends meet, Americans have taken on large amounts of debt and report that their prime concern is not enough money for life's basics (Gallup Poll, 2007). Household debt in the United States "has consistently trended upward," and by 2005 "it was over 130 percent of disposable personal income." About 25 percent of low-income households, and close to

14 percent of middle-income families, had "debt-service obligations that exceeded 40 percent of their income" (Mishel et al., 2007). The deregulation of credit card interest, fees, and aggressive marketing tactics has exposed low- and middle-income consumers to predatory lending practices, which jeopardize their economic future and increasingly lead to bankruptcies (Warren, 2007).

Counting the Poor

Poverty reaches deeply across the United States and is concentrated among the young. Children under 18 years of age represent 24.9 percent of the total population, but account for 35.2 percent of people in poverty. The number of people 65 years and older living in poverty declined from 3.6 million in 2005 to 3.4 million in 2006. (Danziger, 2005). Poverty among America's 100 million people in ethnic minority groups is widespread, and skewed, in ratio to their representation in the population (U.S. Census Bureau, 2007).

Concentrated Poverty

The geographic isolation and concentration of the urban poor population are key determinants of the complexity and persistence of poverty in the United States. Hurricane Katrina exposed the geographic concentration of poverty in what Wilson (2007) called the new urban poverty. "Poor, segregated neighborhoods in which substantial percentages of individual adults are either unemployed or have dropped out or never been a part of the labor force" (Wilson, 2007, p. 93).

The Effects of Welfare Reform

The combination of wages, tax credits, cash assistance, and other benefits such as food stamps, Medicaid, and subsidies for child care and transportation led to a sustainable success in the transition to work for many families. However, some families continued to face barriers to stable employment because they are challenged by a lack of skills or education, or disabling medical, physical, or emotional con-

ditions (Joyce Foundation, 2002). Therefore, a higher level of support is needed to secure stable employment for these families.

Employment Measures

All employment and unemployment measures should be carefully analyzed to obtain a clear understanding of what is being measured. For example, in September 2007, the Labor Department reported that 7.2 million people were unemployed and that an additional 1.3 million people were "marginally attached to the labor force (without jobs, interested in working)." According to the Bureau of Labor Statistics (2007) "marginally attached workers" are considered unemployed, even though they are defined as without jobs. Another confounding measure used by the Labor Department is a subgroup of marginally attached workers known as "discouraged workers": those who want a job, but who are without hope of finding work. In September 2007, discouraged workers accounted for 276,000 of the 1.3 million people reported as marginally attached to the labor force by the Department of Labor. The highest rate of unemployment reported by the Labor Department in September 2007 was 16 percent for teenagers; that number excluded discouraged workers and marginally attached workers (Bureau of Labor Statistics, 2007).

POLICY STATEMENT

NASW supports a national economic policy that invests in "human capital" and recognizes that a nation's well-being derives not only from an economic balance sheet, but also from the well-being of its members. Specifically, NASW supports

■ an economic policy that includes the elimination of poverty and race-based barriers to opportunity, reducing the dynamics of individual and intergroup competition and thus reducing economic sources of discrimination by race, gender, age, and other factors.

■ broad social, economic, and political actions to end poverty and the vast inequalities in wealth and income.

- the full use and development of available, productive, and creative human resources and capacities, and the rejection of the notion that the United States cannot afford economic reform.

- efforts to educate social workers and the public about the unequal distribution of income and wealth, with particular attention to its effects on communities, women, people of color, and those living in poverty.

- efforts to engage the public in understanding that it is in everyone's interest to reduce economic inequalities.

- proposals to protect the long-term viability of economic security programs for all Americans.

- proposals to improve economic programs for low-wage workers, women, children, people of color, people living in poverty, and people with disabilities.

- federal tax, budget, and spending mechanisms that help to narrow gaps in the resources available to people at different levels, as well as an adequate safety net for those unable to provide for themselves.

- economic policies that either avoid recession and inflation or mitigate their impact.

- a policy of full employment at all levels for all those able to work, with a range of alternative work patterns and strategies to address conditions if the economy is unable to sustain full employment.

- income levels that meet or exceed the federal poverty guidelines for anyone who works full-time.

- a federal minimum wage indexed to cost-of-living increases and is a living wage.

- fair labor practices for all workers, including children, youths, and those on public employment programs; equity and enforcement of equal opportunity, and affirmative action legislation.

- national policy that creates a seamless support system for intergenerational well-being, including stable and viable economic and employment policies, and care provisions for dependent family members.

- policies that support compensation for individuals engaged in the care of dependent family members.

- quality, accessible, and affordable child care for those working outside the home

- unstigmatized financial support at a level that enables those who are unable to work to live in dignity.

- federal programs that invest in education and retraining, particularly addressing the need for competence in the global economy, especially for low-income workers, displaced workers, current public assistance recipients, and former public assistance recipients. Such programs should include financial support and tuition subsidies, and opportunities to obtain higher education available to all who can benefit from it, without regard to ability to pay.

- equitable community development and revitalization, including the strengthening of communities through job creation; affordable, accessible, and quality housing; quality public education; affordable and accessible public transportation; safe work sites, neighborhoods, and homes; high-quality and affordable health care, including comprehensive mental health services, and accessible opportunities for training and employment, which lead to better jobs at living wages.

- expanded efforts by the United States at international economic cooperation and development of a comprehensive international industrial policy, including trade agreements that protect the environment, ensure the right to organize and bargain collectively, and provide a living wage.

REFERENCES

Aron-Dine, A., & Shapiro, I. (2007, March 29). *Share of national income going to wages and salaries at record low in 2006: Share of income going to corporate profits at record high.* Retrieved October 9, 2007, from http://www.cbpp.org/8-31-06inc.html

Bureau of Labor Statistics. (2007, September). The employment situation: September 2007. *Employment Situation Summary, NEWS Bureau of Labor Statistics.* Retrieved October 7, 2007, from http://www.bls.gov/news.release/empsit.nr0.html

Danziger, S. (2005). Poverty and low-wage work 40 years after the declaration of the war on poverty. *Poverty Research Insights,* pp. 3–6. Retrieved October 7, 2007, from http://www.npc.umich.edu/publications/newsletter/fall05/

DeNavas-Walt, C., Proctor, B. D., & Smith, J. (2007). *Income, poverty, and health insurance coverage in the United States: 2006* (U.S. Census Bureau, Current Population Reports, P60-233). Retrieved September 27, 2007 from http://www.census.gov/prod/2007pubs/p60-233.pdf

Gallup Poll. (2007, June 19). Seventy percent of Americans say that the economy is getting worse. Retrieved October 9, 2007, from http://www.galluppoll.com/content/?ci=27922

Joyce Foundation. (2002). *Welfare to work: What have we learned?* Chicago: Author. Retrieved October 9, 2007, from http://www.joycefdn.org/pdf/welrept/welfarereport.pdf

Mishel, L., Bernstein, J., & Allegretto, S. (2007). *The state of working America 2006/2007.* Ithaca, NY: Cornell University Press. Data available at http://epi.org

Ozawa, M. N., Kim, J., & Joo, M. (2006). Income class and the accumulation of net worth in the United States. *Social Work Research, 30,* 211–222.

Urban Institute. (2006, July 26). *A decade of welfare reform: Facts and figures: Assessing the new federalism.* Retrieved October 9, 2007, from http://www.urban.org/UploadedPDF/900980_welfarereform.pdf

U.S. Census Bureau. (2007, May 17). *Minority population tops 100 million.* Retrieved October 9, 2007, from http://www.census.gov/Press-Release/www/releases/archives/population

Warren, E. (2007). The vanishing middle class. In J. Edwards, M. Crain, & A. L. Kalleberg (Eds.), *Ending poverty in America: How to restore the American dream* (pp. 38–52). New York: New Press.

Wilson, J. W. (2007). A new agenda for America's ghetto poor. In J. Edwards, M. Crain, & A. L. Kalleberg (Eds.), *Ending poverty in America: How to restore the American dream* (pp. 88–98). New York: New Press.

Policy statement approved by the NASW Delegate Assembly, August 2008. This policy statement supersedes the policy statement on Economic Policy approved by the Assembly in 1999 and referred by the 2005 Delegate Assembly to the 2008 Delegate Assembly for revision., and the policy statement approved by the Assembly in 1993 and 1990. For further information, contact the National Association of Social Workers, 750 First Street, NE, Suite 700, Washington, DC 20002-4241. Telephone: 202-408-8600 or 800-638-8799; e-mail: press@naswdc.org

Professional Impairment

BACKGROUND

Professional impairment among social workers is a significant and growing concern in the profession. Professional impairment has been defined in many ways.

One of the earliest and most widely used definitions cites interference with professional functioning that is reflected in one or more of the following: an inability or unwillingness to acquire and integrate professional standards into one's repertoire of professional behavior; an inability to acquire professional skills to reach an acceptable level of competency; and an inability to control personal stress, psychological dysfunction, or excessive emotional reactions that interfere with professional functioning (Lamb et al., 1987). The *Social Work Dictionary* defines an *impaired social worker* as "one who is unable to function adequately as a professional social worker and provide competent care to clients as a result of a physical or mental disorder or personal problems, or the ability or desire to adhere to the *code of ethics* of the profession. These problems most commonly include alcoholism, substance abuse, mental illness, burnout, stress, and relationship problems" (Barker, 2003, p. 210).

Impaired functioning should be distinguished from incompetence or inexperience by evidence that the social worker has previously functioned acceptably according to standards of social work practice.

Professional impairment can manifest in different ways. The most frequently discussed form of impairment is that of alcohol and other drug (AOD) use (Bissell, Fewell, & Jones, 1980; Fewell, King, & Weinstein, 1993; Siebert, 2003, 2005). One earlier study of alcohol abuse among colleagues and families, using samples of NASW members, confirmed the existence of significant alcohol and drug abuse problems within the social work profession (Fewell et al., 1993). A more recent study, also using a sample of NASW members in a chapter, indicated troubling levels of AOD use among social workers. Twelve percent of the sample was at serious risk of AOD abuse. Of those considered high risk, 53 percent reported some type of impairment and 20 percent reported three or more impairment incidents (Siebert, 2003). Effects of professional impairment reported by respondents included the following: providing inadequate or substandard client care, being late or missing appointments, engaging in inappropriate relationships, missing days from work, being confronted by a coworker, being disciplined by an employer, or being forced to change jobs (Siebert, 2003).

Concern for professional impairment in the field of social work education was highlighted in an article examining commonly occurring ethical dilemmas faced by social work educators in their roles of teaching, scholarship, and service (Strom-Gottfried & D'Aprix, 2006). Alcohol use in master's-level social work students has been explored in one comparison study of graduate MSW students and undergraduate students. Findings indicated that the MSW sample of three universities in the northeastern United States did not drink as aggressively as the undergraduate students. One explanation for the lower rate was that MSW students may enter the social work profession seeking to better understand drinking problems of their own or the problems of members of their families, and to help others with their drinking problems (Gassman, Demone, & Wechsler, 2002).

Mental health conditions may significantly affect a social worker's performance. Depression, as a form of professional impairment, has received little attention in the field of social work. One significant study of depression among social workers, using a sample of NASW members, found that 19 percent reported current symptoms of depression, 16 percent had seriously considered suicide at some time, 20 percent were currently taking medication for depression, and 60 percent self-evaluated as either currently depressed or depressed at some time in the past. However, it was also found that respondents with more years of experience, professional designations, and higher degrees were less likely to report depressive symptoms. But the most alarming finding from the study was that the percentage of respondents self-assessed as depressed represented three times the lifetime depression rate in the general population (Siebert, 2004).

Burnout, compassion fatigue, secondary traumatic stress, and vicarious traumatization are also conditions that may contribute to a form of professional impairment (Bride, 2007; Figley, 1995; Jayaratne & Chess, 1984; Soderfeldt, Soderfeldt, & Warg, 1995). These conditions are often considered to be related to the organizational climate, work stressors, and negative psychological effects of helping.

Impairment often leads to professional mistakes, failure in providing competent care to clients, and violation of the ethical standards of the profession (Berliner, 1989; Houston-Vega & Nuehring, 1997; Lowenberg, Dolgoff, & Harrington, 2000; Reamer, 1992, 1994, 1998). The inability or unwillingness to identify impairment in a colleague's performance and lack of knowledge and guidance on how to respond effectively are stumbling blocks for social work professionals in encouraging their colleagues to seek help. Denial of one's own professional impairment has been documented as a serious concern, especially related to AOD abuse (Siebert, 2003).

Through the efforts of three chapters, New York City, New York State and New Jersey, NASW formally acknowledged the problems of impaired social workers in 1979 in the release of a public policy on alcoholism and alcohol-related problems (NASW, 2006; Reamer, 1992).

In 1980, Social Workers Helping Social Workers was formed to provide mutual support and assistance to social work professionals with impairment issues.

In 1994, NASW formally addressed professional impairment in the *Code of Ethics*, with further revisions in 1996 and 1999 (NASW, 2000, 2006). The *Code of Ethics* addresses impairment issues through four specific standards, which basically mandate action in two significant areas—when social workers suspect impairment in colleagues or when social workers are impaired (NASW, 2000).

Despite the recent increase in attention and organized efforts directed toward the problem of professional impairment, there is still significant work to be undertaken to effectively create awareness about different forms of impairment and to address a serious and growing concern in the profession of social work.

ISSUE STATEMENT

Professional impairment among social workers is a critically important issue to address for a variety of reasons. The ability of social workers to perceive situations clearly and objectively is pivotal to their work. Social workers suffering from AOD abuse disorders, psychiatric stressors and disorders, secondary traumatic stress, and other causal factors of impairment may compromise performance, jeopardizing the rights of their clients and the effectiveness of the treatment provided. Although research on the impairment of social workers is limited, findings suggest that services to clients are affected by the degree of impairment (Siebert, 2003, 2004, 2005). Social workers practicing while impaired are at greater risk of unethical conduct and malpractice (Houston-Vega & Nuehring, 1997; Lowenberg et al., 2000; Reamer, 1998). Impaired social workers may pay inconsistent attention to work requirements, fail to complete assignments, engage in excessive absenteeism, or commit treatment errors that may lead to serious ethical violations.

Professional impairment in social work is also important because of its impact on the profession in general. Although all misconduct is not the result of impairment, highly publicized cases of unethical actions caused by impairment portray social workers in an embarrassing light, damaging the reputation of the profession and causing questions to be raised about the competence of the profession overall.

The issue of impaired practice presents real dilemmas and challenges for the profession that are compounded by little guidance on the issue from regulatory boards and professional organizations. Clients who are affected most by impaired performance generally do not recognize it. Unfortunately, many social workers avoid "interfering" in the lives of their troubled colleagues, despite the ethical mandates to intervene (NASW, 2000). A 1992 study of NASW members indicated that the majority— 41 percent were uncertain about reporting, 36 percent favored reporting, and 23 percent were against reporting (Elpers, 1992). Social workers are often fearful about colleagues' reactions to their confrontation and its effect on their future working relationships, making practitioners reluctant to intervene even when they suspect impairment of their colleagues (Reamer, 1992). Finally, a lack of recognition of their problems makes it unlikely that professionals who are impaired will self-initiate appropriate actions such as seeking treatment, making adjustments in workload, terminating services or practices, or taking other steps necessary to protect clients. Data from one study of NASW members suggested that social workers do not frequently seek help, even when they are considered to be at high risk of AOD use (Siebert, 2005). Reasons for not seeking help included concern about confidentiality and professional consequences, the belief that treatment provider options were unacceptable, feeling uncomfortable because they knew the providers personally or professionally, believing that they could not take time from work to obtain assistance, and viewing counseling as ineffective.

The social work profession must address the needs of its members and protect the welfare of its clients. Addressing the issues that arise from the identification and treatment of professional impairment will continue to present a challenge for those social work professionals who have denied their vulnerability.

POLICY STATEMENT

NASW recognizes that the prevention, identification, and treatment of professional impairment is vital to protect the welfare of clients, practicing social workers, the work environment, and the integrity of the profession. A multisystemic approach, focusing on prevention, identification, and treatment, must be used to address professional impairment among social workers.

Prevention

Recognizing that preventive education is critical, NASW supports social work education programs that enhance awareness through incorporating material about student and professional impairment, and ethical responsibilities related to impairment, into their recruitment, screening, and curriculum.

This material may include evidence-based research on the identification of risk factors associated with professional impairment, the characteristics of impaired functioning, the strategies available for approaching and assisting social work colleagues believed to be impaired, treatment and other options available for professionals with impairments, and the ethical obligations of social workers with regard to professional impairment.

NASW supports

■ mandatory continuing education addressing professional impairment as part of the ethics requirement of each state's regulatory boards.

■ ongoing individual and group services for both social work students and practitioners as a means to discuss workplace stressors and the physical and psychological effect of working within social work settings.

■ advocacy efforts directed toward ensuring that social workers operate in a safe work environment with adequate resources that maximize the efficacy and efficiency of the social worker and that minimize environmental stressors and the resultant negative psychological impact that increase the risk of impairment.

Identification and Treatment

It is imperative that confidential and non-punitive treatment options aimed at identifying and assisting social workers in returning to competent functioning be available to social workers who are impaired. NASW encourages the establishment of colleague-assistance programs that confidentially help to identify colleagues with impairments, encourage them to obtain treatment, identify appropriate treatment options available, and facilitate integration back into the workplace upon recovery.

NASW supports

■ insurance benefits that provide access to comprehensive preventive and treatment services addressing professional impairment issues.

■ programs for at-risk and recovering social workers that offer the opportunity for additional supervision and consultation.

■ fair, nondiscriminatory, and accessible rehabilitative practices, addressing professional impairment, which are enforced by employers, regulatory boards, schools of social work, and other professional organizations.

■ the education of clients on procedures for reporting their concerns regarding potential violations of their rights, resulting from professional impairment.

Macro Level Initiatives

On a macro level, NASW supports

■ additional research on professional impairment, including prevention, assessment, treatment, and help-seeking behaviors among impaired social workers and social work students.

■ updating and dissemination of practical guidelines for social workers to identify colleagues at risk and practical strategies for approaching impaired colleagues.

■ civil immunity laws that protect those who report colleagues believed to be impaired.

REFERENCES

Barker, R. L. (2003). *The social work dictionary* (5th ed.). Washington, DC: NASW Press.

Berliner, A. K. (1989). Misconduct in social work practice. *Social Work, 34,* 69–72.

Bissell, L., Fewell, C. H., & Jones, R. W. (1980). The alcoholic social worker: A survey. *Social Work in Health Care, 5,* 421–433.

Bride, B. E. (2007). Prevalence of secondary traumatic stress among social workers. *Social Work, 52,* 63–70.

Elpers, K. (1992). *Social work impairment: A statewide survey of the National Association of Social Workers.* Evansville, IN: Author.

Fewell, C. H., King, B. L., & Weinstein, D. L. (1993). Alcohol and other drug abuse among social work colleagues and their families: Impact on practice. *Social Work, 38,* 565–570.

Figley, C. R. (Ed.). (1995). *Compassion fatigue: Coping with secondary traumatic stress disorder in those who treat the traumatized.* New York: Brunner-Mazel.

Gassman, R. A., Demone, H. W., & Wechsler, H. (2002). College student's drinking: Master's in social work compared with undergraduate students. *Health & Social Work, 27,* 184–193.

Houston-Vega, M. K., & Nuehring, E. M. (with Daguio, E. R.). (1997). *Prudent practice: A guide for managing malpractice risk.* Washington, DC: NASW Press.

Jayaratne, S., & Chess, W. A. (1984). Job satisfaction, burnout and turnover: A national study. *Social Work, 29,* 448–453.

Lamb, D. H., Presser, N. R., Pfost, K. S., Baum, M. C., Jackson, V. R., & Jarvis, P. A. (1987). Confronting professional impairment during the internship: Identification, due process, and remediation. *Professional Psychology: Research and Practice, 18,* 597–603.

Loewenberg, F. M., Dolgoff, R., & Harrington, D. (2000). *Ethical decisions for social work practice* (6th ed.). Itasca, IL: F. E. Peacock.

National Association of Social Workers. (2000). *Code of ethics of the National Association of Social Workers.* Washington, DC: NASW Press.

National Association of Social Workers. (2006). Professional impairment. In *Social Work* speaks: National Association of Social Workers policy statements (7th ed., pp. 296–300). Washington, DC: NASW Press.

Reamer, F. G. (1992). The impaired social worker. *Social Work, 37*, 165–170.

Reamer, F. G. (1994). *Social work malpractice and liability: Strategies for prevention.* New York: Columbia University Press.

Reamer, F. G. (1998). *Ethical standards in social work: A critical review of the NASW code of ethics.* Washington, DC: NASW Press.

Siebert, D. C. (2003). Denial of AOD use: An issue for social workers and the profession. *Health & Social Work, 28*, 89–97.

Siebert, D. C. (2004). Depression in North Carolina social workers: Implications for practice and research. *Social Work Research, 28*, 30–40.

Siebert, D. C. (2005). Help seeking for AOD misuse among social workers: Patterns, barriers, and implications. *Social Work, 50*, 65–75.

Soderfeldt, M., Soderfeldt, B., & Warg, L. E. (1995). Burnout in social work. *Social Work, 40*, 638–646.

Strom-Gottfried, K., & D'Aprix, A. (2006). Ethics for academics. *Social Work Education, 25*, 225–244.

Policy statement approved by the NASW Delegate Assembly, August 2008. This policy statement supersedes the policy statement on Professional Impairment approved by the Assembly in August 1999 and referred by the 2005 Delegate Assembly to the 2008 Delegate Assembly for revision, and the policy statement on The Impaired Professional approved by the Delegate Assembly in 1987 and reconfirmed by the Delegate Assembly in 1993. This policy statement was previously titled A Colleague-Assistance Program. For further information, contact the National Association of Social Workers, 750 First Street, NE, Suite 700, Washington, DC 20002-4241. Telephone: 202-408-8600 or 800-638-8799; e-mail: press@naswdc.org

Professional Self-Care and Social Work

BACKGROUND

Professional self-care is an essential underpinning to best practice in the profession of social work. The need for professional self-care has relevance to all social workers in the setting within which they practice. The practice of self-care is critical to the survival and growth of the profession. Yet professional self-care has not been fully examined or addressed within the profession.

The profession of social work offers unique challenges that are both rewarding and potentially overwhelming for the professional social worker. Authors such as Munson (2002) and Shulman (1993) discussed the importance of understanding the stress reactions of social workers and the role that supervisors may play in helping social workers to prevent or overcome stress. Some authors specifically emphasize an ongoing self-awareness and urge preparation for our work by seeking and creating supportive networks (Murphy & Dillon, 2003).

It is not often that social workers engage in thoughtful discourse of the unique challenges of our profession and ways of addressing and managing the effect. Numerous stressors are prevalent in the social work arena such as long hours, time constraints and deadlines, large and professionally challenging client caseloads, limited or inadequate resources, crises and emergencies, low pay, safety concerns (Whitaker, Weismiller, & Clark, 2006), and lack of recognition and autonomy. These stressors tend to be related to the organizational structure and operations of agencies, as well as the cultural, community, and political context affecting clients and practice.

The earliest explorations of the effect of helping in social work practice recognized the risk of stress and burnout (Arches, 1991; Edelwich, & Brodsky, 1980; Gillespie, 1987; Powell, 1994; Söderfeldt, Söderfeldt, & Warg, 1995; Um & Harrison, 1998). Many early authors connected with the work of Maslach (1993, 2003) who defined burnout as "a syndrome of emotional exhaustion, depersonalization, and reduced personal accomplishment that can occur among individuals who do 'people-work' of some kind." Later definitions included a loss of enthusiasm for the work, a loss of a sense of commitment to the profession, and a disengagement and distancing from clients (Conrad & Joseph, 2003; Joseph, 1988).

Later research helped to enlighten social workers and other helping professionals about conditions that could result from the process of listening to the clients' stories and the therapeutic conversations, with themes of helplessness and hopelessness. Frameworks have been developed for understanding specific experiences such as compassion fatigue (Figley, 1995, 2002), secondary traumatic stress (Figley, 2002; Stamm, 1999), and vicarious traumatization (McCann & Pearlman, 1990; Pearlman, 1995; Pearlman & Saakvitne, 1995). *Compassion fatigue*, or secondary traumatic stress, is defined "as the natural, predictable, treatable, and preventable unwanted consequence of working with suffering people, that is, the cost of caring" (Figley, 1995; Stamm, 1999). *Vicarious traumatization* refers to a cumulative transformative effect or condition experienced by trauma therapists as they work with specific populations of survivors of traumatic life events (McCann & Pearlman, 1990; Pearlman & Saakvitne, 1995). The common characteristic is that they represent the negative, unwanted, psychological effects of the experience of helping and therefore, uniquely affect the helping professional.

Particular focus of the literature has been on the effect of trauma work on social workers in settings dealing with family violence (Bell, 2003; Bell, Kulkami, & Dalton, 2003), child protective service (Cornille & Meyers, 1999; Dane, 2000; Pryce, Shackelford, & Pryce, 2007; Regehr, Hemsworth, Leslie, Howe, & Chau, 2004), sexual abuse (Couper, 2000; Cunningham, 1999), and grief and loss (Walsh-Burke, 2006). Cunningham (2003) described two types of trauma: human induced trauma, such as sexual abuse, and naturally caused trauma such as cancer. Some studies have examined the effect of disasters on social workers (Adams, Boscarino, & Figley, 2006; Boscarino, Figley, & Adams, 2004) and the incidence of secondary traumatic stress in child welfare (Pryce et al., 2007). Greene (2007) and others have expanded resilience to the workplace, and the risks for those professionals involved with the "occupational hazards that presents for Social Work professionals time and again . . . of taking care of others, both before and more than ourselves" (Fink-Samnick, 2007).

Some attention has been focused on educating social work students about these conditions through classroom experiences where stress management techniques are taught (Dziegielewski, Tumage, & Roest-Marti, 2004) and through lectures exploring vicarious trauma as one of the psychological effects of helping (Cunningham, 2004).

Throughout the explorations and discussions of these stress factors, most authors emphasize the need for social workers and other helping professionals. Some recommend specific strategies that are self-affirming, self-protecting, and self-nurturing (Pearlman & Saakvitne, 1995). Others discuss survival strategies and tools that address the physical, psychological, professional, interpersonal, and spiritual aspects of the practitioner (Figley, 1995). One study, using the strengths perspective in family violence work, identified five distinct characteristics of the more resilient workers as having a sense of competence about coping, maintaining an objective motivation, resolving personal traumas, drawing on positive role models of coping, and having buffering personal beliefs (Bell, 2003).

ISSUE STATEMENT

In light of recent and significant research indicating that social workers engaged in direct practice are likely to develop symptoms of secondary traumatic stress, it is imperative that the social work profession devotes greater attention to and creates greater awareness of these issues.

The critical key to prevention and management of adverse conditions such as stress, burnout, compassion fatigue, and secondary traumatic stress or vicarious trauma is the practice of self-care. Baker (2003) conceptualized self-care as the combination of three processes: self-awareness, self-regulation, and balancing connections between self, others, and the larger community. *Professional self-care* in social work can be defined as a core essential component to social work practice and reflects a choice and commitment to become actively involved in maintaining one's effectiveness as a social worker. Furthermore, in promoting the practice of professional self-care, a repertoire of self-care strategies is essential to support the social worker in preventing, addressing, and coping with the natural, yet unwanted, consequences of helping (Lopez, 2007).

Professional self-care is vital to the profession of social work for several reasons:

- Professional self-care is an essential component in competent, compassionate, and ethical social work practice, requiring time, energy, and commitment.

- Promoting the practice of professional self-care in social work explicitly acknowledges the challenging and often overwhelming nature of our work.

- Professional self-care places emphasis on primary prevention of these unwanted conditions and implies that tools and strategies should be part of one's overall professional self-care plan. Actively preparing social workers with knowledge and skill for overcoming these experiences is key.

- Professional self-care in social work is critical to maintaining ethical and professional behavior and providing competent services to clients across diverse settings.

■ Although the practice of professional self-care applies to all social workers, it is especially critical for social workers providing care to traumatized populations

■ Acknowledging professional self-care in social work is an important first step in preserving the integrity of social workers and in retaining valued professionals in the profession. Actively preparing social workers to effectively face these conditions will support social workers in maintaining their commitment to the profession.

POLICY STATEMENT

NASW recognizes and acknowledges the unique and valuable contributions of the professional social worker. NASW supports the practice of professional self-care for social workers as a means of maintaining their competence, strengthening the profession, and preserving the integrity of their work with clients. Education, self-awareness, and commitment are considered key to promoting the practice of professional self-care. In recognition of social workers as valued professional resources across diverse practice settings, NASW supports

■ the establishment and implementation of organizational policies that promote participatory decision making, interactive coping styles, and environments in which organizational values and conflict can be openly discussed and negotiated.

■ the establishment and enforcement of organizational policies and practices that address and enhance safety in the workplace. Organizations may be supportive by examining the organizational culture, redefining workload, providing essential supervision, encouraging self-care practices, allowing for group support, and creating a supportive work environment.

■ the promotion, support, and modeling of the practice of professional self-care by social work supervisors with social work supervisees.

■ the promotion and support of the practice of professional self-care by social work administrators. Social work administrators can demonstrate support for self-care by reflecting self-care in policies and in the process of evaluation; offering supportive supervision, ongoing processing and debriefing after traumatic or stressful occurrences, staff retreats, team building with a focus on rejuvenating social work staff; and actively sponsoring healthy lifestyle activities within the work environment, such as walking, running, aerobics, healthy eating, encouraging time off, taking breaks and mental health days, and providing relaxing and nurturing environments for meditating.

■ the development of individual professional self-care plans by all social workers that includes a repertoire of personalized strategies for maintaining health, preventing burnout and compassion fatigue, and addressing secondary traumatic stress or vicarious trauma. The plan should also include the development or enhancement of interactive coping styles that deal directly with the management of organizational conflict and differences with colleagues. Social workers should cultivate and maintain self-awareness of their personal and professional limitations and monitor their efforts to promote the practice of professional self-care and to support social work colleagues in these processes as well.

■ the development of continuing education programs on professional self-care and conditions such as stress, burnout, compassion fatigue, secondary traumatic stress, and vicarious trauma.

■ the development of creative and innovative support services for social workers, which may include support groups, professional retreats, Web site resources, online support, and chat groups.

■ the recognition by social work education programs of their critically important roles in educating social work students about the practice of professional self-care by integrating such content into existing student standards, policies, foundation and advanced curriculums, field practicum, and assignments and projects.

■ the training of social work students about professional self-care in their field experiences and the modeling of these behaviors by field instructors.

- further research to continue the exploration of the prevalence of secondary traumatic stress and vicarious trauma among social workers in a variety of settings and to examine resiliency factors and self-care practices among social workers.

- further development of publications that address the issue of professional self-care and social work and that offer tools and strategies for thriving in social work practice.

REFERENCES

Adams, R. E., Boscarino, J. A., & Figley, C. R. (2006). Compassion fatigue and psychological distress among social workers: A validation study. *American Journal of Orthopsychiatry, 76*, 103–108.

Arches, J. (1991). Social structure, burnout, and job satisfaction. *Social Work, 36*, 202–206.

Baker, E. (2003). *Caring for ourselves as psychologists*. Retrieved May 30, 2008, from http://www.google.com/search?hl=en&as_q=Baker+and+2003&as_epq=professional+self-care&as_oq=&as_eq=&num=10&lr=lang_en&as_filetype=&ft=i&as_sitesearch=&as_qdr=all&as_rights=&as_occt=any&cr=&as_nlo=&as_nhi=&safe=images

Bell, H. (2003). Strengths and secondary trauma in family violence work. *Social Work, 48*, 513–522.

Bell, H., Kulkarni, S., & Dalton, L. (2003). Organizational prevention of vicarious trauma. *Families in Society, 84*, 463–470.

Boscarino, J. A., Figley, C. R., & Adams, R. E. (2004). Compassion fatigue following the September 11 terrorist attacks: A study of secondary trauma among New York city social workers. *International Journal of Emergency Mental Health, 6*(2), 57–66.

Conrad, A. P., & Joseph, M. V. (2003). Spirituality and burnout prevention. In *Solid Practice III* (pp. 18–42). Hong Kong: Cosmos Books.

Cornille, T. A., & Meyers, T. W. (1999). Secondary traumatic stress among child protective service workers: Prevalence, severity and predictive factors. *Traumatology, 5*, 15–31.

Couper, D. (2000). The impact of the sexually abused child's pain on the worker and the team. *Journal of Social Work Practice, 14*(1), 9–16.

Cunningham, M. (1999). The impact of sexual abuse treatment on the social work clinician. *Child and Adolescent Social Work Journal, 16*, 277–290.

Cunningham, M. (2003). Impact of trauma on social work clinicians: Empirical findings. *Social Work, 48*, 451–459.

Cunningham, M. (2004). Teaching social workers about trauma: Reducing the risks of vicarious traumatization in the classroom. *Journal of Social Work Education, 40*, 305–317.

Dane, B. (2000). Child welfare workers: An innovative approach for interacting with secondary trauma. *Journal of Social Work Education, 36*, 27–38.

Dziegielewski, S. F., Turnage, B., & Roest-Marti, S. (2004). Addressing stress with social work students: A controlled evaluation. *Journal of Social Work Education, 40*, 105–119.

Edelwich, J., & Brodsky, A. (1980). *Burn-out*. New York: Human Sciences Press.

Figley, C. R. (Ed.). (1995). *Compassion fatigue: Coping with secondary traumatic stress disorder in those who treat the traumatized*. New York: Brunner/Mazel.

Figley, C. R. (Ed.). (2002). *Treating compassion fatigue*. New York: Brunner-Routledge.

Fink-Samnick, E. (2007). Fostering a sense of professional resilience. *The New Social Worker, 14*(3), 24–27.

Gillespie, D. F. (Ed.). (1987). *Burnout among social workers*. New York: Haworth Press.

Greene, R. R. (2007). *Social work practice: A risk and resilience perspective*. Belmont, CA: Brooks/Cole.

Joseph, M. V. (1988, January). The roots of burnout: Implications of church ministries. *Church Personnel Issues*, pp. 1–6.

Lopez, S. A. (2007, July 20). *Professional self-care & social work*. Opening keynote Address—NASW Texas Chapter Sandra A. Lopez Leadership Institute, Austin.

Maslach, C. (1993). Burnout: A multidimensional perspective. In W. B. Schaufeli, C. Maslach, & T. Marek (Eds.), *Professional burnout: Recent developments in theory and* research (pp. 19–32). Washington, DC: Taylor & Francis.

Maslach, C. (2003). *The burnout: The cost of caring.* Cambridge, MA: Malor Book.

McCann, L. L., & Pearlman, L. A. (1990). Vicarious traumatization: A contextual model for understanding the effects of trauma on helpers. *Journal of Traumatic Stress, 3,* 131–149.

Munson, C. E. (2002). *Handbook of clinical social work supervision* (3rd ed.). New York: Haworth Press.

Murphy, B. C., & Dillon, C. (2003). *Interviewing in action: Relationship, process, and change.* Pacific Grove, CA: Brooks/Cole.

Pearlman, L. A. (1995). Self-care for trauma therapists: Ameliorating vicarious traumatization. In B. H. Stamm (Ed.), *Secondary traumatic stress: Self-care issues for clinicians, researchers, and educators* (pp. 51–64). Lutherville, MD: Sidran Press.

Pearlman, L. A., & Saakvitne, K. W. (1995). *Trauma and the therapist: Countertransference and vicarious traumatization in psychotherapy with incest survivors.* New York: W. W. Norton.

Powell, W. E. (1994). The relationship between feelings of alienation and burnout in social work. *Families in Society, 75,* 229–235.

Pryce, J., Shackelford, K., & Pryce, D. (2007). *Secondary traumatic stress and the child welfare professional.* Chicago: Lyceum Books.

Regehr, C., Hemsworth, D., Leslie, B., Howe, P., & Chau, S. (2004). Predictors of posttraumatic distress in child welfare workers: A linear structural equation model. *Ontario Association of Children's Aid Societies Journal, 48*(4), 25–30.

Shulman, L. (1993). *Interactional supervision.* Washington, DC: NASW Press.

Söderfeldt, M., Söderfeldt, B., & Warg, L.-E. (1995). Burnout in social work. *Social Work, 40,* 638–646.

Stamm, B. H. (Ed.). (1999). *Secondary traumatic stress: Self-care issues for clinicians, researchers and educators* (2nd ed.). Baltimore: Sidran Press.

Um, M-Y., & Harrison, D. F. (1998). Role stressors, burnout, mediators, and job satisfaction: A stress–strain–outcome model and an empirical test. *Social Work Research, 22,* 100–115.

Walsh-Burke, K. (2006). *Grief and loss: Theories and skills for helping professionals.* Boston: Pearson Education, Inc.

Whitaker, T., Weismiller, T., & Clark, E. (2006). *Assuring the sufficiency of a frontline workforce: A national study of licensed social workers* [Executive Summary]. Washington, DC: National Association of Social Workers.

Policy statement approved by the NASW Delegate Assembly, August 2008. For further information, contact the National Association of Social Workers, 750 First Street, NE, Suite 700, Washington, DC 20002-4241. Telephone: 202-408-8600 or 800-638-8799; e-mail: press@naswdc.org

Prostituted People, Commercial Sex Workers, and Social Work Practice

BACKGROUND

Since the beginnings of the social work profession, social workers have worked with prostituted people and individuals engaged in commercial sex work. During the 1920s, social workers tried to rehabilitate "fallen women" by changing their personalities through casework and therapy. Social workers used interventions that focused on the individual. The thinking was that as long as the causes of prostitution lay with the individual, then it could be eliminated if only all of the fallen women could be redeemed. For 40 years after World War I, the discourse on prostitution was largely shaped by psychiatrists who theorized that the causes of prostitution could be traced back to the individual neurotic, frigid, or masochistic female (Hobson, 1987). Not until the cultural and social protests of the 1960s and 1970s did prostitution again become an issue of sexual politics or social justice. Ever mired in controversy, however, discourse on prostitution and commercial sex work would continue to stagnate and be dogged by conflicts in class and gender politics (Hobson, 1987).

For the sake of this policy, NASW recognizes a difference between prostitution which is involuntary, and commercial sex work which is voluntary. *Prostitution* is defined as involuntary or forced sexual activity in exchange for remuneration. *Commercial sex work* is a term coined within the past two decades that is inclusive of many activities in which resources are voluntarily exchanged for sexual stimulation, gratification, or other sex acts (World Health Organization [WHO], 1994). *Trafficking* is another term often used interchangeably with prostitution, although trafficking is much broader than sexual trafficking and is defined by the United Nations (2000) as the illegal or illicit movement of people through force or coercion. Trafficking is a separate issue that will not be addressed in this policy.

In the 1970s, commercial sex workers around the world began organizing for safety and respect. Many commercial sex workers argued that their undocumented status increased their vulnerability to violence, exploitation, and disease.

With the rise of the HIV/AIDS epidemic in the 1980s, commercial sex workers again became scapegoats for the spread of sexually transmitted infections (STIs) (Sacks, 1996). However, many prostituted people and commercial sex workers are unable to enforce the use of condoms and therefore are at greater risk of HIV/AIDS and other STIs (WHO, Regional Office for the Western Pacific [ROWP], 2001). Social workers in almost any setting may encounter commercial sex workers, but those active in needle exchange programs, substance abuse treatment programs, HIV/AIDS outreach programs, safer sex education and public health programs for people with HIV/AIDS have the most frequent contact. Although several of the prostitution and sex worker-focused HIV/AIDS education programs and "John Schools" (diversion programs that educate men who are arrested for soliciting a prostitute) in the 1990s were organized and run by current and former prostituted people and commercial sex workers, some employ the services of social workers.

The average age of recruitment into prostitution is between 13 and 16 years; however, nationally, direct care service providers say that the victims they have encountered in the past five years are even younger (Lloyd, 2005; Silbert & Pines, 1981; Spangenberg, 2001). Girls who are exposed to "the life" are put in violent and dangerous situations. Girls are beaten, raped, and threatened by their pimps, clients, or even other prostituted women. One study of 800 prostituted women found that 85 percent had experienced rapes; 95 percent, assaults; and 77 percent, kidnapping by pimps (Council for Prostitution Alternatives [CPA], 1991). Another study found that almost 20 percent of the women interviewed had been assaulted, sexually assaulted, or propositioned by law enforcement personnel (Nixon, Tutty, Downe, Gorkoff, & Ursel, 2002).

Boys and girls are drawn into prostitution; the trauma to them is the same, and the social causes are similar. Both boys and girls who run away from home are at risk of turning to survival sex (exchange of sex for resources): at least 10 percent of shelter youths and 28 percent of street youths reported engaging in survival sex (Greene, Ennett, & Ringwalt, 1999). However, the causes of running away are somewhat different for boys and girls. Girls (20 percent to 40 percent) are more likely than boys (10 percent to 30 percent) to run away because of abuse (Estes & Weiner, 2001), and it is thought that boys are more likely than girls to be "thrown away" or to run away because of negative parental reaction to their sexual orientation (Savin-Williams, 1998). Approximately 25 percent to 35 percent of prostituted boys self-identify as gay, bisexual, or transgender transsexual (Estes & Weiner, 2001). Children with histories of family abuse, drug use, and STIs were more likely to engage in survival sex than those without these histories (Greene et al., 1999). Boys experience health concerns similar to those of girls: drug use, violence, rape, and risk of HIV/AIDS and STIs because of high rates of unprotected sex. Although boys are to be included in this policy statement, it is important to note that the vast majority of studies and research focus on girls, who, more often than boys, are victims of pimps and other traffickers (Estes & Weiner, 2001).

ISSUE STATEMENT

The pressing concerns about prostitution and commercial sex work are nested within a broader cultural context of economic injustice and social inequality. Research indicates that 75 percent to 85 percent of women would leave prostitution if they had secure housing. Although sexual exploitation can affect youths from all backgrounds, it is the "youth from low-socioeconomic backgrounds who are at high risk for recruitment and often find it harder to leave" (Lloyd, 2005, p. 16). The undocumented status of many prostituted people and commercial sex workers increases their vulnerability to violence, exploitation, and disease. Prostituted people and commercial sex workers, who are predominately female, are arrested 10 times more often than their customers, who are predominately male (WHO, ROWP, 2001). Female prostitutes and commercial sex workers of color are disproportionately targeted by law enforcement for prostitution regulation.

Violence is just one of the major problems for prostituted people and commercial sex workers. Although figures vary, an early study of violence against prostituted people and commercial sex workers indicated that 60 percent of the abuse against street prostitutes is perpetrated by clients, 20 percent by police, and 20 percent by domestic partners (Jaget, 1980). A more recent study of 130 street workers (most homeless) who engaged in prostitution or survival sex found that 80 percent had been physically assaulted (Farley & Barkan, 1998). Among prostituted people and commercial sex workers seeking services to leave prostitution at the CPA, a Portland, Oregon, organization, 85 percent of prostitutes and clients reported a history of childhood sexual abuse; 70 percent reported incest (CPA, 1991).

Substance abuse is another oft-cited concern for prostituted people and commercial sex workers. Studies in the United States have found prevalence rates of substance use and addiction up to 84 percent, depending on the exact population being studied (Alexander, 1987; Sloan, 1997; Weiner, 1996). In the United States and Canada, substance addiction is relatively common among street prostitutes who may engage in prostitution or commercial sex work to support their drug habits (Cepeda & Valdez, 2003; Monroe & Sloan, 2004). In addition, some prostitution or commercial sex work venues provide ready access to alcohol and other substances. Substance abuse is less common, however, among "off-street" and legal commercial sex workers in parts of Nevada and much of Canada.

The rate of HIV/AIDS and STIs among prostituted people and commercial sex workers varies on the basis of the rate of infection in the general population, venue, and, the type of sexual behavior in which the prostituted person or commercial sex worker engages. Prostituted people and commercial sex workers who are not able to enforce the use of condoms when engaged in high-risk behavior are placed at increased risk of HIV/AIDS and other STIs (WHO, ROWP, 2001). The experience in many Asian countries suggests that strong antiprostitution laws create barriers for prostituted people and commercial sex workers enforcing 100 percent condom usage programs (WHO, ROWP, 2001). In Thailand, for example, 80 percent of men infected with HIV/AIDS are reported to have contracted the disease from prostituted people or commercial sex workers (WHO, ROWP, 2001). By contrast, in New South Wales, Australia, where condom use is strongly enforced and the rate of HIV/AIDS is low in the general population, prostituted people and commercial sex workers have low rates of HIV/AIDS and other STIs.

One of the most common characteristics of prostituted people is their history of childhood abuse, especially sexual abuse. In 20 recent studies of adult women who were involved in prostitution or commercial sex work, the percentage of those who had been sexually abused as children ranged from 33 percent to 84 percent (Raphael, 2004). These children quickly learn that they and their bodies are only valued for sex. Therefore, they are likely to equate sex with love, and degradation with caring. A profound sense of shame and guilt develops, and often leads to depression and hopelessness. Children who encounter this type of abuse without any protective supports from family or community services will more than likely end up battered and scorned, and are searching for a way to escape their pain (Salvatore, 2002). These individuals become easy targets for sex predators, most notably pimps, who may lure them with romantic promises of a better life. A 1994 National Institute of Justice report stated that children who were sexually abused are 28 times more likely to be arrested for prostitution at some point in their lives than children who were not sexually abused (as reported in Spangenberg, 2001). The earlier-identified risk factors make traumatized children more vulnerable to prostitution and commercial sex work.

Given all of these factors prostitution like ". . . No other 'employment' has comparable rates of physical assault, rape, and homicide, except for war combat. The symptoms of profound emotional distress that result from prostitution . . . are: depression, suicidality, anxiety, posttraumatic stress disorder, dissociation, and substance abuse, and they cannot be ignored" (Farley, 2005, p. 2).

POLICY STATEMENT

NASW supports

■ the right of commercial sex workers and prostituted people to be treated with dignity and respect.

■ vigorous enforcement of laws protecting prostituted people and commercial sex workers from violence, including from partners, customers, or police.

■ policies and services that promote access and remove barriers (like criminal records) to education, housing, health care services (including mental health and substance abuse treatment), and ability to secure employment.

■ access for prostituted people and commercial sex workers to appropriate victim services and criminal justice response to criminal offenses committed against them.

■ the United Nations Convention on the Elimination of all Forms of Discrimination against Women in 1979, and the United Nations Declaration on the Elimination of Violence against Women in 1993. Both of these documents condemn prostitution and support the elimination of sexual exploitation.

■ advocacy for laws which decriminalize prostitution so prostituted people and commercial sex workers are not jailed and can still access services.

- intervention services such as housing, job training, and supports that would enable people to leave a life of prostitution or commercial sex work if they choose.

- services for male and female youths who are at risk of involvement in prostitution.

REFERENCES

Alexander, A. (1987). Prostitution: A difficult issue for feminists. In F. Delacoste & P. Alexander (Eds.), Sex work: Writings by women in the sex industry (pp. 184–214). San Francisco: Cleis Press.

Cepeda, A., & Valdez, A. (2003). Female sex workers and injecting drug use on the U.S.–Mexico border: Nuevo Laredo, Tamaulipas. Journal of Border Health, 7(1), 84–93.

Council for Prostitution Alternatives. (1991). Annual report. Portland, OR: Author.

Estes, R., & Weiner, N. (2001). The commercial sexual exploitation of children in the U.S., Canada, and Mexico. Philadelphia: University of Pennsylvania.

Farley, M. (2005, August). Unequal. Nation Magazine, pp. 1–5. Retrieved November 3, 2007, from www.prostitutionresearch.com

Farley, M., & Barkan, H. (1998). Prostitution, violence, and posttraumatic stress disorder. Women & Health, 27(3), 37–49.

Greene, J. M., Ennett, S. T., & Ringwalt, C. (1999). Prevalence and correlates of survival sex among runaway and homeless youth. American Journal of Public Health, 89, 1406–1409.

Hobson, B. M. (1987). Uneasy virtue: The politics of prostitution and the American reform tradition. Chicago: University of Chicago Press.

Jaget, C. (Ed.). (1980). Prostitutes, our life. Bristol, England: Falling Wall Press.

Lloyd, R. (2005). Acceptable victims? Sexually exploited youth in the U.S. Encounter: Education for Meaning and Social Justice, 18(3), 16–18.

Monroe, J., & Sloan, L. M. (2004, September). The truth about sex work. Paper presentation at the 1st National Conference on Prostitution, Sex Work, and the Commercial Sex Industry: The State of Women's Health. Toledo, OH: University of Toledo.

Nixon, K., Tutty, L., Downe, P., Gorkoff, K., & Ursel, J. (2002, September). The everyday occurrence: Violence in the lives of girls exploited through prostitution. Violence Against Women, 8, 1016–1043.

Raphael, J. (2004). Listening to Olivia: Violence, poverty, and prostitution. Boston: Northeastern University Press.

Sacks, V. (1996). Women and AIDS: An analysis of media misrepresentations. Social Science & Medicine, 42, 59–73.

Salvatore, J. (2002). The prostituted child. Franklin, MA: NESPIN.

Savin-Williams, R. C. (1998). The disclosure to families of same-sex attractions by lesbian, gay, and bisexual youths. Journal of Research on Adolescence, 8, 49–68.

Silbert, M., & Pines, A. (1981). Occupational hazards of street prostitutes. Criminal Justice and Behavior, 8, 395–399.

Sloan, L. M. (1997). A qualitative study of women who work as topless dancers. Unpublished doctoral dissertation, University of Texas at Austin.

Spangenberg, M. (2001). Prostituted youth in New York City: An overview. New York City: ECPAT-USA.

United Nations. (2000). United Nations Convention Against Transnational Organized Crime. Vienna, Austria: Author.

Weiner, A. (1996). Understanding the social needs of streetwalking prostitutes. Social Work, 41, 97–105.

World Health Organization. (1994). HIV/AIDS and sex workers. Retrieved June 2004, from http://www.who.org

World Health Organization, Regional Office for the Western Pacific. (2001). Sex work in Asia. Manila, Philippines: Author.

Policy statement approved by the NASW Delegate Assembly, August 2008. This policy statement supersedes the policy statement on Commercial Sex Workers and Social Work Practice approved by the Delegate Assembly in 2005. For further information, contact the National Association of Social Workers, 750 First Street, NE, Suite 700, Washington, DC 20002-4241. Telephone: 202-408-8600 or 800-638-8799; e-mail: press@naswdc.org

Public Child Welfare

BACKGROUND

Public child welfare services are child centered and family focused and include an array of preventive and support services, as well as protective services out-of-home care, and other permanency options such as placement with relatives/kinship care, and adoption. The public child welfare agencies fulfill society's mandated commitment to help families or family substitutes provide safe, stable, and permanent homes for their children. Decision making about the most appropriate environment for children and youths not only calls for an extensive knowledge of child development and an understanding of where a particular youth may be in the course of development, but also requires an ability to bring together different groups who have interests in the outcome that can be competing and conflictual. The rights of biological parents, the demands of juvenile courts, the requirements of federal and state rules and procedures, and the assessments of other professionals, all must be synthesized into a coherent, consistent, comprehensive plan that will achieve safety, stability, and permanency for each child and youth.

Although professional social work practice in public child welfare exemplifies the profession's values and mission to serve the most vulnerable, high turnover rates, with significant delays in replacement, among professional social workers have increased over the past two decades (Barnes, 2000; Kraus, 2000). Social work students continue to be more interested in social work practice in private clinically oriented settings, health care, education, aged, or employee assistance programs (Barnes). Poor working environments, high rates of ex-

posure to critical events, high levels of accountability to multiple and conflicting stakeholders, poor or inadequate supervision, the widespread practice of splitting clinical intervention from case management work, noncompetitive salaries, few promotional opportunities, and intrusiveness into their personal lives discourage new graduate social workers from entering public child welfare and influence qualified experienced staff to leave the child welfare field (Barak, Nissly, & Levin, 2001; Bednar, 2003; Cyphers, 2001, 2005; Ellett, Ellett, & Rugutt, 2003; GAO, 2003, 2004; Regehr, Chau, Leslie, & Howe, 2002; Rycraft, 1994; Samantrai, 1992). This inability to attract and retain social workers causes concern because the tasks to be accomplished and the critical decisions to be made demand a high degree of professional expertise that is applied consistently over extended periods.

ISSUE STATEMENT

The lifelong effects of child welfare decisions demand highly qualified personnel in public child welfare administration and services who have a thorough knowledge of child and youth developmental needs, comprehensive knowledge of the resources needed to meet those needs, ability to find and develop the necessary resources, and commitment to serving children and youths from impoverished environments (Cyphers, 2001, 2005; Ellett et al.; GAO, 2003, 2004). Decisions made by public child welfare staff are critical; they can alter the future course of a child's life and that of his or her family. Decisions such as whether a child was abused, should be removed from the home, should be placed in a particular type of treatment setting, should be returned home or whether to petition a court for termination of parental rights are typical of those made daily by child welfare workers. In addition, child welfare workers must work with public child welfare agencies, government rules and regulations, private child welfare agencies, courts, and parents and family members, all of whom frequently have competing and conflicting interests in the decisions and who hold the child welfare worker accountable for the decision that is made (Barak et al., 2001; Ellett et al., 2003). Only individuals who have had professional training should be given the responsibility for such important decision making.

The social work profession needs to assert its role in public child welfare by supporting three principles:

1. An undergraduate social work degree should be required for the delivery, and a graduate social work degree should be required for the supervision and administration, of social services in public child welfare to ensure that workers have the necessary skills, knowledge, and values to provide high-quality services.

2. The development of an educational curriculum and professional training is vital to the recruitment and retention of professional social workers in public child welfare.

3. The profession must organize at the local, state, and national levels to promote public understanding of and financial support for the public child welfare system, its services to clients, including equal access of resources to guardians and kinship providers, and its workers.

POLICY STATEMENT

The National Association of Social Workers (NASW) recognizes that effective services to the children and families in public child welfare demand the values, knowledge, and skills that are intrinsic to social work education.

Therefore, undergraduate social work education should be required for the delivery of social services in public child welfare, and graduate social work education should be required for the supervision and administration of social services in public child welfare. NASW supports the initiatives that encourage recruitment, education, and retention of professional social workers (BSWs or MSWs) in the public child welfare system, such as loan forgiveness programs, payment of licensure fees, financial incentives for rural practice, and statewide access to social work education programs.

NASW believes that children and families who are served through the public child welfare system have a right to the same level and quality of services delivered by professional social workers in other fields of practice. Furthermore, because the philosophical base of public child welfare requires both rehabilitative and preventive services, social workers need skill and professionalism to provide these services under the legally mandated authority of the public agency.

The same elements that undergird all professional social work practice should guide social work practice in public child welfare. Nonjudgmental respect for the dignity of the individual child and family, the use of a helping relationship, support for family self-determination, confidentiality, the right to culturally and ethnically sensitive service, and advocacy with meso and macro systems are among the essential elements in social work practice. Social workers also must address the vulnerability of women, people of color, and people with a non-heterosexual orientation in the delivery and receipt of public child welfare services and attempt to resolve their disempowerment.

NASW advocates high standards of professional ethics and practice in child protection, intact family services, kinship care, foster care, group care, and adoption, with an emphasis on keeping children connected to families of origin.

NASW supports increased activities for the recruitment, education, training, and retention of professional social workers in public child welfare. NASW also supports federal funding for education and training programs to prepare social workers for practice in child welfare.

National and local units of NASW will work together to support and promote the use of professional social workers in state and local child welfare agencies.

Public child welfare agencies and workers face unique demands and stresses. Social workers must work with other groups and professional organizations to succeed in the following activities:

■ promoting public understanding of and financial support for public child welfare services to clients, the public child welfare system, including research of that system and services, and public child welfare workers

■ supporting efforts to reform the public child welfare system to keep families strong, increase the safety of children, and ensure quality service delivery

■ creating greater opportunities for the professional development of public child welfare workers

■ securing adequate salary levels for public child welfare workers

■ advocating for loan forgiveness programs for professional social workers in the child welfare system

■ establishing a maximum caseload standard nationwide

■ promoting job flexibility

■ providing supervision that is consultative and supportive

■ promoting evidence-based practice

■ ensuring working conditions that are suitable and professional

■ supporting title protection, which allows only workers with a social work degree to use that title.

Social workers should be allied with leaders in the public child welfare field to develop appropriate public policy in this arena. NASW reaffirms that professional social work practice in public child welfare exemplifies the profession's values and mission to serve the most vulnerable.

REFERENCES

Barak, M.E.M., Nissly, J. A., & Levin, A. (2001). Antecedents to retention and turnover among child welfare, social work, and other human service employees: What can we learn from past research? A review and met-analysis. *Social Service Review, 75*, 625–661.

Barnes, S. W. (2000). Inside story. *Policy and Practice of Public Human Services, 58*(2), 4–5.

Bednar, S. G. (2003). Elements of satisfying organizational climates in child welfare agencies. *Families in Society, 84*, 7–12.

Cyphers, G. (2001). Report from the child welfare workforce survey: State and county data and findings. Washington, DC: American Public Human Services Association.

Cyphers, G. (2005). Report from the 2004 child welfare workforce survey: State agency findings. Washington, DC: American Public Human Services Association.

Ellett, A. J., Ellett, C. D., & Rugutt, J. K. (2003, March). A study of personal and organizational factors contributing to employee retention and turnover in child welfare in Georgia, Athens: School of Social Work, University of Georgia.

General Accounting Office. (2003). *Child welfare: HHS could play a greater role in helping child welfare agencies recruit and retain staff.* Washington, DC: Author.

General Accounting Office. (2004). *D.C. Child and Family Services Agency: More focus needed on human capital management issues for caseworkers and foster parent recruitment and retention.* Washington, DC: Author.

General Accounting Office Report to Congressional Requestors. (2004, April). *Child and family services reviews: Better use of data and improved guidance could enhance HHS's oversight of state performance.* Retrieved from http://www.gao.gov/highlights/d04333high.pdf

Kraus, A. (2000). Changing personnel practices to support health and human service reform. *Policy and Practice of Public Human Services, 58*(2), 19–26.

Regehr, C., Chau, S., Leslie, B., & Howe, P. (2002). An exploration of supervisor's and manager's responses to child welfare reform. *Administration in Social Work, 26*(3), 17–36.

Rycraft, J. R. (1994). The party isn't over: The agency role in the retention of public child welfare caseworkers. *Social Work, 39,* 75–80.

Samantrai, K. (1992). Factors in the decision to leave: Retaining social workers with MSWs in public child welfare. *Social Work, 37,* 454–458.

Policy statement approved by the NASW Delegate Assembly, August 2005. This statement supersedes the statement approved by the Delegate Assembly in November 1987 and reconfirmed in 1993 and referred by the 1999 Delegate Assembly to the 2002 Delegate Assembly to be combined with policy statements on Foster Care and Adoptions and Child Abuse and Neglect, which was not completed for the 2002 Delegate Assembly but was submitted to the 2005 Delegate Assembly for review. For further information, contact the National Association of Social Workers, 750 First Street, NE, Suite 700, Washington, DC 20002-4241. Telephone: 202-408-8600 or 800-638-8799; e-mail: press@naswdc.org

Racism

BACKGROUND

Racism is pervasive in U.S. society and remains a silent code that systematically closes the doors of opportunity to many individuals. Contextually, *racism* is the belief or practice through demonstrated power of perceived superiority of one group over others by reason of race, color, ethnicity, or cultural heritage. This perceived power or right is part of the cultural inheritance of the United States. At the birth of the nation, racism was particularly demonstrated in the intent to conquer Indian nations and the perpetuation of black slavery (Perea, Delgado, Harris, & Wildman, n.d.). "The unresolved legacy of those early racial dilemmas . . . as well as additional, complex issues that we confront today as a result of our demographics" (Perea et al., n.d.) are intertwined with social and economic interests that make it difficult to safeguard contemporary policy based on law. It has been scientifically documented that races are not biological groupings but rather are social constructions (Petit, 1998). Racism is indefensible. Race and ethnicity intersect with a multitude of coexisting cultural identities, including class, religion, gender, sexual orientation, and age, that illuminate and shape the meaning given to racial, social, and economic status. These coexisting identifiers classify, categorize, and construct the social value that is assigned to individuals; position them within society; and legitimize either indignities or privilege (Harley, Jolivette, McCormick, & Tice, 2002). Contexts specific to time, place, and situation also shape racial or ethnic meaning and contribute to the placement of individuals in superior or inferior positions. For example, in the United States, whiteness conveys an ideology of privilege and power. Research has suggested the phenomenon of *white transparency*, which is the tendency among white people to not see themselves in racial terms and their lack of awareness, as an "invisible knapsack of privilege" (McIntosh, 2004). The denial of the effect of whiteness on interactions between individuals and groups contributes to the problem of racism.

Awareness of the changing demographics of racial and ethnic minority groups is important as these numbers have grown dramatically in the United States. In some areas they no longer constitute a numeric minority; yet, they are disadvantaged. Since 1980, the populations of Asian Americans have tripled, Hispanics have doubled, Native Americans have increased by 62 percent, and African Americans have increased by 31 percent; the white population remains almost the same (Ethnic Majority, 2004). By the year 2050 it has been predicted that what are often now referred to as minority populations will comprise half of the U.S. population (Day, 1996). The change in the 2000 Census to capture people of mixed racial and ethnic background has added another factor to the equation. The 2000 census categorized eight mutually exclusive and exhaustive racial and ethnic groups: American Indian/Alaskan Native only, Asian only, black or African American only, Hispanic American, Native Hawaiian/other Pacific Islander only, white only, some other race only, and two or more races. The expanded options allow for 63 confusing categories. For example, the most common multiracial combinations in 2000 were white and American Indian/Alaskan Native (1 million), white and Asian (868,000), white and black (785,000), and black and American Indian/Alaskan Native (182,000) (U.S. Census Bureau, 2001).

To establish consistency in this paper, heuristic reference is made to "oppressed racial and ethnic groups." The terms "oppressed" and "oppression" are used to clarify reference to those who are discriminated against because of their race or ethnicity. Many members of oppressed racial and ethnic groups continue to struggle for equal access and opportunity, particularly during times of slow economic growth, strident calls for tax cuts, dwindling natural resources, inflation, widespread unemployment and underemployment, and conservative judicial opinions within hegemonic structural and institutional systems that are precursors to greater racial oppression and deprivation. Unless curbed, these conditions will lead to greater ethnic and racial disputes and to greater cultural, political, social, and economic discrimination.

NASW has assumed increasing leadership in developing policies and programs to eliminate racism in society and in the social work profession. According to the NASW *Code of Ethics*, "Social workers . . . should advocate for changes in policy and legislation to improve social conditions in order to meet basic human needs and promote social justice. . . . Social workers should act to prevent and eliminate domination of, exploitation of, and discrimination against any person, group, or class" (NASW, 2000, p. 27). NASW will continue to assume a leadership role in developing practice strategies and programs that are culturally proficient.

The major demographic changes for the United States, in the number of individuals from oppressed racial and ethnic groups, "alter and increase the diversity confronting social workers daily in their agencies . . . and the complexities associated with cultural diversity" (NASW, 2001, p. 7). Cultural competence standards have been developed to enhance cultural appropriateness in service delivery to diverse client groups. The *NASW Standards for Cultural Competence in Social Work Practice* (NASW, 2001) encourage "the development of a high level of social work practice that encourages cultural competence among all social workers so that they can respond effectively, knowledgeably, sensitively, and skillfully to the diversity inherent in the agencies in which they work and with the clients and communities they serve" (p. 14).

Education

The educational system in the United States systematically denies equal access and opportunity to racially and ethnically diverse children and adults, especially those who are poor. Inadequate attention is paid to the impact of the societal forces of racism, segregation, language, and racial discrimination (for example, limited English proficiency students, poverty, and urbanization) on educational achievement. Individuals from oppressed racial and ethnic communities, including African Americans, American Indians and Alaskan Natives, Asian Americans and Pacific Islanders, and Latino or Hispanic Americans, are disproportionately represented among the impoverished segments of the population.

More astute attention is needed to address the impact of racial and ethnic discrimination in our education systems. The necessity for comprehensive multilingual and multicultural curriculums is not sufficiently recognized in national policy or local practice. In higher education, racial and ethnic groups are not proportionately represented at staff, student, faculty, or administrative levels. Insufficient financial resources exacerbate these and other problems related to education disparities.

Employment

For many members of oppressed racial and ethnic groups, there is always an economic depression. Often, individuals from these marginalized groups are the last hired and the first fired. As a result, budget cuts, downsizing, outsourcing, and privatization may disproportionately hurt these groups. Furthermore, there is a growing shortage of manufacturing and other jobs that they have historically held. In January 2004 the unemployment rate for African Americans was 10.5 percent; for Hispanics or Latinos it was 7.3 percent, below overall rates of 5.6 percent. Data was not available for American Indians; other groups had rates better than the overall rate (U.S. Bureau of Labor Statistics

[BLS], 2004). A record 120,000 African Americans dropped out of the labor market in February 2004.

The unemployment rate for adolescents from oppressed racial and ethnic groups is approximately four times that of white adolescents (BLS, 2004); it is not surprising that women and men in these groups continue to be underrepresented in decision-making and administrative positions. Affirmative action programs are not sufficiently enforced and supported and in some cases have produced conflict and polarity among employees.

Housing

Many members of marginalized racial and ethnic groups have little choice as to where they live, and they pay higher rents for less adequate housing. Mortgage and lending institutions continue the illegal practice of redlining. An $11 million settlement regarding red lining mortgages in marginalized neighborhoods was agreed to in the metropolitan Washington, DC, area. Studies conducted by the Federal Reserve, the U.S. Department of Housing and Urban Development (HUD), and the Urban Institute have found persistent discrimination against African Americans and Hispanic Americans and other ethnically diverse groups by financial institutions, landlords, and real estate agencies (Congressional Black Caucus Foundation, 1995). A more recent study conducted in 2000 by HUD to measure the extent of housing discrimination in metropolitan areas against people of color found that although generally down, housing discrimination still exists at unacceptable levels (HUD, 2004). The greatest share of discrimination for Hispanic and African American home seekers can still be attributed to being told rental units are unavailable when compared with non-Hispanic white home seekers. Although discrimination is down on most measures for African American and Hispanic homebuyers, "there are worrisome upward trends of discrimination in the areas of geographic steering for African Americans and, relative to non-Hispanic whites, the amount of help agents provide to Hispanics with obtaining financing" (HUD, 2004). The same study found consistent adverse treatment and systematic discrimination against Native Americans and Asian and Pacific Islanders in both the rental and homebuyer fields.

The maintenance of public housing continues to be a serious problem. In the new millennium, homeless shelters too often become the solution for housing millions of men, women, and children. The fact that African Americans and other oppressed groups are disproportionately affected by homelessness further aggravates the reality of the differential treatment of oppressed minority groups.

Health Care and Mental Health Services

Striking disparities exist for Americans of oppressed racial and ethnic groups in access, quality, and availability of health care and mental health services. For example, in the United States life expectancy for these groups is significantly less than it is for white people (Arias, 2004). The infant mortality rate of African Americans is more than twice that of white people (Matthews, Menacker, & MacDorman, 2002). Death from asthma is two to six times more likely to occur among African Americans and Hispanics than among white people (Health Resources and Services Administration, 2000). Suicide rates for American Indians/Alaskan Natives are 50 percent higher than the national rate, and as many as 40 percent of Hispanic Americans report limited English-language proficiency (U.S. Surgeon General, 2001), a factor that has a major impact on both access to and quality of health services.

Discrimination has had a direct impact on the health of minority populations. "Racism in the health care delivery system has a long history. Its impact is felt today in both the experiences individuals have in entering the system and the quality of care they receive" (Grant Makers in Health, 2000).

The dual health care systems of fee-for-service and public care are not meeting the needs of many members of marginalized racial and ethnic groups. Most health care costs continue to increase in the private and public sectors, and for many the quality and accessibility of services decline. "Especially disturbing is that racial and ethnic minorities comprised a disproportionate burden of the uninsured population. Though African Americans are only 12 percent of the population, 20.2 percent of African Americans were uninsured in 2002. Twenty-six percent of blacks in poverty were without health insurance year-round" (Congressional Black Caucus Foundation, 2003). For Hispanics, more than one-third (33.3 percent) under age 65 are uninsured, the poorest rate of any group (National Alliance for Hispanic Health, 2004). African Americans, Hispanics, and Asian/Pacific Islanders comprise 29 percent of the U.S. population and 52.3 percent of the nation's year-round uninsured population (Congressional Black Caucus Foundation, 2003). A majority of the nation's uninsured suffer the highest rates of chronic diseases that could have been prevented with access to quality health care.

Many health care facilities, mental health services, and health care providers tend to be located in areas that are inaccessible to low-income urban neighborhoods and rural districts, where many members of marginalized racial and ethnic groups reside. For example, older African Americans tend to reside in geographical clusters corresponding to racially stratified residential patterns. As a result racial discrimination can occur through a process of "medical redlining" (Rockeymoore & Hawkinson, 2004). With the decline of free public hospitals and of public or low-cost mental health care, the residents of racially stratified residential areas go without care. Public services, such as sanitation, are more likely to be neglected in low-income areas, thus creating additional health hazards. Use of folk wisdom and traditional healing, common practices in diverse racial and ethnic communities, are beginning to be recognized and integrated into the health care arena, yet, they are limited in many communities, and the quality of culturally proficient health care interventions is often considered a low priority or simply neglected.

Public Welfare

Oppressed racial and ethnic groups are overrepresented in the public welfare system because of their overrepresentation in the ranks of poor people. As a result they have received the brunt of the effects of the dismantling of the federal government's commitment to a philosophy of providing support for families impoverished because of unemployment and/or ill health. Stereotypes about poor people negate the reality that the U.S. economy and the job market cannot provide sufficient employment to produce the necessary income for all those who are now dependent on welfare benefits. Although acknowledged to be necessary concomitants to successful reduction of dependence on public welfare, limited services for job training, education, child care, family planning, and health care or unemployment insurance are limited or unavailable. Disregard for personal rights and human dignity, inconsistent policies, and violation of regulations have often characterized the administration and delivery of public assistance and keep people of racial and ethnic backgrounds who apply for assistance at a disadvantage.

Social Services

Social services programs are not staffed to respond to the needs of racial and ethnic oppressed populations. Often, the result is nonuse or underutilization of services by people who confront racial, cultural, and linguistic barriers. Although generally responsive to immediate basic needs, the services provided by social services agencies often dilute the intensity and negative impact of the larger structural problems such as racism, unemployment, illiteracy, and poverty. Too often society "blames the victim" and focuses on adjusting the individual to existing societal conditions, disregarding the need for structural, environmental, and institutional change and responsiveness. Social services workers who do not fully inform their clients of available entitlements or, when appropriate, do not encourage their clients to use those entitlements are an intrinsic element of the system that fails members of racial and ethnic groups.

Criminal Justice

Incarceration rates of individuals from oppressed racial and ethnic populations are so high that criminal justice has become the civil rights movement of this generation (Center on Juvenile and Criminal Justice [CJCJ], 2004). Overrepresentation of oppressed racial and ethnic groups in the justice system exists in every state in the country and at every stage of the process. Racial and ethnic disparities are more pronounced at intake, but they are compounded at each decision point. The CJCJ report indicated that nationwide African Americans are 26 percent of juvenile arrests, 44 percent of those detained, 46 percent of youths who are judicially waived to criminal court, and 58 percent of youths admitted to state prison. Hispanic American and Asian American youths with felony arrests are 3.8 times more likely than white youths with felony arrests to be sentenced to the California Youth Authority. The Juvenile Justice and Delinquency Prevention Act of 2002 (P.L. 107-273) identified disproportionate confinement of individuals of racial and ethnic groups as a condition that continues to exist.

Political Activity

Members of marginalized racial and ethnic groups are grossly underrepresented in federal and local elective and appointed positions. Thus, legislation affecting all people is produced by nonrepresentative legislative bodies. A study found an apparent pattern of harassment against African American elected officials in the United States using tactics of Internal Revenue Service audits, surveillance, phone taps, recall movements, and so forth (Congressional Black Caucus Foundation, 1995).

Hate crimes are violent acts against people, property, or organizations because of the group to which they belong or identify with. The largest determinant of hate crimes is race or ethnicity. Hate crimes are not necessarily random, uncontrollable, or inevitable occurrences, according to current research. There is overwhelming evidence that society can intervene to reduce or prevent violence that threatens whole categories or groups of people. The Violent Crime Control and Law Enforcement Act of 1994 (P.L. 103-322) provides for longer sentences if the offense is determined to be a hate crime and proven to be motivated by race, color, religion, national origin, ethnicity, gender, disability, or sexual orientation. Law enforcement officials, community leaders, educators, researchers, and policymakers need to continue to work together against hate crimes.

Research

Culturally proficient indicators are a major priority for those interested in measuring systems, performance, and outcomes. NASW's (2001) cultural competence standards address ethical responsibilities of the social work profession. Further research to enhance and enrich culturally proficient practice and policy can be an effective way to address social justice, equality, and empowerment.

Social Work Profession

NASW supports and encourages the use of its standards for culturally competent social work practice, and the advancement of practice models that have relevance for the range of needs and services represented by diverse client populations (NASW, 2003).

ISSUE STATEMENT

Racism is the ideology or practice through demonstrated power of perceived superiority of one group over others by reason of race, color, ethnicity, or cultural heritage. In the United States and elsewhere, racism is manifested at the individual, group, and institutional levels. It has been institutionalized and maintained in educational, economic, political, religious, social, and cultural policies and activities. It is observable in the prejudiced attitudes, values, myths, beliefs, and discriminatory practices of many people and institutions in positions of power. Racism is functional—that is, it serves a purpose. In U.S. society, racism functions to maintain structural inequities that are to the disadvantage of individuals in certain racial and ethnic groups.

Organized discrimination against members of certain racial and ethnic groups has permeated every aspect of their lives, including education, employment, contacts with the legal system, economics, housing, politics, religion, and social relationships. It has become institutionalized through folklore, legal restrictions, values, myths, the media, and social mores that are openly supported by a substantial number of people, including those who maintain control of the major institutions of U.S. society.

The history of racism in this country began with the genocide of American Indians and Alaskan Natives and includes the atrocities of slavery, colonialism. The subjugation of individuals of Spanish, Mexican, and American Indian descent in the southwest and along the southern border of the United States, the victimization of Chinese and Asian immigrants during the construction of the U.S. railway system, and the more recent internment of Japanese Americans during Work War II are also a part of that history. This same history has been used to justify the conquering of American Indians and Alaskan Natives, African Americans, Puerto Ricans and other Latinas, and Native Hawaiians and Pacific Islanders to obtain land, promote slavery, and perpetuate exploitation through labor and control over the distribution of resources. These conquered population groups became involuntary U.S. citizens.

Newer immigrants face many of the same stereotypes, myths, and prejudices that the conquered populations had faced. Historically, all immigrants entering the country experience racism and discrimination. The effects of racism are documented in a variety of ways: inadequate physical and mental health care services, low wages, high unemployment and underemployment, racial profiling, overrepresentation in the criminal justice systems, substandard housing, higher rates of school dropout, increased suicide, less access to higher education, and other institutional maladies.

Racism negatively affects both the oppressed and the oppressor. Institutional racism has historical roots in injustices perpetrated by our ancestors on indigenous and other populations in conquering and populating this country. Recognition of historical injustices is the first step in combating racism. It should be acknowledged that the sons and daughters are not responsible for the sins of their parents, but the sons and daughters must analyze the present reality to ascertain the antecedents that have resulted in one group in society being in a more advantageous and favorable position at the expense of other groups. It is incumbent in solidarity and in alliance with groups who are inappropriately considered subordinate to join forces with the social work profession to bring about a more just and equitable society in which power, status, wealth, services, and opportunities, are enjoyed by all. Most common to racism is the unconscious behavior associated with white privilege and the benefits of discrimination against others. Racism limits and minimizes the contributions of many, as well as the contributions that will be made.

Social workers often hold jobs in which they confront the damaging effects of racism at conscious and unconscious levels and at individual and institutional levels. As professional administrators, educators, organizers, planners, case managers, clinicians, supervisors, consultants, caseworkers, and researchers, today's social workers have firsthand knowledge of the difficulties that many encounter in their efforts to combat white privilege, gain access to resources, and obtain a professional education.

Most social workers also witness the scarcity of professional peers from oppressed racial and ethnic groups to act as role models and to provide services to diverse client populations. Furthermore, employment opportunities in the upper echelons of the social work delivery systems and academia historically have been elusive to social workers of oppressed racial and ethnic groups.

POLICY STATEMENT

NASW supports an inclusive, multicultural society in which racial, ethnic, class, sexual orientation, age, physical and mental ability, religion and spirituality, gender and other cultural and social identities are valued and respected. Racism will not be tolerated at any level. Emphasis must be placed on self-examination, learning, and change that encompass an ability to deconstruct racist beliefs and practices to become culturally proficient and to ally with others in the full appreciation of diversity.

NASW (2001) charges social workers with the ethical responsibility to be culturally competent.

The association seeks the enactment of public social policies that will protect the rights of and ensure equity and social justice for all members of diverse racial and ethnic groups. It is the ethical responsibility of NASW members to assess their own practices and the agencies in which they work for specific ways to end racism.

The basic goal should be to involve social workers in education programs designed to bring about measurable changes in provider agencies and in NASW national units, chapters, and local units. This is based on the premise that to engage in constructive intraprofessional relationships and to effectively serve clients, social workers must engage in deconstruction of their own biases and stereotypes and work in concerted alliance with others to enhance social justice and equity for all. Racism is embedded in our society and unless we identify specific instances and work together to remove them, we are part of the problem rather than a mechanism for the solution.

Education

NASW advocates the following:

■ supporting the development and implementation of comprehensive multilingual and multicultural curricula—such curricula must call attention to white privilege, the pain of oppression, the legacy of racism, and the contributions of racially and ethnically oppressed groups

■ implementing programs and policies designed to produce high-quality education through a range of effective approaches

■ addressing and seeking censure against educators and educational systems that practice discrimination against students, faculty, staff, and their families because of their race or ethnicity

■ creating educational systems in which faculties, staff, students, administrators, and boards of education reflect the cultural diversity of neighborhoods and the larger society

■ supporting the highest standard of all educational systems to ensure that fair and adequate treatment of, and funding for, diverse racial and ethnic communities is upheld.

Employment

NASW advocates the following:

■ implementation of a national policy of full and fair employment insurance in times of economic downtimes

■ development of comprehensive job training programs

■ maintenance and strengthening of affirmative action plans so that they have the necessary authority and resources to be implemented successfully as demonstrated by measurable outcomes

■ genuine compliance, rather than tokenism, with affirmative action and equal employment opportunity requirements

■ implementation of an adequate minimum wage that reflects the realities of the cost of living and minimum standards of subsistence

■ providing effective, affordable, comprehensive, multicultural, multilingual, and accessible child care

■ supporting workforce policies that prohibit the negative impact on employees of marginalized racial and ethnic groups.

Housing and Community

NASW advocates the following:

■ enactment and practice of an open housing policy designed to eliminate externally imposed segregation in housing resulting from concentrated public housing, redlining, renovation, and conversion of apartment houses to condominiums

■ establishment of government and support programs that promote revitalization in marginalized racial and ethnic communities.

Health Care and Mental Health Services

NASW advocates the following:

■ empowerment of health and mental health practitioners to learn and use culturally relevant healing practices

■ self-study by health and mental health providers to identify oppressive policies, practices, and strategies and target dates for change

■ accessible, affordable, and culturally proficient health care, mental health services, and private practitioners in all neighborhoods

■ enhanced recruitment and training of marginalized racial and ethnic groups and individuals as health and mental health providers, particularly social workers.

Public Welfare Services

NASW advocates the following:

■ positive regard and respect for each individual's personal rights and human dignity

■ elimination of violations of regulations and inconsistent policies in public welfare that place some members of racial and ethnic groups at a disadvantage

■ use of racial, ethnic, and cultural expertise in the development and delivery of public welfare services

■ elimination of broader problems such as unemployment, illiteracy, and poverty that create the need for public welfare.

Social Services

NASW advocates the following:

■ development of social services that target needs articulated by the community to be served

■ development of model social programs that emphasize empowerment of the community and stress economic independence

■ addressing the underrepresentation of marginalized racial and ethnic groups in the social services professions and policy-making boards of social services agencies.

Criminal Justice System

NASW advocates the following:

■ fair and equitable treatment of individuals from oppressed racial and ethnic groups involved in the criminal justice system

■ monitoring and promoting criminal justice policies, statutes, and laws that do not discriminate against individuals on the basis of race, ethnicity, class, political affiliation, sexual orientation, nationality, ability, age, or place of residence

■ addressing the problem of overrepresentation of marginalized racial and ethnic groups within the criminal justice system

■ striving to end racism and discrimination in recruitment, hiring, retention, and promotion in employment of members of racial and ethnic groups in all levels of the criminal justice system

■ availability and accessibility to professionally trained and culturally proficient interpreters in situations where language differences may inhibit communication

■ developing initiatives to examine and correct policies and regulations of hate crimes.

Civil Rights

NASW advocates the following:

■ developing initiatives to examine and correct the discriminating and inhumane detention and deportation policies and regulations of the U.S. Immigration and Naturalization Service (INS).

■ developing initiatives to rectify the discrimination provisions and civil rights violations of the Patriot Act

■ holding law enforcement agencies accountable when they use racial profiling

■ providing education and training to law enforcement agencies on how to discontinue the use of racial profiling.

Political Activity

NASW advocates the following:

■ passage of legislation that acknowledges, maintains, or enhances the sovereign rights and religious freedom of indigenous populations

■ election and appointment of legislators from underrepresented racial and ethnic groups

■ passage of federal antidiscrimination laws, statutes, and regulations to ensure full legal protection against discrimination and hate crimes

■ programs that offer training for police and victim-assistance professionals in early interventions to help hate crime victims better cope with trauma

■ increase in public interest groups that are racially and ethnically diverse

■ passage of legislation that will have a favorable impact on people of diverse racial and ethnic backgrounds

■ massive voter registration and education

■ campaigns against legislators who sponsor or support bills that are racist in intent or implementation

■ cultural proficiency training for public officials

■ proactive involvement in regional processes that actively promote participation of diverse racial and ethnic communities

■ initiatives that support policies and procedures to sustain affirmative action and equal employment opportunity.

Research

NASW advocates the following:

■ promotion and support of social work research about culturally proficient practice strategies

■ encouragement of representation of and participation by underrepresented racial and ethnic groups in research

■ funding that will enhance research to promote social justice in marginalized racial and ethnic communities.

Social Work Profession

NASW advocates the following:

■ continuously acknowledging, recognizing, confronting, and addressing all forms of racism within social work practice at the individual, agency, and institutional levels and within the broader community

■ full representation of groups oppressed because of race, color, ethnicity, or national origin at all levels of leadership and employment, policy formulation, research, administration, supervision, and direct services in social work agencies and professional organizations and associations.

■ implementation of the concepts of affirmative action in all facets of the profession at both the voluntary and the paid levels of service, especially in practice, education, research, and professional development

■ development of guidelines for multicultural social work curricula that emphasize social work as a profession that strives to empower those with less power because of racial or ethnic identification.

REFERENCES

Arias, E. (2004). *United States life tables 2001* (National Vital Statistics Reports, Vol. 52, No. 14, Table 12). Hyattsville, MD: National Center for Health Statistics.

Center on Juvenile and Criminal Justice. (2004). *Myths and facts about youth and crime.* Retrieved September 10, 2004, from http://cjcj.org/jjic/myths_facts.php

Congressional Black Caucus Foundation. (1995). *The mean season for African Americans.* Washington, DC: Author.

Congressional Black Caucus Foundation. (2003, September 29). *Congressional Black Caucus Foundation denounces rise in the number of uninsured: Census figures reveal minorities hardest hit* [Press Release]. Retrieved September 29, 2004, from http://www.cbcfonline.org/Uninsured.html

Day, J. C. (1996). *Population projections of the Unites States by age, sex, race, and Hispanic origin: 1995 to 2050* (Current Population

Reports, Series p. 25-1130). Washington, DC: U.S. Census Bureau.

Ethnic Majority. (2004). "African, Hispanic and Asian American demographics" [Homepage]. Retrieved October 18, 2004, from http://www.ethnicmajority.com/demographics_home.htm

Grant Makers in Health. (2000). *Strategies for reducing racial and ethnic disparities in health* (Issue Brief No. 5). Washington, DC: Author.

Harley, D. A., Jolivette, K., McCormick, K., & Tice, K. (2002). Race, class, and gender: A constellation of positionalities with implications for counseling. *Journal of Multicultural Counseling and Development, 30,* 216–236.

Health Resources and Services Administration. (2000). *Eliminating health disparities in the United States.* Washington, DC: U.S. Department of Health and Human Resources.

Institute on Race and Poverty. (2002). *Racism and metropolitan dynamics: The civil rights challenge of the 21st century.* Minneapolis: Author.

Juvenile Justice and Delinquency Prevention Act of 2002, P.L. 107-273, 116 Stat. 1869.

Matthews, T. J., Menacker, F., & MacDorman, M. F. (2002). *Infant mortality statistics from the 2000 period linked birth/infant death data set* (National Vital Statistics Reports, Vol. 50, No. 12, Table 1). Hyattsville, MD: National Center for Health Statistics.

McIntosh, P. (2004). White privilege. Unpacking the invisible knapsack. In M. L. Anderson & P. H. Collins (Eds.), *Race, class and gender* (5th ed., pp. 103–108). Belmont, CA: Wadsworth/Thomson.

National Alliance for Hispanic Health. (2004). *Delivering health care to Hispanics* (3rd ed., p. 128). Washington, DC: Estrella Press.

National Association of Social Workers. (2000). *Code of ethics of the National Association of Social Workers.* Washington, DC: Author.

National Association of Social Workers. (2001). *NASW standards for cultural competence in social work practice.* Washington, DC: Author.

National Association of Social Workers. (2003). Cultural competence in the social work profession. In *Social work speaks: National Association of Social Workers policy statements* (6th ed., pp. 71–74). Washington, DC: NASW Press.

Perea, J. F., Delgado, R., Harris, A., & Wildman, S. M. (n.d.). *Race and racism in American law.* Retrieved November 8, 2004, from http://academic.udayton.edu/race/syllabi/race/index.htm

Petit, C. (1998, February 23). No biological basis for race scientists say. *San Francisco Chronicle.* Retrieved February 1, 2005, from http://www.geocities.com/CapitolHill/Lobby/2788/race2.html

Rockeymoore, M., & Hawkinson, L. (2004). *Structured inefficiency: The impact of Medicare reform on African Americans* (Policy Report No. 1, pp. 3–20). Washington, DC: Congressional Black Caucus Foundation, Center for Policy Analysis and Research.

U.S. Bureau of Labor Statistics. (2004). *Labor force statistics from the Current Population Survey: Black or African American, Hispanic or Latino.* Retrieved October 10, 2004, from http://data.bls.gov/cgi-bin/surveymost

U.S. Census Bureau. (2001). *United States Census 2000.* Washington, DC: Author.

U.S. Surgeon General. (2001). *Culture counts in mental health services and research finds new surgeon general report* [Press release]. Retrieved April 4, 2004, from http:www.surgeongeneral.gov/library/mentalhealth

Violent Crime Control and Law Enforcement Act of 1994, P.L. 103-322, 108 Stat. 1796.

SUGGESTED READINGS

Banton, M. (1988). *Racial consciousness.* London: Longman.

Bowser, B. P., Jones, T., & Young, G. A. (Eds.). (1995). *Toward the multicultural university.* Westport, CT: Praeger.

Federico, C., & Sidanius, J. (2001). *Racism, ideology, and affirmative action revisited: The antecedents and consequences of "principled objections" to affirmative action* (Working Paper #183). Retrieved March 1, 2004, from www:russellsage.org

Freire, P. (1998). *Pedagogy of freedom: Ethics, democracy, and civic courage.* Lanham, MD: Rowman & Littlefield.

Gray, W. (1996, May). *Speech for the 100th anniversary of Plessy vs. Ferguson.* Cambridge: Harvard University, W.E.B. Du Bois Institute. (C-Span, August 13, 1996).

Jackson, S., & Solis, J. (1995). *Beyond comfort zones in multiculturalism: Confronting the politics of privilege.* Westport, CT: Bergin & Garvey.

Kivel, P. (2002). *Uprooting racism: How white people can work for racial justice.* Philadelphia: Ingram.

Mahalingam, R., & McCarthy, C. (2000). *Multicultural curriculum. New directions for social theory, practice and policy.* New York: Routledge.

Reeves, T., & Bennette, C. (2003). The Asian and Pacific Islander population in the US: March 2002. In *Current Population Reports* (P20-540). Washington, DC: U.S. Census Bureau.

Policy statement approved by the NASW Delegate Assembly, August 2005. This policy supersedes the policy statement on Racism approved by the Delegate Assembly in 1996 and the policy statement on Racism approved by the NASW national Board of Directors in October 1993 following recommendations by the Delegate Assembly in August 1993, and referred by the 2002 Delegate Assembly to the 2005 Delegate Assembly for revision. For further information, contact the National Association of Social Workers, 750 First Street, NE, Suite 700, Washington, DC 20002-4241. Telephone: 202-408-8600 or 800-638-8799; e-mail: press@naswdc.org

Role of Government, Social Policy, and Social Work

BACKGROUND

Since the colonial beginnings of this country, government has been involved in addressing social problems. As a reaction to the strong central authority of European monarchies from which the founders fled or rebelled, they favored a theory of negative government, meaning the less government, the better. This preference for limited government responsibility for social services led Jansson (2001) to label the United States a "reluctant welfare state" as a way of distinguishing it from the traditional European welfare states. Despite this obvious and strong preference for private and individual solutions, government has mitigated the fallout from an unregulated economy and protected disadvantaged populations. As far back as the early 1700s, Massachusetts's colonists received aid from the general treasury to care for sick and displaced people (Trattner, 1999). Although government assistance goes back to our earliest beginnings, there has always been a struggle over how much government should be involved in helping cure the social ills of the nation.

An infamous instance of the hands-off approach is found in the "Pierce Veto." In the 1850s, Franklin Pierce vetoed legislation that would have designated federal lands to be used to establish psychiatric hospitals. Pierce vetoed the legislation because he feared that the federal government would become the "great almoner" to poor people (Pumphrey & Pumphrey, 1967). He did not want to set an "untenable precedent and draw the federal government into an inappropriate and unconstitutional relationship with the nation's needy" (Hall, 2004, p. 1).

Trends and countertrends addressed the most extreme dimensions of poverty, inequal-ity, and oppression. In the early years of the 20th century, the Progressive Era tempered the harshness of the free market economy and protected the most vulnerable people. The Roaring Twenties returned the country to a time of limited government involvement. This was exemplified by the Hoover administration, which refused to support government intervention into the serious hardship experienced by people at the beginning of the Great Depression.

Ultimately, the Great Depression and response of Franklin Delano Roosevelt's New Deal administration in the 1930s firmly established the responsibility of the federal government to ameliorate a capitalistic system. During the subsequent 40 years, the presidential leadership of both parties further established and expanded at the federal level rights of citizenship that included new social, political, and economic benefits.

Leadership by the federal government in promoting an equality-of-opportunity social agenda peaked in the Kennedy–Johnson era of the 1960s. More socially progressive legislation was passed in the 1960s than at any time in U.S. history, and even continued under the Nixon administration. President Nixon instituted block grants to the states, as part of a "new federalism" without abdicating federal leadership, and instituted Title XX support for a range of social programs. Nixon supported the "federalization" of categorical welfare entitlements eventually enacted as Supplemental Security Income, or SSI, benefits. Finally, he proposed the federal takeover of Aid to Families with Dependent Children and introduced national health insurance legislation that would have extended Medicare- and Medicaid-like health coverage to new categories of citizens.

Although the administrations of Presidents Ford and Carter tampered little with social programs and priorities, the "stagflation" during the 1970s led to increasing calls for limits on taxes and on social spending at both the federal and state levels and a shift from universal to selective approaches to services. Concurrently, public hostility toward poor people and other marginalized groups was captured by the republican party's appeals to the "silent majority" or those who were unwilling participants in government intervention on behalf of these groups.

The Reagan and Bush administrations in the 1980s even more vigorously promoted an ideology of individualism and privatization, challenged many established entitlements, and scaled down the government role in "interfering" with the marketplace and corporate profits. Supply-side economics and tax policies forced real cuts in social program spending, a reversal of social program priorities, and efforts to deregulate businesses. The gap between rich and poor increased dramatically. Both administrations continued the concept of a "safety net" supplemented by private charity for meeting the needs of the "truly needy." Although this safety net was selective, the administrations still considered government as the provider of last resort, and there was no attempt to remove federal protection for special groups, such as abused and neglected children.

President Bill Clinton's victory in 1992 did not lead to a return to the philosophy on which the New Deal was based. Instead, Clinton, a neo-liberal Democrat, announced that the "era of big government is over." Consequently, he signed the 1996 Personal Responsibility and Work Opportunity Reconciliation Act (P.L. 104-193), which limited entitlement to public assistance for children and their families that the Roosevelt administration had established in 1935 with the passage of the Social Security Act. The Clinton administration restricted government provision and reduced record-setting deficits that had deepened during the Reagan–Bush years.

Both parties concurred that government should be reduced in size and scope. In the 1994 national elections, candidates supporting further limitations on government won the majority of congressional seats for the first time in 40 years. A majority of state governors was also elected on a platform of less government and lower taxes. These newly elected leaders sought to curtail the federal government in social program guarantees and funding, in protecting vulnerable populations, in restricting monitoring of business and investments, and in promoting affirmative action and other equity programs. At the same time they sought a greater social control role for government in shaping how families, and women in particular, may behave and in restricting who may come to this country and the rights they could exercise while in residence.

In the 2000 election, George W. Bush described himself as a "compassionate conservative." His social welfare policies were similar to those of his father's and Reagan's with the further elaboration of privatizating social services programs, an emphasis on faith-based initiatives, and profit-making social services programs.

In the early years of the 21st century attacks on the role of the federal government have grown from a preference for limited federal involvement to view recipients of services in ways that are antithetical to social work values in several ways: There is a shift from blaming victims to punishing them. The category of "undeserving poor" has expanded to include almost everyone, even those formerly protected, such as children, veterans, elderly people, and people with mental and physical illnesses. Users of public resources are subject to greater social control measures. Consumers of both market and social services are granted fewer real protections and are simply admonished to "let the buyer beware." Stereotypical views of personal characteristics or behaviors of certain groups by virtue of their racial, ethnic, or citizenship status (in the form of acts of racism, ageism, sexism, homophobia, and xenophobia) are justified under the guise of returning to "a supposed" normalcy or "survival of the fittest."

Consistent with this social agenda are economic tenets that include spending cuts and tax breaks for upper-income groups coupled with balanced budget legislation, shifts of minimum programs back to the states without any entitlement provisions, heavy deregulation of industry, the lifting of consumer and environmental protections, and mandates for personal responsibility legislation.

Results of national elections in the first decade of the 21st century reflect seriously divided public opinion over the role of government. Public policy is the dominant variable in determining the nature of social work practice, and it is profoundly affected by government policy. Although social agencies and social work professionals can help shape policies and practices, the nature of the services delivery system and the legitimacy of social work as a profession is established by public social policy. Changes in government policies affect clients, their eligibility, and their ability to obtain benefits and services. In conclusion, restructuring and limiting government responsibility has profoundly altered the availability and the delivery of social work services and the role and status of social work as a profession.

ISSUE STATEMENT

Advances in science and technology, food production, public health, worker safety, and the environment have resulted in improvements in the quality of life undreamed of in the past. At the same time, dislocations and problems that have accompanied many of these changes have caused considerable misery and inequities for many people and communities. From Franklin D. Roosevelt to Jimmy Carter, the electorate chose representatives who viewed government as a mediating structure that modified the vagaries and inequities found in the marketplace. This view was accompanied by ideologies to create equality of opportunity to fulfill the vision of the United States of America as an open, pluralistic, caring, and inclusive society.

From 1935 to the late 1970s, federal government efforts moved in the direction of sharing the benefits of economic growth among its citizens, moderating the harshness of an unregulated economy, and protecting vulnerable

people. During this period, government has fulfilled this by

■ regulation and oversight

■ designing and funding programs created specifically to meet its policy goals

■ stimulating the economy through industrial, taxation, and other fiscal policies

■ redistributing the wealth of the society through the tax system.

However, regressive "Reaganomics" interrupted the progressive ideals of the government. Recent administrations have replaced fundamental values of the New Deal with their own agendas of privatization, personal responsibility, corporate welfare, and faith-based and profit-making social services.

The combination of severe cuts in funding of social programs to provide tax cuts for the wealthiest citizens, deregulation of legal rights and protections, and devolution of programs to states or private corporations with less funding and little or no regulation and standards with very short notice can cause great harm to our society and especially to its most vulnerable populations.

Since the beginning of social work as a profession and the inception of NASW, two basic assumptions have been made: The social ills of the nation and its citizens need public attention, resources, and solutions, and government has a major role and responsibility to meet human needs. Moreover, there has been increasing recognition that major shifts in the structure and functions of society, including demographic, economic, health, and family factors require universal social welfare benefits and services.

The George W. Bush administration saw problems as being individual in origin rather than social or environmental in nature, and too often the etiology of problems in society is being characterized in moral, racial and cultural, or intellectual terms. The influence of social, economic, or political factors on community and family life has been minimized or ignored. At the beginning of the 21st century, government is no longer regarded as an instrument of problem solution; instead, in some quarters, by some factions, it is portrayed as the problem or an exacerbating factor of the problem. Although state governments have been given more responsibility and opportunities to address these issues with fewer resources, there are yet more requirements that states meet the needs of vulnerable and oppressed populations.

POLICY STATEMENT

It is the position of NASW that federal, state, and local governments must have a role in developing policies and programs that expand opportunities, address social and economic justice, improve the quality of life of all people in this country, with special emphasis on oppressed groups, and enhance the social conditions of the nation's communities. NASW reaffirms its commitment to the promotion of the positive role of federal, state, and local governments as guarantors of the social safety net and as the mechanisms by which people through their elected representatives can ensure equitable and accountable policies to address

■ curbing the excesses of a free market economy

■ entitlements to assist in the elimination of poverty

■ access to universal comprehensive health care

■ standards for public services

■ enabling citizen participation in the development and implementation of social programs

■ taxation that is progressive and fair and promotes a reduction of poverty

■ an income floor for working poor people through earned income tax credits and other mechanisms

■ adequate federal minimum wage laws indexed to annual cost-of-living increases

■ standards and laws for the protection of workers in the workplace

■ standards and laws for the protection of vulnerable populations

■ product safety standards

■ access to legal services

■ commitment to full employment

■ adequate and affordable housing

■ assurance of adequate public education and educational standards for all schools

■ a justice system rooted in law and administered impartially

■ laws that protect and maintain the fragile, natural environment

■ ensuring the civil rights of citizens and noncitizen residents, and the right of all to marry

■ nondiscrimination and affirmative action

■ international initiatives based on collaborative and cooperative relationships with other nations.

The key to accomplishing these policy goals is a view of government as an embodiment of and by the people, rather than an entity above and apart from its citizens. This policy calls for a renewed commitment to civic responsibility by an informed community through participation in democratic forums. This policy can be achieved with civic and political participation by all, and with campaign finance reform that levels the political playing field. It demands open debate on a wide variety of policies and programs while maintaining the basic functions listed. As necessary, such a process would support the reform of government when it is consistent with the social work value base.

NASW reaffirms the essential role of government. The role of the federal government is to ensure uniform standards, adequate resources, equal protection under the law, monitoring and evaluating of outcomes, and provision of technical assistance to state and local governments. NASW also recognizes the role of state and local governments in social programs. State governments are often in better positions to understand the needs of the people in those states. As a part of a national community, states must work together to implement a federal policy that supports the well-being of the people of this nation. Thus, social programs are most effective when there is consistency in federal standards and guidelines with adequate funding and accountability mechanisms for states and localities to administer programs in ways that are best adapted to meet the needs of people, examining the effectiveness, efficiency, and accountability of programs necessary to ensure the success of that role. Laws, regulations, and program guidelines need constant and thorough review. NASW can provide significant leadership in evaluating existing programs and in designing and recommending new ones that advance the goals of the social policy it has reaffirmed.

NASW believes that social workers can be effective at all levels of and in many roles in government. Social workers can fulfill roles as elected officials and leaders in government and as administrators in agencies. The recent reintroduction of block grants is an opportunity for social workers to support the collaborative efforts of government and the people. This policy asserts that government should actively and creatively guide, negotiate, and participate in cooperative efforts with nongovernmental organizations to provide programs that expand and support opportunities, address social and economic justice, and improve the quality of life for all people.

REFERENCES

Hall, P. (2004). *Beyond affliction: Dorothea Dix and Franklin Pierce highlight page.* Retrieved June 21, 2004, from www.npr.org/programs/disability/project.dir/project.html

Jansson, B. (2001). *The reluctant welfare state with infotrac: American social welfare policies—Past, present and future.* Belmont, CA: Wadsworth.

Personal Responsibility and Work Opportunity Reconciliation Act, P.L. 104-193, 110 Stat. 2105.

Pumphrey, R., & Pumphrey, M. (1967). *The heritage of American social work.* New York: Columbia University Press.

Trattner, W. (1999). *From poor law to welfare state.* New York: Free Press.

Policy statement approved by the NASW Delegate Assembly, August 2005. This policy supersedes the policy statement on Role of Government approved by the Delegate Assembly in August 1996. For further information, contact the National Association of Social Workers, 750 First Street, NE, Suite 700, Washington, DC 20002-4241. Telephone: 202-408-8600 or 800-638-8799; e-mail: press@ naswdc.org

Rural Social Work

BACKGROUND

The historical roots of social work are generally traced to urban communities, yet social work practice, which specifically addresses the needs of rural individuals and communities, is equally as important, as nearly 50 million Americans (or 17 percent of the U.S. population) live in rural areas. Rural areas extend across 80 percent of the land area and cover approximately 2,000 counties (U.S. Department of Agriculture Rural Development [USDARD], n.d.).

Social workers practicing in rural areas have historically sought to resolve issues of equity, service availability, and isolation that adversely affect residents. They also work to support and advocate for vulnerable and at-risk people living in rural communities. Individuals and families in rural areas face a host of challenges that often result in inequality and disenfranchisement.

Rural Inequality

Individuals who live in rural areas are more likely than their urban counterparts to have no form of health coverage, to neglect seeing a physician due to cost, to have no dental care, to smoke, to be obese, and to suffer from chronic illness (North Carolina Rural Health Research and Policy Analysis Center, 2010). For those who do seek treatment, it is often a challenging undertaking, as only 10 percent of physicians practice in rural America (National Rural Health Association [NRHA], n.d.).

Rural residents are also more likely to suffer from the consequences of poverty. Great wealth has been extracted from rural America, yet it remains the site of some of the nation's most intense and persistent poverty. According to the USDARD (n.d.), people in rural areas experience lower income levels, higher unemployment, and higher poverty rates than people in urban areas. Rural poverty rose significantly by 2009, reaching 16.6 percent. Residents in some parts of the country, such as Appalachia or along the Texas–Mexico border, experience poverty rates of 30 percent to 50 percent (Ambrosino, Ambrosino, Heffernan, & Shuttlesworth, 2008). Over 400 rural counties had poverty rates of 20 percent or more in 2000, which is well above the national average. Median household income in rural areas now stands at 78.7 percent of the metropolitan median. Areas with high levels of poverty are concentrated in the South, and reflect the relatively low incomes of racial and ethnic minorities, female-headed families, and households with children (USDARD, n.d.).

In addition to significant levels of rural poverty, the past decade has continued a 30-year trend toward rising government transfer payments, such as food stamps and subsidies for health care, to rural residents. These payments now account for 22.7 percent of personal income, compared with 13.6 percent in metropolitan areas. The majority of these transfers were due to the high cost of health care (USDARD, n.d.). Yet Medicare payments to rural hospitals and physicians are dramatically less than those in urban areas for equivalent services. This correlates closely with the fact that more than 470 rural hospitals have closed in the past 25 years. Rural residents are also less likely to have employer-provided health care coverage or prescription drug coverage and rely more heavily on the federal food stamp program (NRHA, n.d.).

Access to Care

Many rural areas are considered health professional shortage areas, as defined by the U.S. Department of Health and Human Services, to have a shortage of primary medical care, dental, or mental health providers (Health Resources and Services Administration, n.d.). There are 2,157 health professional shortage areas in rural and frontier areas of all states and U.S. territories compared with 910 in urban areas (NRHA, n.d.). The geographic distribution of social workers is uneven, resulting in gaps in access for those in rural areas (Whitaker, Weismiller, & Clark, 2006). Rural communities may have fewer formal resources, and those that do exist are taxed beyond their limits (Hepworth, Rooney, & Rooney, 2010). Rural areas may offer public welfare services, mental health and developmental disabilities outreach centers, and public health services. Available services are usually understaffed, offer limited assistance, and often are accessible by traveling long distances (Ambrosino et al., 2008).

With respect toward mental health care, President George W. Bush's New Freedom Commission on Mental Health reported that the vast majority of Americans living in underserved, rural, and remote areas experience disparities in mental health services. The commission concluded that, "rural issues are often misunderstood, minimized, and not considered in forming national mental health policy. Too often, policies and practices developed for metropolitan areas are erroneously assumed to apply to rural areas" (President's New Freedom Commission Report, 2003). Twenty percent of rural areas lack mental health services compared with 5 percent of metropolitan areas (NRHA, n.d.).

Furthermore, the health and human services that do exist in rural areas are diminished by issues related to levels of professional training among staff (Daley & Avant, 1999; Ginsberg, 2005). Rural agencies generally face shortages of professional social workers. Bachelor's-level social workers provide higher proportions of the services in rural communities than in urban communities (Daley & Avant, 1999; Johnson, 1980), and many of their colleagues lack professional social work education. Given the low salaries and high caseloads characteristic of practice in the public sector, particularly in rural areas, it is not surprising that graduates of accredited BSW and MSW programs seek employment opportunities elsewhere, which leaves a void in the public sector that is often filled by people with degrees in disciplines other than social work (Lohmann & Lohmann, 2010).

Another area of great inequality, which has an effect on the health and well-being of residents in rural locales, is the digital divide. Rural areas have historically been the last to receive telecommunication investments and are behind in Internet usage. The Obama administration stated that "Modern technology is critical to the expansion of business, education, and health care opportunities in rural areas and the competitiveness of the nation's small towns and rural communities" (White House, n.d.). In 2007, 63 percent of rural residents compared with 73 percent of urban residents used the Internet somewhere. The cost to provide a rural household with telecommunication services has always been higher than for an urban household. Outside of larger rural towns, cable companies are bypassing rural areas for the most part (USDARD, n.d).

Diversity

Social workers practicing in rural areas must be prepared to work with diverse populations and communities (Davenport & Davenport, 2008). Rural areas are increasingly diverse, which brings with it challenges and opportunities. Many rural areas struggle with the economic and social changes brought about by in-migration and immigration of outside populations. All of these groups bring new and different languages, cultures, and beliefs to the rural communities with the resulting pressure on educational, health, and human services resources and on a community's ability to accept and blend these individuals into the community fabric (Hagan, 2011; Nelson, Lee, & Nelson, 2009).

Racial and ethnic minorities now make up 18.3 percent of rural residents. African Americans are the largest minority group in these areas, however Hispanics and Asians are the fastest growing populations (USDARD, n.d.).

Although rural areas struggle with a disproportionate share of poverty, people of color in rural areas bear an even greater burden. Rural non-Hispanic black Americans had the highest incidence of poverty in 2009, at 32.2 percent. The 2009 poverty rate for rural Hispanics was 27.8 percent. These rates were more than twice the poverty rates for non-Hispanic white Americans at 13.3 percent. Rural Native Americans and black Americans are three times more likely to live in low-income families, and consequently, more likely to use public services than non-Hispanic white Americans (USDARD, n.d.).

In addition, poverty is higher for children in rural areas. The child poverty rate in rural areas was 23.5 percent compared with 20.2 percent in metropolitan areas in 2009. At the other end of the aging spectrum, rural areas have a larger share of older people (15 percent) than the population as a whole (12 percent). Compared with their urban peers, older rural Americans generally have less income, lower educational attainment, and a higher dependence on social security income (USDARD, n.d.).

Finally, a large rural population, with specific needs, are members of the military and veterans. U.S. servicemembers in recent conflicts are increasingly drawn from rural areas and return to live in those areas. More than 44 percent of U.S. military recruits come from rural areas ("Youths in Rural U.S.," 2005), with an opposite trend in larger cities. Veterans who live in rural settings have greater health care needs than their urban counterparts, yet they access health care systems less often. Although rural veterans may use psychiatric services less than their urban counterparts, those who are diagnosed with psychiatric disorders are sicker than urban veterans.

As a result of increasingly diverse rural communities, social workers must continually seek to be culturally competent as they work with individuals from a variety of backgrounds, races and ethnicities, and income and education levels. In different parts of the country, the ability to speak dual languages, particularly Spanish, or have access to interpreter services, is also important.

By recognizing all of these diversity factors, rural social work practice contributes to the social work mission of advocating for social justice and extending access to services for underserved populations. These and other factors raise crucial issues for social work practice and educational preparation for social work practice in rural areas.

ISSUE STATEMENT

In response to the challenges facing rural areas, social workers have a unique and important role to play to help ensure the health and well-being of all rural residents. However, they struggle with numerous workforce challenges that may never be faced, or faced to a lesser degree, by their urban counterparts. Rural social workers must care for the increasing number of clients in need of social work services, while dealing with insufficient numbers of professional social work colleagues to provide care, as well as a lack of sufficient social work supervision, high caseloads, the lowest social work salaries of any geographic location, the tendency for agencies to hire non–social workers who lack professional training to fill social work positions, and complicated ethical challenges (Whitaker et al., 2006).

Professional recruitment and retention issues are, in part, by-products of a social work educational system that developed largely from urban roots. Consequently, most social workers receive little content on rural social work in their professional education. This creates a major barrier to developing a social work labor force prepared to address the needs of rural clients and communities and poses a deficit for social workers practicing in rural areas. Rural social work knowledge is important for all social workers, as rural people migrate to urban centers seeking economic opportunity in the face of joblessness, disaster, and conflict. Social workers practicing in urban areas will benefit from knowledge of practice skills that are most effective with rural individuals, families, and communities.

Rural social work practice requires a sophisticated level of understanding of values and ethics and highly developed skills in applying them. "Many of the skills needed to practice social work are the same as those that urban social workers use, an important difference is the emphasis on informal and personal relationships in rural settings" (Ambrosino et al., 2008, p. 398).

Small communities pose unique service challenges because of the low numbers of professional social workers, the importance of interacting with providers and community members who have limited understanding of professional ethics, and the close-knit nature of rural communities. Rural social workers must learn to practice with a lack of anonymity because it is often the case that everyone appears to know what everyone else is doing (Davenport & Davenport, 2008). Effective rural practice often involves locality-based community development that may make maintaining "professional distance" something that is considered inappropriate and may limit effectiveness. Protecting clients from any negative consequences of dual relationships in rural settings has less to do with limiting social relationships and more to do with setting clear boundaries. In fact, nonsexual dual and multiple relationships may even be seen as a strength, if not a necessity, of a good social worker (Bodor, 2005).

Rural communities often retain traditional structures, both informal and faith-based service delivery systems, that can be either assets or challenges. These structures provide self-monitoring and vigilance, making rural communities sometimes safer than urban areas, and encourage a strong informal helping system. However, the same structures may be less hospitable to those perceived as outside of the mainstream culture, such as people of color, women, or gay, lesbian, bisexual, and transgender people. Residents of rural areas may be judgmental toward clients and services that reflect cultures and lifestyles different from community norms. Social workers who are not from the community may also find it more of a challenge to establish effective working relationships due to the close-knit nature of the rural community. Education of community members requires a sustained effort based on trust.

The overall understanding of rural people and cultures is a pressing issue of cultural competence in the social work profession. All social workers should seek to understand the unique challenges and assets within rural communities. All of the issues previously discussed raise crucial issues for social work practice and educational preparation for social workers in rural areas.

POLICY STATEMENT

NASW supports the following:

■ recognition of the importance of rural populations to the nation's economy and cultural identity by all social workers and society as a whole.

■ legislation and policy that improves rural infrastructure, economic development, and access to health care, transportation, education, and social services.

■ advocacy for social work practice and policy that addresses the unique needs of rural clients, particularly those who are vulnerable and oppressed, while recognizing the strengths and assets of rural communities.

■ culturally competent practice, research, and education specific to rural cultures, diversity, and people in a contextual framework at the bachelor's and master's levels.

■ the development and application of ethical principles for professional practice with rural populations.

■ policies that attract and retain social workers in rural settings by creating incentives, networking, professional development, and role modeling for effective practice.

■ continuing education opportunities for social workers to provide a broad range of services, including clinical and health practice, community organization, administration and management, public welfare, and community-based services for rural people.

■ promotion of the effectiveness of professional social workers in helping rural people to capitalize on their strengths, improve their lives, maintain healthy families, and improve their communities.

- development and extension of expanded technology for professional development as well as for rural clients and communities, and the ethical use of technology in service delivery.

REFERENCES

Ambrosino, R., Ambrosino, R., Heffernan, J., & Shuttlesworth, G. (2008). *Social work and social welfare: An introduction* (6th ed.). Belmont, CA: Brooks/Cole.

Bodor, R. C. (2005). Nonsexual dual and multiple relationships: When urban worldviews define rural reality. In B. Locke & V. Majewski (Eds.), *Finding our voices, having our say: Meeting the challenges of rural communities* (pp. 104–119). Morgantown: West Virginia University Division of Social Work.

Daley, M., & Avant, F. (1999). Attracting and retaining professionals for social work practice in rural areas: An example from East Texas. In I. B. Carlton-Laney, R. L. Edwards, & P. N. Reid (Eds.), *Preserving and strengthening small towns and rural communities* (pp. 335–345). Washington, DC: NASW Press.

Davenport, J. A., & Davenport, J., III. (2008). Rural practice. In T. Mizrahi & L. E. Davis (Eds.-in-Chief), *Encyclopedia of social work* (20th ed., Vol. 3, pp. 536–541). Washington, DC: NASW Press.

Ginsberg, L. H. (2005). The overall context of rural practice. In L. H. Ginsberg (Ed.), *Social work in rural communities* (4th ed., pp. 2). Alexandria, VA: Council on Social Work Education.

Hagan, C. (2011, February 23). Hispanic surge seen in Pacific Northwest. *USA Today*.

Health Resources and Services Administration. (n.d.). *Remarks to the rural voices leadership and policy workshop*. Retrieved http://www.hrsa.gov/about/news/speeches/2011/04042011voices.html

Hepworth, D. H., Rooney, R. H., & Rooney, G. D. (2010). *Direct social work practice: Theory and skills* (8th ed.). Belmont, CA: Brooks/Cole.

Johnson, L. C. (1980). Human service delivery patterns in non-metropolitan communities. In H. W. Johnson (Ed.), *Rural human services* (pp. 69–81). Itasca, IL: F. E. Peacock.

Lohmann, N., & Lohmann, R. A. (Eds.). (2010). *Rural social work practice*. New York: Columbia University Press.

National Rural Health Association. (n.d.). *What's different about rural health?* Retrieved from http://www.ruralhealthweb.org/go/left/about-rural-health/what-s-different-about-rural-health-care/what-s-different-about-rural-health-care

Nelson, P., Lee, A. W., Nelson, L. (2009). Linking baby boomer and Hispanic migration streams into rural America—A multi-scaled approach. *Population, Space and Place, 15,* 277–293.

North Carolina Rural Health Research and Policy Analysis Center. (2010). *Rural health snapshot 2010*. Retrieved from http://www.shepscenter.unc.edu/research_programs/rural_program/pubs/other/RuralHealthSnapshot2010.pdf

President's New Freedom Commission on Mental Health. (2003). *Achieving the promise: Transforming health care in America*. Washington, DC: Author.

U.S. Department of Agriculture Rural Development. (n.d.). About RD. Retrieved from http://www.rurdev.usda.gov/Home.html

Whitaker, T., Weismiller, T., & Clark, E. (2006). *Assuring the sufficiency of a frontline workforce: A national study of licensed social workers. Executive summary*. Washington, DC: National Association of Social Workers.

White House. (n.d.). *Rural issues*. Retrieved from http://www.whitehouse.gov/issues/rural

Youths in Rural U.S. Are Drawn to Military. (2005, November 3). *Washington Post*. Retrieved from http://www.washingtonpost.com/wp-n/content/article/2005/11/03/AR2005110302528.html

NASW Members with Primary Responsibility for Revision of This Policy

First Draft Revision:

Michael R. Daley (AL)

Policy Panelists:

Rilla Murray (VT)
Patricia Findley (NJ)
Iris Carlton-LaNey (NC)
Richard Osburn (MI)
Suzanne Oliver (TX)
Scott Sorensen (UT)

Policy statement approved by the NASW Delegate Assembly, August 2011. This statement supersedes the policy statement on Rural Social Work approved by the Delegate Assembly in August 2002. For further information, contact the National Association of Social Workers, 750 First Street, NE, Suite 700, Washington, DC 20002-4241. Telephone: 202-408-8600; e-mail: press@naswdc.org

School Truancy and Dropout Prevention

BACKGROUND

The outcomes and consequences of school dropout are dramatic and compelling. Each year's class of dropouts costs the country more than $200 billion during their lifetimes in lost earnings and unrealized tax revenue. Students from low-income families have a dropout rate of 10 percent; students from middle-income families have a dropout rate of 5.2 percent, and 1.6 percent of students from high-income families dropout (National Center for Educational Statistics, 2001).

High school graduates, on the average, earn $9,245 more per year than high school dropouts (Employment Policy Foundation, 2002). The unemployment rate for this group was 29.8 percent—almost 12 percentage points higher than the unemployment rate for recent high school graduates who were not enrolled in college (U.S. Department of Labor, 2003). The cost to taxpayers of adult illiteracy is $224 billion per year (National Reading Panel, 1999). U.S. companies lose nearly $40 billion annually because of illiteracy (National Reading Panel, 1999). If literacy levels in the United States were the same as those in Sweden, the U.S. GDP would rise by approximately $463 billion, and tax revenues would increase by approximately $162 billion (Alliance for Excellent Education, 2003a, b, c, d, e). For juvenile offenders involved in quality reading instruction programs while incarcerated, recidivism was reduced by 20 percent or more (Alliance for Excellent Education, 2003a, b, c, d, e).

High school dropouts are 3.5 times more likely than high school graduates to be arrested in their lifetime (Alliance for Excellent Education, 2003a); 75 percent of state prison inmates are high school dropouts (Harlow, 2003). A 1 percent increase in high school graduation rates would save approximately $1.4 billion in incarceration costs, or about $2,100 per year for each male high school graduate (Alliance for Excellent Education, 2003a, b, c, d, e). A one-year increase in average education levels would reduce arrest rates by 11 percent (Alliance for Excellent Education, 2003a, b, c, c, e).

Male and female students with low academic achievement are twice as likely to become parents by their senior year of high school compared with students with high academic achievement (Alliance for Excellent Education, 2003a, b, c, d, e). The U.S. death rate for people with fewer than 12 years of education is 2.5 times higher than the rate of those with 13 or more years of education (Alliance for Excellent Education, 2003a, b, c, d, e).

The U.S. Department of Justice, Office of Juvenile Justice and Delinquency Prevention summarizes the causes and correlates of truancy into the following broad categories (Baker, 2000): family factors, school factors, economic influences, and student variables. Family factors include lack of guidance or parental supervision, domestic violence, poverty, drug or alcohol abuse in the home, lack of awareness of attendance laws, and differing attitudes toward education. School factors include school climate issues, such as school size and attitudes of teachers, other students, and administrators and inflexibility in meeting the diverse cultural and learning styles of the students. Schools often have inconsistent procedures for dealing with chronic absenteeism and may not have meaningful consequences available for truant youths (for example, out-of-school suspension). Economic influences include employed students, single-parent homes, high mobility rates, parents who hold multiple jobs, and a lack of affordable transportation and child care. Student variables include drug and alcohol abuse, lack of understanding of attendance laws, lack of social competence, mental health difficulties, and poor physical health.

Although not mentioned specifically, the community significantly influences the occurrence of truancy as well. Community factors are folded into the four areas mentioned. For example, economic conditions and differing culturally based attitudes toward education are also important factors in the community.

Truancy and dropout constitute a school, family, community, and juvenile justice system problem. Therefore, all segments of the community need to be involved and work collaboratively to have a positive effect on reducing truancy and dropout in that community. Early intervention at the first sign of truancy is essential. Prevention, early and consistent intervention, and individualized flexible and creative educational and youth and family services are all keys to success.

ISSUE STATEMENT

Since 1996 school truancy and dropout have stayed the same or worsened. On average, school truancy and dropout have worsened in urban areas and with special populations (for example, special education students and juvenile delinquents). Preventing school truancy and dropout must become a priority social policy issue. The public and private sectors share equally in providing leadership, resources, and solutions to this important problem. Dropping out is the "quiet killer of the American dream" (National Foundation for the Improvement of Education, 1986). Students are at educational and dropout risk because of limited English proficiency, poverty, race, geographic location, or economic disadvantage. Children living in poverty enter school with health and learning difficulties that may result from inadequate prenatal care or the effects of substance abuse. These conditions correlate to dropping out of school before completion of secondary education. School dropout can pose lifelong challenges for the individual student and concomitant costs for society. Consequently, effective

action in the area of school truancy and dropout prevention has never been greater.

To support student learning and success, NASW's policy on school truancy and dropout prevention is consistent with its mission of enhancing the functioning of individuals, families, and society at large, particularly in light of current social and funding trends: schools' diminished ability to provide for students who require educational services beyond the conventional; a competitive labor market that requires entry-level employees to have not only basic skills, but also advanced technical abilities; increasing political pressure for decreasing and redirecting funding for government educational and social welfare assistance; and imposing financial penalties on those who are poor.

Truancy and dropout prevention programs assist individuals in obtaining self-sufficiency and dignity. These programs help individuals to compete in the global marketplace and therefore are cost-effective and humane. The projected loss in human capital of youths' not completing high school is staggering. Dropouts are more likely than high school graduates to be unemployed and are more likely to be incarcerated.

The social work profession has a special responsibility and possesses the skills to address school truancy and dropout, including expertise in parental involvement, community collaboration, early prevention through strength-based life skills building; enhancing individual, family, and community protective factors; and reducing risk factors.

The Office of Juvenile Justice offers the following promising prevention, reduction, and intervention efforts:

■ consistent attendance policy and practice, known to all students, parents, staff, and community agencies

■ early intervention especially with elementary students after three to five absences; swift, appropriate consequences for students and parents; accountability monitoring of schools and related systems

■ a continuum of prevention and intervention services, along with incentives and graduated sanctions for students and parents

- meaningful parental involvement—the most significant area for success, fun, prevention, and intervention

- special attention to health (for example, providing onsite responses for asthmatic children, meeting special education needs)

- data-driven decision making

- student attendance review boards of all involved systems in collaboration

- quasi-judicial proceedings (for example, truancy "court" or review boards)

- business involvement

- focus on school transition years

- public education and awareness campaigns.

Some flexible, individualized empirical validated interventions include truancy mediation for elementary students and their parents and teachers, twilight or evening school for high school-age youths, the choice of quality community and charter schools, and home-based family services for severe multi-need cases.

POLICY STATEMENT

It is the policy of NASW to promote comprehensive and individualized services to enhance each student's opportunity to successfully complete school and to have the opportunities of a full and productive adult life. Regarding school truancy and dropout prevention, NASW supports the following:

- implement prevention programs, fully funded and staffed student service teams for each school that include school social workers and essential school–community collaborations with parent groups, law enforcement, child protective services, juvenile justice, business and so forth, and adequate school social work resources to meet the needs of the student body.

- student assistance programs to systematically identify and support students with risk factors for truancy and dropout as early as possible in their school experience. Supportive services provided in a way that avoids stigmatization.

- access to alternative education programs for at-risk students, with an adequate number of school social workers to address the myriad problems that this population presents. Appropriate ratios for school social work staff to students depending on the characteristics of the student population to be served. NASW believes that alternative education programs within schools, or separate alternative programs, are to be regarded as a student's right and not a punishment for unproductive and disruptive behaviors. A full continuum of creative programming should be available. Programs should be flexible and address the individual student's social, academic, and future world of work needs.

- recruitment of adults as role model mentors, advocates, and tutors for potential dropouts. It is particularly important that men of African American, Latino/Hispanic and other diverse cultures be recruited as such mentors.

- a substantial role for school social workers in promoting family engagement and empowering parents of at-risk multi-need students to participate more fully in decision making about school programs and services.

- increased public school responsiveness to the needs of at-risk and multi-need students, and incorporation of policies and practices that are respectful of differences among people, including race, gender, cultural heritage, language, sexual orientation, socioeconomic status, and behavior issues.

- inclusion of bilingual education or dual language programs in all schools where there is an identified need.

- taking steps to make schools safe learning environments, particularly those schools located in violent communities.

- collaborative, integrated, holistic, individualized services for at-risk and multi-need students and their families, because the needs of potential dropouts and their families cannot be addressed by the public schools alone. The multiple and interconnected needs of at-risk children and their families demand that health, social, justice, and economic services be delivered in a "timely, coordinated, and comprehensive fashion" (Behrman, 1992).

- school-linked, integrated service programs to meet the varied needs of at-risk and multi-need students and their families. These integrated and coordinated health and social services should be offered in the school and in the child's community and family and should involve school social workers in coordination and delivery of services. Constructive and engaging after-school opportunities on the school campus are essential enhancements.

- early childhood education and elementary school early screening and assessment procedures that identify risk and protective factors, to provide prevention and life skills building services to students, families, and schools, including early literacy development.

- opportunities for at-risk and multi-need students to increase their attachment to and connectedness with their school, while simultaneously working to decrease their alienation and disengagement from school. This can be accomplished by systemic renewal, professional and teacher development, student active learning, educational technology, individualized instruction, and career and technical education.

- implementation of proven transition programs for students as they move into the junior and senior high school grades, with individualized support for students who have struggled academically, emotionally, or socially during earlier grades.

- educational curriculum that specifically helps students to understand, in their own terms, the relationship among the education they receive, their understanding of meaningful adult roles, and the world of work. Students at risk of school dropout often display a "disconnect" between the above factors.

- flexible scheduling, school-based mental health and child care services, and vocational internships for all students.

- social worker support, consultation, and education, when needed, to assist educators with the complexities of meeting the social and emotional needs of students.

- social worker advocacy with local, state and national policymakers to increase educational resources, including, but not limited to, reduced school and class sizes, more school social workers, and increased salaries.

- education of the public and the media about the reasons for school dropouts and needs of at-risk students.

- development of relevant data systems and evaluation of the effectiveness of truancy and dropout prevention programs. Findings should be reported to policymakers so that the most successful truancy and dropout prevention programs can be replicated.

REFERENCES

Alliance for Excellent Education. (2003a, November). *FactSheet: The impact of education on: Crime*. Washington, DC: Author.

Alliance for Excellent Education. (2003b, November). *FactSheet: The impact of education on: Health and well being*. Washington, DC: Author.

Alliance for Excellent Education. (2003c, November). *FactSheet: The impact of education on: Personal income and employment*. Washington, DC: Author.

Alliance for Excellent Education. (2003d, November). *FactSheet: The impact of education on: Poverty and homelessness*. Washington, DC: Author.

Alliance for Excellent Education (2003e, November). *FactSheet: The impact of education on: The economy*: Washington, DC: Author.

Baker, M. L. (2000). *Evaluation of the Truancy Reduction Demonstration Program: Interim report*. Denver: Colorado Foundation for Families and Children.

Behrman, R. E. (1992). Introduction. *Future of Children, 2*(1), 4–5.

Bell, A. J., Rosen, L. A., & Dynlacht, D. (1994). *Truancy intervention. Journal of Research and Development in Education, 57*, 203–211.

Dryfoos, J. G. (1990). *Adolescents at risk: Prevalence and prevention*. New York: Oxford University Press.

Employment Policy Foundation 2002 Report from National Dropout Prevention Center. (2003, October 3), Retrieved from http://www.dropoutprevention.org.

Garry, E. M. (1996). *Truancy: First step to a lifetime of problems* [Bulletin]. Washington, DC: U.S. Department of Justice, Office of Justice Programs, Office of Juvenile Justice and Delinquency Prevention.

Harlow, C. W. (2003, January). *Education and correctional populations* [Bureau of Justice Statistics Special Report]. Washington, DC: U. S. Department of Justice.

Hawkins, J. D., & Catalano, R. (1995). *Risk focused prevention: Using the social development strategy.* Seattle. WrapAround Developmental Research and Programs, Inc.

Huizinga, D., Loeber, R., & Thronberry, T. (1995). *Urban delinquency and substance abuse: Initial findings.* Washington, DC: U.S. Department of Justice, Office of Justice Programs, Office of Juvenile Justice and Delinquency Prevention.

Ingersoll, S., & LeBoeuf, D. (1997). *Reaching out to youth out of the education mainstream.* Washington, DC: U.S. Department of Justice, Office of Justice Programs, Office of Juvenile Justice and Delinquency Prevention.

Kelley, B. T., Loeber, R., Keenan, K., & DeLamarte, M. (1997). *Developmental pathways in boys' disruptive and delinquent behavior.* Washington, DC: U.S. Department of Justice, Office of Justice Programs, Office of Juvenile Justice and Delinquency Prevention.

Mone, M. (2002). *Big reductions in truancy/tardiness prompt state to expand parent/school mediation program.* Columbus: Ohio Commission on Dispute Resolution and Conflict Management.

National Center for Educational Statistics. (2001). *Dropout rates in the United States: 2000.* Retrieved November 28, 2001, from http://nces.ed.gov/pubsearch/pubsinfo.asp?pubid=2002114

National Dropout Prevention Center. (2003, October 3). *Effective strategies.* Retrieved from http://www.dropoutprevention.org/effstrat/family_inv/family_over.htm

National Foundation for the Improvement of Education. (1986). *A blueprint for success.* Washington, DC: Author.

National Reading Panel. (1999). *1999 NRP progress report.* Retrieved January 8, 2004, from http://www.nationalreadingpanel.org

Office of Juvenile Justice and Delinquency Prevention. (2004, January/February). *Truancy reduction: Keeping youth in school and out of trouble* (News @ a Glance, Vol. 3, no. 1). Washington, DC; U.S. Department of Justice.

Rohrman, D. (1993). *Combating truancy in our schools—A community effort.* Bulletin, 76(549), 40–51.

U.S. Department of Education. (1993). *Conditions of education: 199 indicators 32 and 32.* Washington, DC: Author.

U.S. Department of Labor. (2003, June). *College enrollment and work activity of 2002 high school graduates.* Retrieved August 2004, from http://www.bls.gov/news.release/hsgec.toc.htm

SUGGESTED READINGS

Baker, M. L., Nady Sigmon, J., & Nugent, M. E. (2001). *Truancy reduction: Keeping students in school.* Washington, DC: U.S. Department of Justice.

Bernat, F. P. (1996). *Survey evaluation for the Governor's Division for Children: State truancies and unexcused absences* (Final Report). Phoenix, AZ: Governor's Division for Children.

Bureau of Labor Statistics. (2001). *A profile of the working poor, 1999* (Report 947). Washington, DC: U. S. Department of Labor.

Catalano, F. R., Arthur, M. W., Hawkins, J. D., Berglund, L., & Olson, J. J. (1998). In R. Loeber & D. Farrington (Eds.), *Comprehensive community and school based interventions to prevent antisocial behavior in serious and violent juvenile offenders: Risk factors and successful interventions.* Thousand Oaks, CA: Sage Publications.

Catterall, J. S. (1985, September). *On the social costs of dropping out of schools* (Report No. 86). Stanford, CA: Stanford University, Center for Educational Research.

Doland, E. (2001). *Give yourself the gift of a degree.* Retrieved May 2002, from http://www.epf.org/media/newsreleases/2001/nr20011219.htm

Dynarski, M., & Gleason, P. (1999). *How can we help? Lessons from federal dropout prevention programs:* Princeton, NJ: Mathematica Policy Research, Inc.

Heaviside, S., Rowand, C., Williams, C., & Farris, E. (1998). *Violence and discipline problems in U. S. public schools 1996–1997*. Washington, DC: U.S. Department of Education, Office of Educational Research and Improvement, National Center for Education Statistics.

Henderson, A. T., & Mapp, K. L. (2002). *A new wave of evidence: The impact of school, family, and community connections on student achievement*. Austin, TX: Southwest Educational Development Laboratory and the National Center for Family and Community Connections with Schools.

Hennepin County Attorney. (2004). *What's your excuse? Truancy intervention*. Minneapolis: Author.

Howell, J. C. (1995). *Guide for implementing the comprehensive strategy for serious, violence and chronic juvenile offenders*. Washington, DC: U.S. Department of Justice, Office of Justice Programs, Office of Juvenile Justice and Delinquency Prevention.

Loeber, R., & Farrington, D. (2000). *Young children who commit crime: Epidemiology, developmental origins, risk factors, early interventions, and policy implications*.

Loeber, R., & Farrington, D. P. (Eds.). (2001a). *Child delinquents: Development, intervention, and service needs*. Thousand Oaks, CA: Sage Publications.

Loeber, R., & Farrington, D. P. (2001b). *The significance of child delinquency*. Thousand Oaks, CA: Sage Publications.

Minneapolis Public Schools. (2004). *School attendance review board*. Minneapolis: Author.

Morley, E., & Rossman, S. B. (1997). *Helping at-risk youth: Lessons from community-based initiatives*. Washington, DC: Urban Institute.

National Center for Juvenile Justice. (1996). *Easy access to FBI arrest statistics, 1990–1999*. Pittsburgh: Author.

Omni Institute. (1992). *Working together: A profile of collaboration*. Denver: Author.

Reimer, S., & Cash, T. (2003). *Alternative schools: Best practices for development and evaluation*. Clemson, SC: National Dropout Prevention Center Network.

Robins, L. N., & Ratcliff, K. S. (1978). *Long-range outcomes associated with school truancy*. Washington, DC: U.S. Public Health Service.

Roderick, M, Chiong, J., Arney, M., DaCosta, K., Stone, M., Villarreal-Sosa, L., & Waxman, E. (1997). *Habits hard to break: A new look at truancy in Chicago's public high schools* [Research in Brief]. Chicago: University of Chicago, School of Social Service Administration.

Schargel, F. P., & Smink, J. (2001). *Strategies to help solve our school dropout problem*. Larchmont, NY: Eye on Education.

Schorr, L. B. (1997). *Common purpose: Strengthening families and neighborhoods to rebuild America*. New York: Doubleday.

Seoane, M., & Smink, J. (1991, June). *Incentives and education: A series of solutions and strategies*. Clemson, SC: National Dropout Prevention Center.

Sigmon, J. N., Neguen, M. E., & Engelhardt-Greer, S. (1999). *Abolish Chronic Truancy now diversion program: Evaluation report*. Alexandria, VA: American Prosecutors Research Institute.

Snyder, H. N., & Sickmund, M. (1995). *Juvenile offenders and victims: A national report*. Washington, DC: U.S. Department of Justice, Office of Justice Programs, Office of Juvenile Justice and Delinquency Prevention.

Stegelin, D. A. (2003). *Literacy education: First steps toward dropout prevention*. Clemson, SC: National Dropout Prevention Center Network.

Thorstensen, B. I. (2004). *If you build it, they will come: Investing in public education*. Retrieved January 13, 2004, from http://abec.unm.edu/resources/gallery/present/invest_in_ed.pdf

Policy statement approved by the NASW Delegate Assembly, August 2005. This policy supersedes the policy statement on School Dropout Prevention approved by the Delegate Assembly in 1996 and in 1987, and referred by the 2002 Delegate Assembly to the 2005 Delegate Assembly. For further information, contact the National Association of Social Workers, 750 First Street, NE, Suite 700, Washington, DC 20002-4241. Telephone: 202-408-8600 or 800-638-8799; e-mail: press@naswdc.org

School Violence

BACKGROUND

Millions of students in the United States, and worldwide, face violence at school on a daily basis. The National Crime Victimization Survey (U.S. Department of Justice, Bureau of Justice Statistics, 2007) showed that students ages 12 to 18 were victims of 1.5 million nonfatal crimes (theft and violent crime) while they were at school. School violence not only places students in direct harm, but also causes a decrease in students' sense of safety and well-being and disrupts the learning environment. School violence occurs through all age groups and extends into colleges and universities.

Violence in schools appears in many forms ranging from non-physical to physical aggression. Some examples of non-physical aggression are name calling, threats, spreading rumors, and harassment. Examples of physical aggression are pushing, tripping, spitting, hitting, stealing, and property destruction. More extreme cases of physical violence—such as sexual assault, rape, homicide, and suicide—are also present in schools. Bullying and cyberbullying also occur and are recognized as a form of violence within schools. Gang activity is also present in many school systems.

In 2007, students reported being more afraid of encountering dangers at school than on the way to school. Rates of violent crime victimization at school (26 violent crimes per 1,000 students) were higher than those away from school (20 violent crimes per 1,000 students) (Dinkes, Kemp, & Baum, 2009). However, all forms of violence, including bullying and intimate partner violence, can occur outside of school hours and still have a profound effect on students' sense of safety and well-being, and disrupt the learning environment at school. School systems have struggled with how to manage these occurrences that happen outside of school hours and off of school property because jurisdiction is unclear.

School violence is strongly influenced by the community in which the school is located and by the size of the school. Teachers at urban schools were twice as likely to report serious violent crimes as those in suburban towns and in rural locations, and the larger the school, the more likely that incidents of violent crimes have occurred. School violence also extends to college and university campuses, where dating violence remains the most frequent type of violence experienced.

Many groups of students are targeted as victims of school violence, but this problem affects all students, their families, the school environment, and the community as a whole. School violence can affect anyone, but some populations may be at greater risk. According to the Centers for Disease Control and Prevention (CDC) (2011), as a group, lesbian, gay, bisexual, and transgender (LGBT) youths are at increased risk for school violence compared with their non-LGBT peers.

ISSUE STATEMENT

Research scientists have identified a number of variables that put youths at risk of violent behaviors as well as variables that will protect them (Office of the Surgeon General, 2001). A *risk factor* is generally seen as any factor that increases the probability that a person will suffer from harm, and a *protective factor* is something that decreases the potential harmful effect of a risk factor. To effectively develop intervention programs, schools and communities need to consider both variables.

Former Surgeon General Dr. David Satcher's *Report on Youth Violence* (Office of the Surgeon General, 2001) noted that the most effective violence prevention programs combine both individual risk factors and environmental conditions, particularly building individual skills and competencies, providing parent effectiveness training, improving the climate of the schools, and making changes in the type and level of involvement in peer groups. Dr. Satcher's report further suggested that violence prevention initiatives that target change in the social context appear to be more effective than those that attempt to change individual attitudes, skills, and risk behaviors.

The same report supports what social workers have long maintained—that violence prevention starts in the family and the community. To combat the problem, one must provide services to families and communities before and during crises. One such effective, proven prevention program is the Families and Schools Together Program (FAST), developed by social worker Dr. Lynn McDonald. Others are being developed but are too new to have the history needed to prove successful (Dwyer, Osher, & Warger, 1998).

Children who witness violence and abuse, even if they have not personally been the victim of the abuse, can suffer psychological trauma, including posttraumatic stress disorder. These children also can display an array of emotional and behavioral disturbances including, but not limited, to low self-esteem; withdrawal; nightmares; self-blame; and aggression against peers, family members, and property (Peled, Jaffee, & Edelson, 1995).

Several research studies have shown that chronic exposure to violence can adversely affect a child's ability to learn (Barton, Coley, & Wenglinsky, 1998). Children who achieve in school and who develop adequate critical thinking, problem-solving, and communication skills are better able to cope with stressful situations. Academic achievement enhances the development of positive self-esteem and self-efficacy, both of which are necessary for experiencing emotional well-being and achieving success in life (Prothrow-Stith & Quaday, 1995). School social workers and social workers who work with school systems and in communities can play a crucial role in providing counseling and other support services to the victims of violence so that healthy coping

strategies and healthy self-esteem can be developed. This will enable schools to be places where positive growth, learning, and a sense of belonging is fostered.

Given that depression, feelings of isolation, and worthlessness were issues for many assailants of recent school shootings, providing more school social work services along with other support services in school is one way to prevent further tragedies (Office of Juvenile Justice and Delinquency Prevention and the Communities in Schools, 1999). School social workers are uniquely trained to identify students and families at risk, to provide diagnostic assessments, to understand both risk and protective factors for individuals and families, to intervene appropriately with students and families, and to arrange for referrals to appropriate community resources.

POLICY STATEMENT

NASW supports:

■ the position that school violence reflects the social, economic, moral, and ethical challenges of the larger society.

■ all students having the right to attend a physically and emotionally safe school where they can maximize their academic potential.

■ school environments in which all students and staff are respected, nurtured, safe, and supported.

■ each school developing comprehensive violence prevention plans in accordance to the school population's unique needs and including the participation of students, parents, school staff, and community resources.

■ comprehensive approaches to school violence prevention outlining three levels for intervention: (1) schoolwide foundation and primary prevention, (2) early intervention, and (3) urgent response and crisis intervention.

■ intervention plans developed and implemented to meet the needs of the individuals involved rather than uniform interventions.

■ each school developing and regularly reviewing crisis intervention and safety plans in collaboration with community resources and invested parties.

- teachers and school staff receiving ongoing training and evaluation regarding cultural awareness and competency.

- clear guidelines and expectations for student behavior that are consistently taught and enforced by all school personnel.

- recognition of students who make positive choices and positive contributions to the school climate and culture through regularly implemented formal and informal recognition procedures.

- models of intervention that are developmentally appropriate and therapeutic in nature rather than punitive.

- training of all school staff regarding warning signs and risk factors for violent behavior, including clear procedures for assessing students at risk for emotional difficulties including violent behavior.

- a confidential and reliable referral process to ensure students who exhibit warning signs can receive adequate treatment.

- schools using school social workers and other qualified mental health professionals to assess students at risk; to provide a clinical assessment; to provide individual, group, and family counseling; and to identify community resources for those in need.

- providing more intensive services to children experiencing significant emotional or behavioral problems that interfere with the learning process or endanger the health and welfare of others.

REFERENCES

Barton, P. E., Coley, R., & Wenglinsky, H. (1998). *Order in the classroom: Violence, discipline, and student achievement* [Online]. Retrieved from http://www.ets.org/Media/Research/pdf/PICORDER.pdf

Centers for Disease Control and Prevention. (2011). *Lesbian, gay, bisexual and transgender health.* Retrieved from http://www.cdc.gov/lgbthealth/youth.htm

Dinkes, R. Kemp, J., & Baum, K. (2009). *Indicators of school crime and safety: 2009* (NCES 2010-012/NCJ 228478). Washington, DC: National Center for Education Statistics, Institute of Education Sciences, U.S. Department of Education and Bureau of Justice Statistics, Office of Justice Programs, U.S. Department of Justice.

Dwyer, K., Osher, D., & Warger, C. (1998). *Annual report on school safety.* Retrieved from http://www.ed.gov/pubs/AnnSchoolRept98

Office of Juvenile Justice and Delinquency Prevention and the Communities in Schools. (1999, Fall). *Facts you can use: Recognizing and preventing school violence* (Vol. 3, No. 3). Washington, DC: U.S. Government Printing Office.

Office of the Surgeon General. (2001). *Youth violence: A report of the surgeon general* [Online]. Retrieved from http://www.surgeongeneral.gov/library/youthviolence

Peled, E., Jaffee, P. G., & Edelson, J. L. (Eds.). (1995). *Ending the cycle of violence: Community responses to children of battered women.* Thousand Oaks, CA: Sage Publications.

Prothrow-Stith, D., & Quaday, S. (1995). *Hidden casualties: The relationship between violence and learning.* Washington, DC: National Health and Education Consortium for African American Children. (ERIC Document Reproduction Service No. ED390552)

U.S. Department of Justice, Bureau of Justice Statistics. (2007). *National Crime Victimization Survey.* Washington, DC: Author.

NASW Members with Primary Responsibility for Revision of This Policy

First Draft Revision:

Linda Openshaw (TX)
Dana Harader (TX)

Policy Panelists:

Kalina Black (MA)
Sheridan Quarless Kingsberry (DE)
Allison Ledet (AR)
Lydia Montes de Oca (NM)
Emily Bleyl (UT)

Policy statement approved by the NASW Delegate Assembly, August 2011. This statement supersedes the policy statement approved by the Delegate Assembly in August 2002. For further information, contact the National Association of Social Workers, 750 First Street, NE, Suite 700, Washington, DC 20002-4241. Telephone: 202-408-8600; e-mail: press@naswdc.org

Slavery and Human Trafficking

BACKGROUND

Today, between 12.3 million (International Labor Organization, 2005) and 27 million people (Free the Slaves, 2007) are held against their will in violent conditions and forced to work without pay. The U.S. government believes that the majority are women and children (U.S. Department of State, 2007). The phenomenon has grown dramatically over the past several decades, fueled primarily by the large increase in worldwide population and poverty, the economic devastation that globalization has brought to many global communities, and widespread government corruption that turns a blind eye to and even profits directly from slavery (Bales, 1999).

Modern slavery and trafficking represent the commodification of human beings—objects or "goods" to be bought, sold, used, shipped, and traded for money in response to the growing demands for sexual and labor exploitation of children and adults. Slavery exists in every country in the world—including the United States (U.S. Department of State, 2004).

Human trafficking is a component of modern slavery. Although not all slaves are transported from one location to another, criminals take advantage of the ease of modern transport and the growth in global communications and technology to use abduction, violence, threats against family, or the false promise of gainful work to move annually about 800,000 people illegally across borders worldwide. It is estimated that between 14,500 and 17,500 of these victims are trafficked into the United States (U.S. Department of State, 2007).

The United States is both a source and a destination country for thousands of victims of slavery. The precise number of U.S. citizens and legal residents who are enslaved in the United States is unknown, but what is known is that the vast majority are trafficked into the country from East Asia, Eastern Europe, Mexico, and Central America for domestic work, migrant farm labor, or work in the sex industry (U.S. Department of State, 2007).

In terms of prevalence, the largest group works in agriculture. But slaves are used in many other kinds of labor: brick making, mining or quarrying, prostitution, gem working and jewelry making, cloth and carpet making, and domestic service (Bales, 1999). Modern-day slavery also encompasses individuals or families in indentured servitude, including debt bondage and victims captured and used by marauders or in armed conflicts.

The human costs (physical, emotional, and spiritual) to victims of slavery are among the most severe and lasting of any prolonged trauma. The economic costs are equally staggering. According to Interpol, human trafficking is a $44.5 billion business and now ranks among the three largest criminal enterprises, along with the sale of guns and drugs (Interpol, 2007). Without the demand for illegal commodities (including human beings) and associated profit such enterprises would not thrive.

Globalization and the promise of good jobs, economic opportunity, and personal freedom also serve to lure women and men to what they believe will bring them a better life. Determining whether a person has been trafficked or is an illegal migrant is often a complicated process that is based on the presence of three factors: the use or threat of force, fraud, or coercion. Although many people migrate freely and are able to maintain their freedom while being smuggled across borders and after arriving at their destination, trafficking victims may be abducted and are always deceived by false promises of a better existence. Only after trafficking victims arrive at their destination do they realize that the person who transported them will use whatever force or coercion necessary to keep them under his or her control. It is also common practice to sell trafficking victims to someone else who will use the same terror tactics to keep them enslaved.

People are recruited in several different ways, such as through fake employment agencies, acquaintances, newspaper ads, front businesses, word of mouth, or abduction (Freedom Network, 2003). Traffickers, for example, may be neighbors, friends, family members who sell their own children (Harrison, 2007), agricultural operators, owners of small businesses, diplomats, and other people of privilege (Lewis, 2007). Increasingly, however, traffickers are organized crime syndicates, often operating in collaboration with corrupt law enforcement entities, government officials or employers, who may use several intermediaries from the first point of contact to the final destination of the victim. Slaveholders and traffickers are willing to do whatever it takes to maintain their total domination over their victims, isolating them from the public, including family members or support networks. They often confiscate their passports or identification documents and use the threat of violence against family, induce shame, prey on their fear of imprisonment or deportation, and control their money.

Human trafficking has grown in part as a result of the advances in Internet and communication technology, which make information fast, anonymous, and easily accessible to predators and traffickers worldwide. According to Naim (2005) the modern-day slave auction is electronic, wherein local pimps can examine and purchase via e-mail women and girls from wholesalers in other countries and where retail customers can order up the prostitute of their choice. In fact, sex tourism is one of the world's largest industries and has become integrated into the economy of many countries.

Given the many forms that trafficking and modern-day slavery take both worldwide and in the United States, the solutions to this phenomenon need be multipronged, including an educated profession and public, legislative protections for individuals at risk, and, to decrease one's vulnerability to slavery, opportunities for education, sustainable livelihoods, and politically and psychologically empowered local communities.

ISSUE STATEMENT

If social workers are to assume a leadership role in ensuring and promoting human rights, they need to be knowledgeable about human trafficking and modern-day slavery and apply their tools and skills broadly and creatively, taking into account issues of culture, power, privilege, and oppression. This effort includes collaborating across professions; intervening in local, state, and national policy arenas as advocates and thought leaders; recognizing, assisting, and supporting victims and survivors; and galvanizing others to do so as well.

The NASW *Code of Ethics* (NASW, 2000) and existing policy statements provide ample justification for the association to take a position in strong opposition to modern slavery and human trafficking and to propose a series of solutions to eradicate both. The core values enumerated in the code's Preamble emphasize the profession's commitments to social justice and the dignity and worth of each person. It encourages social workers to pursue social change, particularly with and on behalf of vulnerable and oppressed individuals and groups, and specifically targets poverty, unemployment, and discrimination— all of which increase an individual's vulnerability to slavery and trafficking—as worthy targets for intervention.

In the same spirit, standard 6.01 of the code challenges NASW members to exercise their ethical responsibilities to promote the general welfare of society, locally and globally, and to advocate for living conditions conducive to the fulfillment of basic human needs. Standard 6.04(d) is particularly applicable to the eradication of slavery and human trafficking, calling on social workers to "act to prevent and eliminate domination of, exploitation of, and discrimination against any person, group, or class on the basis of race, ethnicity, national origin, color, sex, sexual orientation, age, marital status, political belief, religion, or mental or physical disability" (NASW, 2000, p. 27).

Standard 6.04(a) calls on NASW members to "engage in social and political action that seeks to ensure that all people have equal access to the resources, employment, services, and opportunities they require . . . to develop fully" (NASW, 2000, p. 27), and exhorts social workers to "advocate for changes in policy and legislation to improve social conditions in order to meet basic human needs and promote social justice" (NASW, 2000, p. 27).

Combating slavery and human trafficking is also a logical application of NASW's International Policy on Human Rights, which promotes U.S. ratification of the Universal Declaration of Human Rights (UDHR). The policy exhorts social workers to be especially vigilant about human rights violations related to children's rights and exploitation such as child labor and child prostitution (NASW, 2006). Twenty-four of the UDHR's 30 articles are applicable to eradicating slavery. Article 4 states the following: "No one shall be held in slavery or servitude; slavery and the slave trade shall be prohibited in all their forms," (United Nations, 1948) and article 5 declares that "No one shall be subjected to torture or to cruel, inhuman or degrading treatment or punishment" (United Nations, 1948). In addition, the existence today of human trafficking and slavery runs directly counter to NASW's strong support for human rights as the foundational principle for social work theory and practice (Asamoah, Healy, & Mayadas, 1997; Wetzel, 1993, 1998).

POLICY STATEMENT

NASW supports public awareness and advocacy for legislative and administrative change to end human trafficking and slavery in the United States and around the world, and supports public education efforts that ensure that this perspective has a strong presence in the media and legislatures.

Public Awareness and Advocacy

■ NASW supports public education campaigns that teach communities to recognize the warning signs of all aspects of human trafficking and slavery and to report suspicious behavior to the appropriate social services or law enforcement agency.

■ NASW supports efforts to identify successful initiatives and best practices for freeing slaves, and to help freed individuals to engage in rehabilitation, community reintegration, and the development of sustainable livelihoods.

■ NASW supports the enforcement and strengthening of the Trafficking Victims Protection Reauthorization Act of 2003.

Services to Victims and Survivors

■ NASW promotes social workers taking leadership in compiling and further developing and applying sound clinical practices and in formulating appropriate public policy for helping people emerging from slavery.

■ NASW encourages social workers to help government and community-based organizations to address short-term needs of survivors, including developing mechanisms to protect victims who come forward, and families vulnerable to retaliation and threats by traffickers in their home country or community.

Professional Development and Continuing Education

■ NASW supports the development and implementation of culturally competent social work curriculums that prepare students to meet the psychosocial and empowerment needs of survivors of slavery.

- NASW supports cross-sector training and collaboration among social workers, law enforcement, and community workers and other gatekeepers to freedom in the identification of potential victims and consumers of slavery, helping survivors to safety, protecting them from further harm, and successfully prosecuting slaveholders.

Legal and Political Action/Mobilizing Civil Society/Public Policy

- NASW encourages local, state and national governments to construct, implement, and enforce effective and well-resourced plans to prevent and end slavery within their borders.

- NASW encourages the U.S. government to use diplomacy, trade policy, and foreign aid as leverage in fighting slavery internationally.

- NASW supports the development and implementation of legislation and policies that enforce the prosecution of consumers.

- NASW condemns practices that enable investment in and production of goods and services that use slave labor, in recognition of the rights of people who are enslaved.

- NASW supports greater legal protections and monitoring of workers in sectors particularly vulnerable to slavery.

- NASW advocates for the elimination of incentives in immigration policy for unscrupulous employers to use forced labor.

REFERENCES

Asamoah, Y., Healy, L., & Mayadas, N. (1997). Ending the international–domestic dichotomy: New approaches to a global curriculum for the millennium. *Journal of Social Work Education, 33,* 389–401.

Bales, K. (1999). *Disposable people: New slavery in the global economy.* Berkeley: University of California Press.

Freedom Network. (2003). *Institute on Human Trafficking and Slavery: Tools for an effective response participant tool kit.* Retrieved November 26, 2007, from http://www.castla.org

Free the Slaves. (2007). *Ending slavery.* Retrieved November 26, 2007, from http://www.freetheslaves.net/NETCOMMUNITY/Page.aspx?pid=183&srcid=-2)face

Harrison, D. (2007). *Children for sale: UK's new slave trade.* Retrieved April 24, 2008, from http://www.telegraph.co.uk/news/main.jhtml?xml=/news/2008/01/27/nslave127.xml

International Labor Organization. (2005). *A global alliance against forced labour—Executive summary.* Retrieved November 24, 2007, from http://www.ilo.ru/news/200505/FLGR_ExSum.pdf

Interpol. (2007). *Trafficking in human beings.* Retrieved November 25, 2007, from http://www.Interpol.int/Public/THB/Default.asp

Lewis, L. (2007). *Diplomatic abuse of servants hard to prosecute.* Retrieved April 24, 2008, from http://www.npr.org/templates/story/story.php?storyId=7672967

Naim, M. (2005). *Illicit: How smugglers, traffickers and copycats are hijacking the global economy.* New York: Doubleday.

National Association of Social Workers. (2000). *Code of ethics of the National Association of Social Workers.* Washington, DC: NASW Press.

National Association of Social Workers. (2006). *International policy on human rights* [Abstract]. Retrieved November 26, 2007, from http://www.socialworkers.org/resources/abstracts/abstracts/international.asp

United Nations. (1948). *Universal declaration of human rights.* New York: Author.

U.S. Department of State. (2004). *Victims of Trafficking and Violence Protection Act of 2000: Trafficking in persons report.* Retrieved March 21, 2008, from http://www.state.gov/g/tip/rls/tiprpt/2004/

U.S. Department of State. (2007). *Trafficking in persons report.* Retrieved May 30, 2008, from http://www.state.gov/g/tip/rls/tiprpt/2007/

Wetzel, J. W. (1993). *The world of women: In pursuit of human rights*. London: Macmillan.

Wetzel, J. W. (1998). *Human rights values: An international challenge to social work*. Paper presented at the 15th Annual Social Work Day at the United Nations, New York, March 25; at the International Association of Schools of Social Work symposium, Council of Social Work Education Annual Program Meeting, Orlando, FL, March 8; at the University of Texas "Celebrate International Social Work," Austin, March 27.

Policy statement approved by the NASW Delegate Assembly, August 2008. For further information, contact the National Association of Social Workers, 750 First Street, NE, Suite 700, Washington, DC 20002-4241. Telephone: 202-408-8600 or 800-638-8799; e-mail: press@naswdc.org

Social Services

BACKGROUND

Social services is defined in the *Social Work Dictionary* (Barker, 2003) as the activities of social workers and others

> in promoting the health and well-being of people and in helping people to become more self-sufficient; preventing dependency; strengthening family relationships; and restoring individuals, families, groups, or communities to successful *social functioning*. Specific kinds of social services include helping people [to] obtain adequate financial resources for their needs, evaluating the capabilities of people to care for children or other dependents, counseling and psychotherapy, ... advocating for social causes, informing organizations of their obligations to individuals, facilitating health care provisions, and linking clients to resources. (p. 407)

Social services have been in existence for over 100 years in the United States. During the late 19th century and early 20th century, the Charity Organization Society, for example, assisted new immigrants with issues of poverty and employment. The settlement house movement, provided programs and services to assist individuals with citizenship issues, character building, leadership development, and problem solving (Brueggemann, 2006).

The New Deal era instituted many new social service programs. With the focus of providing relief and other forms of aid to people in need, the Works Progress Administration, the Civilian Conservation Corps, and the Civil Works Administration were among the most prominent of these new programs (Chapin, 2007). The Social Security Act of 1935, perhaps the best-known social service program in modern history, provided support for old-age benefits, financial assistance for older people and those who were blind, dependent children and children who were disabled, maternal and child welfare, public health, and unemployment compensation. The Old Age, Survivors, and Disability Insurance (OASDI) program, assisted surviving family members after a worker's death, and Aid to Families with Dependent Children (AFDC), provided cash assistance for children in need. The Social Security Act and the OASDI were foundational safety net programs (Chapin, 2007). In addition, following World War II, new social services emphasized support for returning veterans. The Servicemen's Readjustment Act, for example, provided loans to veterans for purchasing homes, starting businesses, or attending college (Chapin, 2007).

Challenges to racial segregation and other forms of discrimination in the 1960s and 1970s prompted several social policy initiatives. The passage of the Civil Rights Act of 1964 and the Voting Rights Act of 1965 was particularly effective in bringing awareness to the importance of equality and its relationship to the well-being of individuals, families, and communities. In addition, the Lyndon Johnson administration's War on Poverty led to the Economic Opportunity Act of 1964, establishing a number of programs to provide economic opportunities and empower those living in poverty. Medicare and Medicaid were later added to the Social Security Act to provide health assistance to older adults and poor people (Chapin, 2007).

During the last two decades of the 20th century and most of the first decade of the 21st century, a more politically conservative approach resulted in "New Federalism," devolution, and privatization of social services. As a result, there was a shift of responsibility from the federal government to the states, for the welfare of their citizens (Chapin, 2007). Overall support for low-income people was reduced. An example of this is the Personal Responsibility and Work

Opportunity Reconciliation Act of 1996, replacing AFDC with Temporary Assistance for Needy Families. Despite a conservative political environment, some progress was made, especially in social services to people with disabilities and their caregivers. These are examples of a system of laws that has evolved to ensure equal opportunity and access to and availability of services, as well as mandates for the operation of certain services.

Since the founding of the profession, social workers have been involved with and have enhanced social services. Settlement houses and charity organizations provided social workers with an opportunity to work with individuals and groups and to actively improve the delivery of social services within communities. The enhancement of social services paved the way for organizations to provide social services both equitably and effectively. Evidence-based practice has been a long-endorsed theory within the social work profession, and today that engagement is evident by the utilization of client-based outcomes as a means for appropriate treatment (Krysik & Finn, 2010; O'Hare, 2005).

A prominent and important contribution of the social work profession is the strengths-based perspective. Through this approach, social service planning incorporates existing strengths in organizations, communities, and individuals to enrich the environment and create new opportunities. As such, collaboration with consumer groups, organizations, and associations is emphasized. The focus is on current strengths, capacity building, enhancement of current programs, and prevention (Long, Tice, & Morrison, 2006).

ISSUE STATEMENT

A comprehensive social services system is needed to enhance the health, self-sufficiency, social functioning, and well-being of individuals, families, and communities. Yet there is no national social policy addressing the need, significance, and role of social services in the United States. In addition, there is a lack of acknowledgment of the role of social workers in the provision of social services. Social poli-

cies are continually influenced and bound by social, economic, and political forces on national, state, and local levels. As such, the approach to social services tends to be residual as opposed to institutional. The unique knowledge, skills, and abilities of professional social workers are inadequately recognized and used.

Although some social services are universal and proactive, many others are more residual and reactive. In addition, major events and political power can strongly influence the extent to which social services are supported and enhanced. The extent to which social services are institutionalized, and provided through government, also varies by era, administration, or both.

Too often, services are established and provided in a fragmented manner, resulting in individuals and families becoming compartmentalized by one specific challenge. Because resources are allocated by categories, decisions are made as to who is eligible for services, under what circumstances services are to be offered, and how long services will last, without adequate consideration of the social work values of self-determination and the strengths perspective.

Universal access to and diversity-inclusive services have been a long-standing concern for social workers. Social workers actively work to address these issues yet often find that both policy and funding pose significant barriers to eliminating unequal access and ensuring culturally competent and inclusive services (O'Hare, 2005).

POLICY STATEMENT

NASW advocates the following principles:

Access to Services

Services should be accessible, attainable, and offered in a way that encourages voluntary use. No criteria—including gender, marital status, sexual orientation, disability, religion, political views, race, and ethnic and national origin—shall be used to limit access. Eligibility for social services occurs when a reasonable request is made to a practitioner or social services agency that possesses the required skills to meet the request, subject to the willingness of the recipient to make a reasonable investment in the service. When services are imposed by courts, considered mandatory, or based on needs that may result in significant life changes for an individual or family, such services shall be available in a timely manner and according to best practice standards. Appropriate private administrative review and reasonable subsidy shall be available.

Comprehensive Services

The social services system must develop an organized, broad spectrum of public and private services to meet the short- and long-term service requests and needs of individuals, groups, and families. Consumers should be given alternatives, freedom to move from one service to another, and specific competence to fulfill defined needs in service systems that are supported by public funds. The social services system must include multiple types and levels of providers, as well as prominent roles for federal, state, and local governments, to meet various needs. The professional expertise of social workers, in collaboration with consumers, should be integrated into the decision-making process at all levels.

Informed Consent

Each consumer's decisions should be informed by self-determination regarding choice of services, protection of individuality, and ability to participate in policy matters, if not directly, then through selected or assigned advocates. Confidentiality is not absolute but dictates that sharing of information is done at all times in the best interests of those served.

Simplicity and Efficiency

Systems to establish accountability for social services should be designed to ensure simplicity of procedures and administration. Required documentation should be limited to what is essential. Technological advances should be appropriately used to enhance service delivery.

Establishment of Policies and Priorities

Establishment of policies and priorities for the social services system must include active participation of social work professionals. Policy design and standard setting must include consumers and the community at large, in addition to organizational representatives. Social workers should take the initiative in facilitating broad participation in priority setting and policy design.

Planning and Evaluation

The social services system should ensure maximum accountability. Funding sources, policy-making bodies, administrators, service personnel, and consumers should obtain regular and precise information about the operations, trends, problems, and results of the services delivered and recommend adjustments, wherever needed. Social services should incorporate evidence-based practices whenever possible.

Advocacy

Professional social workers value social justice, alleviating social ills and oppression at all levels of society. As such, they are uniquely qualified to provide advocacy at micro, mezzo, and macro levels of practice.

Financing of the social services system is the joint responsibility of all citizens and all levels of government. Public–private partnerships should be facilitated to enhance these services. Social workers are qualified to take the lead in educating funding communities, both public and private, about the nature and necessity of social services.

REFERENCES

Barker, R. L. (2003). *The social work dictionary* (5th ed.). Washington, DC: NASW Press.

Brueggemann, W. (2006). *The practice of macro social work* (3rd ed.). Belmont, CA: Thompson Brooks/Cole.

Chapin, R. (2007). *Social policy for effective practice: A strengths approach*. New York: McGraw-Hill.

Krysik, J., & Finn, J. (2010). *Research for effective social work practice* (2nd ed.). New York: Taylor & Francis.

Long, D., Tice, C., & Morrison, J. (2006). *Macro social work practice: A strengths pers-* *pective*. Belmont, CA: Thompson-Brooks/ Cole.

O'Hare, T. (2005). *Evidence-based practices for social workers: An interdisciplinary approach.* Chicago: Lyceum Books.

NASW Members with Primary Responsibility for Revision of This Policy

First Draft Revision:

Mark Cederburg (KS)

Policy Panelists:

Zuline Gray Wilkinson (MA)
Laura Eastman-Follis (NYS)
Bettye Bradshaw (FL)
Mary Garrison (IL)
Dawn Lakamsani (TX)
Brian Kaufman (CA)

Policy statement approved by the NASW Delegate Assembly, August 2011. This statement supersedes the policy statement on Social Services approved by the Delegate Assembly in 2002 and 1975 and reconfirmed by the Delegate Assembly in 1993. For further information, contact the National Association of Social Workers, 750 First Street, NE, Suite 700, Washington, DC 20002-4241. Telephone: 202-408-8600; e-mail: press@naswdc.org

Social Work in the Criminal Justice System

BACKGROUND

In 2006, there were 2,245,189 individuals incarcerated in local, state, and federal correctional facilities in the United States (Sabol, Minton, & Harrison, 2007). The United States has the highest incarceration rate in the world, and the rate increased 700 percent between 1970 and 2005 (Public Safety Performance Project, 2007). In addition, up to 60 percent of incarcerated individuals who are released will be reincarcerated within two years (Langan & Levin, 2002). Professionals anticipate that incarceration rates in this country will continue to increase, and this projected increase creates concerns about the social and economic effects of incarceration. Social workers have a unique set of professional skills to assist in addressing both the policy and practice issues surrounding incarceration in the United States.

Statistics clearly indicate that a disproportionate number of individuals of a racial or ethnic minority are incarcerated. Disproportionate arrest rates, racial profiling, discrimination, and denial of vital resources continue to exacerbate this problem. In 2005, 3,145 out of every 100,000 black men, 1,244 out of every 100,000 Hispanic men, and 471 out of every 100,000 white men in the population were incarcerated (Sabol et al., 2007). Although women have lower incarceration rates than do men, women who are racial or ethnic minorities are more likely to be incarcerated. In 2004, black women had incarceration rates two and one-half times higher than did Hispanic women and nearly four times higher than white women. These differences were consistent across all age groups. Among people convicted of drug felonies, white people were less likely than were black people to be incarcerated (33 percent versus 51 percent) (Durose & Lanagan, 2001). In addition to traditionally defined "women" and "men," there is a growing body of evidence documenting the disproportionate effect that criminal justice policies and laws have on transgender communities in the United States. Although studies have been scarce, advocates for the transgendered conservatively estimate that one in three transgender people have been imprisoned, with advocates pointing to systemic discrimination leading to pervasive poverty as the main cause for such high rates of imprisonment (TGI Justice Project [TGIJP], 2007; Sylvia Riveria Law Project, 2007).

Homeland Security and Immigration

An emphasis on homeland security and immigration regulations has affected incarceration rates and trends. Between 1995 and 2003 the number of incarcerated individuals in federal institutions for public offenses increased by 170 percent, and this increase primarily was due to an increase in the number of individuals incarcerated for immigration-related offenses. In 1995, 3,420 individuals were incarcerated because of an immigration-related offense compared with 16,903 individuals in 2003 (Beck & Harrison, 2005).

Substance Use

The number of incarcerated individuals in state correctional facilities for drug-related offenses was 19,000 in 1980 compared with 250,900 in 2003 (Sabol et al., 2007). Mandatory sentencing laws have increased incarceration rates, leading to a correctional system clogged with incarcerated individuals who have a substance dependence disorder. Involvement in a criminal episode frequently occurs following the use of drugs and alcohol (McNeece & Roberts, 1996). The U.S. Department of Justice (Mumola & Karberg, 2006) reported that 32 percent of state prisoners and 26 percent of federal prisoners reported using substances at the time of their offense, with 53 percent of state prisoners and 45 percent of federal prisoners reporting a history of substance abuse and dependence.

Mental Health

Correctional facilities have become the treatment facility of last resort for individuals who have been failed by other systems. The dismantling of the psychiatric hospital system and the fragmentation of community mental health systems has shifted the care of those with chronic mental health issues to the correctional system. Substantial numbers of offenders have mental health disorders that have not been diagnosed or treated. Many of these individuals have comorbid substance abuse issues. Weedon (2005) reported there are five times more persons with mental illnesses in jails than in state psychiatric hospitals. Conservative estimates propose that 10 percent of offenders have a mental illness (Norton, 2005), with rates of mental health problems in incarcerated individuals reported as high as 64 percent (James & Glaze, 2006).

Health Care Needs

Increasing numbers of incarcerated individuals have special health needs, including those who have been exposed to hepatitis, tuberculosis, HIV, and other infectious diseases. The special health care needs of female incarcerated individuals, including care for those who are pregnant, must be considered. The health care needs of aging incarcerated individuals are increasingly important as this population continues to grow in the correctional system. The special needs of those incarcerated individuals with impairments in mobility, vision, hearing, or speech must be considered in correctional facilities, including the health needs of incar-

cerated transgender people (Rosenblum, 2000; Thaler, 2007; Women in Prison Project, 2007).

Family Impact

Incarcerated individuals describe their inability to be involved in the daily lives of their children and other loved ones as a source of great psychological stress (Lanier, 1993). Approximately 70 percent of female incarcerated individuals lived with their minor children before incarceration. In about one-third of such cases, child protective services and other agencies were involved in out-of-home placement of the children (Versay, 1998). In almost all cases, lesbian, gay, bisexual, and transgender prisoners are not allowed conjugal visits from same-sex partners. Studies show that incarcerated individuals who maintain strong family and friendship ties during incarceration and who assume responsible marital and parental roles upon their release have lower recidivism rates (Hairston, 1988).

Privatization

A private correctional facility houses incarcerated individuals for a profit. The operation of private correctional facilities is a point of controversy. The U.S. Bureau of Justice reported that approximately 7 percent of state and federal incarcerated individuals were held in private correctional facilities (Blakely & Bumphus, 2004). Advocates of privatization posit that private facilities operate more efficiently, thereby reducing costs to the public. Opponents argue that the government must retain responsibility for the direct provision of programs for the incarceration and rehabilitation of offenders to safeguard the interests of society and the rights of individuals. Development of standards and continued research are necessary to ensure that the interests of society are protected and that responsible care and rehabilitation occur.

Incarcerated Women

Sabol et al. (2007) reported that there were 111,403 female individuals incarcerated in state and federal correctional facilities and that the population had increased at approximately twice the rate of male incarcerated individuals during the study period. Because correctional facilities tend to be designed for men, the differences in the sexes are ignored, causing increased stress for female incarcerated individuals (Versay, 1998). Transgender women are usually housed in men's facilities and are at risk of sexual propositions, harassment, assault, and infection with HIV.

Female incarcerated individuals frequently have experienced past trauma and abuse. In one study, 48 percent of female incarcerated individuals met diagnostic criteria for posttraumatic stress disorder. Zlotnik (1997) reported that 87 percent of the women experienced at least one assault in their lifetime, with 55 percent experiencing childhood physical abuse, 53 percent experiencing rape in adulthood, and 63 percent experiencing physical assault in adulthood. According to advocates for the transgender community in San Francisco, at least 75 percent of transgender women facing criminal charges in county jail also reported surviving physical or sexual abuse, frequently as children (TGJIP, 2007). Furthermore, transgender women prisoners in California are 13 times more likely to be sexually assaulted than are those in the non-transgender prison population (Jenness et al., 2007).

Juvenile Justice

A dramatic rise in juvenile violence, particularly homicides, which began in the mid to late 1980s and peaked in the early 1990s, generated concern among the public and led to policy changes by federal, state, and local governments. Most states stiffened their laws relating to juvenile justice, including measures that allow, or in many cases mandate, youngsters to be transferred to the adult system at younger ages and for a greater variety of offenses. Sabol and colleagues (2007) reported that there were 2,364 juveniles in state prisons in June 2006. Juveniles are also housed in adult federal correctional facilities. The practice of incarcerating juveniles with adult offenders is especially problematic. Vulnerability to exploitation and abuse is high for these youth. Exposure to offenders with extensive criminal backgrounds may foster a pattern of incarceration rather than successful reentry for this population.

ISSUE STATEMENT

The current incarcerated population has surpassed 2 million individuals. This population is expected to increase by 192,000 by the end of 2011 (Public Safety Performance Project, 2007). The incarcerated population suffers from myriad social, economic, health, mental health, and addiction issues. The provision of services to this population has created an ever expanding need for social work services.

As Showalter and Hunsinger (2007) stated, "in essence our prisons are full of people extremely short on resources and long on problems" (p. 366). Social workers trained in the corrections field are uniquely qualified to provide services addressing all the problem areas. Yet little has been written about delivery of services in this field, and schools of social work rarely address correctional social work and criminal justice. Incarceration needs to be closely analyzed by the profession as the "increasing incidence of severe and terminal physical illness, mental disorder, developmental delays and severe substance abuse problems among these individuals make this need even more pressing" (Ivanhoff, Smyth, & Dulmus, 2007, p. 349). The functioning of the incarcerated person's family is affected as well, resulting in economic burdens, stigma, emotional distress, and an increased risk of children to commit crimes (Rowe & Farrington, 1997), which also cause difficulties for incarcerated individuals, their families, and their communities. Social workers must become involved in corrections and rehabilitation as advocates and treatment providers for this vulnerable population.

Several specific areas are pertinent to the profession of social work. Our mission of promoting social functioning requires us to examine the following:

■ safe and humane environments that protect the public, provide cost-effective services, and are responsive to the needs of the community.

■ the role of social work within the criminal justice system.

- the role of social work in transition planning for successful reentry of incarcerated individuals into their communities.

- ongoing advocacy for the creation and enforcement of policies to protect the basic human rights, safety, and fair treatment of all incarcerated people is essential. Transgender people are at greater risk of physical and sexual abuse by incarcerated individuals, guards, and others in positions of authority. Human rights and safety for transgender people may include the continuation of ongoing hormone treatments first instituted prior to their incarceration.

- the role of social work in advocacy for policies that improve access to services and resources for formerly incarcerated individuals, with special attention to the needs of racial, sexual, and gender minorities, juveniles, elderly persons, and women.

- integrations of social work services within the framework of the criminal justice system.

- prevalence of substance abuse and mental health issues within the correctional system.

- the special issues of sexual offenders within the criminal justice system.

- trends toward incarceration and mandatory sentencing instead of the provision of community-based treatment, particularly their impact on people of color and other vulnerable populations.

- the biopsychosocial needs of all incarcerated individuals, with special attention to the needs of racial, sexual, and gender minorities, juveniles, elderly, and female offenders.

POLICY STATEMENT

NASW recognizes the importance of providing quality social work interventions to the incarcerated population. The provision of an adequate level of professional social work services could reduce the rates of recidivism, reentry, and incarceration for the betterment of the individual as well as society. Thus, NASW supports

- ongoing advocacy to address issues surrounding and leading to disproportionate rates of incarceration for individuals of racial or ethnic minorities, juveniles, women, and undocumented individuals;

- increased use of professional forensic social workers to provide culturally competent treatment and intervention for the growing population of incarcerated individuals, including mental health and substance abuse services;

- safe, humane, and equitable treatment for all incarcerated individuals, including cessation of sexual abuse, sexual harassment, and differential sentencing and treatment;

- access to quality health care, medications, nutrition, treatment, rehabilitation programs and support for incarcerated individuals including resisting all forms of discrimination based on diagnosis in delivery of medical care;

- appropriate educational and vocational opportunities to assist incarcerated individuals with transitioning back into their communities;

- access to affordable and adequate housing to assist incarcerated individuals with transitioning back into their communities;

- establishment of best practice standards for professional social work in criminal justice settings;

- specialized training on the unique application of social work skills and values in a correctional environment for social workers practicing in criminal justice settings;

- research to identify effective alternatives to incarceration, such as diversion programs.

- expansion of prevention, screening, and treatment efforts, including issues such as substance abuse and dependence, mental illness, sexually transmitted disease, blood and airborne pathogens, confidential testing, and domestic violence;

- increased funding for community-based options, especially for those individuals with substance dependence or serious mental illness who may be better rehabilitated by these services;

- identification of and response to the special needs of any individual under the supervision of the criminal justice system, including, but not limited to, racial, sexual, and gender minorities; juveniles; women (including pregnant women); the elderly; and those with impairments;

■ advocacy and social work leadership to establish national policy on criminal justice, issues in collaboration with other organizations.

REFERENCES

Bachrach, L. (1980). Overview: Model programs for chronic mental patients. *American Journal of Psychiatry, 137*, 1023–1031.

Blakely, C., & Bumphus, V. (2004). Private and public sector prisons: A comparison of select characteristics. *Federal Probation, 68*, 27–31.

Ditton, P. (1999). *Mental health treatment of incarcerated individuals and probationers.* Washington, DC: U.S. Department of Justice, Bureau of Justice Statistics.

Hairston, C. (1988). Family ties during imprisonment: Do they influence future criminal activity? *Federal Probation, 52*, 48–52.

Ivanhoff, A., Smyth, N., & Dulmus, C. (2007). Preparing social workers for practice in correctional institutions. In A. R. Roberts & D. W. Springer (Eds.), *Social work in juvenile and criminal justice settings* (pp. 341–350). Springfield, IL: Charles C Thomas.

James, D., & Glaze, L. (2006). *Mental health problems of prison and jail incarcerated individuals.* Washington, DC: U.S. Department of Justice, Bureau of Justice Statistics.

Jenness, V., Maxson, C. L., Matsuda, K. N., & Sumner, J. M. (2007). *Violence in California correctional facilities: An empirical examination of sexual assault. A report submitted to the California Department of Corrections & Rehabilitation, Center for Evidence-Based Corrections.* Irvine, CA: University of California.

Juvenile Justice and Delinquency Prevention Act of 1974, P.L. 93-415, 88 Stat. 1109.

Langan, P., & Levin, D. (2002). Recidivism of incarcerated individuals released in 1994. *Federal Sentencing Reporter, 15*(1), 58–65.

Lanier, C. (1993). Affective states of fathers in prison. *Justice Quarterly, 10*, 49–65.

McNeece, C. A., & Roberts, A. (1996). *Policy and practice in the justice system.* Chicago: Nelson-Hall.

Mumola, C. J., & Karberg, J. C. (2006). *Drug use and dependence, state and federal incarcerated individuals, 2004* (NCJ 213530). Washington, DC: U.S. Department of Justice, Bureau of Justice Statistics.

Norton, S. (2005, February). Successfully managing mentally ill offenders: Thoughts and recommendations. *Corrections Today, 67*, 28–33.

Public Safety Performance Project. (2007). *Public safety, public spending: Forecasting America's prison population 2007–2011.* Retrieved July 1, 2007, from www.pewpublicsafety.org

Rosenblum, D. (2000). 'Trapped' in Sing Sing: Transgendered prisoners caught in the gender binarism. *Michigan Journal of Gender & Law, 6*, 522–526.

Rowe, D., & Farrington, D. (1997). The familial transmission of criminal convictions. *Criminology, 35*, 177–183.

Sabol, W. J., Minton, T. D., & Harrison, P. M. (2007). *Prison and jail incarcerated individuals at midyear 2006* (NCJ 217675). Washington, DC: U.S. Department of Justice, Bureau of Justice Statistics.

Showalter, D., & Hunsinger, D. (2007). Social work within a maximum security setting. In A. R. Roberts & D. W. Springer (Eds.), *Social work in juvenile and criminal justice settings* (pp. 366–375). Springfield, IL: Charles C Thomas.

Sylvia Riveria Law Project. (2007). *It's war in here; A report on the treatment of transgender and intersex people in New York State men's prison.* Retrieved March 19, 2008, from http://www.srlp.org/index.php?sec=03N&page=warinhere

Texeira, M. (2007). Review of 'Women behind bars: Gender and race in U.S. prisons.' *Gender and Society, 21*, 304–307.

Thaler, C. (2007). *Putting transgender health care myths on trial.* Retrieved July 14, 2007, from http://www.lambdalegal.org/our-work/publications/page.jsp?itemID=32007335

TGI Justice Project. (2007). Overview of issues facing transgender, gender variant, & intersex prisoners. Retrieved March 19, 2008, from http://www.tgijp.org/giraldo/protest.html

Versay, B. (1998). Specific needs of women diagnosed with mental illness in U.S. jails. In B. L. Levin, A. K. Blanch, & A. Jennings (Eds.),

Women's mental health services (pp. 368–389). Thousand Oaks, CA: Sage Publications.

Weedon, J. (2005, February). The incarceration of the mentally ill. *Corrections Today, 67,* 16–20.

Women in Prison Project. (2007). *Transgender issues and the criminal justice system.* Retrieved April 24, 2007, from http://www.correctional association.org/WIPP/publications/Trans gender_Issues_2007.pdf

Zlotnick, C. (1997). Posttraumatic stress disorder (PTSD), PTSD comorbidity, and childhood abuse among incarcerated women. *Journal of Nervous and Mental Disorders, 185,* 761–763.

Policy statement approved by the NASW Delegate Assembly, August 2008. This policy statement supersedes the policy statement on Correctional Social Work approved by the Delegate Assembly in 1999 and referred by the 2005 Delegate Assembly to the 2008 Delegate Assembly for revision. For further information, contact the National Association of Social Workers, 750 First Street, NE, Suite 700, Washington, DC 20002-4241. Telephone: 202-408-8600 or 800-638-8799; e-mail: press@naswdc.org

Sovereignty, Rights, and Well-Being of Indigenous Peoples

BACKGROUND

This policy statement focuses on indigenous peoples within the United States, its territories, commonwealths, and Micronesian nation states affiliated through the Compact of Free Association (COFA). Included are the following: First Nations peoples living within the geographical boundaries of the continental United States; Alaska Natives, Kanaka Maoli (Native Hawaiians); CHamorus of Guahan (Guam) (Although both Chamorro and CHamoru can be used, CHamoru is the indigenous spelling of the reference to the CHamoru people and language.); indigenous peoples of the Federated States of Micronesia (FSM), Republic of Palau (ROP), and Republic of the Marshall Islands (RMI); Taino Indians (Puerto Rico); and Samoans (American Samoa). Common to these indigenous peoples are a history of U.S. colonization, dispossession of land and natural resources, and historical trauma (Brave Heart, 2005) that have limited their inherent right to self-determination and sovereignty (United Nations, 2007).

Native Americans (First Nations peoples)

Since the earliest contact with Europeans at the end of the 15th century, Native Americans were subjugated to the laws of colonization and denied tribal sovereignty that is the basis of tribal government (Wilkins, 2009). The number of Native Americans, estimated at about 10 million in 1500, gradually decreased as their food sources disappeared and they fell victim to diseases such as measles, smallpox, and influenza. By 1800 the Native American population was about 600,000, and by 1900 it had been reduced to less than 250,000. Native tribes differed substantially in regard to religious beliefs and practices, language, dress, hairstyles, political organization, social structures, gender roles, worldview, and living conditions in response to the environment, which varied from forests, deserts, mountains, plains, and coasts to subarctic and arctic areas (Hall, n.d.).

U.S. policies ranging from the Indian Removal Act in 1830, various treaties negotiated with individual tribes, the 1887 Dawes Act (or General Allotment Act), the Indian Reorganization Act of 1934 (P.L. 73-383), and the Termination Act of 1953 further stripped away much of the history, geography, political life, and traditions from indigenous people to produce an abstract perception (Konkle, 2008) of the immensely significant cultural, family, and spiritual life that defines Native Americans. Each policy was designed to achieve progressive acculturation and final assimilation of the Native American into the "white" culture. Influenced in part by the Pan-Indian movement of the 1960s and 1970s, the passage in 1978 of both the Indian Child Welfare Act (P.L. 95-608) and the American Indian Religious Freedom Act (P.L. 94-341), and later the Native American Graves Protection and Repatriation Act of 1990 (P.L. 101-601), were attempts to make some reparation for the mistreatment of Native Peoples over the previous 500 years. Today, the estimated 5.2 million Native Americans (Humes, Jones, & Ramirez, 2011) are still burdened with extensive unemployment; health and mental health disparities including diabetes, cancer, substance abuse, and suicide (Indian Health Service, 2007); and remain one of the poorest races as a direct result of the U.S. policy (and subsequent interventions) toward Native Americans (Rodgers, 2008).

Alaska Natives

Beginning in the 1750s, the pattern of exploitation of natural resources first occurred by the Russians, then in the 1850s by the Americans. In 1867, Alaska was purchased by the United States from Russia and the exploitation continued. By 1942, the Native population declined by 75 percent from an estimated 100,000 to 25,000 people from introduced diseases (Lally & Haynes, 1995). The Alaska Native Land Claims Settlement Act of 1971 established a capitalistic structure through which U.S. and international corporations established access to oil deposits in the northern region. The act provided the title of 14 million acres to state-chartered Native corporations, required Native people to set up village and regional corporations, and transferred land ownership to corporations and not individual Alaska Natives. Despite these significant improvements regarding legal and land rights, decisions on sovereignty and subsistence often pit Alaska Natives against state and federal authorities (Hunhdorf & Huhndorf, 2011).

Discrimination and racism still remain, despite gains made through the past four decades. Although 16 percent of Alaska's population identifies as solely Alaskan Native, 84 percent of the state's population are primarily U.S. citizens, often from the lower 48 states (Thompson, 2008). Similar to Native Americans in other U.S. states, four generations of Alaskan Native children were forced to attend mission and government-run boarding schools. The U.S. policy at that time was to remove their cultural identity and make these children a viable workforce for the populations coming into Alaska.

In 2008, 28 percent of Alaska Natives reported not completing high school as compared with less than one out of 12 (7.5 percent) white people in the United States. Unemployment rates are up to three times higher among Alaskan natives (21 percent in some regions) compared with the white population (6.6 percent). The poverty rate is estimated at 22 percent among the Alaskan Native population as compared with 13 percent of all Americans (Martin & Hill, 2009).

Health disparities continue among Alaskan Natives, and even though they have a lower rate of diabetes than the U.S. non-Hispanic population, between 1997 and 2003, the prevalence of diabetes increased by 41 percent in the population served by the Indian Health Service. Fetal alcohol syndrome cases have been reported at a rate of 5.6 per 1,000 in Alaska, well above the rate for other races or ethnicities. Other health conditions associated with mortality rates among Alaskan Natives include heart disease (236.2 in 100,000), malignant neoplasms (183.5 in 100,000), and unintentional injuries (90.1 in 100,000) (Indian Health Service, 2007).

Kanaka Maoli (Native Hawaiians)

The first foreigners to establish themselves in Hawai'i in 1778 were Western traders seeking commercial gain, then Christian missionaries seeking religious conversion. In the first 150 years of contact, Kanaka Maoli faced physical extinction from foreign diseases and cultural genocide from laws and practices that favored foreign interests. Laws were enacted that subverted the traditional system of land tenure from collective stewardship to private property, dispossessing Kanaka Maoli from their source of well-being. In 1893, American industrialists and U.S. Marines overthrew the lawful Hawaiian government, gave lands to the United States without compensation, and imprisoned and dethroned Hawai'i's last ruling monarch, Queen Lili'uokalani (Kaholokula, Nacapoy, & Dang, 2009; Kamau'u, 1989). In 1898, Hawai'i was annexed as a U.S. territory. These many devastating losses caused cultural trauma and are believed to influence many of the social problems experienced by Kanaka Maoli in contemporary times (Ka'opua, Braun, Browne, Mokuau, & Park, 2011; Office of Hawaiian Affairs, 2010).

CHamorus

In 1521, Magellan's arrival on Guahan marked CHamorus's first contact with the Western world. Over the next 200 years, as a result of the introduction of Western diseases and warfare, Guahan suffered a population collapse from 50,000 to 3,500 (Hattori, 2004). Guahan was a spoil of the Spanish–American

War given to the United States in the Treaty of Paris in 1898. At this time, CHamorus were politically divided, with those living in the Commonwealth of the Northern Mariana Islands (CNMI) falling under the administration of the Germans. Hattori reported that on Guahan, language and health reform policies were implemented adversely affecting CHamorus's lives and culture under U.S. rule. Japan occupied Guahan from 1941 to 1944, after which, the United States reoccupied Guahan, seizing 42 percent of the landmass that displaced the CHamoru people. The 1950 Organic Act of Guam granted a limited form of U.S. citizenship. At present, the proposed U.S. military buildup on Guahan threatens further dispossession of CHamorus and continual denial of their inalienable right to self-determination. CHamorus in the CNMI have lived under Spanish, German, Japanese, and American colonial rule. Their current political status is that of a commonwealth of the United States, which was created in 1976. As a commonwealth, U.S. sovereignty is acknowledged; however, certain federal laws have only limited applicability in the CNMI. The federalization of the CNMI's immigration policies in 2009 has resulted in the further colonization of CHamorus living in the CNMI. CHamorus have become a political minority in their homeland, comprising 21.3 percent of the total population (U.S. Census Bureau, 2000).

Peoples of Nations Affiliated with the United States through the Compact of Free Association

The islands now known as FSM, RMI, and ROP, or the Freely Associated States (FAS) catapulted into U.S. view during World War II and confirmed the value of the islands' location to U.S. defense (Hezel, 1995; Ka'opua & Holden, 2010). In 1947, the United States became administrator of the Trust Territory of the Pacific Islands (TTPI), committing to prepare the indigenous people for self-governance and improve their health status. During this period, the United States executed nuclear testing of 84 bombs over Bikini and other atolls. Tests resulted in mass deaths, contamination of land and waters, radiation-related cancers, and birth defects (Ka'popua, 2007; Keever, 2004). Canned food and tobacco were introduced, increasing risk of chronic disease and resulting in mass out-migration to Hawai'i for health care and education (Ka'opua & Holden, 2010). TTPI informed development of COFA, defining U.S. relations with FAS. In exchange for exclusive military access to these nations, the United States provides economic aid and access to health grants. FAS citizens have U.S. citizenship status comparable to that of legal immigrants. In 1996, the Welfare Reform Act (Personal Responsibility and Work Opportunity Reconciliation Act of 1996) (P.L. 104-193) made FAS citizens ineligible for public assistance, while access to Medicaid is uncertain.

Taino

In the early 1800s, the King of Spain granted a Cedula de Bracia (the Document of Bracia) to increase the European population of Puerto Rico by awarding land grants to immigrants from South American colonies, Spain, and other European countries. The Taino Indians almost disappeared early after the Spanish colonization. The main influence in Puerto Rican culture, values, and lifestyles has been the Spanish colonization. During the Spanish–American War, U.S. troops invaded Puerto Rico at Guanica in 1898. At the end the war, the United States demanded Puerto Rico as "war payment" from Spain in the Treaty of Paris. In 1917, all Puerto Ricans were granted full U.S. citizenship.

American Samoans

Dutch explorers made initial contact in 1722. Business and military expansion by other Western powers followed, with social disruption of the indigenous cultural order and warfare. In 1827, the U.S. Navy occupied and began to use Pago Pago (Tutuila Island) as a fueling station. The United States, Germany, and Britain came into conflict during the Second Samoan Civil War, which resulted in the 1899 Treaty of Berlin and established the colony of American Samoa (AS) in the eastern Samoan archipelago. In 1929, the colony was annexed as U.S. flag territory. Through the covenant agreement binding the United States and AS, the latter is subject to U.S. federal laws and has a nonvoting representative in the U.S. Congress. Currently, there are about 68,000 AS residents, 96 percent of whom are of Samoan ethnicity. Economic activity remains strongly linked to the United States. Though culturally rich, AS is resource poor, with about 73 percent of the indigenous population living at or below the U.S. federal poverty level (American Samoa Office of the Governor, 2007).

ISSUE STATEMENT

In April 2010, the United Nations Permanent Forum on Indigenous Issues (UNPFII) held its ninth session. This session focused on indigenous peoples of North America. As background for this meeting, the UNPFII reported "indigenous peoples of North America suffer many social problems, including lack of employment; access to clean water; physical and social isolation; substandard housing; attacks on their cultural identity; and high rates of crime and incarceration" (see http://www.un.org/esa/socdev/unpfii/en/session_ninth.html).

Due to the extensive colonization by the United States, indigenous peoples have been deprived the right to self-governance, to cultural practices and traditional language and lifestyles, and to protection of resources essential to their holistic health and well-being. The oppression of indigenous peoples in their own lands has resulted in their overall burden of poor health and their compromised well-being.

According to the United Nations Declaration on Rights of Indigenous Peoples (United Nations, 2007), indigenous peoples have the equal right to enjoy the highest standard of health. This includes, but is not limited to, the ability of indigenous peoples to have full management of their lands and natural resources as well as possess all the rights inherent in that management. Land and the environment are intrinsic to the health of indigenous peoples. The environment provides the foundation on which indigenous knowledge, cultural practices, and social institutions are based. Management of these resources by indigenous peoples enables the preservation and strengthening of indigenous knowledge, practices, and institutions as well as the promotion of health and

well-being. Indigenous peoples are best positioned to make their own choices in accordance with their own values (United Nations, 2007).

POLICY STATEMENT

NASW recognizes the struggle of indigenous peoples for sovereignty and freedom from oppression, and that their struggle has origins in past practices of genocide and ethnic cleansing implemented as policies of the U.S. government.

NASW condemns oppressive acts (for example, land acquisition with the use of imminent domain, environmental neglect, and degradation) by administering powers of government that exploit indigenous peoples.

NASW supports

■ the development of social policies and practices that promote the health and human rights of indigenous peoples living within U.S. boundaries.

■ the rights of indigenous peoples in their efforts to gain health and self-determination and sustain the physical, emotional, and spiritual health that are consistent with the principles, values, and roles of social work.

■ education and training of all social workers on cultural competence, specifically with regard to value differences between the dominant culture and the cultures of indigenous peoples, and the various social determinants that influence the health and well-being of indigenous peoples.

■ the preservation of traditional spiritual, health, and cultural practices of indigenous peoples.

REFERENCES

American Indian Religious Freedom Act, P.L. 94-341, 92 Stat. 469 (1978).

American Samoa Office of the Governor. (2007). *Health and human services report*. American Samoa: Author.

Brave Heart, M.Y.H. (2005). *Substance abuse, co-occurring mental health disorders, and the historical trauma response among American*

Indians/Alaska Natives. Retrieved from http://www.scribd.com/doc/341457/014 94BPMonograph3#

General Allotment Act, 24 Stat. 388, ch. 119, 25 USCA 331.

Hall, D. (n.d.). *Race and ethnic relations: Native Americans.* Retrieved from http://www. angelfire.com/nv/verbigerate/native americans.html

Hattori, A. P. (2004). *Colonial dis-ease: US Navy health policies and the Chamorros of Guam, 1898–1941.* Honolulu: University of Hawaii Press.

Hezel, F. X. (1995). *Strangers in their own land: A century of colonial rule in the Caroline and Marshall Islands* (Pacific Islands Monograph Series No. 13). Honolulu: University of Hawai`i Press.

Humes, K., Jones, N., & Ramirez, R. (2011). *2010 census briefs: Overview of race and Hispanic origin: 2010.* Washington, DC: U.S. Census Bureau.

Hunhdorf, R. M., & Huhndorf, S. M. (2011). Alaska Natives since the Alaska Native Claims Settlement Act. *South Atlantic Quarterly 110,* 385–401.

Indian Child Welfare Act, P.L. 95-608, 93 Stat. 3071 (1978).

Indian Health Service. (2007). *2006 national summary: Measuring and improving quality healthcare for American Indian and Alaskan Natives.* Washington, DC: U.S. Department of Health and Human Services.

Indian Reorganization Act of 1934, P.L. 73-383, 48 Stat. 984-250 U.S.C. § 461 et seq.

Kaholokula, J. K., Nacapoy, A. H., & Dang, K. (2009). Social justice as a public health imperative for Kanaka Maoli. *AlterNative, 5,* 117–137.

Kamau'u, M. (1994). He alo a he alo: *Hawaiian voices on sovereignty.* Honolulu: American Friends Committee.

Ka'opua, L. S. (2007). *CDC Pacific Islands integration and coordination project. Summary of Information Gathered from the USAPI* [Technical report]. Chamblee, GA: Centers for Disease Control and Prevention, Division of Cancer Prevention and Control.

Ka'opua, L. S., Braun, K. L., Browne, C. V., Mokuau, N., & Park, C.-B. (2011). *Why are Native Hawaiians underrepresented in Hawai'i's older adult population? Exploring disparities of Hawaiian elders.* Manuscript submitted for publication.

Ka'opua, L. S., & Holden, D. J. (2010). Cancer disparities in the Federated States of Micronesia: Funding challenges of a developing nation in epidemiological transition [Special issue]. *Social Work in Public Health, 25,* 296–310.

Keever, B. (2004). *News zero: The New York Times and the bomb.* New York: Consortium Book.

Konkle, M. (2008). Indigenous ownership and the emergence of US liberal imperialism. *American Indian Quarterly, 32,* 297–323.

Lally, E. M., & Haynes, H. A. (1995). Alaska natives. In R. L. Edwards (Ed.-in-Chief), *Encyclopedia of social work* (19th ed., Vol. 1, pp. 194–203). Washington, DC: NASW Press.

Martin, S., & Hill, A. (2009). *The changing status of Alaskan Natives.* Anchorage: University of Alaska Anchorage, Institute of Social and Economic Research.

Native American Graves Protection and Repatriation Act of 1990, P.L. 101-601, 104 Stat. 3048 (1990).

Office of Hawaiian Affairs. (2010). *The disparate treatment of Native Hawaiians in the criminal justice system.* Honolulu: Author.

Personal Responsibility and Work Opportunity Reconciliation Act of 1996, P.L. 104-193, 110 Stat. 2105 (1996).

Rodgers, T. (2008). *Native American poverty: A challenge too often ignored.* Retrieved from http://www.spotlightonpoverty.org/Excl usiveCommentary.aspx?id=0fe5c04e-fdbf-4718-980c-0373ba823da7

Thompson, T. F. (2008). Gone native: Immigrants, natives and the quest for the "real Alaskan." *Journal of Intercultural Studies, 29,* 399–412.

United Nations. (2007). *United Nations declaration on the rights of indigenous peoples.* Retrieved from http://www.un.org/esa/ socdev/unpfii/en/drip.html

U.S. Census Bureau. (2000). 2000 census of population and housing (US Summary File 1, Population and housing profile: Guam, population and housing profile: CNMI). Washington, DC: Author.

Wilkins, D. E. (Ed.). (2009). *Documents of Native American political development: 1500s to 1933.* New York: Oxford University Press.

NASW Members with Primary Responsibility for Revision of This Policy

First Draft Revision:

Palama Lee (HI)

Policy Panelists:

Jeffrey Gaudet (MA)
Ben Sher (NYC)
Teri Cardwell (IN)
Marlene Schulz (SD)
Warren Aoki (HI)

Policy statement approved by the NASW Delegate Assembly, August 2011. This statement supersedes the policy statement on Sovereignty and the Health of Indigenous Peoples approved by the Delegate Assembly in 2002. For further information, contact the National Association of Social Workers, 750 First Street, NE, Suite 700, Washington, DC 20002-4241. Telephone: 202-408-8600; e-mail: press@naswdc.org

Technology and Social Work

BACKGROUND

The seminal contribution of Mary Richmond offers the first mention of technology and social work. Richmond (1917) noted the importance of using the telephone in social work practice. At the turn of the 20th century social workers were somewhat uncertain of telephone technology. However, they eventually accepted the telephone as an important practice tool. More recently, social work has been challenged by the reconciliation of social work values and ethics with the utilization of technology as evidenced by the introduction of the telephone in the 19th century up through our current digital age.

Three unlikely technological streams of historical connections led to useful computer applications for social work practice. First, military applications were the impetus for computers (Burks & Burks, 1988) and the Internet (Marson, 1997). Although these applications were clear improvements for war and defense goals, they were neither user friendly or affordable. Highly specialized university professors produced much of the advances in technological war and defense applications. Because of the second connection, academic freedom, the advances in military technology were spread throughout the academic community—including schools of social work. Although academic social workers were employing computer-related technologies to social service research, these technological advances were not user friendly and could not be efficiently applied to social work practice. Here enters the third connection—commercialization of technology. Starting in the early 1960s (Redin, 2007), technology entrepreneurs were motivated by profit to reduce costs and to make technology user friendly. Even with such rapid advances in reducing cost and increasing user friendliness,

resistance among social workers to use computer technology as a tool for daily practice is well documented (Huff & Edwards, 1998; Lamb, 1990). With his 1981 inaugural issue of a newsletter titled *Computer Use in Social Services Network Newsletter*, Dick Schoech advocated for the integration of technology in social work practice. In 1985, Schoech's newsletter evolved into a practice journal, the *Journal of Technology in Human Services*, and thus had a greater impact. However, unlike military and business uses of technology, social worker applications demanded understanding more than merely when it can be used and how it works.

"Technology has changed the educational landscape in terms of how information is delivered and to whom, the speed of access to information, and in terms of choice of options for courses, programs, and colleges and universities" (Truluck, 2007). Social work education is part of that landscape.

ISSUE STATEMENT

The evolution and proliferation of information technologies has expanded the ways in which social workers provide services to clients, administer agencies, educate practitioners, and conduct research and evaluation. Accompanying these dramatic developments are a number of compelling issues for social workers that include direct practice, management, education, and research.

Direct Practice

Electronically mediated communication technologies make practice possible on a global scale and with all sizes of systems. With improving interactive technology, both direct practice and consultation can take place between people who are separated in space and time. This use of technology poses new challenges for social workers in establishing therapeutic relationships, making appropriate assessments and referrals, monitoring and evaluating interventions, and providing emergency assistance. Information technology use is becoming increasingly frequent for practitioners, which raises ethical issues surrounding their use, such as document loss or interception and lack of privacy, "Confidentiality in an electronic medium can quickly evaporate; jurisdiction, liability, and malpractice issues blur when state lines and national boundaries are crossed electronically" (NASW, 2005).

Management

Managerial uses of various technologies for administrative work, including fiscal planning, scheduling, billing, and human resources have long been a part of agency practice. Such information is valuable for designing agency systems and program planning. Social workers are also challenged to manage information systems related to client data. However, information about client systems and employees must be protected from access and use without the person's knowledge or permission, and in ways that may not be in the best interests of consumers or the profession. Ethical and pragmatic decisions must be made about the collection, storage, retrieval, and protection of client and employee information.

Education

The advances in educational technology systems have now become an alternative to traditional instruction. This has led to significant changes in how social work curriculums are constructed and delivered. Students can now access educational learning in many different environments, for example, interactive television (ITV), Blackboard, interactive bulletin boards, e-mail, software-based program instruction, net meetings, chat rooms, pod-casts and the World Wide Web (East et al., 2006).

Classes that lend themselves to these various instruction modalities are necessary. Miller and King (2003) stated the selection of technologies should be based on appropriateness for the learner and the curriculum. Consideration should be given to student learning styles and to cultural and individual differences.

Faculty development and continued technological skill training benefit not only students but also the faculty member. According to Regan (2005), curriculum committees must provide guidance and supportive processes for faculty who are interested in teaching distance education courses.

Distance education has been an asset to rural communities where technology is promoting new and innovative partnerships. Collaborative higher education programs provide students in rural areas access to online masters' programs with accredited social work programs in other states. Heitkamp (2007) noted low wages and out migration from rural areas have resulted in a workforce shortage in mental health, addiction, and child welfare practitioners, particularly in rural and reservation communities. This technology could allow rural students to remain in their home communities and ultimately practice in rural or underserved areas.

In addition, Web-based continuing education programs are now being offered by many social work professional organizations and universities. "The proliferation of distance learning programs, coursework, and new technologies allows the lifelong learner the ability to continually advance his/her skills in a changing knowledge and digital economy, anywhere, and at any time" (Portugal, 2006).

The use of information technology must also be addressed when designing professional development and in-service trainings. Education and training should include legal, ethical, and competency-based standards.

Research Issues

The social work profession is strengthened when practitioners use the evidence from social work research to guide their choice of practice interventions and to evaluate their effectiveness. Social work researchers contribute to the knowledge base of the social work profession by developing, organizing, and implementing research founded on sound, ethical principles. Although technology has enabled faster access to and use of data, social work researchers continue to safeguard the confidentiality of client records, follow human subjects' protection guidelines, and understand the importance of gathering valid and reliable data. It is also important for social work researchers to disseminate their findings widely and advocate for the advancement of ethical human subjects research in general, and for practitioners to use these findings to help guide their work to improve the quality of life for individuals, families, groups, organizations, and the communities in which all function.

Ethical Issues

Although the last two decades have revolutionized technology in all aspects of social work practice, "social workers should ensure that the use of technology conforms to all practice and regulatory standards addressing ethical conduct and protection of the public" (NASW, 2005).

The NASW *Code of Ethics* (NASW, 2000) also recommends that social workers take precautions to ensure and maintain the confidentiality of information transmitted to other parties through the use of computers, electronic mail, facsimile machines, telephone and telephone answering machines, and other electronic or computer technology.

As technology continues to influence social work knowledge and practice, ethical issues will continue to be monitored and revised.

POLICY STATEMENT

It is important that the use of technology in social work be directed by the social work values and ethics that are the essential principles of the profession. With this in mind, NASW supports

■ the maintenance, review, and revision of competencies for the use of technology in social work practice. These competencies are based in the areas of direct and indirect prac-

tice, management, social work education, and research.

■ a continuing leadership role in using technology to improve service to NASW members and to further the goal and mission of the association.

■ advocacy efforts for the efficiency and efficacy of technology on the profession and its clients.

■ policies that promote informing clients about the process, associated benefits and risks, and their rights and responsibilities when technology is used in practice.

■ adequate resources to ensure the availability and accessibility of basic technology to all members of society, especially in rural and underserved areas.

■ public funding for the advancement of technology.

■ policies that ensure that technology does no harm to people, in particular support of the Internal Review Board process.

REFERENCES

Burks, A. R., & Burks, A. W. (1988). *The first electronic computer: The Atanasoff story*. Ann Arbor: University of Michigan Press.

East, J., Alter, C., Haddow, J., La Mendola, W., Molidor, C., Petrila, A., & Walls, N. G. (2006). *Distance education for social work education: models, technologies, and best practices*. Proposal submitted to the Council on Social Work Education Commission of Reaccreditation.

Heitkamp, T. (2007). *Twenty years later: Lessons learned in administering distance education programs: Preparing the next generation of educators*. Paper presented at the 53rd Annual Program Meeting, Council of Social Work Education: San Francisco.

Huff, M. T., & Edwards, S. L. (1998, March 6). *Using electronic journals in social work education*. Paper presented at the 44th Annual Program Meeting of the Council on Social Work Education, Orlando, FL.

Lamb, J. A. (1990). Teaching computer literacy to human service students. In R. L. Reinoehl & B. J. Mueller (Eds.), *Computer literacy in human service* (pp. 31–43). Binghamton, NY: Haworth Press.

Marson, S. M. (1997). A selective history of the Internet technology and social work. *Computers in Human Services, 14*, 35–49.

Miller, T. W., & King F. B. (2003). Distance education: Pedagogy and best practices in the new millennium. *International Journal of Leadership in Education, 6*, 283–297.

National Association of Social Workers. (2000). *Code of ethics of the National Association of Social Workers.* Washington, DC: NASW Press.

National Association of Social Workers. (2005). *NASW & ASWB Standards for Technology and Social Work Practice.* Washington, DC: Author.

Portugal, L. M. (2006). Emerging leadership roles in distance education: Current state of affairs and forecasting future trends. *Online Journal of Distance Learning Administration, 9*(3). Retrieved February 19, 2008, from http://westga.edu/~distance/ojdla/fall93/portugal93.htm

Redin, J. (2007). *The calculator wars.* Retrieved November 16, 2007, from http://www.xnumber.com/history_pages/history6.htm

Regan, J. R. C. (2005). Faculty issues in distance education. In P. Abel (Ed.), *Distance education in social work* (pp. 119–139). New York: Springer.

Richmond, M. E. (1917). *Social diagnosis.* New York: Russell Sage Foundation.

Truluck, J. (2007, Spring). Establishing a mentoring plan for improving retention in online graduate degree programs. *Online Journal of Distance Learning Administration, 10*(1). Retrieved February 19, 2008, from http://westga.edu/~distance/ojdla/spring 101/truluck101.htm

Policy statement approved by the NASW Delegate Assembly, August 2008. This policy statement supersedes the policy statement on Technology and Social Work approved by the Delegate Assembly in 1999 and referred by the 2005 Delegate Assembly to the 2008 Delegate Assembly. For further information, contact the National Association of Social Workers, 750 First Street, NE, Suite 700, Washington, DC 20002-4241. Telephone: 202-408-8600 or 800-638-8799; e-mail: press@naswdc.org

Transgender and Gender Identity Issues

BACKGROUND

Gender is a human social system of differentiation by sex for roles, behaviors, characteristics, appearances, and identities (for example, "man" or "woman"), which maps cultural meanings and norms about both sex and gender onto human bodies. Everyone has an internal sense of his or her "gender," and this sense is called "gender identity" (Stone, 2004). "Most people's gender identity is congruent with their assigned sex, but many people experience their gender identity to be discordant with their natal sex" (Lev, 2004, p. 397).

"Transgender" is a broad term used to describe those whose gender, gender identity, or gender expression is in some sense different from, or transgresses social norms for, their assigned birth sex. Transgender may include those who identify as being transsexual, cross-dressers, androgynous, bi-gender, no-gender, multi-gender, genderqueer, and a growing number of people who do not identify as belonging to any gender category at all. For some transgender individuals the discomfort with social gender role is accompanied by a profound sense of mismatch of the physical body to their internal bodily experience. This body dysphoria (known as "gender dysphoria") causes significant distress, negatively affects daily functioning and well-being, and requires medical services to realign the body with the self. Although there are many transgender people with medically diagnosed intersex conditions (Xavier, Honnold, & Bradford, 2007) most people with intersex conditions are not transgender (Intersex Society of North America, n.d.; Koyama, n.d.).

In the absence of systematic data collection, estimates vary widely as to the number of transgender individuals in the United States, rang-ing from 3 million to as many as 9 million individuals (Bushong, 1995; Olyslager & Conway, 2007). Prevalence of transgender identities is "likely to be on the order of at least 1:100 (i.e., 1%)" (Olyslager & Conway, 2007, p. 23), and transsexualism is also not rare, with prevalence now being estimated at between 1:2000 and 1:500 (Olyslager & Conway, 2007). Reports now indicate there may be roughly equal numbers of male-to-female and female-to-male transsexual people (Bullough, Bullough, & Elias, 1997; MacKenzie, 1994).

Transgender people encounter difficulties in virtually every aspect of their lives, both in facing the substantial hostility that society associates with those who do not conform to gender norms and in coping with their own feelings of difference. Considerable verbal harassment and physical violence accompany the powerful social stigma faced by transgender people (Clements-Nolles, Marx, & Katz, 2006; Lombardi, Wilchins, Priesing, & Malouf, 2001; Wyss, 2004) and may be accompanied by racial and ethnic discrimination (Juang, 2006). Transgender people also experience dismissal from jobs, eviction from housing, and denial of services, even by police officers and medical emergency professionals (Xavier, 2000; Xavier, Honnold, & Bradford, 2007). Restrooms, the most mundane of public and workplace amenities, often become sites of harassment and confrontation, with access often denied (Transgender Law Center, 2005).

Transgender and transsexual people are often denied appropriate medical and mental health care and are uniquely at risk of adverse health outcomes (Dean et al., 2000; Xavier et al., 2004). Basic services may be denied because of ignorance about or discomfort with a transgender client. To align the physical body with the experienced sense of self, usually as an integral part of social transition away from the sex assigned at birth, transsexuals and some other individuals require medical services (for example, hormone replacement, facial electrolysis, or surgical and other procedures, as appropriate to the individual). Despite ongoing evidence that the vast majority who access such services achieve congruence and well-being (De Cuypere et al., 2005; Newfield, Hart, Dibble, & Kohler, 2006; Pfafflin & Junge, 1998; Rehman, Lazer, Benet, Schaefer, & Melman, 1999; Ross & Need, 1989), medical and mental health providers routinely refuse to provide such services, and health insurance carriers and governmental payers (for example, Medicare, Medicaid, VA, and Tri-Care) routinely deny coverage for them, sometimes under the belief that such care is "experimental" or "cosmetic" (Dean et al., 2000; JSI Research and Training Institute, Inc., 2000; Middleton, 1997; Spack, 2005; Spade, 2006; Thaler, 2007). Access to medically necessary transition-related services is thus largely limited to a privileged few who can pay out-of-pocket for services. Continued barriers to health care may have been shown to contribute to lowered self-esteem and well being, or may be experienced as posttraumatic stress, and may lead some to self-medicate through street hormones or over-the-counter treatments or to resort to high-risk injection silicone use—all without medical supervision (Risser & Shelton, 2002; Xavier, 2000). It is important to underscore the denial of basic health care, and also the extreme race and socioeconomic status disparities: Needs assessments in major cities show that severe marginalization and barriers to transition contribute to high rates of joblessness and disproportionately affect people of color. Lack of employment leaves many without health insurance, and because insurance carriers often deny coverage for transgender individuals' other nontransition-related services, transgender individuals often lack access to all ongoing basic health services, even when employed (Xavier et al., 2004).

Gender identity disorder, or GID (American Psychiatric Association, 2000), a diagnosis often required by providers as a prerequisite to transgender transition-related health services, is also seen as a barrier to health care. GID has been criticized for further stigmatizing nontypical gender expression and reinforcing gender stereotypes, for pathologizing transgender realities as mental illness, and for failing to accurately describe the "symptoms" experienced by transsexual people. The diagnosis is vague regarding the medical necessity for and demonstrated success of treatment, particularly medically assisted transsexual transition, which prevents insurance reimbursements for care and leaves transgender youths and adults vulnerable to so-called "reparative" treatment (Bockting & Ehrbar, 2005; Hill, Rozanski, Carfagnini, & Willoughby, 2005; Lev, 2005; Spack, 2005; Winters, 2005). Although some individuals experience the current diagnosis as a good fit, many transgender health advocates seek either greatly revised language or a medical (physical, nonpsychiatric) diagnosis to replace it (Green, 2004; Lev, 2004; Stone, 2004).

Mental health providers, including social workers, are often positioned as "gatekeepers" in the medical process (for example, as providers of referrals for hormonal therapy and surgery), which may hamper the therapeutic alliance between them and their transgender clients. More recently, many community-based urban clinics and individual providers have developed protocols and practices that do not require a GID diagnosis (Lev, 2004; Tom Waddell Health Center, 2001). Clients benefit from treatment with therapists who have expertise in transgender issues (Lurie, 2005; Rachlin, 2002). Those therapists with little training or familiarity in this arena often require that a diagnosis be assigned, and apply its criteria narrowly, denying access to nontranssexual transgender people or forcing clients to wait months or years before they can obtain medicalized transition services (Califia, 1997; Lev, 2004; Meyerowitz, 2002).

Many transgender children and youths face harassment and violence in school environments, and those who do not feel safe or valued at school cannot reach their potential and may drop out (D'Augelli, Grossman, & Starks, 2006; Gay, Lesbian and Straight Education Network, 2004; Grossman, D'Augelli, & Slater, 2006; Wyss, 2004). Although medical protocols exist for children whose body dysphoria may lead to severe depression and suicidality, including endocrinologic intervention to prevent or delay unwanted puberty (Cohen-Kettenis & van Goozen, 1997; Smith, van Goozen, & Cohen-Kettenis, 2001; Spack, 2005), there are still few support resources for transgender children, their parents, or surrounding social institutions, leaving transgender youths particularly vulnerable to so-called "reparative" treatments. (Menvielle, Tuerk, & Perrin, 2005; PFLAG, 2004).

Although there is no federal law protecting individuals from discrimination on the basis of gender identity or gender expression, a handful of states and a growing number of local jurisdictions, as well as employers, are beginning to extend such protections (Lambda Legal Defense Fund, n.d.). Federal administrations and most states require proof of genital or other surgery before altering the sex marker on passports, birth certificates, or other documents. Such policies reinforce the myth that all transgender people undergo a single "sex change operation," regardless of an individual's need or ability to undergo, or afford, transition procedures (Thaler, 2007). Inaccurate identity documentation is a common barrier to employment, housing, and appropriate services from gender-segregated facilities. The increased vulnerability—to violence and harassment, to loss of social support and mounting despair—suggests that policies that prevent changing documentation to align with gender identity represent serious barriers to health and well-being. Transsexual individuals and their partners may also be denied access to civil marriage on the basis that they are in a same-sex relationship (Minter, 2003) or be denied access to same-sex domestic partnerships or to same-sex domestic partnerships on the basis that they are in an opposite-sex relationship, and thus are denied access to the social status, rights, and privileges of civil marriage or domestic partnerships.

A host of institutional settings in the United States are hostile to transgender people, especially those that are segregated by sex, many of which require transgender individuals to have undergone genital surgery to be placed according to their gender identity. Homeless shelters and other facilities that refuse to house clients with the appropriate gender place individuals at risk of sexual propositions, harassment, and assault. Sex-based dress codes affect youths in particular, who are often disciplined and ejected from the facilities for violating such policies (Mottet & Ohle, 2003; Ray, 2006). Those incarcerated in jails and prisons face similar barriers to accessing gender-appropriate facilities, and in many jurisdictions, transgender people in state custody are also denied access to ongoing hormone therapy and other transgender transition-related procedures, including surgery (Jenness et al., 2007; Rosenblum, 2000; Sylvia Rivera Law Project, 2007; Thaler, 2007; Women in Prison Project, 2007). Although few resources exist regarding aging and the transgender population, residential and care facilities may pose familiar barriers such as sex segregation and lack of culturally competent caregivers at a time of life when transgender individuals may be unable to advocate for themselves; many older transgender people may also fear abuse and neglect (Cook-Daniels, 1997, 2002; Gapka & Raj, 2003).

Lack of appropriately trained service providers, including mental health providers, makes it hard to obtain culturally competent legal, medical, and advocacy services (Lurie, 2005; Xavier et al., 2004). Although social workers are frontline providers of mental health and other services for many transgender individuals, most schools of social work have little in their curriculums on transgender issues.

Transgender individuals and communities are increasingly impatient with a backseat role in shaping policies that affect their lives. In the face of stigma, increasing numbers of transgender individuals are becoming powerful community advocates and are encouraging others to join with them.

ISSUE STATEMENT

Transgender people experience the stigma, prejudice, discrimination, and extreme hostility known as transphobia on a daily basis. Although gender nonconforming experience can be traced across history and the successful social and medical transition of transsexuals is well documented since the middle of the 20th century, only in recent years has this emerged in the public discourse. Unfortunately, most in our society have little or no understanding of the profound discomfort some may feel in trying to conform to rigid gender roles assigned to them by virtue of their physiology. Similarly, ignorance and insensitivity prevail regarding the debilitating distress that accompanies body dysphoria, and the damage done to those left without access to medical and social transition.

Social workers have the responsibility to understand and appreciate the full range of differences that exist among human beings and to explore any and all prejudices that result in oppressive and unjust treatment. It is incumbent upon the social work profession to embrace and explore this domain of human variation and help educate the public in a manner that mitigates stigma and supports the rights of transgender, transsexual, and gender nonconforming individuals, consistent with NASW's *Code of Ethics* (2000) which states the following:

■ "Social workers should not practice, condone, facilitate, or collaborate with any form of discrimination on the basis of race, ethnicity, national origin, color, sex, sexual orientation, age, marital status, political belief, religion, or mental or physical disability." (pp. 22–23)

■ "Social workers should act to expand choice and opportunity for all people, with special regard for vulnerable, disadvantaged, oppressed, and exploited people and groups." (p. 27)

■ "Social workers should promote conditions that encourage respect for cultural and social diversity within the United States and globally. Social workers should promote policies and practices that demonstrate respect for difference, support the expansion of cultural knowledge and resources, advocate for programs and institutions that demonstrate cultural competence, and promote policies that safeguard the rights of and confirm equity and social justice for all people." (p. 27)

Social workers are trained to work with clients who are different along many dimensions of diversity. Gender-diverse individuals should be included among this constituency. As clinicians, social workers must be equipped to provide their clients with education and re-sources on gender experience, gender expression and sexuality, including specific examples of successful role models in society. Social workers must also be prepared to provide services and referrals for those clients who may require social or medical transition to a sex different from that assigned at birth. All legal impediments to the full equality of rights and opportunities for anyone, regardless of that person's gender identity or expression must be eliminated. Individuals, families, schools, and communities should have the resources to welcome and support gender-diverse people. At the community and policy-making levels, inclusive environments and provision for access to services should all be respected, valued, and empowered. Social workers should be partnered with the transgender community to modify laws, medical protocols, research, and policies in ways that preserve and protect the quality of life for transgender, transsexual, and gender nonconforming citizens. In the domain of gender diversity, prejudice and oppression should be replaced with compassion, support, and celebration of difference.

POLICY STATEMENT

NASW recognizes the considerable diversity in gender expression and identity among our population. NASW believes that people of diverse gender—including all those who are included under the transgender umbrella—should be afforded the same respect and rights as that for any other people. NASW asserts that discrimination and prejudice directed against any individuals on the basis of gender identity or gender expression, whether real or perceived, are damaging to the social, emotional, psychological, physical, and economic well-being of the affected individuals, as well as society as a whole, and NASW seeks the elimination of the same both inside and outside the profession, in public and private sectors.

NASW believes that a nonjudgmental and affirming attitude toward gender diversity enables social workers to provide maximum support and services to those whose gender departs from the expected norm. Social workers and the social work profession can support and empower such people in all aspects of their development, helping them to lead fully actualized and engaged lives on the basis of their genuine gender identities. NASW supports the development of supportive and knowledgeable practice environments for those struggling with gender expression and identity issues (both clients and colleagues) and for those who are struggling with prejudices, biases, and transphobia.

Professional and Continuing Education

■ NASW supports curriculum policies in schools of social work that eliminate discrimination against those who are transgender, transsexual, genderqueer, cross-dressers, and of other minority gender identities; provide equal opportunities to all students for investigating issues of relevance to these populations; develop and provide training for classroom instructors, field supervisors, and field advisors regarding gender diversity issues; and seek field opportunities for students interested in working with transgender people.

■ NASW encourages the implementation of continuing education programs on practice and policy issues relevant to gender diversity, to include the distinctive, complex biopsychosocial needs of transgender individuals and their families, legal and employment issues, ethical dilemmas and responsibilities, and effective interventions and community resources.

Antidiscrimination

■ NASW reaffirms a commitment to human rights and freedom and opposes all public and private discrimination on the basis of gender identity and of gender expression, whether actual or perceived, and regardless of assigned sex at birth, including denial of access to employment, housing, education, appropriate treatment in gender segregated facilities, appropriate medical care and health care coverage, appropriate identity documents, and civil marriage and all its attendant benefits, rights, and privileges.

■ NASW encourages the repeal of discriminatory legislation and the passage of legislation protecting the rights, legal benefits, and privileges of people of all gender identities and expressions.

■ NASW encourages all institutions that train or employ social workers to broaden any nondiscriminatory statement made to students, faculty, staff, or clients, to include "gender identity or expression" in all nondiscrimination statements.

Public Awareness and Advocacy

■ NASW supports efforts to provide safe and secure educational environments, at all levels of education, that promote an understanding and acceptance of self and in which all youths, including youths of all gender identities and expressions, may be free to express their genuine gender identity and obtain an education free from discrimination, harassment, violence, and abuse.

■ NASW supports the development of, and participation in, coalitions with other professional associations and progressive organizations to lobby on behalf of the civil rights for all people of diverse gender expression and identity.

■ NASW supports collaboration with organizations and groups supportive of the transgender community to develop programs to increase public awareness of the mistreatment and discrimination experienced by transgender people and of the contributions they make to society.

■ NASW encourages the development of programs, training, and information that promote proactive efforts to eliminate psychological, social, and physical harm directed toward transgender people and to portray them accurately and compassionately.

■ NASW supports the development of programs within schools and other child and youth services agencies that educate students, faculty, and staff about the range of gender diversity and the needs of transgender children and youths.

■ NASW supports the creation of scientific and educational resources that inform public discussion about gender identity and gender diversity, to promote public policy development and to strengthen societal and familial attitudes and behaviors that affirm the dignity and rights of all individuals, regardless of gender identity or gender expression.

Health and Mental Health Services

■ NASW endorses policies in the public and private sectors that ensure nondiscrimination, that are sensitive to the health and mental health needs of transgender people, and that promote an understanding of gender expression and gender identity issues.

■ NASW advocates for the availability of comprehensive psychological and social support services for transgender people and their families that are respectful and sensitive to individual concerns.

■ NASW supports the rights of all individuals to receive health insurance and other health coverage without discrimination on the basis of gender identity, and specifically without exclusion of services related to transgender or transsexual transition (or sex change), to receive medical and mental health services through their primary care physician and the appropriate referrals to medical specialists, which may include hormone replacement therapy, surgical interventions, prosthetic devices, and other medical procedures.

■ NASW encourages the development of an appropriate, non-stigmatizing medical diagnosis for transgender individuals whose self-experienced gender does not match the sex assigned at birth and who require medical services to align the body with the experienced self.

■ NASW supports the collaboration of organizations with the U.S. surgeon general to implement data collection and production of comprehensive reports on prevention of hate crimes against adults and youth violence prevention, including such issues as bullying, prejudice, and discrimination, including violence and discrimination that are based on gender identity, gender expression, or both.

■ NASW advocates for the implementation of programs to address the education, housing, employment, health, and mental health needs of adults and youths who are struggling with gender issues and who are thus at high risk of suicide, vulnerable to violence or assault, at increased risk of HIV/AIDS, or otherwise at risk.

■ NASW supports the creation of a national health survey that incorporates a representative sample of the U.S. population of all ages (including adolescents); that includes questions on gender identity, gender expression, and sexual orientation; and that explores the barriers to health care experienced by transgender people. NASW also supports inclusion of transgender individuals in existing national and state health surveys and data collection, by inclusion of questions on gender identity, to enable research on health and other disparities in the transgender population.

Legal and Political Action

■ NASW advocates for increased funding for education, treatment services, and research on behalf of people of diverse gender expression and gender identity.

■ NASW supports the legal recognition of transgender individuals as members of the gender with which they identify, regardless of assigned sex at birth or subsequent surgical or other medical interventions.

■ NASW supports the legal recognition of marriage, domestic partnership, and civil unions, regardless of either the sex or gender status of the betrothed or partnered individuals.

■ NASW encourages the repeal of laws and discriminatory practices that impede individuals in their identification with, and their expression of, the gender that matches their sense of themselves, in all areas of the public arena, especially employment, health care, education, and housing, including in custodial settings.

■ NASW encourages the adoption of laws that will prohibit discrimination against, protect the civil rights of, and preserve the access to health care and well-being of, individuals who identify with and express their gender identities, in education, housing, inheritance, health and other types of insurance, child custody, property, and other areas. NASW particularly encourages such protections in education; housing, including custodial settings; inheritance and pensions; health coverage and all other types of insurance; provision of health care and medical services; child custody; property; as well as other areas.

■ NASW acknowledges the importance of social group work and community organizing to support transgender community development and help the larger community to overcome ignorance and fear of transgender people, and to move toward inclusion, equality, and justice.

REFERENCES

American Psychiatric Association. (2000). *Diagnostic and statistical manual of mental disorders* (4th ed., text rev.). Washington, DC: Author.

Bockting, W. O., & Ehrbar, R. D. (2005). Commentary: Gender variance, dissonance, or identity disorder? *Journal of Human Sexuality, 17*(3/4), 125–134.

Bullough, V. L., Bullough, B., & Elias, J. (1997). *Gender blending.* New York: Prometheus Books.

Bushong, C. W. (1995). The multi-dimensionality of gender. *Transgender Tapestry, 72,* 33–37.

Califia, P. (1997). *Sex changes: The politics of transgenderism.* San Francisco: Cleis Press.

Clements-Nolles, K., Marx, R., & Katz, M. (2006). Attempted suicide among transgender persons: The influence of gender-based discrimination and victimization. *Journal of Homosexuality, 51*(3), 53–69.

Cohen-Kettenis, P. T., & van Goozen, S. H. M. (1997). Sex reassignment of adolescent transsexuals: A follow-up study. *Journal of the American Academy of Child and Adolescent Psychiatry, 36*(2), 263–271.

Cook-Daniels, L. (1997). Lesbian, gay male, bisexual and transgendered elders: Elder abuse and neglect issues. *Journal of Elder Abuse & Neglect, 9*(2), 35–49.

Cook-Daniels, L. (2002). *Transgender elders and SOFFAS: A primer.* Paper presented at the 110th Convention of the American Psychological Association. Retrieved August 13, 2004, from http://www.forge-forward.org/handouts/TransEldersSOFFAs-web.pdf

D'Augelli, A. R., Grossman, A. H., & Starks, M. T. (2006). Childhood gender atypicality, victimization, and PTSD among lesbian, gay, and bisexual youth. *Journal of Interpersonal Violence, 21,* 1462–1482.

Dean, L., Meyer, I. H., Robinson, K., Sell, R. L., Sember, R., Silenzio, V. M. B., Bowen, D. J., Bradford, J., Rothblum, E., White, J., Dunn, P., Lawrence, A., Wolfe, D., & Xavier, J. (2000). Lesbian, gay, bisexual, and transgender health: Findings and concerns. *Journal of the Gay and Lesbian Medical Association, 4*(3), 102–151.

De Cuypere, G., T'Sjoen, G., Beerten, R., Selvaggi, G., De Sutter, P., Hoebeke, P., Monstrey, S., Vansteenwegen, A., & Rubens, R. (2005). Sexual and physical health after sex reassignment surgery. *Archives of Sexual Behavior, 34,* 679–690.

Gapka, S., & Raj, R. (2003). *Trans Health Project: A position paper and resolution.* Retrieved July 14, 2007, from: http://www.opha.on.ca/ppres/2003-06_pp.pdf

Gay, Lesbian and Straight Education Network. (2004). *2003 National School Climate Survey: The school-related experiences of our nation's lesbian, gay, bisexual and transgender youth.* New York: Author.

Green, J. (2004). *Becoming a visible man.* Nashville, TN: Vanderbilt University Press.

Grossman, A. H., D'Augelli, A. R., & Slater, N. P. (2006). Male-to-female transgender youth: Gender expression milestones, gender atypicality, victimization, and parents' responses. *Journal of GLBT Family Studies, 2*(1), 71–92.

Hill, D. B., Rozanski, C., Carfagnini, J., & Willoughby, B. (2005). Gender identity disorders in childhood and adolescence: A critical inquiry. *Journal of Human Sexuality, 17*(3/4), 7–34.

Intersex Society of North America. (n.d.). *What's the difference between being transgender or* transsexual and having an intersex condition? Retrieved July 15, 2007, from http://www.isna.org/faq/transgender

Jenness, V., Maxson, C. L., Matsuda, K. N., & Sumner, J. M. (2007, April). *Violence in California correctional facilities: An empirical examination of sexual assault.* Report submitted to the California Department of Corrections & Rehabilitation, Center for Evidence-Based Corrections, University of California, Irvine.

JSI Research and Training Institute, Inc. (2000). *Access to health care for transgendered persons in greater Boston.* Boston: Author.

Juang, R. M. (2006). Transgendering the politics of recognition. In S. Stryker & S. Whittle (Eds.), *The transgender studies reader* (pp. 706–717). New York: Routledge.

Koyama, E. (n.d.). *Is gender identity disorder an intersex condition?* Retrieved July 12, 2007, from http://www.intersexinitiative.org/articles/gid.html

Lambda Legal Defense Fund. (n.d.). *The rights of transgender people.* Retrieved May 7, 2007, from http://www.lambdalegal.org/our-work/issues/rights-of-transgender-people/

Lev, A. I. (2004). *Transgender emergence: Therapeutic guidelines for working with gender-variant people and their families.* Binghamton, NY: Haworth Clinical Practice Press.

Lev, A. I. (2005). Disordering gender identity: Gender identity in the DSM-IV-TR. *Journal of Human Sexuality, 17*(3/4), 35–69.

Lombardi, E. L., Wilchins, R. A., Priesing, D., & Malouf, D. (2001). Gender violence: Transgender experiences with violence and discrimination. *Journal of Homosexuality, 42*(1), 89–101.

Lurie, S. (2005). Identifying training needs of health-care providers related to treatment and care of transgendered patients: A qualitative needs assessment conducted in New England. *International Journal of Transgenderism, 3*(2/3), 93–112.

MacKenzie, G. O. (1994). *Transgender nation.* Bowling Green, OH: Bowling Green State University, Popular Press.

Menvielle, E. J., Tuerk, C., & Perrin, E. C. (2005). To the beat of a different drummer: The gender-variant child. *Contemporary Pediatrics, 22*(2), 38–46.

Meyerowitz, J. (2002). *How sex changed: A history of transsexuality in the United States.* Cambridge, MA: Harvard University Press.

Middleton L. (1997). Insurance and the reimbursement of transgender health care. In G. Israel & D. Tarver (Eds.), *Transgender care: Recommended guidelines, practical information & personal accounts* (pp. 215–224). Philadelphia: Temple University Press.

Minter, S. (2003). *Representing transsexual clients: Selected legal issues.* Retrieved August 3, 2004, from: http://www.transgenderlaw.org/resources/translaw.htm

Mottet, L., & Ohle, J. (2003). *Transitioning our shelters: A guide to making homeless shelters safe for transgender people.* Retrieved September 9, 2005, from http://www.thetaskforce.org/reports_and_research/trans_homeless

National Association of Social Workers. (2000). *Code of ethics of the National Association of Social Workers.* Washington, DC: Author.

Newfield, E., Hart, S., Dibble, S., & Kohler, L. (2006). Female-to-male transgender quality of life. *Quality of Life Research, 15,* 1447–1457.

Olyslager, F., & Conway, L. (2007, September). *On the calculation of the prevalence of transsexualism.* Paper presented at the WPATH 20th International Symposium, Chicago.

Pfafflin, F., & Junge, A. (1998). *Sex reassignment. Thirty years of international follow-up studies after sex reassignment surgery: A comprehensive review, 1961–1991.* Retrieved November 22, 2007, from http://www.symposion.com/ijt/pfaefflin/1000.htm

PFLAG North Bay Chapter. (2004). *The transgender umbrella: Parents, Families and Friends of Lesbians and Gays North Bay Chapter.* San Francisco: Author.

Rachlin, K. (2002). Transgendered individuals' experiences of psychotherapy. *International Journal of Transgenderism, 6*(1). Retrieved November 22, 2007, from http://www.symposion.com/ijt/ijtvo06no01_03.htm

Ray, N. (2006). *Lesbian, gay, bisexual, and transgender youth: An epidemic of homelessness.* Washington, DC: National Gay and Lesbian Task Force Policy Institute and the National Coalition for the Homeless. Retrieved July 14, 2007, from http://www.thetaskforce.org/downloads/HomelessYouth.pdf

Rehman, J., Lazer, S., Benet, A. E., Schaefer, L. C., & Melman, A. (1999). The reported sex and surgery satisfactions of 28 postoperative male-to-female transsexual patients. *Archives of Sexual Behavior, 28*(1), 71–89.

Risser, J., & Shelton, A. (2002). *Behavioral assessment of the transgender population, Houston, Texas.* Galveston: University of Texas School of Public Health.

Rosenblum, D. (2000). 'Trapped' in Sing Sing: Transgendered prisoners caught in the gender binarism. *Michigan Journal of Gender & Law, 6,* 522–526.

Ross, M. W., & Need, J. A. (1989). Effects of adequacy of gender reassignment surgery on psychological adjustment: A follow-up of fourteen male-to-female patients. *Archives of Sexual Behavior, 18*(2), 145–153.

Smith, Y. L. S., van Goozen, S. H. M., & Cohen-Kettenis, P. T. (2001). Adolescents with gender identity disorder who were accepted or rejected for sex reassignment surgery: A prospective follow-up study. *Journal of American Academy of Child and Adolescent Psychiatry, 40,* 472–481.

Spack, N. (2005, Fall). Transgenderism. *Lahey Clinic Journal of Medical Ethics.* Retrieved February 13, 2007, from http://www.lahey.org/NewsPubs/Publications/Ethics/JournalFall2005/Journal_Fall2005_Feature.asp

Spade, D. (2006). Compliance is gendered: Struggling for self-determination in a hostile economy. In P. Currah, R. M. Juang, & S. M. Minter (Eds.), *Transgender rights* (pp. 217–241). Minneapolis: University of Minnesota Press.

Stone, M. R. (2004, September 10). *Gender identity is for everyone: Creating a paradigm of change.* Paper presented at the 6th International Congress on Sex and Gender Diversity, Manchester, England.

Sylvia Rivera Law Project. (2007). *It's war in here: A report on the treatment of transgender and intersex people in New York State men's prisons.* Retrieved March 19, 2008, from http://www.srlp.org/index.php?sec=03N&page=warinhere

Thaler, C. (2007). *Putting transgender health care myths on trial.* Retrieved July 14, 2007, from http://www.lambdalegal.org/our-work/publications/page.jsp?itemID=32007335

Tom Waddell Health Center. (2001). *Protocols for hormonal reassignment of gender.* Retrieved July 15, 2007, from http://www.dph.sf.ca.us/chn/HlthCtrs/HlthCtrDocs/TransGendprotocols.pdf

Transgender Law Center. (2005). *Peeing in peace: A resource guide for transgender activists and allies.* San Francisco: Author.

Winters, K. W. (2005). Gender dissonance: Diagnostic reform of gender identity for adults. *Journal of Human Sexuality, 17*(3/4), 71–89.

Women in Prison Project (WIPP). (2007). *Transgender issues and the criminal justice system.* Retrieved April 24, 2007, from http://www.correctionalassociation.org/publications/factsheets.htm

Wyss, S. E. (2004). 'This was my hell': The violence experienced by gender non-conforming youth in US high schools. *International Journal of Qualitative Studies in Education, 17,* 709–730.

Xavier, J. (2000). *Final report of the Washington Transgender Needs Assessment Survey.* Retrieved June 18, 2004, from http://www.gender.org/resources/dge/gea01011.pdf

Xavier, J., Hitchcock, D., Hollinshead, S., Keisling, M., Lewis, Y., Lombardi, E., Lurie, S., Sanchez, D., Singer, B., Stone, M. R., & Williams, B. (2004). *An overview of U.S. trans health priorities: A report by the Eliminating Disparities Working Group.* Retrieved March 26, 2006, from http://www.nctequality.org/HealthPriorities.pdf

Xavier, J., Honnold, J. A., & Bradford, J. (2007). *The health, health-related needs, and lifecourse experiences of transgender Virginians.* Richmond: Virginia Department of Health.

Policy statement approved by the NASW Delegate Assembly, August 2008. This policy statement supersedes the policy statement on Transgender and Gender Identity Issues approved by the Delegate Assembly in 1999 and referred by the 2005 Delegate Assembly to the 2008 Delegate Assembly for revision. For further information, contact the National Association of Social Workers, 750 First Street, NE, Suite 700, Washington, DC 20002-4241. Telephone: 202-408-8600 or 800-638-8799; e-mail: press@naswdc.org

Voter Participation

BACKGROUND

Participating in elections is important, because those elected will ultimately determine the policies that affect us all. Social workers and others have worked for years to ensure that disenfranchised populations have the right to vote. That right was given to women in 1920, and passage of the Voting Right Act of 1965 was a key victory of the civil rights movement of the 1950s and 1960s.

Women's Suffrage and the Voting Rights Act increased the number of individuals with the ability to vote, but in the 1980s people living in poverty, those with less education, and people of color remained overrepresented among U.S. citizens who did not vote. In 1982, Frances Fox Piven and Richard A. Cloward at Columbia University School of Social Work founded Human Service Employees Registration and Voter Education (Human SERVE) to promote voter registration as a routine part of application processes in government and other human service agencies (Piven & Minnite, 2008).

A major objective of Human SERVE's was to make registering to vote easier and more accessible to individuals as they applied for human service benefits. Schools of social work, NASW chapters, and national human service organizations with state and local affiliates were the focus of Human SERVE's activities. Human SERVE was organized to defend against the growing antiwelfare sentiment that led to the cutting of funding to many governmental programs, particularly income support programs. Another reason for mobilizing the political power of the social welfare community was the growing political power of organizations such as in the Moral Majority (Piven & Minnite, 2008). The most lasting legacy of Human SERVE was the National Voter Registration Act

(1993). NVRA made it possible for people to register by mail and eliminated the need to be deputized to register voters. The law permitted self-registration and required certain public welfare programs to register all clients at the point of initial application and at each annual renewal. Nongovernmental social service agencies were encouraged to register clients. In short, NVRA made it much easier to register voters, while actual voter registration requirements remained largely unchanged. There were several legal challenges to the enforcement of NVRA but, in the end, the basic features of the law were upheld and remain in effect (Piven & Minnite, 2008).

The 21st century brought a slight increase in voting in presidential elections, including 51.3 percent of the population voting in 2000, 55.3 percent of the population voting in 2004, and 56.8 percent of the population voting in 2008. The estimated 2010 voter turnout expressed as vote for highest office divided by the voting-eligible population was 40.9 percent (U.S. Elections Project, 2011). According to the *America Goes to the Polls 2010* report, the Latino vote followed its upward trend as a share of the electorate, particularly in western states. "Younger voters are the most racially and ethnically diverse age group in the electorate. Among younger voters in 2010, 65 percent were white, 16 percent black, 14 percent Hispanic, and 5 percent Asian American or "other" (Native, mixed race). Voters 30 and older were 80 percent white, 10 percent black, 7 percent Hispanic, and 3 percent Asian American and other. The larger trend was the partisan swing toward Republican candidates among older, white, and higher-income voters. The age swing was most pronounced. Voters age 65 and over went from a 2 percent gap in favor of Democrats in 2006 to a 21 point gap in favor of Republicans in 2010. Voters ages 45 to 64 had a similar shift. These shifts are not uncommon in midterm elections, especially among 'independent voters' with a history of higher anti-incumbent volatility from election to election (Nonprofit Vote, 2010).

The increase in voting in the 2008 presidential election was significant, especially because much of the increase came from greater participation among young and minority voters. Even with the increases of that year, the 2008 voter turnout continued to illustrate voter turnout disparities. Voter turnout in households making $100,000 or more a year was 79 percent, and of those living in household making less than $25,000, only 54 percent voted. Sixty-six percent of white people voted, and 57 percent of other people voted. Seventy-three percent of those with some college or more education voted, and 61 percent of those with high school education or less voted. Sixty-five percent of those with no reported disability voted, and 57 percent of those with a reported disability voted. Voter turnout for those 30 years of age or older was 67 percent, and for those under 30 years of age it was 51 percent (Hess & Herman, 2009).

The Voting Rights Act (1965), amended in 2006, established that voting rights are guaranteed in federal law, whereas voting procedures are largely controlled by the states .

Some procedures make voter participation difficult and may discourage voting, especially among groups served by social workers (Piven & Cloward, 2000). Many are not able to vote for a variety of reasons including age, immigration, and parole status. Others who do vote are often marginalized because of winner-take-all districting (Amy, 2011; FairVote, 2009; Guinier, 1993), gerrymandering (Amy, 2000; Guinier, 1993), and corporate confiscation of our politics (Avila, Lee, & Ao, 2006; Beaulieu, 1996; Choo, 1999; Clawson, Neustadtl, & Weller, 1998; Francia, Goldberg, Green, Hernson, & Wicox, 1999; League of Women Voters, n.d.).

In the wake of the disputed Bush versus Gore presidential election of 2000, Congress strengthened federal oversight of state and local election with passage of the Help America Vote Act (HAVA) (P.L. 107-252). The law provided guidelines for computerized statewide voter registration systems and provided money to states to modernize voting technology and train elections staff. HAVA also required states to allow voters to cast provisional ballots when there were disputes over whether a voter was eligible to vote or not. This legislation further addressed unresolved voting issues, including requiring all states to accept mail-in voter registration More than a dozen states have enacted major legislation since then, and 27 states now have more comprehensive voter identification requirements than mandated by the federal law. Thirteen states currently request or require voters to show a photo identification (ID); 16 other states require any form of identification. "New laws in Texas and South Carolina were on hold pending U.S. Department of Justice preclearance" (National Conference of State Legislatures [NCSL], n.d.). In Georgia and Indiana, voters without ID cast a provisional ballot and must return to election officials and show a photo ID for their ballots to be counted (NCSL, n.d.).

Following the leadership of Cloward and Piven, social workers have developed voter registration projects, including an effort by one school of social work to have all students organize voter registration projects at their field work agencies (Lane, Humpheys, Graham, Mathews, & Moriarty, 2007).

In the past decade, there have been new methods of increasing voter participation through political movements, social media, radio talk shows, and political talk shows hosted by major TV outlets. Efforts such as Rock the Vote, a nonprofit, non-partisan organization, use music, popular culture, and new technologies to engage and encourage young people to register and vote in every U.S. election (see http://www.rockthevote.org). They give young people tools to identify, learn about, and take action on the issues that affect their lives and to leverage their power in the political process. The 2008 presidential election further demonstrated how the Internet enhanced public opinion and increased voter participation. President Barack Obama's campaign used online tools and social networks to contribute to his victory as the first African American president of the United States (Turner-Lee, 2011).

ISSUE STATEMENT

Elections are the foundation of democracy. Yet those who are young, not white, poor, and less educated are disproportionately unlikely to vote.- (Pew Research Center for the People and the Press, 2006). Increasing voter participation for these groups, many of whom may be the clients of social workers, is important as those elected will make decisions on policies that affect lives of society's most vulnerable populations.

"Get Out The Vote" (GOTV) activities are important to voter participation and support the NASW *Code of Ethics*. Social workers can apply their efforts through community grassroots activities, grassroots advocacy, and volunteer or paid work on campaigns that support social work values and interests. They can also run for office at every level.

Helping clients vote their interests is more difficult but still important. According to the NASW *Code of Ethics*,

> Social workers promote social justice and social change with and on behalf of clients. "Clients" is used inclusively to refer to individuals, families, groups, organizations, and communities. Social workers are sensitive to cultural and ethnic diversity and strive to end discrimination, oppression, poverty, and other forms of social injustice. (NASW, 2008, p. 1)

One of the ethical principles: "*Social workers challenge social injustice*" means

> social workers pursue social change, particularly with and on behalf of vulnerable and oppressed individuals and groups of people. Social workers' social change efforts are focused primarily on issues of poverty, unemployment, discrimination, and other forms of social injustice. These activities seek to promote sensitivity to and knowledge about oppression and cultural and ethnic diversity. Social workers strive to ensure access to needed information, services, and resources; equality of opportunity; and meaningful participation in decision making for all people. (NASW, 2008, p. 5)

Unfortunately, in many places the voting system continues to be discriminatory (Avila et al., 2006). "Every Election Day, several million Americans are unable to vote because of a problem with their voter registration. Some may have missed their state's registration deadline. Others may have submitted their registration card to their Secretary of State or Board of Motor Vehicles, who then failed to forward it on to the local election clerk in time. Still others may have been unaware of particular voter registration rules and procedures in their jurisdiction. An estimated 3.5 million Americans with a felony conviction are barred from voting after completing their prison term" (Nonprofit Vote, 2010). Most states require voters to register before an election, with various deadlines.

Overcoming impediments to vote requires persistence, and strategies that target specific groups with culturally sensitive interventions to lower institutional barriers. Supporting alternative voting procedures such as early voting, voting by mail, online voting, and proportional voting may be effective. As of 2011, 10 states have some form of Election Day voter registration including Idaho, Iowa, Maine, Minnesota, Montana, New Hampshire, North Carolina, Wisconsin, Wyoming, and Washington, DC. Montana began Election Day voter registration in 2006, North Carolina in 2007, and Iowa in 2008. Connecticut also has Election Day registration, but only for presidential elections. North Dakota has no voter registration requirement at all (Demos, n.d.). According to the *America Goes to the Polls* report (Nonprofit Vote, 2010), states that have Election Day registration and allow voters to fix a registration problem or register on Election Day have had consistently higher voter participation rates, even after adjusting for all other turnout factors. This trend continued in 2010. It is estimated that 27 percent to 29 percent of voters cast ballots early in 2010, well above the 19 percent of the electorate who voted early in 2006.

Many local elections of school boards and councils are now using proportional voting and have found this to be helpful in getting more people to participate (Amy, McBride, & Richie, 2000). Other efforts may include instant runoffs, open primaries, cross or multiple endorsements, and Election Day registration.

POLICY STATEMENT

To increase voter participation among social work clients and others, NASW supports

■ nonpartisan voter education programs by nongovernmental and public agencies that inform clients about the positions of candidates and how they are affected.

■ full implementation and enforcement of the National Voter Registration Act, the Help America Vote Act, and the Voting Rights Act of 1965.

■ social workers and social work students who work to increase voter participation by registering voters, organizing GOTV activities through nonpartisan education activities, and assisting the public and clients on Election Day.

■ social workers working at the polls on Election Day and being part of the postelection accountability and monitoring activities.

■ voter privacy, accuracy of the vote count, and assurances that all votes are counted and recorded.

■ continued efforts to reform and modernize voter registration laws that make it easier for people to register and vote.

■ efforts to make Election Day a national holiday.

■ full restoration of voting rights for all convicted felons once they have completed their legal obligations.

■ responsible, accurate, and fair media coverage, and public debate to promote informed voter participation.

■ working with other groups and organizations dedicated to increasing voter participation, especially efforts to help people living in poverty, people of color, those with disabilities, those who experience homelessness, elderly people, single parents, and others who are tra-

ditionally oppressed and often do not participate in elections.

REFERENCES

Amy, D. J. (2000). *Behind the ballot box: A citizen's guide to voting systems.* Westport, CT: Praeger.

Amy, D. J. (2011, November). *Instant runoff voting: No substitute for proportional representation.* Retrieved from http://www.mthol yoke.edu/acad/polit/damy/articles/irv. htm

Amy, D. J., McBride, F., & Richie, R. (2000, November/December). New means for political empowerment: Proportional voting. *Poverty and Race Research Action Council Newsletter, 9*(6). Retrieved from http:// www.prrac.org/display_newsletter.php? text_id=138&item_id=1789&newsletter_id =53&header=November/December 2000%20Newsletter

Avila, J., Lee, E., & Ao, T. (2006). *Voting rights in California: 1982–2006.* Retrieved from http:// www.civilrights.org/voting-rights/vra/ states.html

Beaulieu, D. (1996). The public should finance election campaigns. *U.S. Catholic, 61*(10), 15–20.

Choo, K. Y. (1999). *Influence of money on politics.* Retrieved from http://www.political-reform.net/money_politic.htm

Clawson, D., Neustadtl, A., & Weller M. (1998). *Dollars and votes: How business campaign contributions subvert democracy.* Philadelphia: Temple University Press.

Demos. (n.d.). *Election day registration-state by state information.* Retrieved from http:// archive.demos.org/page93.cfm

FairVote. (2009). *Redistricting.* Retrieved from http://www.fairvote.org/redistricting

Francia, P. L., Goldberg, R. E., Green, J. C., Hernson, P. S., & Wicox, C. (1999). Individual donors in the 1996 federal elections. In J. C. Green (Ed.), *Financing the 1996 election* (pp. 151–152). Armonk, NY: M. E. Sharpe.

Guinier, L. (1993). Groups, representation, and race-conscious districting: A case of the emperor's clothes. 71 *Texas Law Review* 1589.

Help America Vote Act, P.L. 107-252, 1666, Stat. 116 (2002).

Hess, D. R., & Herman, J. (2009). *Representational bias in the 2008 electorate.* Retrieved from http://www.projectvote.org/electorate-composition.html

Lane, S. R., Humphreys, N. A., Graham, E., Mathews, N., & Moriarty, J. (2007). Voter registration: Empowering clients through agency-based voter registration. *Journal of Policy Practice, 6*(4), 79–93.

League of Women Voters. (n.d.). *Money in elections.* Retrieved from http://www.lwv.org/AM/Template.cfm?Section=Campaign_Finance_Reform

National Association of Social Workers. (2008). *Code of ethics of the National Association of Social Workers.* Washington, DC: Author.

National Conference of State Legislatures. (n.d.). *Voter identification requirements.* Retrieved from http://www.ncsl.org/LegislaturesElections/ElectionsCampaigns/StateRequirementsforVoterID/tabid/16602/Default.aspx

National Voter Registration Act, P.L. 103-31, 107 Stat. 77 (1993).

Nonprofit Vote. (2010). *America goes to the polls 2010.* Retrieved from http://www.nonprofitvote.org/voter-turnout-main.html

Pew Research Center for the People and the Press. (2006) *Who votes, who doesn't and why.* Retrieved from http://people-press.org/2006/10/18/who-votes-who-doesnt-and-why/

Piven, F. F., & Cloward, R. A. (2000). *Why Americans still don't vote: And why politicians want it that way.* Boston: Beacon Press.

Piven, F. F., & Minnite, L. C. (2008). Voter education. In T. Mizrahi & L. E. Davis (Eds-in-Chief), *Encyclopedia of social work* (20th ed., pp. 272–277) [Electronic version]. Washington, DC and New York: NASW Press and Oxford University Press.

Turner-Lee, N. (2011). Where do we go from here? *Minority Media and Telecommunications Council's Broadband and Social Justice Summit.* Retrieved from http://broadbandandsocialjustice.org/2011/01/dr-nicol-turner-lee-on-the-2010-elections-where-do-we-go-from-here/

U.S. Elections Project. (2011). *2010 General election turnout rates.* Retrieved from http://elections.gmu.edu/Turnout_2010G.html

Voting Rights Act, 42 U.S.C. §§ 1973–1973aa-6 (1965, amended in 2006).

NASW Members with Primary Responsibility for Revision of This Policy

First Draft Revision:

Nancy Humphreys (CT)

Policy Panelists:

Jason Ostrander (MA)
Renee Koubiadis (NJ)
Karen Franklin (TN)
Joel Rubin (IL)
Mary Bishop (TX)
Natalia Salinas (CA)
Lawanna Barron (GA)

Policy statement approved by the NASW Delegate Assembly, August 2011. This statement supersedes the policy statement on Voter Participation approved by the Delegate Assembly in August 2002 and 1990 and reconfirmed in 1999. For further information, contact the National Association of Social Workers, 750 First Street, NE, Suite 700, Washington, DC 20002-4241. Telephone: 202-408-8600; e-mail: press@naswdc.org

Welfare Reform

BACKGROUND

Enacted in 1996, the Personality Responsibility and Work Opportunity Reconciliation Act dramatically changed the way the federal government provides financial assistance to needy families. This act created Temporary Assistance for Needy Families (TANF), which limited assistance to 60 months and required recipients to work. However, TANF failed to contain appropriate provisions for education and job training. There were strong work requirements, a performance bonus to reward states for moving welfare recipients into jobs, state maintenance of effort requirements, comprehensive child support enforcement, and some supports for families in moving them from welfare to work, including increased funding for child care and guaranteed medical coverage (U.S. Department of Health and Human Services, 2005). Major provisions of the act include the following:

■ Welfare recipients will be required to work after two years.

■ Cash payments will be provided for no more than five years during recipients' lives.

■ Unwed mothers under 18 years of age are ineligible for assistance unless they live in the home of an adult relative or in another adult-supervised arrangement.

■ States will be allowed to deny cash payments to children born into families already receiving assistance.

■ State must comply with mandated work participation rates to maintain block grants (Ozawa & Kirk, 1996).

Although welfare rolls declined by 60 percent between August 1996 and September 2006, from 4.41 million to 1.76 million families, the cycle of poverty and permanent self-sufficiency were not outcomes for the many single mothers and poor families. According to the U.S. Department of Health and Human Services (2007), "Only 32 percent of TANF families with an adult participated for enough hours to count and almost three-fifths of TANF adults had no reported hours in work activities, nevertheless using up their time-limited benefits" (p. 2).

Changes in the law that mandated states to engage TANF families in productive work activities that would facilitate self-sufficiency included the following:

■ First, the law changed the base year of the calculation of the caseload reduction credit from FY 1995 to FY 2005. The caseload reduction credit had inadvertently undermined TANF work requirements.

■ The law included in the work participation rates families in separate state programs, which were previously excluded from the rates. Under prior law and rules, some states moved families to programs essentially identical to their TANF programs but funded with state money used toward the maintenance-of-effort (MOE) requirement.

■ The law eliminated provisions for the High Performance Bonus and the Illegitimacy Reduction Bonus and replaced them with a $150 million-a-year research, demonstration, and technical assistance fund. This fund is for competitive grants to strengthen family formation, promote healthy marriages, support responsible fatherhood, and improve coordination between tribal TANF and child welfare services.

- The DRA expanded a state's ability to meet its MOE requirement. States may now count expenditures that provide pro-family benefits and services to anyone, without regard to financial need or family composition, if the expenditure is to prevent and reduce the incidence of out-of-wedlock births (TANF purpose 3), or encourage the formation and maintenance of two-parent married families (TANF purpose 4).

- It increased federal child care funding by $200 million per year, $1 billion over five years. With the inclusion of state matching funds required to draw down these additional dollars, new funding for child care totals $1.8 billion over five years (U.S. Department of Health and Human Services, 2007).

Because of the drastic increase in families working without a significant increase in earnings, working poverty has replaced welfare. According to Carnevale and Reich (2000), although the overall rate of poverty has declined, poor people are poorer and more working families are living in poverty. Because educational access is inextricably linked to economic security, poor single women and families must have access to education and job training to achieve permanent self-sufficiency and economic security. Education and training programs must not be seen as separate entities from work but as part of a continuum of activities that result in work.

A major facet of welfare reform is supporting healthy marriages and responsible fatherhood. Congress stipulated in the Welfare Reform Law of 1996 that three of the four purposes of the block grant to states should be related to promoting healthy marriages; when the Deficit Reduction Act of 2005 was signed in 2006 to reauthorize welfare reform, $150 million was included for support of programs designed to help couples form and sustain healthy marriages (Dion, 2006).

ISSUE STATEMENT

The social work profession is keenly aware that poverty serves as an impediment to promoting the general welfare of society from the local and global levels. It is an impediment to the development of people, their communities, and their social environments. Recent policy efforts directed at offering a political decision to address a complex issue has not been effective at moving individuals from living in poverty to self-sufficiency. *Self-sufficiency* can be defined as able to provide for your own needs without help from others. It is an ideal. Social workers realize that for some, true self-sufficiency is not attainable to all members of society. There are members of our communities who because of disabilities and limitations cannot achieve this ideal.

The work requirements of TANF and other barriers forced many single-parent recipients to leave school to maintain their welfare payments (Price, 2005). During 1995–1996, more than 650,000 welfare recipients were enrolled in education beyond high school. By 1999 this number decreased by almost one half (U.S. Department of Education, 1999). Many jobs in today's job market require credentials, skills, and cognitive tasks. Welfare recipients with low skills and educational levels are faring poorly in the labor market. The most successful welfare programs use more than one approach, only job search for some and for others, career development, short-term training, and education that are focused on obtaining specific jobs. Even though earnings have been shown to increase with these mixed strategies, recipients still remain in poverty (Gueron & Hamilton, 2002). More attention needs to be placed on poverty reduction strategies that lead to career development. Research demonstrates that mothers' successful educational outcomes significantly affect their children's cognitive abilities and educational achievements (Kates, 2001).

In addressing the effects of poverty, social workers need to acknowledge that poverty imposes an enormous cost on society at large. The lost potential of children reared in poor households, the lower productivity and earnings of poor adults, the poor health, increased crime, and broken neighborhoods all serve as counterproductive to moving individuals, families, and communities toward self-sufficiency.

It is now the responsibility of organizations such as NASW to engage in this policy-making process by campaigning to change voters' stereotypes about poor people, offering a humane and efficacious approach to income assistance programs, and working to modify the impact of the 1996 legislation on poor people and families. As stated earlier, this legislation rests on the assumption that the economy and the job market can provide sufficient employment to produce the necessary income for those who are now receiving welfare benefits.

POLICY STATEMENT

NASW affirms the value and importance of work in a free market economy. We acknowledge the importance of wealth building for all citizens, while being clear that our economic system has structural inequities that keep some individuals and families poor. We reject the perspective that views failure to develop wealth as a personal failure without reference to these structural inequities. As Ozawa and Kirk (1996) noted, "the economic system and the wage structure are . . . changing rapidly. Under these circumstances of social change, it is inevitable that some mothers and their children will be economically dependent. Blaming them for their economic predicament and for other social problems is not only simplistic, it is a cruel hoax." (p. 195)

Key principles include the following:

■ the restoration of a safety net that protects the most vulnerable individuals while supporting their efforts to become economically self-sufficient.

■ universal social welfare system that does not stigmatize, categorize, or pathologize people.

■ entitlement of all people to be treated with dignity, respect, and well-being regardless of their economic status.

NASW supports

■ comprehensive child support for all single custodial parents.

■ universal health care.

■ meaningful employment training (both postsecondary education and skill building) for available employment opportunities.

■ higher education for people on welfare that will provide opportunities for economic security.

■ assistance in obtaining employment at a living wage, including partnerships with the private sector; healthy, safe working conditions; child care; and unemployment insurance.

■ increase in EITC (earned income tax credit) participation in all states.

■ adequate services to address domestic violence, sexual abuse, mental health needs, substance abuse, and literacy problems.

■ the need to address problems that contribute to poverty, such as substance abuse, domestic violence, mental illness, illiteracy, and others.

■ policies to encourage job creation and campaigns to expand definitions of job training and efforts to unionize low-wage jobs.

■ social work redefining itself regarding income maintenance services.

■ an economic system that ensures every person has a job at a livable wage and safe and humane working conditions.

■ the recognition of the economic value of child rearing and caregiving.

■ policies on the administration of welfare benefits and programs that promote national standards and policies for the delivery of benefits and programs that serve as a safety net for all people.

■ advocacy at the state level for the development and improvement of state welfare policies in the various state legislatures and with local officials.

■ collaborative public–private efforts to move welfare recipients into work experiences that offer a living wage, appropriate levels of training, adequate health benefits, and an intentional effort to provide opportunities for economic advancement.

■ policies that protect the entitlement status of Medicaid and food stamps for all who meet eligibility criteria, including immigrants, refugees, and noncitizens.

■ the integration and expansion of professional social work personnel into the delivery of public and private social services for welfare recipients.

- advocacy efforts for legislation and funding for research activities that track recipients who are dropped from welfare programs. Data collection also is essential to document the subsequent policy impact on child development, employment, and increases in child abuse and termination of parental rights. In addition, research must investigate the long-term effects of welfare reform on poverty.

- the integration of welfare policies with housing, child welfare, economic, and mental health policies so there is a holistic approach to reducing and eliminating poverty.

- policies that allow people to receive benefits for as long as they need them and eliminate punitive measures such as full family sanctions and family caps, including sanctions imposed during the time period that health, domestic violence, family, and addiction problems are being addressed.

- the promotion of strategies that enable welfare recipients to build personal and financial assets, such as individual development accounts.

- promotion of intensive work supports for low-income families with children, including child care subsidies, Medicaid and expansion of SCHIP, food stamp program promotion, and EITC availability.

- the promotion and support of intensive case management services to welfare teenagers, elimination of the living-arrangement rule, and relaxation of school attendance requirements as per individual circumstances.

REFERENCES

Carnevale, A. P., & Reich, K. (2000). *A piece of the puzzle: How states can use education to make work pay for welfare recipients.* Princeton, NJ: Education Testing Services.

Dion, M. R. (2006, December). *The Oklahoma Marriage Initiative: An overview of the longest-running statewide marriage initiative in the U.S.* [ASPE Research Brief]. Washington, DC: U.S. Department of Health and Human Services, Office of the Assistant Secretary for Planning and Evaluation, Office of Human Services Policy.

Gueron, J. M., & Hamilton, G. (2002). *The role of education and training in welfare reform.* Brookings Institution.

Kates, E. (2001, Summer). Welfare reform and access to education: Penalizing mothers and children. *CYD Journal, 2*(3).

Ozawa, M. N., & Kirk, S. A. (1996). Welfare reform [Editorial]. *Social Work Research, 20,* 194–195.

Personal Responsibility and Work Opportunity Reconciliation Act of 1996, P.L. 104-193, 110 Stat. 2105.

Price, C. (2005, September). Reforming welfare reform postsecondary education policy: Two state case studies in political culture, organizing, and advocacy. *Journal of Sociology and Social Welfare, 32*(3).

U.S. Department of Health and Human Services. (2005). *1996 Personal Responsibility and Work Opportunity Reconciliation Act.* Washington, DC: Author.

U.S. Department of Health and Human Services. (2007). *The next phase of welfare reform* (pp. 1–7). Washington, DC: Author.

Policy statement approved by the NASW Delegate Assembly, August 2008. This policy statement supersedes the policy statement on Temporary Assistance for Needy Families: Welfare Reform approved by the Delegate Assembly in 1999 and referred by the 2005 Delegate Assembly to the 2008 Delegate Assembly for revision, the policy statement on Aid to Families with Dependent Children Reform approved by the Delegate Assembly in 1990, and the policy statement on Welfare Reform approved by the Delegate Assembly in 1987. For further information, contact the National Association of Social Workers, 750 First Street, NE, Suite 700, Washington, DC 20002-4241. Telephone: 202-408-8600 or 800-638-8799; e-mail: press@naswdc.org

Women in the Social Work Profession

BACKGROUND

The history of social work is a "herstory" of female reformers, suffragists, and charity workers (Vandiver, 1980). A partial list of social work pioneers includes such prestigious names as Grace Abbott, Jane Addams, Sophonisba Breckenridge, Florence Kelly, Julia Lathrop, Lillian Ward, Mary Richmond, Bertha Reynolds, and Francis Perkins. African American reformers were prominent as well and included such luminaries as Mary Church Terrell, Ida B. Wells-Barnett (Peebles-Wilkins & Francis (1990), and Nannie Helen Burroughs (Perkins, 1997).

Although women were prominent in the newly developing profession of social work, men often held managerial positions and directed the frontline, and predominantly female, workforce. As early as 1880 women noted and protested this uneven representation (Vandiver, 1980). Social work frequently has been referred to as a "female-dominated profession," although that supposition has been challenged over the years (Giovannoni & Purvine, 1974; Meyer, 1982). McPhail (2004) contends that a more accurate characterization of social work is a "female majority, male-dominated" profession.

Today women continue to make important contributions to the social work profession while comprising the numerical majority of social workers. For instance, 87.8 percent of students awarded baccalaureate (BSW) degrees and 84.6 percent awarded master's (MSW) degrees in 1999 and 2000 were women (Lennon, 2002). Women represent approximately 73 percent of all social work doctoral degrees (Di Palma, 2005). A recent representative sample of NASW members found that 80 percent were female (NASW, 2005a). In a book celebrating the faces and voices of social work exemplars (Dumez, 2003), 43 percent of the social workers featured are women.

Women in social work, like their male counterparts, demonstrate a range of professional skills; assist people in overcoming some of life's most difficult challenges, such as poverty, discrimination, abuse, and addiction (NASW, n.d.); act in a variety of roles such as academics, clinical practitioners, activists, educators, legislators, and policy analysts; bring knowledge, training, determination, professionalism, energy, and enthusiasm to the complex profession of social work; and epitomize social work values as they work for social and economic justice. The strengths of female social workers are a wonder to behold as they make a difference in the lives of people every day.

However, women in social work face challenges inside the profession. Social workers operate in a world that continues to reflect traditional male bias and power in its institutions, structures, and theoretical models. Dressel (1987) argued that "the numerical dominance of women in social work has not translated into authority, power, and pay equity or equality" (p. 297). Female social workers are not immune from the problems women in many other professions confront in the workplace, including pay inequities, the glass ceiling, sexual harassment, and a problem that has only recently received increased attention, the maternal wall. As a result, female social workers face an ironic situation: working in a profession largely comprised of women, primarily serving women and their children, they are often second-class citizens in the profession they are said to dominate. Although women in the social work profession have made much progress, inequities continue to exist.

Pay Inequities

Gender-based wage disparities in the social work profession have been documented since 1961, when the first labor force study was conducted by NASW (Becker, 1961) and have been reaffirmed in subsequent investigations (Gibelman & Schervish, 1997; Huber & Orlando, 1995). In an analysis of the *Current Population Survey*, a U.S. Census-administered monthly survey of the labor market that allows respondents to make their own determination of whether they are a social worker, the average hourly wage in 1999 for social workers was $15.56 per hour for female respondents and $17.90 per hour for male respondents (Barth, 2003). Surveying a random sample of Pennsylvania social workers in 1994, Koeske and Krowinski (2004) found male social workers' salaries significantly higher than female social workers' salaries, even after controlling for years of experience in social work, job role, and status; female social workers received about 90 cents to the dollar made by male social workers, a difference of more than $3,500 over the course of a year. Among NASW members in 1995, the median income of female respondents was $34,135 compared with $37,503 for male respondents (Gibelman & Schervish, 1997), a difference of $3,368. A random sample of regular NASW members conducted in 2000 revealed that men earned about $10,780 more than women, with a median income for men reported at $54,290 and for women, $43,510 (NASW, 2002).

Comparing salaries by industry and the proportion of women in the industry, Gibelman (2003) found that "the proportion of women in an occupational group has an inverse relationship to weekly salary levels; that is, as the proportion goes up, salaries go down" (p. 25). Although minor exceptions exist, Gibelman noted that the pattern is consistent and strong.

Pay inequities in social work reflect pay inequities across the board in women's employment. For example, the U.S. Census Bureau

(2000) reported that the median annual earnings of year-round, full-time women in the paid labor force were 73 percent of the median annual earnings of year-round, full-time men in the labor force. The numbers show racial as well as gender disparities: African American women earned 65 percent and Latinas earned 52 percent of their male counterparts' earnings.

Glass Ceilings and Escalators

The U.S. Department of Labor defined the *glass ceiling* as "those artificial barriers based on attitudinal or organizational bias that prevent qualified individuals from advancing upward into management-level positions" (cited in Gibelman & Schervish, 1993, p. 443). In a study of NASW members, Gibelman & Schervish (1997) found evidence of a glass ceiling in social work; after accumulating 10 or more years of experience, 32.5 percent of men compared with 22.7 percent of women held management positions. Zunz (1991) found that although female social workers seem to have equal access to education, training, and mentors, they move into management positions at a slower pace than men, often lacking self-confidence and finding it a riskier proposition than do men. Another study, based on interviews with female leaders in human services organizations, identified respondents' greatest barriers to professional advancement as prejudice and discrimination based on race, ethnicity, gender, and heterosexism (Gardella & Haynes, 2004).

In a study of undergraduate directors at accredited BSW programs and deans or chairs of accredited MSW programs from 1985 to 1996, DiPalma and Topper (2001) found that the percentage of women directors of BSW programs increased significantly over the years, from 43.4 percent in 1985 to 57.2 percent in 1996. The number of women deans or chairs of MSW programs also increased during this same time period, from 29.3 percent in 1985 to 44.7 percent in 1996. The researchers attributed the gains to two factors: (1) concerted efforts of the Council on Social Work Education's (CSWE) Commission on the Role and Status of Women, and (2) an increase in the number of women in social work academia. This study is encouraging and, as the title of the article suggests, could mean the glass ceiling is beginning to crack.

In social work academia Petchers (1996) found that although there was an increase in the number of women faculty in graduate social work programs from 1972 to 1993, many of these women were clustered in nontenure-track positions. For instance, from 1983 to 1993 the most common rank for male faculty in graduate programs was full professor, whereas female faculty members were more likely to hold a nonprofessorial rank, such as instructor or lecturer. Petchers noted that "as the status level increased, the percentage of female faculty decreased" (pp. 25–26). Di Palma (2005) found that although women continue to be underrepresented on faculties of colleges and universities across disciplines, in contrast women social work faculty have made greater progress: by the year 2000 in graduate social work education 43 percent of full professors were women, 62 percent of associate professors, and 67 percent of assistant professors. Di Palmer also noted the dramatic increase in the number of positions for both men and women in nontenure-track positions, in a similar gender ratio as the assistant professor position.

In a study women faculty were asked about their perceptions of obtaining tenure, and they noted the following obstacles: Most tenured faculty are men and thereby dominate the tenure review process; female faculty were perceived to be held to a higher standard of work and effort than male faculty; women felt responsible for more of the "organizational housework" or administrative tasks than male faculty; and in the tenure process more emphasis was placed on scholarship (especially quantitative research methods) than teaching and service, which ran counter to the preferences of many respondents (DiNitto, Aguilar, Franklin, & Jordan, 1995). In an informal survey of CSWE women board members, concerns for women in social work education included gender disparities in salaries, conservative backlash and a drift away from affirmative action, the glass ceiling, lack of real power, and rising expectations for promotion, tenure, and assuming administrative tasks (Bentley, Valentine, & Haskett, 1999).

Researchers also have found that men in the profession take on administrative tasks and move into administrative positions more often and at a much faster rate than women, with significant differences appearing three to 10 years after receiving an MSW degree (Gibelman & Schervish, 1993; Lambert, 1994; Zunz, 1991). Koeske and Krowinski (2004) found that men were more likely to occupy administrative roles, whereas women were more likely to be in direct practice positions. In a study that examined the status of men in predominantly female professions (social work, library science, and teaching), Williams (1995) found that men in these professions often received preference in hiring, were closely mentored by other men in the profession, and were actively encouraged to move into leadership positions. In contrast to the glass ceiling facing women moving into traditionally "male professions," Williams described the opposite phenomenon, men moving quickly up the management ladder in the so-called "women's professions," as analogous to riding a "glass escalator."

Maternal Wall

The glass ceiling phenomenon has received increased attention over the past couple of decades, but less attention has been given to the maternal wall, which refers to the problems women face in juggling their roles as employed workers with that of mother and caregiver. In a survey of university faculty in California, Mason and Goulden (2004) found that tenure-track faculty differ from their male counterparts in that they are less likely to marry and have children and more likely to divorce. The authors conclude that, "rather than blatant discrimination against women, it is the long work hours and the required travel, precisely at the time when most women with advanced degrees have children and begin families, that force women to leave the fast-track professions" (p. 90).

This problem has largely been invisible, often seen as a personal rather than political struggle for women based on their "choice" to have children or care for aging parents. This attitude is changing. As Crittenden (2001) said, "What is needed is across-the-board recognition—in the workplace, in the family, in the law, and in social policy—that someone has to do the necessary work of raising children and sustaining families, and that the reward for such vital work should not be professional marginalization, a loss of status, and an increased risk of poverty" (p. 10). This unequal distribution of caregiving between women and men affects women in the social work profession as well as the largely female clientele they serve.

Because most female social work researchers are academicians, not surprising, research on the status of women in social work has primarily focused on women in the academy. Less is known about how female social workers fare outside of the academy. A random sample of 10,000 social workers drawn from social work licensure lists in 48 states and the District of Colombia shed some light on social workers outside academic settings (NASW, 2005b). Female social workers were found in many practice settings with women comprising 90 percent of social workers in the field of aging, 79 percent in behavioral health, 83 percent in children and families, and 87 percent in health care venues. Although other results were not reported by gender, the study found serious challenges facing social workers today. For instance, the social work labor force is older than most professions, the current labor force is expected to decrease significantly over the next two years, the profession is not keeping pace with population trends in its ability to attract social workers of color, and social workers have experienced increased demands in their work in recent years, but decreased resources and supports. How these challenges affect women similarly or differently than their male counterparts is unknown.

Other Inequities

Sexual harassment has been documented in social work at agencies and educational institutions (Risley-Curtiss & Hudson, 1998; Singer, 1989). Across the board men have been the most frequent perpetrators of sexual harassment, and women have been the most common victims. Sexual harassment has been categorized as violence against women and as a form of economic coercion (Hill, 2003). Another serious issue for women in social work is client violence perpetrated against social workers. Newhill (1996) found gender to be a risk factor in client violence, and other studies have documented client threats or physical violence directed toward social workers (Spencer & Munch, 2003).

Publication rates have traditionally been higher among male than female faculty, including among African American scholars (Bentley, Hutchison, & Green, 1994; Rosenblatt, Turner, Patterson, & Rollosson, 1970; Schiele, 1992). In addition, although the majority of social workers and social work clients are female, traditional male-model theories continue to be taught (that is, Freud, Erickson, and Piaget) instead of newer theories that take into account female growth and development and the structural issues that negatively affect women.

Curricular content on women had to be mandated for inclusion in social work education in 1977 (Bentley et al., 1999), and evidence suggests that it still is not fully integrated in the social work curriculum (Figueira-McDonough, Netting, & Nichols-Casebolt, 1998). To more fully integrate gender in the curriculum, Nichols-Casebolt, Figueira-McDonough, and Netting (2000) suggested assessing both the school's resources and culture to plan an effective change strategy that matches appropriate tactics with the school's culture.

ISSUE STATEMENT

Although it may seem ironic that a profession often termed "female-dominated" would need a policy statement on the status of women in the profession, such a statement is necessary. Although some of the greatest social reformers have been women, Jane Addams, Mary Richmond, Ida Wells-Barnett, and Mary Church Terrell to name a few, the personal and structural sexism and discrimination that women face in the larger society exists in the profession as well. Rather than being an exception to the systemic discrimination women face in the world, the social work profession is a microcosm of that world.

This state of affairs may be invisible to many within and outside the social work profession for several reasons (McPhail, 2004). First, the fact that historically women have played an important role in the profession and are frequently (and naively) credited with founding the profession may cause some to overlook the subordinate status of women within the profession. The fact that women comprise the numerical majority of social workers often conceals the power imbalance in the profession. But, as observed in other professions and societies, having the numerical majority may not translate into wielding the majority of the power. In addition, the semantics of calling a profession female-dominated or a "women's profession" can distract or disguise the second-class status of women within the profession.

The background provided in this policy statement systematically makes the case that women do not dominate the profession, and in fact, are often subordinate in terms of salary, prestige, position, and the curriculum. Although the profession has taken helpful and effective steps to document and address some of these inequities, such as NASW's affirmative action stance that places women in leadership positions in proportion to their numbers among the membership, much work needs to be done.

Some might describe the present time period "post-patriarchal" or "post-feminist," however, the research findings presented here challenge such a characterization. Although gains have been made and can be celebrated, social workers must continue to examine and document the status of women in the profession and seek new, innovative ways to support women. Such a stance is necessary, fair, and can be accomplished without blaming or denigrating men.

Some social workers might believe that the focus on women in the profession is misplaced and constitutes a distraction from work with clients. A helpful metaphor to address this potential concern is the preflight emergency instructions given by flight attendants to passengers who are traveling with small children or those needing additional assistance. Passengers are advised to first put on their own oxygen mask before assisting others. Similarly, if female social workers do not advocate for and empower themselves by confronting sexism

and discrimination in their professional lives, it is hard (and hypocritical) to teach those skills and strategies to female clients operating in the larger world. The health and well-being of social work clients should not come at the expense of female social workers.

Although women have made great strides, the successes have been uneven. For instance, although some structural barriers have fallen in the public realm, women struggle with inequality in the home, which affects their lives at work. In addition, although some institutions have changed to accommodate women in the workforce, the underlying institutional structures, theoretical models, and work requirements continue to be imbued with a subtle, and not so subtle, bias that privileges men. The mixed messages women receive and the multiple roles they are expected to play have profound consequences for both female social workers and their clients. In addition, the gains that have been achieved often benefit women differently based on their race, ethnicity, sexual identity, socioeconomic status, caregiving roles, and level of ability.

POLICY STATEMENT

NASW has actively responded to the issues that negatively affect women in the social work profession—in the workplace, in social work education, and in program development and design. According to the *Code of Ethics of the National Association of Social Workers* (NASW, 2000), social workers should act to prevent and eliminate discrimination in organizations and in society. In 1973 NASW adopted a policy to address sexism and sex discrimination in the profession and in society. An affirmative action plan was initiated to ensure that NASW leadership would reflect the racial and gender composition of the membership and that women and people of color would have equal employment opportunities in NASW.

The National Committee on Women's Issues became a standing committee of NASW in 1975 to encourage and monitor activities aimed at the elimination of sexism in the association, the profession, and society. In 1976 NASW's journal *Social Work* published a special issue on women; in 1977 the NASW Delegate Assembly adopted a policy statement on women's issues; in 1980 the first NASW Conference on Social Work Practice with Women was held. In 1987 the Delegate Assembly revised the policy statement on women's issues to express a commitment to increase women's leadership in professional organizations and social services agencies and to ensure equal pay for men and women with similar qualifications and responsibilities. The 1993 Delegate Assembly approved a resolution titled "NASW Personnel Policies on Sexual Harassment" that addressed the need for educational materials, personnel policies, and procedures to protect NASW employees and social workers from sexual harassment. The NASW *Standards for Social Work Personnel Practices* (NASW, 2003) addresses discriminatory hiring and personnel actions, comparable worth, and employer's support of the family responsibilities of caregivers. NASW has made progress in addressing these issues within the organization and the larger society; however, much remains to be done.

Therefore, NASW supports the following:

■ continued attention to and documentation of the status of women in the social work profession, both within and outside of social work academia, including disparities faced by subpopulations of women due to race, ethnicity, disability, and sexual identity, focusing on, but not limited to, pay inequities, leadership and tenure-track positions, sexual harassment, gender inclusion in the curriculum, publication rates in professional journals, disparities in receipt of research funding, and the work–family conflict.

■ identifying and overcoming barriers to the advancement of women in social work, including internal and external obstacles, by teaching female social work students job negotiation, confidence-building, and assertiveness skills; establishing support and networking groups for women planning a managerial career; challenging internalized restrictive gender-role stereotypes; increasing management training for women including financial statement analysis and budget development; educating social workers about pay inequities in the profession; teaching women about legal remedies such as

filing a claim with the Equal Employment Opportunity Commission; using the accreditation process to hold schools accountable for attention to women's issues; continuing to develop mentoring programs for women starting early in their careers; and increasing union membership and the use of comparable worth policies as a way to increase women's salaries.

■ adopting and teaching non-oppressive leadership styles to male and female social work administrators that more congruently fit both social work values and women's preferred style of interactional leadership.

■ continued use of affirmative action programs inside and outside NASW as an effective tool for the advancement of women and other marginalized groups, while countering the current backlash and premature curtailing of such programs across the nation.

■ initiatives that maximize the flexibility of working conditions to support the caregiving roles of both female and male social workers, including tenure-track flexibility, better and less-expensive child care, and improved maternity and paternity leaves.

■ policies and procedures designed to eliminate violence and sexual harassment in social work agencies and educational institutions and research to document the extent of these problems and the outcomes of educational and intervention efforts.

■ working for the advancement of women in academia. Petchers (1996) recommended setting goals and strategies and specific, objective, and quantifiable targets for the proportional representation of women at each academic rank, and strengthening the function of accreditation review to enforce remedial measures. DiNitto and colleagues (1995) recommended greater value placed on qualitative research, teaching, and service; adequate representation of women on promotion and tenure committees; and male faculty taking greater responsibility for organizational tasks.

■ conducting research that more fully examines the reasons for pay and position inequities in social work. For instance, are the barriers internal and external? Are women choosing less well paid and lower status positions to better juggle work and family? And if so, why must women choose between family and work while men are less likely to have to choose between the two? Are the barriers the result of institutionalized sexism and discrimination? How are the barriers similar and different for women of color, lesbian women, and women with disabilities? Research must take the profession beyond documenting the disparities to understanding them more fully and addressing them with change at structural levels.

REFERENCES

Barth, M. C. (2003). Social work labor market: A first look. *Social Work, 48*, 9–19.

Becker, R. (1961). *Study of salaries of NASW members.* New York: National Association of Social Workers.

Bentley, K. J., Hutchison, E. D., & Green, R. G. (1994). Women as social work scholars: An empirical analysis. *Affilia, 9*, 171–189.

Bentley, K. J., Valentine, D., & Haskett, G. (1999). Women's issues and social work accreditation: A status report. *Affilia, 14*, 344–363.

Crittenden, A. (2001). *The price of motherhood: Why the most important job in the world is still the least valued.* New York: Henry Holt.

DiNitto, D., Aguilar, M. A., Franklin, C., & Jordan, C. (1995). Over the edge? Women and tenure in today's academic environment. *Affilia, 10*, 255–279.

Di Palma, S. (2005). Progress for women faculty in social work academia. *Affilia, 20*, 71–86.

Di Palma, S. L., & Topper, G. G. (2001). Social work academia: Is the glass ceiling beginning to crack? *Affilia, 16*, 31–45.

Dressel, P. (1987). Patriarchy and social welfare work. *Social Problems, 34*, 294–309.

Dumez, E. W. (Ed.). (2003). *Celebrating social work: Faces and voices of the formative years.* Alexandria, VA: Council on Social Work Education.

Figueira-McDonough, J., Netting, F. E., & Nichols-Casebolt, A. (Eds.). (1998). *The role of gender in practice knowledge: Claiming half of the human experience.* New York: Garland.

Gardella, L. G., & Haynes, K. S. (2004). *A dream and a plan: A woman's path to leadership in human services.* Washington, DC: NASW Press.

Gibelman, M. (2003). So how far have we come?: Pestilent and persistent gender gap in pay. *Social Work, 48*, 22–32.

Gibelman, M., & Schervish, P. H. (1993). The glass ceiling in social work: Is it shatterproof? *Affilia, 8*, 442–455.

Gibelman, M., & Schervish, P. H. (1997). *Who we are: A second look.* Washington, DC: NASW Press.

Giovannoni, J. M., & Purvine, M. E. (1974). The myth of the social work matriarchy. In *Official Proceedings 100th Annual Forum of the National Conference on Social Welfare* (pp. 166–195). New York: Columbia University Press.

Hill, A. (2003). The nature of the beast: Sexual harassment. In R. Morgan (Ed.), *Sisterhood is forever* (pp. 296–305). New York: Washington Square Press.

Huber, R., & Orlando, B. P. (1995). Persisting gender differences in social workers' incomes: Does the profession really care? *Social Work, 40*, 585–591.

Koeske, G. F., & Krowinski, W. J. (2004). Gender-based salary inequity in social work: Mediators of gender's effect on salary. *Social Work, 49*, 309–317.

Lambert, S. J. (1994). A day late and a dollar short: Persistent gender differences amid changing requirements for organizational advancement. *Journal of Applied Social Sciences, 18(1)*, 89–108.

Lennon, T. (2002). *Statistics on social work education in the United States: 2000.* Alexandria, VA: Council on Social Work Education.

Mason, M. A., & Goulden, M. (2004). Marriage and baby blues: Redefining gender equity in the academy. *Annals of the American Academy, 596*, 86–103.

McPhail, B. A. (2004). Setting the record straight: Social work is not a female-dominated profession. *Social Work, 49*, 323–326.

Meyer, C. H. (1982). Issues for women in a 'woman's profession.' In A. Weick & S. T. Vandiver (Eds.), *Women, power, and change* (pp. 197–205). Washington, DC: NASW Press.

National Association of Social Workers. (2000). *Code of ethics of the National Association of Social Workers.* Washington, DC: Author.

National Association of Social Workers. (2002). *Social work income 2*, PRN 1(6). Retrieved October 14, 2005, from http://www.naswdc .org/naswprn

National Association of Social Workers. (2003). *Standards for social work personnel practices.* Washington, DC: NASW Press.

National Association of Social Workers. (n.d.). General fact sheets: Social work profession. Retrieved October 14, 2005, from http:// naswdc.org/pressroom/features/general/ profession.asp

National Association of Social Workers. (2005a). *Practice Research Network III* (Final Report). Washington, DC: Author.

National Association of Social Workers. (2005b). *Assuring the sufficiency of a front-line workforce: A national study of licensed social workers* (Preliminary Report). Washington, DC: NASW Center for Workforce Studies.

Newhill, C. E. (1996). Prevalence and risk factors for client violence toward social workers. *Families in Society, 77*, 488–495.

Nichols-Casebolt, A., Figueira-McDonough, J., & Netting, F. E. (2000). Change strategies for integrating women's knowledge into social work curricula. *Journal of Social Work Education, 36*, 65–78.

Peebles-Wilkins, W., & Francis, E. A. (1990). Two outstanding black women in social welfare history: Mary Church Terrell and Ida B. Wells-Barnett. *Affilia, 5*, 87–100.

Perkins, L. C. (1997). Nannie Helen Burroughs: A progressive example for modern times. *Affilia, 12*, 229–239.

Petchers, M. S. (1996). Debunking the myth of progress for women social work educators. *Affilia, 11*, 11–38.

Risley-Curtiss, C., & Hudson, W. W. (1998). Sexual harassment of social work students. *Affilia, 13*, 190–210.

Rosenblatt, A., Turner, E. M., Patterson, A. R., & Rollosson, C. K. (1970). Predominance of male authors in social work publications. *Social Casework, 51*, 421–430.

Schiele, J. H. (1992). Disparities between African-American women and men on social work faculty. *Affilia, 7*, 44–56.

Singer, T. (1989). Sexual harassment in graduate schools of social work: Provocative dilemmas. *Journal of Social Work Education, 25*, 68–76.

Spencer, P. C., & Munch, S. (2003). Client violence toward social workers: The role of management in community mental health programs. *Social Work, 48*, 532–544.

U.S. Census Bureau. (2000). *Median earnings in 1999 (dollars) by work experience by sex for the population 16 years and older with earnings by race.* Washington, DC: U.S. Department of Commerce.

Vandiver, S. T. (1980). A herstory of women in social work. In E. Norman & A. Mancuso (Eds.), *Women's issues and social work practice* (pp. 21–38). Itasca, IL: F. E. Peacock.

Williams, C. L. (1995). *Still a man's world: Men who do women's work.* Berkeley: University of California Press.

Zunz, S. J. (1991). Gender-related issues in the career development of social work managers. *Affilia, 6*, 39–52.

Policy statement approved by the NASW Delegate Assembly, August 2005. This policy supersedes the policy statement on Women in the Social Work Profession approved by the Delegate Assembly in 1996. For further information, contact the National Association of Social Workers, 750 First Street, NE, Suite 700, Washington, DC 20002-4241. Telephone: 202-408-8600 or 800-638-8799; e-mail: press@naswdc.org

Women's Issues

BACKGROUND

Throughout history, with rare exceptions, women have been relegated to second-class status, their lives controlled, regulated, and limited. In the United States, women were denied the right to vote, attend school, own property, keep their wages, or obtain custody of their children. Although gains have been realized, largely because of the first and second waves of the women's movement, much remains to be done. There is a measure of water in the glass, although some might view it as half empty and others as half full. Documentation of the current status of women and girls through numerical evidence builds a case for the social work profession to continue to monitor women's issues and progress (or lack thereof), with a special focus on unique populations of women who are disparately affected by discrimination as a result of the intersecting oppressions of race or ethnicity, sexual orientation and gender identity, citizenship status, disability, socioeconomic status, or religious affiliation. The following statistics indicate the continued disparity between men and women:

■ In 2002 there were 144 million females in the United States, 51 percent of the population (U.S. Census Bureau, 2003).

■ In 2002, 60 percent of women were in the labor force compared with 74 percent of men (U.S. Census Bureau, 2003). The majority of women were in occupations traditionally identified as "female." For instance, women held 79 percent of administrative support positions, whereas men held 91 percent of the jobs in precision production, craft, and repair occupations (U.S. Census Bureau, 2003).

■ There continued to be a gender gap in earnings between men and women. Median weekly earnings for women employed in full-time work were $530 in 2002, or 78 percent of the $680 median for their male counterparts (U.S. Department of Labor, Bureau of Labor Statistics, 2003). Also, earnings differed according to race. For instance, the median weekly earnings for white women were $549 compared with $702 for white men; $474 for black women compared with $523 for black men, and $396 for Latinas compared with $449 for Latinos (U.S. Department of Labor, Bureau of Labor Statistics, 2003).

■ Household income varied dramatically by type of family. For instance, in 2001 among married heterosexual-couple families only 2 percent had an income below $10,000 compared with 17 percent for female-headed households with no spouse present, and 8 percent for male-headed households with no spouse present (U.S. Census Bureau, 2003).

■ Women are more likely to live in poverty than men. For ages 18 to 64, the poverty rate for women was 11.6 percent compared with 8.5 percent for men (U.S. Census Bureau, 2003). The differences in rates are more pronounced for older women. For those 65 years and older, the poverty rate for women was 12.4 percent compared with 7.0 percent for men. Poverty, like income, varied by household type. Of families living in poverty in 2001, 50.9 percent were female-headed households with no spouse present, 40.5 percent were married-couple families, and 8.5 percent were male-headed households with no spouse present (U.S. Census Bureau, 2003). Poverty also varies by race. In 2002, 24.0 percent of African Americans lived in poverty compared with 21.8 percent of Hispanics, 10.2 percent of Asian Americans, and 8.0 percent of European Americans.

■ Women are still not represented in government in proportion to their representation in the population. As noted, women are 51 percent of the population, but make up only 14.3 percent of the president's cabinet, 14 percent of the U.S. Senate, 13.6 percent of the U.S. House of Representatives, 22 percent of the U.S. Supreme Court, 20.6 percent of federal judges, 16.0 percent of state governors, 20.8 percent of state senators, 23.0 percent of state representatives, 9.0 percent of state judges, and 20.8 percent of big-city mayors (GenderGap, 2004).

■ The status of women in the area of educational attainment shows substantial progress over the years. In 1978, for the first time, more women were enrolled in undergraduate education in both two- and four-year degree-granting institutions than men. That trend continues today with women's undergraduate enrollment increasing at a faster pace than men's (National Center for Education Statistics, 2004). Since 1976, female enrollment in graduate programs has increased by 73 percent, while male enrollment has increased by only 9 percent. High school completion rates for men and women over age 24 were both 84 percent; men were more likely to have a bachelor's degree or more and women were more likely than men to have some college or have completed an associate's degree (U.S. Census Bureau, 2003).

■ Although more low-income single parents are working after the institution of welfare "reform," more than three-fourths of those workers are concentrated in typically low-wage occupations (Institute for Women's Policy Research [IWPR], 2003b). Low-income single-mother families experienced a decrease in their incomes following welfare reform (from $664 to $647 per month) and a decrease in participation in Temporary Assistance for Needy Families (TANF) (from 27.8 percent to 14.6 percent). As a result, these families slid deeper into poverty.

■ Violence against women remains a continuing problem that affects all women, regardless of race, sexual identity, socioeconomic status, or any other identifying characteristic. One study found that almost 3 percent of college women experienced a completed or attempted rape (Fisher, Cullen, & Turner, 2000). Of the 691,710 nonfatal violent victimizations committed by intimate partners, 85 percent of the incidents were committed against women (Rennison, 2003). In 2000, 1,247 women were killed by an intimate partner in the United States. Between 1992 and 2000, on average for each year, 131,950 females were the victims of completed rapes, 98,970 females were the victims of attempted rapes, and 135,550 females were the victims of completed and attempted sexual assault (Rennison, 2002). Female victims accounted for 94 percent of all completed rapes, 91 percent of attempted rapes, and 89 percent of all completed and attempted sexual assaults.

■ Women face unique health risks, and women's health issues have received increased attention in the past decades. Heart disease kills more women than men each year, although on average women develop the disease 10 years later than men (Society for Women's Health Research [SWHR], 2004). Women are two to three times more likely than men to suffer from depression. Female smokers are more likely to develop lung cancer than male smokers, at the same level of exposure (SWHR). In fact, lung cancer kills more women than breast cancer. Women are two times more likely than men to contract a sexually transmitted disease, and 10 times more likely to contract HIV during unprotected sex with an infected partner (SWHR). Women are 18 percent of the cumulative AIDS cases in the United States with the most common exposure due to heterosexual sex, followed by injection drug use (Centers for Disease Control and Prevention [CDC], Division of HIV/AIDS Prevention, 2003). An estimated 14 percent of the population was without health insurance in 2000, which included more than 18 million girls and women (U.S. Census Bureau, 2001).

■ Almost half (49 percent) of all pregnancies among U.S. women are unintended, and almost half of these end in abortion (Alan Guttmacher Institute, 2002). In 2000, 1.31 million abortions took place, with the rate of abortions slowly decreasing each year since a record high in 1980. At the state and federal levels there are concerted efforts to regulate and restrict legal abortion, including no federal funding of abortion unless the mother's life is in danger; the reinstatement of the global gag rule, which bans federal aid to family planning clinics overseas that counsel on or provide abortions; expanding definitions of children and people that include fetal life; and numerous state regulations such as mandated waiting periods, restriction of minor's access, and restriction of the inclusion of abortion and family planning coverage in insurance plans (IWPR, 2003a). Many women consider the right to control their bodies as fundamental to their rights as free citizens in a democratic nation. The issue is also about health and safety, as risks to women are significantly reduced when abortion remains legal and accessible (IWPR, 2003a). This highlights the necessity to view women's rights as human rights (Jansen, 2000).

ISSUE STATEMENT

Women make up a majority of the U.S. population and clients that social workers serve. Attention to women's issues is essential because of the disadvantages and discrimination women continue to face in many aspects of their lives. Women perform the majority of the world's work but control a disproportionately small share of its resources. Although women in the more prosperous Western nations often fare better in life circumstances than women in many of the less wealthy nations of the world, economic, political, social, and cultural forces in most societies operate to the disadvantage of women and girls. These disadvantages affect education; health care, including reproductive and mental health; crime, especially as victims of violence; employment; and social welfare, especially income maintenance programs. These disadvantages affect the well-being of women and their families at all stages of the life cycle, from girlhood through old age.

The social work profession has a long-standing commitment to the elimination of all forms of discrimination against women. Many efforts have been made to address the disadvantages and discrimination women face. However, continuing efforts to develop social work practices, policies, and services that better meet the needs of women are essential for enhancing the health, development, and well-being of all

U.S. women, especially our clients and others at great risk.

The social work profession's continued leadership in the struggle for women's increased opportunities is essential. Although social work is often mischaracterized as a "female-dominated profession," the profession is more appropriately described as a "female majority, male-dominated profession" (McPhail, 2004). Although the majority of both social workers and social work clients are female, the underlying structures and functions of the profession are often based on male models and theories. Therefore, achieving gender equity is paramount for both the profession and the clients served. The social work profession commits itself to social justice and ending the oppression of all people (NASW, 2000). This statement of belief exemplifies the perspective of women's rights as human rights (Jansen, 2000). In addition, the National Association of Social Workers' *Code of Ethics* incorporates an antidiscrimination clause, which includes the category of sex (NASW, 2000). Also, the Code states, "Social workers should act to expand choice and opportunity for all people, with special regard for vulnerable, disadvantaged, oppressed, and exploited people and groups" (NASW, 2000, 6.04b). In the history of our nation, women as a group are characterized by those adjectives, essentially second-class citizens in a country that holds out the promise of equality and justice. Part of operationalizing this mandate is continuing to monitor and document the status of women while seeking to make and influence policy and practices that improve the status of women and girls in this society.

Because different groups of women experience their gender differently and often in interaction with other oppressions, termed intersectionality (Collins, 2000), special attention must be devoted to women of color, lesbians, women with disabilities, older women, immigrant women, and poor women.

Although women are gaining parity with men in selected areas, often achieving liberal feminist goals, the goal of changing structures and institutions to make them more equitable for both women and men, rather than merely having women join fundamentally flawed institutions in equal numbers as men, has not been realized (Saulnier, 1996). Although women have gained some measure of equity in the public spheres, the private spheres remain largely unchanged. Therefore, social work needs to continue to monitor, assess, and advocate for women's issues in policy and practice.

POLICY STATEMENT

NASW recognizes the wide range of issues that affect women and is committed to advancing policies and practices to improve the status and well-being of all women. Although every issue is a "woman's issue," only a select number of policies and practices are highlighted in this document. More important than a focus on specific issues, it is vital for social workers to develop a critical consciousness about gender (Brown, 2004) or use a feminist policy analysis (McPhail, 2003) that enables the ramifications of gender to be made visible in every issue, in every policy and every practice, at all three levels—micro, meso, and macro.

EMPLOYMENT

NASW supports the following:

■ legislative and administrative strategies that address pay equity and comparable worth initiatives for increasing women's wages in both the public and private sectors, including addressing the pay inequities within the profession of social work (Koeske & Krowinski, 2004)

■ breaking the "glass ceiling," the "Lucite ceiling" for women of color, and the "maternal wall" that affects mothers in the paid labor force, while addressing the "glass escalator" phenomenon for men in social work (Williams, 1995)

■ ending sexual harassment and occupational segregation, which clusters women in low-paying, "pink-collar" occupations

■ initiatives that conceptualize caring as work, to value it socially, legally, and economically, which might include reducing the paid work week, creating more part-time jobs with benefits, equalizing social security for spouses, offer-

ing work-related social insurance programs to all workers (including unwaged caregivers), universal preschool for all three- and four-year-olds, subsidized child care, child allowances, free health care coverage to all children and their primary caregivers, and including unpaid caregiving labor into the calculations of the nation's gross domestic product (Crittenden, 2001).

PUBLIC ASSISTANCE PROGRAMS

NASW supports the following:

■ comprehensive funding of TANF that would address structural causes of poverty as well as provide temporary assistance, which would include creating stable jobs with living wages, with special attention to the inner cities; allowing education (including college) and training as alternatives to work requirements; subsidized child care and health insurance coverage while on TANF and continuing after leaving the program; transportation assistance; and addressing the multiple problems that often affect women and their children who receive assistance, such as mental and physical health issues, learning disabilities, domestic violence, and drug and alcohol abuse (Anderson, Halter, & Gryzlak, 2004; Taylor & Barush, 2004)

■ programs for the enforcement, collection, and distribution of child support

■ initiatives for social security and Medicare reform to provide increased retirement security for women who are disproportionately poor as they age

■ viewing housing as a women's issue and increasing funding to programs that provide affordable housing.

Education

NASW supports the following:

■ adequate and equitable funding for non-sexist public education for all students, including vocational education, special education, and higher education for all women

- curricula that include women's issues, history, and experiences, including social work education, especially theories developed by and about women such as the relational-cultural theory or the "tend-and-befriend" model of stress response (Jordan & Hartling, 2002; Taylor et al., 2000)

- vigorous enforcement of Title IX and other civil rights laws, including affirmative action initiatives that address sexual discrimination in education.

Health and Mental Health

NASW supports the following:

- initiatives to reduce teenage pregnancy, as it has been demonstrated that, intended or unintended, adolescent motherhood truncates the educational, vocational, and economic lives of young women

- adequate funding and increased research on health and mental health services and issues that address the special needs of women, including adolescent women, poor women, women of color, lesbians, older women, and women with disabilities

- access to adequate health and mental health services regardless of financial status, race and ethnicity, age, or employment status, which would require universal health care coverage, although incremental expansions of coverage for low-income women and their children are a first step

- developing practices and programs that empower women and girls, enabling them to resist gender stereotypes; become resilient to shame; critique sexist and misogynist media representations of females; develop positive self-esteem and body image; confront internal and external sexism, racism, and homophobia; and challenge sexual double standards, so girls and women might develop the power and sense of entitlement that fuels self-advocacy

- reproductive freedom and safe access to the full range of reproductive health services for all women, including access to abortion; over-the-counter emergency contraception; comprehensive sexual education; family planning services; education and screening for a variety of sexually transmitted diseases, including HIV, with special attention to groups of women at increased risk, such as African American women

- gender-sensitive and culturally competent substance abuse programs that provide child care and other child services along with integrated substance abuse and mental health services for dually diagnosed women (DiNitto & Crisp, 2002).

- participation in both prevention and intervention efforts that address all forms of violence against women across the life span, including adequate health and mental health services, crime victim assistance, and other social services while educating all social workers about violence, including screening for past and current violence in all psychosocial assessments (Danis & Lockhart, 2004)

- efforts to seek out, study, develop, and disseminate theories of psychosocial development and models of services delivery in the social work curriculum that recognize, and do not pathologize, the unique developmental patterns of women, recognizing the diversity of women's experiences, situations, cultural and ethnic identifications, and sexual orientation and gender identities, including critiques of the gender bias in the *Diagnostic and Statistical Manual of Mental Disorders* (Caplan, 1995).

Global Women's Issues

NASW supports the following:

- ratification by the United States of the Convention to Eliminate All Forms of Discrimination against Women (CEAFDW)

- international programs that address women's rights as human rights, including having women in each country involved in defining their needs, identifying their oppressions, and developing programs that meet their needs

- increased attention by social work education to problems facing women internationally, often due to the effects of globalization and colonization, as well as traditional patriarchal structures.

REFERENCES

Alan Guttmacher Institute. (2002). *Induced abortion: Facts in brief*. New York: Author.

Anderson, S. G., Halter, A. P., & Gryzlak, B. M. (2004). Difficulties after leaving TANF: Inner-city women talk about reasons for returning to welfare. *Social Work, 49*, 185–194.

Brown, B. (2004). *Women & shame: Reaching out, speaking truths, & building connection*. Austin, TX: 3C Press.

Caplan, P. J. (1995). *They say you're crazy: How the world's most powerful psychiatrists decide who's normal*. Reading, MA: Addison-Wesley.

Centers for Disease Control and Prevention, Division of HIV/AIDS Prevention. (2003). *HIV/AIDS Surveillance report*. Atlanta: Author.

Collins, P. H. (2000). *Black feminist thought* (2nd ed.). New York: Routledge.

Crittenden, A. (2001). *The price of motherhood*. New York: Holt, Rinehart & Winston.

Danis, F. S., & Lockhart, L. L. (Eds.). (2004). *Breaking the silence in social work education: Domestic violence modules for foundation courses*. Alexandria, VA: Council on Social Work Education.

DiNitto, D. M., & Crisp, C. (2002). Addictions and women with major psychiatric disorders. In S.L.A. Straussner & S. Brown (Eds.), *The handbook of addiction treatment for women* (pp. 423–450). San Francisco: Jossey-Bass.

Fisher, B. S., Cullen, F. T., & Turner, M. G. (2000). *Sexual victimization of college women* (NCJ 182369). Washington, DC: U.S. Department of Justice, National Criminal Justice Reference Service.

GenderGap. (2004). *Gender gap in government*. Retrieved May 13, 2004, from http://gendergap.com/goverme.htm

Institute for Women's Policy Research. (2003a). *Policy update on safe and legal abortion 30 years after Roe v. Wade* (No. B241). Washington, DC: Author.

Institute for Women's Policy Research. (2003b). *Before and after welfare reform*. Washington, DC: Author.

Jansen, G. G. (2000, Feb.). *Women's rights are human rights: Violence against women redefined*. Paper presented at CSWE 46th APM, New York. (The phrase is part of the Vienna Declaration from the UN sponsored Human Rights Conference in Vienna, 1993.)

Jordan, J. V., & Hartling, L. M. (2002). New developments in relational-cultural theory. In M. Ballou & L. S. Brown (Eds.), *Rethinking mental health & disorder: Feminist perspectives* (pp. 48–70). New York: Guilford Press.

Koeske, G. F., & Krowinski, W. J. (2004). Gender-based salary inequity in social work. *Social Work, 49*, 309–317.

McPhail, B. A. (2003). Feminist policy analysis framework: Through a gendered lens. *Social Policy Journal, 2*(2/3), 39–61.

McPhail, B. A. (2004). Setting the record straight: Social work is not a female-dominated profession [Commentary]. *Social Work, 49*, 323–326.

National Association of Social Workers. (2000). *Code of ethics of the National Association of Social Workers*. Washington, DC: Author.

National Center for Education Statistics. (2004). *The condition of education 2003* (NCES 2003-067). Washington, DC: U.S. Department of Education, Institute of Education Sciences.

National Council for Research on Women. (2004). *Missing: Information about women's lives*. Washington, DC: Author.

National Women's Law Center. (2004). *Slip sliding away: The erosion of hard-won gains for women under the Bush administration and an agenda for moving forward*. Washington, DC: Author.

Rennison, C. M. (2002). *Rape and sexual assault* [Crime Data Brief] (Publication No. NCJ 194530). Washington, DC: U.S. Department of Justice, Office of Justice Programs.

Rennison, C. M. (2003). *Intimate partner violence, 1993–2001* [Crime Data Brief.] (Publication No. NCJ 197838). Washington, DC: U.S. Department of Justice, Office of Justice Programs, Bureau of Justice Statistics.

Saulnier, C. F. (1996). *Feminist theories and social work*. New York: Haworth Press.

Society for Women's Health Research. (2004). *Women and men: 10 differences that make a difference*. Retrieved from http://www.womens-health.org/sbb/10diff.htm

Taylor, M. J., & Barusch, A. S. (2004). Personal, family, and multiple barriers of long-term welfare recipients. *Social Work, 49*, 175–183.

Taylor, S. E., Klein, L. C., Lewis, B. P., Gruenewald, T. L., Gurung, R.A.R., & Updegraff, J. A. (2000). Biobehavorial responses to stress in females: Tend-and-befriend, not fight-or-flight. *Psychological Review, 107,* 411–429.

U.S. Census Bureau. (2001). *Health insurance coverage: 2000.* Washington, DC: U.S. Department of Commerce, Economics and Statistics Administration.

U.S. Census Bureau. (2003). *Women and men in the United States: March 2002.* Washington, DC: U.S. Department of Commerce, Economics and Statistics Administration.

U.S. Department of Labor, Bureau of Labor Statistics. (2003). *Highlights of women's earnings in 2002.* Washington, DC: Author.

Williams, C. L. (1995). *Still a man's world: Men who do women's work.* Berkeley: University of California Press.

Policy statement approved by the NASW Delegate Assembly, August 2005. This policy supersedes the policy statement on Women's Issues approved by the Delegate Assembly in 1996, in 1987, in 1977, and referred by the 2002 Delegate Assembly to the 2005 Delegate Assembly for revision. For further information, contact the National Association of Social Workers, 750 First Street, NE, Suite 700, Washington, DC 20002-4241. Telephone: 202-408-8600 or 800-638-8799; e-mail: press@naswdc.org

Youth Suicide

BACKGROUND

In 1999 former Surgeon General David Satcher, MD, PhD, released "The National Strategy for Suicide Prevention: Goals and Objectives for Action." This document, which reflected national awareness of suicide as a serious public health problem, was also designed to be "a catalyst for social change" by offering a comprehensive and integrated approach to suicide awareness and prevention. (U.S. Public Health Service [PHS], 1999). This approach was based on the growing body of knowledge about the biological and psychological factors that contribute to suicidal behaviors as well as recognition of the critical importance of trained, coordinated interdisciplinary resources for suicide prevention and intervention.

In 2002 the President's New Freedom Commission on Mental Health specifically recognized youth suicide early intervention and prevention as urgent public health priorities. Although suicides account for 1.2 percent of deaths in the United States annually, they comprise 12.8 percent of all deaths among 15- to 24-year-olds. In that age group, suicide ranks as the third leading cause of death, although in several states, particularly in western regions of the nation, suicide is the second leading cause of death in this age group (Centers for Disease Control and Prevention [CDC], 1999). Suicide also ranks as the third cause of death in 10- to 14-year-olds, which reflects a 99 percent increase between 1980 and 1997 (American Association of Suicidology, 2001; Children's Safety Network National Injury and Violence Prevention Resource Center, 2004). Although the suicide rate in this youth cohort remains highest for white males, the rate for African American males ages 15 to 19 is increasing rapidly and has more than doubled from 2.9 per 100,000 to 6.1 per 100,000 from 1981 to 1998. (CDC, 2000). The suicide rate for Native American youths is also exceedingly high compared with the overall rate for males ages 10 to 19 (19.3 per 100,000 versus 8.5 per 100,000) (CDC, 2000).

The rate for youth suicide attempts is difficult to estimate because many attempters may not be treated in a hospital or recorded as self-injury (Miller, Covington, & Jensen, 1998). The potential relationship among homicide, "suicide by cop" (youth intentionally escalates law enforcement into lethal use of force), excessive speed, and driving under the influence to suicide rates for youths warrants further research (Lindsay & Lester, 2004). Self-report data from 1999, however, indicate that 19.3 percent of high school students seriously considered attempting suicide, 14.5 percent made plans to attempt suicide, and 8.3 percent made an attempt in the year preceding the survey (CDC, 2000). This survey's data also indicated that Latino students, both male and female, were significantly more likely than white students to have reported a suicide attempt (12.8 percent versus 6.7 percent), with Latino females almost three times more likely than males (18.9 percent versus 6.6 percent) to have reported a suicide attempt. The most likely explanation for ethnic rate differences is variations in cultural norms related to suicide, including cultural views on adolescence and communication expectation among family members.

Firearms are the most common method for suicide completion by youths across sex, race, and age. More than 60 percent of suicides among youths between ages 10 and 19 in 1998 were firearm-related. The rate of youth suicides involving firearms increased 38 percent between 1981 and 1994, and although there has been a slight decrease since 1994, these numbers remain critically high (CDC, 2000).

Just as in adult suicide, the causation of youth suicide is complex, multidetermined, and reflects an interaction of risk and protective factors (Berman, Jobes, & Silverman, 2005). Risk factors for completion include previous suicide attempts, a family history of suicide, childhood trauma, and a mental health or substance abuse disorder. Studies show that 90 percent of youths who completed suicide were suffering from a diagnosable mental illness at the time of their death (American Foundation for Suicide Prevention, http://www.afsp.org). Other risk factors include exposure to domestic violence, sexual abuse, impulsive and aggressive behavior, family instability, and a recent severe stressor. This stressor is rarely the cause of suicide, but often acts as a precipitating event or trigger for high-risk youths (Gould, Fisher, Parides, Flory, & Shaffer, 1996). A particularly significant trigger is incarceration. One study found that suicide in juvenile detention facilities was more than four times greater than the overall rate for youths in general (Hayes, 2000).

Exposure to the suicidal behavior of others, whether through personal experience or through real or fictionalized accounts in the media, has been shown to increase the suicide risk in vulnerable teenagers. There is also evidence that local epidemics of suicides, known as clusters, can have a contagious effect on youths who were only marginally connected to the suicide completer (Velting & Gould, 1997).

Although there is growing concern that gay and lesbian youths are at an elevated risk of suicide because of sexual orientation, no national statistics exist for completion rates in this group. Part of the challenge in assessing the implications of sexual orientation on suicide risk is that experts disagree about the best ways to measure sexual orientation; in addition, many adolescents may be reluctant to report issues related to sexual identity (National Institute of Mental Health, 1999). Clearly, this area requires further investigation.

Research indicates a positive association between the accessibility and availability of firearms in the home and the risk of youth suicide (Brent et al., 1993). The risk presented by guns is proportional to their accessibility and their number in the home (Kellerman et al., 1992).

In addition to the assessment of suicide risk factors, it is critical to recognize the protective factors that mitigate risk. Protective factors for youths include learned skills in problem solving, impulse control, skills in conflict resolution, family and community support, access to appropriate mental health care and support for help seeking, restricted access to lethal methods of suicide, and life-affirming cultural and religious beliefs that discourage suicide (PHS, 1999).

Despite national recognition of youth suicide as a major public health problem, there has been little systematic evidence on what is effective in regard to prevention (Briss et al., 2000). There has been, however, increasing awareness of the complexity of the problem as well as the implementation of scientific approaches to describing and monitoring youth suicide; understanding risk and protective factors; developing, implementing, and evaluating prevention strategies; and disseminating information about effective strategies (PHS, 1999).

The research on risk and protective factors suggests that a promising prevention strategy among school-age children is to reduce early risk factors for depression, substance abuse, and aggressive behaviors and to implement programs that enhance resilience. A confidential screening instrument has been developed to identify depression, substance abuse, and suicidal ideation among high school youths; subsequent evaluation by mental health professionals can then facilitate referral for appropriate treatment (Shaffer & Craft, 1999).

Other school-based interventions, such as general awareness programs, and dissemination of lists of "warning signs," have been less promising. These programs have sometimes had the unintended effect of suggesting that suicide is an option for many young people (PHS, 1999). Obviously, the need for carefully evaluated program development that is informed by existing research is essential.

ISSUE STATEMENT

The suicide rate has long been understood to correlate with cultural, social, political, and economic forces (Goldsmith, Pellmar, Kleinman, & Bunney, 2002). Because social work values are so intrinsically related to supporting the individual's right to self-determination in a societal context, it has both the responsibility and the opportunity to apply its expertise to the multifaceted, systemic challenges presented by youth suicide. Few professions have as ubiquitous a presence in systems that involve children, from the family and the school to child protective agencies and the juvenile justice system.

Unfortunately, social work education has been slow to include suicide assessment and prevention in graduate coursework or continuing education requirements. Feldman and Freedenthal (2003), in a recent national survey of social workers, reported that 78 percent of respondents felt that they were inadequately trained in suicide prevention in their MSW program. Only 55 percent had some classroom instruction in suicide intervention and of those, 78 percent reported they had received two hours or less of instruction. At the same time, 86 percent recommended required continuing education in suicide management.

The profession of social work is not alone in this oversight. Goal 6 in the National Strategy for Suicide Prevention states that "many mental health professionals are not adequately trained to provide proper assessment, treatment, and management of suicidal patients, nor do they know how to refer clients for specialized assessment and treatment" (PHS, 1999, p. 79). It also indicates that there is lack of awareness of the mental health issues faced by family members of loved ones who have died by suicide. The National Strategy for Suicide Prevention, therefore, recognizes that the training of community gatekeepers, including social workers, must be improved to provide proper assessment, treatment, and management of suicidal people (PHS). The accessibility of current epidemiological data and research information on nationally recognized Internet sites enhances this learning process and is a valuable educational resource.

Given that many social workers serve as community gatekeepers, social workers are in a unique position to address the stigma associated with mental illness, substance abuse, and suicide. Not only does this stigma inhibit help seeking, but it also has contributed to inadequate funding for preventive services and to low reimbursements for treatment (PHS, 1999). Transforming public attitudes requires broad-based support, and the systemic approach of social work can bring community linkage skills to this critical public education need. In fact, because the community is truly at the core of many youth suicide prevention and intervention initiatives, social work networking and community organization techniques can facilitate the coordination of interorganizational communication and service delivery related to youth suicide awareness and prevention.

Social work is also in a position to contribute to the increasing body of knowledge about prevention strategies, treatment interventions, and the enhancement of protective factors that mitigate risk, especially in school and community settings. As in all social problems, the profession plays a vital role in the development of public policy that is theoretically grounded in evidence-based research and is directed toward the development of comprehensive youth suicide prevention plans.

POLICY STATEMENT

NASW is in agreement with the surgeon general's recognition of youth suicide as a major public health problem. It is the position of NASW to address the social and mental health issues related to youth suicide, by supporting the following:

■ undergraduate, graduate, and continuing professional education about the scope of youth suicide and the current evidence-based prevention and intervention strategies.

■ provision of a range of prevention, intervention, and postvention services at the community level for families and others affected by the suicide of children and youths.

- evidence-based research into the unique risk factors of ethnically, sexually, and gender diverse youths.

- involvement of social workers in the development and implementation of youth suicide awareness and prevention (including continuing education programs for and consultation services to non–mental health staff) in schools, child welfare agencies (child protection teams), juvenile detention facilities, courts, and other settings where youths may be at elevated risk.

- media education for the general public and community gatekeepers (including clergy, police, hospital personnel, emergency personnel, and recreation staff) to minimize the risk of suicide contagion and encourage the dissemination of information on mental health resources for youth suicide prevention at the community level.

- interdisciplinary strategies developed in collaboration with professional associations and community agencies to decrease the stigma associated with mental illness, substance abuse, and suicide.

- research concerning posttraumatic stress syndrome and its impact on youth suicide.

- educational and legislative measures that restrict access of youths to firearms

- family, school, and community-based programs that enhance protective factors for families and youths.

- school-based, evidence-based, multifactored screening as an important tool in the identification of at-risk youths. Training on the use of this tool provided to the gatekeepers (including administrators, counselors, coaches, teachers, school social workers). NASW supports the administration of such tools only by qualified mental health personnel.

- development and funding of multidisciplinary research projects aimed at extending the knowledge base about youth suicide and demonstrating which interventions have proven efficacy.

- legislative efforts to provide grants to state and local governments and nonprofit organizations to help develop, coordinate, and expand early intervention and prevention strategies and community mental health services for at-risk youths.

- evaluation of the effectiveness and efficacy of youth suicide prevention and early intervention activities.

- social work involvement in the development of policies, procedures, and protocols that facilitate interdisciplinary collaboration with professional associations and community agencies in the provision of early identification, intervention, and postvention services.

- advocacy on state and local levels, to ensure an appropriate continuum of care, from least restrictive to most restrictive, is available for youths at risk of suicide.

REFERENCES

American Association of Suicidology. (2001). *Youth suicide fact sheet.* Retrieved May 24, 2004, from http://www.suicidology.org

Berman, A. L., Jobes, D. A., & Silverman, M. M. (2005). *Adolescent suicide: Assessment and intervention* (2nd ed.). Washington, DC: American Psychological Association.

Brent, D., Perper, J., Moritz, G., Baugher, M., Schweers, J., & Roth, C. (1993). Firearms and adolescent suicide: A community case-control study. *American Journal of Disease of Children, 147,* 1066–1071.

Briss, P., Zasa, S., Pappaioanou, S., Fielding, J., Wright-de Aguero, L., Truman, B. L., Hopkins, D. P., Mullen, P. D., & Thompson, R. S. (2000). Developing an evidence-based guide to community prevention services-method. *American Journal of Preventive Medicine, 18*(1S).

Centers for Disease Control and Prevention. (1999). *10 leading causes of injury deaths, United States, 1997, all races, both sexes.* Atlanta: CDC, NCIPC.

Centers for Disease Control and Prevention. (2000). Youth risk behavior surveillance— United States, 1999. In *CDC surveillance summaries, June 9, 2000. Morbidity and Mortality Weekly Report, 49* (No. SS-5).

Children's Safety Network National Injury and Violence Prevention Resource Center. (2004). *Youth suicide statistics.* Retrieved May 24, 2004, from http://www.edc.org/HHD/csn

Feldman, B., & Freedenthal, S. (2003). *Social work education in suicide assessment and intervention: An unmet need?* Unpublished manuscript, University of New Hampshire School of Social Work.

Goldsmith, S. K., Pellmar, T. C., Kleinman, W. E., & Bunney, W. E. (Eds.). (2002). *Reducing suicide: A national imperative.* Washington, DC: National Academies Press.

Gould, M., Fisher, P., Parides, M., Flory, M., & Shaffer, D. (1996). Psychosocial risk factors of child and adolescent completed suicide. *Archives of General Psychiatry, 53,* 1155–1162.

Hayes, L. (2000). Suicide prevention in juvenile facilities. *Juvenile Justice, 7*(1), 24–32.

Kellerman, A. L., Rivara, F. P., Rushford, N., Somes, G., Reay, D. T., Francisco, J., Barton, J. G., Podzinski, J., Fligner, C. L., & Hackman, B. B. (1992). Suicide in the home in relationship to gun ownership. *New England Journal of Medicine, 327,* 467–472.

Lindsay, M., & Lester, D. (2004). *Suicide by cop: Committing suicide by provoking police to shoot you.* Amityville, NY: Baywood.

Miller, T. R., Covington, K. L., & Jensen, A. F. (1998). Costs of injury by major cause, United States, 1995: Cobbling together estimates. In S. Mulder (Ed.), *Measuring the burden of injuries: Proceedings of a conference in Noordwijkerhout, Netherlands: May 13–15, 1998.* Unpublished manuscript.

National Institute of Mental Health. (1999). *Frequently asked questions about suicide.* Retrieved May 24, 2004, from http://www.nimh.nih.gov/suicideprevention/index.cfm

Shaffer, D., & Craft, L. (1999). Methods of adolescent suicide prevention. *Journal of Clinical Psychiatry, 60*(Suppl. 2), 70–74.

U.S. Public Health Service. (1999). *National strategy for suicide prevention: Goals and objectives for action.* Rockville, MD: Public Health Service (Document No. SMA 3517). Retrieved May 24, 2004, from http://www.mentalhealth.org/suicideprevention

Velting, D., & Gould, M. (1997). Suicide contagion. In R. Maris & M. Silverman (Eds.), *Review of suicidology* (pp. 96–137). New York: Guilford Press.

SUGGESTED READING

Centers for Disease Control. (1992). *Youth suicide prevention programs: A resource guide.* Atlanta: Author. (Updated 1998).

Policy statement approved by the NASW Delegate Assembly, August 2005. This policy statement supersedes the policy statement on Youth Suicide approved by the Delegate Assembly in 1996 and referred by the 2005 Delegate Assembly to the 2005 Delegate Assembly, and the statement approved in 1987. For further information, contact the National Association of Social Workers, 750 First Street, NE, Suite 700, Washington, DC 20002-4241. Telephone: 2002-408-8600 or 800-638-8799; e-mail: press@naswdc.org.

NASW
CODE OF ETHICS

NASW Code of Ethics

PREAMBLE

The primary mission of the social work profession is to enhance human well-being and help meet the basic human needs of all people, with particular attention to the needs and empowerment of people who are vulnerable, oppressed, and living in poverty. A historic and defining feature of social work is the profession's focus on individual well-being in a social context and the well-being of society. Fundamental to social work is attention to the environmental forces that create, contribute to, and address problems in living.

Social workers promote social justice and social change with and on behalf of clients. "Clients" is used inclusively to refer to individuals, families, groups, organizations, and communities. Social workers are sensitive to cultural and ethnic diversity and strive to end discrimination, oppression, poverty, and other forms of social injustice. These activities may be in the form of direct practice, community organizing, supervision, consultation, administration, advocacy, social and political action, policy development and implementation, education, and research and evaluation. Social workers seek to enhance the capacity of people to address their own needs. Social workers also seek to promote the responsiveness of organizations, communities, and other social institutions to individuals' needs and social problems.

The mission of the social work profession is rooted in a set of core values. These core values, embraced by social workers throughout the profession's history, are the foundation of social work's unique purpose and perspective:

- service
- social justice
- dignity and worth of the person
- importance of human relationships
- integrity
- competence.

This constellation of core values reflects what is unique to the social work profession. Core values, and the principles that flow from them, must be balanced within the context and complexity of the human experience.

PURPOSE OF THE NASW CODE OF ETHICS

Professional ethics are at the core of social work. The profession has an obligation to articulate its basic values, ethical principles, and ethical standards. The *NASW Code of Ethics* sets forth these values, principles, and standards to guide social workers' conduct. The *Code* is relevant to all social workers and social work students, regardless of their professional functions, the settings in which they work, or the populations they serve.

The *NASW Code of Ethics* serves six purposes:

1. The *Code* identifies core values on which social work's mission is based.
2. The *Code* summarizes broad ethical principles that reflect the profession's core values and establishes a set of specific ethical standards that should be used to guide social work practice.
3. The *Code* is designed to help social workers identify relevant considerations when professional obligations conflict or ethical uncertainties arise.
4. The *Code* provides ethical standards to which the general public can hold the social work profession accountable.

5. The *Code* socializes practitioners new to the field to social work's mission, values, ethical principles, and ethical standards.

6. The *Code* articulates standards that the social work profession itself can use to assess whether social workers have engaged in unethical conduct. NASW has formal procedures to adjudicate ethics complaints filed against its members.[1] In subscribing to this *Code*, social workers are required to cooperate in its implementation, participate in NASW adjudication proceedings, and abide by any NASW disciplinary rulings or sanctions based on it.

The *Code* offers a set of values, principles, and standards to guide decision making and conduct when ethical issues arise. It does not provide a set of rules that prescribe how social workers should act in all situations. Specific applications of the *Code* must take into account the context in which it is being considered and the possibility of conflicts among the *Code*'s values, principles, and standards. Ethical responsibilities flow from all human relationships, from the personal and familial to the social and professional.

Further, the *NASW Code of Ethics* does not specify which values, principles, and standards are most important and ought to outweigh others in instances when they conflict. Reasonable differences of opinion can and do exist among social workers with respect to the ways in which values, ethical principles, and ethical standards should be rank ordered when they conflict. Ethical decision making in a given situation must apply the informed judgment of the individual social worker and should also consider how the issues would be judged in a peer review process where the ethical standards of the profession would be applied.

Ethical decision making is a process. There are many instances in social work where simple answers are not available to resolve complex ethical issues. Social workers should take into consideration all the values, principles,

and standards in this *Code* that are relevant to any situation in which ethical judgment is warranted. Social workers' decisions and actions should be consistent with the spirit as well as the letter of this *Code*.

In addition to this *Code*, there are many other sources of information about ethical thinking that may be useful. Social workers should consider ethical theory and principles generally, social work theory and research, laws, regulations, agency policies, and other relevant codes of ethics, recognizing that among codes of ethics social workers should consider the *NASW Code of Ethics* as their primary source. Social workers also should be aware of the impact on ethical decision making of their clients' and their own personal values and cultural and religious beliefs and practices. They should be aware of any conflicts between personal and professional values and deal with them responsibly. For additional guidance social workers should consult the relevant literature on professional ethics and ethical decision making and seek appropriate consultation when faced with ethical dilemmas. This may involve consultation with an agency-based or social work organization's ethics committee, a regulatory body, knowledgeable colleagues, supervisors, or legal counsel.

Instances may arise when social workers' ethical obligations conflict with agency policies or relevant laws or regulations. When such con-flicts occur, social workers must make a responsible effort to resolve the conflict in a manner that is consistent with the values, principles, and standards expressed in this *Code*. If a reasonable resolution of the conflict does not appear possible, social workers should seek proper consultation before making a decision.

The *NASW Code of Ethics* is to be used by NASW and by individuals, agencies, organizations, and bodies (such as licensing and regulatory boards, professional liability insurance providers, courts of law, agency boards of directors, government agencies, and other professional groups) that choose to adopt it or use it as a frame of reference. Violation of standards in this *Code* does not automatically imply legal liability or violation of the law. Such

---

[1] *For information on NASW adjudication procedures, see* NASW Procedures for the Adjudication of Grievances.

determination can only be made in the context of legal and judicial proceedings. Alleged violations of the *Code* would be subject to a peer review process. Such processes are generally separate from legal or administrative procedures and insulated from legal review or proceedings to allow the profession to counsel and discipline its own members.

A code of ethics cannot guarantee ethical behavior. Moreover, a code of ethics cannot resolve all ethical issues or disputes or capture the richness and complexity involved in striving to make responsible choices within a moral community. Rather, a code of ethics sets forth values, ethical principles, and ethical standards to which professionals aspire and by which their actions can be judged. Social workers' ethical behavior should result from their personal commitment to engage in ethical practice. The *NASW Code of Ethics* reflects the commitment of all social workers to uphold the profession's values and to act ethically. Principles and standards must be applied by individuals of good character who discern moral questions and, in good faith, seek to make reliable ethical judgments.

ETHICAL PRINCIPLES

The following broad ethical principles are based on social work's core values of service, social justice, dignity and worth of the person, importance of human relationships, integrity, and competence. These principles set forth ideals to which all social workers should aspire.

Value: *Service*

Ethical Principle: *Social workers' primary goal is to help people in need and to address social problems.*

Social workers elevate service to others above self-interest. Social workers draw on their knowledge, values, and skills to help people in need and to address social problems. Social workers are encouraged to volunteer some portion of their professional skills with no expectation of significant financial return (pro bono service).

Value: *Social Justice*

Ethical Principle: *Social workers challenge social injustice.*

Social workers pursue social change, particularly with and on behalf of vulnerable and oppressed individuals and groups of people. Social workers' social change efforts are focused primarily on issues of poverty, unemployment, discrimination, and other forms of social injustice. These activities seek to promote sensitivity to and knowledge about oppression and cultural and ethnic diversity. Social workers strive to ensure access to needed information, services, and resources; equality of opportunity; and meaningful participation in decision making for all people.

Value: *Dignity and Worth of the Person*

Ethical Principle: *Social workers respect the inherent dignity and worth of the person.*

Social workers treat each person in a caring and respectful fashion, mindful of individual differences and cultural and ethnic diversity. Social workers promote clients' socially responsible self-determination. Social workers seek to enhance clients' capacity and opportunity to change and to address their own needs. Social workers are cognizant of their dual responsibility to clients and to the broader society. They seek to resolve conflicts between clients' interests and the broader society's interests in a socially responsible manner consistent with the values, ethical principles, and ethical standards of the profession.

Value: *Importance of Human Relationships*

Ethical Principle: *Social workers recognize the central importance of human relationships.*

Social workers understand that relationships between and among people are an important vehicle for change. Social workers engage people as partners in the helping process. Social workers seek to strengthen relationships among people in a purposeful effort to promote, restore, maintain, and enhance the well-being of individuals, families, social groups, organizations, and communities.

Value: *Integrity*

Ethical Principle: *Social workers behave in a trustworthy manner.*

Social workers are continually aware of the profession's mission, values, ethical principles, and ethical standards and practice in a manner consistent with them. Social workers act honestly and responsibly and promote ethical practices on the part of the organizations with which they are affiliated.

Value: *Competence*

Ethical Principle: *Social workers practice within their areas of competence and develop and enhance their professional expertise.*

Social workers continually strive to increase their professional knowledge and skills and to apply them in practice. Social workers should aspire to contribute to the knowledge base of the profession.

ETHICAL STANDARDS

The following ethical standards are relevant to the professional activities of all social workers. These standards concern (1) social workers' ethical responsibilities to clients, (2) social workers' ethical responsibilities to colleagues, (3) social workers' ethical responsibilities in practice settings, (4) social workers' ethical responsibilities as professionals, (5) social workers' ethical responsibilities to the social work profession, and (6) social workers' ethical responsibilities to the broader society.

Some of the standards that follow are enforceable guidelines for professional conduct, and some are aspirational. The extent to which each standard is enforceable is a matter of professional judgment to be exercised by those responsible for reviewing alleged violations of ethical standards.

1. SOCIAL WORKERS' ETHICAL RESPONSIBILITIES TO CLIENTS

1.01 Commitment to Clients

Social workers' primary responsibility is to promote the well-being of clients. In general, clients' interests are primary. However, social workers' responsibility to the larger society or specific legal obligations may on limited occasions supersede the loyalty owed clients, and clients should be so advised. (Examples include when a social worker is required by law to report that a client has abused a child or has threatened to harm self or others.)

1.02 Self-Determination

Social workers respect and promote the right of clients to self-determination and assist clients in their efforts to identify and clarify their goals. Social workers may limit clients' right to self-determination when, in the social workers' professional judgment, clients' actions or potential actions pose a serious, foreseeable, and imminent risk to themselves or others.

1.03 Informed Consent

(a) Social workers should provide services to clients only in the context of a professional relationship based, when appropriate, on valid informed consent. Social workers should use clear and understandable language to inform clients of the purpose of the services, risks related to the services, limits to services because of the requirements of a third-party payer, relevant costs, reasonable alternatives, clients' right to refuse or withdraw consent, and the time frame covered by the consent. Social workers should provide clients with an opportunity to ask questions.

(b) In instances when clients are not literate or have difficulty understanding the primary language used in the practice setting, social workers should take steps to ensure clients' comprehension. This may include providing clients with a detailed verbal explanation or arranging for a qualified interpreter or translator whenever possible.

(c) In instances when clients lack the capacity to provide informed consent, social workers should protect clients' interests by seeking permission from an appropriate third party, informing clients consistent with the clients' level of understanding. In such instances social workers should seek to ensure that the third party acts in a manner consistent with clients' wishes and interests. Social workers should take reasonable steps to enhance such clients' ability to give informed consent.

(d) In instances when clients are receiving services involuntarily, social workers should provide information about the nature and extent of services and about the extent of clients' right to refuse service.

(e) Social workers who provide services via electronic media (such as computer, telephone, radio, and television) should inform recipients of the limitations and risks associated with such services.

(f) Social workers should obtain clients' informed consent before audiotaping or videotaping clients or permitting observation of services to clients by a third party.

1.04   Competence

(a) Social workers should provide services and represent themselves as competent only within the boundaries of their education, training, license, certification, consultation received, supervised experience, or other relevant professional experience.

(b) Social workers should provide services in substantive areas or use intervention techniques or approaches that are new to them only after engaging in appropriate study, training, consultation, and supervision from people who are competent in those interventions or techniques.

(c) When generally recognized standards do not exist with respect to an emerging area of practice, social workers should exercise careful judgment and take responsible steps (including appropriate education, research, training, consultation, and supervision) to ensure the competence of their work and to protect clients from harm.

1.05   Cultural Competence and Social Diversity

(a) Social workers should understand culture and its function in human behavior and society, recognizing the strengths that exist in all cultures.

(b) Social workers should have a knowledge base of their clients' cultures and be able to demonstrate competence in the provision of services that are sensitive to clients' cultures and to differences among people and cultural groups.

(c) Social workers should obtain education about and seek to understand the nature of so-cial diversity and oppression with respect to race, ethnicity, national origin, color, sex, sexual orientation, gender identity or expression, age, marital status, political belief, religion, immigration status, and mental or physical disability.

1.06   Conflicts of Interest

(a) Social workers should be alert to and avoid conflicts of interest that interfere with the exercise of professional discretion and impartial judgment. Social workers should inform clients when a real or potential conflict of interest arises and take reasonable steps to resolve the issue in a manner that makes the clients' interests primary and protects clients' interests to the greatest extent possible. In some cases, protecting clients' interests may require termination of the professional relationship with proper referral of the client.

(b) Social workers should not take unfair advantage of any professional relationship or exploit others to further their personal, religious, political, or business interests.

(c) Social workers should not engage in dual or multiple relationships with clients or former clients in which there is a risk of exploitation or potential harm to the client. In instances when dual or multiple relationships are unavoidable, social workers should take steps to protect clients and are responsible for setting clear, appropriate, and culturally sensitive boundaries. (Dual or multiple relationships occur when social workers relate to clients in more than one relationship, whether professional, social, or business. Dual or multiple relationships can occur simultaneously or consecutively.)

(d) When social workers provide services to two or more people who have a relationship with each other (for example, couples, family members), social workers should clarify with all parties which individuals will be considered clients and the nature of social workers' professional obligations to the various individuals who are receiving services. Social workers who anticipate a conflict of interest among the individuals receiving services or who anticipate having to perform in potentially conflicting roles (for example, when a social worker is asked to testify in a child custody dispute or divorce proceedings involving clients) should clarify their role with the parties involved and take appropriate action to minimize any conflict of interest.

1.07   Privacy and Confidentiality

(a) Social workers should respect clients' right to privacy. Social workers should not solicit private information from clients unless it is essential to providing services or conducting social work evaluation or research. Once private information is shared, standards of confidentiality apply.

(b) Social workers may disclose confidential information when appropriate with valid consent from a client or a person legally authorized to consent on behalf of a client.

(c) Social workers should protect the confidentiality of all information obtained in the course of professional service, except for compelling professional reasons. The general expectation that social workers will keep information confidential does not apply when disclosure is necessary to prevent serious, foreseeable, and imminent harm to a client or other identifiable person. In all instances, social workers should disclose the least amount of confidential information necessary to achieve the desired purpose; only information that is directly relevant to the purpose for which the disclosure is made should be revealed.

(d) Social workers should inform clients, to the extent possible, about the disclosure of confidential information and the potential consequences, when feasible before the disclosure is made. This applies whether social workers disclose confidential information on the basis of a legal requirement or client consent.

(e) Social workers should discuss with clients and other interested parties the nature of confidentiality and limitations of clients' right to confidentiality. Social workers should review with clients circumstances where confidential information may be requested and where disclosure of confidential information may be legally required. This discussion should occur as soon as possible in the social worker–client relationship and as needed throughout the course of the relationship.

(f) When social workers provide counseling services to families, couples, or groups, social workers should seek agreement among the parties involved concerning each individual's right to confidentiality and obligation to preserve the confidentiality of information shared by others. Social workers should inform participants in family, couples, or group counseling that social workers cannot guarantee that all participants will honor such agreements.

(g) Social workers should inform clients involved in family, couples, marital, or group counseling of the social worker's, employer's, and agency's policy concerning the social worker's disclosure of confidential information among the parties involved in the counseling.

(h) Social workers should not disclose confidential information to third-party payers unless clients have authorized such disclosure.

(i) Social workers should not discuss confidential information in any setting unless privacy can be ensured. Social workers should not discuss confidential information in public or semipublic areas such as hallways, waiting rooms, elevators, and restaurants.

(j) Social workers should protect the confidentiality of clients during legal proceedings to the extent permitted by law. When a court of law or other legally authorized body orders social workers to disclose confidential or privileged information without a client's consent and such disclosure could cause harm to the client, social workers should request that the court withdraw the order or limit the order as narrowly as possible or maintain the records under seal, unavailable for public inspection.

(k) Social workers should protect the confidentiality of clients when responding to requests from members of the media.

(l) Social workers should protect the confidentiality of clients' written and electronic records and other sensitive information. Social workers should take reasonable steps to ensure that clients' records are stored in a secure location and that clients' records are not available to others who are not authorized to have access.

(m) Social workers should take precautions to ensure and maintain the confidentiality of information transmitted to other parties through the use of computers, electronic mail, facsimile machines, telephones and telephone answering machines, and other electronic or computer technology. Disclosure of identifying information should be avoided whenever possible.

(n) Social workers should transfer or dispose of clients' records in a manner that protects clients' confidentiality and is consistent with state statutes governing records and social work licensure.

(o) Social workers should take reasonable precautions to protect client confidentiality in the event of the social worker's termination of practice, incapacitation, or death.

(p) Social workers should not disclose identifying information when discussing clients for teaching or training purposes unless the client has consented to disclosure of confidential information.

(q) Social workers should not disclose identifying information when discussing clients with consultants unless the client has consented to disclosure of confidential information or there is a compelling need for such disclosure.

(r) Social workers should protect the confidentiality of deceased clients consistent with the preceding standards.

1.08   Access to Records

(a) Social workers should provide clients with reasonable access to records concerning the clients. Social workers who are concerned that clients' access to their records could cause serious misunderstanding or harm to the client should provide assistance in interpreting the records and consultation with the client regarding the records. Social workers should limit clients' access to their records, or portions of their records, only in exceptional circumstances when there is compelling evidence that such access would cause serious harm to the client. Both clients' requests and the rationale for withholding some or all of the record should be documented in clients' files.

(b) When providing clients with access to their records, social workers should take steps to protect the confidentiality of other individuals identified or discussed in such records.

1.09   Sexual Relationships

(a) Social workers should under no circumstances engage in sexual activities or sexual contact with current clients, whether such contact is consensual or forced.

(b) Social workers should not engage in sexual activities or sexual contact with clients' relatives or other individuals with whom clients maintain a close personal relationship when there is a risk of exploitation or potential harm to the client. Sexual activity or sexual contact with clients' relatives or other individuals with whom clients maintain a personal relationship has the potential to be harmful to the client and may make it difficult for the social worker and client to maintain appropriate professional boundaries. Social workers—not their clients, their clients' relatives, or other individuals with whom the client maintains a personal relationship—assume the full burden for setting clear, appropriate, and culturally sensitive boundaries.

(c) Social workers should not engage in sexual activities or sexual contact with former clients because of the potential for harm to the client. If social workers engage in conduct contrary to this prohibition or claim that an exception to this prohibition is warranted because of extraordinary circumstances, it is social workers—not their clients—who assume the full burden of demonstrating that the former client has not been exploited, coerced, or manipulated, intentionally or unintentionally.

(d) Social workers should not provide clinical services to individuals with whom they have had a prior sexual relationship. Providing clinical services to a former sexual partner has the potential to be harmful to the individual and is likely to make it difficult for the social worker and individual to maintain appropriate professional boundaries.

1.10   Physical Contact

Social workers should not engage in physical contact with clients when there is a possibility of psychological harm to the client as a result of the contact (such as cradling or caressing clients). Social workers who engage in appropriate physical contact with clients are responsible for setting clear, appropriate, and culturally sensitive boundaries that govern such physical contact.

1.11   Sexual Harassment

Social workers should not sexually harass clients. Sexual harassment includes sexual advances, sexual solicitation, requests for sexual favors, and other verbal or physical conduct of a sexual nature.

1.12 Derogatory Language

Social workers should not use derogatory language in their written or verbal communications to or about clients. Social workers should use accurate and respectful language in all communications to and about clients.

1.13 Payment for Services

(a) When setting fees, social workers should ensure that the fees are fair, reasonable, and commensurate with the services performed. Consideration should be given to clients' ability to pay.

(b) Social workers should avoid accepting goods or services from clients as payment for professional services. Bartering arrangements, particularly involving services, create the potential for conflicts of interest, exploitation, and inappropriate boundaries in social workers' relationships with clients. Social workers should explore and may participate in bartering only in very limited circumstances when it can be demonstrated that such arrangements are an accepted practice among professionals in the local community, considered to be essential for the provision of services, negotiated without coercion, and entered into at the client's initiative and with the client's informed consent. Social workers who accept goods or services from clients as payment for professional services assume the full burden of demonstrating that this arrangement will not be detrimental to the client or the professional relationship.

(c) Social workers should not solicit a private fee or other remuneration for providing services to clients who are entitled to such available services through the social workers' employer or agency.

1.14 Clients Who Lack Decision-Making Capacity

When social workers act on behalf of clients who lack the capacity to make informed decisions, social workers should take reasonable steps to safeguard the interests and rights of those clients.

1.15 Interruption of Services

Social workers should make reasonable efforts to ensure continuity of services in the event that services are interrupted by factors such as unavailability, relocation, illness, disability, or death.

1.16 Termination of Services

(a) Social workers should terminate services to clients and professional relationships with them when such services and relationships are no longer required or no longer serve the clients' needs or interests.

(b) Social workers should take reasonable steps to avoid abandoning clients who are still in need of services. Social workers should withdraw services precipitously only under unusual circumstances, giving careful consideration to all factors in the situation and taking care to minimize possible adverse effects. Social workers should assist in making appropriate arrangements for continuation of services when necessary.

(c) Social workers in fee-for-service settings may terminate services to clients who are not paying an overdue balance if the financial contractual arrangements have been made clear to the client, if the client does not pose an imminent danger to self or others, and if the clinical and other consequences of the current nonpayment have been addressed and discussed with the client.

(d) Social workers should not terminate services to pursue a social, financial, or sexual relationship with a client.

(e) Social workers who anticipate the termination or interruption of services to clients should notify clients promptly and seek the transfer, referral, or continuation of services in relation to the clients' needs and preferences.

(f) Social workers who are leaving an employment setting should inform clients of appropriate options for the continuation of services and of the benefits and risks of the options.

2. SOCIAL WORKERS' ETHICAL RESPONSIBILITIES TO COLLEAGUES

2.01 Respect

(a) Social workers should treat colleagues with respect and should represent accurately and fairly the qualifications, views, and obligations of colleagues.

(b) Social workers should avoid unwarranted negative criticism of colleagues in communications with clients or with other professionals. Unwarranted negative criticism may include demeaning comments that refer to colleagues' level of competence or to individuals' attributes such as race, ethnicity, national origin, color, sex, sexual orientation, gender identity or expression, age, marital status, political belief, religion, immigration status, and mental or physical disability.

(c) Social workers should cooperate with social work colleagues and with colleagues of other professions when such cooperation serves the well-being of clients.

2.02 Confidentiality

Social workers should respect confidential information shared by colleagues in the course of their professional relationships and transactions. Social workers should ensure that such colleagues understand social workers' obligation to respect confidentiality and any exceptions related to it.

2.03 Interdisciplinary Collaboration

(a) Social workers who are members of an interdisciplinary team should participate in and contribute to decisions that affect the well-being of clients by drawing on the perspectives, values, and experiences of the social work profession. Professional and ethical obligations of the interdisciplinary team as a whole and of its individual members should be clearly established.

(b) Social workers for whom a team decision raises ethical concerns should attempt to resolve the disagreement through appropriate channels. If the disagreement cannot be resolved, social workers should pursue other avenues to address their concerns consistent with client well-being.

2.04 Disputes Involving Colleagues

(a) Social workers should not take advantage of a dispute between a colleague and an employer to obtain a position or otherwise advance the social workers' own interests.

(b) Social workers should not exploit clients in disputes with colleagues or engage clients in any inappropriate discussion of conflicts between social workers and their colleagues.

2.05 Consultation

(a) Social workers should seek the advice and counsel of colleagues whenever such consultation is in the best interests of clients.

(b) Social workers should keep themselves informed about colleagues' areas of expertise and competencies. Social workers should seek consultation only from colleagues who have demonstrated knowledge, expertise, and competence related to the subject of the consultation.

(c) When consulting with colleagues about clients, social workers should disclose the least amount of information necessary to achieve the purposes of the consultation.

2.06 Referral for Services

(a) Social workers should refer clients to other professionals when the other professionals' specialized knowledge or expertise is needed to serve clients fully or when social workers believe that they are not being effective or making reasonable progress with clients and that additional service is required.

(b) Social workers who refer clients to other professionals should take appropriate steps to facilitate an orderly transfer of responsibility. Social workers who refer clients to other professionals should disclose, with clients' consent, all pertinent information to the new service providers.

(c) Social workers are prohibited from giving or receiving payment for a referral when no professional service is provided by the referring social worker.

2.07 Sexual Relationships

(a) Social workers who function as supervisors or educators should not engage in sexual activities or contact with supervisees, students, trainees, or other colleagues over whom they exercise professional authority.

(b) Social workers should avoid engaging in sexual relationships with colleagues when there is potential for a conflict of interest. Social workers who become involved in, or anticipate becoming involved in, a sexual relationship with a colleague have a duty to transfer professional responsibilities, when necessary, to avoid a conflict of interest.

2.08 Sexual Harassment

Social workers should not sexually harass supervisees, students, trainees, or colleagues. Sexual harassment includes sexual advances, sexual solicitation, requests for sexual favors, and other verbal or physical conduct of a sexual nature.

2.09 Impairment of Colleagues

(a) Social workers who have direct knowledge of a social work colleague's impairment that is due to personal problems, psychosocial distress, substance abuse, or mental health difficulties and that interferes with practice effectiveness should consult with that colleague when feasible and assist the colleague in taking remedial action.

(b) Social workers who believe that a social work colleague's impairment interferes with practice effectiveness and that the colleague has not taken adequate steps to address the impairment should take action through appropriate channels established by employers, agencies, NASW, licensing and regulatory bodies, and other professional organizations.

2.10 Incompetence of Colleagues

(a) Social workers who have direct knowledge of a social work colleague's incompetence should consult with that colleague when feasible and assist the colleague in taking remedial action.

(b) Social workers who believe that a social work colleague is incompetent and has not taken adequate steps to address the incompetence should take action through appropriate channels established by employers, agencies, NASW, licensing and regulatory bodies, and other professional organizations.

2.11 Unethical Conduct of Colleagues

(a) Social workers should take adequate measures to discourage, prevent, expose, and correct the unethical conduct of colleagues.

(b) Social workers should be knowledgeable about established policies and procedures for handling concerns about colleagues' unethical behavior. Social workers should be familiar with national, state, and local procedures for handling ethics complaints. These include policies and procedures created by NASW, licensing and regulatory bodies, employers, agencies, and other professional organizations.

(c) Social workers who believe that a colleague has acted unethically should seek resolution by discussing their concerns with the colleague when feasible and when such discussion is likely to be productive.

(d) When necessary, social workers who believe that a colleague has acted unethically should take action through appropriate formal channels (such as contacting a state licensing board or regulatory body, an NASW committee on inquiry, or other professional ethics committees).

(e) Social workers should defend and assist colleagues who are unjustly charged with unethical conduct.

3. SOCIAL WORKERS' ETHICAL RESPONSIBILITIES IN PRACTICE SETTINGS

3.01 Supervision and Consultation

(a) Social workers who provide supervision or consultation should have the necessary knowledge and skill to supervise or consult appropriately and should do so only within their areas of knowledge and competence.

(b) Social workers who provide supervision or consultation are responsible for setting clear, appropriate, and culturally sensitive boundaries.

(c) Social workers should not engage in any dual or multiple relationships with supervisees in which there is a risk of exploitation of or potential harm to the supervisee.

(d) Social workers who provide supervision should evaluate supervisees' performance in a manner that is fair and respectful.

3.02 Education and Training

(a) Social workers who function as educators, field instructors for students, or trainers should provide instruction only within their areas of knowledge and competence and should provide instruction based on the most current information and knowledge available in the profession.

(b) Social workers who function as educators or field instructors for students should evaluate students' performance in a manner that is fair and respectful.

(c) Social workers who function as educators or field instructors for students should take reasonable steps to ensure that clients are routinely informed when services are being provided by students.

(d) Social workers who function as educators or field instructors for students should not engage in any dual or multiple relationships with students in which there is a risk of exploitation or potential harm to the student. Social work educators and field instructors are responsible for setting clear, appropriate, and culturally sensitive boundaries.

3.03 Performance Evaluation

Social workers who have responsibility for evaluating the performance of others should fulfill such responsibility in a fair and considerate manner and on the basis of clearly stated criteria.

3.04 Client Records

(a) Social workers should take reasonable steps to ensure that documentation in records is accurate and reflects the services provided.

(b) Social workers should include sufficient and timely documentation in records to facilitate the delivery of services and to ensure continuity of services provided to clients in the future.

(c) Social workers' documentation should protect clients' privacy to the extent that is possible and appropriate and should include only information that is directly relevant to the delivery of services.

(d) Social workers should store records following the termination of services to ensure reasonable future access. Records should be maintained for the number of years required by state statutes or relevant contracts.

3.05 Billing

Social workers should establish and maintain billing practices that accurately reflect the nature and extent of services provided and that identify who provided the service in the practice setting.

3.06 Client Transfer

(a) When an individual who is receiving services from another agency or colleague contacts a social worker for services, the social worker should carefully consider the client's needs before agreeing to provide services. To minimize possible confusion and conflict, social workers should discuss with potential clients the nature of the clients' current relationship with other service providers and the implications, including possible benefits or risks, of entering into a relationship with a new service provider.

(b) If a new client has been served by another agency or colleague, social workers should discuss with the client whether consultation with the previous service provider is in the client's best interest.

3.07 Administration

(a) Social work administrators should advocate within and outside their agencies for adequate resources to meet clients' needs.

(b) Social workers should advocate for resource allocation procedures that are open and fair. When not all clients' needs can be met, an allocation procedure should be developed that is nondiscriminatory and based on appropriate and consistently applied principles.

(c) Social workers who are administrators should take reasonable steps to ensure that adequate agency or organizational resources are available to provide appropriate staff supervision.

(d) Social work administrators should take reasonable steps to ensure that the working environment for which they are responsible is consistent with and encourages compliance with the *NASW Code of Ethics*. Social work administrators should take reasonable steps to eliminate any conditions in their organizations that violate, interfere with, or discourage compliance with the *Code*.

3.08 Continuing Education and Staff Development

Social work administrators and supervisors should take reasonable steps to provide or arrange for continuing education and staff development for all staff for whom they are responsible. Continuing education and staff development should address current knowledge and emerging developments related to social work practice and ethics.

3.09 Commitments to Employers

(a) Social workers generally should adhere to commitments made to employers and employing organizations.

(b) Social workers should work to improve employing agencies' policies and procedures and the efficiency and effectiveness of their services.

(c) Social workers should take reasonable steps to ensure that employers are aware of social workers' ethical obligations as set forth in the *NASW Code of Ethics* and of the implications of those obligations for social work practice.

(d) Social workers should not allow an employing organization's policies, procedures, regulations, or administrative orders to interfere with their ethical practice of social work. Social workers should take reasonable steps to ensure that their employing organizations' practices are consistent with the *NASW Code of Ethics*.

(e) Social workers should act to prevent and eliminate discrimination in the employing organization's work assignments and in its employment policies and practices.

(f) Social workers should accept employment or arrange student field placements only in organizations that exercise fair personnel practices.

(g) Social workers should be diligent stewards of the resources of their employing organizations, wisely conserving funds where appropriate and never misappropriating funds or using them for unintended purposes.

3.10 Labor–Management Disputes

(a) Social workers may engage in organized action, including the formation of and participation in labor unions, to improve services to clients and working conditions.

(b) The actions of social workers who are involved in labor–management disputes, job actions, or labor strikes should be guided by the profession's values, ethical principles, and ethical standards. Reasonable differences of opinion exist among social workers concerning their primary obligation as professionals during an actual or threatened labor strike or job action. Social workers should carefully examine relevant issues and their possible impact on clients before deciding on a course of action.

4. SOCIAL WORKERS' ETHICAL RESPONSIBILITIES AS PROFESSIONALS

4.01 Competence

(a) Social workers should accept responsibility or employment only on the basis of existing competence or the intention to acquire the necessary competence.

(b) Social workers should strive to become and remain proficient in professional practice and the performance of professional functions. Social workers should critically examine and keep current with emerging knowledge relevant to social work. Social workers should routinely review the professional literature and participate in continuing education relevant to social work practice and social work ethics.

(c) Social workers should base practice on recognized knowledge, including empirically based knowledge, relevant to social work and social work ethics.

4.02 Discrimination

Social workers should not practice, condone, facilitate, or collaborate with any form of discrimination on the basis of race, ethnicity, national origin, color, sex, sexual orientation, gender identity or expression, age, marital status, political belief, religion, immigration status, or mental or physical disability.

4.03 Private Conduct

Social workers should not permit their private conduct to interfere with their ability to fulfill their professional responsibilities.

4.04 Dishonesty, Fraud, and Deception

Social workers should not participate in, condone, or be associated with dishonesty, fraud, or deception.

4.05 Impairment

(a) Social workers should not allow their own personal problems, psychosocial distress, legal problems, substance abuse, or mental health difficulties to interfere with their professional judgment and performance or to jeopardize the best interests of people for whom they have a professional responsibility.

(b) Social workers whose personal problems, psychosocial distress, legal problems, substance abuse, or mental health difficulties interfere with their professional judgment and performance should immediately seek consultation and take appropriate remedial action by seeking professional help, making adjustments in workload, terminating practice, or taking any other steps necessary to protect clients and others.

4.06 Misrepresentation

(a) Social workers should make clear distinctions between statements made and actions engaged in as a private individual and as a representative of the social work profession, a professional social work organization, or the social worker's employing agency.

(b) Social workers who speak on behalf of professional social work organizations should accurately represent the official and authorized positions of the organizations.

(c) Social workers should ensure that their representations to clients, agencies, and the public of professional qualifications, credentials, education, competence, affiliations, services provided, or results to be achieved are accurate. Social workers should claim only those relevant professional credentials they actually possess and take steps to correct any inaccuracies or misrepresentations of their credentials by others.

4.07 Solicitations

(a) Social workers should not engage in uninvited solicitation of potential clients who, because of their circumstances, are vulnerable to undue influence, manipulation, or coercion.

(b) Social workers should not engage in solicitation of testimonial endorsements (including solicitation of consent to use a client's prior statement as a testimonial endorsement) from current clients or from other people who, because of their particular circumstances, are vulnerable to undue influence.

4.08 Acknowledging Credit

(a) Social workers should take responsibility and credit, including authorship credit, only for work they have actually performed and to which they have contributed.

(b) Social workers should honestly acknowledge the work of and the contributions made by others.

5. SOCIAL WORKERS' ETHICAL RESPONSIBILITIES TO THE SOCIAL WORK PROFESSION

5.01 Integrity of the Profession

(a) Social workers should work toward the maintenance and promotion of high standards of practice.

(b) Social workers should uphold and advance the values, ethics, knowledge, and mission of the profession. Social workers should protect, enhance, and improve the integrity of the profession through appropriate study and research, active discussion, and responsible criticism of the profession.

(c) Social workers should contribute time and professional expertise to activities that promote respect for the value, integrity, and competence of the social work profession. These activities may include teaching, research, consultation, service, legislative testimony, presentations in the community, and participation in their professional organizations.

(d) Social workers should contribute to the knowledge base of social work and share with colleagues their knowledge related to practice, research, and ethics. Social workers should seek to contribute to the profession's literature and to share their knowledge at professional meetings and conferences.

(e) Social workers should act to prevent the unauthorized and unqualified practice of social work.

5.02 Evaluation and Research

(a) Social workers should monitor and evaluate policies, the implementation of programs, and practice interventions.

(b) Social workers should promote and facilitate evaluation and research to contribute to the development of knowledge.

(c) Social workers should critically examine and keep current with emerging knowledge relevant to social work and fully use evaluation and research evidence in their professional practice.

(d) Social workers engaged in evaluation or research should carefully consider possible consequences and should follow guidelines developed for the protection of evaluation and research participants. Appropriate institutional review boards should be consulted.

(e) Social workers engaged in evaluation or research should obtain voluntary and written informed consent from participants, when appropriate, without any implied or actual deprivation or penalty for refusal to participate; without undue inducement to participate; and with due regard for participants' well-being, privacy, and dignity. Informed consent should include information about the nature, extent, and duration of the participation requested and disclosure of the risks and benefits of participation in the research.

(f) When evaluation or research participants are incapable of giving informed consent, social workers should provide an appropriate explanation to the participants, obtain the participants' assent to the extent they are able, and obtain written consent from an appropriate proxy.

(g) Social workers should never design or conduct evaluation or research that does not use consent procedures, such as certain forms of naturalistic observation and archival research, unless rigorous and responsible review of the research has found it to be justified because of its prospective scientific, educational, or applied value and unless equally effective alternative procedures that do not involve waiver of consent are not feasible.

(h) Social workers should inform participants of their right to withdraw from evaluation and research at any time without penalty.

(i) Social workers should take appropriate steps to ensure that participants in evaluation and research have access to appropriate supportive services.

(j) Social workers engaged in evaluation or research should protect participants from unwarranted physical or mental distress, harm, danger, or deprivation.

(k) Social workers engaged in the evaluation of services should discuss collected information only for professional purposes and only with people professionally concerned with this information.

(l) Social workers engaged in evaluation or research should ensure the anonymity or confidentiality of participants and of the data obtained from them. Social workers should inform participants of any limits of confidentiality, the measures that will be taken to ensure confidentiality, and when any records containing research data will be destroyed.

(m) Social workers who report evaluation and research results should protect participants' confidentiality by omitting identifying information unless proper consent has been obtained authorizing disclosure.

(n) Social workers should report evaluation and research findings accurately. They should not fabricate or falsify results and should take steps to correct any errors later found in published data using standard publication methods.

(o) Social workers engaged in evaluation or research should be alert to and avoid conflicts of interest and dual relationships with participants, should inform participants when a real or potential conflict of interest arises, and should take steps to resolve the issue in a manner that makes participants' interests primary.

(p) Social workers should educate themselves, their students, and their colleagues about responsible research practices.

6. SOCIAL WORKERS' ETHICAL RESPONSIBILITIES TO THE BROADER SOCIETY

6.01 Social Welfare

Social workers should promote the general welfare of society, from local to global levels, and the development of people, their communities, and their environments. Social workers should advocate for living conditions conducive to the fulfillment of basic human needs and should promote social, economic, political, and cultural values and institutions that are compatible with the realization of social justice.

6.02 Public Participation

Social workers should facilitate informed participation by the public in shaping social policies and institutions.

6.03 Public Emergencies

Social workers should provide appropriate professional services in public emergencies to the greatest extent possible.

6.04 Social and Political Action

(a) Social workers should engage in social and political action that seeks to ensure that all people have equal access to the resources, employment, services, and opportunities they require to meet their basic human needs and to develop fully. Social workers should be aware of the impact of the political arena on practice and should advocate for changes in policy and legislation to improve social conditions in order to meet basic human needs and promote social justice.

(b) Social workers should act to expand choice and opportunity for all people, with special regard for vulnerable, disadvantaged, oppressed, and exploited people and groups.

(c) Social workers should promote conditions that encourage respect for cultural and social diversity within the United States and globally. Social workers should promote policies and practices that demonstrate respect for difference, support the expansion of cultural knowledge and resources, advocate for programs and institutions that demonstrate cultural competence, and promote policies that safeguard the rights of and confirm equity and social justice for all people.

(d) Social workers should act to prevent and eliminate domination of, exploitation of, and discrimination against any person, group, or class on the basis of race, ethnicity, national origin, color, sex, sexual orientation, gender identity or expression, age, marital status, political belief, religion, immigration status, or mental or physical disability.

Index

Health Security Act, 231
Healthy life expectancy, 13
Healthy People 2010, 168
Help America Vote Act (HAVA), 347
High Intensity Drug Trafficking Area Program, 28
Hispanics. *See also* Discrimination; People of color; Racism
    adolescent pregnancy rates in, 4
    in child welfare system, 148
    health insurance for, 3, 169, 283
    HIV/AIDS and, 32
    hospice care and, 189
    housing and, 282
    incarceration of, 321
    juvenile justice and, 211
    language use and, 215, 216
    in rural communities, 298
    statistics regarding, 215
    substance abuse and, 32
    as voters, 346
    workplace discrimination and, 155–157
HIV/AIDS
    adolescents and, 3, 4
    background on, 172–173
    confidentiality and, 60
    effects on individuals, families, and communities, 173
    hospice care and, 188
    issue statement on, 173–175
    policy statement on, 175–176
    political action and advocacy, 176
    prevention of, 175
    prostituted people and, 272–274
    substance abuse and, 32
    testing for, 172, 174–176
    treatment of, 173, 174, 176
    women and, 173, 174
Homeland Security Act, 51
Homelessness. *See also* Poverty
    background on, 178–182
    information sources on, 179
    issue statement on, 182
    policy on, 181–183
    policy statement on, 182–184
Homeless shelters, 180–181, 183
Home schooling, 98
Homicide
    in adolescents, 4
    rates of, 39
Homosexuals. *See* Gays; Lesbian, gay, bisexual, and
        transgender (LGBT) issues; Lesbians; Transgender
        identity
Hopkins, Harry, 105
Hospice care, 117. *See also* End-of-life care
    background on, 187–188
    issue statement on, 188–190
    policy statement on, 190–191
Housing
    affordable, 182, 194
    background on, 193
    community infrastructure and, 194
    employment and, 194–195
    issue statement on, 193–195
    policy statement on, 195
    for populations with special needs, 194
    racism and, 282, 286
    social services and, 194
Housing Act of 1949, 194

Housing and Community Development Act Amendments of
    1981, 22
Housing and Community Development Act of 1974, 22
Human Genome Education Model (HuGEM), 162
Human Genome Project, 162
Human rights
    history of, 203–205
    issue statement on, 205–206
    policy statement on, 206–207
    social work and, 204–205
Human Rights Council (United Nations), 241
Human Service Employees Registration and Voter
        Education (Human SERVE), 346

Illegal Immigration Reform and Immigrant Responsibility
        Act of 1996, 198
Illness. *See also* Health care; HIV/AIDS; Hospice care;
        Mental health
    childhood trauma and, 45–45
    chronic adolescent, 5
    environmental degradation and, 124
    health care access and, 169
Immigrant Reform and Control Act of 1986, 197
Immigrants
    child welfare system and, 151
    health insurance for, 5
Immigration. *See also* Slavery/human trafficking
    background on, 197–199
    imprisonment for offenses related to, 321
    issue statement on, 199
    language use and, 215, 216
    policy statement on, 200–201
    trends in, 137–138
Immigration Act of 1990, 197
Immigration and Nationality Act Amendments (1965), 197
Immigration and Naturalization Service, 198
Incarcerated individuals. *See also* Criminal justice system;
        Prisons
    background on, 321
    child welfare system and, 150
    for drug-related offenses, 321–322
    family issues for, 322
    health care needs of, 322
    for immigration-related offenses, 321
    issue statement on, 323–324
    juveniles as, 323
    mental health and, 231, 322
    policy statement on, 324–325
    statistics regarding, 321, 323
    women as, 321–323
Incompetent, 118
Independent living (IL), 247
Indian Child Welfare Act of 1978 (ICWA), 148
Indian Removal Act of 1830, 327
Indian Reorganization Act of 1934, 327
Indigenous peoples. *See also specific groups*
    background on, 327–330
    family violence and, 143
    issue statement on, 330
    policy statement on, 330
Individuals with Disabilities Education Act (IDEA), 60, 247
Infant mortality rate, 130
Information utilization
    background on, 60–61
    issue statement on, 61–62
    policy statement on, 62–63

Racism (*continued*)
    policy statement on, 285–288
    political activity and, 284, 288
    public welfare and, 283, 287
    research and, 284, 288
    social justice and, 242
    social services and, 283, 287
    social work profession and, 288
Rand Institute for Civil Justice, 232
Randolph, A. Phillip, 21
Reagan, Ronald, 292
Reclassification. *See* Deprofessionalization/reclassification
Recruitment and retention issues
    in child welfare practice, 150
    in rural social work practice, 297, 298
Refugees. *See also* Immigration
    admissions of, 198
    background on, 197–199
    impact of terrorism on, 198
    issue statement on, 199
    policy statement on, 200
Rehabilitation Act Amendments of 1992, 247
Rehabilitation Act of 1973, 88, 246
Reproductive choice
    abortion and, 130–131
    access to services for, 133
    background on, 129–130
    education and research and, 134
    emergency contraception and, 130
    issue statement on, 131–132
    legislation related to, 133–134
    men and contraception and, 131
    policy statement on, 132–134
    violence and, 131
Reproductive health
    in adolescents, 4–5
Reproductive technology. *See* Contraception
Restitution Incorporated, 40
Revelle, Roger, 122
Richmond, Mary, 333
Risk behaviors
    in adolescents, 4–5
Risk factors
    for adolescents, 3, 4
    for families, 144, 150
    in school violence, 308–309
    for youth suicide, 371
Rock the Vote, 347
Roe v. Wade (1973), 53, 133
Roosevelt, Eleanor, 203
Roosevelt, Franklin, 21
Rural communities
    technology and, 297
Rural social work
    background on, 296–298
    issue statement on, 298–299
    policy statement on, 299–300
Rust v. Sullivan (1991), 50

Same-sex marriage, 219, 220
Sanger, Margaret, 129
Satcher, David, 308–309, 370
Saunders, Cicely, 187
Schiavo, Terri, 119
School-based health centers (SBHCs), 6
Schools. *See* Education

School social workers
    privacy and, 61, 62
    violence prevention and, 308–309
School truancy/dropout prevention
    background on, 302–303
    issue statement on, 303–304
    policy statement on, 304–305
School violence
    background on, 308
    issue statement on, 308–309
    policy statement on, 309–310
Secondary traumatic stress (STS), 66–67
Self-care. *See* Professional self-care
Self-determination
    hospice care and, 187, 189, 190
    individuals with disabilities and, 248
    in reproductive decisions, 131–132, 134
Self-help movement, 29
Self-sufficiency, 352
Seniors. *See* Elderly individuals
Servicemen's Readjustment Act, 317
Sex education, 175
Sexual abuse
    adolescent pregnancy and, 8
    health and childhood, 46
    prostitution and, 274
    of transgender individuals, 323
Sexual activity
    in adolescents, 4–5, 8, 9
    HIV/AIDS and, 3, 4
Sexual harassment, 358
Sexual orientation. *See also* Lesbian, gay, bisexual, and
        transgender (LGBT) issues
Sexually transmitted diseases (STDs), 272. *See also* HIV/AIDS
Sexual orientation. *See also* Gays; Lesbians; Transgender
      identity
    cultural identity and, 70–71
    discrimination related to, 138, 219–220
Shalala, Donna, 312
Slavery/human trafficking. *See also* Prostituted people
    background of, 312–313
    issue statement on, 313–314
    policy statement on, 314–315
Small Business Jobs Protection Act of 1996, 149
Social justice. *See also* Capital punishment; Civil liberties
    background on, 241–242
    civil liberties and, 50–54
    human rights and, 203, 204
    issue statement on, 242
    policy statement on, 242–243
    voter participation and, 348
Social policies
    background on, 291–293
    family, 137
    issue statement on, 293–294
    policy statement on, 294–295
Social Security Act of 1935, 14, 44, 60, 292, 317
Social Security Disability Insurance (SSDI), 31
Social services
    background on, 317–318
    family issues and, 139
    housing and, 194
    issue statement on, 318
    policy statement on, 318–319
    privacy rights and, 53–54
    racism and, 283

females and, 156–158, 366
issue statement on, 158
legislation addressing, 155–156
policy statement on, 158–159
World Health Organization (WHO), 13, 112, 129, 130

Youths. *See* Adolescents; Children
Youth suicide
background on, 4, 370–371
issue statement on, 372
policy statement on, 372–373